CULTURAL
ANTHROPOLOGY

CULTURAL ANTHROPOLOGY

SECOND EDITION

Conrad Phillip Kottak
University of Michigan

RANDOM HOUSE/NEW YORK

Second Edition
98765432
Copyright © 1974, 1975, 1978, 1979 by Random House, Inc.

Library of Congress Cataloging in Publication Data

Kottak, Conrad Phillip.
   Cultural anthropology.

   Includes bibliographies and index.
   1. Ethnology.   I. Title.
GN316.K64   1978   301.2   78-15704
ISBN 0-394-32221-5

Text designed by Rodelinde Albrecht
Cover photograph by Jacques Jangoux

Photo credits for part openers: Part I – H. W. Silvester/
   Rapho/Photo Researchers; Part II – Ken Heyman; Part
   III – Ken Heyman; Part IV – Menschenfreund; Part
   V – Ken Heyman; Part VI – Charles Harbutt/Magnum

Manufactured in the United States of America

To my mother,
Mariana Kottak Roberts

PREFACE

The anthropology texts that were available when I decided to write the first edition of this book suffered from one or both of two problems. Most were anthropology cookbooks, encyclopedic works more concerned with cataloging data than with the common interests and organizing principles that tie anthropology together. Those few texts that did provide a coherent, consistent, and — inevitably — selective introduction to the field were written too technically for beginning students. In my first edition I tried to apply a consistent set of ecological and evolutionary principles to data and issues in anthropology. I aimed at a reading level most beginning college students could understand, and I tried to deal with issues that affected them and related to their interests. Anthropology's contributions to such subjects as poverty in the United States and abroad, economic development and underdevelopment, colonialism, ethical issues affecting anthropologists, applied anthropology, and socioeconomic stratification received more attention in my first edition than in traditional anthropology texts.

The second edition of *Cultural Anthropology* retains these attributes and adds others. Again I focus on adaptation, variation and change. Ecological and evolutionary principles are applied to human variation in time and place. Totally new chapters cover such topics of contemporary student interest as sex roles in cross-cultural perspective, primate behavior and sociobiology, "race" and "intelligence," and anthropological analysis of contemporary American culture. Structural and symbolic analysis are explained using familiar examples from contemporary American culture.

Cultural Anthropology is intended for use in introductory courses in cultural anthropology. Its moderate length permits its use in quarter, trimester, and semester-long courses. As was the case with the first edition, I have extracted the second edition of *Cultural Anthropology* from a longer text — *Anthropology: The Exploration of Human Diversity* (Random House, 1978) — which covers all four subdisciplines. Instructors whose courses survey biological and archeological anthropology as well as cultural anthropology and linguistics should use the longer book.

I wrote this book — like the first edition — myself. My editors have improved and tightened my style and helped me remove some unnecessary jargon and technical language, but I am responsible for the writing, including the photo and figure captions and the annotated bibliographies.

The second edition of *Cultural Anthropology* contains several improvements, including new chapters and sections:

☐ In contrast to a decade ago, when more students took general (four-field) anthropology courses, cultural anthropology courses now constitute many students' only exposure to anthropology. Because of this, cultural anthropology textbooks are obliged to pay more attention to how cultural anthropology fits into general anthropology and how findings of the other subdisciplines help resolve some major issues in cultural anthropology. Chapters 1, 2, and 11 address these needs.

☐ Chapter 1's discussion of links between cultural anthropology and the other subdisciplines has been expanded. The concept of culture—particularly the role of culture in human biological evolution—receives fuller treatment than in the first edition.

☐ Chapter 2, which focuses on primate behavior and social life, is totally new. It provides a historical background on Darwinian theory in biology and applies principles of evolution through natural selection to the biology and learned behavior of non-human primates. My own students are always fascinated with similarities between humans and other primates, and this chapter discusses these topics. Recent information about primate communication, behavioral variation, and adaptation to environmental change is discussed in Chapter 2.

☐ The chapters on the implications of food production (3) and chiefdoms and states (4) have been thoroughly revised. Chapter 3's sections on plant cultivation, and especially pastoralism, have been expanded. Chapter 4 discusses theories of state formation more fully, and includes a brief case analysis of the development of an African state (Buganda).

☐ Incorporation of new studies and deletion of overly complicated or outdated material are the major changes in Chapters 5 through 10, 13, and 14.

☐ The chapter on language (12) has been totally rewritten. The sections on transformational/generative theory and sociolinguistics, including contemporary dialects of American English, now make the treatment of linguistics fully consistent with the book's general interest in unity, variation, and change.

☐ The second edition's two most innovative chapters are 11 (Biology, Society, and Culture) and 15 (Anthropological Perspectives on Contemporary American Culture). As far as I know, the topics treated in these chapters, areas that are of major interest to today's students and that anthropology is uniquely qualified to examine, receive no such consistent and detailed treatment in any other text. Chapter 11 examines sociobiology, sex roles and sexual expression in cross-cultural perspective, and "race" and IQ. Contributions from all four subdisciplines are used in this chapter to combat various forms of genetic determinism.

☐ Chapter 15 reflects my belief that one of the most effective ways of combating ethnocentrism is to apply to contemporary American culture exactly the same terms and techniques that anthropologists have used in analyzing other cultures. The interpretations in this chapter of rock music, football, the Disney phenomenon, and fast-food restaurants help American students see themselves as natives, and also illustrate structuralist, symbolic, and etic analysis through familiar examples. My own students' reactions to the material covered in these new chapters, particularly Chapter 15, convince me that they will generate more enthusiasm for anthropology than standard textbook examples.

Although I hope my academic colleagues will find this book competent and like working with it, I have written it for students. The first edition grew out of a dozen trimesters of teaching introductory anthropology at the University of Michigan. Since its publication, I've taught almost another dozen. The experience of teaching introductory anthropology is, I think, an important ingredient in producing a text. Students' interests, experiences, and career plans have changed over the past five years. Through course evaluations, conversations with students and teaching assistants, and other feedback, I've followed some of these changes, and the second edition reflects this.

My colleagues, friends, and former teachers in anthropology may recognize the contribution of their thoughts, words, and works to this book. I mention Ataydes Alves de Souza, Robbins Burling, Napoleon Chagnon, Lambros Comitas, George Condominas, Norma Diamond, Penelope Eckert, Kent Flannery, Richard Ford, Shepard Forman, Morton Fried, Daniel Gross, Marvin Harris, Joseph Jorgensen, Maxine Margolis, Robert Murphy, Jeffrey Parsons, Nan Pendrell, Jean Noel Rakoto, Roy Rappaport, Marshall Sahlins, Elman Service, Eliot Skinner, Julian Steward, Pierre Vérin, Charles Wagley, Leslie White, Eric Wolf, Henry Wright, and Aram Yengoyan as people who have directly influenced my vision of anthropology and hence this book.

I renew my thanks to Robbins Burling for his detailed criticism of the first edition manuscript. In addition to Peter Miller and Ralph Faulkingham, who were prepublication reviewers of the first edition, I now must thank several others. Gerald Berreman, Jeffrey Froehlich, Ruth Houghton,

Stasé McPherron, Phoebe Miller, Michael Seelye, and Charles Weitz will recognize the impact of their reviews of the first edition on the second. In addition to Froehlich and McPherron, I thank John Blank, Vaughn Bryant, and especially Maxine Margolis for commenting on the second edition manuscript. I am also grateful to unnamed reviewers, and to several colleagues who wrote me — after using the first edition — to point out mistakes, suggest changes, or report on their students' reactions. I thank, among many others, Philippa Gordon, Ann Hart Rappaport, Roy Rappaport, Harvey Summ, and Charles Wagley for reading, critiquing and/or arguing with and encouraging me about my analysis of aspects of contemporary American culture (Chapter 15). Special thanks to Aram Yengoyan for criticizing Chapter 1, and to Sylvestre Novak for sharing his subscription to *Rolling Stone*.

Anthropology 101 is taught at the University of Michigan as a course with three hours of lecture and one of discussion/recitation each week. I give the lectures and graduate student teaching assistants teach the sections, make up the exams, and do much of the day-to-day work connected with the course. Consistently, these teaching assistants have helped not just beginning anthropology students, but me — to organize, present, and convey data and ideas in a way that many undergraduates at Michigan seem to appreciate. I thank them for this, and for the other insights and knowledge they share with me. I want to renew my thanks to Catherine Cross, Rohn Eloul, John Omohundro, Verena Haas, Cary Meister, Bea Bigony, Donald Calloway, Susan Stokes, Timothy Earle, Susan Kus, and Marjorie Weiner.

Patricia Johnson and James Wood read and commented on the entire manuscript and wrote about 500 of the more than 750 multiple-choice questions that appear in the new Instructor's Manual. Among the teaching assistants who have worked with me recently, I especially thank, along with Johnson and Wood, John Alden, Dan Caister, Eileen Cantrell, Leslie Dow, Jay Fikes, Laurie Hoffman, Arthur Keene, Connie Ojile, and Michael Peletz.

For helping me choose photos for either or both editions, I thank Paul Doughty, Napoleon Chagnon, Shepard Forman, and Cecilia Wagley. For typing and other labors on either or both editions, I thank Maureen Deegan, Lynda Fuerstnau, Karen Shedlowe, and Marcia Solomon.

No book can have an impact on its discipline without a competent publisher. I renew my thanks to Random House personnel for their efforts on behalf of the manuscripts I have spent years writing. First, I thank Barry Fetterolf. Although he joined Random House as anthropology editor less than a year before the first edition was published, his suggestions for two new chapters immediately improved the first edition manuscript. His impact on the second edition is pervasive. It has benefited enormously from the numerous pre-publication reviews he commissioned, and from his knowledge of the interests of today's anthropology teachers. Most important, Barry Fetterolf — while offering guidance and suggestions — has consistently respected my independence as an author and my image of what this book should be.

My project editor, Betty Gatewood, both for *Anthropology* and *Cultural Anthropology* also deserves special thanks. Once the manuscript was in, Betty Gatewood and I worked closely on an expanded illustration program and final editorial work. Along with R. Lynn Goldberg, picture editor, and Flavia Rando, photo researcher, she is responsible for the improvement in the second edition's photos over the first. I particularly appreciate Betty Gatewood's improvements on the manuscript, the many places where she questioned my choice of an unnecessary technical term, suggesting that an ordinary English word or phrase might do as well. I think that students who read this book will benefit particularly from her labors.

I was particularly pleased that Susan Rothstein, who worked so hard as project editor for the first edition, contributed to the second as copy editor. Again I thank V. Susan Fox, who made several of the line drawings.

I would not have started the first edition of this textbook without the encouragement of publishers, and I remain especially indebted to Hugh Treadwell and Mark Sexton of Random House, and to Raleigh Wilson and Walter Lippincott for their interest and confidence.

Betty, Juliet, and Nicholas Kottak have twice experienced my irritability and occasional irresponsibility as the pressure of meeting deadlines mounted, and I thank them for their patience. This time, Juliet and Nicholas deserve special thanks. They have helped me to appreciate enculturation and to become a native anthropologist. I am indebted to Betty Wagley Kottak not only for discussing with me many of the topics treated in this book but also for her assistance in ethnographic field work in Brazil and Madagascar since 1962. Many of the cases and examples discussed in this book depend as much on her field work as on mine.

This book is dedicated to my mother, Mariana Kottak Roberts, who constantly rekindles my interest in the human condition and who made my conversion to social science inevitable.

Ann Arbor, Michigan
March 21, 1978

CONTENTS

part six
FOCUSING ON
CONTEMPORARY SOCIETY

CULTURAL ANTHROPOLOGY

The EXPLORATION
of HUMAN DIVERSITY

Anthropology: The Exploration of Human Diversity

1

People, members of the species *Homo sapiens,* are the world's most adaptable animals. In the Andes of South America, people who sleep in villages 17,500 feet above sea level wake up each day and trek 1,500 feet higher to work in tin mines. In the central Australian desert, people hold totemic ceremonies and discuss philosophy. Human populations survive malaria and other endemic diseases in forested tropical areas throughout the world. Men have walked on the moon. A message from Earth carried by a human artifact, *Pioneer X,* is journeying beyond our solar system. The model of the *Starship Enterprise* that stands in the Smithsonian Institution represents the desire of many Americans to boldly go where no human has gone before. The human desire to know and manipulate the unknown, to control the uncontrollable, to bring order to chaos, to escape the limitations of ordinary knowledge and the constraints of everyday existence, finds varied expression, often elaborated in religion, among people of all times and places. While constraints do operate and have operated throughout our past—often, paradoxically, resulting in change—flexibility and adaptability are basic human attributes. Human history is founded on these attributes, and such human diversity is the subject matter of anthropology.

Encountering anthropology for the first time, students are often amazed by its breadth. Anthropology is a uniquely *holistic* science: its concern with the whole of the human condition encompasses past, present, and future; biology, society (organized life in groups), and culture. *Culture* consists of traditions that govern the thought and behavior of individuals exposed to them. These traditions, which children learn as they grow up as members of a given society, identify the society's customs and specify its opinions—developed over the generations—about what

3

kinds of behavior are proper and improper. Cultural traditions answer such questions as: How do we do things? How do we view the world? How do we distinguish right from wrong? These traditions tend to promote and maintain consistency in behavior, thought, and activity by members of the same society across the generations. Culture consists not just of the traditions, but of the actual ongoing behavior, thought, and products of members of society. The most critical element of such cultural traditions and behavior is their dependence on and transmission through *learning* and social interaction rather than biological inheritance.

THE CONCEPT OF CULTURE

Humans are animals with a difference, and that difference is culture, a major reason for our adaptability and success. Human groups are equipped with "cultural adaptive kits"—containing customary tasks and activities and tools—that enable them to wrest a living from their environment. The cultural adaptive apparatus of a human population also consists of its ideology—that is, ideas about how things should be done and what things should be done in everyday life.

A simple illustration of adaptation through sociocultural means is provided by the Eskimos, who inhabit the extreme Arctic region of the Western Hemisphere. Over centuries of biological evolution, various mammals that Eskimo men hunt have developed fur coats that enable them to survive in the extreme climate. Eskimo technology, in turn, includes a range of techniques that enable them to hunt and kill these animals and use their skins. While human populations still adapt biologically as well as culturally, reliance on sociocultural means of adaptation has increased during many years of prehuman and human evolution.

Social and cultural means of adaptation are crucially important to human evolution. *Society* is the organization of life in groups. Like humans, many other animals—gorillas, chimpanzees, baboons, wolves, and ants, for example—live in organized groups. The daily life of the baboons that live on the plains, or *savannas*, of eastern Africa is organized through the *troop*. In this social group, dominance hierarchies, juvenile play groups, and a variety of coordinated movements and daily activities regulate contacts between members. Human populations, however, are organized not only by the group's activities and relationships, but also by exposure to a common cultural tradition.

The concept of culture has long been basic to anthropology. In his book *Primitive Culture* (1958; orig. 1871), British anthropologist Sir Edward Burnett Tylor argued correctly that systems of human behavior and thought were not random, but were subject to certain natural laws, and therefore could be interpreted scientifically. Tylor's definition of culture gives a good overview of the subject matter of anthropology and is still widely quoted. "Culture . . . , taken in its widest . . . sense, is that complex whole which includes knowledge, belief, arts, morals,

Like humans, many other animals, including the chimpanzees shown here, live in organized groups. Although our nearest relatives, chimpanzees and gorillas, have at least a rudimentary precultural ability, no genus has elaborated cultural abilities—to learn, to communicate, to store and process information—to the same extent as **Homo**. (Anthro-Photo)

law, custom, and any other capabilities and habits acquired by man as a member of society" (1958; orig. 1871). The crucial phrase here is "acquired by man as a member of society." Tylor's definition focuses on capabilities that a person acquires not through biological heredity but by growing up in a particular society, where he or she is exposed to a specific cultural tradition.

Culture and Symbolic Thought

Anthropologist Henry Selby (1975) defines culture as "a set of ideas that is learned, patterned, and transmitted from generation to generation." Anthropologist Clifford Geertz (1973) points out that a critical feature in human evolution is dependence on a particular kind of learning—cultural learning—which allows people to create and deal with concepts and to grasp and apply specific systems of symbolic meaning. He defines culture as "a set of control mechanisms—plans, recipes, rules, constructions, what computer engineers call programs for the governing of behavior."

An individual born in a specific human population begins immediately, through a process of conscious and unconscious learning involving interaction with others, to internalize, or incorporate, the culture of that population through the process of enculturation. The individual learns to deal with a previously established system of meaning and symbols in terms of which people define their world, express their feelings, and make their judgments.

Anthropologist Leslie White (1959) also stresses the unique and critical significance of symbolic thought. White defines culture as "an extrasomatic (nongenetic, nonbodily), temporal continuum of things and events dependent upon symbolling. . . . Culture consists of tools, implements, utensils, clothing, ornaments, customs, institutions, beliefs, rituals, games, works of art, language, etc." For White, culture, and therefore humanity, came into existence when our ancestors acquired the ability to symbol: "the ability freely and arbitrarily to originate and bestow meaning upon a thing or event, and, correspondingly, the ability to grasp and appreciate such meaning." A symbol is something that arbitrarily stands for something else. There is no obvious, natural, or intrinsic link between the two. White uses holy water to illustrate the human capacity to symbol. Water is not intrinsically holier than milk, blood, or other liquids, nor is holy water chemically different from ordinary water. Holy water is a category of a cultural system in which a thing in nature is arbitrarily associated with a particular human meaning or value. For perhaps 500,000 years, people have shared the abilities on which culture rests: to think symbolically, to learn, to manipulate language, to employ tools and other products of cultural traditions in organizing their lives and in adapting to their environments.

Culture rests on human biology, but it is not biological. Every contemporary human population has the ability to symbol, and thus to create and to maintain the things and events dependent on symbolling that White has listed. However, there is growing evidence that chimpanzees share with humans at least basic abilities not only to learn from experience and from others, to fashion tools with specific purposes in mind, and to learn systems of symbolic communication based on human language, but also to symbol. Although our nearest relatives appear to have at least a rudimentary precultural ability, no genus has *elaborated* cultural abilities—namely, to learn, to communicate, and to store, process, and use information—to the same extent as *Homo.*

Culture is an attribute of the genus *Homo,* but anthropologists also use the term "culture" to describe the different and varied cultural traditions of specific human populations. Humanity shares a capacity for culture, but people live in different cultures, are encultured by different cultural systems. Humans, wherever they may be, grow up in the presence of and learn those rules or programs of behavior that compose their particular cultural tradition. All human populations share this ability to acquire and continue specific cultural traditions—American, Italian, French, Armenian, Bugandan, Japanese, or whatever. All members of *Homo sapiens* grow up in the presence of cultural rules that are learned, patterned, shared, and transmitted from generation to generation. The varied and diverse rules associated with specific populations represent the *cultures* that anthropologists study.

Emic and Etic Research Strategies

To study different cultures, anthropologists have advocated two approaches, the *emic* (actor-oriented) and *etic* (observer-oriented). The emic approach views a culture as mental or ideational and assumes that it can be described only by getting into the heads of the people studied. An emic strategy tries to un-

Human populations are organized not only by the diverse activities and relationships of group life, but also by exposure to a common cultural tradition. Kinship, which rests on language, links the three generations shown here. Kinship, language, and reliance on tools are essential features of human life. (Louis Goldman/Rapho/Photo Researchers, Inc.)

derstand how the natives think; how they view and categorize the world; how they use, follow, and manipulate shared rules for behavior; how they conceptualize and explain their behavior. The anthropologist seeks the "native viewpoint" and relies on the culture-bearers, or actors, to judge whether something they do, say, or think is significant or not.

The etic (observer-oriented) approach implies different goals for the anthropologist. When describing, interpreting, and analyzing a culture, the anthropologist relies on his or her own extended observations and gives more weight to the trained scientist's criteria of significance than to those of the culture-bearers. Choice of the etic research strategy rests on the assumption that, as a trained and objective scientist, he or she can take a less involved, more

impartial, and larger view of what is going on. The etic approach realizes that culture-bearers are often themselves too involved in what they are doing to evaluate their cultures impartially.

Most anthropologists actually combine emic and etic strategies in their research. Native viewpoints aid the anthropologist in understanding how different cultural systems work, are interesting in themselves, and enlighten the anthropologist's usually Western view of the world. However, anthropologists are scientists as well as humanists, and as such, in their task of placing particular cultures in broader comparative and historical perspective, they must be aware that natives may fail to admit, or even to recognize, certain aspects and results of their behavior. In describing a culture, the anthropologist should strive to escape both his or her own cultural biases, or *ethnocentrism*, and the biases of the culture-bearers under study. One of the main goals of anthropology is to combat ethnocentrism—people's tendency to apply their own cultural values in judging the behavior and attitudes of people raised in other cultural or ethnic traditions. One example of ethnocentrism is middle-class Americans' assumption that kinship means the same thing to members of other groups as it does to them. Anthropology's comparative approach demonstrates and explains tremendous diversity in human behavior and life styles.

BIOLOGY, SOCIETY, AND CULTURE

Anthropologists agree that culture is uniquely elaborated among humans, that culture is the major reason for human adaptability, and that the capacity for culture is shared by all humans. Anthropologists are also united in their acceptance of a doctrine originally proposed in the nineteenth century as "the psychic unity of man." Anthropology assumes *biopsychological equality* among all human groups: *individuals* may differ in emotional, intellectual, and other psychological and biological tendencies and capacities, but all human *populations* have equivalent capacities for culture. Regardless of physical appearance and genetic composition, human groups have equivalent genetic capacities that can be molded through learning to internalize *any* cultural tradition.

To illustrate this point, consider that contemporary Americans, participants in shared features of American culture, are the genetically diverse descendants of migrants from all over the world. Their ancestors were biologically diverse, lived in a variety of places, and participated in a multitude of cultural traditions. Yet the earliest colonists, later immigrants, and their descendants have been active participants in American life and have come to share a host of cultural features.

To recognize biopsychological equality is not to deny biological and cultural differences among human populations. In studying biological and cultural diversity in time and space, anthropologists must distinguish between the universal, the generalized, and the particular. Certain biological, psychological, social, and cultural features are *universal*—shared by all human populations. Others are merely *generalized*—common to several, but not all,

human groups. Still other traits are *particular*—not shared at all; they lend uniqueness and distinctiveness to certain populations and cultural traditions.

Universality

Universal traits, whether biological, psychological, social, or cultural, are those that are shared by all humans and that more or less distinguish *Homo sapiens* from other species. Among the biological universals are a long period of infant dependency; year-round sexual activity; and a large and complex brain that enables us to create and maintain elaborate symbolic systems, languages, and cultures. Since all human populations have large and complex brains, some anthropologists and linguists believe that these regularities must be responsible for certain universal features of learning and thinking, which are revealed in culture and language. Some psychologists also believe that certain psychological universals reflect experiences common to all human development—growth in the womb, birth itself, and interaction with parents and parent substitutes.

Among the social universals are life in groups and in some sort of family. Since culture organizes human life in groups and depends on human social relationships and interactions to be expressed and continued, many anthropologists find little value in rigidly distinguishing between society and culture. Throughout this book, the term *sociocultural* will refer to human behavior, products, interactions, and interrelationships *and* the cultural traditions, programs, and rules that organize group life and are transmitted through learning from generation to generation. Such human universals as family living and food sharing, which embody cultural traditions and organize groups, should be considered sociocultural universals.

Among the most significant sociocultural universals are exogamy and the *incest taboo*. Humans everywhere consider some people (various cultures differ about *which* people) too closely related to marry and prohibit (taboo) mating or marriage between them. The violation of this prohibition is *incest*, which is discouraged and punished in a variety of ways in different cultures. If incest is prohibited, exogamy—marriage outside of one's group—is inevitable. Because it links human groups together into larger networks, exogamy has been crucial in human evolution. Like other sociocultural universals, exogamy now appears to be an elaboration on tendencies observed among other primates. Recent studies of wild populations of monkeys and apes have shown that these animals avoid mating with close kin (male with mother or possibly sister; female with brother — usually fathers are unknown) and tend at least sometimes to mate outside of their native groups.

Particularity

Biological and sociocultural uniqueness and particularity are at the opposite extreme from universals. Some human groups are biologically unique in possessing particular genetically determined characteristics, such as a particular blood chemistry. Cultures display tremendous variation and diversity, too. Unusual and exotic beliefs and practices lend distinctiveness to particular cultural traditions. Contemporary American culture provides a good example: football. After research involving field work among the Pittsburgh Steelers, and more than 5,000 hours of watching television, anthropologist William Arens (1976) concluded that football is not just a preoccupation of "Middle America," but of all America. It is a particular cultural attribute that is both shared by and peculiar to Americans. Arens notes that football is one of the few interests that Americans share with almost everyone within our borders, but with few outside them. Is football popular because it provides an outlet for our innate aggression (that is, biological determinism) or because of particular aspects of contemporary American culture? Arens's analysis illustrates particularly well differences between biological determinism, which he rejects, and cultural determinism, which he accepts.

To understand why, we must look at *ethology*, the study of the biological basis of animal behavior. Ethological perspectives and findings, particularly their simplistic and usually erroneous applications to humans, are well known. Among the popular examples of this approach are books by scientists Konrad Lorenz (*On Aggression*, 1966) and Lionel Tiger (*Men in Groups*, 1969); by playwright and scientific popularizer Robert Ardrey (*African Genesis*, 1961; *The Territorial Imperative*, 1966; *The Social Contract*, 1970; and *The Hunting Hypothesis*, 1976); and by zoologist Desmond Morris (*The Naked Ape*, 1967; *The Human Zoo*, 1970).

The ethological perspective usually starts with the observation that other animals are sometimes or often aggressive; argues that aggression has a genetic, instinctive base; and concludes that since humans are animals, they must be instinctively aggressive as well. The argument totally ignores abundant evidence (such as will be presented in later chapters) that human aggression is variable: some human populations are quite fierce, and others are gentle and peaceful. Furthermore, the ethological perspective disregards the fact that for more than a million years, humans have drawn upon culture, as well as biology, in adapting to their environments. Certain features of culture, for example, its emphasis on group life, cooperation, and sharing, clash with aggressive tendencies. A variant of the ethological argument (also discussed later) is that human aggression, blood lust, and desires to kill, dismember, and maim, while universal, have not been inherited from our remote, prehuman ancestors, but developed within the genus *Homo* itself and have been inherited from our hunting ancestors. Ethological perspectives view aggression as a universal element of human behavior and psychology and give it a genetic basis. Anthropologists have provided a variety of good arguments for aggression and warfare, where they occur, which is certainly not everywhere, and these are discussed later in the book.

To return to football. Americans, even those who secretly relish football, commonly express the view that the players are brutes, that football is a violent game, and that watching it provides a means of expression for the pent-up aggressive feelings of the spectators. It makes more sense, however, to look to our daily lives instead of to the genes of our hunting ancestors to explain why contemporary Americans are frustrated and why such aggressive feelings arise. Arens denies that an innate tendency toward violence is the sole, or even primary, reason for football's success. Witness the fact that boxing, a much bloodier sport than football is less popular than football in the contemporary United States.

Rather than using aggression, which may or may not be universal, to explain football, which certainly is not, Arens relates the popularity of football to the total pattern of late-twentieth-century American culture, society, and economy. Specifically, he sees football as combining qualities of group coordination through a complex division of labor with highly developed specialization — all attributes of American technology, economy, and society, which provide football's cultural context. (Like Arens, I reject explanations based on instinctive violence or aggression and give my own anthropological analysis of football in Chapter 15.)

Another example of particularity is the culturally conditioned preference for homosexuality among several tribes in the Trans-Fly region of New Guinea. Although homosexuality has been approved or at least tolerated as a sexual alternative in a wide variety of cultural contexts, it is rare to find it as a cultural preference. Trans-Fly sexuality illustrates once again the contrast between biologically based and culturally based explanations of human behavior. Humans are born without established sexual identities and preferences. During the first years of life, children's sexuality is plastic; sexual drives are undifferentiated and indiscriminate—they might be called bisexual. That heterosexual relations are far more frequent than homosexual expressions among humans and other animals is no doubt attributable to reproductive necessity. While most cultures mold infantile bisexuality toward adult heterosexuality, Trans-Fly tribes like the Etoro (Raymond Kelly, 1976) and Marind-anim (J. van Baal, 1966) do not.

The Etoro actually prohibit heterosexual intercourse for between 205 and 260 days per year. They believe that the male life force resides in semen, a not uncommon belief in different cultures. Contact in general, but especially sexual relations, between men and women is considered dangerous and depleting. The Etoro believe that because boys share a common source of depletion through contact with females—development in the mother's womb—not only must they be physically separated from women and girls, they must also acquire semen, which confers the male life force, from another man. To accomplish this, a boy is expected to form a homosexual relationship with a kinsman.

Most cultures have *population policies* (see Wagley, 1969)—cultural practices and beliefs that regulate and stabilize population size, usually toward zero population growth. Abortion and infanticide are common forms of population regulation. Taboos on heterosexual relations also serve to limit population growth. Lindenbaum (1972) has linked the level of institutionalized avoidance and hostility between males and females in the highlands of New Guinea to degree of population pressure. Taboos on heterosexual relations are usually of limited duration and apply at specific times, for example, for one or two years after a child is born, or before hunting and raiding expeditions. The Trans-Fly tribes, by inten-

sifying heterosexual avoidance and segregation of the sexes, have followed a widespread cultural belief and practice to an extreme conclusion. Because of homosexuality and other practices, the birth rate among the Marind-anim of the Trans-Fly (van Baal, 1966) is so low that to perpetuate their population, they must raid their neighbors. Many children who grow up to be Marind-anim have been captured rather than born into Marind-anim society.

Neither Trans-Fly homosexuality nor American football are inevitable outgrowths of instincts. Both illustrate cultural elaborations on the basic biological plasticity of *Homo sapiens*.

Anthropology aims both to impart knowledge and skills and to broaden understanding. By focusing on and trying to explain alternative life styles, it liberates us by forcing a reappraisal of familiar ways of thinking and acting. Its contribution is to demonstrate not only the amazing number and variety of human ways of life, but also that aspects of contemporary American culture can be seen as merely variants, which are no more natural than others.

Generality

Anthropologists do not deal only with the description of universals and a demonstration of their importance in human evolution or with the description and analysis of diversity and uniqueness. They try to explain differences and similarities as well. Anthropologists concern themselves with those biological and cultural regularities, which, while not universal, do recur in different times and places. In their examination of human biology, for example, they have found striking similarities in physiological adaptations of high-altitude groups living in the South American Andes and the South Asian Himalayas. Also generalized, though not universal, are similarities in shades of skin color that have developed independently among populations in different areas of the world for similar reasons.

An example of a sociocultural similarity that occurs in some, but not all, societies is the *nuclear family*, a kinship unit made up of parents and children. Although middle-class Americans ethnocentrically view the nuclear family as a proper and "natural" group, it is in fact merely generalized—not universal. The nuclear family is prominent among many of the technologically simple societies that live by *foraging*—hunting and collecting wild vegetable produce. It is also the most significant kinship unit among contemporary middle-class Americans and Western Europeans. Anthropologists have concerned themselves with explaining why this particular kinship group exists in such different societies. An explanation of the nuclear family as a basic kinship unit in specific *types* of society will be given in Chapter 5.

A PANORAMA OF CHANGE

The subject matter of anthropology is bound neither by time nor by space. The discipline confronts major questions: Where did we come from? What is our peculiar origin and history? What are we now and where are we going? Charles Darwin suggested, and modern genetics demonstrates, that all life forms are ultimately related. Anthropology confirms that much of the diversity we see in cultures, as in nature, reflects adaptation to a variety of different natural circumstances. In culture as in life, variation and change are natural and constant. *Homo* has changed in the past and humans are changing today. We know that we are closely related to other animals, and recent genetic, laboratory, and behavioral studies demonstrate that we are much closer to our nearest relatives, chimpanzees and gorillas, than was imagined even a decade ago.

When did our ancestors begin to diverge from those remote great-aunts and great-uncles whose descendants are contemporary chimpanzees and gorillas? By studying the remote past, by examining the fossilized bones and tools of our ancestors, anthropologists attempt to answer such questions as: Where and when did the genus *Homo* originate and how has it changed? How has biological change interacted with and been affected by changes in culture and society? Anthropological study of the past demonstrates a gradual but continuous addition of sociocultural to biological means of adaptation to the environment. The rate of cultural change has also speeded up, particularly during the past 10,000 years.

About 40,000 years ago, people who looked essentially like modern humans were living in Africa, Asia, and Europe. By 25,000 years ago, physically modern humans were colonizing the New World and Australia. But while their appearance was modern, their ways of life recalled the past. Until about 10,000 years ago, people everywhere lived by foraging. Economically, and probably culturally as well, they were more similar to their physically different ancestors than to their physically similar descendants.

However, in the Near East of 12,000–10,000 B.P. (before present)—and somewhat later in other parts of the world—a major shift in social and economic life began. Humans became food producers—planting and domesticating crops, tending and stockbreeding animals—rather than simply reaping the provisions of nature. The rate of cultural change increased further. Between 6000 and 5000 B.P. the first civilizations, or states, arose in the Near East. In the much more recent past, industrialism had profoundly affected the lives of people throughout the world. Each major economic shift has rapidly spread at the expense of earlier economies and social types. It took only a few thousand years for food production to retire foraging—our ancestors' pattern for millions of years—as the major human subsistence strategy. Soon thereafter, state organization was born and grew quickly. Today—after just a few centuries—industrial economies draw raw materials from and provide manufactured products for people everywhere.

Occasionally, however, glimmers of the past come to light. A few years ago, the Tasaday, a small group of forest people isolated from their neighbors and subsisting through foraging, were discovered in the Philippines. Because the Tasaday lived in caves, the news media were quick to proclaim them "living fossils," purportedly living like ancient "cave men," a popular stereotype of the foragers who lived before the advent of food production. Reflection on anthropological knowledge dispels the image of the Tasaday as representatives of the past. Their jungle environment, isolation, and tiny population size contrast sharply to past ways of life based on foraging. Similarities between their language and the languages of groups who live outside the forest suggest that the Tasaday's ancestors were refugees who moved into the forest fairly recently, perhaps during the past five hundred years, long after food production had spread throughout most of the world. Their ancestors may even have been cultivators who reverted to foraging once in the forest. Only a press uninformed about anthropology could turn the Tasaday into unique reminders of our past.

GENERAL ANTHROPOLOGY

Although anthropology is a relatively recent addition to the curricula of many colleges and universities in

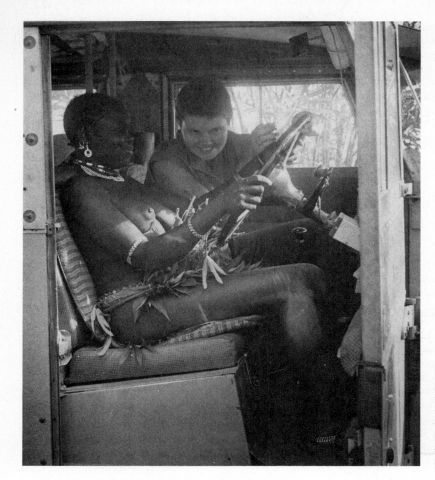

Today's industrial economies draw materials from and provide manufactured goods for people everywhere and have profoundly modified their lives. Here, a woman in northern Kenya is being shown the fundamentals of truck driving. (George Rodger/Magnum Photos)

the United States, it can contribute to the resolution of many significant public issues. Its four subdisciplines—sociocultural, archeological, biological, and linguistic anthropology—are interrelated areas of specialization united by a common concern with human populations. Most anthropologists are expected to acquire a general background. University departments of anthropology usually include at least one representative of each subdiscipline. Most American anthropologists, the author included, specialize in sociocultural anthropology. However, all anthropologists must be familiar with the basics of all the subdisciplines that together compose *general anthropology*. There are several historical reasons for the incorporation of four subdisciplines into a single science in the United States. American anthropology grew up in the late nineteenth and early twentieth centuries out of a concern with natural

history and with the native populations of North America. Over time, related interests in the origins and diversity of Native Americans brought together the study of customs, social life, language, and physical traits. A historical concern with the origins of, and relationships among, the native populations of the New World was combined with an interest in describing, reconstructing, and cataloging the variety of Indian customs and ways of life.

There are also logical reasons for the unity of the four subdisciplines. Each is concerned with variations in time as well as in space, that is, different geographic areas. Sociocultural and archeological anthropologists are both interested in historical problems—changes in social life and customs of specific groups of people. Biological anthropologists have provided data about the major changes in human physical form and means of adaptation over long periods. Anthropological linguists have reconstructed languages and events of the past from the study of contemporary languages.

This common concern with variation in time may be stated differently: the study of evolution unifies the four subdisciplines of anthropology. Defined simply, evolution is change in form over generations. According to Charles Darwin, it is descent with modification. (An evolutionary approach, supplemented by an interest in ecology, orients this book. The terms "evolution" and "ecology" are clarified below.)

Furthermore, subdisciplinary specialization does not lead to compartmentalization. The findings of one subdiscipline filter into the others as anthropologists talk to one another, read some of the same books and journals, and participate in many of the same professional associations. In addition, anthropologists share certain overarching interests. Anthropology is united in its insistence that conclusions about "human nature" cannot be drawn from a single cultural tradition, such as our own. In the face of biological and sociocultural variation, the collaboration of the subdisciplines is necessary to unravel the essentials of human biology, psychology, society, and culture. The nature of unity and the reasons for diversity, then, are questions that engage anthropologists regardless of their subdiscipline.

Understanding many contemporary problems and issues requires a knowledge of the interrelations between biology, society, and culture. For example, several important issues currently before the public involve the "genetics versus environment" controversy. One issue in the controversy concerns differences between the sexes. Anthropology can often make more informed statements than other sciences about whether differences in male and female capacities, attitudes, and behavior reflect biological or sociocultural variation. Are females naturally less aggressive and egoistic than males? Are there emotional and intellectual differences between the sexes? Is male dominance a human universal? By examining the nature of social, emotional, and intellectual differences—if any—between males and females in a variety of cultural contexts, anthropology demonstrates that culture has more to do with a person's destiny than anatomy. In other words, most social and psychological differences between the sexes reflect cultural tradition rather than inherent biological differences.

Another "genetics versus environment" debate, already discussed, involves the cultural or biological determinants of human aggression. Anthropology has demonstrated that there is tremendous variation in aggressive behavior among cultures of different times and places—from untrammeled violence to extreme docility. If aggression is a universal, genetically determined tendency, its relatively minor force is confirmed by the large number of cultures that have managed to block its manifestation.

Anthropologists have also been called upon to comment on assertions that differences in the quantity or quality of intellectual capacities among human groups—between males and females, blacks and whites, rich and poor, and so on—are genetically determined. Drawing on studies of biology, psychology, society, and culture, anthropologists have found no evidence for intergroup differences in innate intellectual capacities. They have provided environmental explanations for differences in measured intelligence among human groups by showing cultural biases inherent in standard intelligence tests and testing situations. Anthropology, then, is not simply a specialized science of the exotic carried on by scholars in ivory towers—it is a discipline with a lot to tell the public. One of its principal contributions is its broadening, liberating role in a liberal undergraduate education.

THE SUBDISCIPLINES OF ANTHROPOLOGY

Sociocultural Anthropology

The sociocultural anthropologist focuses on human social life, that is, on the relationships of individuals to other individuals, of individuals to groups, and of groups to other groups. Sociocultural anthropologists are also concerned with particular, generalized, and universal social and cultural phenomena. Sociocultural anthropology is traditionally divided into two parts: ethnography and ethnology, which are usually combined by any sociocultural anthropologist in his or her work.

Ethnography is the primary, data-gathering part of sociocultural anthropology, that is, field work in a given society. My own field experience has been in two different parts of the world: among ocean-going fishermen of northeastern Brazil and among rice farmers of central Madagascar, a large island off the southeast coast of Africa. My approach to field work was typically ethnographic. I lived in small communities of peasants. I studied their everyday behavior, their normal social life, their economic activities, their relationships with their relatives and in-laws, their relationship to the nation-state in which they live, their rituals and ceremonial behavior, and their notions about appropriate social behavior.

Ethnographers are in a position to recognize, and indeed are themselves often caught up in, the web of personal relations and problems encountered by those they study. Perhaps this is the reason why most sociocultural anthropologists tend to be humanists.

Like the people studied by many anthropologists, those I worked with were relatively poor and powerless in the context of their total society, the nation that enclosed them. Ethnographers are in a position to see the kinds of discriminatory practices that are directed toward such people in many contemporary nations. They are able to see poverty in terms of dietary deficiencies. Their perspective sometimes differs radically from those of economists and political scientists, who have traditionally been concerned with organizations at the national level, and who have been forced by the nature of their inquiries to work with political and economic elites. On the other hand, the anthropological perspective is not necessarily better — it merely examines a different aspect of the same problem. Political scientists see programs that nations develop; anthropologists see how these programs work on the local level. Both are probably necessary for us to arrive at an understanding of human life in the twentieth century.

In ethnology, the other division of sociocultural anthropology, data not from a single society but from several are considered and compared. The ethnologist attempts to make generalizations, to explain social and cultural differences and similarities. It is in this aspect of the anthropological endeavor that the distinction between universal, generalized, and particular is relevant. Data that enter ethnological formulations come from monographs (reports) and books published by ethnographers about their field work. Data of relevance to ethnology also come from the other subdisciplines of anthropology, particularly from archeology.

Archeological Anthropology

Archeological anthropology, which might be called *paleoethnography,* is concerned with the analysis, description, and interpretation of the ways of life of peoples who no longer exist. Archeologists attempt to infer as much as possible about these people from the remains they have left. Study of material things that have endured over several centuries or even millenniums enables the archeologist, familiar with ethnological theory, to make inferences about the nature of life in the community that existed on the archeological site he or she is excavating.

Several kinds of material remains are of interest to archeologists. Garbage dumps often reveal a great deal about diet; analysis of coprolites (fossilized feces) also gives information about the ingredients of meals and about whether foods were eaten raw or cooked. Examination of animal bones reveals such things as the average age of animals slaughtered and provides other information useful in determining whether species were wild or domesticated. From such data, archeologists can reconstruct an amazing amount about the economy of the people they study. They can tell whether prehistoric populations were primarily hunters or whether they domesticated and bred animals, killing for food only those animals of a certain age and sex. They can tell if most vegetable food came from collecting wild plants or from sowing, tending, and harvesting crops, that is, plant cultivation. At the site of long-abandoned settlements, archeologists find *artifacts,* manufactured items. They examine the materials that were used to make these things and discover whether these materials were available locally. If they were not, archeologists attempt to determine where they were available. From such information, ancient trade routes can be reconstructed.

Archeologists have spent a great deal of time studying *potsherds,* fragments of earthenware that can provide a great deal of information about the archeological population. The range of pottery types, for example, may indicate the level of technological complexity. Furthermore, the quantity of pottery fragments in a given area may permit inferences about population size and density. The discovery that pottery was made with materials not locally available suggests systems of interregional trade. Archeological interest in pottery also reflects the fact that potsherds are more durable than many other artifacts — textiles and wooden objects, for example. For many years archeologists have used pottery as an indication of the presence of sedentary populations with food-producing economies, those of cultivators, for example, rather than of people who subsisted on foraging. Finally, many archeologists have been especially interested in pottery styles, arguing that similarities in manufacturing techniques and decoration at different sites can be taken as evidence for cultural connections. Peoples with similar pots and similar decorative techniques have been assumed either to be historically related—for example, offshoots of a common ancestral population—or to have been in contact, perhaps through trade networks or by inclusion in the same political system.

The inferences archeologists have made and can make are not limited to the local economy or even to regional trade patterns. By dating sites, making regional surveys, taking aerial photographs, and using other techniques, archeologists can plot the range of variation in the sizes of villages and the distances between them at a given time. From this they can estimate the population of local and regional units of the society. From examining certain types of structures and buildings, they can say a great deal about the political organization of the people. Some societies of the past have mobilized large groups of people to work together on public works projects. Where temples, pyramids, and other special-purpose sites and buildings endure, one might infer that the society in question was a state with a central authority and an administrative structure whose edicts, backed by the threat of force, convoked public works parties, slave or free.

Archeology has contributed a tremendous amount to ethnology and promises to contribute even more. Many archeologists are interested in *paleoecology*. *Ecology* is the study of interrelationships among living things in a given environment. The living organisms and their environment together constitute an *ecosystem*, a patterned arrangement of energy flows and exchanges. Human ecology studies the ecosystems of which human populations are part. Paleoecology is concerned with ecosystems of the past. Archeologists with this interest can considerably expand our knowledge of the kinds of relationships human populations have established with their environments at different times and in different places.

Archeologists are also able to chart changes in a society by an intensive excavation of particular sites through a succession of levels or layers. By analyzing the presence and time of year of human occupation at each level, they can uncover similarities and differences in activities and life styles. Archeology is therefore also vital to ethnology because it reveals evolution or change of form—in this case, change of

settlement form and purpose; change in the interrelationships between settlements; and, in a larger sense, change in the forms of basic economic, social, and political activities. Ethnographers have traditionally done their field research among nonliterate people. To know about the past of prehistoric populations—those who have no written records of that past—archeology is essential. Comparison of temporal sequences in different parts of the world has enabled anthropologists to formulate certain laws and generalizations, for example, about the influences of environment and economy on social and political organization. In fact, one might reasonably argue that archeology and ethnography have contributed equally to the comparative science of ethnology.

Biological, or Physical, Anthropology

Biological, or physical, anthropologists, as the names suggest, are principally, though not exclusively, interested in humans as biological organisms. They relate human biological variation in time and space to variation in environment—which includes both abiotic factors (for example, temperature, rainfall, and elevation), and biotic factors (for example, plants, animals, and other humans). A common interest in describing and explaining variation unites several more specialized areas of study, including human evolution as revealed by the fossil record; human genetics; the biology, evolution, and behavior of monkeys, apes, and other subhuman primates; human growth and development; and the relevance of human biological plasticity to environmental adaptation. These interests link biological anthropologists to several other disciplines, including zoology, anatomy, physiology, medicine, biology, geology, and public health.

Knowledge of *osteology*, the study of bones, aids those biological anthropologists who examine fossilized skulls, teeth, and other bones to document long-term changes in human morphology, or physical form. The fossil record enables a biological anthropologist to reconstruct the major changes in physical form of the genus *Homo*, to identify our remote ancestors, and to make inferences about their ways of life. Because fossils are often found with tools, and because certain kinds of stone tools are characteristically associated with certain groups of fossils, the study of the fossil record brings about a collaboration between biological anthropologists and archeologists that enriches our understanding of the past. Often the anatomical changes that are found can be linked to changes in technology, environment, or social life. New discoveries and interpretations often lead students of the fossil record to ponder issues that have traditionally been the concern of sociocultural anthropologists: the nature and origin of a human pattern of life distinct from that of other primates; and the origins of such sociocultural universals as exogamy, tool making, and speech.

The study of human genetics is also necessary to understand human variation in time and space. When Charles Darwin proposed natural selection as the major reason for evolution (descent with modification) among life forms, he argued that the variation encountered in any population meant that some individuals would be better able than others to survive and reproduce in that environment. Genetics enlightens us about the biochemical and mechanical causes of variation. It addresses such questions as how variety originates, how it is preserved, and how it is reduced among populations of interbreeding organisms. By seeking reasons for biological changes in populations over time, genetics contributes importantly to the study of evolution. It attempts to explain genetic similarities and differences among populations in terms of natural selection and other causes of genetic evolution and variation.

Biological anthropologists are aware, however, that not all biological differences between individuals and between populations have a genetic basis. Accordingly, a growing number of scholars are investigating, through experiments and field research, the effects on biology of such environmental factors as nutrition, altitude, temperature, and disease. Studies of human growth and development demonstrate the effects of a host of specific environmental variables on adult physical characteristics. *Phenotype,* the manifest physical characteristics of an organism, reflects not only *genotype* — hereditary makeup — but the totality of environmental forces that influence the organism's growth and development. Focusing on specific characteristics, biological anthropologists increasingly understand how genetics and environment interact to produce human biological variation.

Finally, biological anthropologists have traditionally been interested in *primatology,* the study of our closest nonhuman relatives. Studies of primates involve their morphology, genetics, and evolution. Primatologists also undertake studies of primates in the wild, their natural environment. Field work among baboons, gorillas, or chimpanzees, for example, is similar to the ethnographer's study of the behavior of specific human populations. Many anthropologists believe that the study of primate behavior may shed some light on the behavior of our own remote ancestors.

Anthropological Linguistics

Although we do not know — perhaps cannot know — when the genus *Homo* or the species *sapiens* began to speak, all contemporary humans do speak languages. Linguists study languages of the present and make inferences about languages of the past. Linguistics, like other subdisciplines of anthropology, examines variation in time and space. Linguistic techniques are especially useful to ethnographers doing field work, for they enable them to rapidly learn languages that in some cases have never been written.

Descriptive linguistics is the analysis of systems of sound, grammar, and meaning in particular languages. *Historical linguistics* is the study of linguistic variation and change over time, for example, the changes in sound system, grammar, and vocabulary that occurred between Middle English and modern English. It is also concerned with variation among speakers of the same language at a given time. Linguistic variation may reflect geography, as do regional dialects of American English. It is also associated with social divisions; for example, the bilinguality of members of many ethnic groups in the contemporary United States, or variant speech habits of members of different social classes and ethnic groups. Such studies of relationships between social contrasts and linguistic variation are conducted in a growing subfield know as *sociolinguistics.* They provide an exciting framework for understanding the relationships between language and society and between linguistic change and social change.

The process of historical change is revealed in variation on a single time-level; both geographical and social barriers as well as distance are responsible for changes in languages. Given sufficient time, variants of one language can develop into separate languages. Once languages themselves have separated, linguists can use a technique called the comparative method to examine a group of languages that have developed over time out of a common ancestral language, called the *protolanguage.* The Indo-European language family is probably the most prominent example. There are several languages that exist today following a long period of differentiation from proto-Indo-European. Examination of contemporary languages enables the linguist to reconstruct much of the parent language. Historical linguistics is also useful to anthropologists because it provides historical information about other aspects of culture. Some of its specific uses will be explored in Chapter 12.

Anthropologists have recently become interested in a more general linguistic approach that attempts to determine linguistic universals, features common to all languages. Both linguistic and cultural anthropologists are also increasingly interested in how the structure and use of languages are related to other aspects of cultures. Some have argued that studying how people conceive of and talk about their world tells a great deal about their psychological makeup. Certainly, the study of language and culture promises to contribute to the understanding of human behavior.

ANTHROPOLOGY AND THE OTHER HUMAN SCIENCES

The basic distinction between anthropology and other academic disciplines that study human existence has to do with anthropology's *holism,* its study of humanity from a biological, sociocultural, and linguistic point of view. But there are also important distinctions between sociocultural anthropology, specifically, on the one hand, and the other social sciences and the humanities, on the other.

Although anthropologists once concentrated on nonindustrial societies, studies of the United States and other complex societies are increasingly common. Of particular interest to contemporary anthropologists are socioeconomic problems and ethnic diversity within modern nations. Here an anthropologist (seated) uses a tape recorder to interview an informant in Mesa, Arizona. (Michal Heron/Woodfin Camp & Assoc.)

Sociocultural Anthropology and Sociology

Anthropologists are often asked about the distinction between sociocultural anthropology and sociology. The anthropologist (throughout this discussion I will be referring to the sociocultural anthropologist) and the sociologist share a common interest in human society, in the organization and behavior of humans in groups, and in patterns of social relations. However, many differences between the practices of the two disciplines result from the different kinds of societies each has traditionally studied. Sociologists are best known for their studies of only one kind of society, the industrial West; and in the United States, they have principally studied American life. Anthropologists, on the other hand, have tended to concentrate on nonindustrial societies.

The different kinds of societies are approached through different techniques of data collection and analysis. Sociologists make extensive use of questionnaires and other means of gathering quantifiable, or countable, data. Accordingly, expertise in sampling, statistical techniques, and other formal methods of analysis is widely valued in sociology. Sociologists have concentrated on societies in which their informants or respondents—the people who answer their questions and are their objects of study—are often literate. Thus, sociologists can ask respondents to fill out questionnaires. Anthropologists, on the other hand, have worked most often with informants who live in nonliterate societies or who, as peasants in a nation-state, are illiterate.

Anthropologists traditionally have worked among small populations, whereas sociologists have been concerned with analyzing nation-states, which are usually much more complex. Anthropologists have developed techniques of data collection applicable to small communities. They live among local people, observing their everyday behavior—the things they do, the people they see, and the web of relationships that unite them. They gather data through personal contact with the people. One traditional technique of ethnographic field work is participant observation: anthropologists actually take part in the events they are observing and analyzing.

This is a somewhat oversimplified description of the difference between disciplines. Often it has not been so clear-cut. Today there is increasing convergence between anthropology and sociology, both in subject matter and techniques. Sociologists now do research in areas of the world that were once al-most exclusively within the anthropological orbit, and anthropologists study areas of industrial society, for example, ethnic groups and urban neighborhoods in the United States. Anthropologists are subjecting such aspects of American culture as football, soap operas, television commercials, amusement parks, movies, markets, and fast-food restaurants to the same kinds of analysis they use when they study other cultures. And as they extend the scope of their studies, they are adopting many of the techniques of data collection used by sociologists. In my own ethnographic work in Madagascar, for example, I used mimeographed *interview schedules* (a series of questions that I asked each informant) as a basis for formal interviews. By asking a large sample of people the same questions, I was able to determine how widespread certain behavior patterns and social relationships were. My knowledge of the people I studied in Madagascar is not based on my impressions and unstructured observations alone. Rather, the information I gathered permits me to say definitely what is typical or atypical and to assess the range of variation. Similarly, sociologists have found that there is something of value in anthropological techniques and are increasing their use of informal interviews and intensive work with informants.

Anthropology, Economics, and Political Science

Economics and political science concentrate on particular areas of human behavior, usually in industrial nations. In the societies that anthropologists have traditionally studied, politics and economics often do not stand out as distinct areas of human activity amenable to separate analysis, as they do in modern nations. In fact, in technologically primitive societies the political and economic orders are usually submerged in the social order. Many of the societies studied by anthropologists have nothing comparable to the political structure of nation-states. There is no government or central authority. Authority is vested in kinship statuses; parents and grandparents may be the only individuals who can exercise authority over their children and grandchildren; or authority may be a function of age or sex, so that all men or all women can hope to exercise similar authority when they have reached a certain age.

People in nonindustrial societies often conceive of a social world with only two broad categories of people: insiders (friends) and outsiders (potential or actual enemies). One's friends are those people with whom one has a personal relationship. They include one's actual relatives and those who are regarded as relatives because of some ceremonial, such as blood brotherhood; they also include one's in-laws and potential in-laws and those of their relatives. Those who lack such personal connections are considered to be outsiders until such alliance-creating mechanisms as ceremonials, marriages, or trading partnerships convert them into friends.

Statements by anthropologists about the economy — the system of production, distribution, and consumption of material resources — usually result from ethnographic field work. Given the holistic approach of anthropology, anthropologists try to deal with as many aspects of human behavior as possible in the society they are studying. The comparative study of economics has been enriched by anthropologists who have revealed differences between societies in the principles that regulate the distribution of resources. Anthropologists have also added to the comparative study of political systems by analyzing means of preserving order and preventing or resolving conflict in stateless societies. As a result, the findings of economists and political scientists about Western nations can be placed in a broader perspective.

Anthropology and the Humanities

Such academic disciplines as art, literature, and music — the humanities — are traditionally concerned with the "fine arts," the appreciation of which is viewed as one of the attributes of a "cultured person" in our own society. But anthropology goes beyond the concept of culture in its common meaning of "cultured" — that is, cultivated, sophisticated, proper, and tasteful — and in so doing broadens the study of such creative expressions as art, dance, music, and literature.

The humanities typically emphasize works of fine art that have been produced for an elite segment of society in Western civilization. Anthropology broadens the study of creative expression in a variety of ways. Through research in remote and small-scale communities, ethnographers provide comparative data about such nonelite expressions as popular or folk art, music, and literature. They try to relate both the expressions and their creators to their social and cultural contexts. In remote areas of northeastern Brazil, for example, ethnographers have found rich social documents in popular ballads that recount the frustrations of everyday life and describe attempts to reform oppressive social institutions. Of equal anthropological interest are such sources as American "country music" — with its tales of ordinary people, their legal and family problems and their emotions, which often have a social or economic basis. For young Americans, protest songs have expressed collective dissatisfaction with American society and government. Motion pictures draw upon themes of American life, and changes in their subject matter reflect changes in the society at large.

For anthropologists, culture is not confined to one segment of society — an elite, let us say — but is imparted to all members of the society through enculturation. In this view, the creative expressions of all segments of society have the same potential value; and anthropologists are concerned with all the manifestations of creative expression in a society. At the same time, students of the humanities are enlarging their subject matter. Anthropologists and humanities professors alike are now exploring ethnic art, music, and dance; folklore and oral literature; and even such aspects of American "pop culture" as comic books, science fiction, television programs, protest songs, soap operas, and detective stories. Anthropology reveals that such expressions are not only interesting in themselves, but are also social documents produced in a cultural and social context and incorporating cultural themes and social issues.

Anthropology and Psychology

Anthropology and psychology are both concerned with human behavior. Anthropology has the greatest relevance for those psychologists interested in motivation, personality structure, and the tenor of social relationships. Like other social scientists, psychologists tend to gather data and make observations in the society of which they are themselves members. Anthropology can contribute to psychology by providing comparative data for psychological statements previously based on the observation of behavior in a single society or a single type of society.

The subdivision of sociocultural anthropology known as psychological anthropology, or culture and personality, is closely tied to psychology. Anthropologist Margaret Mead, in her books *Coming of Age in Samoa* (1928), *Growing up in New Guinea* (1930), and others, has shown that as cultures differ in what they regard as normal and appropriate, so too do the personality types of individuals in those cultures. Thus anthropologists have shown that cultures interested in inculcating different values train their children differently and that the personalities of adults in a culture reflect its child-rearing practices.

One of the most famous contributions by an anthropologist to the cross-cultural study of human psychology was made by Bronislaw Malinowski, well known for his studies of the population of the Trobriand Islands in the South Pacific. Like many other peoples, the Trobrianders reckon kinship and descent matrilineally—that is, the individual (a male, in this case) is considered to be related to his mother and her relatives, but not to his father. At birth the individual is incorporated into his mother's rather than his father's group. As Malinowski pointed out, in the Trobrianders' matrilineal society, the relative who exercises authority over an individual is not his father, who is, after all, not even considered a relative, but his mother's brother, his maternal uncle. The uncle rather than the father is the disciplinarian. Furthermore, one inherits from one's mother's brother rather than from one's father. Marked respect is shown toward one's uncle, with whom one often has a cool and distant relationship. In contrast, the father-son relationship among the Trobrianders typically involves free and easy, friendly behavior and considerable affection.

Malinowski's work among the Trobrianders suggested some modifications in Sigmund Freud's famous theory of the universality of the Oedipus complex. According to Freud, boys around the age of five are universally attracted sexually to their mothers. The Oedipus complex is resolved, in Freud's view, as the boy overcomes his sexual jealousy of, and identifies with, his father. Freud, however, lived in the patriarchal Austria of the late nineteenth and early twentieth centuries, a social milieu in which the father was a strong authoritarian figure. In Freud's society the father played a dual role as primary authority figure to the child and as the mother's sexual partner. In the Trobriand Islands, on the other hand, the two roles were separated: the father was only the mother's sexual partner. If the Oedipus complex everywhere produced social distance based on jealousy toward the mother's sexual partner, it would have shown up in the father-son relationship among the Trobrianders. It did not. Malinowski's data therefore suggested that the nature of the authority structure was as important a de-

terminant in producing a cool and distant relationship between father and son in Freud's society as was sexual jealousy. Individual behavior depends on the sociocultural context in which it occurs.

An additional contrast between anthropology and psychology is apparent in their differing attitudes toward the individual. Psychologists are interested in the individual as an individual but anthropologists often are not. Rather, many anthropologists study individual behavior to identify behavior typical of particular positions and relationships within a society. Ethnographers observe several cases of interaction between fathers and sons, husbands and wives, old women and young women, and so forth, to build up a picture of the operation of the total social system and the social divisions and contrasts that are essential parts of it. Some areas of psychology—for example, psychoanalysis—assume that each individual's personality is structured or integrated in a unique way, although generalized psychological processes and problems are, of course, revealed by examining a variety of individual cases. But most anthropologists are concerned with the structure, integration, and consistency of a culture or society rather than of an individual personality. The anthropologist, when examining a single case—typically a community or other social unit—attempts to discover how individuals are organized into groups as well as how these groups interrelate and how they are organized into a single social system.

A final tie between anthropology and psychology is the former's interest in universal, generalized, and particular psychological, as well as sociocultural, phenomena. Links between anthropology, biology, and psychology are especially apparent in the study of aggression, sexuality, sex roles, and intelligence.

Anthropology and History

The subject of anthropology and history leads logically into Chapter 2. A broad statement about history would define it as the study of the past, of changes through time. However, like many historians, anthropologists recognize two approaches to temporal change. The first approach concentrates on individuals as individuals. Imagine, for example, any stable society. Individuals enter this social system at birth and leave it at death—its personnel changes. The second approach studies individuals as representative of something larger. A stable social system, perhaps because of changes in its physical environment, an invention, or a change in its relationships with neighboring societies, can become unstable. *A social system can change its form.* This temporal process involving change of form is evolution. Most anthropologists are interested in change in form rather than change in personnel.

For those who have studied history in high school and primary school the contrast should be easy to understand: learning history involved memorizing names and dates. The emphasis was on individuals as individuals. Of course, some major changes in social or governmental form were also mentioned — the French and the American revolutions, for example. Obviously, archeologists cannot study changes in personnel in prehistoric societies, for it is usually impossible to identify specific individuals who lived at a given site. Similarly, biological anthropologists, who study human evolution through the fossils of our remote ancestors, cannot concern themselves with changes in personnel, even if they want to.

The distinction drawn here between personnel change and change in social form does not necessarily reflect a distinction between professors of history and those of anthropology. Many historians are principally interested in changes in social form and often call themselves macrohistorians or social historians. Their work parallels that of anthropologists.

SUMMARY

Anthropology, the study of human biological and cultural similarities and differences in time and space, is a uniquely holistic discipline. Culture, which is transmitted through learning and social life rather than through biological inheritance, is a major reason for human adaptability and success. Culture rests on the universal human capacity to think symbolically — arbitrarily to bestow meaning on a thing or an event. A symbol is something that arbitrarily stands for something else and that has a particular meaning or value to participants in the same cultural tradition. Some anthropologists adopt an emic research strategy, studying native viewpoints and accepting informants' opinions about what things are or are not significant within a given culture. Some other anthropologists pursue etic research strategies; they give less weight to informants' criteria of significance and more to those of the trained, and presumably more impartial, scientific observer.

Anthropology finds no evidence that genetic differences can explain cultural variation. Adopting a broad comparative perspective, anthropology examines biological, psychological, social, and cultural universals and generalities — as well as unique and distinctive aspects of the human condition. In its consideration of varied cultural elaborations on the fundamental biological plasticity of *Homo sapiens,* anthropology has come to demonstrate that American cultural traditions are no more proper or natural than any others.

Anthropologists share a common interest in origins of and changes in aspects of the human condition. Among their concerns are the origin of humankind from subhuman primate ancestry and the major changes in biology and culture glimpsed through the fossil record; the origin and evolution of food production out of foraging economies; the origin and differentiation of groups of related languages; variations in speech patterns over short time spans; the origin and evolution of distinctive cultures and the impact on them of changes in world power relationships.

All four subdisciplines of general anthropology — sociocultural, biological, and archeological anthropology, and anthropological linguistics — share a common interest in variation in time and space. All study evolution: change in form over generations. All are concerned with identifying and explaining universal, generalized, and distinctive aspects of the human condition. Sociocultural anthropology examines the diversity of the present and very recent past. Archeological anthropology approaches the diversity of the past by reconstructing social, economic, religious, and political patterns of prehistoric populations. Biological anthropology relates biological diversity in time and space to variation in environment — through study of fossils, human genetics, human biological plasticity, and nonhuman primates. Anthropological linguistics documents diversity among contemporary languages and studies ways in which speech habits change in different social situations and over time spans of various lengths.

A concern with the past and present — with biology, society, culture, and language—links anthropology to other sciences. Sociocultural anthropology is closely related to sociology; the principal difference has been that sociologists have studied urban and industrial populations, while anthropologists have studied rural, non-Western peoples. Economics and politics are also of interest to anthropologists, who bring a comparative perspective to these domains of Western society. Anthropologists often study art, music, and oral literature, but their concern is with the esthetic expressions of common people rather than with art commissioned and appreciated mainly by elites. Anthropologists view creators and their products in their social context. In the study of culture and personality, which attempts to relate personality structure to social and cultural variables, anthropology and psychology have a common interest. By introducing a comparative dimension, anthropology is able to broaden understanding of this field. Like historians, anthropologists study the past, although they often deal with a more remote past and are less concerned with individuals and individual events than with major changes in forms of human adaptations and social institutions.

SOURCES AND SUGGESTED READINGS

ARDREY, R.
  1961   *African Genesis.* New York: Atheneum. Playwright Ardrey interprets the early human fossil record in terms of the street gang conflict in *West Side Story;* trendsetting popular work linking human behavior to biology and our animal heritage.

  1966   *The Territorial Imperative.* New York: Atheneum. Ardrey's second attempt to link human behavior (defense of property) to genes that we supposedly share with other animals.

  1970   *The Social Contract.* New York: Atheneum. Here Ardrey suggests a biological basis for social inequality.

  1976   *The Hunting Hypothesis.* New York: Atheneum. How the genes of our hunting ancestors influence our everyday lives today.

ARENS, W.
  1976   Professional Football: An American Symbol and Ritual. In *The American Dimension: Cultural Myths and Social Realities,* ed. W. Arens and S. P. Montague, pp. 3–14. Port Washington, N.Y.: Alfred.

BAAL, J. VAN
  1966   *Dema: Description and Analysis of Marind-anim Culture (South New Guinea).* The Hague: M. Nijhoff. Field study of homosexual tribe in New Guinea.

FREUD, S.
  1950   (orig. 1918). *Totem and Taboo,* trans. J. Strachey. New York: W. W. Norton. Speculative account of the origin of the Oedipus complex, which Freud believed to be a human universal.

FRIED, M. H.
  1972   *The Study of Anthropology.* New York: Crowell. Anthropology as a field, and anthropologists as teachers and researchers; intended for college students.

GEERTZ, C.
  1973   *The Interpretation of Culture.* New York: Basic Books. In a series of essays, a prominent contemporary anthropologist examines the nature of culture and cultural diversity.

KELLY, R. C.
  1976   Witchcraft and Sexual Relations: An Exploration in the Social and Semantic Implications of the Structure of Belief. In *Man and Woman in the New Guinea Highlands,* ed. P. Brown and G. Buchbinder, pp. 36–53. Special Publication No. 8. Washington, D.C.: American Anthropological Association. Links homosexual behavior among the Etoro of New Guinea to an elaborate set of beliefs about birth, growth, parenthood, senility, and death.

LINDEN, E.
  1974   *Apes, Men, and Language.* New York: Penguin. Fascinating popular account of recent evidence for chimpanzee linguistic abilities; discusses language-using chimpanzees and their human teachers.

LINDENBAUM, S.
  1972   Sorcerers, Ghosts, and Polluting Women: An Analysis of Religious Belief and Population Control. *Ethnology* 11: 241–253.

Links antagonism between the sexes to population density in the New Guinea highlands.

LORENZ, K.
1966   *On Aggression.* New York: Bantam. In this popular work a prominent ethnologist, citing studies of other animals, argues that human aggression is universal and genetically based.

MALINOWSKI, B.
1927   *Sex and Repression in Savage Society.* London and New York: International Library of Psychology, Philosophy and Scientific Method. Examination of a society with no Oedipus complex.

MEAD, M.
1928   *Coming of Age in Samoa.* New York: Morrow. Field study of Samoan female adolescence.

1930   *Growing Up in New Guinea.* New York: Blue Ribbon. Enculturation in the South Pacific.

1935   *Sex and Temperament in Three Primitive Societies.* New York: Morrow. Sex-role differences in three New Guinea societies.

MORRIS, D.
1967   *The Naked Ape.* London: Jonathan Cape. Writing for a lay audience, a zoologist focuses on behavior in the United States of the sixties to illustrate humans' animal heritage.

1969   *The Human Zoo.* London: Jonathan Cape. A host of contemporary social ills are attributed to overcrowding, as in experiments with rats.

NANCE, J.
1975   *The Gentle Tasaday: A Stone Age People in the Philippine Rain Forest.* New York: Harcourt Brace Jovanovich. Popular account of recently contacted population of foragers in the Philippines.

SELBY, H. A.
1975   *Social Organization: Symbol, Structure, and Setting.* Dubuque, Iowa: Wm. C. Brown. A brief introduction to the anthropological study of kinship and other principles that organize human society.

TIGER, L.
1969   *Men in Groups.* New York: Random House. The sociability of males—here seen as greater than that of females—is linked to human biology.

TYLOR, E. B.
1958   (orig. 1871). *Primitive Culture.* New York: Harper Torchbooks. Classic early statement of anthropology's subject matter; argues for scientific study of culture.

WAGLEY, C.
1969   (orig. 1951). Cultural Influences on Population: A Comparison of Two Tupi Tribes. In *Environment and Cultural Behavior,* ed. A. P. Vayda, pp. 268–279. Garden City, N. Y.: The Natural History Press. Supernatural sanctions are important in the population policy of the Tapirape, one of the two tribes discussed.

WHITE, L. A.
1959   *The Evolution of Culture: The Development of Civilization to the Fall of Rome.* New York: McGraw-Hill. Modern classic; stresses critical significance of symbolic thought in distinguishing humans from beasts.

BIOLOGY and BEHAVIOR
as ADAPTIVE MEANS

Primate Behavior and Social Life

2

EVOLUTION

During the seventeenth, eighteenth, and nineteenth centuries, natural scientists were concerned with classifying the array of plant and animal species found on earth and explaining the origins of the diverse genera and species. The commonly accepted explanation for the origin of species was the one outlined in Genesis, that God created the species during the original six days of Creation. During the seventeenth and eighteenth centuries, Biblical scholars James Ussher and John Lightfoot, through calculations based on genealogies included in the Bible, purported to trace Creation to the year 4004 B.C., specifically to October twenty-third of that year, at nine o'clock in the morning. The belief was that God had created the animals and plants found on earth in a series of individual acts.

One who accepted the Biblical account of Creation was Carolus Linnaeus (1707–1778), who developed the first comprehensive taxonomy for categorizing living plants and animals. He grouped living things on the basis of similarities and differences in their overall physical characteristics. He used such structural traits as the presence of a backbone to distinguish vertebrates from invertebrates, and the presence of mammary glands to distinguish mammals from such other categories as birds. Linnaeus viewed the differences between contemporary life forms as structural details in the Creator's orderly plan. Differences between life forms were established at Creation and did not reflect different degrees of genetic relationship. As such, they were immutable—set once and for all, they could not change.

Linnaean classification is still used by scientists today. However, in contrast to Linnaeus, contemporary scholars see an evolutionary basis for taxonomy. Animals included within any category are assumed to be more closely related to one another than to any animal outside that category. The similarities that lead to their common taxonomic placement rest on their more recent common ancestry.

The Biblical doctrine of *creationism* was placed in some doubt as important fossil discoveries were made during the eighteenth and nineteenth centuries. The fossil evidence demonstrated that forms of plant and animal life no longer found on earth had existed in the past. How were the absence of past species on earth now and the absence of contemporary species from the fossil record to be explained?

A modified explanatory framework combining creationism with *catastrophism* soon arose to replace the original doctrine. The catatrophists interpreted the fossil record by arguing that many of the species that had once lived had been obliterated from the face of the earth as a result of major catastrophes — fires and floods, for example. The French natural scientist Georges Cuvier (1769–1832), the principal proponent of catastrophism, argued that the Biblical flood involving Noah's ark was merely the last of these cataclysms. Following such destructive events, God embarked on new creative enterprises, bringing into existence the species of plants and animals now found on earth. However, to explain similarities between fossil and modern animals, Cuvier and other catastrophists recognized that some species had managed to survive. Noah's two of each kind, for example, later spread out, migrating to other parts of the world from the isolated areas where they had been able to avoid extinction.

The alternative to creationism and catastrophism was *transformism,* also called evolution. Transformists held that over the course of time species had arisen gradually from others through a process of transformation, or descent with modification. Charles Darwin has become the best known of the transformists, but he was influenced by earlier scholars, including his own grandfather, Erasmus Darwin, who, in a book called *Zoonomia,* published in 1794, had argued for an ultimate relationship of common descent among all animal species. Charles Darwin was also influenced by Sir Charles Lyell, generally considered the father of geology. During his famous voyage to South America aboard the *Beagle,* Darwin read Lyell's controversial book *Principles of Geology,* which exposed him to Lyell's principle of *uniformitarianism.*

According to uniformitarianism, the present is the key to the past: the explanations for past events should be sought in factors that continue to work today. In his book Lyell argued that geological formations such as mountain ranges had been caused by the same natural forces that work in the modern world — rainfall, soil deposition, and earthquakes, for example. Lyell asserted that the earth's physical structure was gradually transformed through the operation of natural forces.

Lyell's uniformitarianism became a vital building block in the development of evolutionary theory. It cast serious doubt on James Ussher's Bible-based calculation of the age of the world. For such natural forces as rain and wind to have produced major geological features, the world would have to have come into existence long before 4004 B.C. The longer time span required by Lyell's theory also provided sufficient time for major changes in life forms — such as those being revealed by fossil discoveries during the eighteenth and nineteenth centuries — to have occurred. Darwin, on the basis of these implications of Lyell's work, applied transformism through natural forces to living things.

Like other transformists, Darwin argued that all life forms were ultimately related. Differences between contemporary species, said Darwin, have arisen gradually as a result of modification and branching out of ancestral forms. In contrast to proponents of divine creation, Darwin argued that the number of species is not immutable, and has, in fact, increased over time. To explain this process of descent with modification, Darwin developed the doctrine of *natural selection* as a single principle capable of explaining the origin of species, biological diversity, and similarities among related life forms. Charles Darwin's major contribution was not therefore, transformism or the theory of evolution. Rather, it was his postulation of natural selection to explain evolutionary change in life forms.

Natural selection was not Darwin's unique discovery. Working simultaneously, naturalist Alfred Russel Wallace had reached essentially the same conclusion about how biological change occurs. In a joint paper read to the Linnaean Society in 1858, Darwin and Wallace made their discovery public. Darwin's book, *On the Origin of Species,* published in 1859, offered fuller documentation, but engendered great controversy. Essential to the doctrine of evolution through natural selection is the assumption that nature selects the forms most fit to survive and reproduce in a given environment. Darwin postulated that for natural selection to operate on a particular population, there must be variety within it, as there always is.

Natural selection would operate, argued Darwin, in situations where competition for resources strategic to life, such as food or space, existed among members of a population. Darwin was acquainted with the work of Thomas Malthus, an English economist and social theorist who, in his famous "Essay on the Principles of Population," had argued that competition was the natural result of a universal tendency for populations to increase faster than their food supply. Malthus intended his essay to apply principally to human populations. He saw such stresses as war, disease, and other means of limiting or reducing population as fundamental to human life. Darwin extended this struggle for existence to the entire biological realm. In a situation of competition, those individuals whose attributes render them most fit to survive and reproduce in their environment will, in fact, survive and reproduce in greater numbers than others. Over the years, the less fit individuals gradually will die off, and the favored ones will survive.

Darwin recognized that, for natural selection to operate, there must be variety in the population undergoing selection. Documentation of variation is a major concern of modern anthropology; more important, however, is the *explanation* of variability. Genetics, a science that grew up after Darwin's work, is responsible for much of our knowledge of the hereditary causes of variation within populations. We now know that several kinds of biochemical changes (mutations) in the DNA (deoxyribonucleic acid) molecules that compose the genes and chromosomes—the hereditary material—represent the principal source of variety on which natural selection operates. Over millions of years, natural selective forces associated with particular environments have worked on genetic variety to produce differences between humans and our nearest relatives—the great apes.

THE PRIMATE ORDER

Similarities between humans and apes are obvious in their anatomies, DNA, brain structure, and body chemistry, including protein construction and reactions to disease. These resemblances are recognized in *zoological taxonomy*, the assignment of organisms to categories (*taxa;* singular, *taxon*). Figure 2.1 demonstrates that humans and apes are included in the same zoological superfamily, *Hominoidea,* whereas monkeys are assigned to two others. Thus, humans and apes are more closely related to each other than either are to monkeys.

The systematic classification of life forms dates to the eighteenth century and Carolus Linnaeus. As noted, Linnaeus thought that similarities between species reflected not their common evolutionary development out of a single ancestral population (their *phylogeny,* or *phylogenetic relationship*), but an orderly structural plan devised by the Creator. On the basis of structural resemblances, many of which we now know to reflect degrees of phylogenetic relationship, Linnaeus assigned a group of formally similar species to the same *genus* (plural, *genera*); structurally similar genera to the same *family;* similar families to the same *superfamily;* similar superfamilies to the same *suborder;* similar suborders to the same *order;* similar orders to the same *class;* and similar classes to the same *kingdom.* The highest taxonomic distinction is the kingdom; at that level animals are distinguished from plants.

Modern biology uses a modified version of Linnaean classification and recognizes that the similarities and differences indicated in taxonomy are generally based on different degrees of phylogenetic relationship. The species placed in the same genus, for example, are the diversified descendants of one former species; the same applies to the genera included within the same family and the families included in the same superfamily, but the common ancestral species lived in the ever more distant past. The lowest level taxa in zoological taxonomy are species and subspecies. A species is a population whose members are capable of interbreeding and producing viable and fertile offspring whose own offspring will be viable and fertile. Speciation occurs when—after a sufficient period of reproductive isolation—subpopulations that once belonged to the same species can no longer interbreed. When this occurs, two closely related species, assigned to the same genus, will have evolved out of one. At the very lowest level of zoological taxonomy, a species may be divided into subspecies—its more or less, but not yet totally, isolated subpopulations.

The similarities that permit two or more taxa to be assigned to the same higher-level taxon are *homolo-*

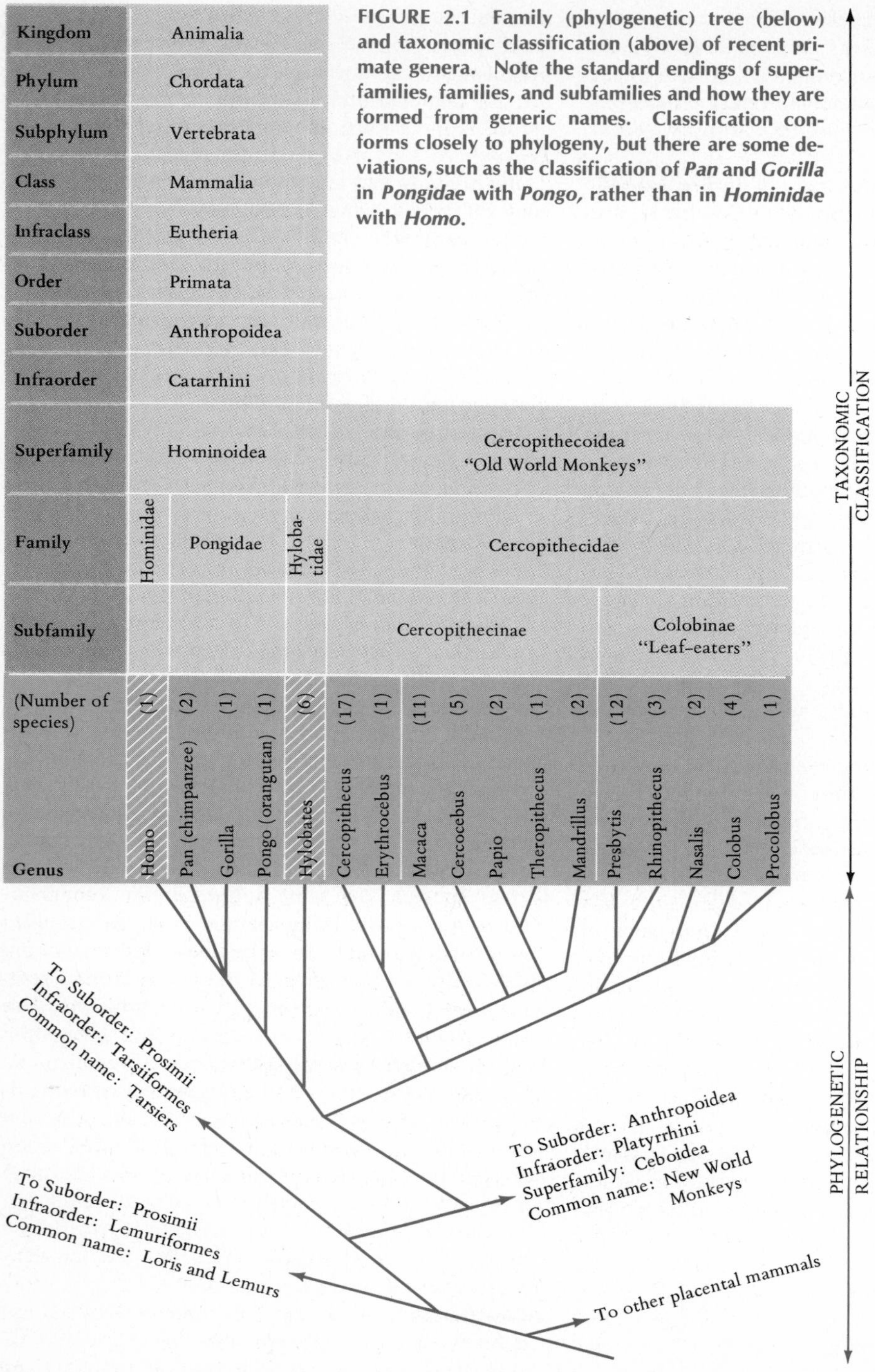

FIGURE 2.1 Family (phylogenetic) tree (below) and taxonomic classification (above) of recent primate genera. Note the standard endings of superfamilies, families, and subfamilies and how they are formed from generic names. Classification conforms closely to phylogeny, but there are some deviations, such as the classification of *Pan* and *Gorilla* in *Pongidae* with *Pongo,* rather than in *Hominidae* with *Homo.*

Kingdom	Animalia	
Phylum	Chordata	
Subphylum	Vertebrata	
Class	Mammalia	
Infraclass	Eutheria	
Order	Primata	
Suborder	Anthropoidea	
Infraorder	Catarrhini	
Superfamily	Hominoidea	Cercopithecoidea "Old World Monkeys"
Family	Hominidae / Pongidae / Hylobatidae	Cercopithecidae
Subfamily		Cercopithecinae / Colobinae "Leaf-eaters"

Number of species / Genus:

- (1) Homo
- (2) Pan (chimpanzee)
- (1) Gorilla
- (1) Pongo (orangutan)
- (6) Hylobates
- (17) Cercopithecus
- (1) Erythrocebus
- (11) Macaca
- (5) Cercocebus
- (2) Papio
- (1) Theropithecus
- (2) Mandrillus
- (12) Presbytis
- (3) Rhinopithecus
- (2) Nasalis
- (4) Colobus
- (1) Procolobus

TAXONOMIC CLASSIFICATION

PHYLOGENETIC RELATIONSHIP

To Suborder: Prosimii
Infraorder: Tarsiiformes
Common name: Tarsiers

To Suborder: Anthropoidea
Infraorder: Platyrrhini
Superfamily: Ceboidea
Common name: New World Monkeys

To Suborder: Prosimii
Infraorder: Lemuriformes
Common name: Loris and Lemurs

To other placental mammals

gies, traits they have jointly inherited from their common ancestral species. Figure 2.1 shows the place of humans in zoological taxonomy and our relative structural, biochemical, and phylogenetic relationships to other animals. *Homo sapiens,* like many other species, is a member of the class *Mammalia,* one of the major subdivisions of the kingdom *Animalia.* All mammals share certain structural traits, including mammary glands, that set them apart from members of other classes of *Animalia* (for instance, birds, reptiles, amphibians). These structural traits rest on the distinct common ancestries of mammals versus, say, birds. Below the level of class, humans are assigned to the zoological order *Primata.* All primates share certain structural and biochemical resemblances that set them apart from members of such other mammalian orders as *Carnivoria* (dogs, cats, foxes, wolves, badgers, weasels) and *Rodentia* (rats, mice, beavers, squirrels). The resemblances that primates share are homologies that they have inherited from the common early primate ancestors after they had become reproductively isolated from the ancestors of the rodents and the carnivores.

HOMOLOGIES AND ANALOGIES

The larger question in a discussion of taxonomy is: Why do similarities in biology or behavior exist among members of different species? Different taxa are assigned to the same higher-level taxon on the basis of similarities called homologies: traits inherited by members of lower-level taxa from their common ancestor. For example, similarities in the genetic codes and body chemistry of apes and humans are some of the homologies that confirm our common ancestry and lead to our joint classification as hominoids. Still other kinds of similarities between species are *analogies:* traits that have evolved independently in two or more distantly related species because the natural selective forces associated with their environments were similar and produced equivalent adaptive responses. The process whereby analogies are produced is known as *convergence,* or *convergent evolution.* Similarities between fish and dolphins illustrate convergent evolution. In adapting to an aquatic ecological niche, dolphins, which are mammals, have developed many similarities (analogies) with fish, including such anatomical characteristics as hairlessness, fins, and streamlining for efficient locomotion in the water.

Certain analogies (wings, small size, light bones) between birds and bats also illustrate convergent evolution in an airborne ecological niche.

It is possible for similarities to be both homologies *and* analogies. This occurs when two or more closely related groups adapt to similar environments. Because the natural selective forces to which they must adapt are similar, they retain many of the traits they have inherited from their common ancestor. Because they are biologically close to begin with, they are also likely to change in similar, or parallel, ways. The process whereby closely related groups develop or retain the same traits or modify their traits in similar directions is known as *parallelism,* or *parallel evolution.*

In theory, only homologies should be used as a basis for zoological classification, but in practice, especially if there is doubt about whether structural resemblances reflect common ancestry rather than convergence or parallelism, analogies sometimes influence zoological classification. For example, consider how the *Hominoidea,* the superfamily that includes humans and apes, is divided into lower-level taxa. *Hominoidea* includes three families; *Hominidea* and *Pongidae* are two of them. There is no doubt that humans, gorillas, and chimpanzees are more closely related to one another than any of the three is to orangutans, Asiatic apes. Since humans, chimps, and gorillas share a more recent common ancestor than they do with orangutans, their phylogeny suggests that they should be assigned to a single taxon distinct from orangutans. Accordingly, a few scientists do assign gorillas, chimps, and humans to *Hominidae.* However, on the basis of structural analogies between gorillas, chimpanzees, and orangutans — reflecting convergent evolution — other taxonomists place orangutans, along with chimpanzees and gorillas, in a great ape family (*Pongidae*) and make humans the exclusive occupants of the category *Hominidae.* Here, analogy rather than homology determines zoological classification. A third family of *Hominoidea* consists of gibbons and siamangs, small arboreal (tree-living) apes of Asia.

PRIMATE TENDENCIES

Most scholars agree that it is difficult to point to a single feature that distinguishes the primates from other zoological orders like insectivores and carnivores, whose dietary specializations justify their

The South American marmoset, which normally gives birth to twins, is an exception to the primate tendency toward single births. Here, a male marmoset is shown with its two offspring. (San Diego Zoo)

zoological classifications. Primates have adapted to a variety of ecological niches. Some primates are active during the day, others at night, others at twilight. Primates display a host of dietary combinations and specializations: some eat mainly insects, others mainly fruits, others mainly bulk vegetation, others mainly seeds or roots; and still others are best described as omnivorous. Some are *terrestrial:* they spend all their time on the ground. Others are totally arboreal; and there are intermediate adaptations. All primates, however, share an ancestral arboreal heritage that, subsequent specializations aside, explains certain similarities present in varying degrees among most, if not all, primates.

Trends in primate evolution can be identified. Many of them are most clearly exemplified by the anthropid primates—monkeys, apes, and humans—which belong to the primate suborder *Anthropoidea.* The other primate suborder, *Prosimii,* in-

cludes lemurs, loris, and tarsiers—the prosimian primates.

1. Grasping Adaptation. Recalling the arboreal niches of the remote ancestors of all primates are features of the hands and feet that reflect adaptation to arboreal movement by grasping. Primates retain the primitive five-digited hand/foot anatomy of the earliest mammals. Primates' ecological niches have selected for neither hooves nor fins. Many primates (the reader included) have opposable thumbs; the thumb can touch all the other digits on that hand. Many primates also have grasping feet, some with a tendency toward opposable big toes. Hominids, in adapting to upright bipedalism, eliminated most of the foot's potentiality as a grasping organ. Any reader who is turning the pages of this book with one foot while smoking a cigarette with the other is unlikely to be a hominid. Mobility of the digits of both hands and feet—needed to encircle and grasp branches—was an important part of the early primates' arboreal adaptation. Scholars have also speculated that thumb opposability and the resulting *precision grip* (grasping an object between index finger and thumb) may have been selectively favored by inclusion of insects in the early primate diet. These features would certainly aid the capture of insects attracted to the abundant flowers and fruits of an arboreal environment.

2. Olfactory to Visual Shift. Several changes in anatomy reflect a shift from smell to sight as primates' major means of gaining information vital to adaptation and survival. The anthropoid primates in particular have depth and color vision. The portion of the brain devoted to vision expands, while the olfactory region of the brain is reduced.

3. Nose to Hand Shift. Information is also conveyed by touch, through an organism's tactile organs. Both cats and dogs have moist tactile skin on their noses that transmits information. Cats also have tactile hairs—whiskers—that perform this function, too. In primates, the sense of touch shifts from the face to the hands—the sensitive pads of the "fingerprint" region of the fingers.

4. Brain Complexity. Among the primates, the proportion of brain tissue concerned with memory, reflection, and association increases. The ratio of brain size to body size also exceeds that of most other mammals.

5. Litter Size. Most primates give birth to a single offspring rather than to a litter. Young primates thus receive more individual attention and have more learning opportunities than do other mammals. Learned behavior becomes a vital part of primate adaptation.

6. *Social Groups.* Many primates are social animals, living with other members of their species. Longer and more attentive child care places a selective value on social relations — support by other members of a primate's social group.

Studies of primate behavior and social life have become especially popular since the late 1950s, when primatologists, following the example of the ethnographer, began to study their subjects in the field — in natural settings — rather than in zoos. Behavioral primatologists have tremendously increased our knowledge of the societies and habits of our closest relatives, and they have corrected some misleading impressions about the nature of primate society that were based on observations of primates in zoos.

SIMILARITIES BETWEEN HUMANS AND OTHER PRIMATES

Anthropologists have commonly stressed the differences, rather than the similarities, between subhuman primates and humans. There are differences, to be sure, but studies of primate behavior under a variety of conditions are making it increasingly clear that the similarities are more extensive than was once supposed. Formerly, it was argued that our reliance on learned behavior rather than instinct made us distinct from all other animals. We now know that other primates, especially monkeys and apes, also rely a great deal on learned behavior. The differences between humans and subhuman primates are differences in degree rather than kind; that is, they are quantitative rather than qualitative. Humans rely on learned behavior as a principal means of adapting to their environments. Monkeys and apes also rely on learned behavior, but more of their adaptive behavior appears to be genetically programmed. Both chimpanzees and humans make tools, but human reliance on tools is much more complete and pervasive. Because humans rely more on tools and learned behavior than do other primates, they have been successful in terms of reproduction (there are more humans than any other primate) and the range of environments they inhabit and exploit. Let us consider some of the major similarities between humans and their nearest relatives.

Tools

Anthropologists have traditionally distinguished humans from other animals by calling us "tool-using" animals. It is certainly true that *Homo* employs tools far more extensively than any other animal and that the tool kit of no other animal rivals our in complexity. However, it is now apparent that tool use is a basic part of the adaptive kits of several nonhuman species. In the Galapagos Islands, located off western South America, lives a woodpecker finch that regularly uses, and sometimes chooses between, cactus spines and twigs to ferret out insects or grubs from their holes beneath the bark of trees. Sea otters use rocks to break open mollusks, which form an important part of their diets. American beavers are famous for their abilities in construction. Recognizing that people are not the only tool-using animals, anthropologists have argued more recently that only humans manufacture tools with foresight, that is, with a specific end in mind. However, even this qualitative distinction between ourselves and other animals can be challenged.

Our knowledge of the behavior of chimpanzees in their natural setting has been increased tremen-

In the Galapagos Islands, the woodpecker finch uses cactus spines and twigs to ferret out insects. Not just tool use, but tool manufacture, is a hominoid ability and was basic to development of a human way of life. (Miguel Castro/Photo Researchers, Inc.)

Two Gombe chimpanzees, named Fifi and Flo by Jane Goodall, are using primitive tools—specially prepared twigs—to obtain a termite dinner. (© National Geographic Society)

dously by the field research of Jane Goodall (1968a), who since 1960 has observed free-ranging chimpanzees in the Gombe Stream National Park in Tanzania, East Africa. It is now clear that chimpanzees, more than any other ape, share our tendency toward deliberate tool manufacture. In *Homo,* of course, the tendency is fully developed, whereas among chimps, one of our closest relatives, it is expressed only in rudimentary form. Nevertheless, there are several examples of tool manufacture by chimps in their natural settings. Faced with the problem of obtaining water from sources that they cannot easily reach with their mouths, thirsty chimps have been observed to pick leaves, chew and crumple them, and then dip them into the water. They have, with a specific end in mind, devised primitive containers—chimpanzee "sponges." Even more impressive than the manufacture of these primitive sponges is chimpanzee behavior in catching termites. Chimps have been observed manufacturing tools to probe termite hills, or nests. They choose twigs appropriate for termiting and modify them by removing the leaves and peeling off the bark so as to expose the sticky surface beneath. They then carry them to the termite holes, make holes in them with their fingers, and insert the twigs. When

they remove the twigs they eat the termites that have been attracted to the sticky surface.

Chimps have also been seen using sticks for prying, crumpling leaves to make "toilet paper," and aiming and throwing stones and other objects. One can probably regard this aiming as a behavioral carryover from the common ancestor of chimpanzees and people. However, in our case this behavior has been considerably elaborated, serving as a basis for projectile technology and weaponry.

Among nonhuman primates, chimpanzees are by far the most proficient tool makers. Although other apes, including the gorilla, build nests and under certain conditions throw branches, grass, vines, and other objects, none that we know of now approaches the tool-making ability of the chimp. Moreover, when chimpanzees are removed from their natural habitats and trained by humans, their manipulatory skills flower, as anyone who has ever seen movie, circus, or zoo chimps knows.

Communication Systems

Like deliberate tool manufacture, language has been cited by many students of human behavior as one of the distinctive attributes of human beings. It is true that only humans speak languages, but evidence is accumulating that our linguistic ability, like our tool-manufacturing ability, is quantitatively rather than qualitatively different from that of other primates, especially the great apes.

Among no other living animal population has anything approaching the complexity of human languages evolved. Yet observations of the natural communication systems of chimpanzees and other primates (call systems) are revealing a far greater complexity in verbal signals than was once supposed. Furthermore, while no nonhuman primate has been taught to speak a human language, recent research has shown that gorillas and chimpanzees have the ability to understand and to manipulate nonverbal symbols based on human language. In other words, current research on communication systems is confirming once again that other hominoids are more similar to people than was once supposed. Chimpanzees and gorillas share with us, apparently through genetic inheritance from our common ancestor, a tendency toward linguistic ability, toward complex communication systems. Among wild apes the tendency has just not been elaborated into true language.

Because of the obvious similarities that apes share with us, could they be taught to speak? Prior to the 1960s experiments seemed to suggest that apes lacked linguistic abilities. In the 1950s a couple raised a chimpanzee, Viki, from infancy as a member of their family, and although they made a great effort to teach her to speak, Viki was able to learn only three words. In an early–twentieth-century experiment an orangutan had managed only two words. The human vocal apparatus permits us to talk, but the apparatus of other primates apparently denies this capacity to them.

After several years of research, Goodall and her associates at the Gombe National Park have demonstrated that wild chimpanzees communicate in a natural setting through a combination of gestures and a large number of distinct calls. Goodall has identified at least twenty-five acoustically distinct calls used by Gombe chimps; each of the twenty-five carried a distinct meaning and was evoked in certain broad situations. Goodall also noted that chimpanzees, like other primates, including people, communicate through a rich array of facial expressions, noises, and bodily movements.

Other apes and monkeys also have call systems; they seem to communicate through a limited number of acoustically distinct calls evoked by environmental stimuli. The calls convey discrete messages to *conspecifics* — other members of the primate's species. It is difficult to identify the extent to which nonhuman primate calls are instinctive or learned. Many of them — for example, those uttered by monkeys when threatening conspecifics and those emitted by gibbons in situations of danger — may vary in intensity. Variation in intensity, duration, and repetition of a given call increases the amount of information conveyed to conspecifics about the environmental stimulus.

Primate calls may reflect socialization as well as genetic predisposition. That some learning is involved is suggested by the fact that primates raised apart from conspecifics do not automatically emit all the calls characteristic of their natural communication systems. This is similar to findings in laboratory experiments that such aspects of monkey (rhesus macaque) social behavior as sexual intercourse and the formation of dominance relationships depend not only on biology but also on social interaction.

Regardless of whether the genetic or learning component is greater in call systems, calls are far less flexible than language because calls are automatic and discrete, that is, they cannot be combined. When nonhuman primates encounter two environmental stimuli simultaneously — for example, food and danger — for which calls are available, they will choose only one call. They cannot combine the calls for food and danger into a single call signifying that both food and danger are present. If by chance they did, the message would probably not be understood by the primate's conspecifics. At some point in the evolutionary line leading to humans, however, such call combinations began to take place and to be understood. It is likely that there was also an expansion in the number of calls; the number of meaningful verbal forms uttered and understood has increased throughout human evolution. Eventually, the number of calls became far too great to be transmitted even in part genetically, and the ability to communicate became almost totally a function of learning. Still a subject for speculation is the matter of when in human evolution this shift occurred.

Wild apes' and monkeys' communication may be based on call systems, but recent experiments in which humans have raised apes show that chimpanzees and gorillas can learn to use, though not to speak, true language. Experiments with young apes since 1966 have produced startling evidence contradicting traditional notions of humans' unique linguistic capabilities. Several young apes have learned to converse with humans. This has been accomplished through a variety of media other than speech, which, because of apes' vocal apparatus, will continue to elude them. A few chimpanzees have been taught to use American Sign Language, Ameslan, the most widespread system of communication used by deaf Americans. Like English or any spoken language, Ameslan exhibits a feature that linguists consider essential to language: *duality of patterning*. Any language has two structures: a phonological structure—the sound system; and a grammar, or formal structure—a system of verbal forms with meaning. Our ability to connect phonology and grammar is learned, not instinctive. In the phonological system are a limited number of sounds that lack meaning by themselves but that distinguish between meaningful units. Consider the English words "pit" and "bit." They vary only in their initial sounds, *p* and *b*. Neither *p* nor *b* has meaning in itself, but preceding the sound represented by *-it*, they serve to differentiate meaning, to keep meanings distinct. Within the second structure, the grammar, or formal system, are the words and other verbal forms that carry meaning by themselves. "Pit" and "bit" are verbal forms that designate things and events in the real world. They are meaningful forms composed of certain conventional arrangements of sounds. Similarly, with Ameslan a limited number of rudimentary gesture units, analogous to the sounds in the phonological system, combine to form words and other larger units with meaning in themselves, and these words can be strung together in sentences.

The first chimpanzee to be taught Ameslan was Washoe, a female. Captured in the wild in West Africa, Washoe was turned over to R. Allen Gardner and Beatrice Gardner, scientists at the University of Nevada in Reno, in 1966, when she was about a year old. She now lives near Norman, Oklahoma, on a farm that has been converted by its owner, psychologist William Lemmon, into the Institute for Primate Studies. Washoe's learning experiences during her early years at Reno have revolutionized our understanding of the language-learning abilities of apes. Under the care of the Gardners and their former research assistant, Roger Fouts, who now works with Washoe and other chimps in Oklahoma, Washoe lived in a trailer and was isolated from spoken language. The Gardners and their associates always used Ameslan when communicating with one another in Washoe's presence. Washoe gradually learned to distinguish between more than two hundred Ameslan gestures representing English words. Even more impressive than Washoe's vocabulary, which is, of course, far more extensive than that of her cousins in the wild, is the fact that when she was two years old, she independently began to combine the different signs she had learned into rudimentary sentences such as "Give me water." Washoe then learned to combine as many as four symbols into sentences or statements. At first it seemed that Washoe demonstrated no notion of grammar; during her first few years of learning Ameslan, she seemed to arrange her gestures at random: she might as easily say "The table is on the book" as "The book is on the table." However, more recent experiments with other Ameslan-using chimps, along with Washoe's subsequent progress, have demonstrated the ability among chimps to distinguish between subject and object and to converse grammatically.

Lucy, Washoe's junior by one year, has shown an even greater language-learning ability. Lucy has been raised by human foster parents Maurice and Jane Temerlin and foster brother Steve Temerlin since she was two days old in the Temerlins' home near Norman, Oklahoma. The house has been furnished with a rambunctious and inquisitive chimpanzee "daughter" in mind. When the Temerlins are home, Lucy enjoys the run of the house, even sleeping in Jane Temerlin's bedroom. When they are out, Lucy stays in specially designed indoor-outdoor quarters that include a roof playground. Fouts, who works most of the time at the nearby Institute for Primate Studies, reserves two days a week for testing and improving Lucy's knowledge of Ameslan. During the rest of the week, Lucy uses the language to converse with her foster parents. Lucy began to learn Ameslan at six years and has now mastered more than one hundred words. Lucy has learned Ameslan's grammar even more rapidly than Washoe did. Washoe and Lucy, since acquiring language, have revealed a number of remarkably human characteristics: swearing, joking, telling lies, and trying to impart their language to others. When irritated, Washoe has referred to a macaque coresident and at least one human worker at the Institute for Primate Studies as "dirty monkey" and, say,

"dirty Sam." Lucy has been seen gesturing about a "dirty cat." Wrestling with Fouts, Washoe urinated on her human friend, then gestured "funny." Fouts once arrived at the Temerlins' for his session with Lucy only to find a pile of suspicious looking dung on the living room floor. When he asked the chimp what it was, she replied "dirty, dirty," her expression for excrement. Asked whose "dirty, dirty" it was, she first named a human acquaintance, Sue, and, when Fouts refused to believe her, blamed it on Fouts himself. She finally admitted that the dung was her own and apologized.

Cultural transmission, the spread and perpetuation of a communication system through learning rather than through genetics, is one of the fundamental attributes of language use, and it will be discussed further below. Both Washoe and Lucy have tried to teach Ameslan to other animals, and researchers hope that they will eventually teach it to their offspring. Washoe has taught a few meaningful gestures to other chimps at the Institute, and Lucy has been observed trying to mold the paws of her pet cat into Ameslan gestures. The Oklahoma researchers hope eventually to introduce Ally—a male chimp being raised in another Oklahoma home—to

Lucy, and other chimps to Washoe and the other Ameslan-users at the Institute for Primate Studies. On an island in the Institute's artificial lake, they plan to establish the first colony of Ameslan-using chimps and to test several attributes of language use, including its maintenance as a means of communication and its cultural transmission.

The great size and strength of gorillas render them less likely subjects of such experiments than chimpanzees. Adult male gorillas weigh 400 pounds, and even full-grown females weigh between 150 and 250 pounds. Thus psychologist Penny Patterson's work with gorillas at Stanford University seems even more daring than the chimp experiments. Patterson's five-year-old female gorilla, Koko, who presently weighs about eighty pounds, lives in a house trailer in a courtyard next to Stanford's art museum. On the basis of Patterson's reports, Koko's vocabulary is larger than any chimp's. She now regularly uses more than 250 Ameslan signs and recognizes about 400. Her Ameslan sentences also appear to be more complex than Lucy's and Washoe's. Asking, in the evening, to be let into the bedroom of her trailer home, Koko will gesture, "Penny, open key hurry bedroom"; what she is saying, when this is translated into English, is "Unlock my bedroom door and be quick about it."

Koko, Lucy, and Washoe also have demonstrated that another linguistic capacity hitherto considered confined to humans is also shared with the apes. Traditionally, the limited nature of the call systems of subhuman primates has been contrasted with the *productivity* associated with language. We are able to use the rules of sound and meaning in our language to bestow meaning arbitrarily, to create entirely new expressions. It is possible, for example, to coin the word "baboonlet" to refer to a baboon infant by borrowing from other words in which the suffix "-let" is used to designate the young of a species. Anyone who speaks English can immediately understand the meaning of the new form. However, until Koko, Washoe, and Lucy demonstrated otherwise, it was believed that no ape could duplicate such a feat. Using already familiar gestures, Lucy coined the word "drinkfruit" to name a newly discovered food source—a watermelon. Washoe, seeing a swan for the first time, created "waterbird." Koko, who knew the gestures for "finger" and "bracelet," formed "finger bracelet" when she was given a ring. Similarly, she dubbed a mask an "eye hat." The Ameslan-using apes' creativity and productivity have gone beyond combining such already familiar gestures. Washoe independently invented the Ameslan gesture for "bib" to describe her own, when even her teachers were unfamiliar with the appropriate gesture.

These experiments seem to demonstrate that chimps and gorillas have the mental capacity to communicate through language. Although, to the best of our knowledge, they have never invented such a meaningful gesture system in the wild, one such a vehicle of communication is available, they show many humanlike abilities in learning and using it.

No one will dispute that such language use by apes is a product of human intervention and teaching. These experiments have not indicated that apes can independently invent language (nor, it should be pointed out, has any human ever been faced with that task). However, like human children, young apes gradually master a fully developed language, Ameslan, and employ it productively and creatively. While no confirming data yet exist, it seems possible that apes, like humans, can transmit their language culturally. The colony of Ameslan-using gorillas planned by Patterson and the chimp colony projected for the Institute for Primate Studies will, if the personalities of the somewhat pampered apes permit, provide necessary data on cultural transmission, as will observation of how Lucy or Washoe interacts with any eventual offspring.

Researchers at the Institute for Primate Studies also plan to use their chimp colony to test whether chimps have the capacity for linguistic *displacement*. Each of the calls emitted by nonhuman primates is tied to an immediate environmental stimulus—food, danger, and so forth—and is uttered only when that stimulus is present. Humans, on the other hand, can speak of danger or food when neither is present. We need not perceive the actual referents before we emit the verbal forms. Our conversations are not bound by place; we can talk of the past, of the future; we can convey our own experiences to others and profit from theirs. Fouts plans to find out whether colony-dwelling chimps will exhibit the capacity for displacement. Both attractive and repugnant objects will be shown to one chimp, who will then be taken back to the others. Fouts will then investigate the extent and manner of transmission of information about such displaced objects.

As shown by recent work with apes, the ability to remember and to combine a large number of meaningful expressions is latent in hominoids other than humans. In the evolutionary line leading to *Homo,* a comparable latent ability was probably elaborated and eventually became the basis for language. Although differences in the verbal communication systems of contemporary human and nonhuman primates are great, they are, nevertheless, differences of degree. Human linguistic ability did not develop either spontaneously or miraculously; it emerged over millions of years of evolution, as call systems similar in many ways to those of contemporary apes were transformed, gradually, into language.

Language represented a tremendous adaptive advantage for the genus *Homo.* Along with manufacture and use of tools, language is a basic part of our nonbodily, or extrasomatic, means of adaptation. Because of language, the amount of information stored by any human group far exceeds that of any nonhuman primate group. Language is a uniquely successful vehicle of learning. Because we can speak of things and events that we have never experienced, we can anticipate responses before stimuli are encountered. Use of language increases learning ability, our uniquely developed capacity to adapt through learned behavior patterns rather than solely through biology. Adaptive change can therefore occur more rapidly in *Homo* than in the other primates because our adaptive means are more flexible.

Behavioral Adaptation to Environmental Stress: Predation and Hunting

Anthropologists commonly attribute the emergence of the earliest members of our own (hominid) zoological family to ecological differentiation, arguing that while the ancestors of the apes were adapting to a variety of forested and woodland environments, our ancestors were spending more and more of their time on the tropical savannas of the Old World. In adapting to a savanna environment, early hominids took some of their inherited hominoid tendencies — for example, learning and linguistic and tool-making abilities — and perfected them as means of survival in open country. To illustrate factors involved in producing divergent evolution between *Homo* and other anthropoids, consider contrasts between humans and terrestrial monkeys — baboons and macaques. In terms of sheer numbers and extent of geographic range, *Homo* is the most successful member of the hominoid superfamily, and baboons and macaques represent the most successful of the Old World monkeys. The expansion of all three — humans, baboons, and macaques — reflects their ability to survive away from trees and forests. However, the reasons for their success are different, as is the nature of their adaptations to terrestrial environments.

Through tightly knit, hierarchical group organization and sexual dimorphism (marked differences in the anatomies and temperaments of males and females), baboons and macaques have adapted to environments with predators. Adult males protect troop members from various threats. Among humans, whose sexual dimorphism is far less marked, adaptation to predators has involved reliance on tools and weapons.

There is a fundamental reason for these differences between humans and terrestrial monkeys. Baboons might have adapted even more successfully to terrestrial life if they had developed tool manufacture as early humans did. However, necessity is not the mother of invention; a trait does not develop merely because it is needed. The ancestral baboons were monkeys, and as such, their posture and characteristic mode of locomotion was *pronograde,* on all fours. The ancestors of humans, however, had a tendency toward *orthograde,* or upright, posture, as do chimpanzees and gorillas, who knuckle-walk when on the ground. This tendency toward upright posture, as well as tendencies toward aimed throwing and use and manufacture of tools, were favored in the savanna environment and formed the basis for *Homo*'s successful adaptation away from the trees.

Early hominid adaptation to the savanna proceeded on the basis of a number of interrelated changes in anatomy, behavior, and social organization. The process of adaptation involved long-term *positive feedback* relationships: as changes gradually occurred, they altered selective forces and mutually reinforced one another. For example, the hominoid tendency toward orthograde posture permitted the use of tools and weapons against savanna predators. Increasing reliance on tools and weapons fed back on anatomy, conferring a selective advantage on animals with more upright posture. It is thought that tools and weapons were valuable in repelling attacks by predators, but humans could also have used them as offensive weapons. Several anthropologists have speculated, in fact, that given upright posture and tool use, early hominids were becoming cooperative hunters of other savanna animals. Traditionally, the presumed importance of hunting has been used to distinguish the activities of early hominids from those of other primates.

However, as in the case of tool use and language, research among other primates is demonstrating that what was previously thought to be a difference of kind is merely a difference of degree. We now know that dietary habits of other terrestrial primates are not exclusively vegetarian, as was once thought. As early as 1959 anthropologists Sherwood Washburn and Irven DeVore observed savanna-dwelling baboons killing and eating young antelopes. Recent work among chimpanzees demonstrates that given appropriate environmental conditions, predation also occurs among even closer relatives. Several researchers have observed predation by chimpanzees, but the most detailed report has been provided by Geza Teleki (1973a), who spent twelve months in 1968 and 1969 observing predation among the chimpanzees of Gombe Stream National Park. Prior to Teleki's systematic study, Goodall and other Gombe researchers had witnessed several cases of chimpanzee predation involving a variety of small animals:

insects, birds' eggs, young bushpigs, and several kinds of monkey. During his own field work Teleki recorded thirty cases of chimpanzee predation, twelve of which resulted in a kill. He found that one kill per month was not out of line with previous estimates of the frequency of chimp predation. About a hundred kills were recorded in the decade from 1960, when Goodall first began research at Gombe.

Although in most of the cases Teleki observed, the chimps simply lunged at and seized their prey, he also witnessed more complex hunting procedures involving chasing and stalking. A chase typically involved the chimp's rapid pursuit of prey, followed by a lunge and an attempt at seizure. Stalking, however, was most similar to human hunting. Teleki and other researchers have observed groups as large as five or six chimps carefully and patiently stalking a prey animal. Teleki was unable to determine how such a hunt was coordinated. Stalking was silent, vocalization typically breaking out only when the prey was actually seized. Nor did the chimps seem to be coordinating their hunting with gestures. Seizure accomplished, the successful chimp dispatched its prey by biting or wringing its neck or by bashing its head against the ground or a tree. Occasionally infant baboons were ripped apart as two chimps seized them simultaneously. Teleki also describes how meat is divided. He found that for a few moments after the kill was made, even chimps who had not taken part in the hunt were allowed to grab some part of the carcass. Once this initial division had occurred, however, meat sharing became a more intricate process. Chimps used a variety of gestures to request meat from their fellows. Dominance did not seem to be a factor in the distribution of meat. Even the most dominant chimp at Gombe was observed requesting meat from a less dominant male. Requests were granted about one-third of the time.

The observations of Teleki, Goodall, and several others are important in revising notions of differences and similarities between humans and other primates. Coordinated hunting and meat sharing by primates, previously considered exclusively human traits, are now, like linguistic ability, tool manufacture, and reliance on learning, demonstrated to be more generalized hominoid capacities. As with the other shared tendencies, these abilities have been uniquely elaborated among humans through early hominid adaptation to savanna life.

Related to this are reports of highly aggressive interactions between gibbons in areas of Malaysia where human encroachment is gradually destroying the natural habitat of these small tree-living apes. Although the potentiality for predation may be generalized among monkeys and apes, its expression also reflects environment. Just as aggression and defense of territory among gibbons can be linked to pressure on strategic resources, so, too, is there evidence that chimpanzees are more or less predatory depending on their environment. Anthropologist Vernon Reynolds (1975), who himself did nine months of field research among wild chimps in Uganda's Budongo Forest, observed no predation in a tropical rain-forest habitat, nor did an early researcher, H. W. Nissen (1931), note such activity among woodland West African chimpanzees in Guinea. Field work even more recent than Teleki's, however, has confirmed chimpanzee predation both in woodland and forest habitats, as well as in the mixed woodland-forest-grassland setting of the Gombe Stream National Park (Teleki, 1973b). Clearly, then, the presence and degree of predation cannot be related only to type of habitat (forest, woodland, grassland, or whatever).

Populations adapt, through learned behavior and biology, not to broad environmental types, but to specific natural selective forces associated with particular environments. What specific environmental conditions might trigger predatory behavior among chimpanzees? Curiously, although chimpanzee predation observed in previous years had involved several small mammals, all the kills witnessed by Teleki were of baboons. Reynolds (1975) has focused on Teleki's report to argue that the Gombe chimps, while certainly free-ranging, are far from wild. Reynolds argues that *interspecific* (between different species) aggression, of chimpanzees against baboons, is a behavioral response to an artificial feeding situation present at Gombe just before Teleki's study. Particularly during 1967 and 1968, the Gombe researchers had attracted both chimpanzee and baboon subjects by daily banana feeding. Reynolds argues that such artificial feeding can stimulate aggressive tendencies; he had, himself, observed a consistent rise in aggressive interactions as feeding time approached for a group of thirty chimps living in an admittedly artificial environment—an Air Force base in New Mexico. Indeed, at least one incident of a chimp attack on a young baboon reported by Teleki (1973a) seems clearly related to tension surrounding the Gombe feeding situation.

Recent observations by Goodall also tend to confirm Reynolds's argument that chimp aggression and predation are related to the distribution of food and other strategic resources. Most significantly, Goodall relates *intraspecific* predation among Gombe chimps to human encroachment on their natural habitat (Cox, 1976). The chimpanzees of Gombe are divided into a more populous northern group and a smaller group of southerners. Goodall reports that small parties from the northern group (she calls them "border patrols") have taken to invading southern territory and have killed as many as four of the southern chimps. Three other cases of murder—infanticide—of chimp by chimp were observed during a two-year period. Two of the victims were partially eaten by their assailants (Cox, 1976).

Observations by Teleki, Goodall, Reynolds, and a variety of other primatologists demonstrate once more that other hominoids share a variety of abilities and tendencies with human beings. Again, it is clear that primate behavior is flexible, not simply genetically programmed, but able to vary widely as environmental forces shift and vary. Gibbons in Malaysia and chimps in Gombe illustrate that intensity of aggression and predation increases as humans encroach on the natural environments of our primate relatives. Among contemporary humans, too, aggression seems to increase when necessary resources are threatened or scarce. Although we shall never know just how aggressive or predatory our savanna-dwelling early hominid ancestors were, on the basis of what we now know about other primates, we can safely assume that early hominids were neither uniformly aggressive nor consistently meek. Their aggression and predation were related to environmental variation. We can only speculate about how much of their diet came from vegetation, hunting, or scavenging. Current evidence suggests, however, that our ancestors between 5 and 1 million years ago ate more vegetation than meat and probably obtained more meat from scavenging the kills of savanna predators than from hunting cooperatively.

Behavioral Adaptation to Environmental Stress Among Orangutans

We have at Gombe only one of many examples of human encroachment on another primate's natural habitat. Pressure on the strategic resources of primate ecological niches does not, however, inevitably result in predation and cannibalism, as observations by primatologist John MacKinnon confirm. Beginning in 1968, MacKinnon did field research among free-ranging orangutans on the Indonesian islands of Borneo and Sumatra, where they survive today only in isolated, forested, hilly country. A combination of climatic changes, hunting by humans, and forest burning has now confined them to the tropical forests of these two islands, but fossil evidence confirms that their range once extended as far north as China.

Marked sexual dimorphism among orangutans means that females, as well as the young, can exploit an arboreal niche more efficiently than males. Among wild orangutans, the average adult male weighs between two hundred and three hundred pounds. As among gorillas, such massive size poses obstacles to arboreal adaptation, limiting males to substantial trunks and branches. Zoologist Hans Kummer (1971) has speculated that sexual dimorphism may be related more to feeding habits and to diet than to defense. Kummer reports that, because of their smaller size, female baboons are able to feed in areas of trees that adult males cannot reach. The same is true of orangutans, mainly fruit-eating animals whose diet also includes acorns, shoots, leaves, bark, and wood pith.

MacKinnon found orangutans to be solitary animals. In contrast to the fluid troop organization of chimpanzees and gorillas, and the tightly knit gibbon primary group (a permanently bonded male and female and their subadolescent offspring), male orangutans typically travel and feed alone, and females are accompanied by their offspring. MacKinnon attributes differences in the behavior and social organization of orangutans in Borneo and northern Sumatra to environmental variation. Specifically, the Sumatran orangutans share their forest habitat and fruit diet with many other primates, including siamangs, gibbons, and several species of monkey. Bornean orangutans, on the other hand, are encountering human encroachment in the form of farming and timbering operations.

It is MacKinnon's belief that the presence of siamangs, larger members (twenty to twenty-five pounds) of the gibbon family, accounts for certain aspects of orangutan social organization and breeding behavior in Sumatra. Having initially assumed that the orangutan's larger size would confer first-feeding rights, MacKinnon was surprised to discover that in the intense competition between orangutans and siamangs for the same foods, the smaller apes, cooperating in tightly knit primary groups, used their physical quickness and agility to drive orangutans from feeding sites. Responding to the siamang threat, Sumatran males and females formed courting relationships for a few months. Furthermore, Sumatran male orangutans often remained with their mates for a while after an infant's birth.

MacKinnon observed neither type of association in Borneo, where, in adapting to human encroachment—deforestation through timbering and farming—orangutans had developed a pattern of sexual antagonism. Sexual liaisons were rare and, when they occurred, were brief; they were rapes, which often occurred with screaming infants clinging to their mothers throughout the ordeal. During MacKinnon's field work in Borneo, logging operations sent emigrant orangutans whose own territory had been destroyed into his research area, swelling the population it had to support. The response to sudden overpopulation was a drastic decline in birth rate. According to MacKinnon's observations, no orangutans were born in 1970. Predation and defense of territory are, therefore, not the only primate responses to population pressure. Alterations in interactions between the sexes may also, if they affect birth rate, act to check population pressure on the resources of an ecological niche.

Other than rape, MacKinnon found antagonism between orangutans to be rare. In fact, encounters and territorial encroachment were usually altogether avoided by the use of warning cries. The roar of the adult male warns others to stay away, and also tells them where he is feeding, so that once he has moved on, others—particularly females and young who can feed in less sturdy trees and on slighter branches—can locate the spot.

DIFFERENCES BETWEEN HUMANS AND OTHER PRIMATES

In the preceding section, similarities rather than differences between humans and other primates were emphasized. Although this discussion pointed out differences as well, these were differences in degree rather than kind. Certain tendencies and abilities that humans share with other anthropoids, especially the great apes, have developed to a much greater extent in *Homo* than in other primates. It is a unique concentration and combination of characteristics that makes us distinct. Along with elaborations of those abilities we share with other anthro-

poids, the savanna niche in which our ancestors evolved also required the development of some adaptive traits that are not as obviously foreshadowed by our nearest relatives.

Sharing, Cooperation, and Division of Economic Labor

The average adult woman carries about 89 percent of the weight of an adult man, whereas the baboon, gorilla, or orangutan female weighs about half as much as the average adult male of her species. Among human populations who live in small social units known as bands and have economies based on foraging, the strongest and most aggressive members do not dominate, as they do in the baboon troop. In fact, aggression and dominance are typically discouraged. If within the same band there are men who are more successful hunters than others, they are expected to be generous and are not permitted to hoard food for themselves. Observations among those hunter-gatherers who have survived into the twentieth century have shown that sharing and curbing of aggression are as intrinsic to human foragers as dominance and threat are to savanna-dwelling baboons.

Like terrestrial monkeys in their social units, human males and females in these bands of foragers play different roles. In baboon and macaque troops this involves differences in the defensive roles of males and females, but among humans it is more basically a division of economic labor. After a monkey infant is weaned, it learns to fend for itself in the quest for food, foraging for the vegetation and insects that form its natural diet. Humans, on the other hand, regularly share food. Among foragers, males generally hunt and females normally gather. In the evening, or after a successful hunting foray, the resources garnered by the women and the men are brought back to the camp, where they are shared. A man shares with his wife and children, a woman with her husband and children. When hunters have brought in a large animal, they share it with everyone else in the camp. The older people who did not engage in the food quest that day, but stayed home to take care of children, are also fed. Because of this division of economic labor, and the possibility of freeing some individuals from the subsistence quest, greater adaptability is possible. Old people, protected and nourished by younger members of their band, live past reproductive age, and they are respected for their age and knowledge. They transmit culture by carrying on the traditions of the band. The amount of information stored in a human band is far greater than in the social unit of any other primate. Sharing, cooperation, and language are intrinsic to information storage.

Observations of chimpanzee predation suggest that, as among human foragers, males tend to be the hunters. While female chimps have been observed seizing prey, only males have been seen cooperatively stalking. Food sharing among chimps is weakly developed, and only some meat is distributed after a successful hunting episode. By far the greatest part of the diet of any hominoid but *Homo* comes from individual foraging efforts—usually for vegetation. The rarity of meat eating and the concentration on vegetation are basic features distinguishing the ecological niches of contemporary apes from humans'. Over millions of years of adaptation to an omnivorous diet, hominids have relied on meat eating as well as food sharing and other cooperative behavior as universal and basic parts of their adaptive strategies.

Mating, Exogamy, and Kinship

Another major difference between humans and other primates is related to mating. Sexual relationships among baboons and chimpanzees depend on the periodic sexual receptivity of the female. When receptive, the female forms temporary bonds with males of her group. Her partner is not permanent. In contrast, humans have neither periodic receptivity nor a mating season; sexual activity occurs throughout the year. To regulate their more constant sexuality, all human societies have some form of *marriage,* an institution that places mating on a relatively permanent basis and grants to each spouse relatively exclusive sexual rights to the other.

With marriage comes another major difference between human and nonhuman adaptations: exogamy and kinship systems. Most human populations have a cultural rule, a custom sanctified by tradition, that directs people to seek their spouses from different groups. This rule is *exogamy,* and, coupled

with the recognition of kinship, it confers adaptive advantages. It creates ties between an individual and his or her spouse's group of origin. For their children, it means that they have relatives in two bands rather than one. Extension of ties through kinship with other bands means that individuals increase the number of allies upon whom they may call for help. Exogamy and kinship, along with tool manufacture and language, represent major adaptive advantages that have led to the success of *Homo.*

Maintenance of affective ties to related individuals who join other social groups appears to be lacking among hominoids other than *Homo.* A common tendency among nonhuman primates is dispersal at adolescence, most notably of males. Both male and female gibbons and siamangs leave their parents when they become sexually mature, and, once they locate their own mates and establish their own territories, affective ties with their native groups cease. Some long-term studies of macaques suggest that most males born within a troop leave near the age of puberty, eventually winning places in other social units. The troop's stable core, we are now learning, often consists of females, sometimes forming *uterine groups*—mothers, sisters, daughters, and those of their male offspring who have not yet joined other troops. In a ten-year study of rhesus macaques, Donald Sade (1972) found that no male had remained a member of its troop for more than four years. Dispersion of males at adolescence or just prior to the mating season also reduces the incidence of incestuous matings. In his longitudinal study of rhesus macaques begun in 1960, Sade (1972) observed only a few out of several possible incidents of mother-son sexual intercourse. While affective ties are often, therefore, maintained among female primates, no affective links based on kinship are preserved through males. A troop's core of females mates with males who have joined the troop in, and after, adolescence. Although in all human societies people commonly choose their mate outside their own native group, and at least one spouse moves to the other's group, affective ties are maintained with sons as well as daughters through kinship systems.

SUMMARY

Since the seventeenth century, natural scientists have been concerned with classifying life forms. Scientific taxonomy can be traced to Carolus Linnaeus, who viewed structural differences and similarities between life forms as part of the Creator's orderly plan, rather than as evidence for phylogenetic relationships and evolution. Influenced by earlier transformists, Charles Darwin and Alfred Russel Wallace proposed the doctrine of natural selection to explain the origin of species, biological diversity, and similarities encountered among related life forms. Darwin recognized that for natural selection to operate there must be variety within the population undergoing selection.

Humans, apes, monkeys, and prosimians all belong to the *Primate* zoological order. This order is subdivided into suborders, infraorders, superfamilies, families, subfamilies, genera, species, and subspecies on the basis of several criteria. In general, organisms included within any subdivision, or taxon, of a zoological taxonomy are assumed to share more recent common ancestry with one another than with organisms in other taxa. They are therefore assumed to share more homologies, reflected in their appearance, structure, physiology, and genetic make-up. Because of difficulties in distinguishing homologous similarities, which reflect common ancestry, from analogies, which reflect convergent evolution, controversy surrounds the placement of certain groups within the same taxonomic class in the *Primate* order. For example, most scientists doubt that orangutans, gorillas, and chimpanzees (placed together in the family *Pongidae*, rather than in the family *Hominidae*, which includes humans) are more closely related to one another than to humans.

Diverse primates are assigned to the same zoological order on the basis of several trends that are most obvious among the anthropoids. The involve grasping, vision, touch, brain complexity, litter size, and social organization.

Anthropologists and others have often stressed differences rather than similarities between humans and other primates. However, recent research has demonstrated that similarities are far more extensive than was once supposed. Several differences are quantitative rather than qualitative. A unique concentration and combination of ingredients makes humans distinct; some of these traits are foreshadowed in other primates, particularly the African apes. For example, chimpanzees make tools for several purposes, an endeavor once thought to be characteristic of humans only. Furthermore, it is now apparent that learning ability, the basis of culture, confers adaptive flexibility on other primates.

Although other primates communicate through call systems, recent research has demonstrated the ability of chimpanzees and gorillas to understand and manipulate creatively a large number of nonverbal symbols based on language. Primate calls are tied to specific environmental stimuli and are uttered only when these are encountered; they cannot be combined if two or more stimuli are present simultaneously. At some point in human evolution, however, our ancestors attained the capacity for displaced speech. Other contrasts between language and nonhuman primate call systems involve productivity, duality of patterning, and cultural transmission—all of which the former have and the latter lack. Over time, call systems gradually developed into true language. The transition occurred as call systems grew too complicated to be transmitted genetically and became instead a function of learning.

Recent observations of wild primates also suggest that other primates are cooperative hunters. Chimps, more omnivorous than once was thought, cooperate in hunting and share meat. Hunting and killing of chimp by chimp, like sexual antagonism among orangutans, seem linked to pressure on strategic resources—human encroachment on their natural habitat. Like humans, chimpanzees, baboons, and orangutans are flexible animals that can increase or reduce their aggression as environmental conditions warrant. Their social organization also varies. Orangutan males care more for their mates and young when siamangs share their habitat.

Although many contrasts are of degree rather than kind, important differences between humans and other primates remain. Aggression and dominance relationships are vital to the adaptation of many baboons and macaques; sharing and cooperation are equally significant among primitive human populations. Related to sharing is traditional division of subsistence labor on the basis of age and sex. Finally, humans maintain kinship ties with their relatives who marry and reside elsewhere. Although other primates avoid incest through male dispersal at adolescence, only humans use explicit linguistically expressed incest taboos to promote exogamy as a means of linking themselves to other social groups.

SOURCES AND SUGGESTED READINGS

ALLAND, A., JR.
1973 *Evolution and Human Behavior: An Introduction to Darwinian Anthropology.* Garden City, N.Y.: Anchor Books. Evidence for evolution and several illustrations that natural selection operates only on the evolutionary material at hand.

BRAMBLETT, C. A.
1976 *Introduction to Primatology.* Palo Alto, Calif.: Mayfield. Social organization, behavior, anatomy, taxonomy, and history of primate studies.

CHEYFITZ, K.
1975 Ape Fluent in Sign Language. *Detroit Free Press,* Sept. 14, pp. 1A, 10A. Similar to other newspaper accounts of Koko's progress in Ameslan.

COX, V.
1976 Jane Goodall: Learning from the Chimpanzee. *Human Behavior,* March, pp. 25–30. Goodall's recent work at Gombe, including the results of human encroachment.

CUVIER, G.
1811 *Recherches sur les Ossements Fossiles.* Paris: G. Dufour and E. D'Ocagne. Original statement of catastrophism.

DARWIN, C.
1958 (orig. 1859). *Origin of Species.* New York: New American Library. Foundation stone of biology and anthropology.

DARWIN, E.
1796 (orig. 1794). *Zoonomia, Or the Laws of Organic Life.* 2nd ed. London: J. Johnson. Nature discussed and classified by an early transformist.

DEVORE, I.
1963 A Comparison of the Ecology and Behavior of Monkeys and Apes. In *Classification and Human Evolution,* ed. S. L. Washburn, pp. 301–319. Chicago: Aldine. Influential article arguing that ecological niche (arboreal versus terrestrial) determines more about primate behavior than does phylogenetic relationship (New World versus Old World).

EATON, G. G.
1976 The Social Order of Japanese Macaques. *Scientific American,* October, pp. 96–106. Well-illustrated, readable account of recent findings on these terrestrial monkeys.

EIMERL, S., AND DEVORE, I.
1965 *The Primates.* New York: Time-Life Books. Introduction to primate behavior; well written and illustrated.

EISELEY, L.
1961 *Darwin's Century.* Garden City, N.Y.: Doubleday Anchor. Lyell, Darwin, Wallace, and other major contributors to natural selection and transformism.

ELLEFSON, J. O.
1968 Territorial Behavior in the Common White-Handed Gibbon, *Hylobates lar Linn.* In *Primates: Studies in Adaptation and Variability,* ed. P. C. Jay, pp. 180–199. New York: Holt, Rinehart and Winston. Field study of gibbons in their natural habitat; anthology contains interesting but technical articles.

GARDNER, B., AND GARDNER, R. A.
1971 Two-Way Communication with an Infant Chimpanzee. In *Behavior of Non-Human Primates,* ed. A. Schrier and F. Stollnitz. New York: Academic Press. Meet Washoe; see Washoe use sign language.

GARDNER, R. A., AND GARDNER, B.
1969 Teaching Sign Language to a Chimpanzee. *Science* 165: 664–672. Washoe learns to communicate.

GOODALL, J. VAN LAWICK
1968a The Behavior of Free-Living Chimpanzees in the Gombe Stream Reserve. *Animal Behavior Monographs* 1: 161–311. A report based on several years of firsthand observation.

1968b A Preliminary Report on Expressive Movements and Communication in Gombe Stream Chimpanzees. In *Primates: Studies in Adaptation and Variability,* ed. P. C. Jay, pp. 313–374. New York: Holt, Rinehart and Winston. Technical report on field study of chimpanzee communication.

1971   *In the Shadow of Man.* Boston: Houghton Mifflin. Popular account of author's life among the chimps.

HARLOW, H.
1966   Development of Patterns of Affection in Macaques. *Yearbook of Physical Anthropology* 14: 1–7. Experiment on maternal care, socialization, and other aspects of macaque behavior.

HINDE, R. A.
1974   *Biological Bases of Human Social Behavior.* New York: McGraw-Hill. What observation of nonhuman primate behavior might tell us about our own.

HOCKETT, C. F., AND ASCHER, R.
1964   The Human Revolution. *Current Anthropology* 5: 135–168. Influential article on differences between human and nonhuman primate communication and the origin of language.

JOLLY, A.
1972   *The Evolution of Primate Behavior.* New York: Macmillan. Behavior and social life of primates; examines variation in time and space.

JOLLY, C. J., AND PLOG, F.
1976   *Physical Anthropology and Archeology.* New York: Random House. More detailed treatment of primate evolution, classification, and adaptations than in this chapter.

KAWAMURA, S.
1963   The Process of Sub-Culture Propagation among Japanese Macaques. In *Primate Social Behavior,* ed. C. Southwick, pp. 82–90. Princeton, N.J.: Van Nostrand. Sweet-potato washing and other subcultural variations in colonies of Japanese macaques.

KUMMER, H.
1971   *Primate Societies: Group Techniques of Ecological Adaptation.* Chicago: Aldine. Good introduction to primate social organization.

LINDEN, E.
1974   *Apes, Men, and Language.* New York: Penguin. Meet Washoe, Lucy, Sarah, and other communicating chimps.

LYELL, C.
1850   (orig. 1830). *Principles of Geology.* 8th ed. London: J. Murray. Influential application of natural principles to landforms; early statement of uniformitarianism.

MACKINNON, J.
1974   *In Search of the Red Ape.* New York: Ballantine. Fascinating nontechnical account of his field research on orangutans.

MALTHUS, T.
1803   (orig. 1798). *An Essay on the Principle of Population.* London: J. Johnson. Classic demographic essay. Asserts that while human population increases geometrically, its food supply increases only arithmetically.

MAYR, E.
1970   *Animal Species and Evolution.* Cambridge: Harvard University Press. Good discussion of evolutionary principles, speciation, and taxonomy.

MICHAEL, R. P., AND CROOK, J. H., EDS.
1973   *Comparative Ecology and Behavior of Primates.* New York: Academic Press. Useful collection of articles offering theory and new data.

NISSEN, H. W.
1931   A Field Study of the Chimpanzee. *Comparative Psychology Monographs* 8: 1–22. Early field study.

POIRIER, F., ED.
1972   *Primate Socialization.* New York: Random House. Mothers, fathers, troops, and the transmission of primate social life.

REYNOLDS, V.
1971   *The Apes.* New York: Harper Colophon. Readable introduction to our nearest relatives.

1975   How Wild Are the Gombe Chimpanzees? *Man* 10: 123–125. Suggests that chimpanzee predation on baboons may be the result of artificial feeding situation at Gombe.

ROWELL, T.
1972   *The Social Behavior of Monkeys.* New York: Penguin. Interesting introductory survey.

SADE, D.
1972   A Longitudinal Study of Social Behavior of Rhesus Monkeys. In *The Functional*

and *Evolutionary Biology of Primates,* ed.
R. Tuttle. Chicago: University of Chicago
Press.

SAVAGE, J. M.
1969   *Evolution.* 2nd ed. New York: Holt,
Rinehart & Winston. Readable introduction to biological evolution; includes a
typology of evolutionary events according
to the rate and magnitude of change.

SCHALLER, G., AND EMLEN, T., JR.
1974   (orig. 1963). Observations on the Ecology and Social Behavior of the Mountain
Gorilla. In *Man in Adaptation: The Biosocial Background,* ed. Y. Cohen, pp. 91–
99. Chicago: Aldine. Diary of field observations of gorillas in East Africa.

SIMPSON, G. G.
1960   (orig. 1949). *The Meaning of Evolution.*
New Haven: Yale University Press. Classic introduction to biological evolution.

SMITH, J. M.
1966   *The Theory of Evolution.* 2nd ed. Baltimore: Penguin. Introduction to biological evolution.

TELEKI, G.
1973a   *The Predatory Behavior of Wild Chimpanzees.* Lewisburg, Pa.: Bucknell University Press. Full report of field study of
hunting by Gombe chimpanzees.

1973b   The Omnivorous Chimpanzee. *Scientific American,* Jan., pp. 32–42. Brief,
well-illustrated and -written report of
author's findings about Gombe chimpanzee predation.

WASHBURN, S. L., AND DEVORE, I.
1975   (orig. 1961). The Social Life of Baboons.
In *Biological Anthropology, Readings
from Scientific American,* ed. S. H. Katz,
pp. 79–89. Early field study; interesting
account.

WEISS, M. L., AND MANN, A. E.
1975   *Human Biology and Behavior: An Anthropological Perspective.* Boston: Little,
Brown. Excellent introduction to biological anthropology; much more detailed than the treatment in this chapter.

FOOD PRODUCTION
and the STATE

The Implications
of Food Production

3

Sometime around 12,000 to 10,000 years ago people gradually began to produce, through animal domestication and plant cultivation, their own food. Before this, throughout the world and during millions of years of hominid evolution, our ancestors had supported themselves by foraging—gathering and hunting. At first—during the Ramapithecine phase of hominid evolution, which spanned the period between about 14 million and 8 million years ago—the coarse, gritty, fibrous vegetation of the tropical savanna was the dietary mainstay. Savanna vegetation remained important during the next evolutionary stage—that of the Australopithecines, who lived in tropical Africa from perhaps 6 million years ago until their evolution into the first true humans (*Homo erectus*) between 2 and 1 million years B.P.

A major change in the foraging profession—greater reliance on hunting made possible by interrelated anatomical and cultural (particularly technological) changes—seems to have been the major reason for the evolution of *Australopithecus* into *Homo*. Over more than one million years thereafter, *Homo erectus* perfected the hunting-gathering mode of existence. Fossils identified as the first members of our own species, *Homo sapiens,* have been dated to the period between 300,000 and 200,000 years B.P. Initially, they represented an early subspecies, *Homo sapiens Neanderthalensis.* Although for years the Neanderthals have served as stereotypical "cavemen," scientists now stress their similarities to contemporary humans rather than the anatomical differences. By ca. 40,000 B.P. the Neanderthals had evolved into anatomically modern people, members of our own subspecies, *Homo sapiens Sapiens.* Nevertheless, people continued the foraging strategies of their ancestors until—beginning around 10,000 years ago in the Near East

49

(the area of modern Iran and Iraq)—they gradually turned to food production. A convergent transition took place in areas of the New World, for example, Mesoamerica (Mexico, Guatemala, Belize), some 4,000 years later. In both the Near East and the highlands of Mexico, food production gradually evolved out of hunting and gathering as human populations incorporated early domesticates (for example, wheat and barley in the Old World; maize, manioc, and potatoes in the New) into the broad spectrum of resources they relied on for subsistence. The transition to food production led to major modifications in human life, as the pace of change in society and culture increased enormously. Throughout the rest of the book, these and other sociocultural changes will be emphasized. The concentration will be on sociocultural diversity, and differences and similarities in social life and cultural traits among human populations of the present and more recent past will be examined.

This chapter examines some of the social and political implications of food production. It also provides a framework for applying certain evolutionary principles to the sociocultural adaptive mechanisms of human populations, particularly those of the present and the recent past. Accepting the Darwinian model of evolution through natural selection, the unit of study is the population. Like our primate relatives and other animal populations, humans have developed adaptive means whose function is to maintain them in their immediate environments. We have seen that natural forces select both biological traits and learned behavior patterns that are adaptive in terms of specific environments. Once a viable and stable relationship with the immediate environment has been established, natural selection operates to maintain that relationship until selective forces change.

Such alterations may involve a seemingly minute difference; for example, one or more mutations in a plant or animal species important to the population's subsistence, or a gradual change in the pattern of alliances between a group and one of its neighbors. When an environmental factor changes, selection may favor new adaptive means. Possessing sociocultural as well as biological means of adaptation neither frees human populations from nature nor guarantees a population's ability to adapt to changing circumstances. Extensive reliance on extrasomatic adaptive means merely allows *Homo sapiens* to adjust to changed circumstances more

quickly and more flexibly than other species. It is always possible, however, for the environmental change to be so severe, or for the adaptive potentialities of the group to be so limited or so inflexible, that extinction rather than evolution results.

EVOLUTION: VARIOUS APPROACHES

It is important to understand the difference between general evolutionary statements and specific evolutionary statements about human populations. *General evolutionary statements* concern the genus *Homo* as a whole. They designate long-term evolutionary trends: broad changes, accomplished over thousands—even millions—of years, in the adaptive means employed by members of the genus without regard for special adaptive problems associated with particular environments. Such generalizations abstract certain broad changes by considering populations of that genus from several different periods and several different geographical areas. *Specific evolutionary statements*, on the other hand, refer to particular human populations living in specific environments of various sizes—for example, Mexico's Valley of Oaxaca, western Iran, the upper Nile region of Africa, Australia, the northwestern shores of Lake Victoria. A study in specific evolution involves documentation of changes in adaptive relationships between particular environments and the human populations within them over an extended time period. An archeologist's detailed analysis of changes in the kinds of site inhabited at different times during a 10,000-year period in a particular Mexican valley exemplifies one specific evolutionary sequence. Others are given below.

General Evolutionary Statements

The identification of trends in the evolution of the stone tools used by our hunting and gathering ancestors prior to the emergence of food production illustrate general evolutionary statements. For example, through the successive stages of human evolution, our reliance on tools has increased. Tools have become more numerous; tools have become functionally differentiated and have been designed for ever more specialized tasks; and tool types have diversified. Other general evolutionary observations are that over millions of years of hominid evolution there has been increasing reliance on sociocultural means of adaptation; populations representing later stages of human evolution have been more successful in a reproductive sense than earlier populations; and the range of environments occupied by members of the genus *Homo* has expanded through time.

Means of harnessing nonhuman energy sources for human use have become more complex, if not always more efficient. Muscle power is human energy. Fire, on the other hand, is an indirect energy source that was brought under human control perhaps a million years ago and that conferred on *Homo* adaptive advantages: the ability to adapt to a wider variety of environments and, because of cooking, the ability to consume a wider variety of foods. Plants and animals are indirect sources of energy. Through photosynthesis, plants capture and transform solar energy to manufacture carbohydrates. Some animals eat plants. Some animals eat other animals. When people gather plants or hunt animals they exploit, directly or indirectly, some of this solar energy to keep themselves alive. However, when humans grow plants or supervise the mating and survival of their animal herds, they are able to concentrate and control the stores of nonhuman energy at their disposal. So, too, do they concentrate and control when they harness a steer to a plow or to a cart; when they tap the wind to sail boats or rivers to run industrial plants; or when they put the atom or solar radiation to use.

Enlarging our frame of reference from the evolution of *Homo* to the evolution of all life, certain general trends are also apparent. There has been, for example, a proliferation of parts and subparts. Multicelled plants and animals have evolved out of single-celled antecedents. One observes a similar trend in human social and cultural evolution. The Ramapithecines and Australopithecines probably lived in small bands that, like baboon troops, were part of no larger social unit. Each band was probably like any other, in the same way that one amoeba resembles another. By the time of *Homo erectus,* however, larger units formed seasonally as subparts, microbands, congregated for communal hunting. With the appearance of *Homo sapiens Sapiens,* the number of human populations, the size of each, and their degree of association with others had increased, as documented archeologically, for example, by increasing population in southwestern France between 17,000 and 12,000 B.P. Much more obvi-

ously, food production accelerated the general evolutionary trend toward proliferation of parts and subparts, subpopulations of the species *Homo sapiens.* Although sedentary life predated food production in certain favored areas — for example, where varied resources packed closely together in space supported year-round settlement of diversified foragers — domestication of plants and animals paved the way for widespread village life. Throughout the world, food production sustained an increase in population and an expansion in range of the genus *Homo.*

In addition to the proliferation of parts and subparts, other trends observable in the general evolution of life also apply to human evolution. As parts and subparts have proliferated, they have also become functionally specialized. From unicellular plants and animals in which a single structure performs a variety of functions have evolved more generally advanced organisms with specialized systems and subsystems — alimentary, reproductive, circulatory, and excretory, for example. And among many food-producing populations, functionally specialized systems and subsystems — military, judicial, administrative or, in broader terms, economic, political, and ritual — have arisen out of less differentiated forms.

Another trend in the general evolution of life that may be extended to *Homo* is the development of more effective means of integrating the functionally specialized parts and subparts, systems and subsystems. Central governments play integrative roles comparable to that of the central nervous system in the coordination of bodily parts and systems.

Several anthropologists have suggested that general evolutionary trends — the proliferation of parts and subparts, their functional differentiation, the development of more effective means of integration, reproductive success as revealed by sheer numbers, and adaptability as revealed by environmental and geographic range — may be used as bases for comparative statements about human populations, present and past. Stated in terms of trends, the comparison has temporal implications. On the basis of the five criteria just listed, early populations of *Homo* must be judged as less *advanced* than later ones. Furthermore, one or more of the five criteria may be used as a basis for comparing human populations of the present and recent past. As we shall see, each of the general evolutionary trends is less developed in most foraging populations than among most food producers.

Specific Evolutionary Approaches

Specific evolutionary statements describe changes experienced by a human population in a specific area of the world. It is possible, for example, to focus study on the French or on the Ganda, a population living on the shores of Lake Victoria in East Africa, rather than on the genus *Homo*. We can describe changes in means of adaptation and other traits and behavior over an extended time period. Comparison of the specific evolutionary sequences in different human populations, once the reasons for these changes have been understood, informs us about the reasons for evolution in human populations of the present and recent past. By examining many specific evolutionary sequences, we can see whether there are some broadly similar trends in development—in other words, whether analogous selective forces operating in broadly similar environments have produced convergent or parallel evolutionary sequences among human populations in different parts of the world. And by delineating the kinds of conditions and stimuli that produce specific changes, we can attempt to generalize about how and why human populations modify their behavior and milieu.

Unilinear Evolution

Anthropologists have used the term "evolution" to refer to still other developmental trends. For example, in Britain and the United States during the latter half of the nineteenth century, social scientists were making *unilinear* evolutionary statements: all human societies were thought to have evolved in the same order through a ranked series of stages, and any society that had attained one of the "higher" stages was assumed to have passed through all the "lower" stages. Twentieth-century ethnographic and archeological research has demonstrated the limitations of a unilinear evolutionary framework. It is possible for societies to develop the same traits but in different order and for developments consisting of different stages to lead to broadly similar results. Human groups may even evolve from a more to a less complex condition because of changes in natural selective pressures.

Leslie White and the Evolution of Culture

In the present century, two sociocultural anthropologists, Leslie White and Julian Steward, used evolu-

tion to refer to still other concepts. White's understanding of the term "evolution" was similar to general evolution as defined above, but for him the evolving unit was not the genus *Homo* but the most distinctive adaptive apparatus of that genus—namely, culture. According to White, the evolution of culture, or cultural advance, was directly proportional to, and therefore could be measured by, the amount of energy harnessed per capita per year or improvements in the means of controlling energy. White's views on cultural evolution were most completely developed in his book *The Evolution of Culture* (1959). In this modern anthropological classic, White discussed major developments in culture from early hunters and gatherers through the fall of Rome. The panoramic movement he described involved a transition from primitive society, which relied almost exclusively on human energy, to the complex societies that emerged following what White called the "Agricultural Revolution," encompassing the domestication of plants and animals. Out of food-producing economies came civilization.

White applied his grand movement view of evolution not only to development over time from early foragers through prestate food producers to civilization, but also to contemporary sociocultural systems. In White's evolutionary scheme, those populations of foragers and prestate food producers that survived into the twentieth century served as present-day representatives, living fossils, of early sociocultural systems because of their relatively simple means of harnessing energy.

A kind of technological or economic determinism seemed to inhere in White's work. Culture advanced as improvements in technology or economy permitted greater energy capture by humans. White recognized, however, that technological, economic, and social developments were associated and interrelated. For example, social, political, and legal changes followed the Agricultural Revolution. Private property, distinctions involving wealth and class, and other social relations unknown in the sociocultural systems of 10,000 years ago arose in food-producing societies. It was therefore to technological, to economic, and to associated sociopolitical forms that White's observations on the evolution of culture applied most directly. His comparison of sociocultural systems, his use of the terms "primitive" or "simple" versus "complex" or "civilized," did not contain moral judgments. Nor did they denote increase in happiness. In fact, White was explicit in arguing that the simpler type of social system based on non–food-producing economies represented the most satisfying kind of social environment that humans had ever experienced. While it was therefore possible to speak of evolutionary advance, measured according to certain trends or criteria, "progress" was too value-laden a term to apply either to the evolution of culture, which was White's concern, or to the long-term evolution of the genus *Homo*.

"Pygmies" of the Ituri Forest, Zaire. Foragers like the "pygmies" and the Tasaday of the Philippines have survived in such isolated forest areas. Like most other foragers, the "pygmies" live in small groups. Shown here is a segment of one "pygmy band." (George Holton/Photo Researchers, Inc.)

Julian Steward and Convergent Evolution

Julian Steward used the term *multilinear evolution* to refer to the sociocultural phenomena he studied. *Multi* means "many," and multilinear evolution referred to the fact that many different lines of development had taken place in different human populations. The study of any one of these brings us back to specific evolution. Steward, however, chose a middle ground between general and specific evolutionary studies. He concentrated on examples of convergent evolution involving historically, genetically, and geographically unrelated populations. One of Steward's best-known articles, "Cultural Causality and Law: A Trial Formulation of the Development of Early Civilizations" (1949), compared the specific evolutionary sequences leading from foraging to nation-state organization in five separate world areas— Peru, highland Mexico, Egypt, Mesopotamia, and

China. Steward found that not only did the human populations in each of these regions complete an analogous evolution from foraging to agricultural economies, with convergent social forms and other adaptive means throughout the sequence, but they also passed through roughly similar stages and generally in the same order. He attributed the five examples of convergent evolution to analogous, long-term interactions between the human populations and broadly similar natural selective forces associated with the five geographically distant but ecologically similar environments.

Steward wrote his 1949 article to demonstrate noteworthy similarities in five specific transitions from foraging to civilization or nation-state organization. According to Steward, the convergent sequences did not occur by chance. In fact, given long-term adaptations to similar environments and analogous selective forces, there was a certain amount of inevitability in the order and development of sociocultural forms in these five areas. It seemed to Steward, therefore, that natural law determined human behavior and evolution as surely as it did other organic and inorganic forms and phenomena.

Along with other anthropologists, Steward was interested in constructing sociocultural typologies. A *typology* is a system of classification that takes similar units and subdivides them, assigning some to category or type A, others to B, and so on. In 1949 Steward proposed that the five areas of the world he had examined belonged to a single *developmental type.* This type involved convergent evolution over long time periods, but was limited to arid areas. Thus, unlike unilinear evolution and other formulations, it was not composed of universal stages. Steward believed that different developmental types, involving different long-term interactions between human populations and their environments, would have prevailed in nonarid areas—regions of tropical rain forest, for example.

Steward, then, contributed to our understanding of evolution in relatively recent human populations by calling attention to parallel changes in sociocultural forms and other adaptive means that had taken place repeatedly and independently of one another in different parts of the world. These are *parallels through time.* In numerous articles, he also directed the attention of anthropologists to examples of sociocultural *parallels in space*, observed at a single time. Compare several of the human populations that have been studied by ethnographers during the twentieth

century, and you will be struck by certain similarities —certain parallel sociocultural forms. Steward explained such parallels in space the way he explained parallel evolutionary sequences. He pointed out that many sociocultural similarities could be shown to reflect convergent evolution. If, in the case of a developmental typology, parallel selective pressures associated with analogous environments had interacted with human populations over thousands of years to produce a similar sequence of sociocultural forms, evolutionary convergence involving only a single time level was even more obvious. For example, in examining a large *sample,* or study group, of foraging societies from all over the world, Steward was able to show that similar sociocultural forms represented convergent adaptation to similar environmental variables such as rainfall patterns, distribution of wild plants, habits of game animals, and others. But Steward did not find that there was a single type of foraging society. Rather, differences in ecological relationships involving particular groups of foragers and their specific environments produced a variety of types, which he called "patrilineal bands," "composite bands," "multi-family predatory bands," and "the family level of sociocultural integration." Since the specific evolutionary sequences leading to them may have been different, the types that were abstracted from observations on a single time level were obviously not developmental types, although they were the convergent end results of specific evolutionary sequences. These might be called *ecological types.* While many of the specifics of Steward's comparative studies must be rejected in view of recent archeological and ethnographic research, his interest in comparing sociocultural variation in time and space remains basic to contemporary anthropology.

Steward never developed an extensive typology based on the examples of cross-cultural convergence he studied and described, but another anthropologist, Yehudi Cohen (1974), has. Like Steward, Cohen is interested in cross-cultural similarities observable at a single time. These represent analogous sociocultural forms that have developed independently among widespread unrelated populations. Cohen argues that the most important determinant of these similarities is a group's strategy of adaptation to its environment. For example, he points to striking similarities between most contemporary populations that have a *foraging* strategy of adaptation. Like Steward, Cohen emphasizes broad similarities in certain features of subsistence and technology, and in ecological relationships. From these similarities, other sociocultural features are shown to follow. Cohen's types are, however, much broader than Steward's and pay less attention to contrasts associated with particular environments. Steward and Cohen have been interested primarily in *similarities* that are observable cross-culturally. However, simply because sociocultural similarities exist that can be related to analogous adaptive problems, it does not mean there are not also differences between the units included within a type. In fact, ecological and evolutionary principles can be used to explain sociocultural divergence and differentiation as well as convergence and parallelism, as this and later chapters will document.

Yehudi Cohen identified six strategies of adaptation: foraging, horticulture, agriculture, pastoralism, mercantilism, and industrialism. Confining our attention to the first four, which are most characteristic of the groups anthropologists traditionally have studied, let us examine some of the social and cultural traits and patterns associated with each. (Trade and industrialism are considered in later chapters.)

FORAGING

Until men and women began to cultivate plants and domesticate animals, human populations throughout the world relied on foraging for subsistence. Of course, the particular resources associated with specific environmental niches dictated differences in foraging strategies. Some early foragers focused on big game animals, whereas others pursued a broader spectrum of wild plants and animals. But a basic feature was shared: people relied on natural reserves for their food and for other materials essential to their lives. In both the Old World and the New World, food production, once begun, spread rapidly, and most hunting and gathering populations eventually came to orient their economies around plant cultivation, animal domestication, or a combination of the two.

Foraging economies held on, however, in certain parts of the world. Today there remain two broad zones of foraging adaptations in Africa. They are the Kalahari Desert of southern Africa, home of the !Kung, and the equatorial forest of central and eastern Africa, where the "pygmies" survive. In Southeast Asia, Malaya, and on certain islands off the Indian coast live other foragers. Like the recently

Bushwomen gathering in the Kalahari. Among tropical foragers, women's productive labor in gathering often provides at least two-thirds of the diet. (Shostak/Anthro-Photo)

discovered Tasaday, foragers of the Philippines, they survive generally in forests or on isolated islands. Some of the most famous contemporary hunters and gatherers are the aborigines of Australia, who, during the more than 20,000 years they have lived on their island continent, have never cultivated plants or domesticated animals. To the south, the island Tasmanians were also hunters and gatherers.

In the New World, the Eskimos are probably the hunters and gatherers most familiar to you. The native populations of California, the Northwest Coast of North America, interior Canada, and the northern Midwest were still foragers when Europeans began to colonize North America. Near the southern tip of South America lived three hunting and gathering populations: the Ona, the Yahgan, and the Alacaluf; and on the grassy plains of Argentina, southern Brazil, Uruguay, and Paraguay lived others.

Foragers persisted in certain areas while food

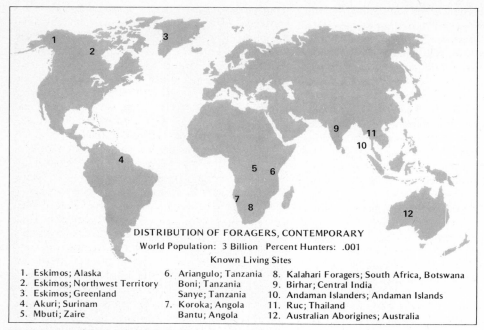

DISTRIBUTION OF FORAGERS, CONTEMPORARY
World Population: 3 Billion   Percent Hunters: .001
Known Living Sites

1. Eskimos; Alaska	6. Ariangulo; Tanzania	8. Kalahari Foragers; South Africa, Botswana
2. Eskimos; Northwest Territory	Boni; Tanzania	9. Birhar; Central India
3. Eskimos; Greenland	Sanye; Tanzania	10. Andaman Islanders; Andaman Islands
4. Akuri; Surinam	7. Koroka; Angola	11. Ruc; Thailand
5. Mbuti; Zaire	Bantu; Angola	12. Australian Aborigines; Australia

FIGURE 3.1 Distribution of contemporary foragers. Foragers have been able to survive the expansion of food production in such marginal and isolated areas as certain islands, tropical forests, deserts, and the Arctic. (From *The Emergence of Man*, Revised and Enlarged Edition, p. 349, by John E. Pfeiffer. Copyright © 1969, 1972 by John E. Pfeiffer. By permission of Harper & Row, Inc.)

production was spreading throughout most of the world for several reasons. Certain environments pose major obstacles to food production and, in fact, to any nonindustrial economic base other than foraging. The environmental obstacles to plant cultivation in the Arctic are obvious. Yet the combination of environmental limitations with rudimentary technologies is not the only reason for the survival of ways of life based on foraging. Though their range of specific environments is large, the niches of contemporary hunters and gatherers share one feature in common: their marginality. This means that they are not of immediate interest to other strategies of adaptation. It is most accurate to think of foragers not as choosing where they live, but as surviving in areas into which neither food production nor industrialism has yet penetrated. Furthermore, some foraging groups have lived in areas that could be cultivated and have had contact with cultivators but — supporting themselves adequately by hunting and gathering — have not become food producers.

The Correlates of a Foraging Economy

Typologies are useful because they suggest correlations, that is, associations or covariations. A specific constellation of other sociocultural features is generally characteristic of each of Yehudi Cohen's strategies of adaptation. Many foragers have been characterized as *band-organized* populations because their basic unit of social organization is the band. A band is a small group of people — fewer than one hundred — related by ties of actual or believed kinship and/or marriage. The typical band size varies from one foraging population to another, and often from one season to another in any one population. Band size reflects the specific environment that the population exploits and the seasonal appearance of resources used by the band's members. Thus in some hunting and gathering societies, band size stays about the same year-round. In others, however, during part of the year the band breaks apart, as smaller units, often family groups, leave to take advantage of seasonally available resources that are better exploited by only a few individuals. During one season of the year, the band fragments will recongregate to engage in cooperative economic or ceremonial activity. Several examples of such seasonal dispersal and recongregation are known from both archeological and ethnographic research. Among some foraging populations, annual congregations may even involve several bands. Even going back 300,000 years to the late *Homo erectus* period of human evolution, bands may have congregated in autumn to prey on large mammals migrating south for the winter. These larger units are called macrobands. Seasonal fragments of a band may be either microbands or individual families.

Of interest in the discussion of band organization are the !Kung (Lee, 1969, 1974; orig. 1968; Draper, 1975) and the Mbuti "pygmies" (Turnbull, 1961, 1965), among whom band size does not appear to vary significantly during the year. Although !Kung bands do not fragment seasonally into family groups, there is great variation in their composition. A !Kung or Mbuti may shift his or her band membership many times during a lifetime. One may be born, for example, in a band where one's mother has kin. Later, one's father, mother, and siblings may move to a band where the father has relatives. !Kung bands tend to be exogamous units. As a result, a father and mother will come from two different bands, and grandparents may have come from four different bands. Foragers apparently enjoy the possibility of affiliating with any of these grandparental bands or, in fact, with any band with which they can show a personal connection.

Personal connections may be based on kinship or on marriage. When a !Kung couple marries, they have the option of residing in either the husband's or the wife's band. Later they may decide to move and join the band of the other spouse for a while.

Finally, one may affiliate with a band through *fictive kinship*: special personal relationships modeled on kinship or genealogy, for instance, godparents and godchildren. !Kung have a limited set of personal names, and they believe that a special relationship links individuals who share a name. Such individuals treat one another like siblings. Furthermore, !Kung have the same right to hospitality in bands where they have namesakes that they do in bands where their real siblings are living. By virtue of their common name, namesakes share a sociological identity. Thus people call everyone in their namesake's band by the kin terms that their namesake uses, and band members will use the same terms to refer to either namesake. Thus through kinship, marriage, and fictive kinship ties, the !Kung has, throughout life, the opportunity to join many bands, and individuals change band membership many times before they die. Membership in a given band thus varies tremendously from year to year.

All human societies have established some sort of division of labor on the basis of gender. The pattern in many foraging societies is for men to hunt and

In small-scale nonindustrial societies, old people are often specially valued as teachers and guardians of tradition. Shown here, an old man of the Joti tribe in Venezuela offers affection and instruction to his grandchild. (Jacques Jangoux)

women to collect, but the specific economic tasks allotted to each sex depend on the environment and the traditions that, over time, the human population has developed for dealing with it. Thus among some foragers, women are the major collectors, and their labor provides more than two-thirds of the calories consumed by band members. Among other foraging populations, men do some collecting as well as hunting, and their contribution to the diet is greater. In still others, women gather vegetation, insects, slow-moving game, and some marine and fresh-water fauna, while men hunt, collect, and fish for different types of food. Division of labor on the basis of gender among foragers and in other societies is examined more completely in Chapter 11.

As there are differences in people's activities because of their sex, so, too, are there differences related to their age. Among many foragers, old people receive great respect as guardians of myths, legends, stories, and traditions of the band. Because of their contributions during their active years, old people may be the objects of considerable affection and admiration. Their knowledge of ritual as well as of practical matters is highly regarded.

All human societies allocate varying degrees of respect to different people. In foraging societies the amount of respect attached to any individual depends on a variety of factors, but particularly on personality attributes. Many kinds of individual talent may serve as a reason for respect—a person can sing or dance well, is an especially good storyteller, or has the ability to go into a trance and communicate with supernatural forces. There is, however, an important difference between band organization and other forms of social organization. Among foragers there is very little differential authority, and no differential power. There are band leaders in many foraging societies, but they are leaders in name only. They serve as focal points for the bands that they head; they are usually more permanent band members than the others. Their position in band life makes them first among equals, and they are sometimes asked for advice or information, which they give. Sometimes they make decisions. However, they have no means of enforcing their decisions.

THE PLANT-CULTIVATING CONTINUUM

Cohen has distinguished between three major strategies of adaptation based on food production in nonindustrial populations. They are horticulture, agriculture, and pastoralism. Each strategy is not an absolutely different, ideal, or pure type but refers to a population's *main* economic activity. As the examples throughout this chapter demonstrate, people typically carry out not just one, but a variety of economic pursuits. Foragers, though lacking control over the reproduction of plants and animals, obtain animal protein through hunting, fishing, and collecting small game, birds, and insects, and they diversify their diet by gathering a variety of plants and their products. Pastoralists, as you will see, live not just on the milk, butter, blood, and meat of their herds—though these may be mainstays of their diet—but commonly obtain grains and other plant products by cultivating some land or trading with their neighbors. Cultivators who irrigate, terrace, or manure their fields to grow their caloric staple—say, rice—may grow several other crops using other, less labor-intensive techniques. Depending on their environments and customs, food producers often gather and hunt to supplement diets based on domesticates, or for trade or relaxation. A strategy of adaptation, therefore, refers only to the main activity.

Horticulture and Agriculture

Cohen has drawn a useful distinction between two broadly different types of plant cultivation—horticulture and agriculture. *Horticulture* refers to non-mechanized systems of plant cultivation that make intensive use of neither land nor human labor. Characteristic cultivating tools of horticulturalists are hoes or digging sticks. Horticulture is sometimes called *swidden,* or slash-and-burn, cultivation. Horticulturalists customarily clear a tract of land that they wish to cultivate by cutting down primary or secondary forest or bush, or by setting fire to the grass that covers the plot. The felled vegetation is burned, and the ashes remain to fertilize the soil. The crops are then sown, tended, and harvested. Use of a given plot is not continuous, and often a plot is cultivated for only one year. This depends, however, on specific environmental factors, including soil fertility and rapidity of invasion of plots by weeds and grasses that compete with cultivated plants for vital nutrients.

Whether the reason for abandoning a plot is soil exhaustion or difficulty in cultivation because of thick stands of weeds and grasses, once the plot is

Toward the horticultural end of the plant-cultivating continuum, people use the slash-and-burn technique. Shown here are cultivators burning off the plant cover and working the soil with hoes before planting. Ashes from the burnt-off plants will also help fertilize the plot. (Arthur Tress)

withdrawn from cultivation, the cultivator clears another stretch of land. The original plot is allowed to revert to forest. Normally, after a fallow period of several years (the duration varies for different horticultural populations), the cultivator returns to the same land and cultivates it again.

Because the relationship between people and plot is not permanent, anthropologists also use the term *shifting cultivation* to refer to horticultural systems. Formerly it was thought that shifting cultivation meant also that whole villages of horticulturalists shifted sites because of declining yields. Yet anthropologist Robert Carneiro (1956) has demonstrated that large and permanent villages may exist with horticultural strategies. For example, among the Kuikuru of the tropical forest of South America, whom he studied, a village of 150 people had remained in the same spot for ninety years. In fact, he calculates that there was sufficient arable land located within walking distance of the village to maintain a permanent population of some 2,000 people. Carneiro found that permanent village sites seemed to be the rule rather than the exception for South American horticulturalists.

A situation of true shifting cultivation might occur if the amount of cultivable land controlled by a village were insufficient to support a permanent settlement. After a few harvests, it would be necessary for the village to move to seek new lands to clear and farm. Eventually, the population might return to the original site after having occupied one or more in between. It appears rare, however, that shifts in village sites are prompted by exhaustion of soil fertility. Rather, one must examine the interaction, mediated by specific sociocultural means of adaptation, between the human population and its immediate environment. For example, the houses in a Kuikuru village are large and well made and, since the toil involved in rebuilding them is great, the Kuikuru would rather walk farther to their plots than construct a new village. On the other hand, Carneiro (1968; orig. 1961) describes horticultural populations of the *montaña* (Andean foothills) of Peru who live in small villages of about thirty people. In contrast to the Kuikuru's, their houses are small and simply constructed. After a few years' residence at a site, these horticulturalists typically construct new villages near virgin land. Because their houses are so simple, they

The Implications of Food Production 59

prefer this alternative to walking even a half-mile to their fields.

Agriculture refers to nonindustrial systems of plant cultivation that require greater labor input and use land intensively and continuously. Labor demands associated with agricultural systems reflect their use of domesticated animals, irrigation, or terracing. Animals may be used as a means of production in several ways in agricultural economies. They may be attached to carts for transport or used as cultivating machines. Among the Betsileo, rice cultivators of central Madagascar, rice is sown in nursery beds. When seedlings are big enough, they are transplanted to flooded rice fields. The Betsileo keep humped zebu cattle. When the rice fields have been flooded and tilled, they let the cattle into them. By yelling at them and switching them, young men drive the cattle into a frenzy so that they will trample the fields, breaking up the clumps of earth and thoroughly mixing the water with the earth to form a smooth mud in which women can transplant the rice seedlings. Like many other agriculturalists, too, the Betsileo collect the manure of their domesticated animals and use it to fertilize their plots, thereby increasing yields.

"Trampling" among the Betsileo of south central Madagascar. (Conrad P. Kottak)

The Betsileo also irrigate their rice fields with water that they bring in canals from rivers, streams, springs, and ponds. To an extent, irrigation frees farmers from the vagaries of nature. They do not have to wait for rainfall before planting, for they control sources of water. Furthermore, irrigation makes it possible for a given plot of land to be cultivated year after year. It is a means of soil enrichment. The irrigated field is a unique ecosystem in which several species of plants and animals, many of them minute organisms, live. Their organic wastes, the products of metabolism and decomposition, fertilize the land. The Betsileo, like other agriculturalists throughout the world, have been farming the same fields for generations, and yields do not appear to have fallen off since the days of their ancestors. In fact, it takes an irrigated field some time to get going. It reaches full productivity only after having been cultivated for several years. In some agricultural areas, however, the accumulation of water-borne salts may render fields unusable after fifty or sixty years.

Terracing is another agricultural technique that the Betsileo have mastered. Many agriculturalists wrest their livelihoods out of rugged countryside. Some areas of central Madagascar are very hilly, with small valleys separated by steep hillsides. If cultivation is to proceed in densely populated areas, it is necessary

to farm these hills. If one simply plants on the steep hillsides, however, crops and good soil will be washed down during the rainy season. So the Betsileo cut into the hillside and construct stage after stage of cultivable field rising from the valley floor. These terraced fields are irrigated from springs above them, and the same advantages associated with irrigation in any field accrue to them. The amount of labor involved in building and maintaining a terrace system is great. The walls of the terraces crumble every year and must be partially rebuilt. The canals and outlets that convey water from terraces above to those below also demand attention.

Continuous Variation

Because horticulture and agriculture are ideal types, many economic systems have features of both. It is useful therefore to discuss cultivators as arranged along a plant-cultivating continuum (PCC). Horticultural systems stand at one end, the "labor-extensive—shifting plot" end, while agricultural strategies lie at the other, the "labor-intensive—permanent-plot" end. Foraging might be placed just before the horticultural end of the PCC, since archeological research has confirmed that historical transitions from foraging to food producing were typically gradual; furthermore, many contemporary horticulturalists continue to depend on foraging for a substantial part of their food supply.

To understand continuous variation in intensity of labor and land use, we focus first on the horticultural end of the continuum. Although some horticulturalists farm a plot only once before fallowing it, the Kuikuru of the tropical forest of South America grow two or three crops of the edible tuber manioc (cassava) before abandoning the plot. People cultivate more intensively in certain densely populated areas of New Guinea. Plots are planted for two or three years in succession, allowed to rest for three to five years, and then recultivated. The plot is abandoned for a longer time only after several of these plant-fallow cycles. Anthropologist Eric Wolf (1966) calls such systems *sectorial-fallowing systems* and points out that, in addition to New Guinea, they have been found in both the Old World and the New World—in West Africa and highland Mexico, for example. In all cases, they are associated with denser populations than the extensive horticultural systems often found in tropical forests, where weed

invasion and declining productivity of delicate soils prohibit intensive cultivation.

Strategies of adaptation that represent the horticultural end of the continuum and those that are intermediate between horticulture and agriculture characterize many human populations. The first food-producers in the Near East and Mesoamerica were horticulturalists. Nonagricultural cultivation was until recently the predominant form of plant cultivation in most of Africa; in large areas of Southeast Asia and Indonesia, especially highland and tropical forest regions; in many parts of the Philippines; in Oceania, including most of Polynesia, Melanesia, and Micronesia; among many native groups in Middle and Central America; and in the South American tropical forest. Examination of a large sample of nonindustrial populations in which plots are still fallowed indicates that some use land much more intensively than others. Even when we limit our attention to a sample of cultivators representing only one area of the world, we see a continuum in intensity of land use and human labor invested in cultivation. For example, Jacques Barrau (1958) demonstrated continuous variation in cultivation techniques among seventeen Melanesian populations—from rudimentary, extensive slash and burn through sectorial fallowing to long-term use of the same plot requiring soil turning, drainage techniques, terracing, composting, and crop rotation.

Viewing horticulture and agriculture as contrasting positions on a continuum both focuses attention on tremendous worldwide variation in cultivating techniques and returns us to the evolutionary models based on natural selection introduced previously. If we compare human populations in terms of particular, assessable variables—which, in their totality, compose the specific environments to which the populations must adapt—we are in a better position to see how such variable sociocultural forms as kinship or political organization help humans solve adaptive problems within their environments. The PCC provides a framework for certain generalizations. As labor intensity increases and as land use becomes more permanent, a variety of demographic, social, and political correlates usually follow. People live in larger and more permanent communities located closer to other settlements. As populations grow, they segment into subgroups. Increase in population size, density, and stability means more interactions among individuals, between individuals and groups, and among groups. If society is not to

The straw hut of the Amahuaca, who prefer to move their small settlements rather than walk to distant fields. Compared with the Kuikuru, the Amahuaca illustrate diversity among shifting cultivators. (Cornell Capa/Magnum Photos)

dissolve, expanding interpersonal relations and the potentially conflicting interests of individuals and groups must be managed, or *regulated;* allocation of land, labor, and other productive resources must be coordinated in economies that have to support more people. A variety of social and political changes — discussed at length in this chapter and in Chapter 4 — often follow as responses to new regulatory demands. Through the examples of plant cultivators and pastoralists that follow, we see how authority structure changes in the presence of such regulatory problems. The relationship between the plant-cultivating continuum — or, more generally, food production — and the larger structure of human life is not simple. It must be demonstrated by considering specific adaptations of human populations to their environments.

We know that both in Mexico and in the Near East, the historical transition from foraging to food production involved a gradual increase in the proportion of domesticates included in the diet. Populations were not hunters and gatherers one year and food producers the next. Rather, plant cultivation began as only part of a broad spectrum of activities in prehistoric economies. Gradually, it contributed more and more to the diet. According to Cohen, when cultivation contributes only about one-tenth of a group's diet, as was the situation when food production first began in prehistoric populations, it may be impossible to maintain sedentary, permanent villages. After all, it is not attributes of the soil, but the distribution and seasonal appearance of wild plants and animals that are critical in determining the movement and settlement patterns of the human population. People may assemble, plant, and disperse soon after, then forage and come together again for the harvest. Depending on the environment and the specific human adaptation to it, they may spend a few months together after the harvest, consuming the plant foods they have harvested. Foraging resumes for the remainder of the year.

When cultivation makes a larger contribution to the diet, sedentary village life is possible, especially if the local ecosystem includes sufficient quantities of other resources for a balanced diet. Although all twenty essential amino acids can, in theory, be obtained from plant products, animal protein becomes essential when a particular population's plant diet is deficient in one or more amino acids. Among many populations of the Old World, domesticated animals supplement a diet of cultivated plants. Since animal protein is usually part of a balanced diet, hunting, fishing, and collecting may still go on. When less than half of the diet comes from cultivated plants, unless natural food resources are particularly concentrated and abundant, population densities are low, and village populations do not exceed two hundred people. Often there will be only one hundred or even fewer inhabitants.

Headmen and Big Men as Regulators

The tremendous variation among plant-cultivating societies in terms of intensity of use of land and labor, relative importance of cultivation in the group's diet, and plant species cultivated makes it difficult to generalize about other sociocultural correlates of plant-cultivating strategies of adaptation. However, a few generalizations about power, authority, and social organization among cultivators can be attempted.

The authority structure of foraging societies and of societies at the horticultural end of the PCC is relatively egalitarian compared with that of most other human societies. Egalitarianism generally wanes as village size and population density increase. When cultivation is extensive and foraging activities are still important, villages are usually small, population density is generally low, and everyone has unimpeded access to strategic resources. Age, sex, and personality determine the respect people receive and the amount of support they are able to obtain from others if they make plans or decisions. The authority roles assigned on the basis of gender in plant-cultivating societies are variable and are discussed in Chapter 11.

At the horticultural end of the PCC, villages usually have *headmen*—rarely, if ever, headwomen. The headmen of horticultural villages are sometimes erroneously called chiefs, a term whose proper meaning is discussed in Chapter 4. The headman's authority, like that of the band leader, is severely limited. If a village headman wants something done, he must lead by example and persuasion. In his book *Yanomamo: The Fierce People* (1977), anthropologist Napoleon Chagnon describes the way in which the headman gets his covillagers to prepare for a feast that will bring outsiders to their village. The headman lacks the right to issue orders. He can only persuade, harangue, and try to move public opinion. If he wants people to clean up the central plaza, he must get out and begin sweeping it himself, hoping that his covillagers will take the hint and relieve

him. When conflict erupts, the Yanomamo headman may be called on to listen to both sides of a dispute. He will render his opinion and offer his advice. If one of the parties is unsatisfied, however, the headman can do nothing. He has no power to back his decisions; he has no way to impose punishments or other kinds of physical sanctions. Like the band leader, he, too, is first among equals.

In many areas of the Melanesian Islands and in New Guinea, populations somewhat further along the PCC have a type of political leader that anthropologists call the *big man*. The big man—again, almost always a male—is an elaborate version of the Yanomamo headman, with some of his same characteristic personality attributes and limitations. Consider the Kapauku Papuans of western New Guinea, who have been described ethnographically by Leopold Pospisil (1963). Like most other New Guineans and Melanesians, the Kapauku cultivate plants (the sweet potato is their staple) and raise pigs. The varied cultivating practices of the Kapauku are far too complex, however, to be described as simple horticulture. Beyond the household, the only political figure encountered among the Kapauku is the big man, known as a *tonowi*. Like the Yanomamo headman, he achieves his status because he works hard—in this case, to amass wealth in pigs and other native riches. Pospisil states that the attributes that separate the Kapauku big man from his fellows include wealth, generosity, eloquence, verbal daring, and physical fitness, and, in some cases, bravery in war and supernatural powers.

Even among peoples representing the intermediate part of the PCC, political prominence is generally achieved by virtue of personality attributes. In this, the similarity to foragers is clear. Among the Kapauku, wealth depends on successful pig breeding and trading of wealth. But any male who is determined enough can become a big man, since people create their own wealth through hard work and good judgment rather than by inheriting it. The big man's wealth and charisma attract supporters, make his reputation, and give him influence. He extends interest-free loans; he sponsors pig feasts in which pigs are slaughtered ceremonially and their meat distributed to his guests.

The big man enjoys one advantage the Yanomamo headman does not. His wealth, created by his own work, is superior to that of his fellows. His supporters, in recognition of past favors and anticipation of future rewards, recognize him as a leader and accept his decisions as binding. The adaptation of 45,000 Kapauku to their environment involves more regulation than is the case with 10,000 Yanomamo. The big man is an important regulator of events in Kapauku life. He helps determine proper dates for feasts and markets; persuades people to sponsor feasts, which distribute meat and other wealth; regulates intervillage contacts by sponsoring dance expeditions to other villages; and initiates large projects that require the cooperation of the entire community.

From the example of the Kapauku big man a generalization can be made about leadership in relatively egalitarian societies: if people manage to achieve wealth and prestige, to command respect and support beyond their fellows, they are expected to be generous. The big man characteristically works hard to be able to give away the fruits of his labor, to convert wealth into prestige and gratitude from fellow members of his group. Should an individual who aspires to become a big man renege on his obligations to be generous, he is soon deserted by his supporters, and his reputation plummets. The Kapauku, in fact, take even more definite measures against big men who hoard. Pospisil reports that in some areas of Kapauku country, selfish and greedy rich men are frequently executed by their fellows, often including their own close kin.

There are also differences in the decision-making authority and influence over other group members between the Yanomamo headman and the Kapauku big man. One can generalize that the authority of political figures is a function of the complexity of regulatory problems encountered in the population's adaptation to its environment. The cultivating economy of the Kapauku Papuans is much more complex than either the Yanomamo's or the Kuikuru's, involving more varied techniques and specialized cultivation practices for specific tracts of land. In addition to two types of shifting cultivation, called by Pospisil *extensive* and *intensive,* the Kapauku practice labor-intensive cultivation of the valley floors. This involves mutual aid of individual cultivators in turning the soil prior to planting. An even more complex regulatory problem is the joint effort of the entire community to construct long drainage ditches in the valley fields. Kapauku plant cultivation supports a larger and denser population than either Kuikuru or Yanomamo horticulture.

Whatever the reasons promoting increased population density and larger villages in the area, these demographic changes represent environmental modifications that pose new regulatory problems and require new adaptive means. As villages grow, as the number of people regularly living together increases, interpersonal conflicts also increase. In Nigeria, in western Africa, there are villages of sectorial-fallowing cultivators whose populations exceed 1,000 people located in areas where population densities exceed 200 people per square mile. In Amazonia, Carneiro (1968; orig. 1961) found documentation for a village of 1,400 inhabitants in 1824, supported by extensive slash-and-burn cultivation. When village size exceeds 1,000, there may be several, and perhaps ten or more, descent groups in the same village instead of one or two.

The *descent group* is a basic social group in many food-producing societies. Descent groups are composed of people who are all descended—or believe they are descended—from a common ancestor. There are normally several descent groups in a given society. Any one of them may be confined to a single village, but usually they will span more than one village. Any branch of the descent group that resides together is called a *localized descent group.* One of the things that keeps one descent group distinct from others in that society is its *estate.* This refers to possession and control over land and herds or, more generally, to a variety of rights that have been inherited from the ancestral members of that descent group.

In large villages, not only are there myriad interpersonal relationships to worry about, there are intergroup relationships as well. In societies with a well-developed descent-group structure, a person's allegiance is principally to his or her descent group, only secondarily to village and tribe. People are expected to take the side of their own group in any dispute with another group that resides in the same village.

If disorder is not to be a day-to-day characteristic of these large-scale cultivating societies, it is necessary to have someone to regulate conflict, to arbitrate disputes among individuals and groups. The functions of the headman and his manner of selection vary among larger-scale nonagricultural cultivators, but the task of this political figure as regulator is fairly demanding. He may have to direct military actions or hunting expeditions. He arbitrates disputes between villagers. He may have to reallocate land used by villagers if, because of different rates of population increase, some descent groups have grown too big for their ancestral estates while others are still too small to exploit their own. He and other elders in the community may resolve conflicts over land or other matters from time to time.

Note another difference. In the smaller-scale societies a person's position rests on age, sex, and personality characteristics. When human populations are organized into descent groups, another basis for status develops—descent-group leadership. In villages with multiple descent groups, each of these has a head. All heads together may form a council of advisers or, normally, a council of elders to assist the headman. Cooperating, they represent the local power structure: the authority of the headman is supported by his council of elders, and it is up to them to make sure that decisions reached through their deliberations are carried out by the members of their individual descent groups. The headman must obtain agreement by all council members on decisions that apply to the village population. Sometimes, however, it is difficult to reach agreement, since decisions good for the community at large may adversely affect the interests of one or more of the descent groups— and descent groups are still important. Societies that rely heavily on nonagricultural plant cultivation are rarely nation-states (see p. 66); they are, instead, *tribal societies*. Although when compared to foraging, such food-producing economies generally support more permanent settlements, larger populations, and more complex forms of sociopolitical integration, there is still no centralized rule. Decisions made by such political bodies as headmen and councils of elders cannot be enforced through any constituted physical means. If the head of one descent group is recalcitrant, the only means of coercion that the other heads and the headman can employ are persuasion and public opinion. And if individuals do not wish to follow the advice of their descent group elders, they may be asked to leave the village; but, again, in tribal societies as in bands, community opinion and persuasion are usually brought to bear.

Despite their enlarged powers, the descent-group leaders and the headman are still expected to be generous. The wealth and life styles of these political figures are normally not very far above those of their fellow villagers. They take part in subsistence activity. They are only part-time political specialists. If they control more land and larger and more productive households, they are expected, like Kapauku big men and other headmen, to give more feasts and support more dependents than ordinary

cultivators. Social classes do not exist in most large-scale nonagricultural societies unless the societies are also involved in long-distance trade networks.

The manner of choosing the village headman varies from one tribal society to another. In some cases, in villages where there are several descent groups, the headmanship rotates among them. In other societies, there are elections among descent-group leaders. In still other cases, the office of headman is confined to one of the several descent groups, perhaps the largest, but the incumbent relies on the support and approval of representatives of the other descent groups. Finally, choice of the headman may be associated with ritual. He may be chosen because of supernatural powers that he is believed to possess. His abilities may be the result of training in ritual matters, or people may believe that they are inherited or have come through divine revelation. In some tribal societies, the headman's supernatural associations support his general authority. Among the Kapauku, shamanistic expertise, although not essential to headmanship, does enhance its power.

Intensive Cultivation and Complex Regulation

At the agricultural end of the continuum, as will be seen in Chapter 4, regulatory problems proliferate. Often they are handled (and sometimes increased) by governmental structures of nation-states. Human labor must be deployed to construct and maintain irrigation and terrace systems. Domesticated animals must be fed, watered, and cared for. Given intensive labor investment and appropriate management, the same land can produce one or more crops a year for several years and even for generations. Sedentary populations, which grow up around the permanent fields, are always characteristic of agricultural cultivators. Agricultural techniques do not necessarily increase annual crop yields over those produced horticulturally. The first crop cultivated by horticulturalists after clearing new or long idle forest land may have a higher yield than a plot of the same size that is cultivated agriculturally. Relative to the amount of labor invested, too, the yield of the nonagriculturalist is usually higher. In terms of crop production, the major difference between agriculture and other nonindustrial systems of cultivation is that the long-term yield per unit area is far greater under agricultural systems. A single area continuously supports its cultivators. Thus it is un-

Cooperative work among women in China. The labor-intensive, permanent cultivation end of the plant-cultivating continuum—often associated with large, dense populations and state organization. (Marc Riboud/Magnum Photos)

derstandable that populations of agriculturalists are usually denser than those of other cultivators.

As human control over nature increases, the range of environments open to human use and settlement becomes greater. Agricultural populations exist in many areas of the world that are too arid for nonirrigators or too hilly for nonterracers. Many of the world's ancient civilizations in arid lands arose on an agricultural base. The demographic, social, and political trends of the PCC are stronger among agriculturalists. Most, but not all, agricultural peoples live in complex *nation-states*—sociopolitical systems possessing governments and encompassing acute contrasts in wealth, prestige, and power. In such contexts, cultivators themselves become merely one part of a socioeconomically differentiated, functionally specialized, and tightly integrated sociopolitical system. Not just agriculturalists, but pastoralists too, are often caught up in and dependent on such state systems.

PASTORALISM

In the Near East and North Africa, in several eastern European and Asiatic regions, and in sub-Saharan Africa live human populations whose activities are centered on the care of such domesticated animals as cattle, sheep, goats, and camels. They are called *pastoralists*. East African pastoralists, like many others, live symbiotically with herd animals and obtain food and other necessities, such as leather, from their herds. Herds supply East Africans with milk, other dairy products, and meat. Cattle blood is often consumed as well. Cattle are slaughtered at funerals and as part of other ceremonies. Since these occur throughout the year, beef is available on a fairly constant basis.

Stockbreeding populations differ in their use of herd animals. In the adaptive strategies of some, animals are a means rather than an end of production. Among the Native Americans of the Great Plains, for example, the horse was not consumed as food but was used within a foraging economy to pursue the large bison herds, which were major subsistence resources. In many agricultural economies, too, animals are used as a means rather than an end of production. In contrast to such use of domesticated animals as productive machines in other adaptive strategies, pastoralists typically make direct use of their herds as subsistence resources, consuming their milk—from which they make yogurt and butter—meat, and blood. Some populations rely on their herd animals more completely than others. It is impossible, however, for people to base subsistence exclusively on animals; most pastoral populations supplement their diet by hunting, gathering, fishing, cultivating plants, or trading.

For pastoralists, animals are storehouses "on the hoof." These Ugandan herders regularly add vital nutrients to their diet by bleeding their animals. Cooked blood and milk are only two of several dairy products used by stockbreeders. (George Rodger/Magnum Photos)

Remember that pastoralism, like all of Cohen's adaptive strategies, is an ideal type. No economy is pure; diets include both plant and animal resources. The mixed nature of pastoral economies is, however, particularly obvious. To gain access to crops, pastoralists either trade with plant cultivators or invest some of their own labor in cultivating or gathering. Because herding and cultivation are, and always have been, interdependent, neither the historical emergence and spread of pastoralism nor contemporary pastoralists can be understood if plant cultivation is ignored. Nineteenth-century anthropologists, lacking today's archeological knowledge, speculated about which came first, plant cultivation or animal domestication. We now know that pastoralism and cultivation emerged and spread together as interrelated parts of a general pattern of increasing human intervention in nature.

In contrast to the previously discussed strategies, which were of worldwide importance before the Industrial Revolution, pastoralism was almost totally confined to the Old World. Before the European conquest, the only New World pastoralists lived in the Peruvian Andes. Typically, however, Andeans maintained their herds of llamas and alpacas not just for subsistence but for a variety of uses in agriculture and transport. More recently, the Navajo of the southwestern United States developed a mixed pastoral economy based on sheep, brought to the New World from Europe. The Navajo have become the major pastoral population of the New World, and today make up between one-third and one-fourth of the Native American population of the United States.

Two characteristic patterns of movement are associated with pastoralism: *nomadism* and *transhumance*. Like horticulture and agriculture, they differ quantitatively rather than qualitatively. With nomadism, the entire herding group—women, men, and children—moves with its animals throughout the year. With transhumance, only part of the population goes along when the herds move seasonally; the other part stays put, carrying out a variety of nonherding activities. Following their herds throughout the year, nomads trade with more sedentary groups, which provide them with crops and other products. Because only part of the population accompanies the herds, transhumants can maintain year-round villages, where they can plant and harvest their own crops. The annual activities of the Jie of Uganda, a transhumant population of some 18,000

In Kenem, Chad, a group of nomadic pastoralists start another leg of their annual trek. With nomadic pastoralism, everyone moves with the herds, while with transhumance, part of the population—usually women, children, and old people—stays put. (Jacques Jangoux)

people (Gulliver, 1955, 1974), for example, are conducted within a territory about 104 km. (65 miles) long by 40 km. (25 miles) wide. The western part of their homeland is better watered than the east, and it is toward the west that the Jie have their villages and cultivate their crops using horticultural techniques. As the rainy season begins, many adult men and some of the boys take the herds to the eastern pasturelands. Later, as the rainy season ends, they move west to an area that can still be grazed after the east is dry. When even the western pastures are exhausted, men, boys, and herds return to the village to spend the rest of the year in the best-watered area

of all. While men and boys move with the herds, women, older men, and most of the children stay home, taking part in a variety of village activities. Transhumance is also practiced in the Alpine areas of western Europe. Movement of people and herds to highland spring and summer pastures is familiar to anyone who has read the children's book *Heidi*. Transhumance and nomadism represent, once again, the idea of continuous variation—since the proportion of the population accompanying the herds, the length of time spent in one place, and the amount of productive labor devoted to activities other than herding are all quantitative matters.

Interethnic Symbiosis

Within the contemporary United States, different states specialize in supplying specific products. Michigan produces cars; Florida, citrus fruits; and California, a variety of fruits, vegetables, and wines.

In both industrial and nonindustrial nations, various *ethnic groups*, that is, people whose customs and cultural heritage differ from other such groups and from the main body of society, are often included within the same national or provincial boundaries. Although each may specialize in particular activities, and therefore occupies its own ecological niche, neighboring ethnic groups are often interdependent. In ecological terms, their associations may involve *mutualism*, also known as *symbiosis:* an obligatory interaction beneficial to both groups—neither could exist without the other. Ecologists use still another term, *protocooperation,* to refer to nonobligatory but still beneficial interactions (see Clapham, 1973). Since the distinction between mutualism and protocooperation is a matter of degree—to what extent could one group survive without the other?—ethnic interactions can sometimes be categorized as either or as fitting someplace in between.

Such ethnic interactions in the state of Swat, Pakistan, have been described by anthropologist Fredrik Barth (1974; orig. 1958). The three ethnic groups—Pathans, Kohistanis, and Gujars—whose interactions Barth describes coexist in the same general area by specializing in different resources and activities. These three groups are also distinguished by different languages and customs. The Pathans are agriculturalists, the Gujars are pastoralists, and the Kohistanis have a mixed economy involving agriculture and herding. Pathans cultivate the same land twice annually; Kohistanis, only once. Pathans live in the fertile valleys of the Swat and Indus rivers, where they rely on river floodwaters in cultivating wheat, rice, and maize. Kohistanis live at higher altitudes where cooler weather limits cultivation to a single growing season. Cooler temperatures also dictate different crop staples for the Kohistanis—maize and millet rather than rice and wheat. Because their habitat is hillier, the Kohistanis must construct terraces and elaborate irrigation systems that tap mountain streams. With limited agricultural productivity, the Kohistanis keep sheep and goats that they herd in a transhumant pattern. Shepherds journey to mountain pastures in spring and return to their villages during fall and winter after these grazing lands are exhausted. Gujars, whose economy is exclusively pastoral, maintain mutualistic or protocooperative relationships with both Pathans and Kohistanis.

Pathan society is divided on the basis of wealth and prestige into several groups: an elite, a class of poor peasants, and several intermediate categories. Gujars have been assimilated into Pathan society as one among many *castes*—endogamous groups differentiated socially and economically. The Gujar economy exists as one specialized part of the complex Pathan economy: Gujars herd Pathan animals, along with their own, in hillsides surrounding Pathan valleys. They also trade with the Pathans. In exchange for clarified butter (ghee) and other animal products, Pathans offer grains and land-use rights to the Gujars. Interactions between Kohistanis and Gujars include similar trade relationships, but no similar social ties.

The example of mutually beneficial interactions among Gujars, Pathans, and Kohistanis has a larger significance. The transition to food production in the Near East and subsequently in other parts of the Old World spawned a variety of ecological niches, some involving specialization of social groups within complex regional systems such as Swat, Pakistan. Similar mutualistic interactions have arisen between *foragers* and food producers in several places, including Zaire in equatorial Africa. Turnbull (1961, 1965) has described exchanges between Mbuti "pygmies" of the Ituri Forest and their horticultural neighbors. With population increase engendered by the spread of food production, African horticulturalists have penetrated the tropical forest and come into contact with the Mbuti and other indigenous foragers. Contemporary Mbuti no longer exist exclusively on foraging, but depend on symbiosis with the horticulturalists, who provide crops in exchange for game, honey, and other forest products. Just as Gujars are specialized herders for the Pathans, many Mbuti today actually live in the horticultural villages as a specialized group of hunters, making occasional forays into the forest to provide game for their hosts. The spread of food production has created, therefore, not simply interdependence between kinds of food producers, but also interdependence between food producers and foragers.

Regulation and Political Organization

Among such foragers as the !Kung and the Mbuti, little regulation is necessary. Small group size and low population density limit the number of interpersonal and intergroup relationships; an economy whose tasks are known by all and in which there is little human intervention in nature also limits regulatory concerns. Along the plant-cultivating continuum, however, problems associated with increasing population and special interests must be managed, and regulatory institutions gradually develop. The extent to which such regulatory mechanisms as differential authority relationships are developed among pastoralists also reflects population density and pressure on scarce resources. Demonstrating this is a study by anthropologist Philip Salzman (1974), who has focused on six populations of increasing density: the Turkana of Uganda (80,000 people), the Jie of Uganda (18,000), the Somali of Ethiopia (3,250,000), the Basseri of Iran (16,000), the Bakhtiari of Iran (100,000), and the Qashqai of Iran (400,000).

The Turkana and the Jie of Uganda are culturally divergent descendants of a single population that split sometime in the past. The extremely arid pastureland on which the Turkana live make their population density lowest among the six groups. The neighboring Jie, with better-watered land, practice pastoral transhumance and horticulture. The Turkana are more nomadic, fragmenting into small groups of men, women, and children who lead the herds from one grazing area to another. Fragmentation into family groups in pursuit of scarce and dispersed resources coupled with low population density and extreme mobility make the Turkana similar to many foraging populations. The major difference, of course, is the intervention of energy-converting machines—domesticated animals—between humans and plants.

Although the total Jie population is less than one-third that of the Turkana, their territory is also much smaller and their population correspondingly denser (about one person per square mile). Like many other tribal populations practicing horticulture, the Jie maintain their villages, though they shift and fallow their horticultural plots. During the times of year when pasturage is lowest, the Jie remain near their villages; their crops are an important part of their diets. Because they grow their own crops, the Jie are less dependent than the Turkana and pastoral nomads generally on trade with other ethnic groups. All grain in the Turkana diet is acquired through trade with their neighbors.

The Somali of Somalia, Ethiopia, and Kenya extend over a far larger area than either the Jie or the Turkana. Their homeland becomes drier from south to north, and economic activities reflect the climatic shift. Horticulture is important in the south; moving north, pastoralism, first as transhumance, then as nomadism, becomes an increasingly significant part of the Somali economy. As is true of many food producers, there is no one-to-one correlation between cultural heritage and economy. As the environment changes, so, too, do their adaptive strategies. In the most arid areas, the Somali, like the Turkana, are pastoral nomads who cultivate no crops of their own and rely on trade for grain.

Differential political authority among the Somali, Jie, and Turkana is not developed much beyond the scale of leaders in foraging societies or village headmen in sparsely populated horticultural societies. Like many nonagricultural cultivators, they live in tribal societies; their social groups are larger than among foragers, but they are not regulated by any government. On the basis of aridity, sparsity of pasture, and low population density, the Turkana, Jie, and Somali contrast with the three Iranian populations. Turning to the Basseri, Bakhtiari, and Qashqai, we see that the scope of political authority among pastoralists expands considerably in response to regulatory problems that arise in densely populated regions. Regional populations are often made up of several ethnic groups, and regulatory problems reflect their interactions.

The three groups of Iranian pastoralists annually traverse a pastoral nomadic route more than 480 km. (300 miles) long. Starting their annual migration from a low plateau near the coast, they herd their animals at altitudes between 600 m. (2,000 ft.) and 5,400 m. (18,000 ft.). The Basseri, Bakhtiari, and Qashqai share their nomadic route with one another and with several other ethnically different pastoral populations. They confront a regulatory problem common to nomads in other areas of similar density and ethnic complexity: several ethnic groups must share access to land and resources. Use of the same pastureland at different times must be carefully scheduled; ethnic-group movements must be tightly coordinated. Expressing this scheduling is *il-rah*, a concept common to Basseri, Bakhtiari, Qashqai, and other Iranian nomads. A group's *il-rah* is its customary path in time and space. It is the schedule, different for each group, of when specific areas will be used in the annual trek between low plateau and upland pastures.

Prior to twentieth-century intervention by the Iranian national government in administering nomadic migrations, such groups as the Basseri, Bakhtiari, and Qashqai each had its own leader, known as the *khan* or *il-khan*. The prerogatives and functions of this political figure contrasted strongly with those of such essentially limited authority figures as !Kung band leaders, Yanomamo village headmen, or even Kapauku big men. The Basseri *khan,* because he dealt with a smaller population, faced fewer problems in coordinating its movements than did the leaders of the Bakhtiari and Qashqai. Correspondingly, the rights, privileges, duties, and authority of the Basseri *khan* were less developed. Nevertheless, his authority exceeded that of any political figure in any nonagricultural society so far discussed. As in the case of the Kapauku big man, however, the Basseri *khan*'s authority was charismatic, emanating from his person rather than from his office. The Basseri followed a particular *khan* not because of the office he happened to fill, but because of personal allegiance and loyalty to him as a man. Personalism and charisma were less characteristic of the relationship between subject and *khan* in Bakhtiari and Qashqai society, where allegiance appears to have been to the office rather than to the man. The Basseri *khan* relied most immediately on the support of the heads of the descent groups into which Basseri society is divided. In contrast to the Bakhtiari and Qashqai, few levels of authority intervened between *khan* and ordinary herder. The *khan* influenced the descent-group heads, each of whom then mobilized support of descent-group members.

Multiple levels of authority and more powerful *khans* distinguished Bakhtiari and Qashqai political organization from that of the Basseri. The Bakhtiari political hierarchy consisted of three levels. Like the Basseri, Bakhtiari belonged to descent groups, which had their own leaders. In contrast to Basseri, however, the Bakhtiari descent groups were grouped into tribes, each of which had a leader, called a *khan.* The Bakhtiari tribe was like the Basseri—regulated only by *khan* and descent-group heads. At the top of Bakhtiari political organization stood the *il-khan,* head of all the tribes and their constituents and supreme political figure over 100,000 subjects.

Regulating 400,000 Qashqai necessitated a still more complex hierarchy. It was headed by the *il-khan,* assisted by a deputy, under whom were the heads of the constituent tribes, under each of whom were descent-group heads. A case cited by Salzman illustrates just how developed the Qashqai authority structure was. A hailstorm prevented a group of nomads from joining the beginning migration at the appointed time. Although it was recognized that

they were not responsible for their delay, the *il-khan* assigned them less favorable grazing land for that year only in place of the excellent pasture to which they were ordinarily entitled. The tardy herders and other Qashqai considered the judgment fair and did not question it. The *il-khan*'s traditional authority was confirmed by an adage that states in effect that neither rain nor snow nor storm can excuse action that contradicts orders from higher authorities.

The functions of these various authority figures extended beyond the planning and managing of the annual migration. They also regulated interpersonal relations within the ethnic group by adjudicating disputes between individuals and between tribes and descent groups.

On the basis of these six pastoral populations, we can generalize that, as regulatory problems increase, political hierarchies become more complex, and political organization becomes less personal, more formal, and less kinship-oriented. The pastoral strategy of adaptation dictates not a particular political organization, but rather a variety of authority structures that manage regulatory problems associated with specific environments. Several generalizations can be made about other strategies of adaptation—namely, that most foragers have band organization and little differential authority; that horticulturalists and other nonagricultural cultivators live in tribal societies with village headmen, descent-group heads, and big men, but rarely chiefs; and that most nonindustrial nation-states have an agricultural base. But the relationship between pastoralism and political organization is far more complex. Some pastoralists live in tribal societies; others have powerful chiefs and live in nation-states. This reflects pastoralists' need to interact with other populations—a need that is less universal among populations with the other adaptive strategies. As both the Swat and Iranian cases illustrate, pastoralism is often just one among many specialized economic activities within complex nation-states and regional ecosystems. As parts of a larger whole, the interests and affairs of pastoral groups are constantly pitted against those of other groups. Ethnic interactions may be regulated by authority structures within the ethnic group, as for the traditional Basseri, Bakhtiari, and Qashqai, or by central governments like Iran, which now appoints *khans* and oversees scheduling of ethnic *il-rahs*.

The nature, scope, strength, and complexity of political organization depend on regulatory problems at several levels involving interpersonal, intergroup, and interethnic interactions. Looking beyond the six populations just used to exemplify certain correlations between political organization and specific environments, we can generalize that pressure on strategic resources, often reflecting population density, is one of the main reasons why regulatory problems increase.

Confronting examples known from archeological and ethnographic study, we would suspect that the genesis of state organization rests not just on problems associated with agriculture, but on regional regulation of a variety of socially and ethnically different groups performing specialized activities within expanding social and economic systems. The regulation of interethnic interaction is an important variable in the process of state formation, which we now examine.

SUMMARY

Two different kinds of evolutionary statements can be made about humans: general evolutionary, which apply to the genus *Homo,* and specific evolutionary, which apply to particular human populations adapting to changing environments. The doctrine of unilinear evolution, a general evolutionary doctrine, was proposed by nineteenth-century scientists. More recently, anthropologist Leslie White has written of the evolution of culture, an approach similar to general evolution but concentrating on changes in *Homo*'s basic adaptive apparatus, culture. Anthropologist Julian Steward has advocated studies of multilinear evolution, examination of cases involving convergent evolution, comparison of specific evolutionary sequences among widespread populations.

Anthropologist Yehudi Cohen has proposed six strategies of adaptation to the environment: foraging, horticulture, agriculture, pastoralism, mercantilism, and industrialism. The first four are examined in detail in this chapter. Foraging was the only strategy of adaptation pursued by humans until the advent of food production 10,000 years ago. Food production replaced foraging throughout most of the world, but foragers survive today in marginal areas. Correlates of a foraging strategy reflect the nature of specific environments. The band is often the basic social unit among foragers. Sometimes band members remain together throughout the year; other times they fragment seasonally into foraging microbands or families. Ties of kinship and marriage, trade, and other arrangements link members of bands. In most foraging societies, tasks are assigned on the basis of sex and age; men generally hunt, and females gather. Old people often retire partially from subsistence activities and care for children. Foragers characteristically form the most egalitarian of all human socie-

ties; there is little differential authority and no differential power among band members, and prestige reflects age, sex, and individual achievements.

Like other strategies of adaptation described, horticulture and agriculture are ideal types. They are viewed here as representing different ends of a plant-cultivating continuum, reflecting increasing labor intensity and continuity of cultivation of the same land. Horticulture refers to nonindustrial systems of plant cultivation that do not use either land or human labor intensively. Horticulturalists generally cultivate a plot of land for one or two years, then abandon it. Further along the plant-cultivating continuum, horticulture uses more intensive techniques, but there is always a fallowing period. Horticulturalists may shift their plots while remaining in the same village. The first plant-cultivating economies were horticultural, and this strategy of adaptation still occurs in many areas of both the Old and New Worlds.

The social and economic correlates of plant cultivation reflect the amount of food that cultivation contributes to the diet and the intensity and yields of productive labor. Cultivation is often combined with other strategies of adaptation—for example, pastoralism or foraging. Cultivators normally live in villages and often belong to descent groups. Cultivating societies span a wide range in terms of village size and population density, reflecting the differential productivity of their economies.

Egalitarianism generally wanes as village size and population density increase, since with more people more interpersonal relationships must be regulated. Horticultural villages generally have a headman; however, his authority is very limited. He must lead by example and persuasion and has no sure means of enforcing his decisions. Authority associated with political figures in cultivating societies generally increases as population size and density and the scale of regulatory problems grow.

Agriculture describes nonindustrial systems of plant cultivation in which the same land is used continuously. Agricultural systems also characteristically demand intensive use of human labor. Agricultural systems are often associated with one or more of the following practices: irrigation, terracing, use of domesticated animals for labor, and manuring. Because the same land is used permanently, agricultural populations are commonly denser than those supported by other strategies of adaptation. There are some tribal agriculturalists, but agriculture is often associated with complex regulatory systems, including state organization. Implications of agriculture are examined more fully in Chapter 4.

Pastoralists often participate in systems of interethnic symbiosis, coexisting in the same general areas as other ethnic groups, each specializing in different resources and activities. The Gujars, Kohistanis, and Pathans of Pakistan provide one example. Considering several pastoral populations, we see that the development of differential authority relationships within a pastoral society reflects population size and density, interethnic relationships, and the regulation of access to scarce resources. In arid habitats with sparse pasture and low population density, for example, the homelands of the Jie, Turkana, and Somali, political authority—as among foragers and horticulturalists—is rudimentary. All these are tribal societies. Regulatory problems increase, and political organization grows stronger, however, among the Basseri, Bakhtiari, and Qashqai of Iran. Each group shares its nomadic route and its strategic resources with several other ethnic groups. As a particular ethnic group's population increases in a densely populated region, its political hierarchy becomes increasingly complex.

SOURCES AND SUGGESTED READINGS

BARRAU, J.
1958   *Subsistence Agriculture in Melanesia.* Bulletin 219. Honolulu: Bernice P. Bishop Museum. French ethnobotanist examines variations in cultivation techniques in Melanesia.

BARTH, F.
1961   *Nomads of South Persia.* Boston: Little, Brown. Field study of the Basseri, Iranian pastoralists.

1974   (orig. 1958). Ecologic Relationships of Ethnic Groups in Swat, North Pakistan. In *Man in Adaptation: The Cultural Present.* 2nd ed., ed. Y. A. Cohen, pp. 378–385. Chicago: Aldine. Classic study of interethnic relations.

BOSERUP, E.
1965   *The Conditions of Agricultural Growth.* Chicago: Aldine. Influential book linking population increase, agricultural intensity, and level of sociopolitical development.

CARNEIRO, R. L.
1956   Slash-and-Burn Agriculture: A Closer Look at Its Implications for Settlement Patterns. In *Men and Cultures,* Selected Papers of the Fifth International Congress of Anthropological and Ethnological Sciences, pp. 229–234. Philadelphia: University of Pennsylvania Press. Influential article that suggests that shifting cultivation may be compatible with permanent villages.

1967   On the Relationships between Size of Population and Complexity of Social Organization. *Southwestern Journal of Anthropology* 23: 234–243. Comparative and evolutionary study.

1968   (orig. 1961). Slash-and-Burn Cultivation among the Kuikuru and Its Implications for Cultural Development in the Amazon Basin. In *Man in Adaptation: The Cultural Present,* ed. Y. A. Cohen, pp. 131–145. Chicago: Aldine. Intriguing comparison of different slash-and-burn adaptations in South America, with implications for understanding the origin of the state.

1974   The Four Faces of Evolution: Unilinear, Universal, Multilinear, and Differential. In *Handbook of Social and Cultural Anthropology,* ed. J. J. Honigmann, pp. 89–110. Chicago: Rand McNally. Different meanings of sociocultural evolution.

CHAGNON, N.
  1977 *Yanomamo: The Fierce People.* 2nd ed. New York: Holt, Rinehart & Winston. Chagnon updates introductory anthropology's most popular ethnography with information on recent changes affecting Yanomamo life.

CLAPHAM, W. B., JR.
  1973 *Natural Ecosystems.* New York: Macmillan. Brief introduction to basic terms and principles of ecology.

COHEN, Y.
  1974 Culture as Adaptation. In *Man in Adaptation: The Cultural Present.* 2nd ed., ed. Y. A. Cohen, pp. 45–68. Chicago: Aldine. Sets forth his typology of strategies of adaptation and uses it to organize the uniformly interesting essays in this reader in cultural anthropology.

COLE, J. W., AND WOLF, E. R.
  1974 *The Hidden Frontier: Ecology and Ethnicity in an Alpine Village.* New York: Academic Press. In this excellent ethnographic and historical study, two anthropologists assess economic and cultural effects of ethnic divergence in two ecologically similar communities.

DRAPER, P.
  1975 !Kung Women: Contrasts in Sexual Egalitarianism in Foraging and Sedentary Contexts. In *Toward an Anthropology of Women,* ed. R. R. Reiter, pp. 77–109. New York: Monthly Review Press. Excellent study of relationship between economy, settlement, and gender roles.

GEERTZ, C.
  1963 *Agricultural Involution: The Process of Ecological Change in Indonesia.* Berkeley: University of California Press. Includes often-cited chapter contrasting horticultural and agricultural adaptations in Java.

GOULD, R. A.
  1968 Living Archaeology: The Ngatatjara of Western Australia. *Southwestern Journal of Anthropology* 24: 101–122. How study of contemporary foragers helps archeologists understand the past.

GULLIVER, P. H.
  1955 *The Family Herds: A Study of Two Pastoral Peoples in East Africa, the Jie and Turkana.* New York: Humanities Press.

Classic study of cultural variation among closely related pastoralists.
  1974 The Jie of Uganda. In *Man in Adaptation: The Cultural Present.* 2nd ed., ed. Y. A. Cohen, pp. 323–345. Chicago: Aldine. An interesting article, followed by a selection on the Turkana, also by Gulliver.

HAINES, F.
  1976 *The Plains Indians: Their Origins, Migrations and Cultural Developments.* New York: Crowell. Readable account of native Plains groups from prehistory to modern times.

HARNER, M. J.
  1970 Population Pressure and the Social Evolution of Agriculturalists. *Southwestern Journal of Anthropology* 26: 67–86. Some of the demographic implications of the plant-cultivating continuum.

HARRIS, M.
  1968 *The Rise of Anthropological Theory.* New York: Crowell. Provocative account of the history of anthropology.

LEE, R. B.
  1969 !Kung Bushman Subsistence: An Input-Output Analysis. In *Environment and Cultural Behavior,* ed. A. P. Vayda, pp. 47–49. Garden City, N.Y.: Doubleday. Unexpected leisure among the !Kung and other foragers.
  1974 (orig. 1968). What Hunters Do for a Living, or, How to Make Out on Scarce Resources. In *Man in Adaptation: The Cultural Present.* 2nd ed., ed. Y. A. Cohen, pp. 87–100. Chicago: Aldine. Comparative study of foragers, highlighted by the !Kung.

LEE, R. B., AND DEVORE, I., EDS.
  1977 Kalahari Hunter-Gatherers: Studies of the !Kung San and Their Neighbors. Cambridge: Harvard University Press. Long-term interdisciplinary study of well-known foragers.

MARSHALL, L.
  1976 *The !Kung of Nyae Nyae.* Cambridge: Harvard University Press. Ethnographic account based on author's twenty-five-year study of the !Kung.

MORGAN, L. H.
  1967 (orig. 1877). *Ancient Society.* Cleveland: World. The transition from sav-

agery to civilization. Although many specific arguments are now discounted, Morgan has influenced generations of anthropologists.

OLIVER, S. C.
1974   (orig. 1962). Ecology and Cultural Continuity as Contributing Factors in the Social Organization of the Plains Indians. In *Man in Adaptation: The Cultural Present.* 2nd ed., ed. Y. A. Cohen, pp. 302–322. Chicago: Aldine. Classic study of cultural persistence and change.

POSPISIL, L.
1963   *The Kapauku Papuans of West New Guinea.* New York: Holt, Rinehart & Winston. Interesting case study; includes a discussion of the Kapauku *tonowi.*

SAHLINS, M. D.
1963   Poor Man, Rich Man, Big-Man, Chief: Political Types in Melanesia and Polynesia. *Comparative Studies in Society and History* 5: 285–303. Compares political and authority figures in Polynesian chiefdoms and Melanesian tribes.

SAHLINS, M. D., AND SERVICE, E. R.
1960   *Evolution and Culture.* Ann Arbor: University of Michigan Press. Application of evolutionary principles to cultural anthropological data a century after Darwin.

SALZMAN, P. C.
1974   Political Organization among Nomadic Peoples. In *Man in Adaptation: The Cultural Present.* 2nd ed., ed. Y. A. Cohen, pp. 267–284. Chicago: Aldine. This unrivaled reader includes several articles about pastoralists, along with other adaptive strategies.

SPENCER, P.
1965   *The Samburu.* Berkeley: University of California Press. Pastoralists in an arid region of Kenya.

SPOONER, B., ED.
1972   *Population Growth: Anthropological Implications.* Cambridge: MIT Press. Relationships between demography and changing adaptive strategies in several world areas.

STEWARD, J.
1949   Cultural Causality and Law: A Trial Formulation of the Development of Early Civilizations. *American Anthropologist* 51: 1–27. Brilliant essay synthesizing archeological and cultural data to show comparable evolution through analogous stages of the state in five areas of the world.

1955   *Theory of Culture Change.* Urbana: University of Illinois Press. Modern anthropological classic; Steward argues for studies of convergent sociocultural evolution, suggests ecological approaches to sociocultural data, and offers techniques for the anthropological study of complex societies.

TURNBULL, C.
1961   *The Forest People.* New York: Simon and Schuster. Popular account of the Mbuti "pygmies" of central Africa and their relationships with horticultural villagers.

1965   The Mbuti Pygmies of the Congo. In *Peoples of Africa,* ed. J. L. Gibbs, Jr., pp. 279–318. New York: Holt, Rinehart & Winston. More complete account of Mbuti subsistence.

WHITE, L. A.
1959   *The Evolution of Culture: The Development of Civilization to the Fall of Rome.* New York: McGraw-Hill. Modern classic; major statement of general evolution and its application to culture.

WOLF, E. R.
1966   *Peasants.* Englewood Cliffs, N.J.: Prentice-Hall. Best introduction to the cross-cultural studies of peasants.

YENGOYAN, A. A.
1968   Demographic and Ecological Influences on Aboriginal Australian Marriage Sections. In *Man the Hunter,* ed. R. B. Lee and I. DeVore, pp. 185–199. Chicago: Aldine. In this anthology about foragers, Yengoyan explains some puzzling features of Australian section (marriage) systems in terms of demography and other ecological factors.

The Emergence
of Chiefdoms and States:
Theory and Practice

4

DIFFERENTIAL ACCESS

We are ready now to examine in more detail forms of sociopolitical organization that appeared later in human evolution—the chiefdom and the archaic or nonindustrial state. Both in chiefdoms and in states one encounters *differential access* to strategic and socially valued resources. This means that some people enjoy privileged access to power, prestige, and wealth; others do not. The privileged commonly control access even to strategic resources such as food and water. There are also similarities in the economies of chiefdoms and states. In many chiefdoms and most archaic states, the economy is based on intensive cultivation. Furthermore, both chiefdoms and states are usually forms of sociopolitical organization that administer populations occupying a variety of diverse ecological niches. Associated with this diversity are systems of regional exchange.

There are also significant differences between chiefdoms and archaic states. The most basic is that in chiefdoms, social relations and individual membership in sociopolitical groups are regulated—as in band or tribal society—by principles of kinship, marriage, fictive kinship, descent, age, generation, and sex; in states, they are *also* regulated by common residence and relationship to a government. Because the chiefdom retains the kinship emphasis of tribal society while simultaneously assigning to its members differential access to strategic resources, it may be considered a transitional form between tribal and state organization. This is, of course, a general evolutionary statement. The first chiefdom appeared before the first state. In general, there has been a chiefdom phase—that is, one in which kinship and differential access were both important—in the specific evolutionary sequences that led to most archaic states. Let us consider more fully the chiefdom before turning to varieties of states.

THE CHIEFDOM

We owe a great deal of our knowledge of how a particular group of chiefdoms worked to ethnographic studies carried out in Polynesia, where chiefdoms were especially numerous at the time of European explorations. A description of Polynesian chiefdoms will indicate some of the features that have characterized chiefdoms in general. Polynesian chiefs often kept long genealogies, sometimes tracing their ancestry back as far as fifty generations. Everyone in a given chiefdom was related to everyone else, and all were believed to be descended from the common founding ancestor. To become chief it was necessary to demonstrate seniority in descent. The chief was usually a man, but, depending on the island, sometimes a woman.

So intricate was the calculation of relative seniority in some areas of Polynesia that there were virtually as many gradations in rank as there were people. For example, the third son would rank below the second, who, in turn, would rank below the first. If their father was an eldest son, however, all three would rank above the children of their father's next younger brother, whose children would, in turn, outrank those of the older brothers in order of birth. Because everyone was related, when Polynesian chiefs addressed even the lowest ranking person in the chiefdom, they were still dealing with a relative. Therefore, the principle determining access to rank, power, prestige, and strategic resources was based on kinship and descent. Although other chiefdoms calculate seniority differently and have shorter genealogies than Polynesia, the concern for genealogy and seniority and the absence of sharp gaps between elites and commoners are usual attributes of any chiefdom.

Since they lived in a kin-based society, chiefs were expected to be generous. However, their generosity was different from that of tribal big men. In a tribal society, the status of big man was created. Big men arose on the basis of personality. When someone wanted to establish himself as a big man, he set about doing it. Sometimes there were no big men. In Polynesian societies as in other chiefdoms, chiefs, in contrast, occupied an office, a permanent position in the social structure. Someone would replace them

when they died. With close relatives and advisers, the chief managed the entire system. Included in the organization of any chiefdom were means of regulating production, distribution, and consumption of produce and products. Chiefs were normally full-time political specialists; unlike tribal big men, they were divorced from labor for subsistence. Other people supported them.

Chiefs could influence production by declaring taboos on certain crops or on cultivating certain areas of land, or by directing that certain crops be grown. They were important in regulating distribution and consumption because their office had means of collecting products and services from the population at large. At certain times during the year, members of the population turned over some of what they had produced to the chief. They might, for example, offer to the chief or a representative (called a *steward*) the first fruits or some more substantial portion of their harvests. These products were transferred from lower-level to higher-level stewards until eventually they reached the chief. Once or more during the year, chiefs might sponsor a feast or giveaway in which they redistributed to the people some of what they had received. The flow of goods into and out of such a central office or storehouse is known as *redistribution*. A chief was still expected to demonstrate some of the generosity associated with big men, headmen, descent-group leaders, and other figures of prestige in tribal societies.

There are certain obvious economic advantages associated with redistribution. Since chiefdoms commonly administer an ecologically diverse population, different areas grow different crops and provide different goods and services. The chief, through redistribution, made the specialized products of diversified zones available to the whole population of the chiefdom. Redistribution also provided a central storehouse for goods that might be scarce in some zones because of famine.

Differences Between Chiefdoms and States

The chiefdom and the state, like many other categories used by anthropologists, are ideal types. There is in reality continuous variation from tribe to chiefdom to state, which we see if our sample of societies in time and space is large enough. The emergence of differential access and subsequently of state organization have been gradual evolutionary processes, often retarded by temporary collapses of developing political machinery. Because of this, it is often a matter of arbitrary judgment whether a particular society with political regulation and differential access should be classified as a chiefdom or as a state. Nevertheless, there are some major contrasts between chiefdoms and fully developed states.

First, states are not formally organized on the basis of kinship or descent. Their populations are divided into socioeconomic classes, or *strata* (singular, *stratum*). Archaic states typically draw at least a broad distinction between upper and lower strata — elites and common people — and kinship ties do not extend from the former to the latter. Generally, there is a tendency toward stratum endogamy. Most peasants marry other peasants; members of the elites marry other members of their own stratum. Second, although many archaic states have redistributive systems, generosity is underplayed in the state compared with the chiefdom. Why should this be so?

In the chiefdom, everyone, depending on his or her particular line of descent, has a different status. The oldest child of the second child of an oldest child has a status different from the second child of the oldest child of the oldest child. Individual gradations in rank are gradual and continuous. It is difficult to draw a line dividing elites and common people. Yet states have done so, and, since chiefdoms often develop into states, at many times and in many areas of the world where chiefdoms eventually have become states, chiefs have been converted into kings by demoting the chief's progressively more distant relatives to the status of commoners.

In archaic states, the division between elites and common people is maintained by a tendency toward stratum endogamy. Furthermore, the elite class in states is more clearly demarcated in terms of its privileges and activities from the common people than are chiefs and their close relatives in

The trappings of high office. The King of Ashanti, a major West African state, now part of Ghana. (Ian Barry, Magnum Photos)

chiefdoms. Most members of the elite take no part in subsistence activities. They have become state personnel with specialized functions to perform. They are administrators, tax collectors, judges, advisers, and law makers; they may be military officials or members of a scholarly or priestly subsystem of the society. As the state grows, the elite group, the part of the population freed from direct concern with subsistence, also grows. In the archaic state, it is up to the population at large to support the elites. As in the chiefdom, this is accomplished through administrative intervention in production, distribution, and consumption of goods and services. The state decrees that a certain area is to produce certain goods. It forbids certain economic activities in other areas. It expropriates the produce and labor of members of the lower stratum.

In contrast to redistribution in the chiefdom, much of what the state receives does not flow back to the population at large. Its wealth is used to feed, clothe, and generally support the members of the elite. Rulers may enlist peasants to build them tombs that will mark their position in the afterlife. Peasants are sometimes called on to fight for territory that will provide the elites with items of no interest at all to the common people. The elite groups in states always enjoy *sumptuary goods*—jewelry, certain kinds of foods and drink, and clothing that is reserved for those of their rank. As we shall see in Chapters 8, 13, and 14, when peasants are discussed, the dietary needs of the common people often suffer because state officials force them to cater first to the needs of the state and its elite. Life in a state is not necessarily a more fulfilling or happier experience for the majority of the population than is life in a band or tribe.

The major contrast between chiefdom and state, then, is between a kin-based society in which generosity is still associated with prestige and a stratified society in which the needs of the elite take precedence over those of the common people. With this in mind, let us consider some attributes of archaic states.

THE STATE

The first states (or *civilizations*, a term often used as a near synonym for state) appeared in the Old World —in southern Mesopotamia (Iraq and western Iran) around 5,500 years ago and slightly later in the lower (northern) Nile region of Egypt. Subsequently, early states were to develop in the Indus River

In stratified, state-organized societies, wealth is retained in families, so that one person may be born into a rich family, another into poverty. Shown here, an extended family in Appalachia. All live in the same house and descend from the standing couple. Socioeconomic strata always include people of both sexes and all ages. (Arthur Tress)

Valley of Pakistan and India, in northern China, and in two areas of the New World—Mesoamerica and the central Andes (Peru-Bolivia).

The contrasts between early states and all previous forms of human social organization were huge. To clarify the tremendous differences, some definitions are needed. Anthropologists traditionally distinguish between ascribed and achieved status in any society. A *status* is simply a position in a social structure. Every society may be said to have a form—its social structure. As individuals mature, they occupy different positions in the social structure. When they die, these positions are vacated, and others fill them. The status endures, even though the individual occupants change.

Some statuses are *ascribed;* this means that individuals have no say in the status they occupy. Gender is an obvious ascribed status (even though there are societies, including our own, in which people can change their gender). Age is also an ascribed status; an individual has little to say about growing older. In chiefdoms, chiefly status is usually ascribed by birth order and seniority of descent. *Achieved* status, on the other hand, is not gained automatically; it is based on the individual's personal traits and activities. In every foraging band, for example, there is a status called "best hunter" that indi-

viduals achieve through hunting skill. People in tribal societies may differ in wealth and power, but usually these differences are achieved rather than ascribed. As in the band society, where a man can make his reputation as a good hunter, in the tribal society, a man may make his reputation as a big man. As we have seen, generosity and the ability to attract supporters are important personality attributes of the big man.

In populations where social organization is more complex, there are marked differences in wealth, prestige, and power. In many instances these are ascribed. Wealth is retained in families, so that one person may be born into a rich family, another into poverty. In many archaic states there was a paramount ruling status known as king, queen, or sovereign. This status conferred on its occupant great prestige and inspired great respect, not because the sovereign was a good ruler, but merely because he or she was sovereign. Often, too, people were taught that the sovereign was divine, or that royal rule was divinely approved. Hereditary differences in wealth, power, and prestige represent a common form of stratification—differential access to strategic resources—which is a universal attribute of state organization.

Perhaps the most useful definition of state has

The contrast between ascribed and achieved status is illustrated by Queen Elizabeth and former Prime Minister Heath. Elizabeth gained office through ascription—a formal rule of succession—whereas Heath achieved his status by his election as a member of Parliament and as head of Britain's Conservative Party. While Elizabeth will remain ruler until her death or abdication, prime ministers routinely come and go, depending on which party has a majority in Parliament. Both Elizabeth and Heath, however, occupy *offices* that survive as their occupants change. (© Bill Beck, *Daily Telegraph*/Woodfin Camp & Assoc.)

been given by anthropologist Morton Fried. Fried (1960) presents what he calls a "bare but essential list of state functions and institutions." The primary functions of any state are to maintain order and support the order of socioeconomic stratification. All states are stratified societies. That is, their populations are divided into two or more duosexual (both sexes), multiage (all ages) groups—strata that contrast in social status and economic prerogatives. One group, the *superordinate* stratum, enjoys privileged access to wealth, power, and other valued resources. The other is *subordinate,* and its members' access to strategic resources is limited by members of the privileged group.

States are complex political regulators. They develop means of accomplishing their primary functions that involve the creation of special-purpose parts and subsystems with a variety of secondary functions. Among them are the following: (1) population control, including the fixing of boundaries, establishment of categories of membership, and census taking; (2) the disposal of trouble cases, encompassing a system of civil and criminal laws, regular legal procedure, the appointment of judges and other regular officers of adjudication; (3) the protection of sovereignty, including maintenance of military and police forces; (4) taxation and conscription to support the foregoing functions.

In comparison with kin-based societies, states tend to extend over larger territories with denser populations. They can organize and manage larger and denser populations because their means of organization—parts and subsystems that fulfill Fried's secondary functions of state organization—are more advanced. Special-purpose subsystems commonly found in states include the following: military, religious, administrative, legal, judicial, fiscal (tax collecting and others), and informational (spies may roam the land to gather information for the ruler). The functionally specialized subsystems, in turn, are integrated and regulated by a ruling subsystem, which may be composed of civil, military, and/or religious functionaries.

In states, membership in politically significant groups is based on residence as well as on kinship. This is one of the most important differences, in human terms, between kin-based societies and states. In the kin-based society, people reside with their relatives. In the band and tribe and even in the chiefdom, a person's social world consists of only two kinds of people: allies and potential or actual enemies. People's allies are their relatives. Nonrelatives who are potential or actual enemies may be converted into friends by the creation of alliances. Common ways of establishing alliances are marriage, rites that convert nonrelatives into (fictive) kin, and trading partnerships. In a state-organized society, on the other hand, people are born in a village, province, district, town, ward, or city. People who live in the same territorial or political subdivision share common obligations to the state; ultimate decisions about their behavior and their lives are made and enforced not only by their older relatives but by state officials.

The individual's social world expands in the state-organized society. In markets, one meets strangers—peasants and other food producers from different areas as well as a host of specialists. *Markets* are economic hubs of far-flung exchange networks typical of states and are subject to at least some administrative control. Occasionally, even the most insignificant peasant must deal with government officials. The closed and often comfortable world in which kinship, marriage, and other personal relationships formed the locus of interaction is gone.

States collect goods and services in taxes and labor from their subjects. States manage the funds they take in, reallocating part for the public good and another part (often larger) to satisfy the needs and aspirations of the elite. Forced public labor is often used to construct monumental public works. Some of these public works may form part of a managed economy—irrigation systems, for example. Others, like temples, palaces, and tombs, can best be understood as shelters for the elite, standing as constant reminders of their prestige. State fiscal officials also supervise manufacturing, marketing, and other exchange activity, standardizing weights and measures, supervising distribution, and extracting taxes on goods that pass through the state.

Within their borders, state officials grant safety to traveling caravans, to itinerant vendors, and to artisans—thus permitting exchange of goods and services over long distances. Often, in addition to regulation of occupational specialization by, for example, setting standards for artisanry and manufacturing, state officials must supervise ecologically diverse and productively specialized niches located in different areas of the state.

In many ways, then, states contrast with kin-based

State organization erodes the kinship basis of residential groups. In states, people are born in towns, provinces, cities, and communes. Shown here, a work cooperative in the People's Republic of China. (Marc Riboud/Magnum Photos)

societies. As a relatively new form of social organization (little more than 5,000 years old), states have competed successfully with populations organized on the basis of kinship, descent, and marriage in many parts of the world. They continue to supplant them. Their military organization undoubtedly enables states to compete successfully with neighboring tribes and chiefdoms. Yet this is not the only explanation for the spread of the state. In view of the hardships it imposes on its populace, state organization must have certain advantages. The most obvious is that its special-purpose subsystems permit order and peace to prevail within the state's boundaries. States curb feuding, often characteristic of tribal societies, and in so doing allow, and indeed encourage, higher levels of production. These, in turn, support massive, dense populations that can be deployed as armies and as colonists to promote the state's expansion.

THE ORIGIN OF THE STATE

Prime Movers

Many scholars have turned their attention to the problem of the origin of the state. Several have offered what are basically *unicausal* explanations, suggestions that a single variable, a *prime mover*, has contributed more to state formation than anything else. Even when they recognize that a prime mover cannot explain every instance of state formation, these scholars still argue that their causal variable generally has been determinative. Most of the prime movers that have been suggested are ecological, economic, or demographic. Let us examine some of them.

HYDRAULIC SYSTEMS Karl Wittfogel (1957) has been foremost among those who argue that state organization emerges to organize the interrelationship between humans and water in an agricultural economy. In simplified form, Wittfogel's position is that state organization arises in arid areas to control large-scale hydraulic networks—systems of irrigation, drainage, and flood control, for example. Ac-

River basin development project in contemporary Pakistan. Wittfogel, Steward, and other scholars link hydraulic programs in arid areas to the rise of ancient states. Although irrigation does not always lead to state formation, it is associated with permanent settlement, dense population, and differential access. (United Nations)

cording to the argument, state organization arises to regulate several problems and activities associated with large-scale hydraulic agriculture: the construction, enlargement, repair, and maintenance of hydraulic works; the allocation of water; the regulation of possible conflict between upstream cultivators, who are in a position to withhold water, and those downstream.

Casting doubt on hydraulic agriculture as a prime mover, anthropologists have investigated and described specific evolutionary sequences in which state organization has appeared before large-scale hydraulic systems and in which states have emerged without irrigation. However, although hydraulic agriculture is not the single cause of the evolution of the state, irrigation does have certain implications for state formation. First, irrigation is associated with permanent cultivation, sedentary communities, and dense human population. Second, irrigation is essential to productive plant cultivation in arid areas. In arid areas where irrigated land is limited, irrigation is correlated in complex ways with differential access to land and other strategic resources and with the emergence of territorial political organization. Even such simple techniques of water control as small-scale canal systems, and pot irrigation (using accessible ground water to pour on field plants) permit productive agriculture in arid lands. Irrigated agriculture typically supports population growth. Population growth may lead to the enlargement of the hydraulic system. Growing emphasis on hydraulic agriculture and its expansion supports increasingly larger and denser concentrations of people. Given such a process, problems involved in regulating interpersonal relations will increase. Conflicts over access to water, for example, will be more frequent. In this context, territorywide means of controlling interpersonal relations and access to water and other strategic resources may arise. Thus a gradual growth in hydraulic systems may be associated with the evolution of political organization on a nonkin, supracommunity basis.

REGULATION OF ECOLOGICAL DIVERSITY It has also been suggested that states and the ruling systems and special-purpose subsystems associated with them arise in areas of ecological diversity. It is argued that states emerge to regulate the production and distribution of diverse products from a variety of environmental niches within the area the state administers. Central coordination, once established, is assumed to be a more efficient adaptation to conditions of ecological diversity than other sociopolitical means; thus, it tends to grow.

Like other prime movers suggested, ecological diversity *is* often associated with state formation. Interzonal regulation does strengthen state organization. Ecological diversity is not, however, sufficient in itself to explain state formation. States have originated in geographical areas where environmental diversity is not marked—ancient Egypt, for example. Furthermore, in other areas of environ-mental diversity, states have never emerged. Finally, one could argue that ecological diversity is as much a product of, as a prime mover in, the evolution of the state. As states grow, they typically create ecological and economic diversity, promoting specialization by particular areas in the production of certain goods.

CONTROL OF LONG-DISTANCE TRADE ROUTES This prime mover is similar to ecological diversity. It has been suggested that states originate to regulate exchange of raw materials, manufactured products, and subsistence or luxury items produced in different areas. It has also been argued that states develop at supply or distributive nodes of long-distance trade networks—for example, at crossroads of caravan routes or in areas that are in a position to halt trade between two supply centers. Although long-distance trade has been important in the evolution of many states, long-distance trade has come after, rather than prior to, the origin of the state in some cases. Regulation of *local* trade and manufacture seems to have been more significant than control over long-distance trade routes in the formation of the Mesopotamian Elamite state of southwestern Iran (Wright and Johnson, 1975). There are also instances of long-distance trade without state organization. New Guinea provides several examples. Nevertheless, developed trade seems to be universally associated with state organization.

Building an irrigation canal in Java. As population density increases in arid areas, more and more people rely on the same source of water for irrigation. Here agents of a contemporary nation-state have summoned several villagers to build a large canal. (United Nations/C. Purcell)

Multivariate Approaches

POPULATION GROWTH, WARFARE, AND ENVIRONMENTAL CIRCUMSCRIPTION Anthropologist Robert Carneiro (1970) has proposed a theory that incorporates three variables acting in conjunction rather than a single prime mover to explain state formation. He argues that wherever and whenever the three conditions — environmental circumscription, increasing population, and warfare — obtain, a process of state formation will begin.

Environmental circumscription may be physical or social. Examples of physically circumscribed environments include small islands, and, in arid areas, alluvial plains and spring-fed valleys. Social circumscription exists when neighboring populations block expansion, migration, or access to resources. When strategic resources are confined to limited areas — even when no impediments to people's moving are present — the effects are similar to environmental circumscription. As an example of such *resource concentration* Carneiro describes the fertile *varzea* soils that line the Amazon River in Brazil. *Varzea* was rich enough to be cultivated year after year, whereas inland plots had to be fallowed. Furthermore, not only could riverfront populations rely on good crops each year, they also had access to riverine resources, including fish, shellfish, and aquatic mammals. Given this difference in productivity between riverfront and inland habitats, people preferred to live near the river. When compared with other parts of the Amazonian region, riverfront land supported dense populations, continuous cultivation, and sociopolitical organization more complex than the tribal societies dispersed throughout the plains and forests of Amazonia. However, Amazonian sociopolitical organization never surpassed, even in the *varzea* habitat, the chiefdom level.

To illustrate the interaction of environmental circumscription, warfare, and population increase in the process of state formation, Carneiro uses another area, coastal Peru. The Peruvian coast is one of the world's most arid areas. Early food production was limited to arable land confined to seventy-eight short, narrow spring-fed valleys, each of which was sharply circumscribed by the Andes to the east, the Pacific Ocean to the west, and desert on either side. Carneiro speculates that the transition from foraging to food production triggered population increase in these valleys (see Figure 4.1). In each

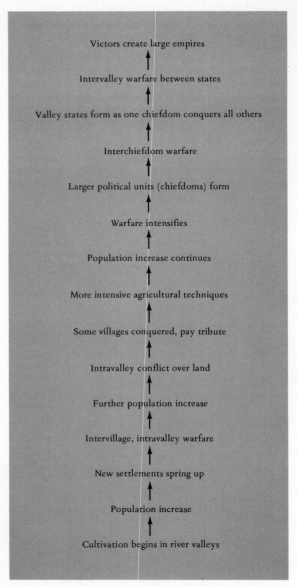

FIGURE 4.1 Carneiro's multivariate approach to the origin of the state, as applied to coastal Peru. In a very arid area, food production emerged in narrow river valleys where water for cultivation was available (resource concentration). With the shift to cultivation, population increased. With eventual population pressure on land, warfare led to the conquest of some villages by others. Physical circumscription (an arid area) meant that losers had no way of escaping their conquerors. The process accelerated as population grew, and as warfare and cultivation intensified. Chiefdoms, states, and empires eventually developed.

valley, old settlements grew more populous, and colonists split off from the old villages and founded new ones. Carneiro believes that rivalries developed between villages in the same valley. Intervillage raiding and warfare were conducted at first for a variety of noneconomic reasons: to capture women; to gain prestige; and to avenge wrongs committed against individuals, kin groups, and villages.

As settlements spread and valley population grew, villages eventually came into competition over access to land. Because these valleys were circumscribed, when one village conquered another, the losers had to submit to the winners. Because land was scarce throughout the valley, there was no room for victims, even in the villages of friendly neighbors. Since the only arable land was in the valleys, and since population was increasing and competition over land developing in the other valleys, a conquered village could keep its own land only by paying tribute to its conquerors. Carneiro argues that by adopting new agricultural techniques, villagers were able to feed themselves while meeting these demands for tribute. Villagers farmed their plots more intensively and brought new areas under cultivation by irrigation and terracing, thus generating a surplus.

Once established, these trends accelerated. Population grew, warfare intensified, and conquered villages were joined together as subordinate parts of larger political units—chiefdoms. Carneiro sees the first Peruvian states emerging as valleywide political domains formed when one of the chiefdoms in a valley conquered all the others. Eventually, the states that had emerged and grown in several valleys came into conflict with others. Again, victors incorporated victims in growing territorial units. In time, the process extended from coast to highlands, and by the time of the Incas it had culminated in one of the major empires of the tropics.

Although Carneiro's formulation is useful, the association between population density and state organization is generalized, not universal. Growth in population size and density *is* associated with state organization; anthropologist Robert Stevenson (1968) has demonstrated a correlation between high population density and state organization in sub-Saharan Africa. Yet increase in population and its density within a circumscribed environment is not the only factor in the origin and growth of states. Consider highland New Guinea, where, in certain valleys that are socially or physically circumscribed

environments, population densities are comparable to those of many states. Warfare is also present. Nevertheless, no states have developed.

It is doubtful that environmental circumscription, resource concentration, population increase, and warfare are necessary and sufficient conditions for all instances of state formation, but Carneiro's theory does enlarge our understanding of state formation. Comparison of several specific evolutionary sequences illustrates that the combined effects of these four conditions *are* often important in the rise of the state. Also, because Carneiro focuses on several variables rather than on a single prime mover, he is on the right track, and his theory of state formation is thus more generally valid than the others.

From my own research (Kottak 1972; 1977) I have become convinced that states have originated in different areas of the world for a variety of reasons. In each case, the origin and evolution of the state involved a unique example of specific evolution in which interacting variables have magnified the effects of one another. To explain the formation of a particular state, we must look for those specific changes in the scale of regulatory problems and systems that have brought stratification and state machinery into being. The following points, however, are important in the consideration and comparison of different cases: (1) Although several different paths to statehood exist, many of the same factors contributed to the emergence of the state in different world areas. (2) In each instance, several variables, rather than a single prime mover, helped determine the development of complex society. (3) Although state formation is more rapid in some cases than in others, it is always a gradual, evolutionary process that depends on both local and regional factors.

THE EMERGENCE OF THE STATE: ARCHEOLOGICAL RECONSTRUCTION

Comparison of actual processes of state formation in different parts of the world demonstrates that interacting variables are often comparable, that analogous causes produce similar effects, and that specific evolutionary sequences are often convergent in broad outline. Just as biological and archeological anthropologists often work together in unraveling problems about early human evolution, both archeological and sociocultural anthropologists are interested in the origin and evolution of the state. Typically, archeological research reveals interrelated changes in settlement types, population size and density, economy, sociopolitical organization, and other variables involved in state formation over long periods of time. Sociocultural anthropologists generally use ethnography, oral history, and written documents to clarify shorter-term changes in more recent instances of state formation.

Archeological research in two different parts of the world—Mesopotamia in the Old World and Mesoamerica in the New—has demonstrated that comparable (convergent) processes of state formation unfolded, independently of one another, thousands of years and thousands of miles apart. State formation can be traced to around 5500 B.P. in Mesopotamia. Comparable events took place in the arid highlands of Mexico more than 3,000 years later; the first Mexican states formed around 2,200 years ago, about 200 B.C. What were some of the specific parallels in state formation in these two arid areas? In each, domesticates had gradually been added to a broad spectrum of resources that sustained human life. Before states could form, a generalized subsistence strategy based on foraging had gradually evolved into a specialized economy based on food production. Simultaneously, patterns of ecological symbiosis and exchange had grown stronger. Early food production had been based on horticulture. However, as population grew in areas especially favorable to horticulture and spilled over into adjacent zones, arid areas were gradually colonized. They became sites of irrigation agriculture and the new centers of population growth.

But the shift was not a radical departure from the past; it incorporated the existing patterns of interregional symbiosis. Population increase in environments circumscribed physically by limited resources or socially by growing populations in neighboring areas produced conflict. Regulatory problems associated with population growth, management of an agricultural economy, interregional trade, manufacture, and patterns of conflict arose gradually and resulted in the evolution of managerial personnel. Differential access to strategic resources emerged and gave rise to differences in life styles—differentiation of the elite from the commoners. Early in the evolution of socioeconomic differentiation, elite status and political authority were intimately associated with ceremony. Monumental architectural structures attest to the functions and authority of the religiously based elites. Over time, as the system grew, special-purpose personnel arose to accom-

plish state functions. From priests, warriors, and rulers came a priesthood, a military organization, and a hereditary monarchy. Urban centers were linked together, through growth, submission, and conquest, into macroregional states. They rose and fell, as did the empires that succeeded them. Differential access became hereditary, and stratification became more complex.

Thus, in two areas of the ancient world, chiefdoms, states, and cities emerged independently. In other arid areas—the central Andes in the New World; Egypt, the Indus Valley, and northern China in the Old World—the sequence was also broadly parallel, though differences may be noted in each case.

Nevertheless, the similarities were striking. They indicate that long-term interactions of human populations with similar ecological variables will produce convergent social, political, economic, and religious institutions. This is not to say that there is a single path to statehood. The lowland Maya of Mesoamerica, using slash-and-burn cultivation as an economic base, developed a state. States have evolved through the interaction of different constellations of ecological variables in nonarid areas, as the following case—Buganda—illustrates.

RECONSTRUCTION BASED ON HISTORICAL, ETHNOHISTORICAL, AND ETHNOGRAPHIC DATA

Populations of precolonial Africa exhibited a rich diversity in their sociopolitical complexity and range of adaptation to a variety of environments. Some of the world's most complex and tightly organized preindustrial civilizations, including Buganda in the Great Lakes (*interlacustrine*) area of eastern Africa, developed in the African tropics. The developments in Buganda, and indeed the very existence of this important state, are unfamiliar to most Americans. The case that follows has been reconstructed on the basis of written historical documents; native oral traditions and genealogies (or *ethnohistorical* sources); and ethnographic data gathered in field research by sociocultural anthropologists. The Buganda sequence again illustrates the gradual, multivariate nature of the process of state formation. Furthermore, many of the same variables that contributed to the prehistoric emergence of complex society in different world areas recur in this African sequence.

Knowledge perpetuated over the generations by African oral historians touched millions of Americans in 1977 with the television series *Roots*. Here, Alex Haley, author of the book on which the series was based, visits distant cousins—descendants of Kunta Kinte's brothers in Gambia, western Africa.

Written historical records about precolonial Africa are rich when compared with those from the aboriginal New World. Centuries of accounts written by Arab, European, and Chinese merchants, travelers, explorers, and missionaries are available. Also, even in the absence of writing in most sub-Saharan African societies, the elites and sometimes the common people have developed elaborate oral traditions, one of the major concerns of which is tracing genealogies.

The use of ethnohistorical accounts as historical sources requires a brief defense. Anthropologists have long recognized that there are risks involved in using oral traditions to reconstruct history. In any society, present realities color memories, and history is often fictionalized in various ways and for various ends. However, many ethnohistorical sources contain valuable and accurate historical data. The use of such sources must be judicious. Still, informed speculation is preferable to total neglect of the past since it allows us to suggest reconstructions and to frame hypotheses that can be tested later—for example, by archeological research. Fortunately, anthropologists have comparative ethnology and archeology to aid them in evaluating events recalled in oral history and in reconstructing the past. Cross-cultural regularities established on the basis of better-documented sequences can be used as standards to judge the probable validity of oral accounts.

In the case that follows, for example, ethnohistory suggests several parallels to processes of state formation reconstructed archeologically for other world areas. These parallels suggest that the outlines sketched in oral accounts are valid.

Although the formation of Buganda was more rapid than the rise of the earliest civilizations, many of the same interacting variables were involved. In this sequence, too, we see that the process of state formation is neither miraculous nor accidental. Given certain conditions, it is inevitable; given their absence, impossible. Also, Buganda, a more recent case, permits a different, but equally important, perspective on the question of how states form and grow. The emergence of the state in Buganda is still remembered in oral traditions, and thus we can focus on more specific changes in behavior, culture, and social organization than in archeological reconstructions. The perspectives of both archeology and sociocultural anthropology are necessary to round out our understanding of how and why complex societies develop.

THE PROCESS OF STATE FORMATION IN BUGANDA

The former kingdom of Buganda, which is now a province of the nation of Uganda, grew up on a plateau about 4,000 feet above sea level. During

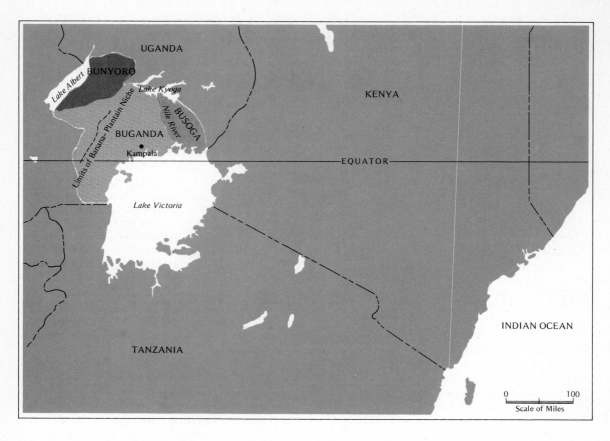

FIGURE 4.2 Map of precolonial Buganda. Borders fluctuated but increased through militarism as Buganda extended its influence to the north (Bunyoro), east (Busoga), and west.

the nineteenth century its territory extended about 200 miles along the northern and western shores of Lake Victoria and about 80 miles inland (Southwold, 1965). When the English travelers Speke and Burton, searching for the source of the Nile, visited Buganda in 1862, it was the most populous and powerful state in the interlacustrine area. (Figure 4.2.) To the north lay the less populous kingdom of Bunyoro (today there are about 1 million Ganda, compared with about 100,000 Nyoro). Since Buganda and Bunyoro were close neighbors, and since developments in the two kingdoms were linked, they will be compared at certain points below. The description of Buganda begins at the height of its power and influence, just before British intervention in the 1860s. A reconstruction of the process of state for-

mation then follows; a variety of sources, including oral traditions, are relied upon.

Local Subsistence Economy

The region north and northwest of Lake Victoria was one of ecological contrasts, important in the emergence of the Gandan state. Subsistence in this area was tied to the amount and seasonal distribution of rainfall. Buganda's rainfall was not only heavier than Bunyoro's, it was more evenly distributed throughout the year. This difference permitted the Ganda, but not the Nyoro, to grow such perennial crops as the banana and the closely related plantain, an important factor in the emergence of the Gandan state.

As the most important crops in the Gandan diet, bananas and plantains presented several advantages. They were not harvested all at once, but throughout the year, as needed. Like intensively cultivated agricultural crops, they could support dense sedentary populations. Once planted, banana and plantain trees yielded for many years—some trees in Buganda produced fruit for as long as forty years. In sharp contrast to intensive cultivation, however, human labor investment was low. Dependence on bananas and plantains was eminently compatible with a sociopolitical system in which a great deal of labor could be marshalled from villages and put to work for higher-level authorities. Men were withdrawn from local subsistence pursuits to take part in public works, warfare, and other activities, and the cultivation was done by women.

Nutritional balance required that bananas and plantains be supplemented with other foods, particularly sources of protein. This had profound implications for the development of an interregional network of exchange and distribution and for the emergence of the Bugandan state. Gandans hunted, fished, and kept sheep, goats, cattle, fowl, and buffalo to provide protein. Particularly near Lake Victoria, fish were an ordinary part of the Gandan diet. The distribution of the fish inland seems to have been one way in which peripheral areas were kept under the control of the central administration.

In drier Bunyoro, the staple was millet. Although it was superior to plantains and bananas in calories, protein, and other nutrients for its weight, it did not yield continuously and for several years. Because land was fallowed, Nyoro cultivation was closer to

the horticultural end of the plant-cultivating continuum than Buganda's. However, the Nyoro invested much more labor in cultivating their millet than the Ganda did in cultivating their bananas and plantains. Because of its greater nutritional value, millet did not need to be supplemented with so many other foods, although the Nyoro did cultivate some other crops. Bunyoro was also better suited to cattle grazing than Buganda, and the Nyoro invested their labor in stockbreeding and herding domesticated animals as well as plant cultivation.

One of the distinguishing attributes of all states is specialization in economic roles. This means that some people are not engaged in subsistence activities, and instead work as artisans, city administrators, or other specialists. In Buganda there was an even more obvious specialization—one based on gender. It is rare in plant-cultivating societies for men to be freed totally from agricultural tasks. But in Buganda, men served as soldiers or worked in craft production, canoe manufacture, or public works and transportation projects. Women functioned in food production, men in production and distribution of goods and services to the hierarchical levels above the village household. In Bunyoro, in contrast, more men worked at clearing land, cultivating plants, and caring for animals. Nyoro men, because of their role in the local subsistence economy, had less time to spend in the service of chiefs,

In contemporary Uganda, a Gandan woman negotiates sales of surplus bananas. Bananas and plantains remain cornerstones of the Gandan diet today. Their cultivation and exchange played a major role in Gandan state formation. (United Nations)

kings, and their agents. Furthermore, the greater uncertainty of relying on annual rather than perennial crops meant that Bunyoro's food supply was not as dependable as Buganda's.

Nineteenth-century Buganda possessed the four-level settlement and administrative hierarchy used by Wright and Johnson (1975) to distinguish states. The lowest level was the peasant village, actually a string of households along a ridge. Administering villages were subchiefs, whose settlements were somewhat larger. Chiefs lived in still larger villages, some with over 1,000 people, where their estates supported a large retinue: several wives, musicians, artisans, bodyguards, and other dependents. The highest level was the capital, which had a population in 1862 estimated at 77,000 — the largest city in interior Africa.

The Buganda Sequence

As in the sequences mentioned earlier, the process of state formation in Buganda ultimately can be traced to the transition to food production. From archeological research we know that plant cultivation, accompanied by an Iron Age technology, spread rapidly in eastern Africa during the first few centuries A.D. The emergence of plantain and banana cultivation in the interlacustrine region was part of this general change in subsistence economy. Reliance on plantains and bananas did not replace — but merely added a secure source of calories to — diversified economies previously based exclusively on foraging around the shores of Lake Victoria. Hunting, fishing, and gathering continued alongside cultivation. The early Ganda, with their Iron Age technology, and plantains and bananas, were free to expand until their further spread was blocked by neighboring groups or until they had reached the natural limits of the banana and plantain niche — in other words, until they encountered factors that would lead to either social or physical circumscription.

As population grew over several centuries, villages were gradually established farther from the lake shores. To maintain a diversified diet including fish, people farther from the lake traded with lakeshore communities. A basis for ranking of descent groups probably arose through their differential population growth during the general population increase. Given warfare, and there is evidence for it

by at least A.D. 1600, the larger descent groups had more members, and hence more support. They also had been sending out migrants and thereby occupying a larger geographic and environmental range than smaller groups. Members of the largest descent groups gradually gained differential access to political leadership because of their military prowess and to strategic resources because of the volume of trade goods their descent groups controlled.

In prestate Buganda trade between shore and inland communities was probably regulated by village headmen, personal trading partners, descent-group heads, and big men. However, the scale, diversity, and volume of trade eventually became too great for these figures to handle. Political regulation on a scale larger than the single village or descent group and its territory was stimulated simultaneously by warfare and trade. Special-purpose subsystems of an emerging state gradually replaced traditional tribal figures in coordinating the provision and movement of products. Thus it was not just warfare, but the regulation of ecological diversity and interregional trade, that contributed to the emergence of complex society in Buganda (see Figure 4.3).

The regulation of interregional exchange had become a major function of the Gandan administration by the eighteenth century. An interregional economic system linking Buganda with other zones took time to develop, as did a sociopolitical system to oversee it. Throughout the emergence of the Gandan state, interregional trade and warfare were interrelated and mutually reinforcing. State organization helped protect the growing trade network against pastoralists in Bunyoro and other neighbors. Once a defensive pose was adopted, Buganda's subsistence base favored its ultimate advancement over neighboring populations, as did its geographical position near water transport and trade routes. Most vital, the men of Buganda could be mobilized into an army without endangering its subsistence economy. By the eighteenth century this army had been converted into an offensive force that was progressively extending Buganda's boundaries at the expense of neighboring populations. As they expanded, the trade network and the military relied more and more on public works projects, also managed by the emerging state. To facilitate movement of people, troops, and goods, roads and bridges were built and maintained. A fleet of canoes — the Gandan navy — allowed Buganda to subjugate other lakeshore popu-

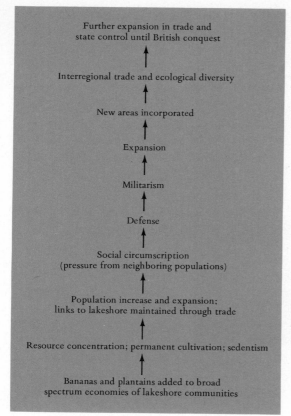

Further expansion in trade and
state control until British conquest

↑

Interregional trade and ecological diversity

↑

New areas incorporated

↑

Expansion

↑

Militarism

↑

Defense

↑

Social circumscription
(pressure from neighboring populations)

↑

Population increase and expansion;
links to lakeshore maintained through trade

↑

Resource concentration; permanent cultivation; sedentism

↑

Bananas and plantains added to broad
spectrum economies of lakeshore communities

FIGURE 4.3 The process of state formation in Buganda.
The major variables in Gandan state formation actually interacted throughout the sequence. Permanent cultivation based on plantains and bananas enabled Gandan men to be diverted to military operations—thus favoring conquest and further expansion. Military expansion and conquest continued to add new areas, contributing to ecological diversity and interregional trade.

lations and, thereafter, to regulate lake commerce. By the eighteenth century the state was requiring peasants to participate in these and other public works projects.

Buganda's history from the eighteenth century on can be reconstructed more precisely from oral traditions, particularly royal genealogies. By examining events during successive reigns, one observes the gradual process of state formation and its temporary setbacks. The oral history of the Gandan kings was collected by Sir Apolo Kagwa in his book *Customs of the Baganda* (1934). Kagwa lists the size of each

king's court retinue—wives, concubines, servants, and resident officials. Growth in the court is associated with increases in royal authority and with changes in Buganda's interregional economy.

Let us begin the sequence with Buganda's sixteenth king, who appears to have ruled around 1700. According to royal history, this reign was associated with an increasing emphasis on raiding and war. The king rewarded military officers with political office and landed estates for their descendants to hold in perpetuity. Kagwa lists the court retinue of the sixteenth king as 309 people. (Figure 4.4.)

The retinue leaps to 508 with Buganda's twenty-first king, who separated church and state, allocating ritual duties that previously had been the king's to one of his sons, whose descendants thereafter did not rule but provided Buganda's high priests. The king's power seems at this point to have been secure enough so that a ritual status was no longer necessary to buttress royal authority. However, the emerging Gandan state experienced setbacks. Buganda's twenty-second king, recalled as a tyrant who was eventually killed by his sister, was notable only for his lack of authority. But by the twenty-fourth reign, centralized rule was once again growing stronger. The twenty-fourth ruler, whose court retinue numbered 510, conquered neighboring areas and replaced traditional chiefs with war heroes.

Other areas were added during the twenty-eighth reign. One of them, along a route to the south that would eventually link Buganda to the East African coast, paid annual tribute in cowrie shells and in trade goods imported from areas still farther south. The court retinue of Buganda's twenty-eighth king rose to 600.

As measured by the increase in court retinue—a jump from 600 to 8,500—Buganda's twenty-ninth reign witnessed a truly dramatic change in scale, paralleling a major expansion of interregional trade. Cotton goods, presumably from the coast, were introduced to Buganda, and elephant hunters, who provided ivory for export, became a professional group. Along with ivory, prisoners of war were traded as slaves to the coast. Lake commerce, particularly with the south, increased with the enlargement of the canoe fleet. Several groups of craft specialists, including blacksmiths, ax makers, and canoe builders, are reported for this reign. The American newspaper reporter Stanley estimated that the Gandan navy numbered between 16,000 and 20,000

Reign Nos. and Dates	Size of Court Retinue	Major Events
31–32 A.D. 1810 to A.D. 1860	20,000	Expansion and tightening of royal control; Arab traders enter Buganda Firearms exchanged for ivory and slaves Buganda controls major interregional trade network
29–30	8500	Expansion of military operations and interregional trade Trade of slaves (prisoners of war) and ivory for cotton goods Local manufacture, craft production, economic specialization, and lake commerce expand
22–28	510–600	Increasing militarism, conquest, tribute, trade, and growth in royal authority tempered by rebellions and temporary setbacks
21	508	Separation of King's ritual and political duties
16–20 ca. A.D. 1700	309	Increasing militarism

FIGURE 4.4 Summary of major events associated with reigns of kings of Buganda from around 1700 until the British conquest in the 1860s. From oral history of Buganda.

men. Buganda's twenty-ninth ruler jealously guarded his authority by having his half-brothers — potential rivals — murdered.

Growth in royal power stalled again during the thirtieth reign — a time of territorial conquests, but also of rebellions and civil disturbances; this setback, as in earlier reigns, was temporary. The court retinue of the thirty-first king, who ruled from 1810 to 1844, increased to 20,000. A change in the scale of the interregional economy was again responsible. Around 1845 coastal traders were admitted to Buganda; they brought firearms and gunpowder, which were exchanged for ivory and slaves. The growth of Buganda's military to 50,000 men, many with rifles, enlarged and strengthened its boundaries and guaranteed prisoners for the slave-firearms trade network. A sanitation system in the capital was begun by public works parties to serve a growing urban population.

Buganda's thirty-second reign was the culmination of its development as an autonomous state. With firearms acquired through trade, Buganda's territory was progressively extended and made more secure. Beginning in the 1860s, however, British intervention and the establishment of missionary posts resulted in conflicts and changes that shook the foundations of royal authority and ended Buganda's autonomy.

Variables in Bugandan State Formation

As in other cases, a *set* of interacting variables determined the evolution of social stratification and the state in Buganda. In combination, these variables gave rise to socioeconomic differentiation and to an administrative subsystem to allocate and reallocate land, people, and products. Another special-purpose subsystem — the military — developed for defensive, and ultimately offensive, functions. Finally, both subsystems interacted to maintain themselves and to strengthen and maintain general order and the order of stratification.

The variables responsible for the evolution of the Gandan state may be briefly summarized. Unlike many African societies, Buganda had a subsistence economy based on permanent cultivation rather than shifting cultivation or pastoralism. The same land could be used from year to year; settlements could be permanent, and a large and dense population could be supported. The heartland and birthplace of Buganda lay in a fertile zone. Resources necessary for banana and plantain cultivation were concentrated in a limited region between the shore of Lake Victoria, where fishing was a vital part of subsistence, and a short-grass zone suited to cattle herding. Population increase led to differential descent-group growth and expansion, but trade continued to link the people and products of different environments. Social circumscription—competition from neighboring societies—led Buganda to adopt a defensive pose. The banana economy allowed men to leave subsistence tasks and form a defensive subsystem. The military developed out of the need for defense eventually became a fully developed special-purpose subsystem oriented toward offensive activities. It allowed expansion, the incorporation of new ecological zones, and the control by the Gandan state of products originating in such zones. The exchange network managed by the Gandan state in the mid-nineteenth century began in Bunyoro and stretched—through coastal traders—to the East African coast. In no other state in this region were all these variables present. This is the explanation for Buganda's power in the East African lake region in the nineteenth century.

SUMMARY

Tribal societies based on horticultural and pastoral economies accompanied the advent of food production in many areas. As food-producing techniques grew more productive, and as new environments, including arid areas, were occupied, new types of human organization—chiefdoms, states, and cities—appeared and spread. All are based on differential access to strategic and other socially valued resources. Chiefdoms differ from states in several respects. Retaining the kinship emphasis of tribal and foraging societies, chiefdoms often recognize genealogical ties between chiefs and all other members of their circumscription. Some of the generosity associated with descent-group elders and big men in tribal societies remains associated with chiefs, who are expected to redistribute produce and products gathered from the population they administer. In a general evolutionary sense chiefdoms are intermediate and transitional between tribal and state organization.

Ancient states evolved independently in Mesopotamia around 5500 B.P. and in the Mexican highlands around 2200 B.P. States sever the kinship relationships between those who enjoy favored or unimpeded access to strategic resources, the elites, and members of subordinate strata. The primary functions of states involve maintenance of order and of socioeconomic stratification. States accomplish these functions in a variety of ways: through population control (census), disposal of trouble cases (legislative and judicial subsystems), the protection of sovereignty (military and enforcement subsystems), and fiscal support (taxation). States manage large and dense populations; promote occupational, economic, and ecological diversity and specialization; participate in long-distance trade; and, of course, have a ruling or administrative class that oversees the entire system.

Several anthropologists have linked the origin of the state to such single variables, or prime movers, as hydraulic agriculture, ecological diversity, and trade routes. These factors undoubtedly have contributed to state formation in some instances, but the origin of the state is actually a complex evolutionary process that involves the interaction of multiple variables that differ from one sequence to another. Proposing a multivariate theory for the origin of the state, Robert Carneiro suggests that states will arise given increasing population, warfare over land, and either environmental circumscription or resource concentration. Although these variables do contribute to state formation in many cases, highland New Guinea shows that they do not inevitably produce states. Actual cases studied by archeological and sociocultural anthropologists demonstrate that many different paths to statehood exist, but that convergent evolution involving many of the same variables does operate. Multiple local and regional factors always operate in state formation.

On the basis of ethnohistorical and ethnographic sources, the process of state formation has been reconstructed for Buganda, on the northwestern shores of Lake Victoria in eastern Africa. During the first few centuries A.D., the ancestors of the Ganda added plantain and banana cultivation to a diversified economy based on lakeshore foraging. As banana-plantain cultivation spread to the natural limits of its ecological niche, populations grew and spread. Trade and warfare contributed to the emergence of stratification and ultimately of state organization. Because bananas and plantains offered long-term and reliable yields for little labor, the men of Buganda could be diverted from subsistence activity to military service, trade, and manufacture. Again, several variables—trade, warfare, and permanent cultivation prominent among them—contributed to the process of state formation in Buganda.

SOURCES AND SUGGESTED READINGS

BEATTIE, J.
1960   *Bunyoro: An African Kingdom.* New York: Holt, Rinehart and Winston. Short and interesting ethnographic study of the Ganda's northern neighbors.

CARNEIRO, R. L.
1970   A Theory of the Origin of the State. *Science* 169: 733–738. Multivariate approach to the origin of the state; a reasonable argument.

CLAIBORNE, R., AND THE EDITORS OF TIME-LIFE BOOKS
1973   *The First Americans.* New York: Time-Life Books. Prehistoric, historic, and contemporary diversity among Native Americans; good section on Woodland and Mississippian times.

EARLE, T., AND ERICSON, J., EDS.
1977   *Exchange Systems in Prehistory.* New York: Academic Press. Several essays examine techniques and results in the study of prehistoric trade networks.

FALLERS, M. C.
1960   *The Eastern Lacustrine Bantu: Ganda, Soga.* London: International African Institute. Essential ethnography of the Ganda and their eastern neighbors, the Soga.

FLANNERY, K. V.
1972   The Cultural Evolution of Civilizations. *Annual Review of Ecology and Systematics* 3: 399–426. Survey of theories of state origins, organized from an original perspective.

FORD, R. I.
1974   Northeastern Archeology: Past and Future Directions. *Annual Review of Anthropology* 3: 385–413. Survey of knowledge about the East and Midwest of the United States from foraging economies to complex society.

FOWLER, M. L.
1974   *Cahokia: Ancient Capital of the Midwest.* Addison-Wesley Module in Anthropology. Menlo Park, Calif.: Cummings. Survey of Cahokia's growth and significance and the archeology done there.

FRIED, M. H.
1960   On the Evolution of Social Stratification and the State. In *Culture in History,* ed. S. Diamond, pp. 713–731. New York: Columbia University Press. Reviews theories of the origin and evolution of the state.

GROSS, D. R., ED.
1973   *Peoples and Cultures of Native South America: An Anthropological Reader.* Garden City, N.Y.: Natural History Press. Excellent reader with articles covering diverse South American cultural adaptations.

HULL, R. W.
1976   *African Cities and Towns Before the European Conquest.* New York: Norton. The range of traditional African urbanism demonstrated through text and illustrations.

KAGWA, A.
1934   *The Customs of the Baganda.* New York: Columbia University Press. A Gandan scholar records his people's oral tradi-

tions, including information about rulers and their reigns.

KOTTAK, C. P.

1972   Ecological Variables in the Origin and Evolution of African States: The Buganda Example. *Comparative Studies in Society and History* 14: 351–380. The full argument for factors in Gandan state formation.

1977   The Process of State Formation in Madagascar. *American Ethnologist* 4: 136–155. Sociopolitical evolution in Madagascar, with a focus on the Betsileo.

LAMBERG-KARLOVSKY, C. C., AND SABLOFF, J. A., EDS.

1974   *The Rise and Fall of Civilizations: Modern Archaeological Approaches to Ancient Cultures: Selected Readings.* Menlo Park, Calif.: Cummings. Good reader on the rise of state organization and the nature of ancient civilizations in different world areas.

MILLON, R., ED.

1973   *Urbanization at Teotihuacan, Mexico, Volume I: The Teotihuacan Map.* Austin: University of Texas Press. A major archeological achievement, incorporating results of a project begun in 1957. Includes numerous maps and other illustrations as well as a reconstruction of residential and public space. Presents the diversity of Teotihuacan during the Classic.

PARSONS, J.

1974   The Development of a Prehistoric Complex Society: A Regional Perspective from the Valley of Mexico. *Journal of Field Archaeology* 1: 81–108. Regional perspective on sociopolitical evolution in the Valley of Mexico.

PFEIFFER, J.

1977   *The Emergence of Society.* New York: McGraw-Hill. A journalist with considerable anthropological expertise surveys the implications of food production and the rise of complex society throughout the world.

SAHLINS, M. D.

1958   *Social Stratification in Polynesia.* Seattle: University of Washington Press. Study of adaptive radiation through sociocultural means among related Polynesian populations, many of them chiefdoms.

SANDERS, W. T., AND PRICE, B. J.

1968   *Mesoamerica: The Evolution of a Civilization.* New York: Random House. State origins, evolution, and variations in Mesoamerica.

SERVICE, E. R.

1971   *Primitive Social Organization: An Evolutionary Perspective.* 2nd ed. New York: Random House. Provocative introduction to social and political organization of bands, tribes, and chiefdoms from a general evolutionary point of view.

1975   *Origins of the State and Civilization: The Process of Cultural Evolution.* New York: Norton. State formation assessed through several case studies.

SMITH, B. D.

1974   Middle Mississippi Exploitation of Animal Populations: A Predictive Model. *American Antiquity* 39: 274–291. Concentration on certain animal resources in human subsistence in Middle Mississippian times.

SOUTHWOLD, M.

1965   The Ganda of Uganda. In *Peoples of Africa,* ed. J. L. Gibbs, pp. 81–118. New York: Holt, Rinehart & Winston. Ethnographic account of the Ganda today and during recent history.

STEVENSON, R. F.

1968   *Population and Political Systems in Tropical Africa.* New York: Columbia University Press. Population density and state organization in sub-Saharan Africa.

STRUEVER, S., ED.

1971   *Prehistoric Agriculture.* Garden City, N.Y.: Natural History Press. Although the emphasis is on early food-producing systems, some of the articles in this excellent reader deal with the origin of the state.

STRUEVER, S., AND VICKERY, K. D.

1973   The Beginnings of Cultivation in the Midwest-Riverine Area of the United States. *American Anthropologist* 75: 1,197–1,220. Argues the independent origin of plant domestication in aboriginal North America.

UCKO, P. J., ET AL., EDS.

1972   *Man, Settlement and Urbanism.* London: Duckworth. Collection examines demography, settlement patterns, and urbanism in comparative and evolutionary perspective.

VANSINA, J.

1965   *Oral Tradition,* trans. H. M. Wright. Chicago: Aldine. A distinguished historian of Africa reconstructs history from oral traditions.

WITTFOGEL, K. A.

1957   *Oriental Despotism: A Comparative Study of Total Power.* New Haven: Yale University Press. Classic presentation of argument linking despotic states to tightly regulated hydraulic systems.

WRIGHT, H. T., AND JOHNSON, G. A.

1975   Population, Exchange, and Early State Formation in Southwestern Iran. *American Anthropologist* 77: 267–289. Evidence for state organization and the role of local trade in the rise of the state.

WYNNE-EDWARDS, V. C.

1962   *Animal Dispersion in Relation to Social Behavior.* Edinburgh: Oliver and Boyd. Influential work in animal ecology. Observations of animal behavior suggest that animal populations are never limited by starvation, since means of dispersal intervene before pressure on strategic resources becomes critical.

YARNELL, R. A.

1969   Contents of Human Paleofeces. In *The Prehistory of Salts Cave, Kentucky,* ed. P. J. Watson. *Reports of Investigations* 16: 41–54. Springfield: Illinois State Museum. Early domesticates within broad spectrum economy.

part
FOUR

SOCIOCULTURAL
ADAPTIVE MEANS

Kinship and Descent

5

Students in introductory anthropology courses are often bewildered by what they perceive to be an overemphasis on kinship. Kinship symbols, charts, and genealogies of the sort that appear in this and subsequent chapters pervade the study of anthropology. The charge that anthropologists have paid too much attention to kinship is perhaps not totally unfair. The cultural tradition of anthropology emphasizes kinship analysis. Such analysis has become an essential part of anthropology and continues to distinguish it from other disciplines.

Concern with systems of kinship and marriage arises naturally from the kinds of society anthropologists have traditionally studied. Kinship is vitally important in everyday life in bands, tribes, and chiefdoms. In many state-organized societies, too, kinship is important, although, as will be shown in Chapter 13, its functions may be very different. Kinship is essential to anthropologists because of its importance to the people whom they study. Therefore, to regard the analysis of kinship systems as merely an intellectual game would be unwarranted. Furthermore, it would be ethnocentric. Anthropologists use the term *ethnocentrism* to describe the universal human tendency to interpret and evaluate foreign beliefs and practices in terms of the values of one's own cultural tradition. Because kinship is not particularly important for many Americans, American students often ethnocentrically believe that it is not important in other societies.

KINSHIP GROUPS

Ethnographers soon recognize social divisions within any population they study. In the course of their field work, they learn about socially significant groups by observing their activities and composition in much the same way that students of primate behavior observe troops of nonhuman primates. Ethnographers, however, enjoy an advantage in the field that is not available to behavioral primatologists. Ethnographers can ask their primates questions. They can, for example, ask Sam why he is helping Harry, or why they live in the same village. In such a way, ethnographers can discover whether there are genealogical, or kinship, links between Sam and Harry and, if so, the nature of these links. The ethnographer may discover, for example, that socially significant groups are composed of all the descendants of a common grandfather. Members of such a group may live in adjacent houses, farm adjoining fields, and help each other in a variety of everyday tasks. Other groups, the ethnographer learns, come together less frequently. Socially significant groups based on actual or fictive kinship include families and descent groups.

THE NUCLEAR FAMILY

The *nuclear family,* which is only one of several kinds of kinship groups found in different human populations, is usually established by marriage and consists of parents and children. Some anthropologists also call it the elementary family or the biological family. Some other kinds of kinship groups are extended families and descent groups—lineages and clans. A *descent* group, remember, consists of people who believe, assert, or demonstrate that they all descend from a common ancestor. Descent groups are found in tribal societies, chiefdoms, and in some nonindustrial states, among populations whose strategies of adaptation are based on plant cultivation and pastoralism.

There are major differences between the nuclear family and descent groups. Descent groups are permanent units that continue to exist even though their membership changes. The nuclear family, on the other hand, is impermanent. It lasts only as long as parents and their children live together. When the parents die or all the children move away, the nuclear family breaks up.

There is another contrast between the nuclear family and descent-group organization. Status as a member of a descent group is often ascribed at birth. Individuals are born members of a given descent group and remain members throughout life. On the other hand, people are usually members of at least two different nuclear families at different times

in their lives. They are born into one consisting of their parents and siblings. Anthropologists call this the *family of orientation.* When people reach adulthood, they usually marry and establish a nuclear family that includes their spouse and eventually their children. Anthropologists call this the *family of procreation.* Since divorce exists in most human societies, some people may establish more than one family of procreation.

The Definition of Marriage

For a nuclear family to come into existence, a marriage must usually take place. Marriage is difficult to define. Reams have been written by anthropologists attempting to provide a definition of marriage that will apply to all human societies, but there is no universally accepted definition—and perhaps there never will be. One of the most frequently quoted definitions comes from a basic book in anthropology, *Notes and Queries in Anthropology* (1951): "Marriage is a union between a man and a woman such that the children born to the woman are recognized as legitimate offspring of both partners." Although it certainly seems to accommodate marriage in the contemporary United States, this definition is not universally applicable. As you will see in Chapter 6, it is not uncommon for marriages to involve the union of more than two spouses. When this is the case, we speak of *plural marriages.* In some parts of the world, for example, a group of brothers may marry the same woman. This arrangement is called *fraternal polyandry.* Furthermore, in a few cultures that place a heavy premium on having heirs who will continue lines of descent, it is possible for one woman to marry another. In such a society, the father of one of the women, having no male heirs, may declare his daughter a sociological male and arrange for her to take a bride. There is no sexual relationship between the two women. The bride is allowed to have sexual relations with men until she becomes pregnant. Her children are recognized as the legitimate offspring of her husband, who is biologically a woman but sociologically a man, and the descent line does not die out.

It would be possible to frame a revision of the *Notes and Queries* definition of marriage to take these deviations into account; however, the revision would be extremely cumbersome. British social anthropologist Edmund Leach (1955) despaired of ever arriving at a universally applicable definition of marriage. Instead, he suggested that, depending on the social context, several different classes of rights may be transmitted by institutions that have been loosely termed "marriage." The rights transmitted vary from one society to another, and no single right is so widespread as to provide a basis for defining marriage.

Among these rights, marriage can establish the legal father of a woman's children and the legal mother of a man's. It can give the husband a monopoly in the wife's sexuality and the wife a monopoly in the husband's. Marriage can also give either or both spouses rights to the labor services of the other. It can give either or both spouses rights over property belonging or potentially accruing to the other. It can establish a joint fund of property—a partnership—for the benefit of the children of the marriage and a socially significant "relationship of affinity" between each spouse and the relatives of the other.

Although Leach's discussion of these rights is useful in focusing attention on specific aspects of marital relationships in different societies, a loose definition at least is necessary to identify an institution that is found in some form in every human society. I suggest the following: marriage is a socially recognized relationship between a socially recognized male (the husband) and a socially recognized female (the wife) such that the children born to the wife are socially accepted as the offspring of both husband and wife. Furthermore, the husband may be the actual genitor of the children, or he (or she) may be only the socially recognized father (*pater*, in anthropological parlance).

THE NUCLEAR FAMILY: NOT A CULTURAL UNIVERSAL

Since marriage exists in all human societies, and since it is necessary before a nuclear family can come into existence, some anthropologists have argued that the nuclear family is also a cultural universal. The intent of this section is to demonstrate that nuclear family organization is not a universal but a variable form of human social organization.

In most societies, adult men and women marry, live together, and have children. However, in some contemporary societies, particularly in the socioeconomically heterogeneous nations of the contemporary New World, many households are headed by a woman, with no permanent husband-father in residence. These are called *matrifocal* families or households, because the mother (*mater*) is the stable and constant parent and the household head. In many other societies, including most tribal societies and chiefdoms, larger kinship groups may overshadow the nuclear family.

In fact, there are only two kinds of society in which the nuclear family tends to be the most important kinship group: industrial nations and foraging societies. Why should these economies—so dissimilar—be associated with nuclear family organization?

Industrialism, Stratification, and Family Organization

For most middle-class Americans, the nuclear family is not only the most important kinship group, it is the only well-defined kinship group. The isolation of the nuclear family is a product of the geographical mobility associated with an industrial economy and, as such, is equally characteristic of many other industrial nations. Typically, middle-class Americans are born into a family of orientation; they grow up and leave home to go to work or college; the break with their parents is underway. Eventually most Americans marry, establishing a relationship that in most cases culminates in a family of procreation. Today, only about 5 percent of the American population works in farming. Most Americans are not tied to the land, to specific localities. Like most people in other industrialized nations, most Americans sell their labor on the market and move where jobs are available. A married couple often lives several hundred miles from the parents of either spouse. The place where one or both of the spouses work determines where they will live. This practice may be described as a cultural preference for *neolocal* postmarital residence. A couple is expected to establish a new place of residence—a home of their own—after they marry. For middle-class Americans, neolocal residence is both a cultural rule and a statistical norm. Most middle-class Americans strive to establish households and nuclear families of their own.

It has been stressed that nuclear family organization and neolocal postmarital residence are cultural rules of the American middle class. Because most Americans are members of this group, its values are often accepted as typical, especially in the media. This should be obvious to anyone who has watched American television. Yet in socioeconomically heterogeneous nations, that is, stratified societies, value systems do vary to some extent from class to class,

Neolocality: Most middle-class American couples start post-marital households of their own. (Mimi Forsyth/Monkmeyer Press)

and so does kinship organization. It is possible, for example, to point to significant differences in kinship values and relationships between middle-class and poorer Americans. For reasons indicated below, many poorer Americans deem it perfectly appropriate for a newly married couple to live with relatives. Thus among members of the lower class in the United States and other stratified nations, the incidence of expanded family households is significantly greater than it is among the middle class.

Expanded family households are of several types. They usually involve coresidence and mutual dependence of relatives representing at least three generations. If so, they are called *extended family* households. However, they may also be *collateral households,* involving siblings and their spouses and children. Joseph Jorgensen (1972) and many other anthropologists who have done field work in the contemporary United States have interpreted the high incidence of expanded families in the lower class as an adaptation to poverty. Unable to survive as independent nuclear family units, relatives band to-

gether in a single household and pool their resources (see also Stack, 1975).

A long history of poverty and powerlessness has caused the kinship values and attitudes of lower-class Americans to diverge from those of the middle class. Thus, when an American who has been raised in poverty achieves financial success, he or she often feels obligated to assist less fortunate relatives. This can involve inviting poorer relatives to join his or her own household. Kinship obligations may also be met through financial contributions to the households of less successful relatives. Upper-class households, residing in larger homes supported by greater wealth, also diverge frequently from the middle-class nuclear family norm. The upper-class household may lodge and feed such relatives of the individual or couple who heads the household as parents, siblings, married children, children's spouses, or grandchildren, as well as frequent guests and, perhaps, servants.

Neolocal postmarital residence and household composition are therefore linked not only to geographical mobility, but also to the distribution of income and other sources of wealth, and to opportunities for achieving and maintaining financial independence. Neolocal residence isolates the nuclear family and makes it the only well-defined kinship group for most contemporary middle-class Americans. The relationship between these factors and the composition of lower- and middle-class households is summarized in Figure 5.1, in which the arrows indicate the direction of causality.

Although the nuclear family is the only important group based on kinship for most middle-class Americans, Americans still include among their kin other relatives, such as grandparents, uncles, aunts, and cousins. Despite this, American kinship calculation is underdeveloped when compared with that of most nonindustrial societies. How many people do most of us consider to be relatives? How extensive is our knowledge about exactly how we are related to the people we count among our kin? How much do we know about our ancestors? How many of the people with whom we associate regularly are related to us? Systematic differences in answers to these questions by people who live in industrial and nonindustrial societies confirm the declining importance of kinship in the former, particularly for contemporary middle-class Americans. Kinship calculation reflects the importance kinship has in everyday life. Most of the people whom middle-class Americans see and in-

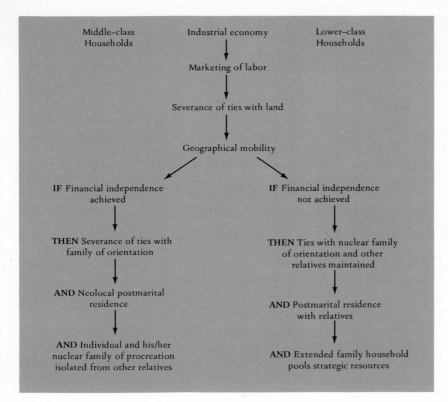

Middle-class Households	Industrial economy	Lower-class Households

Marketing of labor

Severance of ties with land

Geographical mobility

IF Financial independence achieved	**IF** Financial independence not achieved
THEN Severance of ties with family of orientation	**THEN** Ties with nuclear family of orientation and other relatives maintained
AND Neolocal postmarital residence	**AND** Postmarital residence with relatives
AND Individual and his/her nuclear family of procreation isolated from other relatives	**AND** Extended family household pools strategic resources

FIGURE 5.1 The relationship between industrial economy and kinship group organization.

teract with daily are either nonrelatives or members of their nuclear family. Carol Stack's (1975) study of welfare-dependent families in a ghetto area of a middle-sized midwestern city, on the other hand, shows that regular sharing with relatives outside the nuclear family is an important strategy used by the urban poor in adapting to poverty. She shows that contact and sharing among kin are much more significant for poor than for middle-class Americans. In this sense, lower-class kinship patterns in America are more like those of nonindustrial societies than those of the middle class, as you will see below.

The Nuclear Family among Foragers

Far removed from industrial societies on the general evolutionary continuum are populations that pursue foraging strategies of adaptation. Yet, here again the nuclear family is often the most significant group based on kinship. However, in no foraging society is the nuclear family the only group based on kinship. Cross-cultural study shows that the two basic social units of most foraging societies are the nuclear family and the band. People who belong to the same band may be related by kinship, marriage, or fictive kinship.

In contrast to middle-class couples in industrial nations, couples in foraging societies do not typically reside neolocally. In societies with band organization, they join a band where either husband or wife has relatives. A couple may shift from one band to another several times during their married years. Their nonadult children, and sometimes their adult children, follow them. Though nuclear families are ultimately as impermanent among foragers as they are in any other society, they are often more stable social groups than bands.

Many ethnographically and archeologically documented foraging societies lacked year-round band organization. The Native American Shoshone of the Great Basin are an example. Among these people, strategic resources were so meager that during most of the year nuclear family units traveled alone through the countryside hunting and gathering. At certain times of the year, these families came together to take part in cooperative hunts. After a few months together as a seasonal band, they dispersed again.

Although industrial and foraging strategies of adaptation are different, they have something in common. In neither case are people tied permanently to a specific area of land. The consequent mobility and the emphasis on small, economically self-sufficient family units selects for the nuclear family as a basic kinship group in both types of societies.

Functional Alternatives to the Nuclear Family

The point of view of anthropologist George Murdock (1949) is different from those described above. Murdock believes that the nuclear family *is* a cultural universal. He has argued that it is so widespread in human society because its component relationships —wife-husband and parent-child—fulfill four essential social functions: sexual, economic, educational, and reproductive. However, in the following discussion of each of these functions, it will be shown that in tribal societies, chiefdoms, and nonindustrial states, other social units—descent groups and extended families, in particular—can assume many of the functions generally associated with the nuclear family. In other words, there are alternatives to the nuclear family.

SEX AND THE NUCLEAR FAMILY   Murdock argues that because the nuclear family includes the husband-wife relationship, it fulfills a sexual function. It would be more accurate to attribute this function to marriage. Marriage institutionalizes and grants social approval to mating on a regular basis between a couple. However, there are very few human societies in which sexual intercourse is limited to the married pair. It could be argued that the institution of marriage has been selected for over many millenniums of human evolution because humans, unlike other primates, are sexually receptive all year round. Marriage is one way of establishing stable mating patterns and thus preventing conflicts that might result if it were necessary for a new partner to be found every time there was a sexual urge. While I agree, therefore, with Murdock that marriage is a cultural universal, I would dispute his contention that it everywhere gives rise to nuclear family organization.

THE ECONOMIC FUNCTION AND THE NUCLEAR FAMILY   The universality of the nuclear family has also been attributed to its economic function. In all cultures there has been some kind of division of labor on the basis of sex. This is especially clear among foragers, where women usually gather and men usually hunt. A sex-based division of labor also characterizes most industrial societies, including the United States, where males outnumber females in the work force 3 to 2, and where less than two-thirds of all married women work outside the home (see also Chapter 11).

The economic function of the nuclear family is especially important in those societies where it is a self-contained unit of production and consumption. In tribal societies, chiefdoms, and nonindustrial states, the division of labor is often more complex. Among the agricultural Betsileo in Madagascar, certain duties are traditionally performed by women and others by men. But there are also jobs assigned on the basis of age and generation: grandfathers are expected to do certain jobs, adolescent boys and girls, others. There is thus a more complex division of labor on the basis of age, sex, generation, and general social status. In such societies, the nuclear family does not encompass in microcosm all significant economic roles, as it typically does in a foraging economy. Other people are necessary to keep the economy functioning. In such societies, larger kinship groups linking at least three generations are characteristic.

THE EDUCATIONAL FUNCTION AND THE NUCLEAR FAMILY   Before discussing the educational function, it is necessary to distinguish between education and enculturation. *Enculturation* refers to the process whereby children learn about their culture and how they are supposed to act, and cultivate the abilities and habits appropriate in their society. *Education,* on the other hand, refers to the process whereby more formal knowledge is acquired. Education normally goes on in a place called a school. Education requires people to become familiar with relatively esoteric matters, a body of formal knowledge or the lore of their society. In studying education cross-culturally, we note that it is often a correlate of state organization. Many nation-states maintain educa-

tional systems, but not everyone in the society is exposed to them. Knowledge imparted through the educational system is not of the sort that everyone must have to survive in the society.

There are exceptions to the general association between educational systems and state-organized societies. Certain populations in West Africa, and also the Tiwi, a hunting and gathering group of northern Australia (Hart and Pilling, 1960), traditionally maintained bush schools in the hinterland where youths were taken for several years to receive instruction in tribal lore. Having completed bush school, these youths would be accepted as full adult members of their society. This was a kind of passage rite, a period during which individuals passed from one socially significant stage of their life to another.

It is apparent from this that education is not usually a function of the nuclear family but of some state or church organ. Nor is enculturation in any society an exclusive function of the nuclear family. In American society, it is not simply parents and siblings who teach a child how to be an "American," but friends, schoolmates, age peers, teachers, and neighbors. It should be obvious, too, that the enculturative function of the nuclear family is most developed in those societies that isolate it. Among the Betsileo of Madagascar and in many other societies, grandparents, uncles, aunts, and other relatives play con-

Enculturation in Japan. (Grete Mannheim/D.P.I.)

Education—schooling—in Japan. Although enculturation, by definition, is a cultural universal, education is characteristically found in state-organized societies. (Fujihira/ Monkmeyer Press)

stant and important roles in enculturating children. In Madagascar, grandparents sometimes spend more time with a child and have more to say about his or her upbringing than do the child's parents.

THE REPRODUCTIVE FUNCTION AND THE NUCLEAR FAMILY Murdock and others have argued that it is through the nuclear family that the population of a society is perpetuated. It seems that reproduction is more a function of marriage, a cultural universal, than of the nuclear family. Marriage does legitimize the status of children and thus provides offspring who will enjoy full legal rights in the society into which they are born. There are some exceptions, however, which should be noted.

In the Trans-Fly region of New Guinea ethnographers have studied several tribes in which homosexuality, rather than heterosexuality, is the cultural preference. Anthropologist Raymond Kelly (1977) has studied one of these groups, the Etoro, who taboo heterosexual intercourse for more than 200 days during the year. Dutch anthropologist van Baal (1966) has studied their neighbors, the Marind-anim. For various reasons, most notably because homosexual relations are considered ideal, the birth rate is very low in both tribes. So low is it among the Marind-anim that to perpetuate their population they must raid their neighbors. A large percentage of the children who grow up to be Marind-anim have been captured rather than born into Marind-anim society.

Another exception is provided by the Nayars, a group who live on the Malabar Coast in southern India. The Nayar kinship system is *matrilineal* (descent is traced only through females), and their marriage ceremonies are mere formalities. A woman, in adolescence, goes through a marriage ceremony with a man. Afterward, she returns home, in many cases without ever having had sexual intercourse with him. He goes back to his own household. Adult women then receive a succession of sexual partners. Children are automatically admitted as full members of their mother's household and descent group. They are not considered to be relatives of their biological fathers, and some cannot be sure who their biological fathers are. However, for children to be considered legitimate, a man, not necessarily their actual genitor, must go through a ritual acknowledging paternity. Thus Nayar society reproduces itself biologically, but not through the nuclear family.

In summary, in certain populations the nuclear family is the most important or the *only* significant kinship group. When this is the case, its sexual, economic, enculturative, and reproductive functions stand out. Yet enculturation never proceeds exclusively within the nuclear family, and in most societies there are economically important tasks that devolve on groups larger than the nuclear family. In a host of tribal societies, chiefdoms, and nonindustrial states, kinship groups larger than the nuclear family share, and in some cases, take over, functions associated with it in others.

THE SOCIAL ORGANIZATION OF TRIBAL SOCIETIES, CHIEFDOMS, AND NONINDUSTRIAL STATES

Lineages and Clans

The nuclear family is an important kinship group among many foraging populations and in most industrial states; the analogous group in tribal societies, chiefdoms, and many nonindustrial states is the descent group. Anthropologists recognize the existence of two principal varieties of descent groups— *lineages* and *clans*. Common to both is the belief that members all descend from the same apical ancestor, the individual who stands at the apex, or top, of their common genealogy.

There are some significant differences between lineages and clans. A lineage is based on *demonstrated descent*. Members of the descent group will cite the actual or believed descendants in each generation from the apical ancestor through the present. Clans, on the other hand, are based on *stipulated descent*. Clan members believe or assert that they are descended from the same apical ancestor, but they do not trace the genealogical links between themselves and that ancestor. In populations whose social organization includes both lineages and clans, clans generally have a larger membership and are distributed over a larger geographical area than lineages. Several lineages may belong to the same clan.

Sometimes the apical ancestor that distinguishes members of one clan from those of another is not a human at all, but an animal or plant. Whether human or not, the common ancestor symbolizes the social unity and discrete identity of members, marking them off from others. Often, descent groups are exogamous. Thus the common ancestor also serves

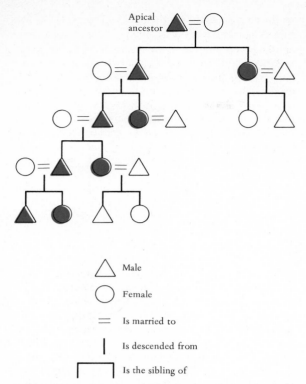

Apical ancestor

△ Male

○ Female

= Is married to

| Is descended from

⌐⌐ Is the sibling of

FIGURE 5.2 A corporate patrilineage five generations deep. Lineages are based on demonstrated descent from an apical ancestor. With patrilineal descent, children of males (shaded) are included as descent-group members. Children of females are excluded; they belong to their father's descent group. Also notice descent-group exogamy.

again, however, anti-kinship, individualistic themes of middle-class American culture disapprove of company officials who occupy their positions because they are the boss's son, daughter, or spouse, rather than through their own competence. Americans can also affiliate with industrial corporations by buying stock on the open market. In contrast, descent rules regulate membership in corporate lineages, determining at birth who is to be a member and who is to be excluded. By virtue of descent rules, one enjoys or is excluded from access to the descent-group estate.

Another attribute shared by industrial corporations and corporate descent groups is *perpetuity.* Descent groups, unlike nuclear families, are permanent and enduring units. New people become descent-group members in every generation and eventually enjoy access to the corporate estate. Unlike the nuclear family, the descent group lives on even though specific members die.

Unilineal Descent Groups and Unilocal Postmarital Residence

Several principles may serve as cultural rules for admitting certain individuals as descent-group members while excluding others. The descent rule may be *patrilineal* or *matrilineal.* With matrilineal descent, individuals of both sexes belong to their mother's group automatically at birth, and they usually remain members of that group throughout their lives. The descent group is composed, therefore, of individuals who have been recruited through the group's female members. (See Figures 5.2 and 5.3.)

When the descent rule is patrilineal, males and females belong automatically at birth to their father's descent group, and they normally remain members of this group throughout their lives. The children of all male members of the descent group become members and the children of female members are excluded. Matrilineal and patrilineal descent are varieties of *unilineal descent,* because descent is based on one line only, either the female or the male.

Matrilineal descent is far less common than patrilineal descent. In a sample of 564 societies, Murdock (1957) found that there were about three times as many societies with patrilineal descent (247 to 84). Why should this be? To answer this question we must first consider *postmarital residence rules.*

as a reference point, forcing people to seek their mates among members of other descent groups.

Among many populations, lineages are *corporate groups.* Like financial corporations in industrial nations, corporate descent groups manage an estate, a resource pool. In an agricultural society, this estate might include fields, rights to irrigation water, and house sites. Among pastoralists, herds might constitute the most significant estate item. Often, descent-group members trace creation of their joint estate to their common apical ancestor.

In a modern industrial society, people become managers in a corporate enterprise by virtue of their own achievements or because of kinship ties. Here

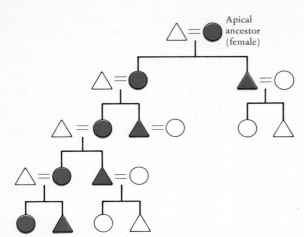

FIGURE 5.3 A corporate matrilineage five generations deep. With matrilineal descent, children of females (shaded) are included as descent-group members. Children of males are excluded; they belong to their mother's descent group. Also notice descent-group exogamy.

In most societies there is some prevailing opinion about where it is proper for a couple to live after their marriage. Neolocality, as we have seen, is the culturally appropriate postmarital residence rule for middle-class Americans. However, neolocality is not very common outside of the United States, western Europe, and European-derived cultures of contemporary Latin America. Far more common is *virilocality* (*vir* in Latin is "husband"), whereby the couple is expected to reside with the husband's relatives after marriage. Virilocality is often associated with patrilineal descent. This makes sense. If only children of male members of the group are to be descent-group members and to have rights in the descent group's estate, then it is well to bring them up on that estate. This can be done if males bring their wives to, and raise their children on, the man's estate rather than the woman's.

A less common postmarital residence rule, but one often associated with matrilineal descent groups, is *uxorilocality* (*uxor* in Latin is "wife"). This means that the couple is expected to live with the wife's group after marriage. Together, virilocality and uxorilocality are known as *unilocal* rules of postmarital residence.

However, there is a problem involved with uxorilocal residence and matrilineal descent that is not

so pressing in patrilineal societies. It relates to the role of men and women in either society. In patrilineal societies, once a female member of the group marries out of her own and into her husband's group and bears children who will be members of that group, she usually has little say in the administration of her own descent-group estate. Its affairs are the concern of the men who have remained at home. In matrilineal societies, too, men make many—or at least some—of the major decisions and are expected to concern themselves with the affairs of their own descent groups.

How is this reconciled with a uxorilocal residence rule that tells men to leave their descent-group estate when they marry? A common way of solving the problem is to maintain descent-group exogamy and village endogamy. Endogamy refers to marriage within a specified group, in this case the village of one's birth. Imagine a matrilineal society in the tropical forest of South America. There are two descent groups living in its village. The village is a circular settlement, with an open central area and houses along the periphery. Each of the two descent groups is associated with its own side of the village. When a man marries, he moves to his wife's place, but this merely involves picking up his things and walking across the village. He is residing uxorilocally, but he is close enough to home to take an active part in the affairs of his own descent group.

In societies with patrilineal descent, on the other hand, there is no major obstacle to a woman's leaving her own village entirely, and she normally does. More restricted residence possibilities for matrilineal than for patrilineal societies may help explain the greater frequency of the latter.

Although matrilineal societies are not numerous, they are proportionately more common among populations toward the horticultural end of the plant-cultivating continuum than among other groups.

It has long been argued that the reason for this lies in the subsistence role of women in horticultural societies. The argument typically runs as follows: since women have an important role in plant cultivation and since they often engage in cooperative economic activities, it is advantageous for them to be able to work together smoothly. Therefore, kinswomen should be kept together. A good way to keep them together permanently is through uxorilocal residence and matrilineal descent. Note, however, that this argument does not explain why more than half the world's horticultural societies are not matrilineal. Nor does it face the fact that raiding and other forms of warfare are not uncommon in horticultural societies. One could just as well argue that since cooperation among males is advantageous for warfare, patrilineal descent should be favored. The problem deserves further study, and the roles of men and women in a variety of social contexts will be examined more fully in Chapter 11.

Flexibility in Descent-Group Organization

In addition to patrilineality and matrilineality, still other principles of descent may assign individuals to corporate or other socially significant groups. Anthropologists have described many societies with nonunilineal, or *ambilineal,* rules of descent. There are descent groups in such societies. Members are recruited on the basis of descent from a common apical ancestor. However, ambilineal groups differ from unilineal groups in that they do not automatically exclude either the children of sons or the children of daughters. It is easier to understand ambilineal descent groups if we regard them as merely being especially flexible instances of unilineal descent organization. In fact, most ambilineal descent groups tend to be either patrilineal or matrilineal. The difference is that the descent rule does not apply to individuals automatically. With unilineal descent rules, descent group membership is an ascribed status. People are born members of their father's group in a patrilineal society or of their mother's group in a matrilineal society. They have no choice; they are members of that descent group for the rest of their lives.

There is a dispute among anthropologists over how much difference there is between ambilineal and unilineal descent groups. Before 1950, descent groups were generally described simply as patrilineal or matrilineal. If a society tended toward patrilineality, the anthropologist classified it as patrilineal and left it at that. The recognition of ambilineal descent represented a formal admission that there is often a great deal of flexibility involved in descent systems. In even the most strictly patrilineal societies, there will always be cases where there are only daughters in a given generation. Something has to be done or the descent line will die out. From this one suspects that all descent systems are flexible, although some are more flexible than others.

Adaptation, Descent Rules, and Descent-Group Composition

In order to explain variations of descent rules more clearly, we must distinguish between the ideology of descent—descent rules—and the composition of descent groups in a society. Here we are talking about a difference between cultural rules or preferences, on the one hand, and actual behavior, on the other. For reasons that are still poorly understood, descent rules and descent-group composition are not always concordant. In cultures with strong ideological emphasis on patrilineal descent, deviations away from patrilineal descent-group composition may nevertheless be common. On the other hand, in populations whose ideology of descent is ambilineal, composition may be strongly patrilineal. The descent ideology of the Betsileo is, for example, very flexible. Betsileo assert that people should join their father's descent group, that the father's side is stronger. Yet they also say that all a man's descendants through his daughters, as well as through his sons, have rights in his group. Descent ideology is flexible among the Betsileo and tends toward ambilineality, but the composition of groups tends toward patrilineality. In contrast, among the Nuer, who live in the Sudan in East Africa, there exists a fairly rigid ideological emphasis on patrilineal descent. Nuer descent groups, however, are actually considerably less patrilineal and more ambilineal in composition than those of the Betsileo and other populations with flexible ideologies.

The major lesson to be learned from this discussion of descent rules and descent-group composition is that most systems of social organization are not totally inflexible. Previous chapters have stressed that flexibility is one of the major keys to the adaptive success of *Homo.* Culture provides human populations with rules to live by. However, if conditions make it impossible to obey these rules all the time, people will violate them. If conditions continue to select for violation of a rule over time, then the ideology will probably change. In this case, cultural evolution has occurred. The selecting influences have changed, and the ideology has changed accordingly.

ECOLOGY AND DESCENT IN MADAGASCAR The population of Madagascar is now more than 7 million people. They belong to twenty different populations or ethnic units. Similarities in their languages, as well as other evidence, suggest that the twenty ethnic groups of Madagascar can be regarded as divergent descendants of an original population that began to settle the island around 2,000 years ago. Over time, the original population grew and dispersed; its offshoots settled in contrasting environments. In the process, the population of Madagascar underwent an *adaptive radiation* (see Glossary), through changes in social and cultural means of adaptation. As the people of Madagascar occupied new niches, they modified some of their customary behavior and beliefs. Whereas their ancestors had been a relatively homogeneous people with the same sociocultural heritage, the contemporary populations of Madagascar now differ from one another in noteworthy social and cultural features.

Variations in descent ideology and in composition of descent groups reflect this divergence. Some Malagasy populations have strict patrilineal ideologies and a very high incidence of patrilineal affiliation. Other ethnic units have more flexible descent rules, and their descent groups include significant numbers who are descended through females. Such variations in ideology and descent-group composition are related to differences in population density and pressure on strategic resources in Madagascar. Patrilineal ideology is strongest, and descent groups are most patrilineal in composition, in some of the most densely populated agricultural areas. With land resources limited, strict ideological emphasis on patrilineal descent limits access to the land only to *agnates*, descendants through male links only, and thus full members of the patrilineal descent group. If the children of female members do not inherit sufficient agricultural land from their fathers, they have to emigrate and seek their fortunes elsewhere. Patrilineal descent rules therefore function in such areas of Madagascar as a means of dispersing excess population that the land cannot support.

The Betsileo, too, are agriculturalists. However, pressure on agricultural land and other strategic resources does not appear to be as great for them. Population densities are typically lower. The Betsileo countryside is rugged and hilly. The most valuable agricultural land is located in valleys. Since the Betsileo irrigate their rice crop, sources of water are also valuable parts of descent-group estates. Betsileo descent ideology is flexible. If a father's descent group cannot grant sufficient farmland to sustain a family because land is scarce, children have the option of joining their mother's group, where land may be more abundant. So flexible, in fact, is Betsileo ideology that individuals can join the descent groups of any one of their four grandparents if need arises and thus have access to their estates. In the case of the Betsileo, flexible descent-group ideology acts to distribute the population over the land by permitting people a larger number of options in terms of descent-group affiliation and inheritance rights.

A third example of descent rule adaptation comes from the Bara, a population who live in a more arid area to the south of the Betsileo and whose strategy of adaptation is based on herding zebu, humped cattle. Population densities among the Bara are less than one-fifth that of the Betsileo. Bara orient their lives around their herds rather than permanent plots of agricultural land. There is no problem of limited access to land, as there is when agriculture is the economic base and population is dense. The Bara are even more flexible than the Betsileo in their descent ideology and descent-group composition. They can accurately be described as ambilineal. Individuals have full rights to affiliate with their father's or their mother's descent group or, in fact, with any group to which they can demonstrate a genealogical relationship.

Descent, Ecology, and Evolution

Some generalizations about relationships between descent groups, ecology, and the evolution of human populations are in order. There is a definite relationship between ecological factors and principles of social organization, including kinship and descent. Because foraging societies live off nature rather than control it, there is no permanent tie between them and specific areas of land. In foraging populations with band organization, nuclear families may move from band to band during the year and throughout their lives. In populations whose strategy of adaptation has changed from cultivation to industrialism, the relationship between humans and specific plots of land is also severed. Nuclear family organization becomes a cultural ideal when ties with the land are cut and the economy rewards geographical mobility of individuals and their dependents.

Descent-group — particularly lineage — organization is especially characteristic of populations whose strategies of adaptation involve a relatively permanent relationship between humans and estates. Descent, by admitting some and excluding others, is a means of regulating access to these estates. Descent must be understood as a flexible sociocultural means of adaptation. If there are too many people for a given estate to support, descent rules become stricter; if, on the other hand, the population exploiting the estate begins to fall, descent rules become less rigid. Principles such as descent that serve in the long run to maintain stable relationships between human populations and their resource base are known as *homeostats* because they maintain equilibrium, or homeostasis. Sociocultural homeostats are not limited to descent rules. Others are examined in subsequent chapters.

With these generalizations in mind, we might expect to find the most rigid descent rules operating in societies where there is great pressure on estates, for example, densely populated agricultural societies. Where the human population does not approach *carrying capacity* (the largest number of people that the environment *could* support, given the society's needs and its techniques of satisfying them), however, or where other means of regulation are employed, descent rules should be weaker. We would therefore expect descent ideology generally to be more flexible and descent-group composition more varied in sparsely populated pastoral and horticultural societies where the relationship between the human population and specific plots of land is less permanent than it is among agriculturalists.

However, the matter of descent is not simply one of population pressure and ties with the land. Descent rules and descent-group organization can serve other functions. The utility of descent as a means of political organization, for example, will be examined in Chapter 7, where we will see that factors other than population pressure on scarce resources can select for descent organization.

EGOCENTRIC KINSHIP STUDIES

In addition to the identification of kinship *groups* that are significant in a given society, anthropologists are also interested in *kinship calculation,* the system according to which individuals in the society reckon kin relationships. In the *egocentric* kinship charts that follow, shaded egos, or I's, identify the individual whose kinship calculation is being examined. The study of kinship calculation requires the ethnographer to concentrate on individuals rather than groups. The ethnographer asks informants questions like "Would you tell me the names of all your relatives?" The ethnographer then poses additional questions to determine whether there are, in fact genealogical relationships between these "relatives" and the individual who has named them. By asking the same questions of several informants, the ethnographer develops a model of the extent and direction of kinship calculation in that society. Furthermore, he or she begins to understand the relationship between kinship groups and kinship calculation, seeing, for example, how individuals use kinship calculation to gain admission into groups and to create networks of personal ties with others outside their groups. The ethnographer also sees that there are some biological kin types who are considered to be relatives and others who are not.

Biological Kin Types and Kinship Calculation

At this point it is necessary to distinguish between relatives and biological kin types. Anthropologists designate biological kin types with letters and symbols such as those shown in Figure 5.4.

FIGURE 5.4 Kinship symbols and biological kin type notation.

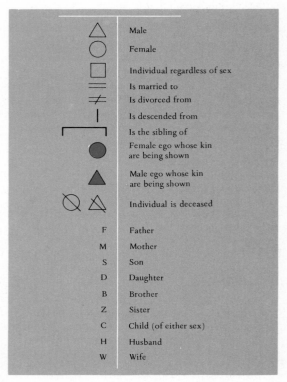

The terms for biological kin types are usually not equivalent to those used for relatives in a given language. For example, in English we use the term *father* to refer to only one biological kin type, the genealogical father (although the word may also be used for an adoptive father). However, when you consider the term *cousin,* you will see that it lumps together several different kin types. We distinguish between first, second, and third cousins, and so on; first cousin once removed, second cousin once removed, and so on. But even the term *first cousin* includes several biological kin types. It includes one's mother's brother's son (MBS), mother's brother's daughter (MBD), mother's sister's son (MZS), mother's sister's daughter (MZD), father's brother's son (FBS), father's brother's daughter (FBD), father's sister's son (FZS), and father's sister's daughter (FZD). Thus "first cousin" lumps together eight biological kin types. There are other Indo-European languages — Portuguese, for example — that distinguish between first cousins on the basis of sex. In Portuguese, there are two terms, each lumping together four biological kin types: *primo* for all male first cousins and *prima* for all female first cousins.

Avoiding ethnocentrism about kinship means understanding that people with different cultures do not define their relatives in the same way that you do. Contemporary Americans believe that people are equally related to all their first cousins, to their father and mother, to their uncles and aunts, to all four grandparents, and to all their grandchildren. This belief is related to the cultural and actual preference for nuclear family organization in the contemporary United States.

KINSHIP TERMINOLOGY

Just as people with different cultural orientations define their relatives differently, they also use different patterns of kinship terminology to refer to them. Consider kinship terminology in the United States. Our term *uncle* lumps together at least two kin types: mother's brother and father's brother. Our term *aunt* applies equally to a mother's sister and a father's sister. *Uncle* and *aunt* are also used for spouses of "blood" aunts and uncles. *Grandfather* includes mother's father and father's father.

In any society, the terminology used to designate relatives is a classification system, a taxonomy or typology. However, it is not a classification system that has been developed by an anthropologist. Rather, it is a native taxonomy, a classification system developed over generations by the people who live in that society. (Wide cross-cultural variation in other native classification systems — including colors, plants, animals, and the stars — is examined in Chapter 12.) The way we classify our relatives is also an American convention, although convergent systems do exist among other populations with prominent nuclear family organization.

A native classification system is based on how people perceive similarities and differences in the things being classified. When Americans use the term *uncle* to refer both to mother's brother and father's brother, it must be because we perceive both as being basically the same kind of relative. By lumping together these two biological kin types under the term *uncle,* we are distinguishing between these two kin types and another, F, whom we call "Father," "Dad," or "Pop." We never, however, use the same term for our father and our uncle. You may be surprised to learn that in many other societies it is common to call a father and a father's brother by a single term. This section examines several systems of kinship terminology encountered in different populations and attempts to suggest explanations for some of the differences and similarities among them.

To clarify the matter, let us return to the distinction between our terms *uncle* and *father.* The nuclear family has been described as the only important group based on kinship for middle-class people in many contemporary industrial nations. Its organization was explained in terms of an industrial economy, geographical mobility associated with lack of permanent ties to the land, sale of labor for cash, financial success, and neolocal postmarital residence. In this social context, it is perfectly reasonable for middle-class Americans to distinguish between those who belong to their nuclear families of orientation and procreation and those who do not. We normally grow up living with our mother and father, but not with our aunts or uncles. We normally see our parents every day and our uncles and aunts less frequently. Often, uncles and aunts live in different towns and cities, perhaps hundreds or thousands of miles from us. We expect to inherit our parents' property. The children of our uncles and aunts, our cousins, have first claim to inherit property from their parents.

Similar observations apply to the family of procreation. We raise and live with our children, see them virtually every day until they leave our households; they are our heirs. We are closer to them than we are to our nieces and nephews. We mean more to them than their aunts and uncles; they mean more to us than our nieces and nephews.

Native classification systems are based on differences and similarities as native members of the society perceive them. The term *uncle* distinguishes between the kin types MB and FB, on the one hand, and the kin type F, on the other. Yet it also lumps together; it uses the same term for MB and FB, two different kin types. Why? American kinship, particularly middle-class kinship, is *bilateral;* it extends equally on the mother's and the father's side. Both kinds of uncle are siblings of our parents. We think of both as roughly the same kind of relative. "No," you may object, "I feel closer to my mother's brother than to my father's brother." That may be. But in a large sample of American college students, we would probably find that approximately equal numbers favor each side. This is what the term *bilateral kinship* means: in the population as a whole, kinship is calculated equally on both sides, through males and females.

Similar observations apply to such things as interaction with, residence near, and rights to inherit property from more distant relatives. Americans usually do not inherit from uncles on either side. However, on the whole, if they do inherit, there is as much chance that they will inherit from one as from the other. Middle-class Americans usually do not live near or in the same household with either of their uncles, but, if they do, the chances are approximately the same that it will be their father's brother as their mother's brother. The same rule applies to other aspects of social life based on kinship in this society.

Several considerations will determine differences in the way people treat, interact with, and classify their biological relatives in different societies. For example, do two biological kin types customarily live together or apart? If they live apart, how far apart? How often do they see each other? What kind of behavior is appropriate between them? What kinds of rights do they have in each other? What benefits do they derive from each other, and what are their obligations? Are they members of the same, or different, descent groups? With these questions in mind, let us examine other systems of kinship terminology.

Kinship Terminology on the Parental Generation

Figure 5.5 applies to biological kin types on the generation above ego, the first ascending generation. Letters at the top serve to identify six biological kin types. Numbers indicate the manner of classification. Where the same number appears in a line under two biological kin types, they are called by the same term. The American system of kinship clas-

	MB	MZ	M	F	FB	FZ
Lineal	3	4	1	2	3	4
Bifurcate merging	3	1	1	2	2	4
Generational	2	1	1	2	2	1
Bifurcate collateral	3	6	1	2	5	4

FIGURE 5.5   Types of kinship classification on the first ascending generation.

sification is called the *lineal system.* The number 3, which appears below the biological kin types FB and MB, stands for the term *uncle,* which is applied both to FB and to MB (see Figure 5.6).

Lineal terminology is found in societies where the nuclear family is the only or the most important social group based on kinship.

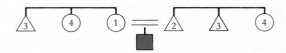

FIGURE 5.6   Lineal kinship terminology.

BIFURCATE MERGING KINSHIP TERMINOLOGY   Bifurcate merging kinship terminology is the most common way of classifying biological kin types on the first ascending generation (see Figure 5.7). It is found in societies with unilineal (patrilineal or matrilineal) descent rules, unilocal (virilocal or uxorilocal) residence patterns, or a combination of these rules.

FIGURE 5.7   Bifurcate merging kinship terminology.

When the population has both a unilocal rule of postmarital residence and a unilineal rule of descent, the logic of bifurcate merging kinship terminology is fairly obvious. With unilineal descent groups, every individual in that society is a member of one descent group. In a patrilineal society, ego's father and father's brother are members of the same descent group, the same sex, and the same generation. Since most patrilineal societies also have rules of virilocal postmarital residence, father and his brother also will be permanent residents of the same local group. Since they share so many attributes that are socially relevant in the society in question, ego regards them as sociological equals and calls them by the same kinship term — 2. The mother's brother belongs to a different descent group, resides somewhere else, and is called by a different term — 3.

What about the mother and the mother's sister in a society with patrilineal descent? As full siblings, they are members of the same descent group, their father's. They are also of the same sex and the same generation. In many cases, though not always, they marry into the same village. These factors in conjunction may be sufficient to explain the use of the same term — 1 — for both.

Similar observations apply to societies with matrilineal descent groups. Consider a society with two matrilineal clans, called the Ravens and the Wolves. Ego is a member of his mother's clan, the Raven clan. Ego's father is a member of the Wolf clan. His mother and her sister are both Ravens of the same sex and generation. If there is uxorilocal residence, as there often is in matrilineal societies, they will also reside in the same local group after they marry.

The father's sister, on the other hand, belongs to a different descent group, the Wolves, resides elsewhere, and is called by a different term — 4. Ego's father and father's brother are both Wolves; they are of the same sex and generation. The fact that they share these attributes may be sufficient to explain why ego uses a single term to describe them. Marrying women of the same clan and residing after marriage in the same local group will serve to reinforce this usage.

GENERATIONAL KINSHIP TERMINOLOGY Like bifurcate merging, generational kinship terminology merges parents and their siblings, but the lumping is more complete (see Figure 5.8). There are really only two terms for relatives on the parental genera-

FIGURE 5.8 Generational kinship terminology.

tion. We may translate them as "father" and "mother," but more accurate translations would be "male member of the parental generation" and "female member of the parental generation." Of interest in generational kinship terminology is the fact that it does not distinguish between mother's side and father's side. It lumps together father, father's brother, and mother's brother. Note that in neither a matrilineal nor a patrilineal society are all three kin types members of the same descent group. Similarly, generational kinship terminology uses a single term for mother, mother's sister, and father's sister, relatives who, in a unilineal society, would never be members of the same descent group. Yet the terms suggest closeness between ego and relatives in the first ascending generation, much more closeness, in fact, than exists between aunts and uncles and nephews and nieces in America. From this we might expect generational terminology to be found in societies where kinship is much more important than in our own, but where there is no rigid distinction between father's side and mother's side.

It is no surprise, then, that generational kin classification is the typical kinship terminology of populations with ambilineal descent. Recall that in such societies there are descent groups centered around estates. Members of the descent group have access to its estate. However, in contrast to unilineal descent, ambilineal descent is not fixed at birth. People have a choice about which descent group they will join. Still other kinds of flexibility are characteristic of societies with ambilineal descent. In some, people may change their descent-group membership during their lifetimes. Furthermore, they may belong to two or more descent groups simultaneously.

How does generational terminology fit in with these conditions? Individuals' use of kin terms allows them to maintain close personal relationships with all relatives on the first ascending generation. In a rough way, people exhibit the same kind of behavior to aunts and uncles that they exhibit to their biological parents. Someday they will have to make a choice about the descent group they will join. Relevant, too, is the fact that in societies with ambilineal descent, postmarital residence is not usually unilocal but *ambilocal*—the married couple can reside either with the husband's or the wife's group.

Consider the implications of cultural rules that allow individuals choice in where they can live after they marry. Ego's father and mother may be living in ego's father's natal community. If a man decides to join his father's descent group and live in his father's local group, he may become a permanent resident of the village where his father and his father's mother are living. However, his father's sister, like his father, may have brought her spouse to her own village. His father's brother may or may not be living in the village where he was born. Possibly he has moved to his wife's community. Similarly, if ego decides to join his mother's descent group, his father and mother may be there if they decided to reside uxorilocally after marriage. His mother's brother may be living there with his wife, or he may have joined her in her village. His mother's sister may be there with her husband, or she may have followed her husband to his own community. In short, because of ambilocal residence and ambilineal descent, it is impossible for ego to know during his childhood which of his relatives on the first ascending generation will be closest to him throughout most of his later life. By calling everyone on that generation either father or mother, he can avoid the problem.

It is also significant to note that generational principles appear in the kin classification systems of some foraging populations with band organization, for example, certain Kalahari groups and several of the native populations of North America. Why? There are certain similarities between hunting and gathering bands and ambilineal descent groups in both their composition and rules of affiliation. In either type of social organization, people have a choice about which group they will join. Furthermore, individuals shift their band affiliations quite commonly. When adults establish their own family of procreation, they may decide to join a band other than their parents'. During their lives, they may be members of several different bands. As in ambilineal, ambilocal societies, generational kinship terminology in populations with band organization establishes close personal relationships with several relatives whom ego may in time use to gain entry into different bands.

BIFURCATE COLLATERAL KINSHIP TERMINOLOGY Of all the systems designating relatives on the parental generation, bifurcate collateral is the most specific: it

FIGURE 5.9 Bifurcate collateral kinship terminology.

has separate kin terms for each of the six kin types on the first ascending generation (see Figure 5.9). Bifurcate collateral kinship terminology is not as common as the others that have been discussed. In fact, a large number of the populations employing this variety of kin terminology are concentrated in a specific part of the world—northern Africa and the Near and Middle East. Many are related genetically, that is, they are offshoots of the same ancestral group. They are geographically close, and in many cases, they have been affected by the same events.

How, then, is bifurcate collateral kinship classification to be explained? Could it be that the kinship terminology simply arose as a quirk in one society in this region and was subsequently transmitted to all the others? Such an explanation assumes that a cultural practice has been *diffused* from one society (or by way of neighboring societies) to others. Or could it be that bifurcate collateral kinship terminology arose accidentally in an ancestral group and now exists in several offshoots that share a common cultural heritage? In other words, was bifurcate collateral terminology invented by the remote ancestors of these populations and culturally transmitted over generations to their descendants? If this is so, it exemplifies what anthropologists call a *genetic* explanation. (Note that this use of *genetic* has nothing to do with DNA, but refers to cultural inheritance—that is, transmission by learning.) Genetic and diffusional explanations are grouped under a common category: *historical* explanations. Social institutions or cultural practices exist among two or more different societies because they shared a period of common history or were exposed to common sources of information.

Anthropologists have thus far come up with no satisfactory explanation for bifurcate collateral kinship terminology. It is possible, however, to suggest a *functional* explanation, which is similar to those that have been offered for the other kinds of kinship terminology. Functional explanations attempt to relate specific practices to other aspects of behavior in the society being examined. Are certain aspects of human behavior so closely related that when one of them changes, the others will change too? What are the social correlates of bifurcate collateral kinship terminology?

Descent-group organization is found among many of the North African and Near Eastern populations who employ bifurcate collateral kinship terminology. Descent rules are generally patrilineal, but this is only a tendency. In composition, many of the descent groups could be classified as ambilineal. I suggest therefore that bifurcate collateral kinship terminology can serve some of the same functions that generational terminology serves. With generational terminology, people maintain the same formal relationship with all members of the parental generation. In bifurcate collateral, they maintain distinctive but close relationships with all their kin on the parental generation. In either case, they have established and maintained, through kin terms, close relationships based on kinship. They may change their descent-group or local-group affiliation at different times during their lives. Establishing close and distinct kinship relations with kin on the generation above will facilitate such changes in group affiliation.

Classification of Same Generation Relatives

Some of the same principles that determine the system of kinship terminology for parental generation kin types also affect the classification of relatives on ego's own generation. Consider a few examples.

FIGURE 5.10 The distinction among lineals, collaterals, and affinals as perceived by ego.

ESKIMO KINSHIP TERMINOLOGY   Eskimo terminology on ego's generation—the system that Americans use to classify their siblings and cousins—is similar to lineal terminology on the first ascending generation. Eskimo kinship terminology separates members of the nuclear family from other kin types. The most important thing about Eskimo terminology, however, is that it clearly distinguishes lineal relatives from collateral relatives (see Figure 5.10). A *lineal relative* is an ancestor or descendant, anyone on the direct line of descent that leads to and from ego. Thus ego's lineal relatives are his or her direct ancestors: parents, grandparents, great-grandparents, great-great-grandparents, and so forth. Equally lineal relatives are one's children, grandchildren, great-grandchildren, and so forth. Collaterals are any other biological kin types. They are ego's own siblings and their descendants, and the siblings of his or her lineals and the descendants of those siblings. One's brothers and sisters, nieces and nephews, aunts and uncles, are collateral relatives. Eskimo terminology has two terms comparable to *brother* and *sister* in English for siblings. It lumps together under a single term analogous to *cousin* the children of parents' collaterals, who are members of different nuclear families.

IROQUOIS KINSHIP TERMINOLOGY   Iroquois kinship terminology is found among many of the populations who employ bifurcate merging kin terms for kin types on the first ascending generation. Recall that bifurcate merging kinship terminology uses the same term for mother and mother's sister. People also refer to their father and their father's brother by a

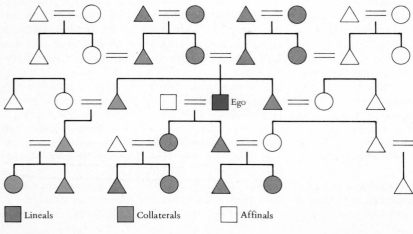

Lineals   Collaterals   Affinals

common term. It is easy to understand Iroquois terminology if you think of it in the following way. You call your mother and your mother's sister by the same term, "mother," a loose translation. You also call your father and father's brother by the same term, "father." The child of anyone whom you call "father" is "brother" or "sister." The child of anyone you call "mother" is also "brother" or "sister." Thus your mother's sister's children and your father's brother's children are called "brother" and "sister," that is, the same terms you use to refer to your own siblings. You use a different term for the children of your father's sister and your mother's brother, your *cross cousins*. In Iroquois terminology the same term (or terms if a sex distinction is made in referring to male and female children) is used for father's sister's children and mother's brother's children. In many populations, however, kin terms distinguish between the father's sister's children and the mother's brother's children. Two variants of Iroquois terminology, known as Omaha cousin terminology and Crow cousin terminology are found respectively among populations with strongly corporate patrilineal and matrilineal descent groups.

HAWAIIAN KINSHIP TERMINOLOGY   If you call all your uncles and aunts by the same terms you use for your father and mother, you have only fathers and mothers on the first ascending generation. The children of any father or mother are your brother and sister. You therefore use one term for your brothers and male first cousins and another for your sisters and female first cousins. This system of classifying relatives on ego's own generation is known as Hawaiian kinship terminology, and it resembles generational kinship terminology on the parental level. The logic of such kinship terminology is clearly to bring people in close relationship with all their kin and to enable them to create especially close ties with any one of them they choose.

DESCRIPTIVE KINSHIP TERMINOLOGY   Ego may employ separate terms for each kin type on his or her own generation: B, Z, MBS, MBD, MZS, MZD, FBS, FBD, FZS, FZD. The first filial generation can also illustrate this descriptive principle (bifurcate collateral), with distinct terms for S, D, BS, BD, ZS, ZD, and perhaps the sons and daughters of each first cousin. When kinship terminology is this descriptive, people usually refer to many of their kin by their names rather than by any kinship term. Kin-

ship terms are used by ego to identify kin when someone asks about a specific relationship.

Relevance of Kinship Terminology

There are many good reasons why anthropologists spend a great deal of time analyzing the kinship terminology of the people they study. Kinship is extremely important in the societies traditionally of interest to anthropologists. Most anthropologists assume that a population's kinship terminology will reveal information of value in understanding its social relationships and interactions. If two biological kin types are designated by the same term, it is probable that they share some attribute of significance in that population's social structure. The anthropologist attempts to determine how categories employed in language are significant in social life.

Several scholars who have studied principles of social organization cross-culturally have found that kinship terminology is one of the slowest-changing aspects of social organization. Ownership and inheritance patterns, postmarital residence rules, and descent principles all appear to change more easily and more rapidly. Because patterns of nonverbal and verbal behavior change at different rates, anthropologists expect to find some cases in which the association between kinship terminology and other aspects of social structure does not hold. If we find generational kinship terminology in a society with virilocal postmarital residence and patrilineal descent groups, for example, we may have to conclude that changes in kinship terminology are lagging behind changes in residence and descent. In such a case the expectation is that the kinship terminology of the society will change ultimately to bifurcate merging.

A final observation about the relationship between kinship terminology and social structure is in order. Certain correspondences between kinship terminology on the first ascending generation and on ego's own generation have been discussed. Often, however, anthropologists encounter societies in which the classification systems for these generations do not correspond. Bifurcate merging, for example, may be used for the parental generation and Hawaiian principles may be used for ego's own, rather than the Iroquois system we would normally expect. Such anomalies may indicate that both kinship terminology and the social and economic factors that influence it are undergoing a change of form—that is, an evolution.

SUMMARY

In the societies that anthropologists have traditionally studied, kinship is extremely important. A distinction is made between kinship groups, whose composition and activities can be observed and charted in the field, and kinship calculation, the manner in which individuals identify and designate their relatives. A kinship-based group encountered in many societies is the nuclear family, which consists of a married couple and their children. Examples of functional alternatives to the nuclear family—social forms that replace or overshadow the nuclear family by assuming functions that would devolve on it in other societies—have been discussed.

In this chapter it has been argued that the nuclear family is best viewed not as a cultural universal but as a variable form of social organization important in foraging and industrial societies. Among nonindustrial cultivators and pastoralists, on the other hand, there exist more definite kinship-based ties with the land, and other kinds of social groupings based on kinship and descent may overshadow the nuclear family in importance. In many contemporary nations, including the United States, the nuclear family is the characteristic kinship group for members of the middle class, while other kinship groups assume greater importance in different strata. Expanded family households and sharing with nonnuclear family kin, for example, are more typically encountered among disadvantaged minorities in contemporary America. The greater significance of kinship in the lower class can be interpreted as an adaptation to poverty that involves pooling of strategic resources by people whose access to such resources is limited.

The descent group appears as the most important kinship group in many tribal societies, chiefdoms, and nonindustrial states. In contrast to nuclear families, descent groups are perpetual units; they endure over several generations. Often, members of the same descent group share access to and manage a common estate. Because of this, anthropologists compare descent groups to modern industrial corporations and call them corporate descent groups. Ethnographic studies have revealed several types of descent groups. Anthropologists distinguish between lineages and clans, the former based on demonstrated descent, the latter on stipulated descent. Different varieties of descent rules also exist: unilineal and ambilineal. Unilineal (patrilineal and matrilineal) descent is often associated with unilocal (respectively, virilocal and uxorilocal) postmarital residence rules.

Like other aspects of culture and social organization, descent rules may be seen as helping people adapt to their environments. Descent rules usually do not rigidly govern the lives of people in a society; rather, their observance often reflects considerable flexibility. The amount of flexibility, the extent of departure from the rules, and the variable functions of descent and descent groups can often be attributed to ecological differences associated with specific environments.

To study kinship calculation, we must distinguish between biological kin types and kinship terminology in a given society. Kinship terminologies, as distinct from biological kinship designations, represent native taxonomies, cultural ways of dividing up the world based on perceived characteristics. Although kinship terminologies belong to specific cultures, comparative research has demonstrated that different cultures always employ one of a limited number of classification systems. Anthropologists' interest in kinship classification reflects the importance of kinship-related institutions in societies that they have traditionally studied. Furthermore, comparativists have discovered general relationships between kinship terminology and other aspects of social organization. To a certain extent, we may predict kinship terminology from knowledge of other aspects of culture and social organization.

We have examined four basic classification systems, each widely distributed throughout the world, that categorize kin types on the parental generation. Lineal terminology, associated with importance of the nuclear family, is the characteristic kinship terminology of many foraging and industrial populations. Bifurcate merging kinship terminology, perhaps the most common, is found among populations with unilocal rules of postmarital residence and unilineal descent groups. Generational terminology is associated with ambilineal descent-group organization and ambilocal postmarital residence, while bifurcate collateral kinship terminology, a system concentrated in the Near East and northern Africa, may also be associated with ambilineal descent.

A limited set of kinship classification systems also exists for relatives on ego's own generation. Eskimo terminology, employed by contemporary Americans, makes a distinction between lineal and collateral relatives. Iroquois terminology is characteristically associated with bifurcate merging on the parental generation. Hawaiian terminology is normally associated with generational terminology on the parental generation. Descriptive kinship terms are often associated with bifurcate collateral.

Anthropologists have demonstrated that kinship terminology usually changes more slowly than other aspects of social organization, such as inheritance patterns, patterns of postmarital residence, and descent-group organization. Thus there is often an incomplete correlation between kinship terms and social structure and between the classification principles that operate for different generations. The study of kinship terminology reveals differences and similarities in the social categories deemed important in human populations, suggesting research problems and increasing knowledge about such variations.

SOURCES AND SUGGESTED READINGS

ASCHENBRENNER, J.
1975   *Lifelines: Black Families in Chicago.* New York: Holt, Rinehart & Winston. Competent ethnographic account, focuses on kinship relations and individual autobiographies.

BAAL, J. VAN
1966   *Dema: Description and Analysis of Marind-anim Culture (South New Guinea).* The Hague: M. Nijhoff. Field study of homosexual tribes in New Guinea.

BOHANNAN, P., AND MIDDLETON, J., EDS.
1968a   *Kinship and Social Organization.* Garden City, N.Y.: Natural History Press. Classic articles on kinship and kinship terminology.

1968b   *Marriage, Family and Residence.* Garden City, N.Y.: Natural History Press. Articles on marriage and postmarital residence rules in several cultural settings.

BUCHLER, I. R., AND SELBY, H. A.
1968   *Kinship and Social Organization: An Introduction to Theory and Method.* New York: Macmillan. Introduction to comparative social organization; several chapters on interpretations of kinship classification systems.

CLARKE, E.
1957   *My Mother Who Fathered Me.* London: George Allen and Unwin. More personal than the average account of matrifocal family organization.

COHEN, Y. A.
1969   Schools and Civilizational States. In *The Social Sciences and the Comparative Study of Educational Systems,* ed. J. Fischer. Scranton, Pa.: International Textbooks. Anthropology's relevance for education.

DAVENPORT, W.
1959   Nonunilineal Descent and Descent Groups. *American Anthropologist* 61: 557–572. Suggests similarities and differences between unilineal and ambilineal descent groups.

EVANS-PRITCHARD, E. E.
1940   *The Nuer: A Description of the Modes of Livelihood and Political Institutions of a Nilotic People.* Oxford: Clarendon Press. Classic study of social structure (including lineage organization) and environment of a Nilotic population.

FORTES, M.
1953   The Structure of Unilineal Descent Groups. *American Anthropologist* 55: 17–41. Classic synthesizing article on corporate attributes of certain kinds of descent groups.

FRIED, M. H.
1957   The Classification of Corporate Unilineal Descent Groups. *Journal of the Royal Anthropological Institute* 87: 1–29. Comparative analysis of descent-group organization in several societies approximating different general evolutionary types.

GOUGH, K.
1959   The Nayars and the Definition of Marriage. *Journal of the Royal Anthropological Institute* 89: 23–24. Unusual marriage customs among the matrilineal Nayars of India. Definition of marriage

offered that, author argues, includes the Nayar and all other known societies.

GRABURN, N., ED.
1971   *Readings in Kinship and Social Structure.* New York: Harper & Row. Several important articles on kinship terminology.

HART, C. W. M., AND PILLING, A. R.
1960   *The Tiwi of North Australia.* New York: Holt, Rinehart & Winston. Case study of unusual population of polygynous and gerontocratic foragers.

JORGENSEN, J. G., ED.
1972   *Reservation Indian Society Today: Studies of Economics, Politics, Kinship and Households.* Berkeley: University of California Press. Anthology with articles on the expanded household as an adaptation to poverty among contemporary inhabitants of reservations in North America.

KEESING, R. M.
1975   *Kinship and Social Structure.* New York: Holt, Rinehart & Winston. Brief, but comprehensive, introduction to comparative kinship.

KELLY, R. C.
1977   *Etoro Social Structure: A Study in Structural Contradiction.* Ann Arbor: University of Michigan Press. Kinship, ideology, and sexual expression in a small New Guinea group.

KOTTAK, C. P.
1971a   Cultural Adaptation, Kinship and Descent in Madagascar. *Southwestern Journal of Anthropology* 27: 129-147. Relates variations in kinship calculation and descent-group organization to population pressure on strategic resources and other ecological variables.

1971b   Social Groups and Kinship Calculation among the Southern Betsileo. *American Anthropologist* 73: 178–193. Variations in descent-group organization and kinship calculation according to socioeconomic stratum within an agricultural society of highland Madagascar.

KROEBER, A.
1909   Classificatory Systems of Relationship. *Journal of the Royal Anthropological Institute* 39: 77–84. Classic analysis of kinship terminologies. Article provided inspiration for the componential analysis approach (see Chapter 18) to kinship terminology.

LEACH, E. R.
1955   Polyandry, Inheritance and the Definition of Marriage. *Man* 55: 182–186. Polyandry in South Asia; argues against the cultural universality of marriage.

LOWIE, R. H.
1948   *Social Organization.* New York: Rinehart. Useful attempt to update his 1920 book; good introduction to kinship terminology included.

1961   (orig. 1920). *Primitive Society.* New York: Harper & Brothers. Classic that examines use of kinship terms and offers a classification of kinship terminologies.

MURDOCK, G. P.
1949   *Social Structure.* New York: Macmillan. Influential statistical examination of kinship, marriage, and descent; includes Murdock's well-known typology of systems of classification of kin on ego's own generation.

1957   World Ethnographic Sample. *American Anthropologist* 59: 664–687. Data on social organizational variables, including kinship terminology, for 565 cultures.

RADCLIFFE-BROWN, A. R.
1950   Introduction to *African Systems of Kinship and Marriage,* ed. A. R. Radcliffe-Brown and D. Forde, pp. 1–85. London: Oxford University Press. Excellent introduction to kinship and classification systems.

1965   (orig. 1952). *Structure and Function in Primitive Society.* New York: Free Press. Includes essay on the study of kinship systems.

ROSENBERG, G. S., AND ANSPRACH, D. F.
1973   *Working Class Kinship.* Lexington, Mass.: D. C. Heath. Study of kinship among working class Philadelphians.

ROYAL ANTHROPOLOGICAL INSTITUTE.
1951   *Notes and Queries on Anthropology.* 6th ed. London: Routledge and Kegan Paul. For years ethnographers have carried this manual into the field; includes a comprehensive list of questions about matters of interest to social anthropologists.

SAHLINS, M. D.
1965   On the Ideology and Composition of Descent Groups. *Man* 65: 104-107. Some similarities and differences between ambilineal and unilineal descent groups.

1968   *Tribesmen.* Englewood Cliffs, N.J.: Prentice-Hall. Kinship, descent, and marriage in tribal societies.

SCHNEIDER, D. M.
 1968   *American Kinship: A Cultural Account.* Englewood Cliffs, N.J.: Prentice-Hall. Impressionistic but often insightful account of American kinship as a cultural system.

SCHUSKY, E. L.
 1965   *Manual for Kinship Analysis.* New York: Holt, Rinehart & Winston. Good elementary introduction to systems of kinship terminology.

SERVICE, E. R.
 1971a   *Cultural Evolutionism: Theory in Practice.* New York: Holt, Rinehart & Winston. Collection of essays; see especially "Kinship Terminology and Evolution" for an innovative approach to kinship terminology in general evolutionary perspective.

 1971b   *Primitive Social Organization: An Evolutionary Perspective.* 2nd ed. New York: Random House. Includes theoretical discussion, from general evolutionary point of view, of kinship terms in bands, tribes, and chiefdoms.

SKINNER, E. P.
 1964   The Effect of Co-residence of Sisters' Sons on African Corporate Patrilineal Descent Groups. *Cahiers d'Etudes Africaines* 16: 467-478. Widespread ambilineal elements in many supposedly patrilineal descent systems in Africa.

STACK, C. B.
 1975   *All Our Kin: Strategies for Survival in a Black Community.* New York: Harper & Row. Well-done ethnographic study of fluidity in household and residence patterns and the importance of nonnuclear family kin in an urban ghetto.

WHITE, L. A.
 1939   A Problem in Kinship Terminology. *American Anthropologist* 41: 566-573. Association of Crow and matrilineal descent; Omaha and patrilineal descent.

 1959   *The Evolution of Culture.* New York: McGraw-Hill. Kinship terminologies in general evolutionary perspective.

Marriage as Alliance

6

In previous chapters it has been suggested that in stateless societies a person's social world consists of two main social categories—friends and strangers, who are potential or actual enemies. Marriage is one of the principal social institutions that converts strangers into friends, that creates and maintains alliances. The incest taboo forces people to be exogamous, to seek their mates outside their own social groups. Exogamy has adaptive value. A child has peaceful relations with the social groups and relatives of both parents, and of different grandparents. Exogamy links individuals to a wider network of people who will nurture, assist, and protect them in times of need.

THE TABOO AGAINST INCEST

Incest involves having sexual relations with, or marrying, a close relative. In all societies there are taboos against it. However, although the incest taboo is a cultural universal, specific cultures define it differently. As an illustration, consider some implications of the distinction between two kinds of first cousins, cross cousins and parallel cousins. Children of siblings of the same sex are *parallel cousins*. Children of siblings of the opposite sex are *cross cousins*. Thus your mother's sister's children are your parallel cousins—the children of two sisters. Your father's brother's children are also your parallel cousins—the children of two brothers. Your father's sister's children are your cross cousins—the children of two siblings of the opposite sex. For the same reason, your mother's brother's children are also your cross cousins (see Figure 6.1).

The American kinship term *cousin* does not distinguish between cross and parallel cousins, but in many cultures, especially those in which there are

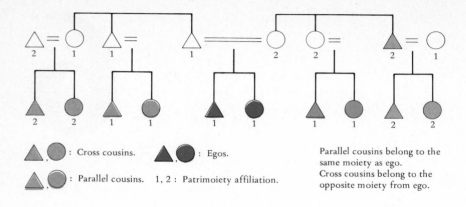

: Cross cousins.   : Egos.

: Parallel cousins.   1, 2 : Patrimoiety affiliation.

Parallel cousins belong to the same moiety as ego.
Cross cousins belong to the opposite moiety from ego.

FIGURE 6.1 Parallel and cross cousins and patrilineal moiety organization.

unilineal descent groups, this distinction is essential. A community in which there are only two descent groups has what is known as *moiety* organization—from the French *moitié*, meaning half—because the society is divided by descent rules, and everyone is a member of either one half or the other. Some societies have patrilineal, others matrilineal, moieties. Figure 6.1 depicts a society with patrilineal moieties. In Figure 6.2, representing another society, the moieties are matrilineal. Notice that in both patrilineal and matrilineal societies, all cross cousins are members of the opposite moiety and all parallel cousins are members of the individual's own moiety. In a patrilineal system, all individuals take their descent-group affiliation from their father. In the matrilineal society, all people take their mother's descent-group affiliation. You can see from these diagrams that your (ego's) mother's sister's children (MZC) and your father's brother's children (FBC), that is, all your parallel cousins, belong

to your group, while your father's sister's children (FZC) and your mother's brother's children (MBC) belong to the other moiety. In such societies, people consider their parallel cousins to be like siblings, and they cannot have sexual intercourse with, or marry, them. Parallel cousins thus lie within the incest taboo of these societies. In fact, people in such societies normally use Iroquois kinship terminology; they call their male and female parallel cousins by the same kinship terms that they use for their own brothers and sisters—indicating the closeness of the relationship. Although this is completely foreign to the American kinship system, parallel cousins are, after all, members of the same generation and the same descent group as ego's own siblings. Like siblings, they are considered too closely related to marry. Thus they are classified with brothers and sisters.

In such societies, cross cousins are members of the opposite group and not relatives. In fact, in many societies, people are expected to marry either their actual cross cousin or someone from the same social category as their cross cousin. In the case of moiety

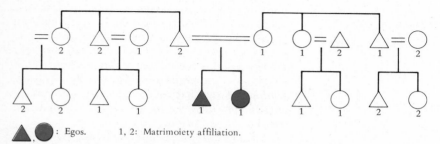

: Egos.   1, 2: Matrimoiety affiliation.

Parallel cousins belong to the same moiety as ego.
Cross cousins belong to the opposite moiety from ego.

FIGURE 6.2 Matrilineal moiety organization.

organization, spouses must belong to different moieties. Among the Yanomamo of Venezuela and Brazil (see Chagnon, 1968, 1974, 1977), men anticipate the fact that they may one day marry their female cross cousins by calling them "wife" and their male cross cousins "brother-in-law." From early childhood, women, too, call their male cross cousins "husband" and their female cross cousins "sister-in-law." For the Yanomamo, as for many other societies with unilineal descent groups, sex with cross cousins is considered perfectly proper, but with parallel cousins it is deemed incestuous.

A rarer phenomenon will further illustrate that people treat their biological kin types differently in different societies. In societies where the principle of unilineal descent is very strongly developed, people do not regard the parent who does not belong to their own descent group as a relative. In a strictly patrilineal society, ego's mother is not a relative but a kind of in-law who has married a member of ego's group, that is, ego's father. And in a strictly matrilineal society, ego's father may not be considered a relative, since he is a member of a different matrilineal descent group.

The social organization of the Lakher of Southeast Asia is strictly patrilineal (Leach, 1961). Using the male ego in Figure 6.3, let us suppose that ego's father and mother have been divorced. Each has remarried and had a daughter by this second marriage. A Lakher always belongs to the father's group, and all members of this group are considered to be relatives. The Lakher consider agnates to be

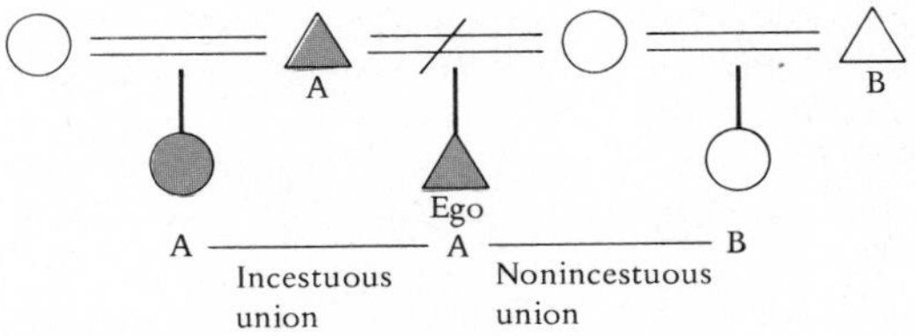

⧺ : Separation or divorce.
FD by second marriage is a comember of
   ego's descent group and is included
   within the incest taboo.
MD by second marriage is not a comember
   of ego's descent group and is
   not tabooed.
A,B: Descent-group affiliation.

FIGURE 6.3 Patrilineal descent-group identity and incest among the Lakher.

too close to marry. Therefore, ego cannot marry his father's daughter by his second marriage. On the other hand, ego's mother's daughter by her second marriage is fair game for him, since she is a member of her own father's descent group and not ego's. The Lakher illustrate particularly well that definitions of relatives differ from culture to culture. In the United States both half-sisters would be too close for mating and marriage. Among the Lakher, only one is considered a close relative and included within the Lakher version of the incest taboo.

We may extend the observations based on the Lakher to strict matrilineal societies. If a man's parents divorce and his father remarries, ego may marry his paternal half-sister. On the other hand, if his mother remarries and has a daughter, she is ego's close relative and sexual relations are taboo. People therefore regard relationships that are equivalent in a biological and genetic sense differently, according to the structure of their social organization and their culturally defined rules.

EXPLANATIONS OF THE INCEST TABOO

Instinctive Revulsion

There is no simple explanation for the fact that all cultures prohibit incest. Recent research on nonhuman primates demonstrates that male, and sometimes female, dispersal at or prior to adolescence is common. In Chapter 2 you saw how this reduced the potentiality and frequency of incestuous unions. Its cultural elaborations aside, human avoidance of mating with close relatives may express a generalized theme of primate—and indeed animal—behavior. Anthropologists Edward Westermarck (1894), L. T. Hobhouse (1915), and Robert Lowie (1961) argued that since the incest taboo is found in all human societies, and since it is concerned with a biological act, sexual intercourse, it is a codification of instinctive revulsion. According to this reasoning, people everywhere have an instinctive aversion to mating with close relatives. Thus, in all human societies, incest is intrinsically repulsive and is considered a crime.

There are several grounds on which to reject this explanation, as Lowie himself did later. First, the mere fact that an institution is culturally universal does not mean that it is instinctually based. Fire making, for example, is also a cultural universal, and it is certainly not an ability transmitted by the genes. Furthermore, if there were indeed an instinctive horror of mating with close relatives, a formal taboo against incest would be unnecessary. No one would ever do it. Social workers, judges, psychiatrists, and psychologists in our own society, however, know that cases of incest are by no means rare. Often they are hushed up; sometimes, they are brought to the attention of the courts and punished.

The final objection to the instinctive revulsion theory is that it cannot explain why in some societies people can marry their cross cousins but not their parallel cousins, or why the Lakher can marry their maternal, but not their paternal, half-siblings. There is no known instinct capable of distinguishing between parallel and cross cousins. The specific kin types included within the incest taboo as well as the taboo itself have a cultural rather than a biological basis. Even among nonhuman primates there is no evidence for an instinct against incest, and adolescent dispersal does not prevent — but merely limits — the frequency of incestuous unions. In human societies, not only do cultural traditions define the specific relatives with whom sex is incestuous, they also punish individuals who violate these prohibited relationships in various ways. Banishment, imprisonment, death, and the threat of supernatural retaliation are some of the punishments imposed.

Biological Degeneration

Nineteenth-century anthropologist Lewis Henry Morgan (1963; orig. 1877) argued that the incest taboo originated because people came to recognize that biological deterioration — the appearance of abnormal or otherwise undesirable offspring — resulted from incestuous unions. To discourage such unions, early humans banned incest. So successful was the stock produced by human populations once the taboo came into existence that the ban spread everywhere. It is this argument against incest that most contemporary Americans accept.

Laboratory experiments with fruit flies, mice, and other animals that reproduce faster than humans confirm that consistent inbreeding, for instance, brother-sister mating across several generations, is accompanied by a decline in the viability and fertility of offspring. Limiting potential incest is evolutionarily

older than Morgan believed. Adolescent dispersal among nonhuman primates and other animals ensures genetic mixture, thus discouraging inbreeding and these potential results. However, despite the possibly harmful biological effects of systematic inbreeding, the universal human taboo against incest is certainly more than simply cultural buttressing of a biologically adaptive and generalized primate pattern. Marriage patterns in various human societies reflect specific cultural rules rather than concerns about biological degeneration several generations in the future. Certainly, neither instinctive revulsion nor fear of biological degeneration can account for the widespread custom of marrying a cross cousin. Nor can fears of biological deterioration explain why breeding with parallel, but not cross, cousins is so often tabooed.

Marry Out or Die Out

Among anthropologists, perhaps the most widely accepted explanation for the incest taboo is that it forces people to marry outside their immediate kinship group. The incest taboo is an adaptive means selected early in the evolution of *Homo*. Since to marry a member of a group with whom one is already on peaceful terms would be, in a sense, counterproductive, for an alliance already exists, there is more profit in extending peaceful relations to a wider group. As indicated previously, exogamy also ensures flow of genetic material among human populations and guarantees a single human species.

The first anthropologist to relate the universality of the incest taboo, and its expression in exogamy, to its role in creating alliances was Sir Edward Burnett Tylor, foremost British anthropologist of the late nineteenth century. More recently, the American ethnologist Leslie White and the French social anthropologist Claude Lévi-Strauss have also emphasized the role of marriage in forming and maintaining alliances among social groups. White (1949, 1959) stated the matter very simply: a group faces the choice of marrying out or of dying out. By forcing its members to marry out, a group increases its allies. Marriage within the group, on the other hand, would isolate that group and ultimately lead to extinction. Exogamy and the concomitant taboo against incest are among the best explanations for the adaptive success of the genus *Homo*.

Familiarity Breeds Attempt

Anthropologist Bronislaw Malinowski (1927), whose numerous books and articles based on his extended field work among the Trobriand Islanders were published in the 1920s and 1930s, explained the universality of the incest taboo in terms of its relationship to enculturation and the family. Malinowski believed that the nuclear family was a cultural universal. Although he recognized that larger kinship groups existed and were important in several societies (including the Trobrianders), he stressed his belief that their functions were secondary. He emphasized instead the primacy of nuclear family relationships. Accordingly, Malinowski argued not only that the nuclear family was universal, but also that it was the essential agency through which the knowledge and sentiments upon which culture was based were transmitted across the generations. Smooth transmission of knowledge and values—that is, enculturation—required family emotions of reverence, dependence, and respect; strong affective bonds to the mother; and submission to the leadership of the father. The formation of the family of procreation accommodated what Malinowski believed to be instinctive parental feelings of both the mother and the father.

Malinowski's view of the family as a complex of emotions, sentiments, and individual attachments reflects his interest in psychology, and particularly his reading of Freud and other early–twentieth-century psychologists. He rejected what Freud had regarded as universal attributes of the human mind, arguing instead that parent-child attitudes varied with different cultural traditions. Malinowski also rejected the significance of sexual emotions prior to puberty. Instead, he stressed that sentiments like reverence, respect, and nonsexual affection were important within the family context. It was only at puberty, according to Malinowski, that sexual urges developed. Believing as he did in the closeness of family bonds, Malinowski argued that it would be natural for children to seek to gratify their emerging sexual urges with people who were already emotionally close to them. In other words, they would naturally seek out members of their nuclear family as sexual partners. To phrase it with a bad pun, familiarity breeds attempt. Malinowski argued that the incest taboo arose to repress and direct outward what he regarded as a universally encountered temptation toward incestuous unions. Were sexual urges of pubescent and postpubescent individuals to be satisfied within the family of orientation, conflict would be engendered that would halt its normal functioning. As Malinowski asserted, the fundamental pattern of all social bonds—the normal relationship of child to mother and father—would be destroyed, and it would be impossible for cultural transmission to continue.

There is much that seems reasonable in Malinowski's argument. As a child grows up, he or she learns that the roles of father, mother, brother, and sister within the family are different. A boy's attempt to emulate his father by having sexual relations with his mother would, in fact, destroy the role structure and the cohesion on which the family is based. You will note, however, that Malinowski's interpretation is not so satisfactory when it comes to the taboo against sexual intercourse between siblings. A more complete and satisfactory explanation of the incest taboo must combine elements of several scholarly contributions. Exogamy and the alliances it engenders and maintains do have adaptive value and biological results. Close relatives do provide enculturative models for role differentiation on the basis of age and sex. Incestuous gratification of sexual urges *would* threaten relationships among close relatives and would lead to conflict. Exogamy establishes alliances, extends peaceful relations beyond the group, promotes genetic mixture, and guards against conflict.

ENDOGAMY

The function of the incest taboo and of rules of exogamy in creating and maintaining alliances among groups has been stressed. Exogamic rules push social organization outward, establishing and preserving bonds among groups. Endogamic rules force people to choose mates from their own social groups. Such rules are less frequently encountered, but are still familiar to anthropologists. Most human societies are, in fact, endogamous units, although there may be no formal cultural rule that individuals should choose as a mate someone from their own society. Note here the distinction between these cultural rules and the actual occurrence of exogamic and endogamic marriages in society.

It is perhaps obvious that in populations whose cultures include both exogamic and endogamic rules, these rules cannot apply to the same social unit. In stratified societies many people are to some degree enjoined to marry members of their own stratum.

Yet each stratum may be divided into several descent groups or other social subdivisions, and each of these may be an exogamous unit. Exogamy links groups together; endogamy isolates groups and maintains them as distinct and exclusive units. Rules of endogamy are often found in stratified societies. Along with other devices, they act to maintain social, economic, and political distinctions, to preserve differential access to strategic and other culturally valued resources.

Caste

An extreme case of endogamic prescriptions is India's traditional caste system, which is undergoing considerable change today. Castes are stratified groups in which membership is ascribed and lifelong. Castes are usually endogamous groups. However, endogamy is not the critical feature in the definition of caste. More significant is the fact that a caste system has rules that automatically and unambiguously classify a person at birth. People have no choice about their caste affiliation. The major difference between castes and unilineal descent groups, which also automatically and unambiguously recruit members at birth, is that castes are stratified.

Indian castes are grouped into five major categories (*varna*), each of which is ranked relative to the other four. These categories are found throughout India and are not confined to certain regions. Each *varna* is composed of a large number of castes (*jati*), each of which is made up of people within a given region or area who may actually intermarry or who have the potential to do so. All the castes within a single *varna* in a region are ranked with respect to one another, just as the *varna* themselves are ranked.

Occupational specialization often serves to demarcate one caste from another. A community may include castes of agricultural workers, merchants, artisans, priests, sweepers, and others. The untouchable *varna*, which is found throughout India, includes castes whose ancestry, ritual status, and occupations are considered so impure that members of higher castes consider even casual contact between themselves and untouchables to be defiling.

Important in maintaining caste endogamy is the ideology that intercaste sexual unions result in a state of ritual impurity for the higher-caste partner. A man who has sexual relations with a lower-caste woman may restore his ritual purity with a bath and

This woman is a member of India's "untouchable" caste. She holds a broom used for cleaning toilets. Occupational specialization has been an aspect of the caste system. (Marilyn Silverstone/Magnum Photos)

perhaps a prayer. However, a woman who has intercourse with a man of lower caste has no such recourse. Her defilement cannot be undone. Note that, since the women have the babies, these differences protect the purity of the caste line, ensuring the pure ancestry of the child. Note also that although Indian castes are endogamous groups, many of them are internally subdivided into exogamous groups. Indians are expected to select as their mate a member of another descent group within their own caste.

A long history, an elaborate ideology that includes notions of ritual purity and contamination, and intricate occupational and economic distinctions buttress the Indian caste system. Yet the principle of caste, with these cultural and historical embellishments absent, is widely encountered in stratified societies. Two ethnic groups, black and white, that are known as "races" in the folk taxonomy of contemporary American culture, for example, have been castelike groups. A dual hierarchy has existed in the United States. The American class structure consists of the lower, middle, and upper classes and their subdivisions. To a certain extent, class status in the United States is achieved. The American ideal of the self-made rugged individualist, the rags-to-riches stories we have all heard, stress and value individual achievement as a means of moving up in the class structure. Yet there has been a second dimension of the American stratification system—the black-white dimension—in which membership has been ascribed rather than achieved. Many American states once prohibited marriages between blacks and whites. However, the really critical cultural and legal rule that created and perpetuated the American system of "race" relations is the rule of hypodescent. Disregarding both the actual physical appearance of the children of black-white unions and the fact that equal shares of their DNA come from each parent, this arbitrary rule automatically assigns them to the socioeconomically disadvantaged group —to the black ethnic group.

Royal Incest

Similar to caste system endogamy in traditional India is privileged royal incest. Well-known examples are provided by the Incas of Peru, the ancient Egyptians, and the royalty of traditional Hawaii. In these states, royal brother-sister marriages were allowed. Privileged endogamy, a violation of the incest taboo that applied to the commoners in these societies as elsewhere, was a means of differentiating between rulers and subjects.

MANIFEST AND LATENT FUNCTIONS   To understand why rulers and their near relatives did not observe the same prohibitions as others against marrying their close relatives, it is necessary to distinguish between manifest functions of behavior patterns and latent functions. The *manifest function* of an institution or custom refers to the reasons that people in the society give for that behavior. The *latent function* refers to an effect that that behavior has for the society, which people do not mention or may not recognize. Anthropologists may discover the manifest and latent functions of customs in the culture they study through, respectively, the emic and the etic research strategies discussed in Chapter 1.

The institution of privileged royal incest illustrates the distinction between manifest and latent functions. Aboriginal Polynesians believed in an imper-

sonal force or substance distributed throughout the world, which they called *mana*. Mana could reside in things or people, in the latter case marking them off from other people and making them divine. In ancient Hawaiian ideology, no other human concentrated as much mana in his or her person as the ruler. The amount of mana depended on closeness of genealogical connections. The individual whose concentrated mana was surpassed only by the king's was his sibling. Thus the most appropriate spouse for a king was his own full sister. Note that brother-sister marriage also meant that the children born of the marriage were as mana-ful, or divine, as it was possible to be. The manifest function of royal incest in ancient Hawaii was related to notions of mana and divinity.

It is also possible to point out certain latent functions of royal incest. Royal sibling marriages had repercussions in the political domains of these ancient states. The ruler and his spouse had the same parents. Since mana was transmitted from parents to child, they were almost equally divine. When the king and his sister married, their children were indisputably divinest in the land. No one could contest their right to rule the kingdom. If, on the other hand, the king had taken a wife who was not his sister, and the sister a husband who was not the king, the children of the two couples would present problems. Both sets of children could argue that they were equally divine and that they had equally valid claims to rule. Royal sibling marriage thus served to limit conflicts over succession by restricting the number of people with valid claims to rule. This political function has, of course, been accomplished differently in other states. It is possible, for example, to specify that only the eldest son of the reigning monarch will succeed. Commonly, too, rulers can kill or banish claimants to succession who rival their favorite heirs.

Royal incest also has a latent function in economic spheres. If both ruler and his sibling had equal rights to the ancestral estate, their marriage to each other, again by limiting the number of heirs, tended to keep it intact. Power often rests on wealth, and royal incest tended to ensure that royal wealth remained concentrated in the same line.

Brazilian Plantation Society

Cases of royal incest are extreme examples of the functions of endogamy as a means of limiting and preserving access to wealth and power. Cases of marriages between close relatives, although not as a rule sister and brother, mother and son, or daughter and father, are not infrequent. In Brazilian plantation society as recently as the nineteenth century, it was common for first cousins to marry. In fact, among families owning sugar and coffee plantations, cousin marriages were often considered ideal unions. Plantation society was composed of ambilineal descent groups centered around estates consisting of land, slaves, equipment, and other resources. Brazilian inheritance law granted estate rights both to sons and daughters and to their descendants. Marriages of heirs to the same estate, including cousins and, on occasion, uncles and nieces, represented conscious attempts to keep estates intact. In the case of Brazilian society, the function of endogamous unions in limiting access to wealth was therefore manifest. Note, however, that it was only partially successful. Endogamous unions only slowed down, they did not stop, the breakup of estates. With laws granting equal inheritance rights to all descendants of large plantation families, severe fragmentation has taken place.

Patrilateral Parallel Cousin Marriage

Functionally similar to marriage of close relatives in Brazilian society is parallel cousin marriage among Islamic, or Moslem, populations of the Near East and North Africa, particularly the Arabs. Arabic society is structured by patrilineal descent. All Arabs ultimately trace their descent patrilineally from Abraham in the Bible. This common genealogy provides a basis for the Arabs' distinctive ethnic identity in the form of a huge patrilineage. Although the origin of their cultural preference for marriage between patrilateral parallel cousins—the children of two brothers—has not been explained, Arabs say that men marry their father's brother's daughter in order to keep property in the family. Such a manifest function follows from the imposition of Islamic inheritance laws on a social organization in which inheritance was formerly patrilineal. Islam stipulates that daughters and sons must share in their parents' estates. However, daughters' shares are only half those of sons. In some Islamic areas, patrilateral parallel cousin marriage does function to prevent fragmentation of estates.

As Fredrik Barth (1954) has pointed out, patrilateral parallel cousin marriage may also serve a politi-

cal function, cementing solidarity among brothers in factional disputes. Furthermore, anthropologists Robert Murphy and Leonard Kasdan (1959) have suggested still another function for such a marriage preference. They argue that because it closes small social groups—brothers and their children—in on themselves, it functions to maintain political factionalism and disunity among the Arabs. Endogamy isolates social groups and contributes to an atmosphere of factionalism. On the other hand, the function of exogamy, which has been repeatedly stressed in this book, is to extend social ties outward, to establish and maintain peaceful intergroup relations.

EXOGAMY

Here we leave the discussion of endogamy, which isolates social groups, and return to exogamy, which incorporates them into larger networks. Among many populations, rules of exogamy are flexible, but in tribal populations, the rules regulating exogamy are often rigid and specific. For example, certain populations with strongly developed unilineal descent organization not only strictly prohibit descent-group endogamy, but also dictate exactly where people are to seek their spouses.

Generalized Exchange

French anthropologist Claude Lévi-Strauss (1969) has been most instrumental in directing anthropological attention toward such societies. He has described and analyzed exogamic rules that give rise to what he calls *generalized exchange* systems. Among populations who practice generalized exchange, there is a set marital relationship among exogamous descent groups. For any descent group B, there is a group C of wife receivers and a group A of wife givers. A, B, and C are each different descent groups. The men of B always take as their wives women of group A, and women of group B always marry men of group C. Note, too, that generalized exchange is associated with patrilineal descent organization and virilocal postmarital residence. The assumption is that the men stay put and the women marry out. A system of generalized exchange may arrange several descent groups in a closed circle, so that women of A always marry men of B, women of B always marry men of C, women of C always marry men of D, and so on through n, the number of descent groups in the circle. The women

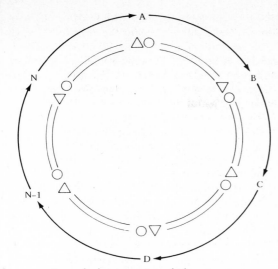

Arrows lead to groups into which women marry.

FIGURE 6.4 Circulating connubium.

of n − 1 will marry the men of n, and the women of n, the men of A; and so the circle continues. This variety of generalized exchange system is often called *circulating connubium* (see Figure 6.4).

Note that if men of B always marry women of A and if descent is patrilineal, a man, who shares his father's descent-group affiliation B, will also take his wife from group A. This is, in fact, his mother's descent group. Aside from his mother, another female member of his mother's descent group is his MBD (mother's brother's daughter). In some societies with generalized exchange systems, cultural preferences actually favor a man's marriage to his own

FIGURE 6.5 Generalized exchange system (male marries his MBD and female her FZS).

MBD. Far more commonly, however, a man is expected to marry either his true MBD or any other female of his mother's group who is of appropriate age. A hypothetical generalized exchange system involving marriage of men to their MBD is shown in Figure 6.5. Note that from a woman's point of view, she is marrying her FZS (father's sister's son). Recall from Chapter 5 that virilocal postmarital residence keeps men who belong to the same localized patrilineage together, as uxorilocal residence does for women in a matrilineal society. Note that generalized exchange, in combination with patrilineal descent, may simultaneously accomplish both of these advantages. Male agnates remain at home after marriage, but, if generalized exchange works in practice as in theory, their wives will all come from a single descent group, and therefore also will be related to one another patrilineally. Some anthropologists use the term *matrilateral cross cousin marriage* to describe such systems. The use of the term "generalized exchange" is preferable, since it avoids viewing marriage from only the man's point of view and implying that actual first cousins are supposed to marry.

MARRIAGE IN NONINDUSTRIAL FOOD-PRODUCING SOCIETIES

Among people who do not live in industrial societies, marriage is often more of a relationship between groups than individuals. In American society, marriage is an individual matter. Certainly, the bride and groom often look to their parents for approval, but the final choice is with the marrying pair. It is they, after all, who plan to spend their lives together. The concept of love in industrial societies symbolizes this relationship between an individual female and an individual male.

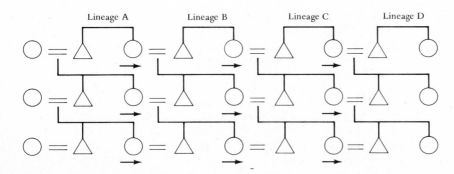

Lineage A   Lineage B   Lineage C   Lineage D

In nonindustrial societies, marriage is a group concern. People do not simply take a spouse; they assume important obligations to a whole group of in-laws. In a society where typical postmarital residence is virilocal, for example, a woman must leave the community where she was born; she must leave her relatives and members of her own descent group. She faces the prospect of living the rest of her life in her husband's village, with her husband's relatives. She may even transfer her major allegiance from her own group to her husband's. Thus, if there are disputes between her group and her husband's, she may side with him.

Bridewealth

Typically in societies with descent groups, people cannot enter marriage alone. They call on other members of their descent group for help. In many societies there is an institution known as bride price, or *bridewealth*. Wealth of some sort is passed from the husband's group to the wife's. The term "bride price" is unfortunate, since it suggests that the wife is

being sold. In most societies with bridewealth institutions, people do not regard the transfer of such wealth as a sale. Certainly, they do not think of marriage as a relationship between a man and an object that can be bought and sold. Alternatively, several explanations are offered for the custom. Sometimes it is said that payment compensates the bride's group for the loss of her companionship and economic labor. Far more often, however, people point to the role of bridewealth in making children born to the woman full members of her husband's group. It is for this reason that some anthropologists prefer to call the institution *progeny price*. It is the children whom the woman will bear, rather than the woman herself, who are being permanently transferred to the husband's group.

Whatever we choose to call it, such an exchange of wealth on the occasion of marriage is common in tribal societies and in some chiefdoms and nonindustrial states. It tends to be found in societies with patrilineal descent. In matrilineal societies, where children are automatically members of the mother's group, there is no reason to pay a progeny price. Although the institution of bridewealth exists in many different parts of the world, there are differences in the nature and quantity of goods transferred at marriage. In many African societies, cattle are the major item in bridewealth payments. There are, however, variations from society to society in the number of cattle given. The following discussion should illustrate some reasons for bridewealth. As the value of bridewealth increases, marriages become more stable; bridewealth may be good insurance against divorce.

Imagine a patrilineal society, represented in Figure 6.6, in which a marriage normally involves the

FIGURE 6.6 Bridewealth. The majority of cattle entering group A from daughter Cynthia's marriage are initially collected by Cynthia's father, Mortimer, and subsequently used as the major part of Sam's bridewealth payment for Zelda. Other close agnates also contribute to Sam's bridewealth payment. The cattle pass to Zelda's group, B, where the majority are conserved by Zelda's father to be used as bridewealth when Desmond marries. The cattle then pass to group C, where Tricia's father (not shown) stores most of the herd until it is needed for bridewealth payment for the marriage of his own son or another of Tricia's close agnates. Ā = not A, descent group other than A; B̄ = not B, descent group other than B; ①= number of cattle received.

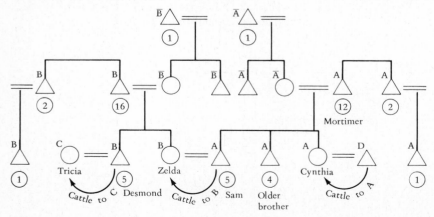

transfer of twenty-five cattle from the groom's group to the bride's group. Figure 6.6 demonstrates where the cattle come from and where they go to. Sam, a member of descent group A, and Zelda, a member of descent group B, are going to get married. Sam must seek the assistance of his relatives in assembling bridewealth. He expects help from his close agnates, that is, his older brother, his father, his father's brother, and his patrilineal parallel cousin. Representatives of Sam's mother's group, his mother's father or his mother's brother, may also contribute as a token of a continuing alliance established one generation earlier when Sam's father and mother got married. Sam's marriage is the con-cern of his entire corporate lineage, and especially of his father. His father or, if his father is dead, his older brother or his father's brother, may actually assemble the cattle. Some of the cattle have come from natural increase in the herds of Sam's descent group. Others have come in as bridewealth for female members of Sam's descent group, for example, Sam's sister Cynthia and other sisters and his father's sisters.

The distribution of the cattle once they have been turned over to Zelda's group mirrors the manner in which they were assembled. Zelda's father, or oldest brother if her father is dead, receives Zelda's bridewealth. Most of the cattle remain with him; he will use them as bridewealth to acquire wives for his sons and other close agnates. However, a share in Zelda's bridewealth also goes to those whom her father will expect to help him when one of his sons gets married.

When Zelda's brother Desmond gets married, therefore, many of the same cattle may pass to a third group, C, his wife's group. Similarly, they are trans-

Exchange of bridewealth (the items in the center). Bridewealth, or progeny price, establishes the legitimacy of marriage and the membership of children in their father's descent group in many patrilineal-virilocal societies, such as the one shown here. Note the larger number of men, members of husband's and wife's descent group, discussing the offering. (M. Glasse)

In industrial society, marriage becomes primarily a relationship between individuals rather than groups. Compare the small number of direct participants in this Jewish wedding in the contemporary United States with the two local descent groups in the bridewealth photo. (Ken Heyman)

mitted through the institution of bridewealth to still other groups, as men use bridewealth derived from their sisters' marriages to obtain wives of their own. In a decade, the cattle that Sam's group gave to Zelda's group may have been dispersed among so many different groups and over so large a territory that Sam's group may have lost track of their whereabouts.

With marriage, there is a covenant between two descent groups. Various cultural traditions define the roles of husband and wife differently. The marriage covenant is an understanding between the two groups that neither Zelda nor Sam will deviate too far from behavior expected of a married couple. The covenant also specifies what Zelda owes to Sam's group and what she can expect from Sam and his agnates. In populations whose members think of bridewealth principally as a device that entitles a woman's children to full membership in her husband's descent group, the woman's major obligation is to bear children, to ensure the continuity of her husband's group.

Several problems may threaten the fulfillment of the marriage covenant between the two groups. Zelda, for example, may find that Sam is not at all what she expected in a husband; she may not be able to get along with him or his agnates. She may consider leaving him and returning home. If she convinces her relatives that she has been treated badly, if the amount of bridewealth was small and is within their means, her relatives may return it. Thus a divorce takes place. However, marriages in such societies are not usually so soluble. It is common for a woman's relatives to try very hard to convince her to return to her husband. This is especially true if the amount of bridewealth was large and it has been distributed among a number of Zelda's agnates and other relatives, or if most of it has been used to obtain a wife for Zelda's brother or another close male agnate. In such a case, Zelda may try again to get along with her husband. To generalize, the more difficult it is to reassemble bridewealth, the more stable is marriage and the rarer divorce.

If Zelda and Sam try again and again to make their marriage a success but fail, both sets of agnates may conclude that the marriage cannot survive. In such circumstances it becomes especially obvious that marriage in bridewealth societies is a relationship between groups as well as individuals. If Zelda has a younger sister, or her brother a daughter, either is a member of Zelda's descent group. To avoid the return of the bridewealth, Zelda's and Sam's descent groups may agree that Zelda is to be replaced by one of these women. There is another possibility. When a woman divorces a man, he may claim her brother's wife. And why not? After all, the cattle that Sam gave to Zelda's father may have been used subsequently to obtain a wife for Zelda's brother Desmond. Since Sam's cattle served as her bridewealth, Sam has a claim on Desmond's wife (Figure 6.6). Such a custom exists among the Ba-Thonga of Mozambique in Southeast Africa.

Marital problems other than incompatibility occur in populations with the institution of bridewealth. It may turn out that Zelda bears no children. Clearly, in this case, neither she nor her group has fulfilled their part of the marriage contract. If the relationship between groups is to be maintained, Zelda's group must furnish a woman, perhaps her younger sister, perhaps another female agnate, who can have children. So important is this consideration among the Betsileo that it is often only after a young woman has become pregnant that the marriage takes place and bridewealth is transferred. There is a period of trial marriage in which the young woman lives in her husband's village. During this time she demonstrates her fertility and also learns whether she and her husband and others in his village are compatible. If after she becomes pregnant, the couple does not wish to get married, the child has the right to become a full member of its mother's descent group.

Among populations whose social organization includes descent groups and bridewealth, any marriage is a contract between descent groups. If a woman cannot have children, her group will be obliged to return the progeny price or to provide a substitute wife. The original wife may sometimes elect to remain in her husband's village. Perhaps she will

someday have a child. Perhaps, in recognition of her companionship and labor and because it has received two women rather than only one, her husband's group will add a bit to the bridewealth. If the first wife stays on, her husband will now be involved in a plural marriage. Most tribal societies, chiefdoms, and nonindustrial states, unlike most foraging societies and industrial nations, allow plural marriages, or *polygamy*. There are two varieties, one common, the other very rare. Common is *polygyny*, in which a man has more than one wife. Rare is *polyandry*, in which a woman has more than one husband. Therefore, if an infertile wife remains married to her husband after he has taken a substitute child bearer provided by her descent group, this is polygyny. Reasons for polygyny other than infertility are discussed shortly.

Durable Alliances: Sororate

It is possible to exemplify the group alliance nature of marriage in such societies by examining still another common practice—continuation of group marital alliances when one spouse dies. What would happen if Zelda died young? Again, Sam's group might call on Zelda's to provide a substitute, perhaps the sister of his deceased wife. This custom is known as the *sororate*. What, you may wonder, happens if Zelda has no sister, or if all her sisters are already married? Quite simply, another marriageable female member of Zelda's group may be available—Zelda's older brother's daughter or some other patrilineal kinswoman. Sam marries her; there is no need to return the bridewealth; and the alliance between the two groups continues. The sororate is found both in matrilineal and patrilineal societies. In a matrilineal society with uxorilocal postmarital residence, a widower may remain with his wife's group by marrying her sister or some other female member of her matrilineage (see Figure 6.7).

Levirate and Other Arrangements

So far, marriage as a relationship between groups rather than individuals has been illustrated only by cases in which the wife reneges on the marriage contract. Obviously, however, a breach can also originate with the husband. What happens, for example, if the husband dies? In many societies, a woman will marry a brother of her deceased husband, or a man, the widow of his deceased brother. This custom is

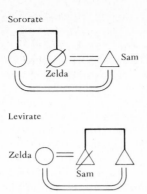

FIGURE 6.7 Sororate and levirate.

known as *levirate,* and like sororate, it represents a kind of continuation marriage. It continues the alliance between descent groups by replacing the deceased husband with another member of his group.

The implications of the levirate vary with the age of the widow. Returning to Sam, Zelda, and company, what happens if Sam dies after Zelda's childbearing years are over? When Sam and Zelda married, it was understood that Sam's group would be obliged to care for Zelda if Sam died. She has fulfilled her part of the marriage contract: she has borne children for Sam's descent group. Now that Sam is dead and gone, who is to care for her? The levirate assigns her to one of Sam's brothers. If he already has a wife, he will now become polygynous. He is obligated to care for Zelda and to treat her as his wife. Depending upon the difference in their ages, their marriage may or may not involve sexual relations.

Alliances End, Conflict Begins

The relationship between groups is not always maintained. Particularly in populations that exchange bridewealth, divorce may not only end an alliance, it may actually trigger conflict. Consider what could happen if Sam argues that Zelda is not behaving like a good wife and Zelda argues that Sam is mistreating her. Sam's group believes and supports him, and Zelda's group believes and supports her. Zelda's group may refuse to provide another woman for a louse like Sam; or Sam's group may declare that it does not want another wife from a group that has done such a bad job in raising its women. With both groups convinced that not only the individual marriage but the group relationship should end, the matter of the bridewealth comes up. Zelda's group may be reluctant to return it, since they feel that the fault lies with Sam. To his group, Zelda is clearly to blame. In societies that lack judicial systems to settle such disputes, open conflict between the two groups may break out.

PLURAL MARRIAGES

In the contemporary United States, as in most industrial nations, polygamy is against the law. Perhaps this is partly because divorces are fairly easy to obtain. Relationships between individuals may break up more easily than those that ally social groups. As divorce becomes more common, both men and women may become involved in what anthropologists call *serial monogamy:* individuals have more than one spouse, but never, legally, more than one at the same time.

As was stated earlier, there are two forms of polygamy: polygyny and polyandry. Polygyny is far more common than polyandry, which is accepted in very few societies. Populations of the Marquesas Islands in Polynesia, and certain groups in Tibet, India, and other parts of southern Asia provide some of the rare examples of polyandry in practice.

Polygyny

Before examining some of the reasons for polygyny, it is necessary to distinguish between the social approval of plural marriage in a given society and its frequency in that society. People in many societies attach no stigma to polygynous unions; in fact, it may be considered good to have more than one wife. However, even in societies where polygyny is encouraged, most men and women are involved in monogamous unions. Polygyny is characteristic of only a fraction of the marriages in that society. Why?

EQUAL SEX RATIOS In the contemporary United States, approximately 105 males are born for every 100 females. However, by adulthood the ratio of men to women is equalized, and later it is reversed. In the United States, the average female lives longer than the average male. In some nonindustrial societies, the sex ratio, if it favors males at birth, may be reversed by adulthood. This is because in many societies the activities allocated to males are more dangerous than those deemed appropriate for females. Men have to climb coconut trees; repair roofs; hunt tigers or sea mammals; take part in raiding parties and warfare; fish, sail, and travel, possibly into alien territory. Populations such as the Eskimos, which assigned especially dangerous jobs to males, often practiced female infanticide. The practice of killing female infants ensured that there were approximately equal numbers of adult female and male Eskimos.

Infanticide is a means of population control common among populations who do not employ birth control. For example, the horticultural Tapirapé of Brazil customarily controlled their population by killing the fourth baby born in each family (see Wagley, 1971). Each couple was allowed to have two girls and a boy or two boys and a girl. If the third child was of the same sex as the previous two, it was killed. The fourth child was always killed. This custom permitted the Tapirapé population to maintain itself, for infant mortality and death from natural causes further reduced the population.

There are some demographic reasons why polygyny is more common than polyandry. If there is no female infanticide and male tasks are more dangerous, there are more adult females, and polygyny is the cultural adaptive result. Polygyny is also found in populations where men marry later than women. Among the Kanuri of Bornu in Nigeria (Cohen, 1967), men customarily marry for the first time between the ages of eighteen and thirty. Many women, on the other hand, marry between twelve and fourteen. Because of the age difference between

spouses, there are more widows than widowers. Most of the widows remarry, some in polygynous unions. Among the Kanuri, and in other polygynous societies, widows make up a large number of the women involved in polygynous unions (see Hart and Pilling, 1960).

SOME EXPLANATIONS FOR POLYGYNY Shifting from anthropologists' to natives' explanations, we find that the reasons people give for practicing polygyny vary from society to society. Perhaps the most common response is a variant of the following: "We are polygynous because our ancestors were polygynous, and that is the way things should be." Related to this is the answer: "It is the custom of our people for men to marry as many women as they can support." Among many populations, including the Kanuri, the number of wives a man has is a measure of his prestige and social position. The Kanuri live in composite households headed by men. Also residing in the household are the man's wives and unmarried children, and, because residence after marriage is virilocal, his married sons and their wives and children (see Figure 6.8). The household is the major productive unit among the Kanuri. The more wives, the more productive workers in a household. Increased productivity means more wealth for the household head; more wealth attracts additional wives. Wealth and wives mean greater prestige for the household and its head, and were it not for the fact that Kanuri marriages are highly unstable, with a high incidence of divorce, there would be a progressive differentiation of Kanuri households.

Informants in several societies have told ethnographers that the additional wife or wives have been obtained at the request of the first wife to help her with household work and other burdens. In such

FIGURE 6.8 A Kanuri household. Note polygyny of household head and three-generation extended family that lives in this household.

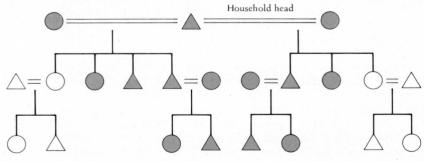

Household head

▲,●: Possible household residents.

cases, the status of the second wife is commonly below that of the first: there are a senior wife and junior wives. Often, it is actually the senior wife who chooses the second wife. She may be a close kinswoman who has not yet married—a younger sister, for example, whom the senior wife is reasonably sure that she can control.

When I asked some of my Betsileo informants in Madagascar about their ancestors' reasons for practicing polygyny, they pointed out that the different wives always lived in different villages. A man's first and senior wife, called "Big Wife," lived in the ancestral village where he cultivated his principal rice field and spent most of his time. However, the Betsileo inherit from several different ancestors and cultivate rice fields in several different areas. Prestigious men with several rice fields customarily established wives and households in hamlets near each rice field. They spent most of their time with their senior wife, but visited the others throughout the year.

Plural wives often play political roles in nonindustrial states. The king of the Merina, a population of more than 1,500,000 located in the highlands of Madagascar north of the Betsileo, established official residences for each of his twelve wives in different provinces. He stayed with them as he traveled throughout his kingdom, and they were his local agents, overseeing and reporting on events in the provinces. The king of Buganda took his wives from among all the commoner clans in his nation. The child of one of his wives would eventually become the new king. Thus all clans in the state were in-laws of the king, and all had a chance to provide the next king. This seems to have been an effective way of giving the common people a stake in the government.

Polygyny. In western Nigeria, the senior wife of the King of Akure is greeted by her co-wives. Only the senior wife may dress like modern western Nigerian women; junior wives must wear special robes traditionally associated with their status. Differences in the rights of junior and senior wives are found in many cases of polygyny. (Marc and Evelyne Bernheim/Woodfin Camp & Assoc.)

From these examples, it should be clear that it is foolhardy to seek a single explanation for polygyny. Its function varies from society to society and even within the same society. Some men are polygynous because they have inherited a widow from a brother or another close kinsman. Others take plural wives because they seek prestige or greater productivity for their households. Still others establish wives in different areas to supervise their estates in those regions. Recall, too, that marriage is a political tool, and it may also be a means of economic advancement. Men with political and economic ambitions cultivate alliances that serve their aims. Polygyny by a monarch to increase his power is a very different matter from polygyny by a commoner who is obliged to care for his older brothers' widows.

Polyandry

Because polyandry is so rare, it is necessary to point to the very specific conditions under which it is practiced. The great majority of ethnographically documented polyandrous marriage systems come from South Asia—from Tibet, India, Nepal, and Sri Lanka. In contemporary India, the most consistent practitioners of polyandry are certain groups that live in the lower ranges of the Himalayas in northern India. Collectively, these people are known as Paharis, which means "people of the mountains," and they have been studied by the anthropologist Gerald Berreman. In particular, Berreman (1962, 1975) has completed a comparative study of two Pahari groups, one located in Jaunsar Bawar in the western foothills of the Himalayas, the other in Garhwal in the central foothills. Berreman noted a high percentage of polyandrous marriages in Jaunsar Bawar, but no cases at all in Garhwal.

The western and the central Paharis are historically, genetically, and linguistically related. They speak dialects of the same language. Western and central Paharis may be viewed as divergent descendants of a common ancestral population that has undergone an adaptive radiation. The polyandrous people of Jaunsar Bawar represent adaptation to an area of the lower ranges of the western Himalayas, those of Garhwal to the lower ranges of the central Himalayas. Noting many similarities in their cultural traditions and social organization, including caste stratification and patrilineal clans, Berreman addressed himself to the question of why one group practiced polyandry while the other did not.

Related to these differences in marriage customs are demographic contrasts. The sex ratios of the two areas were very different. In Jaunsar Bawar, the polyandrous area, there was an unusually great shortage of females (789 females per 1,000 males); in nonpolyandrous Garhwal, the ratio favored females (1,100 females per 1,000 males). Berreman was unable to explain the shortage of females in Jaunsar Bawar. Female infanticide had not been documented in the area. He thought that neglect of female children (*covert* female infanticide) might be a more likely explanation.

Berreman's work documents that there is variation among polyandrous marriage systems as there is among polygynous systems, and such systems occur for different reasons. Polyandry in Jaunsar Bawar is exclusively fraternal; multiple husbands are always brothers. Typically, the oldest brother arranges the marriage. The marriage ceremony establishes all the brothers as socially recognized husbands of the wife. Subsequently, the brothers may marry additional women. All such wives, however, are considered wives of all the brothers. Brothers have equal sexual access to their common wife or to all other wives, and all wives have sexual access to each brother. Children born to the wives call all the brothers "father," disregarding biological paternity.

Furthermore, Berreman (1975) found considerable variation in the marital arrangements of households in Jaunsar Bawar. In one village, 9 percent of the marriages were polyandrous, 33 percent involved multiple brothers married to multiple wives, 25 percent were polygynous, and 34 percent were monogamous. Variation in marriage patterns and household composition reflected such factors as household wealth, age of brothers, and divorce. Berreman found that household composition changed through a developmental cycle. Consider the following example. In 1910 a group of three brothers took their first wife; in 1915 an additional wife was added—changing an arrangement of simple fraternal polyandry into a polyandrous-polygynous household. A few years later, a third wife was added, and later a fourth. A decade later, one of the brothers had died, and two of the wives had left—to divorce and remarry. By 1955 the household had become monogamous, as only one husband and one wife survived.

Comparing marital patterns and household composition in upper and lower castes, Berreman (1975) also found that poorer Paharis are more likely to be monogamous (43 percent) than upper-caste, land-owning Paharis (26 percent). Options about marriage, like the flexible descent rules discussed in Chapter 5, work as homeostats—allowing Paharis to regulate how people and their labor are allocated with respect to land and other strategic resources. Berreman found that the number of working adults, and therefore of spouses, was proportional to the amount of farmland available to the household. Because women were as productive in agricultural work as men, given the same amount of land, two brothers might require and support three or four wives, whereas three or four brothers might have only one or two wives. The incidence of plural marriages was lowest in landless households, whose resources and labor requirements were lowest.

Among the related people of Garhwal, where the sex ratio favors females over males, 85 percent of the unions in Berreman's sample were monogamous, and 15 percent were polygynous. Despite prohibitions against polyandry in Garhwal, Berreman found striking similarities in the actual operation of polyandry in Jaunsar Bawar and monogamy in Garhwal. In Garhwal as in Jaunsar Bawar, a group of brothers jointly contribute to the bridewealth given for the wife of any brother. Furthermore, in Garhwal brothers also have sexual access to one another's wives. The major difference seemed to be that children in nonpolyandrous Garhwal recognize only one father. Needless to say, with the common sexual rights of brothers, children's socially recognized fathers are not necessarily their true genitors.

In other areas of South Asia, informants and ethnographers have pointed to other reasons why polyandry may be selected for. Among some polyandrous groups, marriage of more than one man to a single woman has been interpreted as adaptation to geographical mobility associated with male economic tasks. When men travel a great deal to engage in trade, commerce, or military operations, polyandry ensures that there is usually a male at home. In certain contexts, simple fraternal polyandry may be an adaptive strategy where strategic resources are scarce. Like Americans plagued with poverty, a group of brothers who have inherited access to a limited patrimony may pool their resources in expanded households. In these cases, polyandry, by restricting the number of wives, may also limit the number of heirs who must compete for the same meager estate. In still other cases, the practice of polyandry appears to be related to a distribution of wealth in which women as well as men are property owners, and dowry, a parcel of property rights, is brought into a marriage by the wife. Given such conditions, the anthropologist E. R. Leach (1955) has argued that polyandry serves to keep property of the husbands and wife intact, to be passed on to children with minimal fragmentation. Note, therefore, that fraternal polyandry can serve as a functional alternative to endogamy.

The selecting conditions for polyandry were different among the Marquesan Islanders of Polynesia. In contrast to polyandry in South Asia, however, Marquesan polyandry was typically nonfraternal. During the nineteenth century, following contact with Europeans, the Marquesan population fell drastically. Intertribal skirmishes and warfare with the European explorers appear to have played a part in population decline. However, smallpox and famine were even more devastating (Otterbein, 1968). Population decline affected males and females differently. By the end of the nineteenth century the sex ratio was about six males to five females. Polyandry, in a variety of guises, was the cultural adaptive response.

Otterbein has identified four types of Marquesan marital arrangements: (1) monogamous; (2) simple polyandrous unions involving a woman and multiple husbands; (3) polygynous-polyandrous households in which a married man married a married woman (the new wife and her husband joined the household of the new husband, who was always a richer man, and all spouses had sexual rights to the spouses of the opposite sex); (4) composite households including a core representing one of the other three marital arrangements, to which unmarried males had attached themselves. They did not marry, but had sexual access to the wife or wives of the household.

The Marquesan case represents an example so rare as to be considered only as a curiosity. Like marriage in South Asia, however, it does serve to illustrate that there is no simple trichotomy of monogamy-polyandry-polygyny. All three marriage types can coexist in the same society as part of a flexible set of traditional rules. The practice of polygyny or polyandry among different populations represents a kind of convergence—the appearance of similar forms albeit with different selecting conditions. Cultural forms like polyandry may be adaptive solutions that serve functions analogous to those that other forms, such as endogamy, serve in different cultures.

SUMMARY

Taboos against incest exist in all human societies. However, incest taboos in different societies prohibit marriage with different biological kin types. Various reasons have been suggested for the taboo's universality: (1) it codifies instinctive human revulsion against such unions; (2) it results from recognition of biological degeneration that follows from such unions; (3) it possesses a selective advantage because of the exogamic alliances it promotes; and (4) it is necessary to maintain the role structure of the nuclear family and thus the cohesion of society. Although no single explanation can totally account for the taboo's universality, anthropologists Edward Tylor, Leslie White, Claude Lévi-Strauss, and Bronislaw Malinowski have offered valuable clues to understanding it. The incest taboo does promote exogamy, therefore increasing networks of friends and allies. Furthermore, mating between close relatives, especially parents and children, would create conflict that could impair sociocultural cohesion and continuity.

The major adaptive advantage associated with exogamy is the extension of social ties outward. This is confirmed by a consideration of endogamy, marriage within the group. Endogamic rules are often encountered in stratified societies. Perhaps the most familiar example is traditional India, where castes, though endogamous units, are often subdivided internally into descent groups that are themselves exogamous. People can therefore follow both endogamic and exogamic prescriptions in the same society, but with reference to different groups to which they belong. The American system of "race" relations is structurally similar to the Indian caste system, although it lacks many of the cultural embellishments.

In certain nonindustrial states, royal incest was allowed and even encouraged, even though the incest taboo applied to commoners. The manifest functions of royal incest in ancient Hawaii, for example, were related to the idea of mana. However, royal incest also served latent functions in the political and economic spheres—limiting succession struggles and keeping royal wealth intact. Marriage of close relatives in Brazilian plantation society demonstrates some of the same functions. Preferential marriage of brothers' children in the Near East and North Africa, particularly among Arabs, illustrates some additional functions and effects of endogamy.

Cultural rules in many tribal societies not only forbid people from marrying within their own group, but also rigidly dictate their choice of spouses. What Lévi-Strauss has called generalized exchange is a common variant of such prescriptive exogamic marriage systems. Generalized exchange links exogamous descent groups in a set series of marital relationships, such that women from group B always marry men from group C, while men from group B always take their wives from group A.

Especially among populations with descent-group organization, marriage must be understood as a relationship between groups as well as between spouses. Populations with descent-group organization often follow a custom known as bridewealth, whereby wealth of some sort is assembled by the groom and his relatives and transmitted to the bride and her relatives before marriage. A relationship between bridewealth and divorce has been suggested: as the value of the bridewealth increases, the frequency of divorce declines. The amassing and distributing of bridewealth demonstrates that marriages in tribal societies, chiefdoms, and many nonindustrial states ally groups, as do other customs such as sororate, whereby a man marries the sister of his deceased wife, and levirate, whereby a woman marries the brother of her deceased husband. Certain replacement marriages in the event of incompatibility of specific spouses also confirm the importance attached to maintenance of group alliances.

Among many populations, plural marriages are considered culturally appropriate. Two varieties of polygamy are recognized: polygyny, marriages involving multiple wives; and polyandry, marriages involving multiple husbands. No single reason can account for the practice of polygyny or polyandry in the variety of social and cultural contexts in which they occur. Polygyny occurs far more commonly than polyandry. Demographic, economic, and ecological reasons for plural marriage systems have been discussed.

SOURCES AND SUGGESTED READINGS

BARTH, F.

1954 Father's Brother's Daughter Marriage in Kurdistan. *Southwestern Journal of Anthropology* 10: 164–171. Argues for a political function of marriage of children of brothers among the Kurds.

BERREMAN, G. D.

1962 Pahari Polyandry: A Comparison. *American Anthropologist* 64: 60–75. Similarities and differences in the marriage systems of two related Himalayan populations.

1975 Himalayan Polyandry and the Domestic Cycle. *American Ethnologist* 2: 127–138. Relationships among marriage type, household composition, age, caste, and wealth.

BOHANNAN, P., AND MIDDLETON, J., EDS.

1968 *Marriage, Family and Residence.* Garden City, N.Y.: Natural History Press. Articles on variant forms of marriage, incest, and exogamy, and family and household organization.

BUCHLER, I. R., AND SELBY, H. A.

1968 *Kinship and Social Organization: An Introduction to Theory and Method.* New York: Macmillan. One of the best general works on social organization; includes a good discussion of descent and alliance.

CHAGNON, N.

1968 Yanomamo Social Organization and Warfare. In *War: The Anthropology of Armed Conflict and Aggression,* ed. M. H. Fried, M. Harris, and R. F. Murphy, pp. 109–159. Garden City, N.Y.: Natural History Press. Relationships of Yanomamo marriage and trade patterns to their warfare.

1974 *Studying the Yanomamo.* New York: Holt, Rinehart & Winston. Chagnon's field techniques, including quantitative analysis of kinship and marriage.

1977 *Yanomamo: The Fierce People.* 2nd ed. New York: Holt, Rinehart & Winston. Readable case study of remote, warlike Venezuelan population.

CHANCE, N. A.

1966 *The Eskimo of North Alaska.* New York: Holt, Rinehart & Winston. Case study of contemporary Eskimos.

COHEN, R.

1967 *The Kanuri of Bornu.* New York: Holt, Rinehart & Winston. Case study includes interesting discussion of virilocal, polygynous households and marital instability.

FIRTH, R.

1940 The Analysis of Mana: An Empirical Approach. *Journal of the Polynesian Society* 49: 483–510. Variations in the *mana* doctrine in Oceania.

FREUD, S.

1950 *Totem and Taboo,* trans. J. Strachey. London: Routledge and Kegan Paul. Contains fanciful reconstruction of early human social organization and the origin of the incest taboo.

FREYRE, G.

1956 *The Masters and the Slaves: A Study in the Development of Brazilian Civilization,* trans. S. Putnam. New York: Knopf. Idealistic examination of social relations in plantation society of northeastern Brazil.

GOODY, J., AND TAMBIAH, S. T.

1973 *Bridewealth and Dowry.* Cambridge: Cambridge University Press. Marital exchanges in comparative perspective.

HART, C. W. M., AND PILLING, A. R.

1960 *The Tiwi of North Australia.* New York: Holt, Rinehart & Winston. Case study of unusual degree of polygyny among North Australian foragers.

HOBHOUSE L. T.

1915 *Morals in Evolution.* Rev. ed. New York: Holt. Comparative view of social organization by an early anthropologist.

HOMANS, G., AND SCHNEIDER, D. M.

1955 *Marriage, Authority and Final Causes.* Glencoe, Ill.: Free Press. Interprets marriage of a man to his mother's brother's daughter as following from the affection he feels first toward his mother, and then extends to his mother's brother, and finally to the latter's daughter.

HUTTON, J. M.

1951 *Caste in India: Its Nature, Functions and Origins.* 2nd ed. London: Oxford University Press. Classic study of caste, based on personal knowledge of India.

JONES, R. L., AND JONES, S. K.

1976   *The Himalayan Woman.* Palo Alto, Calif.: Mayfield. Marriage, divorce, and sex roles among the Limbu of Nepal.

LEACH, E. R.

1955   Polyandry, Inheritance and the Definition of Marriage. *Man* 55: 182–186. Argues that marriage is not a cultural universal.

1961   *Rethinking Anthropology.* London: Athlone Press. Stimulating collection of articles; most deal with marriage systems.

LÉVI-STRAUSS, C.

1969   (orig. 1949). *The Elementary Structures of Kinship.* Boston: Beacon Press. Classic account of marriage, particularly generalized exchange, in non-Western societies.

LOWIE, R. H.

1961   (orig. 1920). *Primitive Society.* New York: Harper & Brothers. Classic, chapter-by-chapter attempt to negate Morgan, 1963 (orig. 1877). Origins of clan organization and of age- and sex-based groups; descent, marriage, and kinship terminology.

MALINOWSKI, B.

1927   *Sex and Repression in Savage Society.* London: International Library of Psychology. Role of the father among the matrilineal Trobrianders of the South Pacific.

MERTON, R. K.

1957   *Social Theory and Social Structure.* Rev. ed. Glencoe, Ill.: Free Press. Sociological discussion of manifest and latent functions included.

MORGAN, L. H.

1963   (orig. 1877). *Ancient Society.* Cleveland: World Publishing. Classic contribution to social and political theory by an early American anthropologist.

MURPHY, R. F., AND KASDAN, L.

1959   The Structure of Parallel Cousin Marriage. *American Anthropologist* 61: 17–29. Links marriage of children of brothers in the Near East and North Africa to factionalism; exemplifies in inverse form the alliance functions of exogamy.

OTTERBEIN, K. F.

1968   (orig. 1963). Marquesan Polyandry. In *Marriage, Family and Residence,* ed. P.

Bohannan and J. Middleton, pp. 287–296. Garden City, N.Y.: Natural History Press. Using secondary sources, author reconstructs four household types, some including polyandrous marriages, among this Polynesian population.

TYLER, S. A.

1973   *India: An Anthropological Perspective.* Pacific Palisades, Calif.: Goodyear. An overview of major features of Indian rural and urban life.

TYLOR, E. B.

1889   On a Method of Investigating the Development of Institutions: Applied to Laws of Marriage and Descent. *Journal of the Royal Anthropological Institute* 18: 245–269. Classic article advocating quantitative approach to anthropological comparison, particularly in the study of marriage and other aspects of social organization.

WAGLEY, C.

1969   (orig. 1951). Cultural Influences on Population: A Comparison of Two Tupi Tribes. In *Environment and Cultural Behavior,* ed. A. P. Vayda, pp. 268–279. Garden City, N.Y.: Natural History Press. Cultural means of limiting population growth among two related South American native populations.

1971   *An Introduction to Brazil.* Rev. ed. New York: Columbia University Press. Social organization of a complex society, particularly kinship and marriage of upper- and middle-class Brazilians.

WESTERMARCK, E.

1894   *The History of Human Marriage.* London: Macmillan. Interesting early work; relates the incest taboo to instinctive revulsion.

WHITE, L. A.

1949   *The Science of Culture.* New York: Farrar, Straus. Includes famous essay on the adaptive functions of the incest taboo and exogamy.

1959   *The Evolution of Culture.* New York: McGraw-Hill. Alliance functions of exogamy and variation in social organization among several non-Western populations examined from a general evolutionary viewpoint.

Political Organization and Conflict in Comparative Perspective

7

Anthropologists and political scientists share an interest in political organization. Using data gathered from populations outside the industrial West to provide a framework for the comparative study of such organization, anthropologists have speculated about such matters as the differences between law and cultural rules, between crime and deviation from social norms; the nature of relationships among groups in societies; reasons for disputes and means of resolving them in different social and cultural contexts; variations in power and authority systems of different peoples.

In the mid-nineteenth century, anthropologist-sociologists such as Lewis Henry Morgan, Herbert Spencer, and Sir Henry Maine wrote extensively about the evolution of political organization. Their works, particularly Maine's *Ancient Law,* published in 1861, and Morgan's *Ancient Society,* published in 1877, related also to the evolution of society in general.

In such early work, it is difficult to distinguish contributions to political anthropology from general contributions to social and cultural anthropology because in many nonindustrial populations, particularly those that lack state organization, the *polity,* the political order, does not exist as a separate institution as it does in our own. Rather, it is submerged in the total social order, and it is difficult to characterize an act or event as political rather than merely social.

Recognizing that political organization is but an aspect of social organization, Morton Fried (1967) has offered the following definition: "Political organization comprises those portions of social organization that specifically relate to the individuals or groups that manage the affairs of *public policy* or seek to control the appointment or activities of those individuals or groups [italics added]."

147

This definition certainly applies to political organization in the contemporary United States. Under "individuals or groups that manage the affairs of public policy," you can fit in the whole apparatus of federal, state, and local governments; and those who "seek to control the appointment or activities of those individuals or groups" includes a mass of interest groups and individuals, for example, labor unions, corporations, consumer groups, religious organizations, and their leaders. Fried's definition is, however, weak in terms of societies that lack state organization. Indeed, is there any "public policy" in certain kinds of society, particularly among most foragers? It is also difficult to apply the word "manage" to most of what goes on in everyday life among foragers.

At the risk of overgeneralizing, it may be preferable to delineate the area of study of the political anthropologist more broadly and more loosely: *political anthropology* is the study of the interrelationships among groups or their representatives. Imagine yourself an anthropologist who plans to study the political organization of a society, or who is undertaking a cross-cultural study of political organization. What do you do? First, you identify the groups that are significant in the society or societies included in your sample. Second, you determine what kind of people represent those groups on particular occasions. Now you are well on your way to the central question: What kinds of relationships prevail among these groups and their representatives?

In the remainder of this chapter, we will examine populations representing different general evolutionary types and strategies of adaptation. For each, we will indicate the significant social groups, their local or dispersed nature, the means of tying them together, how they represent themselves to one another—in short, their system of interrelationships. The discussion of each population will also be concerned with the nature of leadership roles; reasons for disputes, if any; means of resolving these disputes; presence or absence of a public policy embodied in a law code; means of enforcing this code; and legal sanctions, rewards, and punishments. All these concerns are included within the traditional subject matter of political anthropology.

Two distinctions are paramount here: (1) disputes over property are confined to certain kinds of society and (2) there is a tremendous contrast between bands and tribes, on the one hand, and states, on the other, in aspects of political organization, law, and order.

Here we recall Fried's definition: in states the individuals and groups who manage the affairs of public policy stand out from other members of the population. Furthermore, as you saw in Chapters 3 and 4, many of them are full-time political functionaries occupying permanent offices. Other implications of state organization will become apparent as individual cases are considered.

The first step in studying political organization is to identify the groups that are significant. The kinds of groups that exist in a society will depend on its general evolutionary type and its strategy of adaptation. For example, in most foraging societies, only two kinds of groups are significant: the nuclear family and the band. Among many foragers, the band does not remain a group all year long but forms seasonally, as its component nuclear families, which vary from year to year, assemble.

POLITICAL ORGANIZATION IN BAND-ORGANIZED SOCIETIES

Among foragers bands or local groups are typically linked together through the webs of personal relationships established by individuals rather than through group ties. Individuals generally marry outside their band, which creates personal ties between people living in different bands. Bands are also tied together through bilateral kinship networks. Since an individual's mother and father, and perhaps all four grandparents, come from different bands, he or she may be related to several different bands. Trade between individuals from different bands also links local groups together.

Finally, fictive kinship may connect individuals residing in separate bands. The !Kung namesake system was mentioned in Chapter 3—individuals with the same name are regarded as relatives. Sam I and Sam II are like brothers. The relatives of Sam I call Sam II by the same kinship term that they apply to Sam I. Sam II also uses the same kinship terms that his namesake uses to refer to the latter's relatives. Among the Eskimos, men had trade partners, whom they treated as quasi-brothers, in different bands. A man extended the hospitality of his home, including sexual access to his wife, to his trading partner. The aborigines of Australia had an institution known as the section system that served similar linking functions.

Descent groups are rarely found among foragers, and thus the political organization of band-organized societies is rudimentary. Bands usually have an unstable membership. Leaders in a foraging society are usually simply the most permanent members of a particular band. They represent a social core around whom other individuals and their families may group for various lengths of time.

The Eskimos: Personalistic Disputes

Among foragers, there is nothing that could accurately be called law in the sense of a legal code, including trial and enforcement. In some foraging societies, there may be a great deal of disorder. The aboriginal Eskimos, as described by E. A. Hoebel (1954, 1968) are a good example. A native population of approximately 20,000 Eskimos extended over approximately 6,000 miles in the extreme north, the Arctic region from eastern Siberia to eastern Greenland. The only significant social groups among Eskimos were the nuclear family and the local band. Bands were tied together through individually established personal relationships. Some of the bands had headmen, and there were also shamans (part-time religious specialists). These positions conferred little power on those who occupied them.

Most disputes that arose among the Eskimos involved males, and most originated over females, commonly over wife stealing and adultery. Although it was acceptable for one man to have intercourse with another man's wife, access was by invitation only. If a man discovered that his wife had been having sexual relations without his sanction, he considered himself wronged and was expected to retaliate against the male offender. (The manner of retaliation will be examined below.)

The Eskimos, as mentioned in Chapter 6, practiced female infanticide to regulate the size and adult sex ratio of the population. In contrast to most foragers, where gathering—usually a female role—is more important, the man's hunting and fishing role in Eskimo subsistence activity was primary, since the diverse and abundant plant foods available in warmer areas were absent in the Arctic. Traveling on land and sea in a bitter environment, Eskimo men faced much more dangerous tasks than did women. Since the male role in the division of labor took more men's lives, women would have outnumbered men considerably if a proportion of female infants had not been killed. Even with female infanticide, however, slightly more women survived than men. This demographic imbalance allowed polygyny. Some men

took two or three wives. The ability to support more than one wife conferred a certain amount of prestige —yet, it also encouraged envy. If a man seemed to be marrying additional wives just to enhance his reputation, he was likely to have one of his wives stolen by a rival. This, like adultery, could lead to conflict.

A wronged man had several alternatives. Community opinion would not let him ignore the offense; one way of avenging his tarnished honor was to kill the man who had stolen his wife. However, if he did this, he could be reasonably sure that one of the close kinsmen of the dead man would try to kill him in retaliation. One dispute could escalate into several deaths.

Although no government existed to intervene and stop such a *blood feud,* an aggrieved individual did have the alternative of challenging the offender to a song contest as a means of regaining lost honor. The contestants made up insulting songs about each other. The audience judged, and at the end of the match, one was declared the winner. However, if the man whose wife had been stolen won, there was no guarantee that his wife would return. Sometimes she decided to stay with her abductor.

Several acts of killing that are deemed crimes in the contemporary United States were not considered criminal among the Eskimos. Individuals who felt that, because of age or infirmity, they were no longer useful might kill themselves or ask others to kill them. Old people or invalids who wished to die would ask a close relative, a son perhaps, to end their lives. It was necessary to ask a close relative to be sure that the relatives of the deceased did not take revenge on the killer.

In our own society, theft is a major source of conflicts, but this was not a problem for the Eskimos. By virtue of membership in a band, everyone had access to resources needed to sustain life. Every man had the right to hunt and fish and to manufacture all the tools he needed for subsistence activities. Individuals could even hunt and fish within the territories of other local groups. Conspicuously absent was the notion of private ownership of strategic resources.

To describe the property notions of people who live in nonstratified societies, anthropologist Elman Service (1966) coined the term *personalty.* Personalty describes items other than strategic resources that are strongly linked to a specific individual, things like the arrows one makes, the pouch one uses to carry tobacco, one's clothes or personal or-

"Personalty" describes the relationship between material items, such as those depicted in this surrealist painting by Magritte, and the individual who owns them. René Magritte, Personelles, 1952/Collection of Harry Torczyner, New York. (Photo courtesy Marlborough Gallery, New York)

namentation. Service chose this term to point to the personal relationship between material items and the individual who owns them. Personalty items are so tied to specific individuals in public opinion that for another to steal them would be inconceivable. It may be that the grave goods found so often in archeological sites prior to the emergence of food production represent items of personalty, things that could not be passed on to heirs, so definite and inseparable was their association with the deceased.

Thus, in band-organized society, there is no differential or impeded access to strategic resources. According to Hoebel (1968), one of the basic postulates of Eskimo life was that "all natural resources are free or common goods." The only private property is personalty, and if people want something that someone else has, they simply ask for it and it is given.

POLITICAL ORGANIZATION IN TRIBAL SOCIETIES

The Yanomamo: Village Raiding

In his books *Yanomamo: The Fierce People* (1977) and *Studying the Yanomamo* (1974), anthropologist Napoleon Chagnon has described the political sys-

tem of the Yanomamo of southern Venezuela and adjacent Brazil. The approximately 15,000 Yanomamo live in about 125 dispersed villages, each with a population of between 40 and 250 people.

The Yanomamo are tribal horticulturists whose staples are bananas and plantains. More social groups are significant for Yanomamo than for the Eskimos and foragers generally. There are nuclear families; local patrilineal descent groups; groups of two intermarrying local descent groups; villages; and geographically dispersed patrilineages. Yet there is no state, no central government capable of maintaining order. In fact, the Yanomamo appear to be exceedingly bloodthirsty. Warfare involving raids in which as many males as possible are killed and as many females as possible are captured is endemic.

The shortage of females in Yanomamo society appears to maintain the intensity of warfare. Frequent raiding occurs to capture women. The Yanomamo practice female infanticide, but, according to Chagnon, they do not realize that this selects against females. In fact, an overarching theme in Yanomamo society is male supremacy. The Yanomamo prefer sons to daughters, especially as first-born children. If the first-born is a girl, it is killed, but a boy is allowed to live. Females are also killed in warfare, as Chagnon (1977) shows, so that in the adult population, too, there are more males than females (449 to

Yanomamo tribesmen of southern Venezuela arguing over a trade item. Among these male chauvinist forest horticulturalists, trade is the first step in alliance formation. Feasting and marriage are the second and third steps. (Napoleon Chagnon)

391 in seven villages he studied). Furthermore, despite the fact that there are too few Yanomamo women to provide even one mate for each man, 25 percent of the men are involved in polygynous unions. The way in which the pattern of Yanomamo warfare perpetuates itself is summarized in Figure 7.1.

FIGURE 7.1 Continued selection for warfare among the Yanomamo.

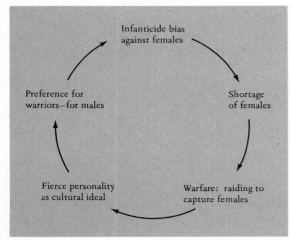

The Yanomamo illustrate in extreme form earlier statements that in stateless societies the world is divided into two categories: allies and potential or actual enemies. The Yanomamo use several social mechanisms — trading, feasting, and marriage — to convert potential or actual enemies into allies. Marriage is the strongest (and trading the weakest) alliance that may link two villages. Only after a relationship based on trade and feasting has been established, however, will two villages begin to intermarry. On the other hand, feast and trade do not always lead to marriage.

Notable in Yanomamo social organization is the absence of solidarity based on descent. Demonstrated descent does not extend very far into the past, and lineages are not named. Lineage membership is usually spread out among multiple villages, and it may cover a large territory. Membership in the same lineage is no basis for friendly relations or solidarity. In fact, disputes break out frequently even among close kin. Chagnon documents several disputes involving full brothers and a case of a violent fight between son and father.

In most other societies, kinship establishes peaceful relationships, but this is not the case among the Yanomamo. Again, this is related to the shortage of women. Among the Yanomamo, brothers determine whom their sisters will marry. To the Yanomamo, the ideal form of marriage is brother-sister exchange (see Figure 7.2). Sam, a member of patrilineage A, gives his sister to Joe, a member of patrilineage B, and Joe gives his own sister to be Sam's wife. What happens, however, if Sam and Joe have brothers? Each of the brothers is competing with the other to give away their sisters in marriage, so as to gain wives for themselves. Sam's father, too, may undertake to pledge some of his daughters, Sam's sisters, in marriage. The father's motives may be different; presumably, he already has a wife. He may simply use his daughters to establish a personal alliance with another village. Or his motives may be the same; he may be seeking a second wife. In either case, he is competing with Sam. It is no wonder then, that, as Chagnon observed, groups allied by marriage enjoy friendlier relationships than those allied by descent. Members of a descent group compete to dispose of the same women in order to obtain wives. On the other hand, two lineages who regularly exchange women have everything to gain from one another.

The fact that alliances are based on marriage

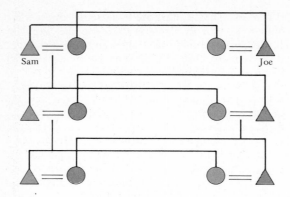

FIGURE 7.2   Brother-sister exchange.

rather than on descent is also important in determining the way a single village divides. Imagine a village in which there are two exogamous descent groups, A and B. Each descent group is divided into two branches, A_1 and A_2, B_1 and B_2, respectively. A_1 exchanges women with B_1, and A_2 with B_2. When the village fissions, A_1 and B_1 move to a new site together, while A_2 and B_2 remain in the original village or settle a new site on their own. In some cases, according to Chagnon, it only takes a few years for the two villages to begin raiding one another. Solidarity results from exchange of women; hostility results from competition over them.

Each Yanomamo village has a headman. As is characteristic of many tribal societies, his role in influencing others is very limited. Because he is expected to be more generous than any other villager, the headman cultivates more land. His plot will supply a great deal of the food consumed when his village hosts a feast for another village. He gets nothing from his position other than the right to give away more. His ability to issue commands is strictly limited. He may issue orders to his wives, children, and younger brothers but not to his brothers who are his age peers (full adults who are "already fierce," as the Yanomamo say) or to other adults in the community.

The Yanomamo headman represents his village in its dealings with other villages. Sometimes he may travel to another village to arrange a feast. He hosts feasts held in his village. Chagnon stresses that the headmanship is an office devoid of authority. The way a given individual conducts himself in the headmanship is a function of his personality and the num-

ber of supporters he can muster among the villagers. Chagnon relates a case in which one village headman, Kaobawa, intervened in a dispute between a man and his wife and prevented the husband from killing the wife. The same headman also guaranteed safety to a delegation from a village with which one of his covillagers was eager to initiate war. Kaobawa is probably a particularly effective headman. He has a large number of brothers and other supporters in his village. He has demonstrated his fierceness in battle. Chagnon points out that he diplomatically exercises his influence in such a way as not to offend other villagers. No one in the village has a better personality claim to the headmanship nor more supporters. If certain segments of the village population are dissatisfied, they have open to them the option of leaving the village and founding one of their own.

The Yanomamo believe that a shortage of women is the principal reason for the frequency of their raids. Most disputes that arise between and within villages are related to women. As villages grow larger, according to Chagnon, the incidence of adultery also increases. There is nothing to stop an enraged husband from killing both his wife and the adulterer. If he is not killed, the adulterer may leave the village. As village size increases, intravillage feuding over women and other matters will eventually increase to such a point that the village will break up.

Warfare between villages arises in several ways. Raiding may begin when people from one village attack individuals or small groups outside the territory of another village. Individual women may be abducted, their husbands killed. If an epidemic kills many people in one village but few in another, people in the former may believe that people in the latter are practicing sorcery against them. This may precipitate raids. People from village A may raid the unprotected gardens or the fruit trees of village B, again leading to revenge raiding. In any event, there is no outside authority that can stop intervillage warfare once it has begun. There is no law, no threat of legal sanctions, no means of keeping peace — in short, no state among the Yanomamo.

WARFARE AMONG TRIBAL CULTIVATORS Anthropologists William Divale and Marvin Harris (1976) believe that the Yanomamo provide a classic illustration of what they see as a prevalent male supremacist complex among tribal cultivators. They argue that warfare, which they define as "all organized forms of intergroup homicide involving combat teams of two or more persons, including feuding and raiding," is the major cause of this widespread male supremacist complex. In their study of warfare, ethnologists Divale and Harris used the Human Relations Area Files (HRAF), a voluminous set of cross-cultural data based on ethnographic reports about 300 different cultures. From the reports, Divale and Harris (1976) found 112 societies, generally band-organized and tribal, in which there was good information about warfare. In 55 (49 percent) warfare was still going on at the time of the report; in 34 (30 percent) warfare had stopped five to twenty-five years before; and in the remaining 23 (21 percent), warfare had stopped twenty-six or more years before data were gathered.

On the basis of the cross-cultural data, Divale and Harris argue that warfare is the most common way of regulating population size among tribal cultivators. They maintain that warfare regulates population size *indirectly* by leading, in a complex way, to female infanticide, *not* by causing deaths in battle. To understand how, consider Figure 7.1. According to Divale and Harris, among the Yanomamo, and tribal cultivators in general, warfare produces and maintains a cultural preference for fierce warriors, thus favoring boys over girls, and leading to female infanticide. Wherever preindustrial warfare exists, they argue, groups that raise large numbers of aggressive warriors will enjoy an advantage — given intergroup warfare — over those that do not. Divale and Harris suggest that in nonindustrial societies men always do the fighting because, on the average, they are taller and heavier than female members of their own population and that this confers an advantage in hand combat with muscle-powered weapons. Any nonindustrial society that had assigned defense to women would have been routed by neighboring societies in which men were the fighters. This argument applies only to nonindustrial societies. A few American women wielding rifles, or even handguns, could easily best a party of Yanomamo raiders.

Given a selective advantage in nonindustrial societies in assigning the fighting role to men, the male supremacist complex, with its stress on fierceness, pervades the rest of culture. Divale and Harris note that in such societies males typically control access to natural resources, capital, and labor power. Accordingly, virilocal postmarital residence and patrilineal descent, which emphasize and maintain male solidarity and control over estates, are far more common than other arrangements. The male supremacist complex is also expressed in polygyny. Divale and Harris suggest that this practice is directly related to the intensity of warfare, since the sexual favors of multiple wives are rewards that go to the fiercest warriors. Furthermore, as we have seen among the Yanomamo, polygyny intensifies the shortage of females that already exists, thus stimulating further fighting to capture women. As a result — as Figure 7.1 shows — fierceness is reinforced as a cultural idea, as are the preference for boys and the practice of female infanticide. Thus, in the 55 societies in which warfare was still going on, the ratio of males to females among juniors (fourteen years and under) was 127:100, whereas in the societies in which warfare had stopped, junior sex ratios approached that of our own society (106:100). Female infanticide is not always direct; preferential treatment of boys and neglect of girls are also factors.

Divale and Harris link the spread of warfare to the emergence and expansion of plant cultivation. Food production, as we have seen in previous chapters, increased the rate of population growth. To understand why, we must examine relationships between diet and fertility. Foragers typically have diets that are relatively high in protein and relatively low in fats and carbohydrates; plant cultivators have the opposite. Diet affects the ratio of body fat to total body weight. Foragers typically have less fat per unit of body weight than food producers. The phenotypical results of diet affect fertility in two ways. High-fat diets promote earlier puberty and, for women, lengthen the childbearing period of their lives. Second, high-fat diets favor conception.

Foragers, with low ratios of body fat to total weight, are partially able to delay conception by nursing their infants for several years. Lactation keeps body fat down, and sexual intercourse is less likely to result in conception. However, long nursing periods are only partially effective as means of limiting population growth among foragers, and infanticide does occur as an additional means among the Eskimos and other foragers. The high-fat and high-carbohydrate diet among plant cultivators means a long nursing period is less effective insurance against conception. If population growth is to be regulated other measures are inevitable, and several have been reported. Often, for example, women with infants are tabooed from having intercourse for one or more years after a child is born. Another cultural means of regulating population — a homosexual orientation—exists among the Etoro and other Trans-Fly tribes of New Guinea. The Trans-Fly tribes represent one extreme elaboration of the preference for males in societies in which warfare is endemic.

Divale and Harris argue, however, that, in the absence of effective contraception and abortion, the most effective and widespread cultural means of regulating population growth among tribal cultivators is intensification of female infanticide, the result of warfare and the male supremacist complex it engenders. As L. L. Cavalli-Sforza and W. Bodman (1971) have pointed out, the reproductive potential of most sexually reproducing species largely reflects the rate of female survivorship. Thus, reducing the percentage of sexually active, fertile females is the most effective means of population control. A human population with a life expectancy of forty-seven years will stabilize if about one-third of all females who are born never survive to reproductive age, and if each woman who survives has an average of three live births. If the number of births increases and if new resources are not added, the population's health and life expectancy will decline or the number of female survivors will be reduced (Divale and Harris, 1976). In summary, Divale and Harris argue that warfare, because it leads to a preference for males and a bias against females expressed in infanticide, represents the most common and effective response to population growth among tribal cultivators.

Data gathered by various ethnographers working among the Yanomamo offer some support for the position of Divale and Harris. Yanomamo population seems to have been expanding as a result of an economic shift from a more generalized strategy of adaptation to greater reliance on plantains and bananas. Divale and Harris (1976) suggest that it is in those Yanomamo areas where population is increasing most rapidly that warfare, the male supremacist complex, and female infanticide are most intense. They cite the following figures to support their point. For eleven villages in the central Yanomamo region, where warfare was most intense and population appeared to be growing fastest, the junior sex ratio was 148 males per 100 females. In twelve peripheral Yanomamo villages, however, the junior sex ratio was 118 males per 100 females, and warfare was also less intense. Divale and Harris believe that variation in the intensity of Yanomamo warfare also reflects a shortage of protein necessary to maintain an expanding Yanomamo population. Although

Chagnon (1977) remains skeptical that Yanomamo warfare can best be explained by shortages of protein, he, his associates, and other ethnographers are now gathering data in different parts of Yanomamo territory to test this hypothesis. A lively controversy seems likely to continue over reasons for warfare among the Yanomamo and other tribal cultivators.

The Tiv and the Nuer: Segmentary Lineage Structure

A different system of political organization regulates intergroup relations among the Nuer, a population numbering some 200,000 people who inhabit the region of the upper Nile River in the Republic of the Sudan. They are one of many Nilotic populations. The Nuer were studied ethnographically by British social anthropologist E. E. Evans-Pritchard in the 1930s and are described in his book *The Nuer* (1940) and in other books and articles by him. Their economy revolves around cattle pastoralism, but they also cultivate some crops horticulturally. Their social organization includes many institutions typically found among tribal populations, including descent groups, marriage relationships that emphasize group alliance, and progeny price. The Nuer have attracted considerable attention among anthropologists because of their type of patrilineal descent structure, known as *segmentary lineage organization*.

The Nuer's segmentary lineage structure is not unique. The Tiv, a Nigerian population numbering approximately 1 million, share this form of descent organization, as did certain populations of North Africa and the Near East including the Arabs and the ancient Jews. In societies with segmentary lineage systems, political organization is based on descent rules and genealogical reckoning. Descent rules of populations with segmentary lineage systems tend toward patrilineality. In the ideology of these populations, an individual should be a member of his or her father's group.

The Tiv believe that all Tiv are ultimately descended from the same apical ancestor, a man called Tiv who settled their present homeland, Tivland, several generations ago. The Tiv trace the line of descent leading from Tiv to the present, listing lineal descendants in each intervening generation. While the Nuer do not claim to be able to demonstrate patrilineal ancestry that far back, they do believe that they have a common ancestry that distinguishes them from the neighboring Dinka and other Nilotic populations.

Evans-Pritchard reports that several levels of descent-group segmentation are significant in Nuer social organization. Nuer clans are composed of segments called lineages. The segments of *maximal* lineages are known as *major lineages*. Major lineages are composed of several *minor lineages*, and the latter are subdivided into *minimal lineages,* whose members are descended over three to five generations from the same man. In contrast to the larger descent groups, which are territorially dispersed, minimal lineages are usually coresident groups, that is, members of the same minimal lineage usually reside in the same local group.

Over time, minimal lineages grow into minor, minor into major, and major into maximal. The genealogy in Figure 7.3 illustrates the segmentary principle. The core of Figure 7.3 is a major lineage founded by an individual called Anthony Smithley-Nurnspratt. Anthony is dead and has become the common apical ancestor for two minor lineages known, respectively, as the Smithleys and the Nurnspratts. Kaobonga Smithley, dead too, has become the apical ancestor for two minimal lineages, the Smiths and the Lees, who reside in separate but neighboring villages. Mo'valuta Smith is now the leader of the Smiths, and Rooster Lee heads the Lee homestead. Once Mo'valuta Smith and Rooster Lee die, and as their descendants increase, their sons and grandsons will become apical ancestors for new minimal lineages, and the former minimal lineages will become minor, the minor major, the major maximal.

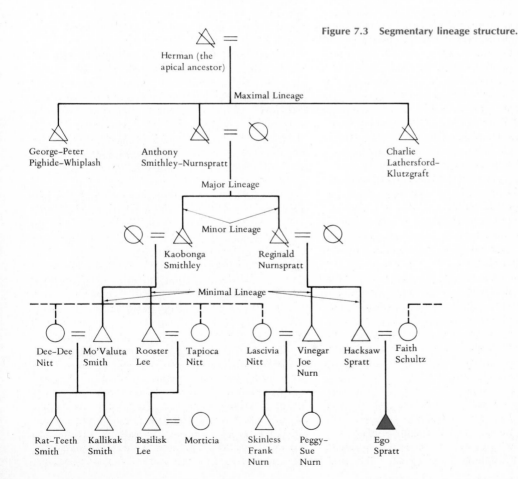

Figure 7.3 Segmentary lineage structure.

Note that while the Smithleys have been segmenting into Smith and Lee minimal segments, the Nurnspratts have been doing the same thing. Vinegar Joe Nurn is the apical ancestor of the newly formed Nurn segment, and Hacksaw Spratt heads the Spratt minimal lineage.

The lineage illustrated in Figure 7.3 is somewhat idealized. In fact, new minimal lineages form only when individuals move away from the local groups where they were born and establish new settlements. In Figure 7.3, all the male agnates in each generation have founded new settlements. In reality, most or perhaps all sons in some generations would stay in the parental settlement, and new and discrete minimal lineage segments would bud off only after a few generations of common residence.

Unlike the Yanomamo, the Nuer seem to suffer no shortage of women. Moreover, the relationship between brothers appears to be very close in societies with segmentary descent organization. This is especially true when the father is still living. He is the manager of his sons' joint estate and attempts to curb quarreling among them. He also uses the bridewealth that his daughters bring in to obtain wives for his sons. When the father dies, the brothers may continue to live together, or one may choose to take his share of the herds and found a settlement of his own. His brothers remain, however, his closest allies. Thus he will establish his local group as close as possible to his brothers'. Even if the brothers stay together following their father's death, segmentation may take place in the next generation, as some of the grandchildren establish new homesteads. Each of the grandsons, however, will try to remain as close to home as possible, settling nearest to his full brothers but nearer to his agnatic first cousins than to any more distant relative.

The basic principle of solidarity among the Nuer is that the closer the agnatic relationship, the greater the solidarity. The more distant the shared patrilineal apical ancestor, the greater the potentiality for hostility. This extends right up the genealogy; there is a greater chance that maximal lineages will engage in disputes than there is in the case of major lineages.

Anthropologist Marshall Sahlins (1961) has argued that segmentary lineage organization and belief in a common apical ancestor represent cultural adaptive means that have enabled Nuer and Tiv to expand at the expense of their neighbors. The common genealogy, Sahlins argues, provides a basis for tribal solidarity, enabling Nuer and Tiv to present, when need arises, a common front against outsiders — people who claim different ethnic identity. According to Sahlins, in the absence of the centralized coordination provided by chiefdoms and states, segmentary lineage structure is the most effective political device encountered in tribal societies. It has a selective advantage in terms of increase in numbers and expansion of range where several tribal populations are competing for the same living space.

The Arabs, who also have segmentary lineage structure, claim to demonstrate their descent patrilineally from Biblical Ishmael. There is an Arab adage, "I and my brother against my cousin [father's brother's son]; I, my brother, and my cousin against all other Arabs; I, my brother, my cousin, and all Arabs against all the world [cf. Murphy and Kasdan, 1959]." Jews believe themselves to be descended from Isaac, half brother of Ishmael. So one generation up, the Jews and the Arabs share a common ancestor, Abraham, the father of both Ishmael and Isaac.

Among Nuer, Tiv, and other populations with segmentary lineage organization, then, there are correlations between closeness of common agnatic ancestry, geographical proximity, and degree of social solidarity. Belief in common descent may serve as the basis for a political structure and provide a means of unifying one tribal population against others that lack such belief. Principles of segmentary descent are also important in understanding the nature of disputes and their resolution.

If a dispute breaks out between two Nuer men who share a common, living patrilineal ancestor, he intervenes to settle the dispute. As head of the minimal descent group that includes the disputants, he backs his authority with the threat of banishment. When there is no common, living agnatic ancestor of the two disputants, the possibility of a blood feud exists.

Most disputes among the Nuer do not appear to arise over shortages of strategic resources. An individual acquires land and cattle as a member of a lineage. Belonging to a minimal descent group, he has a right to its estate. Adultery, however, does often lead to disputes. Furthermore, if an individual murders or brings bodily harm to another, a feud may develop. Conflicts also arise over the disposition of progeny price in the event of divorce. If a woman leaves her husband before providing his group with what they regard as an adequate number of children, her husband's group may press for return of part of the bridewealth. If her own group is unwilling to meet these demands, a dispute may ensue.

Figure 7.3 can be used again to illustrate different ways in which disputes are resolved depending on whether or not the disputants share a common, living patrilineal ancestor. The common ancestor of Rat Teeth Smith and Kallikak Smith is alive. He is Mo'valuta Smith, their father. Should Kallikak kill his brother, Rat Teeth, all members of their group will be shocked. It is, after all, unthinkable for a Nuer to kill his brother or another close relative. However, should such an event take place, Kallikak will not be killed in retribution. The group's rationale for letting him live is that one member has already been lost; it cannot afford to lose another.

Now consider a dispute involving the Smiths and the Lees. Their common ancestor, Kaobonga Smithley, is dead. The dispute developed after Basilisk Lee found his wife, Morticia, committing adultery with Rat Teeth Smith. There is no common ancestor to settle the dispute, but the fathers of the disputants are brothers, and they will probably be able to work out a settlement. The adulterer will probably pay damages in cattle to Basilisk.

Now assume that Basilisk commits adultery with the wife of Skinless Frank Nurn, and Skinless Frank learns of it. He is furious and kills Basilisk. What happens? The nearest common ancestor of Basilisk and Skinless Frank is Anthony Smithley-Nurnspratt, their common great-grandfather. The Lees, who have lost Basilisk, may be willing to forgo a revenge killing and accept damages in cattle from the Nurns. They can use the cattle to acquire a wife for a man of their lineage; she will provide children to replace the dead Basilisk. The Nurns and the Lees may be able to work out an arrangement satisfactory to both, and the dispute may thereby be settled. On the other hand, should they find themselves unable to come to terms, there is then the possibility of a blood feud between the Lees and the Nurns.

The importance of close common agnatic ancestry as a basis for sociopolitical solidarity emerges here. The Smiths are expected to help the Lees since they share a more recent common ancestor, Kaobonga Smithley, than any Smith or Lee does with any Nurn or Spratt. The Spratts, for the same reason, will help the Nurns.

There is an alternative to a blood feud. The parties may consult the leopard-skin man, so-called because he wears a leopard skin over his shoulders. Leopard-skin men perform certain ritual duties, but

A leopard-skin man, mediator among the Nuer, who are tribal cattle herders and horticulturalists. The Nuer mediator has recourse only to supernatural sanctions to arbitrate descent-group feuds. (Kay Lawson/Rapho/Photo Researchers, Inc.)

their most important functions involve mediation of disputes. Skinless Frank Nurn and the elders of his lineage may ask a leopard-skin man to mediate the dispute, to try to convince the close agnates of Basilisk Lee to accept a certain number of cattle as recompense for their murdered kinsman. While the mediator attempts to get the parties to agree to a peaceful settlement, the murderer, Skinless Frank, may take refuge in the leopard-skin man's homestead, which offers him sanctuary until the leopard-skin man resolves the dispute or withdraws.

The leopard-skin man, like the Yanomamo village headman, must rely primarily on his talents for persuasion. He cannot make a decision imputing right or wrong to either side, nor can he hold up the threat of physical enforcement. He merely uses the threat of supernatural retribution. If, after seeking the mediation of a leopard-skin man, the parties to the dispute remain recalcitrant, the mediator may withdraw his services. If one of the segments is especially adamant, he may, in disgust, threaten to curse that segment. The ethnographer of the Nuer, however, was unable to discover a single case in which a leopard-skin man's curse had been invoked. Presumably, this is because once both parties submit their quarrel to his mediation, they are genuinely interested in reconciliation. Negotiations involve the individual parties to the dispute, the elders of their segments, and other close agnates. Disputes involve full and free discussion, and normally there is considerable agreement among the discussants before settlement is made. Such negotiations provide a way out for the individual parties to the dispute, who may be readier to modify their positions in accordance with the collective opinion of the mediator and the elders than they had been previously.

Should the mediator withdraw, however, Skinless Frank would lose his sanctuary and wander out into a world of bloodthirsty Smiths and Lees. In the ensuing feud to avenge the murder of Basilisk, a Smith or Lee might kill a Nurn or Spratt. A Nurn or Spratt might then kill a Smith or Lee, and so on, until the feuding groups grew tired of conflict and settled the dispute themselves or called on the leopard-skin man again. By that time each party would be more willing to resolve their differences.

In the event of a dispute, then, each Nuer is expected to help his closest patrilineal relatives against more remote agnates. All the descendants of Anthony Smithley-Nurnspratt would, for example, band together as allies against all the descendants of Charlie Lathersford-Klutzgraft if the dispute involved Skinless Frank Nurn and Winston Klutz, great-grandson of Charlie Lathersford-Klutzgraft. And so it goes, each one allied against another, up to the maximal lineages of Nuer society. Finally, the Nuer as a group would also unite against neighboring populations on the basis of their belief in common descent.

Among populations with segmentary lineage organization, alliance is relative. No one has a set group of allies. Rather, one's allies vary from one dispute to another, depending on the genealogical distance of the parties to the dispute. Although the peace-making abilities of the leopard-skin man are greater than anything found among either Yanomamo or Eskimos, the blood feud still exists among the stateless Nuer.

The Ifugao: Property Disputes among Stateless Agriculturalists

The Ifugao are a population of wet rice cultivators living in the northern part of Luzon, one of the islands in the Philippines. Their political organization, particularly their law, was the subject of a book by R. F. Barton in 1919. The Ifugao may be classified as agriculturalists because they cultivate their rice on permanent, irrigated plots within monumental terracing systems. The Ifugao countryside is extremely rugged, and generations of Ifugao have carved their terraces into the steep mountainsides.

In contrast to the populations considered previously, the Ifugao, numbering some 120,000 people around 1920, do conceive of private property in strategic resources. Individuals hold access to agricultural land and water used in irrigation. The Ifugao have no descent groups. The most basic kinship group is the nuclear family, and inheritance is equal among sons and daughters, with preference, however, given to the eldest child. The only other significant social groups are hamlets or villages, which are located on the hillsides near the rice terraces. Ifugao are linked to other Ifugao as individuals, through networks based on bilateral kinship.

Among the Ifugao disputes related to individual property in strategic resources are encountered. Since individual plots are limited in size and all children may inherit, disputes may arise over fragmented shares that each heir receives. Furthermore, owners of different rice fields often share access to the same source of water, perhaps a spring high on the hillside. Cultivators who are located at a higher elevation, eager to transplant their own rice, may divert the water first into their own fields. Other disputes arise over murder, bodily injuries, and debts.

The Ifugao also contrast with the other societies just examined by virtue of their well-formulated ideas about crime and its consequences. Over the centuries, the Ifugao have developed an unwritten code of justice, stipulating a range of damage compensations due victims of criminal acts. Thus if a murder has taken place, the Ifugao know precisely what is due the closest bilateral relatives of the victim.

The problem, however, is deciding on the nature of the crime. Similarly, in the United States, a given act may be judged self-defense, manslaughter, second- or first-degree murder, and the punishment will vary with the classification in which the act is placed. When there is a dispute between two Ifugao, the plaintiff, the defendant, and their close relatives may first try to negotiate a settlement. If they are unable, however, to assign fault or agree on the nature of the crime, they may call in a mediator. Usu-

An Ifugao village, built on a hillside near the rice terraces cultivated by the villagers. The rugged terrain inhibits state organization among these stratified agriculturalists. (John Launois/Black Star)

ally, mediators have reputations as successful warriors. The Ifugao were head hunters; successful warriors were men with many heads to their credit. The usefulness of prowess in warfare for the role of mediator will be seen in a moment.

The mediator's job is to travel back and forth between the defendant and the plaintiff and try to get them to agree to a solution. If the dispute is settled peacefully, he will receive a part of the damages paid the plaintiff. Like the Yanomamo headman and the Nuer leopard-skin man, the mediator relies on his abilities to persuade the parties to agree.

By the time the plaintiffs bring in a mediator, they have also notified their bilateral relatives that they are involved in a dispute. The plaintiff's relatives know that they must ready themselves in case mediation fails and a blood feud breaks out. Defendants also inform their kin of the dispute. During his visits back and forth, the mediator conveys to each party just how many are pledged to defend the other. This may have some influence on both parties' decision to

settle. Sometimes, there is a negotiated peace. However, the mediator may possibly decide he has done all he can do and withdraw from the affair.

If he does this, the blood feud can begin. Although the Ifugao lack descent groups, they regard close kin as substitutes for themselves in cases of dispute. Thus if Daryl is the plaintiff and Joe the defendant, Daryl or one of his relatives may kill Joe or one of his kin. The matter is, of course, not settled here. One death breeds desire for revenge. The blood feud is in full swing. According to Barton, such feuds were terminated only by a marriage linking the disputants or their relatives, or by a ritual involving animal sacrifice. The blood feud continually reinforced the pattern of warfare and head taking among the Ifugao. It is possible to speculate that, as among tribal horticulturalists, warfare has been an essential part of the Ifugao's adaptation to their environment. It would appear to have checked population increase in a region where population is dense and there is great pressure on strategic resources. A state organization can regulate internal feuding, but there are obstacles to state control in the rugged terrain where the Ifugao live. Other means of population control—or expansion of the Ifugao territory—would have to emerge in the context of state organization, for, as you are about to see, the blood feud is anathema to state organization.

LAW AND ORDER: THE STATE

It could reasonably be argued that the state ranks alongside exogamy, symbolic communication, and tool making as a major achievement of human evolution. This is not to say that the state is a good thing. It is merely a very significant thing. There are tremendous differences between state-organized societies and tribal and band societies. As an inhabitant of an industrial state, you would find that life in any state-organized society is far more familiar to you than life in a band or tribal society.

Attributes that define the state, discussed more fully in Chapter 4, will be recalled briefly here. All societies with state organization also have socioeconomic stratification, although, as the Ifugao document, the converse is not always true. Certain individuals and groups in states enjoy unimpeded access to strategic resources; others are deprived of such access. Morton Fried (1960) regards the state as a form of sociopolitical organization that has two principal functions. First, the state apparatus acts to maintain the socioeconomic contrasts within the population it governs, to preserve the stratified order. The major concerns of its rulers are defense of the idea of hierarchy, property relations, and the power of the law. We know the last two in our own society as private property and law and order.

The second principal function of the state is to maintain the entire social order for the population it rules. This function is expressed in: (1) suppression of internal disorder; control of the state's population; and (2) defense of the state against external threats. There are subsystems that guard against and suppress internal threats—police, secret services, and the FBI are examples—and those that guard against external threats—the army, the navy, and the Department of Defense are examples. Sometimes, however, the duties of the agents of internal and external order overlap, as, for example, when the National Guard, theoretically a military organization, is used to suppress domestic uprisings.

To accomplish its two major functions, the state has special-purpose subsystems that assume additional, secondary functions. There are four broad categories of these, according to Fried: census and boundary-maintenance subsystem; judicial subsystem; enforcement subsystem; and fiscal subsystem.

The state controls its population by knowing

The National Guard, agents of the military subsystem, on parade in Peru in 1964. (Paul L. Doughty)

whom it governs; it takes censuses and enumerates the population. It also establishes and maintains boundaries to demarcate its territory from that of other populations. Customs officials and coast guard, for example, are stationed at these boundaries to regulate passage from one state to another. Even in nonindustrial states, there may be boundary-maintenance forces. In Buganda the king rewarded faithful military commanders with estates in outlying provinces. These leaders and their followers who settled in such areas acted as guardians against intrusions by alien populations.

The state also controls population through administrative circumscriptions: provinces, districts, "states," counties, subcounties, parishes, and so forth. Specific officials oversee the population and territory of each of the subdivisions.

Finally, the state controls its population by establishing categories of citizenship. The principal contrast is between the citizen and the noncitizen, each of whom has different rights and obligations with respect to the state. In the United States, specific governmental agencies oversee the activities of aliens. Distinctions among the native-born population of the state are also common. In many early states, state nationals included at least three socially distinct categories of people: nobles, commoners, and slaves. The rights and obligations of each group were different. Those familiar with the history of the United States before the Emancipation Proclamation are aware that the same laws did not apply to enslaved and free people. Furthermore, in areas where European colonial rule was established, there were usually separate courts to judge disputes involving only natives and those that involved Europeans.

Among the Merina of central Madagascar, the state's laws were very clearly aimed at maintaining the social categories of the state. Merina legal codes made it a crime against the state for nobles to marry commoners or for any free people to marry slaves.

In the United States, there is no division into nobles, commoners, and slaves, but there are differences in, for example, the rights and obligations of civilians and members of the armed forces. A military code of justice and a military court system exist alongside the civil judicial hierarchy.

Fried's second broad category of secondary functions includes aspects of the judicial system. In all states there is a body of rules and precedents that tends toward codification. In other words, there are legal rules based on precedent and on proclamations of the state's legislative bodies. In states that lacked writing, laws were preserved in oral tradition. The king's chief justices or council of elders might be the officials charged with remembering the laws. An oral tradition is also true of some societies that have had writing for a long time. England is the most familiar example.

We are told in the United States that laws are made to be observed, to regulate conduct in society. Violation of the legal code constitutes a crime. Specified punishments or ranges of punishments are attached to conviction for any crime. However, as among the Ifugao, it is possible here for a given act, for example, the killing of one or more human beings, to be treated legally in different ways. Furthermore, those in the lower socioeconomic strata tend to receive more severe punishments if convicted.

To deal with crimes and disputes, all states have courts and judges. Courts exist at different levels. In the United States there are city courts, county courts, state courts, federal courts, and the Supreme Court. In certain African states there were sub-county courts, county or district courts, and finally, a court consisting of the king and his advisors. In most states, appeals are possible to higher-court officials, though often people are encouraged to resolve their disputes on the local level.

Important in the contrast between states and band or tribal societies is intervention in family matters. The state intervenes to stop blood feuds, to maintain internal order, and it has the ability to do this. Private matters enter the domain of public law, as they are subjected to the adjudication of state-appointed officials.

Decisions of judicial systems, once appeals have been exhausted, are binding. The governmental agencies charged with carrying out court decisions belong to the third of Fried's categories of secondary functions of the state: the enforcement subsystem. For crimes punished by death, executioners are needed; for confinement, jailers are needed. State officials supervise confiscation of property and collect fines.

Fried's fourth category is the fiscal subsystem. Kings, presidents, nobles, officials, and specialists of various sorts constitute a large body of non–food-producers that must be supported. Taxation supports these state officials by feeding them; but it also supports the political structure, the offices of the state itself. Kings use taxes to make state control more secure by expanding its civil and military apparatus. States also call on their subject population for labor. Forced labor has been used in different states to build public works, to maintain irrigation and drainage canal systems, to build great walls, and to erect pyramids.

The attributes just discussed, which Fried regards as a "bare but essential list," collectively define the state as a different form of society. One advantage of the state over the band or tribal society is that the blood feud is ended. Should a Yanomamo state come into existence, no longer would Yanomamo fierceness be allowed to find expression in internal raids. However, although states curb internal conflict, they are certainly not warless societies. War, a side effect of the food-producing revolution, continues, with states fighting other societies. Industrial states, in fact, carry on the most virulent forms of warfare known to humanity. Lacking world government, individual states today are like Yanomamo villages—locked in conflict they seem unable to stop. They fight over economic interests, political empires, and sometimes ideological issues—to maintain certain philosophies of government, to subdue the infidel, to stop the threat of creeping communism, to halt capitalist imperialism. People who live in nation-states enjoy little respite from war.

Other disadvantages are associated with life in states. Stratification is constant; individuals born in lower strata may have very little chance to move up socially or economically. Taxation and state labor demands often deprive members of the subject population of basic resources. In band and tribal societies, individuals typically share their labor and wealth with kin, in-laws, and fictive kin—people who mean something to them personally. In states, people often share labor and its fruits with unknown bureaucrats and rulers. The state does not mean greater freedom or greater leisure for most of its population.

In a work first published in 1877, anthropologist Lewis Henry Morgan characterized stateless society as *societas,* distinguishing it from state organization, which he called *civitas.* Morgan pointed to an important distinction in social relations between the two. In *societas* people interact daily and throughout their lives within a limited social world. They work and spend their leisure hours with their kin, in-laws, and fictive kin—people with whom they have personal relationships. Potential or actual enemies are those people who are not included within these close categories.

With the advent of *civitas,* there is a change. States promote geographical mobility, which often actively severs ties between people and the land. In Buganda, for example, kings could transfer heads of descent groups from their ancestral estates to distant villages. Some of their followers went with them. Over the years, however, descent-group members became widely dispersed throughout the state's territory. Administrative units subject to state rule—hamlets, villages, wards, towns, and cities—became significant social groups, and the importance of descent as a means of sociopolitical organization diminished. The people living in such settlements were not necessarily, or even usually, relatives or in-laws. They were neighbors, people living and working together not on the basis of kinship, marriage, or other personal associations, but because state organization had somehow placed them together. With impersonal and external, rather than personal and internal, bases for association, solidarity often waned. In contemporary industrial nations, where geographical mobility is accentuated, people identify themselves by nationality, dwelling place, occupation, political party affiliation, religion, team or club affiliation, but less usually with reference to kinship.

Despite similarities that enable us to classify states within the same sociopolitical category, all states are not equally successful in terms of effective control over their territory and their subject population. In some states, the government supervises the economic order; in others, like ours, private economic interests jockey for political power and can exercise considerable influence on governmental decisions.

There is a certain amount of truth to the popular American belief that government is strong and is continually growing stronger. Means of control used by various branches of the American government, including computers and other aspects of industrial and atomic technology, are more sophisticated than anything previous states have employed. But consider the recent past: the nineteenth century and the Wild West. Many western towns were virtually ruled by local marshals, who were more like Yanomamo headmen than law officers in some ways. And in the Appalachian Mountains in the early decades of this century, the Hatfields and McCoys engaged in a blood feud that would put the Nuer to shame.

SUMMARY

Since the nineteenth century, anthropologists have compared political organization in different kinds of societies, concerning themselves with the kinds of groups significant in the different societies, the determinants of leadership, the nature of interrelationships among groups or individuals, the reasons for disputes between individuals or groups, and the means available for resolving these disputes. Human populations representing different general evolutionary types and strategies of adaptation are contrasted to illustrate some characteristic differences in political organization.

Bands and nuclear families are characteristic social groups among foragers. Individuals, families, and bands are linked together through personal networks. There is little differential power among foragers; band leaders are merely first among equals and can employ no means of enforcing decisions. Among the Eskimos, as among foragers in general, disputes do not arise over individuals' access to strategic resources, since the means of production are open to all. Rather, most Eskimo disputes originate in cases of adultery or wife stealing. Aggrieved individuals may kill offenders, but their actions will trigger blood feuds, in which a kinsman of the victim may kill a murderer, only to face the prospect of being killed by one of the murderer's kinsmen. Although no governmental authority existed to intervene and halt such blood feuds, there were certain customary means of resolving disputes among the Eskimos.

The Yanomamo Indians of Venezuela and Brazil are tribal horticulturalists. Because of the intensity of their raiding and warlike behavior, they value aggressive male personalities. Their principal ethnographer, Napoleon Chagnon, links Yanomamo disputes to a shortage of females and demonstrates that the pattern of raiding and killing perpetuates itself through cultural mechanisms. Yanomamo sociopolitical organization includes a larger variety of significant groups: villages, localized and dispersed patrilineal descent groups, and groups of intermarrying descent groups. Descent ties provide no basis for solidarity. Differential authority is more developed among the Yanomamo than among foragers, yet village headmen, their major political figures, have no absolute power; they must lead by example and have no way of ensuring that their wishes will be followed. Divale and Harris (1976) have suggested that the Yanomamo illustrate a pattern of warfare that is widespread among tribal cultivators. They link warfare, with the male supremacist complex and female infanticide it engenders, to population control in food-producing societies, particularly horticulturalists.

The Nuer, tribal pastoralists of the Upper Nile, along with the horticultural Tiv of Nigeria, have a different kind of sociopolitical organization based on the segmentary lineage. Like the Yanomamo, they are organized into patrilineal descent groups; however, unlike the Yanomamo, Tivs' or Nuers' closest allies are their agnates. The term *segmentary* describes the organization of descent groups into segments at different genealogical levels. Nuer belong to minimal lineages, which are residential units: groups of these units constitute minor lineages; groups of minor lineages make up major lineages; groups of major lineages make up maximal lineages; and groups of maximal lineages make up clans. Although Nuer clans do not trace descent from the same ancestor, they do believe that they share a common ethnic origin separate from that of their neighbors. Among populations with segmentary descent organization, alliance is relative, depending on genealogical distance. Social solidarity is directly proportional to the closeness of common agnatic ancestry and to geographical proximity. The Nuer have disputes over murder and bodily injuries, adultery, and disposition of bridewealth in cases of divorce, but not individual access to strategic resources. If a dispute involves two agnates, other agnates will support the individual with whom they share a more recent common ancestor. Disputes may be mediated by figures who can invoke only supernatural sanctions. Again, without state organization, there is no sure way of halting blood feuds.

Like the Nuer, the Ifugao, stateless agriculturalists of the Philippines, have mediators. But unlike the Nuer and the other populations discussed here, they have differential access to strategic resources, and many of their disputes are related to the disposition of land and water. The Ifugao do not belong to descent groups; their significant social groups are villages, hamlets, and nuclear families. However, individuals reckon kinship bilaterally, and an Ifugao may rely on kin in the event of a dispute. If mediation does not succeed, a blood feud may erupt.

State organization makes private disputes a matter of public concern, subject to state authority. States, societies characterized by socioeconomic stratification, include administrative and territorial subdivisions in addition to the villages and kinship groups characteristic of the other societies examined. States maintain special-purpose subsystems; a census and boundary-maintenance subsystem that enumerates population and defines and maintains boundaries and internal subdivisions; a legal subsystem with laws and law officers to adjudicate disputes; an enforcement subsystem to ensure that laws are obeyed and penalties are carried out; and a fiscal subsystem to support the officials and special machinery of state organization.

SOURCES AND SUGGESTED READINGS

BAILEY, F. G.
1969   *Stratagems and Spoils: A Social Anthropology of Politics.* New York: Schocken. Influential work.

BALANDIER, G.
1970   *Political Anthropology.* New York: Vintage. Power, culture, and religion in comparative perspective.

BARTON, R. F.
1969   (orig. 1919). *Ifugao Law.* Berkeley: University of California Press. Classic ethnographic study of legal custom among stateless agriculturalists in the Philippines.

BOHANNAN, P., ED.
1967   *Law and Warfare: Studies in the Anthro-*

pology of Conflict. Garden City, N.Y.: Natural History Press. Good collection of articles on law, custom, conflict, and war.

BURCH, E. S., JR.
1975   *Eskimo Kinsmen: Changing Family Relationships in Northwest Alaska.* The American Ethnological Society Monograph 59. New York: West. Changes affecting Eskimo kinship since 1850; an interesting historical and ethnographic work.

CAVALLI-SFORZA, L. L., AND BODMAN, W.
1971   *The Genetics of Human Populations.* San Francisco: W. H. Freeman. Basic text; examines means of regulating population increase.

CHAGNON, N.
1968   Yanomamo Social Organization and Warfare. In *War: The Anthropology of Armed Conflict and Aggression,* ed. M. H. Fried, M. Harris, and R. F. Murphy, pp. 109–159. Garden City, N.Y.: Natural History Press. Relationship between warfare, economy, and social and political organization among horticultural Indians of Venezuela and Brazil.

1974   *Studying the Yanomamo.* New York: Holt, Rinehart & Winston. Detailed account of Chagnon's field methods; of interest to students beyond the introductory course.

1977   *Yanomamo: The Fierce People.* 2nd ed. New York: Holt, Rinehart & Winston. Account of the Yanomamo, who are more aggressive than most tribal peoples; fascinating to most beginning anthropology students.

COHEN, R., AND MIDDLETON, J., EDS.
1967   *Comparative Political Systems: Studies in the Politics of Pre-industrial Societies.* Garden City, N.Y.: Natural History Press. Political organization in different parts of the world.

COLSON, E.
1973   *Tradition and Contract: The Problem of Order.* Chicago: Aldine. Political organization and social control in comparative perspective.

DIAMOND, A. S.
1971   *Primitive Law Past and Present.* London: Methuen. Includes historical summary of known legal codes.

DIVALE, W. T., AND HARRIS, M.
1976   Population, Warfare, and the Male Supremacist Complex. *American Anthropologist* 78: 521–538. Links widespread warfare among horticulturalists to population regulation through female infanticide.

EVANS-PRITCHARD, E. E.
1940   *The Nuer: A Description of the Modes of Livelihood and Political Institutions of a Nilotic People.* Oxford: Clarendon Press. Classic field study of people with segmentary lineage organization.

FOGELSON, R. D., AND ADAMS, R. N., EDS.
1977   *The Anthropology of Power: Ethnographic Studies from Asia, Oceania, and the New World.* Forms of power illustrated through comparative ethnography.

FRIED, M. H.
1960   On the Evolution of Social Stratification and the State. In *Culture in History,* ed. S. Diamond, pp. 713–731. New York: Columbia University Press. Major contribution to the theory of state origins and development; argues against the existence of law in stateless societies.

1967   *The Evolution of Political Society: An Essay in Political Anthropology.* New York: Random House. Valuable introduction to political anthropology.

1975   *The Notion of Tribe.* Menlo Park, Calif.: Cummings. Problems with this loosely used term.

GROSS, D.
1975   Protein Capture and Cultural Development in the Amazon Basin. *American Anthropologist* 77: 526–549. Effects of relative scarcity of protein on warfare, social and political organization among Amazonian horticulturalists.

HARRIS, M.
1974   *Cows, Pigs, Wars, and Witches: The Riddles of Culture.* New York: Random House. Fascinating popular anthropology; the down-to-earth factors that affect food taboos, warfare, and other cultural features.

HARRISON, R.
1973   *Warfare.* Basic Concepts in Anthropology Series. Minneapolis: Burgess. Very brief comparative study of the anthropology of warfare.

HOEBEL, E. A.
1954   *The Law of Primitive Man.* Cambridge:

Harvard University Press. Counters Fried's view that law exists only in state-organized societies; "legal" customs of several societies discussed, case by case; unique in its field.

1968   (orig. 1954). The Eskimo: Rudimentary Law in a Primitive Anarchy. In *Studies in Social and Cultural Anthropology*, ed. J. Middleton, pp. 93–127. New York: Crowell.

KOCH, K.-F.
1974   *The Anthropology of Warfare*. An Addison-Wesley Module in Anthropology. Reading, Mass.: Addison-Wesley. Survey of different theories of warfare, with ethnographic focus on Jale of New Guinea.

MAINE, H. S.
1861   *Ancient Law*. London: J. Murray. Classic comparison of ancient and modern legal systems; a major evolutionary work of the nineteenth century.

MEGGITT, M.
1976   *Blood Is Their Argument*. Palo Alto, Calif.: Mayfield. Political and ecological dimensions of warfare among the Mae Enga, New Guinea horticulturalists.

MORGAN, L. H.
1963   (orig. 1877). *Ancient Society*. Cleveland: World Publishing. Classic treatment of social and political evolution, including private property and the state.

MURDOCK, G. P.
1967   *Ethnographic Atlas*. Pittsburgh: University of Pittsburgh Press. Compendium of comparable quantitative data on different cultures; useful for statistical testing of cross-cultural hypotheses.

POSPISIL, L.
1971   *Anthropology of Law*. New York: Harper & Row. Survey of "law" cross-culturally; viewpoint more similar to Hoebel (1954) than to Fried (1967).

SAHLINS, M. D.
1961   The Segmentary Lineage: An Organization of Predatory Expansion. *American Anthropologist* 63: 322–345. The role of the segmentary lineage as an effective means of political organization in stateless societies.

1968   *Tribesmen*. Englewood Cliffs, N.J.: Prentice-Hall. More general treatment of political organization among tribal peoples.

SERVICE, E. R.
1966   *The Hunters*. Englewood Cliffs, N.J.: Prentice-Hall. Survey of social and political organization of several contemporary or recent foraging populations.

TURNEY-HIGH, H. H.
1971   *Primitive War: Its Practice and Concepts*. 2nd ed. Columbia, S.C.: University of South Carolina Press. Basic cross-cultural survey.

Economic Systems
in Comparative Perspective

8

Economic anthropology is a subdivision of sociocultural anthropology, and its relationship to economics is similar to the one between political anthropology and political science. Anthropologists traditionally study nonindustrial societies, whereas economists concentrate on modern nations, and principally on the capitalist, or "free enterprise," systems found in the United States and western Europe, and on the managed economies found in the Soviet Union and other socialist states. It has remained for the anthropologist to broaden economics by gathering data on nonindustrial economies.

To understand economic anthropology, definitions of "economy," "economics," and "comparative economics" are needed. Anthropologists have argued for several different meanings. The ones often found to be most useful are the following: the *economy* of a population is its system of production, distribution, and consumption of material resources. *Economics* is the study of such systems. *Comparative economics* is the study of such systems in different societies. It is in this last area that anthropologists have made the greatest contribution.

To economic anthropologists of different "schools," one or the other of these two questions is viewed as paramount: (1) What are the differences and similarities in the organization of production, distribution, and consumption between different societies? Here the focus is on systems of human behavior and the organization of these systems. (2) What motivates people in different societies to produce, to distribute or exchange, and/or to consume? Here the focus is not on systems of behavior but on the individuals who participate in these systems. Motivation is a concern of psychologists, but it has also been, implicitly or explicitly, a concern of anthropologists and economists. Anthropologists, of course, are interested in culturally conditioned motivations: traditional systems of beliefs and values that orient personality formation and cause individuals to behave in different ways.

ECONOMIZING AND MAXIMIZATION

Although the relevance of motivation to economics may not be immediately clear, assumptions about motivations are basic to economic theory. In fact, the subject matter of economists is often defined as "economizing"—that is, the allocation of scarce means or resources to alternative ends or uses. What does this mean? Classical economic theory assumes that human wants are infinite and that human resources are always limited. Since means to ends are always scarce, individuals have to make choices. They must decide to what uses they will put their scarce resources—their time, labor, money, capital. Because Western economists have concentrated on capitalist systems, they have tended to assume that, when confronted with alternative ends, individuals usually choose the one that maximizes profit. In other words, the profit motive is supposed to be the principal motivation of Western people.

That individuals usually act to maximize profits was a basic assumption of the classical economists of the nineteenth century, and one that is still held by many contemporary economists in the United States. However, during the twentieth century, certain economists have come to recognize that individuals in Western societies may be motivated by many other ends—the enhancement of their prestige, for example. Anthropologists have shown that in many non-Western societies, as in our own, a variety of considerations and motivations may guide individual choices on how to use scarce resources.

Depending on the society, people may strive to maximize several things: profits, wealth, reputation, overall prestige, pleasure, social harmony. In short, their efforts in producing and exchanging material resources may be directed at many different ends. Again depending on the social context, individuals may strive to realize their personal ambitions or those of some social group to which they belong.

Alternative Ends

To illustrate some of the factors that may determine how individuals allocate their scarce resources, differences between tribal and peasant societies will be discussed. The following statements about tribal societies also apply to populations with band organization. *Peasants* are cultivators, usually using agricultural techniques, who live in nonindustrial states. Occasionally, however, peasants may use strategies of adaptation other than agriculture—less intensive cultivation, for example. In northeastern Brazil the economic activities of certain ocean fishermen revolve around fishing, but these rural Brazilians and their families share many aspects of their culture and social organization with rural cultivators living in nearby communities. They can therefore be considered peasants. Later on, they will be discussed in this context. *Peasant* also includes the small-scale rural farmers of the industrial nations of contemporary western Europe. Despite differences in their economic activities, all peasants share two things in common: (1) they live in state-organized societies; and (2) they produce food without the elaborate industrial technology—chemical fertilizers, tractors, airplane crop spraying, and so on—of modern American agribusiness. Peasants live off their own produce and sell it for profit as well.

To what ends do people in tribal and peasant societies allocate their scarce resources? In his book *Peasants* (1966), Eric Wolf points out that throughout the world people devote some of their time and energy toward building up what he calls a *subsistence fund*. In other words, they have to work to eat, to replace the calories they expend in daily activity. People must also invest their limited resources in a *replacement fund*. A hoe or plow breaks; they must invest their own time and energy or part of their capital in repairing or replacing it. People must maintain their technology. They must also replace items essential not to production but to everyday life: clothing and shelter, for example.

Both tribal peoples and peasants also have to invest in a *social fund*. They have to help their relatives, their fictive kin, their affinals, and, especially among peasants, their unrelated neighbors. In many societies it is useful to distinguish between a social fund and a *ceremonial fund*. The latter refers to expenditures of scarce resources on ceremonies or rituals. To prepare a festival honoring the ancestors, for example, requires time and often the outlay of wealth.

In state-organized societies, individuals must also allocate their time, energy, and wealth to what Wolf calls a *rent fund*. Americans think of rent as a payment, usually in money, for the use of someone else's property. To Wolf, however, *rent fund* has a wider meaning. It refers to scarce resources that a subordinate is required to render to a superordinate. In all states citizens must allocate part of their time, energy, and wealth to the controllers of resources, the agents of administration, and the wielders of power. Subordinates can be tenant farmers or sharecroppers who either pay rent or allocate a portion of their produce to the owner of the land they farm. Peasants generally have to worry not only about providing rent to landlords, but also about obligations to the state. They pay taxes in money or in kind, and often the state appropriates their time and labor for its ends. The major distinction between life in a band or tribal society and in a state (and, though to a lesser extent, a chiefdom), is the existence of the rent fund, the requirement that individuals must allocate part of their scarce resources to superordinates.

The rent fund is not simply an additional obligation for peasants; often, it becomes their primary obligation. There is no evidence that peasants enjoy better nutritional standards than people in tribal societies. Peasants' foremost and unavoidable obligation is to pay rent, and sometimes, to meet this obligation, their own subsistence needs, their intake of basic nutrients, may suffer. Demands of superordinates may divert scarce resources from the subsistence, replacement, social, and ceremonial funds.

The social and ceremonial funds may also assume new and different functions in the state. States often convert ceremonial events into occasions for gathering rent. Consider an example. Today the government of Madagascar levies a tax on every steer sacrificed in a ceremony. In the Merina state, circumcision, a ritual and social event, also became a device for collecting taxes and carrying out a census. In prestate times, circumcision had involved the boy, other members of his household, and his close relatives on his mother's and father's sides. Among the Betsileo, southern neighbors of the Merina, the ritual of circumcision affirmed kinship between the boy, usually a member of his father's group, and his maternal relatives. Traditionally, the maternal uncle was expected to swallow the foreskin. There are indications that the ritual of circumcision was similar among the early Merina. As the Merina state developed, however, the king institu-

Sharecroppers in the United States. The obligation to pay rent—wealth that passes from subordinates to superordinates—often forces poor people to neglect the subsistence and replacement funds, and prevents them from maximizing their own profits in state-organized societies. (Kenneth Murray/Nancy Palmer)

tionalized circumcision and made it a concern of the state. All boys every seventh year were circumcised. Their circumcision sponsors, similar to Western godparents, had to pay a sponsoring fee to the agents of the state. Other examples of ways in which states have modified the functions of social and ceremonial events will be examined in Chapter 13.

Thus among different societies, several factors may determine how individuals dispose of their scarce resources. Because of obligations to pay rent, peasants may be investing in ends that are not their own at all but those of the managers of the state. Motivations differ from society to society, but often individuals lack freedom of choice in allocating scarce resources.

The transplanting cycle of wet rice cultivation by the Betsileo. The collective, seasonal labor of Betsileo women is an important part of their traditional rice production. (Conrad P. Kottak)

PRODUCTION

Organization in Nonindustrial Populations

In previous chapters, certain aspects of production and some aspects of exchange systems, particularly those related to interethnic symbiosis and marriage, have already been discussed. For example, the strategies of adaptation and plant-cultivating continuum are actually based on the system of production that predominates in a particular population. Generalizing about the production systems of societies employing the same broadly defined adaptive strategy is difficult and requires detailed study of the specific environments of these societies.

Among foraging populations, cooperative hunting is rare in some, whereas in others it is frequent. The social organization of production often depends on the habits of the game exploited, whether herds or solitary animals. Gathering is often a more individualistic activity than hunting. Fishermen may be solitary, or they may fish in crews. It is also difficult to generalize about organization of production among cultivators or pastoralists. While a division of economic labor on the basis of age and sex is characteristic of all human societies, the specific tasks assigned to each sex and to individuals of different ages vary. The cultures of some horticulturalists assign a major productive role to women, and others make

male labor primary. Similarly, among pastoralists, men generally tend large animals, but in some cultural traditions milking is considered a woman's task. Tasks that are accomplished among certain cultivators by cooperative work parties consisting of relatives, age peers, and neighbors are carried out in others by smaller groups or people working individually over a longer time.

Within a given population, the organization of production may change over time. Among the Betsileo, there are two stages of cooperative labor in the cycle of wet rice cultivation: transplanting and harvesting. Both activities involve work parties, which vary in number according to the size of the field. Within these work parties, there is a marked division of labor on the basis of age and sex. The first group activity in the transplanting stage is the trampling by cattle of a flooded rice field. Young men and boys drive humped zebu cattle around and around in the plot. This mixes the earth and water into a soil of even consistency for transplanting. As the tramplers leave the plot, older men move in and with their spades break up the clumps of soil that the cattle have missed. Meanwhile, owners of the land or other adult members of their households have pulled the seedlings from the nursery bed and transported them to the field. Women then plant the seedlings in the now trampled and spaded plots. At harvest time, four to five months later, young men cut the rice on the stalk; young women transport it to a cleared area above the field; older women arrange and stack it; and old men and women stand on the stack, stomping and thus compacting it. Three days later, young men thresh the rice, beating the stalks against a rock to remove the grain. Older men beat the threshed stalks with sticks to make sure that all the grains have fallen off.

Most of the other tasks involved in Betsileo rice cultivation are accomplished by owners and members of their households. Adult males maintain and repair the irrigation and drainage systems and the earth walls that separate one plot from the next. Men also till, with spade or plow, and harrow. All noninfant members of the household help weed the rice field.

Nowadays, the Betsileo do not use cooperative labor in maintaining the hydraulic systems essential to rice cultivation. Instead, each man cleans the sections of the canals that irrigate and drain his own rice field. But in the past hydraulic work was cooperative. Irrigation systems, consisting of stone dams built across shallow parts of rivers and canals sometimes seven miles long and irrigating the rice fields of as many as thirty individuals, were originally constructed by work parties organized by political officials. Local officials also convoked male labor to repair these hydraulic systems during the year. These hydraulic systems formerly regulated by political officials can be maintained without cooperative labor in the present-day Betsileo system.

Factors of Production: Territory

Some significant contrasts between industrial and nonindustrial economies involve the factors of production. In band, tribal, and peasant societies there is a more intimate relationship between the worker and the factors of production—land, labor, technology, capital—than in industrial nations. Among foragers ties between individuals and specific areas are usually less permanent than in food-producing societies. Though bands are associated with territories, boundaries are not typically marked, and there is no way that they can be enforced. The hunter's stake in the game animal he is stalking or has hit with a poisoned arrow or spear is more important than territorial considerations—that is, where the animal finally dies. A man acquires the right to exploit the band's territory, to hunt—and a woman, to gather—by being born a member of the band or by joining it through some tie of kinship, marriage or fictive kinship. Among the !Kung, women, whose labor provides over half the diet, may have access to a tract of berry-bearing trees or some other specific area of wild vegetation. But when a woman moves from one band to another, she will acquire a new gathering area.

In tribal societies individuals also acquire rights to land and other factors of production as members of social groups and through marriage. All people born into a descent group have rights to use the estate of their group. If the adaptive strategy is horticultural, the estate includes garden and fallow land essential to shifting cultivation. By virtue of birth and membership in a local group, individuals and their spouses also acquire access to an estate where they may engage in hunting, gathering, and other, secondary economic activities. As members of a descent group, pastoralists have access to animals to start their own herds, to grazing land, to garden land, and to other factors of production.

An individualistic economic activity: camel herding in Kenya. Very arid areas, such as this part of Kenya, can support no social groups larger than extended families. Thus individual, rather than cooperative, labor is characteristic of these pastoralists. (Georg Gerster/Rapho/Photo Researchers, Inc.)

In states the factors of production are unequally distributed. Differential access to strategic resources means the existence of a rent fund. Depending on the state, several factors may be involved in the allocation and distribution of lands owned or used by peasants. In many African states land and other factors of production continue to be allocated on the basis of membership in a descent group or other local group. Often, the estate cannot be alienated, that is, pass from descent-group hands. Among the Betsileo, for example, after two centuries of life in nation-states, descent still plays a role in allocating land, although it has weakened considerably. In the past, rice fields were part of a descent-group estate to which individuals normally gained access through patrilineal ties. Today, estates in rice land are held in common by, and distributed among, members of minimal descent groups, individuals who share the same grandfather. Betsileo do have the legal right to terminate the condominium (joint holding) at any time and register their share of the rice field as private property. They may then also sell their rice field. However, Betsileo continue to discourage sale of rice fields to individuals who are not members of the owner's descent group. If Betsileo wish to sell their rice fields and still maintain good relations with their kin, they will sell them to another member of their own descent group.

Labor and Specialization

Labor is, in addition to land, a factor of production. In band, tribal, and peasant societies access to both is acquired through social position. Coworkers are kin, affinals, fictive kin, and, in peasant societies, neighbors. Mutual aid in production is merely one aspect of a continuous social relationship expressed on different occasions in ongoing social life.

Band, tribal, and peasant societies also contrast with industrial nations in terms of another factor of production—technology. In fact, it is because their technologies are simple that some anthropologists have applied the term "primitive" to certain human populations. In band and tribal societies manufacture of tools and other material items is generally regulated on the basis of age and sex. Depending on the society, women may weave and men manufacture pottery, or vice versa. Most people of a given age and sex share the technical knowledge associated with that status. If married women customarily make baskets, most married women know how to make baskets. Neither technology nor technical knowledge is specialized as it is in states. However, there are certain exceptions to this generalization.

In some tribal societies, there is specialization in local units. Among the Yanomamo, for example, certain villages specialize in the manufacture of clay pots, others in the preparation of different items. Although one might suppose that villages specialize because the raw materials from which their products are made are located near their villages, Chagnon (1977) asserts that this is not the case. Clay suitable for making Yanomamo pottery is available in all villages. People in most villages know how to make pots—but they do not do so. Chagnon relates craft specialization to the social and political environment rather than the natural environment. Trade is the first step in creating an alliance that may eventually convert enemy villages into allies. Village specialization promotes trade, which, like marriage, promotes alliance.

Among the Trobriand Islanders studied by Malinowski (1961), only two of many villages manufactured certain ceremonial items important in a regional exchange network. As with the Yanomamo, this manufacturing specialization did not appear to be related to the natural occurrence of raw materials. Rather, the existence of traditionally specialized villages was part and parcel of an exchange system known as the Kula-ring, which ultimately linked the inhabitants of several different communities and islands.

Alienation and Impersonality in Industrial Economies

What are some of the major contrasts between industrial and nonindustrial economies? It is often—and accurately—said that factory workers in the contemporary United States and western Europe, producing for sale and their employer's profit rather than for their own use, are alienated from the items they make. That is, they feel no strong pride in or personal identification with their products. Among nonindustrial populations there is no such alienation. The manufacturers, that is, the individual workers, usually see their work through from start to completion and feel pride, or at least accomplishment, in the finished item.

In nonindustrial societies, the economic relationship between coworkers is merely one aspect of the social relationship. In the industrial nation, people

In industrial societies, the relationship between workers and what they produce is usually impersonal, as in this poultry processing plant in Georgia. (Ron Sherman/ Nancy Palmer)

usually do not work with their kin and neighbors. If, however, their colleagues are also their friends, the relationship is usually founded on their common occupation rather than on a broader tie of kinship or fictive kinship.

Factory workers have impersonal relationships with what they produce and with their coworkers and employers—the last called "employer-employee relationships" in industrial nations. People sell their labor for cash. They do not give it to their relatives or other members of their personal networks as readily or as frequently as they would in tribal societies.

They do not, without remuneration, give their time and energy to fulfill an obligation to a landlord or political official, as they would in peasant societies. Even privates in the American army receive monetary compensation. In tribal societies people work for their relatives and share community goals. In some peasant societies, where people work for the state, this is also true. The goals of the factory owner, however, often seem to have little bearing on the goals of the factory worker or the consumer.

To summarize: in industrial societies the economic domain stands apart from ordinary social life. In

In contrast to the factory worker, this woman in North Carolina manufactures a product from start to finish and feels pride in her work. (Bruce Roberts/Rapho/ Photo Researchers, Inc.)

nonindustrial societies, however, the relations of production, distribution, and consumption are social relationships with economic aspects. The economy is not a separate entity; rather, it is, in the words of many anthropologists, *embedded* in the society.

THE COMPARATIVE STUDY OF DISTRIBUTION OR EXCHANGE

In addition to studying production cross-culturally, economic anthropologists have also investigated exchange or distribution systems. Economist Karl Polanyi has provided the impetus for the comparative study of exchange. Chief among the exponents of his theories have been anthropologist-economist George Dalton and anthropologist Paul Bohannan. To study exchange cross-culturally, Polanyi defined three principles orienting exchanges: *the market principle, redistribution,* and *reciprocity.* These principles may all be present in the same economy, but they will govern different kinds of transactions. However, in a specific society, one of them usually predominates. The principle of exchange usually considered to be predominant is the one that allocates the factors of production.

The Market Principle

In the industrial West the market principle is dominant. Thus in the United States, the factors of production—land, labor, natural resources, technology, and capital—are distributed by the operation of this principle. "Market exchange refers to the organizational process of purchase and sale at money price" (Dalton, 1968). When exchanges are governed by the market principle, the value of an exchangeable item is determined by the "law of supply and demand." Items enter the market to be bought and sold, their value determined by supply and demand, a variable related to such factors as inflation and summed up in such economic concepts as the gross national product (GNP). Characteristic of exchanges oriented by the market principle is bargaining—involving a kind of behavior that Po-

A Sudanese market. Occasional markets may be found in tribal societies and chiefdoms as well as in states. In states, however, the market principle allocates the factors of production and influences most exchanges. (George Rodger/ Magnum)

lanyi called "higgling-haggling." Both buyer and seller try to get their "money's worth." However, bargaining does not necessitate a verbal exchange between buyer and seller. It may merely involve "shopping around."

Redistribution

Redistribution is the major exchange mode in chiefdoms and some nonindustrial states. This principle operates when goods, services, or their equivalent move from the local level to a center. In states, the center is often a capital or regional collection point. In chiefdoms, it may be a storehouse near the chief's residence. Goods move up through a hierarchy of officials to be stored at the center. Some are consumed along the way and at the center by state or chiefly personnel and dependents. But the principle of exchange here is *re*distribution. Goods also flow out from the center, down through the hierarchy, and back to the common people. An exchange principle similar to redistribution predominates in contemporary managed economies.

Reciprocity

Reciprocity is exchange between social equals not governed by the market principle. Since it is between social equals, you would expect it to be the characteristic form of exchange in relatively egalitarian societies—foragers, cultivators, and pastoralists living in band and tribal societies that lack the office of chief.

Anthropologists Marshall Sahlins, in his books *Tribesmen* (1968) and *Stone Age Economics* (1972) and elsewhere, and Elman Service, in his book *The Hunters* (1966), have identified three degrees of reciprocity: generalized reciprocity, balanced reciprocity, and negative reciprocity. These may be considered as areas on a continuum. *Generalized reciprocity* is characteristic of exchanges between closely related individuals; in *balanced reciprocity,* social distance increases; and at *negative reciprocity,* social distance is greatest. In our own society, even though the market principle is dominant, generalized reciprocity does occur, but it is usually limited to exchanges between spouses and close relatives.

In generalized reciprocity, one party gives to the other and may expect nothing concrete or immediate in return. People view such exchanges not as economic transactions but as normal parts of a personal relationship. They often expect no immediate repayment; affection, respect, or loyalty will suffice. Good parents ultimately breed good children who will, as adults, honor their culture's conventions regarding obligations to aging parents.

Among most foraging populations, all exchanges are governed by reciprocity, usually generalized reciprocity. The cultural conventions of such populations dictate reciprocal exchanges and other forms of sharing. Richard Lee (1974) reports that among the !Kung of Botswana, South Africa, about 40 percent of the population contributed little to the food supply. Children, adolescents, and people over sixty relied on the foraging labor of other band members for their food. Generalized reciprocity also characterized exchanges between members of the working population. Lee found that despite the high proportion of dependents, the average !Kung band member needed to work about half as many hours (twelve to nineteen per week) as the average American. Nonetheless, food flowed at a constant rate into the band since different adults hunted or gathered on different days. Meat from any kill was distributed among everyone in the band. So normal is the expectation of reciprocity that most foragers lack an expression for "Thank you." To offer thanks would be considered impolite or improper, implying that a particular act of sharing—which is the keystone of egalitarian society —was unusual. Robert Dentan (1968), for example, reports for the Semai, a foraging population of central Malaysia, that expressing gratitude for meat would suggest surprise at the hunter's generosity or at his success. To paraphrase a famous line from *Love Story:* generalized reciprocity means never having to say "Thank you." (For additional discussions of reciprocity in band-organized societies, see Lee [1969] and Harris [1974].)

Balanced reciprocity governs exchanges between individuals who are more distantly related than members of the same band or household. In a tribal society, for example, a man presents a gift to someone in another village—perhaps a lineage mate, a trading partner, a brother's wife's brother, or a brother's fictive kinsman. The bestower expects something in exchange for his gift—perhaps not immediately—but the social relationship will be strained and may terminate if, ultimately, there is no return.

People in foraging and tribal societies also practice negative reciprocity. Exchange is still usually between social equals—free trade, freely entered—but it is impersonal. At this end of the continuum belongs intertribal trade, as well as exchanges between distant or hostile groups in the same tribal society. To people whose lives are mostly lived in a world of close personal relations, exchanges on the fringes are permeated with ambiguity and distrust. Trade is a form of alliance, but such alliances are tentative and as close to being purely economic as any exchanges that ever take place in tribal society. Not only do people expect to receive something in return for what they have to offer, but, as in the market-oriented economy, they are concerned with getting their money's worth. Polanyi's term "higgling-haggling" could certainly describe this behavior.

By recognizing three degrees of reciprocity, it is possible to see how negative reciprocity shades into behavior characteristic of economies oriented by the market principle. However, in reciprocity the partners to the exchange are social equals. This is the major contrast with market economies, in which exchanges are not only impersonal and characterized by a concern with getting one's money's worth, but also often involve individuals who are unequal in social status and economic position.

Ethnographers have observed exchanges characterized by negative reciprocity among many tribal populations. One of the most frequently cited examples of intertribal trade is the silent trade or barter between groups of "pygmy" foragers of the African equatorial forest and neighboring horticultural villagers. In silent trade, the potential for hostility in face-to-face economic transactions involving members of two culturally different populations is recognized. There is no personal contact involved in the exchange. A hunter leaves game, honey, and other forest products at a site. Villagers then come to collect the offering and leave horticultural produce in exchange. A bit of silent bargaining may take place in these exchanges. If one party feels that the return is not equivalent to the contributions, that party may reject it by simply leaving it at the trading site. If the other party wishes to continue the relationship, the offering will have to be augmented in time for its collection the following day.

Sahlins and Service regard their three varieties of reciprocity as quantitatively rather than qualitatively different. As people exchange with more and more distantly related individuals, they move along the continuum from generalized reciprocity toward negative reciprocity. But because the differences are in degree rather than kind, exchange relationships may shift as personal relationships change. A good example, which also illustrates the role of exchange in establishing alliances, comes from the Yanomamo. Chagnon reports that two hostile villages may initiate an alliance by beginning to engage in reciprocal exchange. The first step is exchange of products in which each of the villages specializes. The next step involves the exchange of food and hospitality, with each village inviting people of the other to a feast. By this time, intervillage exchanges have moved from the domain of negative reciprocity, in which immediate return and equivalence were characteristic, toward balanced reciprocity, in which gifts may be returned later. Certainly, it takes time to reciprocate a feast. However, there may still be bargaining in the relationship. Anyone who doubts this should see Chagnon's excellent ethnographic film *The Feast*. In it, a reluctant old man must be persuaded to bestow his dog on a man from another village as a village feast comes to an end.

Mutual feasting does not guarantee that an alliance between Yanomamo villages will last, but it represents a closer relationship than one based on intervillage trade of arrows, pots, and hammocks. The final stage in establishing an alliance between two villages comes when they begin to intermarry. As noted previously, many Yanomamo marriages result from an arrangement called sister exchange. If two men have unmarried sisters, they may exchange them, each losing a sister but gaining a wife. The notion of equivalence is involved in sister exchange: a sister is exchanged for a wife. Once the marriages have taken place, however, subsequent exchanges between brothers-in-law fall in the domain of generalized reciprocity, for a close personal relationship has been established. Chagnon's data indicate that people could fall out of alliance the way individuals in our own society fall out of love. Villages may split and stop exchanging women with groups they once married into. They continue to feast for a while and to engage in trade. Finally, one village may invite the other to what Chagnon calls a "treacherous feast," in which the hosts attack and try to kill their guests. The alliance terminated, no longer is there even negative reciprocity. Instead, there is open hostility and a state of feud.

Coexistence of Modes of Exchange

In the United States, the market principle predominates, governing the distribution of factors of production and most other exchanges, for example, those involving consumer goods. On the other hand, there is also redistribution in our society, though it is underdeveloped. We pay federal taxes to the Internal Revenue Service. Many states also levy an income tax; they maintain their coffers at the state capital. A great deal of our tax money goes to support governmental apparatus, but some of it does come back to taxpayers in the form of social services, educational funds, transit funds, and other goods and services.

There are also reciprocal exchanges in our society. Generalized reciprocity is characteristic of most exchanges between parents and children, although even here the American market mentality is strong. Evidence can be found in such newspaper columns as "Dear Abby" and "Ann Landers." For example, in the early 1970s a mother wrote "Dear Abby" to ask how much she should charge her son, a serviceman returning from Vietnam, for his room and board. Exchanges of gifts, cards, and dinner invitations are examples of American reciprocity, though usually of balanced reciprocity. Who has not heard remarks like, "Since they invited us to their daughter's wedding, when our daughter gets married, we'll have to invite them to hers"? Or, "Herman, we gave Gail Smith fifty dollars for a wedding present, and the Smiths only gave our Susan a fruit bowl. I don't think we should invite them to our dinner party next week." Such calculations, which express the overwhelming importance of market principle and profit motive in American society, would be totally out of place in a foraging band, where resources are common to all, and where sharing of the products of human labor is an essential ingredient of social life and of survival.

MONEY AND SPHERES OF EXCHANGE

Money is of such overwhelming importance in the contemporary United States that it is difficult for us to conceive of societies without it. In their attempt to ascertain what money is, some economic anthropologists have argued, plausibly, that it is not a cultural universal: there are many moneyless societies and economies.

Anthropologist Paul Bohannan (1963) has pointed out that money has several different functions. First, money may be a means of exchange—in the United States, the most common means. We don't give food to a bank teller and expect our accounts to

be credited; nor do we give the cashier a dozen roses in exchange for a sirloin steak; we do give money to the supermarket in exchange for food. Second, money may function as a standard of value—the principal standard that Americans use to evaluate relative worth. A washing machine is worth $200, not 225 chickens, 4 pigs, or 40 hours of work. Third, money functions as a means of payment. We pay money to the government, often not in exchange for anything but simply to satisfy some obligation, for example, a parking ticket.

In discussing things that seem to serve as money in different populations, we have to examine the functions they are serving. American money, like the currency of other contemporary nation-states, serves all the functions just mentioned. Paul Bohannan calls such currency *general-purpose money*. Any currency that does not serve all three functions is *special-purpose money*. Among many populations, for example, a cow can be used as a means of exchange but not as a standard of value. In some societies with the institution of progeny price, it would be ridiculous to question people about how many cattle a wife and two children are worth.

Still another complication arises in the cross-cultural study of money. Anthropologists have encountered many populations whose exchange systems are *multicentric* (organized into different categories or spheres). One of the most thoroughly analyzed examples of a multicentric economy comes from Bohannan's (1955) work among the Tiv of Nigeria. Items that Tiv exchanged were evaluated and divided into three spheres. First, items within the *subsistence sphere* were normally exchanged for one another. Included within this sphere were foods, small livestock, household utensils, some tools, and raw materials used to produce any item in this category.

The second sphere was the *prestige sphere*. Within it were slaves, cattle, bolts of large white cloth, and metal bars. The third sphere of exchangeable items was what Bohannan (1955) called the "supreme and unique category of exchange values." It included only one "item"—women.

Although the number of ranked spheres and the particular items within each one vary from society to society, multicentric economies are common in tribal societies and chiefdoms.

How do such exchange systems work? Normally, items in a given sphere are exchanged only for other items in that sphere. Bohannan calls such exchanges *conveyances*. Among the Tiv, examples would be yams for pots, an exchange within the subsistence sphere; cattle or brass rods for slaves, an exchange within the prestige sphere. Tiv believed that in the highest ranked sphere, the only appropriate exchange item for a woman was another woman. The exchange of women was not based on sister exchange, as it is among the Yanomamo, but on what appears to have been a rather elaborate system of wardship whereby men tried to obtain as many female wards as possible and to arrange marriages for them. In return, the men received wives.

With ranked spheres of exchangeable items, exchange becomes a moral problem. Whereas conveyances are considered right, proper, and normal, people try to avoid exchanging higher-sphere for lower-sphere items. Bohannan calls exchanges between spheres—for example, brass rods for food—*conversions*. Although the Tiv apparently considered conveyances to be normal and conversions abnormal, individuals who had been able to convert their subsistence goods into prestige items were very pleased with their luck in the exchange. Of course, those who had to trade prestige items for subsistence items, or women for prestige items, were sorry that circumstances had forced them to make these downward exchanges.

Although their exchange system was multicentric, the Tiv also had a general-purpose money. It was, according to Bohannan, metal bars, which were used simultaneously as a means of exchange, a standard of value, and a means of payment. However—and here is the difference between multicentric economies and our own—use of the general-purpose money was restricted to the prestige sphere. In conversions, metal rods sometimes functioned either as a means of exchange or as a standard of value, but not as both.

THE ADAPTIVE RELEVANCE OF MULTICENTRIC ECONOMIES

How does maintenance of normally distinct spheres of exchange help humans adapt to their immediate environments? Multicentric exchange systems are usually divided into at least prestige and subsistence spheres. Most exchanges are conveyances, but conversions do take place. The following discussion should demonstrate that in societies that lack banks, the higher spheres assume some of the functions that

these institutions serve in industrial nations. On the one hand, individuals may convert momentary surpluses in subsistence resources into higher categories. On the other hand, in times of need they may reconvert into subsistence. Thus in multicentric economies, as in our own, people save for a rainy day. However, the context of saving is personal, and the situations in which deposits and withdrawals take place are social and ceremonial. Consider the following ethnographic case.

One of the most famous of the institutions described by ethnographers is the *potlatch,* or blowout, of the native populations of the northern Pacific Coast of North America. Potlatching tribes included the Coast Salish of Washington and British Columbia and the Kwakiutl, who live farther north. The potlatch was generally a festive event. Assisted by other members of their communities, potlatch sponsors gave away food and blankets, pieces of copper, and other items. In return for this, they received prestige. To give a potlatch was a socially recognized means of enhancing a person's reputation, and the sponsor's prestige grew directly with the magnitude of the potlatch, the volume of goods given away in it.

The tribes on the north Pacific Coast, and especially the Kwakiutl, began to trade extensively with Europeans during the nineteenth century. There is every indication that the volume of their wealth increased while trade was going on. At the same time, Kwakiutl population size appears to have declined drastically because of European diseases. The effect of increased wealth and reduced population was to extend the prerogative of sponsoring a potlatch to a larger segment of Kwakiutl society than had been the case in the past.

Both the Salish and the Kwakiutl had multicentric economies in which it is possible to recognize a subsistence sphere and above it what may be called a sphere of wealth. Finally, the supreme sphere contained a nonmaterial item—prestige. Included in the subsistence sphere were several varieties of food. Although these tribes were hunters and gatherers, compared with such foraging populations as the !Kung, Shoshone, and Eskimos, they were more like food producers. Anthropologists usually speak of tribal or chiefdom rather than band organization when referring to these populations. For one thing, their natural environments were not marginal. In fact, they tapped a wide variety of naturally occurring resources on the land and sea. The most important foods of the Kwakiutl appear to have been salmon, herring, candlefish, and berries, and, to a lesser extent, mountain goats, seals, and porpoises (Piddocke, 1969).

Because of microenvironmental variations, there appear to have been minor differences in the types of food consumed by the Salish and the Kwakiutl. Likewise, the items included in their spheres of wealth differed. Among the Salish, blankets, shell ornaments, hide shirts, and fine baskets were wealth items. The Kwakiutl wealth sphere included slaves, canoes, dressed elk skins, blankets, and pieces of copper. Finally, among both tribes, people could convert wealth into prestige by giving away, on the occasion of the potlatch, wealth items. With European trade, increased wealth, and decreased population among the Kwakiutl during the nineteenth century, people could also convert wealth into prestige by destroying wealth items such as slaves and pieces of copper (Vayda, 1968).

Until recently, most anthropologists who described the potlatch interpreted it as an example of uneconomic, irrational, and competitive behavior — the result of a culturally inspired drive for prestige and status. The destruction of property in the potlatch was stressed to support the contention that in some societies individuals are much more interested in maximizing their prestige and social status than in preserving economically valuable resources.

Ecologically oriented anthropologists, on the other hand, have developed a different interpretation, which also applies to similar blowouts and multicentric economies elsewhere. Wayne Suttles, Stuart Piddocke, and Andrew Vayda, among others, have determined that there are significant fluctuations from year to year and from place to place in the natural resources available to the foragers on the north Pacific Coast. Salmon and herring runs up rivers, for example, are not equally abundant from year to year in a given locality. Furthermore, one village may be enjoying a good year while another village is experiencing a lean one. Later, however, the situations of the two villages may be reversed. Thus while the overall natural environment is more favorable for foraging than elsewhere, there are microenvironmental and microecological variations in time and place.

In this context, the potlatch and the multicentric economies of the Kwakiutl and Salish had adaptive value. A village enjoying an especially good year had a surplus of items in the subsistence sphere, which it could then exchange for wealth items. Among the Salish, potlatch sponsors, drawing on their own wealth and contributions from other members of their communities, gave away food and wealth to people from other communities who needed it. In return, sponsors and their communities were attributed prestige. The decision to potlatch was related to the economic situation of the community in the year the blowout was given. If there had been a surplus of subsistence items and, thereby, a build-up of wealth over several good years, it could afford a potlatch converting food and wealth into prestige.

The adaptive value of this behavior becomes clear when we consider what happened when a community that had enjoyed a good foraging period encountered a lean year. At this point, its members began to accept invitations to attend potlatches in other communities that were faring better. People in the unfortunate community would now accept wealth items and food from potlatching communities. In doing so, they lost some of the prestige they had formerly accumulated, because they became recipients rather than bestowers of gifts. Later, if the community's fortunes continued to decline, its people could exchange their wealth items for food, for example, slaves for herrings or canoes for cherries (Vayda, 1968). They hoped that in time their fortunes would be reversed, and the process of converting up could resume. Note, too, that such intercommunity exchanges, coupled with fluctuations in resources, also prevented the build-up of socioeconomic stratification, since wealth was given away and converted into a nonmaterial item — prestige — rather than being hoarded or invested to create more wealth.

Thus multicentric economies have adaptive value. Like our banks, their wealth and prestige spheres enable people to store a surplus. Multicentric economies also provide for other communities in need. As fortunes fluctuate, food is converted into wealth and prestige, wealth into prestige, prestige back into wealth and food, and wealth back into food. Potlatching linked together the local groups along the north Pacific Coast, establishing an alliance system and an interdependent relationship that in the long run had adaptive value. Potlatching and multicentric exchange had an ecological function, regardless of the motivations of the individual participants. The anthropologists who stressed prestige and status rivalry among the Kwakiutl were not wrong in doing so; they merely emphasized the motivational rather than the systemic aspect of the behavior they were describing.

The use of feasts to enhance individual and community reputations and to redistribute wealth within a population is not peculiar to the Kwakiutl and the Salish. There are numerous other ethnographic examples, particularly from tribal populations. In fact, we might accurately classify the adaptive blowout as an institution of tribal society. Among foraging populations living in marginal environments, resources are too meager to support intercommunity feasting on this level. Further along the general evolutionary continuum, in chiefdoms or states, there are more effective and permanently established means of redistributing strategic resources among local groups. There are storehouses and administrative hierarchies. In Chapter 13, some of the very different functions that blowouts or community feasts assume in nation-states will be considered.

THE FUTURE OF ECONOMIC ANTHROPOLOGY

As a result of work by Polanyi, Dalton, Bohannan, Sahlins, Service, and various ecological anthropologists, comparative understanding of exchange systems is now well established. Anthropologists know that in populations with non-Western cultural traditions, individual behavior is influenced by motivations, incentives, and considerations that may not be the same as our own. They also know that many populations lack the unitary exchange system that money makes possible in the industrial world. And they understand ways in which the institutionalized exchange systems of different societies assist populations in adapting to their environments. But despite their knowledge about the sociocultural factors that motivate people in different cultures to produce and exchange, anthropologists need research designed to establish a firmer basis for the comparative study not of motivations but of economic systems. In concluding this chapter, some of the research problems in comparative economics that have begun to engage anthropologists will be mentioned.

There are signs that future ethnographers will be more concerned with gathering quantifiable data on production, distribution, and consumption, as well as on other matters of interest to anthropologists, for example, aspects of social organization. During my own field work among the Betsileo, I became interested in their economic system and did the following

in studying production: measured rice fields and plots where the Betsileo grew their secondary crops; weighed harvests and was able to determine yields of different crops and soil types; computed the nutritional value of food produced by the Betsileo in terms of calories, protein, vitamins, and minerals; observed work patterns and obtained information on the number of personnel, their ages and sex, and the hours they worked at different tasks involved in rice cultivation. On the basis of these and other inquiries, I can make much more than an impressionistic assessment of the Betsileo system of production and its ramifications throughout the rest of their culture.

As comparable data become available from other societies, it will be possible to determine more precisely differences and similarities between human populations in terms of several questions traditionally of interest to economic anthropologists. The output of an economy in terms of calories can be measured if the caloric value of each food is known and the total yield of all foods produced is approximated. Likewise, the calorie can be used as a unit to measure energy expended in production. Some tasks are harder than others, requiring the expenditure of more energy, more calories. Field workers do have devices to measure the calories expended in different kinds of tasks. If we know how many people work for how many hours on what kinds of productive activities, we can establish the total cost, in calories, of production in a given population. With estimates of energy expended and energy produced, we can answer such questions as, What is the ratio of input to output and of labor invested to yield in different populations? Computer technology will help us in analyzing and manipulating comparative data as well as data gathered from a single society.

Such data will enable us to answer several other comparative questions. Is productive labor allocated on the basis of kinship, marriage, or other ties? How does the amount of labor contributed vary with genealogical or other social distance? What is the relative contribution of males and females, of people of different ages and statuses, to production in the different societies of our sample? By gathering quantifiable data about several !Kung bands, Lee (1974) was able to dispel two previously widespread misconceptions about foragers. First, he demonstrated that gathering—not hunting—was the mainstay of these foragers' diet. Second, he showed that foragers' work, rather than a constant fight against starvation, was much less time-consuming than, and supported at least as many dependents as, the average American's job. When quantitative data are also available on other aspects of life in populations being compared, it will be possible to pinpoint relationships among such areas as economic, social, and political organization.

Similarly, a quantitative approach will increase our knowledge of exchange systems in different societies. Ethnographers must begin to monitor exchanges in the populations they study. Answers to questions such as the following will help to resolve some of the problems raised and confirm some of the generalizations made here. What is exchanged, between whom, how often, and in what way? What is the value of the goods or services exchanged (in terms of, say, energy in calories or time required to produce)?

Finally, quantitative ethnographic research will raise and help to resolve questions about the third aspect of economy, consumption. As in most anthropological discussions of comparative economics, consumption has been neglected in this chapter in favor of production and exchange. Ethnographers are beginning to gather quantitative data on consumption of subsistence items and other resources in the societies they study. Lee's work among the !Kung corrects still another misconception about living conditions in hunting and gathering societies. Lee (1974) found that the !Kung diet, rather than being marginal, was as nutritious and adequate as that enjoyed by middle-class Americans; and that !Kung food output exceeded their minimum daily requirements (1965 calories and 60 grams of protein per person per day—given their size and level of activity) by 165 calories and 33 grams of protein. He also found evidence that the !Kung, who worked only two or three days per week, on the average, could even have increased production a bit—gathering more calories and proteins—without danger of degrading their environment. They did not do so, simply because there was no need to work harder.

Recall from Chapter 7 that Divale and Harris (1976) have linked intensity of warfare, the male supremacist complex, and female infanticide to protein shortage among the Yanomamo. If their hypothesis is to be evaluated, and if the scarcity of protein—or any other vital nutrient—is to be linked to warfare or other aspects of human behavior, then ethnographers must, like Lee, gather quantifiable data on produc-

tion and consumption. In Chapter 14 an example of collaboration between an ethnographer and a nutritionist (Gross and Underwood, 1971) that demonstrates a relationship between diet and social structure will be discussed.

An ethnographic study of production will overlap but usually not totally coincide with a study of consumption. Even if we know the total yield of all food resources in a given household, for example, we cannot be sure that all the food produced is also consumed within that household. A portion may be sold; another part may be converted into a nonsubsistence sphere; some items may end up in state coffers. Goods produced by members of household A may be consumed in household B. Ecologically oriented ethnographers have gathered information about diet by monitoring, during their field work, all food consumed by members of sample households (cf. Rappaport, 1968). Ideally, studies of production and consumption should extend over several years so that seasonal, annual, and longer-term fluctuations in yield and diet can be determined. Although there are obvious limitations to these types of studies, they are needed to confirm many of our generalizations about links between production, consumption, and other aspects of culture.

Collecting quantitative data has not traditionally been the major aim of ethnographers. Thus descriptions of particular societies, and the data that enter cross-cultural studies, have had a qualitative, often impressionistic, basis. Many of the generalizations made in this book are based on qualitative data and cannot be validated statistically at this time. Such generalizations are, however, common in ethnology, and it would be incorrect to suggest that anthropologists should wait until all the data have been collected before they dare to generalize. Because new data raise new problems for research, anthropology will never see a time when all the data have been gathered. The present suggestion is merely that anthropologists pursue new research problems and employ quantitative techniques more extensively. It is probable that, as the fruits of this new strategy are circulated and compared, a surprisingly large number of generalizations based on impressions and qualitative data will turn out to be valid. After all, people could tell the difference between a gorilla and a chimpanzee before geneticists began to measure the contrasts.

SUMMARY

Economics focuses on the economies of industrial nations; economic anthropology studies systems of production, distribution, and consumption of material resources in cross-cultural perspective. Economists commonly define economics as the science of allocating scarce means to alternative ends. Western economists often assume that in choosing alternatives, individuals strive to maximize profit — that they obey the "profit motive." However, in nonindustrial contexts, as, indeed, in our own society, people may attempt to maximize values other than individual profits. Furthermore, people often do not have free choice in allocating their scarce means.

Among populations with band and tribal organization, individuals must invest their time, energy, and wealth into funds described as subsistence, replacement, social, and ceremonial. In states there is also a rent fund: individuals must render a portion of their labor or its fruits to religious or secular authorities or to other superordinates. The rent fund often becomes primary, and subsistence may suffer. In addition, social and ceremonial obligations may serve different functions in state and tribal societies.

The adaptive strategies discussed in Chapter 3 are actually productive strategies. Among nonindustrial populations, production proceeds in a personal context; relations of production are merely aspects of continuous social relationships. A person acquires rights to strategic resources through membership in bands, descent groups, villages, and other social units, and not impersonally through purchase and sale. Labor, too, is recruited through personal ties, and the sharing of labor is merely one aspect of social relationships that are expressed in a variety of social and ceremonial contexts. Although manufacturing specialization is not as developed as it is in states, it may exist in tribal societies, serving to promote trade and alliance between groups. In nonindustrial societies there is typically a personal relationship between producer and commodity, in contrast to the alienation of labor, product, and management in industrial economies.

In addition to studying production, economic anthropologists have been concerned with description, analysis, and comparison of systems of exchange. Economist Karl Polanyi introduced a distinction between three principles of exchange — the market principle, redistribution, and reciprocity. The market principle, governing exchanges dictated by supply and demand, is the dominant principle in the United States and other industrial societies, as well as in many nonindustrial states. It involves impersonal purchase and sale, getting one's money's worth, and exchanges among social unequals; and it allocates the factors of production in industrial nations. Redistribution is the characteristic exchange mode in chiefdoms and some nonindustrial states. It is also present in the United States and in many modern nations. Goods are collected at a central place, and part of what is collected is eventually given back, or redistributed.

Reciprocity, a principle governing exchanges among social equals, is the characteristic mode of exchange in band and tribal societies. Anthropologists Marshall Sahlins and Elman Service have suggested that there are different degrees of reciprocity that ultimately shade into exchange behavior characteristic of the market principle. With generalized reciprocity, there is no immediate expectation of return. With balanced reciprocity, characteristic of exchanges involving more distantly related people, individuals expect their gifts to be returned but not immediately. Exchanges on the fringes of the social systems in band and tribal populations are governed by negative reciprocity, reminiscent of the market principle but involving social equals. There is concern about immediate return of exchanged items and getting one's money's worth. Reciprocity, redistribution, and the market principle may coexist in a society, but the primary exchange mode in any society is the one that allocates the factors of production.

Economic anthropologists distinguish between general-purpose monies — currencies that serve simultaneously as standards of value, means of exchange, and means of payment — and special purpose monies — currencies that do not assume all these functions. They have also described multicentric economies, organized into different spheres of exchange. Ranked spheres including subsistence items, wealth items, and prestige are usually characteristic of multicentric economies. Such spheres are most often found in populations with tribal organization. Multicentric economies have adaptive relevance: conversions of subsistence goods to wealth or prestige and reconversions to subsistence represent ways of saving in tribal societies. Conversions to such nonmaterial items as prestige also impede the emergence of socioeconomic stratification.

In concentrating on production and exchange, anthropologists have slighted systems of consumption. However, ecologically oriented anthropologists have recently monitored diets of sample households and other social units. With similar quantitative data on production and distribution, anthropologists are laying a basis for a statistical approach to economic anthropology, one that will make it possible to compare inputs and outputs in different societies and to confirm or invalidate some of the existing generalizations in economic anthropology and in ethnology in general.

SOURCES AND SUGGESTED READINGS

BELSHAW, C. S.
1965   *Traditional Exchange and Modern Markets*. Englewood Cliffs, N.J.: Prentice-Hall. Exchange systems in cross-cultural perspective.

BOHANNAN, P.
1955   Some Principles of Exchange and Investment among the Tiv. *American Anthropologist* 57: 60–70. A multicentric economy in Nigeria.

1963   *Social Anthropology*. New York: Holt, Rinehart & Winston. Useful statements of many central problems in economic anthropology, including multicentrism, money, and modes of exchange, contained in Chapters 13–15.

BURLING, R.
1962   Maximization Theories and the Study of Economic Anthropology. *American Anthropologist* 64: 802–821. Economic and noneconomic motivations.

CHAGNON, N.
1977   *Yanomamo: The Fierce People*. 2nd ed. New York: Holt, Rinehart & Winston. Discussion of political functions of specialization in the manufacture of trade items is especially interesting.

CLAMMER, J., ED.
1976   *The New Economic Anthropology*. New York: St. Martin's Press. Essays link economic anthropology to problems affecting Third World nations and to Marxist analysis.

CODERE, H. S.
1950   *Fighting with Property*, monograph 18. New York: American Ethnological Society. History of potlatch.

COOK, S.
1966   The Obsolete "Anti-Market" Mentality: A Critique of the Substantive Approach to Economic Anthropology. *American Anthropologist* 68: 323–345. Provocative criticism of view of economic anthropology espoused by P. Bohannan, G. Dalton, and K. Polanyi.

COOK, S., AND DISKIN, M., EDS.
1975   *Markets in Oaxaca: Essays on a Regional Peasant Economy of Mexico*. Austin: University of Texas Press. Study of contemporary peasant life; essays focus on intercommunity exchanges.

DALTON, G.
1968   (orig. 1961). Economic Theory and Primitive Society. In *Economic Anthropology: Readings in Theory and Analysis*, ed. E. E. LeClair and H. K. Schneider, pp. 143–167. New York: Holt, Rinehart & Winston. Defines the "substantive" approach in economic anthropology, and advocates concentrated study of exchange systems in different societies.

DALTON, G., ED.
1967   *Tribal and Peasant Economies*. Garden City, N.Y.: The Natural History Press. Articles on production and distribution in different societies.

1968   *Primitive, Archaic and Modern Economies: Essays of Karl Polanyi*. Garden City, N.Y.: Doubleday. Essays with considerable influence on economic anthropology, especially Polanyi's typology of modes of exchange.

DENTAN, R. K.
1968   *The Semai: A Nonviolent People of Malaya*. New York: Holt, Rinehart & Winston. These Asian foragers are just the op-

posite of the Yanomamo, and illustrate reciprocal exchange.

DIVALE, W. T., AND HARRIS, M.
1976   Population, Warfare, and the Male Supremacist Complex. *American Anthropologist* 78: 521–538. Links widespread warfare among cultivators to population regulation through female infanticide.

DRUCKER, P.
1965   *Cultures of the North Pacific Coast.* San Francisco: Chandler. Survey of the potlatching groups.

FIRTH, R., AND YAMEY, B. S., EDS.
1963   *Capital, Savings and Credit in Peasant Societies.* London: Allen. Articles discussing these institutions in varied peasant contexts.

FORMAN, S.
1970   *The Raft Fisherman: Tradition and Change in the Brazilian Peasant Economy.* Bloomington: Indiana University Press. Field study of Brazilian raft fishermen, their systems of production, and their exchanges with the outside world.

1975   *The Brazilian Peasantry.* New York: Columbia University Press. Study of economy, society, politics, and religion among Brazilian peasants; examines impediments to change.

GODELIER, M.
1972   *Rationality and Irrationality in Economics.* New York: Monthly Review Press. Not for the novice; a French "structural Marxist" anthropologist looks at economy in comparative perspective.

GROSS, D., AND UNDERWOOD, B.
1971   Technological Change and Caloric Costs: Sisal Agriculture in Northeastern Brazil. *American Anthropologist* 73: 725–740. The nutritional costs of economic development; quantitative data support a persuasive argument.

HALPERIN, R., AND DOW, J.
1976   *Peasant Livelihood: Studies in Economic Anthropology and Cultural Ecology.* New York: St. Martin's. These articles, based on ethnographic research, examine peasant economies, emphasizing Latin America.

HARRIS, M.
1974   *Cows, Pigs, Wars, and Witches: The Riddles of Culture.* New York: Random House. Good discussion of different exchange systems and general evolution.

HERSKOVITS, M. J.
1952   *Economic Anthropology.* New York: Knopf. Thorough textbook statement of one position in economic anthropology, from one of its major proponents.

LEE, R. B.
1969   (orig. 1966). !Kung Bushman Subsistence: An Input-Output Analysis. In *Environment and Cultural Behavior,* ed. A. P. Vayda, pp. 47–79. Garden City, N. Y.: The Natural History Press. Creative analysis of subsistence among these famous foragers.

1974   (orig. 1968). What Hunters Do for a Living, or, How to Make Out on Scarce Resources. In *Man in Adaptation: The Cultural Present.* 2nd ed., ed. Y. A. Cohen, pp. 87–100. Chicago: Aldine. Comparative study of foragers, highlighted by the !Kung.

MALINOWSKI, B.
1961   (orig. 1922). *Argonauts of the Western Pacific.* New York: Dutton. Classic ethnographic examination of the behavior of Trobrianders on a trading expedition; as rich in data about ritual and myth as about economic behavior.

MAUSS, M.
1954   (orig. 1925). *The Gift: Forms and Functions of Exchange in Archaic Societies.* New York: The Free Press. Uses comparative data to emphasize the positive value of giving. Influence on the theoretical work of Lévi-Strauss and generations of anthropologists, especially French.

MEILLASSOUX, C.
1964   *Anthropologie Economique des Gouro de Côte d'Ivoire.* Paris: Mouton. Classic study of the economic organization of the Gouro of the Ivory Coast.

NASH, M.
1966   *Primitive and Peasant Economic Systems.* San Francisco: Chandler. Short introduction to economic anthropology.

PIDDOCKE, S.
1969   The Potlatch System of the Southern Kwakiutl: A New Perspective. In *Environment and Cultural Behavior,* ed. A. P. Vayda, pp. 130–156. Garden City, N.Y.: The Natural History Press. Ecological interpretation of potlatching.

POLANYI, K.
1968   (orig. 1958). The Economy as Instituted Process. In *Economic Anthropology: Readings in Theory and Analysis,* ed. E. E. LeClair and H. K. Schneider, pp. 122–143. New York: Holt, Rinehart & Winston. Most comprehensive reader on economic anthropology; this article is a clear statement of Polanyi's position on the comparative study of exchange.

RAPPAPORT, R. A.
1968   *Pigs for the Ancestors: Ritual in the Ecology of a New Guinea People.* New Haven: Yale University Press. Quantitative data on production provide a sound background for this classic study.

SAHLINS, M. D.
1968   *Tribesmen.* Englewood Cliffs, N.J.: Prentice-Hall. Exchange and other issues in economic anthropology.

1972   *Stone Age Economics.* Chicago: Aldine. A major authority in economic anthropology offers a collection of his ideas, new and old.

SERVICE, E. R.
1966   *The Hunters.* Englewood Cliffs, N.J.: Prentice-Hall. Economies based on hunting and gathering.

SUTTLES, W.
1960   Affinal Ties, Subsistence and Prestige among the Coast Salish. *American Anthropologist* 62: 296–305. Innovative view of the potlatch as an adaptive institution.

VAYDA, A. P.
1968   (orig. 1961). Economic Systems in Ecological Perspective: The Case of the Northwest Coast. In *Readings in Anthropology.* 2nd ed., vol. 2, ed. M. H. Fried, pp. 172–178. New York: Crowell. Brief but persuasive attempt to interpret the potlatch in ecological terms.

VEBLEN, T.
1953   (orig. 1899). *The Theory of the Leisure Class.* New York: New American Library. The potlatch used as a comparative case to bolster argument of the importance of prestige in human motivation.

WOLF, E. R.
1966   *Peasants.* Englewood Cliffs, N.J.: Prentice-Hall. Fascinating theoretical and comparative introduction to peasants.

Religious
and Ritual Behavior

9

Before considering some of the speculations of social scientists and philosophers on the origin, nature, and functions of religion, we need a definition of religion. Anthropologist Anthony F. C. Wallace (1966) has provided an adequate one. Religion is "a kind of human behavior . . . which can be classified as belief and ritual concerned with supernatural beings, powers, and forces."

This definition has several implications. First, religion is a kind of human behavior. Religious behavior may be verbal or nonverbal. The nonverbal aspects of religious behavior can involve religious rites, religious personnel, and specific religious acts and activities. The verbal aspects of religious behavior can include beliefs, mythology, ethical standards, conceptions of the supernatural, and religious ideology. Second, religion is broad enough to apply to all populations of *Homo sapiens;* religious behavior, as described, is encountered in all human societies. Religion, then, is a cultural universal. Finally, religion is concerned with the supernatural. The supernatural is the nonordinary, the more than natural, a realm outside the everyday world, the strange, the mysterious, that which is inexplicable in ordinary terms. Supernatural beings—gods and goddesses, ghosts, and souls—are beings not of this world. Extraordinary powers and forces are those that people believe affect them, perhaps control them. Some are personal, wielded by supernatural beings. Others are impersonal; they simply exist. These powers are beyond the ordinary forces controlled by human beings. In some societies, people believe that humans can gain a measure of control over supernatural forces, that individuals can benefit from, become imbued with, or manipulate supernatural powers.

SPECULATIONS ABOUT THE ORIGIN OF RELIGION

When did religion originate? The fact that Neanderthals buried their dead and often interred objects in their graves has convinced many anthropologists that *Homo sapiens Neanderthalensis* was a religious creature concerned about the afterlife. The earliest archeological suggestion of religion dates from the Neanderthal burials. There is no way of knowing if religion predates the Neanderthal, however. Any statement about when, where, why, and how religion first arose, or about its nature, is pure speculation. Nevertheless, although such speculations are inconclusive, many reveal some of the more important functions of religious behavior. Several of these undemonstrable theories — some probable, others not — will be examined now.

Tylor, Animism, and Explanation

Sir Edward Burnett Tylor was one of the founders of the anthropology of religion. He linked the emergence of religion to attempts to comprehend events that could not be explained by daily experience. Tylor believed that our ancestors, along with contemporary nonindustrial peoples, were particularly intrigued with death, dreaming, and trance. In dreams and trances people experience a form of suspended animation; yet on waking, they recall events, people, animals, places, and things from their dream or trance.

Tylor (1873) argued that speculation among early humans about the events associated with dreams and trances led them to the notion that two entities inhabited the body, one active during the day and the other — a double or soul — active during sleep and trance states. They are in complementary distribution. Although they never meet, they are essential to one another. When the double, the soul, permanently leaves the body, the whole personality, the human being, dies. Death is thus the departure of the soul. From the Latin for soul, *anima*, Tylor named what was in his opinion the most primitive form of religion: *animism*.

Tylor also applied a unilineal evolutionary model (see Chapter 3) to his speculations about religion. Out of simple animism came "higher" religious forms: polytheism and, ultimately, monotheism. Tylor thought that religion, which he defined as the belief in spiritual beings, had been invented by hu-

mans to explain things they could not understand in terms of their experiences in the natural world. He thought that religion would diminish in importance as science encroached on its explanatory domain. To an extent, he was right. We now accept without thinking scientific explanations for events that religious doctrines explained during the nineteenth century. Yet religion persists. Why? Religion must do something more than explain the mysterious. It must, and in fact does, have other functions. Other early contributions clarified some of them.

Marett, Mana, and Animatism

Another early speculator about the origin of religion, Robert R. Marett (1909), took issue with Tylor's as-

In Belem, Brazil, a woman enters a trance as part of a festival honoring the deity Xangó. In the Afro-Brazilian cults known as *batuque* (shown here), *candomble*, and *macumba*, participants — usually women — are possessed by spirits known as "saints" (*santos*). Tylor viewed the belief in spirits, manifested in trance and spirit possession, as the earliest religion. (Jacques Jangoux)

sumption that animism was the most primitive form of religion. According to Marett, early humans and contemporary "primitives" conceived of the supernatural as a domain of raw, impersonal power, influencing them but, under certain conditions, able to be controlled. For Marett, this conceptualization of the supernatural, which he called *animatism,* was the most rudimentary form of religious conception. It was only later in human evolution that people added souls, doubles, and other spiritual beings to their theologies.

Marett's belief that animatism was the original form of religion reflected his reading of a work by British missionary Robert Codrington (1891), who had from 1864 spent twenty-four years in Melanesia, an area of the South Pacific that includes New Guinea and such smaller islands and island groups as Fiji, the New Hebrides, and the Torres Straits islands. Like the aboriginal Polynesians discussed in Chapter 6, Melanesians believed in *mana,* an impersonal force that existed in the universe and could reside in people, animals, plants, and sometimes inanimate objects. In some ways Melanesian mana was like our own notion of luck. Melanesians explained the success of individuals in their society by their possession of quantities of mana. Individuals could acquire mana in different ways. When they performed magical rites, they enlisted mana on their behalf to accomplish what they had in mind. Objects containing mana could change people's luck. A charm or trophy that had belonged to a successful

In the contemporary United States, these "Jesus freaks" use this basement as a place of worship. The behavior that expresses religious fervor may be similar (compare the Jesus freaks and the *batuque* dancer) despite differences in belief. The effervescence that often accompanies ritual comes just as easily no matter whether mana (sacred force) or spirits are believed to be causing it. (Thomas Höpker/Woodfin Camp & Assoc.)

hunter was believed to convey his mana to the next individual who possessed it. A woman might place a rock in her horticultural garden and find that yields suddenly improved dramatically. The explanation was believed to be mana, the sacred force contained in the rock.

Mana-like notions exist in several different parts of the world, though the specifics of the religious doctrines vary. The difference between Polynesian and Melanesian mana is related to the greater socioeconomic differentiation that is characteristic of many Polynesian societies. It is like the distinction between ascribed and achieved status. In Melanesia, individuals had approximately equal access to mana; one could acquire it by chance or by working harder at getting it than others. In Polynesia, mana was attached to political offices. Mana is analogous to electricity in that it can flow from one person or thing to another.

Rulers and other members of the nobility were believed to have greater concentrations of mana than ordinary people. In fact, so charged with mana were members of the royal family that contact with them was dangerous to commoners. Polynesians believed that the mana of the king flowed out of his person everywhere he walked; it could infect the ground, making it dangerous for ordinary mortals to walk in his footsteps. It could flow from his person to the containers and utensils he used in eating. Bodily contact between king and commoner was dangerous to the commoner because mana could have an effect very like electrical shock. Ordinary people simply could not support as much sacred current as royalty. Rites to purify exposed individuals were necessary.

Mana is related to the notion of taboo. Because of the mana residing there, the king's person was considered taboo. There was an injunction against contact between royalty and commoners. The concept of mana has also been found—in varied cultural expressions—in aboriginal North America, Africa, and Japan.

Although it is, of course, impossible to say whether animism or animatism was the original form of religion, Marett, like Tylor, in speculating about the origin of religion, increased our understanding of the nature of contemporary religions. Wallace incorporated the contributions of both men in his definition of religion quoted at the beginning of this chapter. Religion consists of behavior related to supernatural beings, forces, and powers. For Tylor

the supernatural world of the primitive was peopled with spiritual beings. For Marett it consisted of an impersonal force or power. In fact, both spirits and impersonal forces are found in the supernatural conceptions of most populations of the present and the recent past.

Frazer, Magic, and Religion

One of the most famous treatises on comparative religious customs and on the origin of religion is *The Golden Bough* (1911–1915), by British anthropologist Sir James Frazer. In abridged form, this monumental work has long been one of the anthropological studies most familiar to the public. Frazer denied that early humans had religion. He argued that religion evolved out of magic, that early humans first approached the supernatural through magical means. Frazer thought that magic among nonindustrial populations was analogous to the science of civilized nations. Magic was a body of techniques designed to accomplish specific aims. Included among the techniques of the magician were such things as spells, formulas, and incantations. Frazer further argued that religion was born when humans finally discovered that magic was ineffective. Instead of continuing to try to control supernatural forces through spells and formulas, humans now began to supplicate, to pray to, to cajole, and, in general, to make themselves subservient to, the supernatural.

Frazer drew a distinction—which is still accepted as valid today—between two types of magic: imitative and contagious. *Imitative magic* is based on what Frazer called the "Law of Similarity." Magicians believe that they can produce the desired effect merely by imitating it. If one wishes a person injured or dead, he or she may imitate the injury or death on an image representing the person. Sticking pins into effigies is an example of such behavior. *Contagious magic* is based on what Frazer called the "Law of Contact or Contagion." Whatever is done to a material object will affect the person who was once in contact with it. In some cases magicians use body products from their victims—their nails or hair, for example. The spell performed on the body product is believed eventually to reach the person and to work the desired result.

Frazer is important for introducing a classification of magical techniques, but most anthropologists reject his speculations about the evolution of religion out of magic. There are several reasons for this.

Aspects of magic and religion may, for example, be found in the same society, and even in the same rites. Contrary to Frazer's argument, too, magical beliefs and practices are neither simpler nor more primitive than animism or animatism.

The speculations of Tylor, Marett, and Frazer are similar in one respect: all are concerned with the role of supernatural conceptions within cognitive systems, that is, within the world views, the ideologies, of human populations. For Tylor and Marett, religious doctrines and beliefs serve to explain. The belief in souls explains what happens in sleep and after death, and how the supernatural world becomes populated. Mana, especially in Melanesia, explains differential success that people are unable or unwilling to explain in ordinary, natural terms. It places success on a supernatural level. Some individuals are less successful at hunting, warfare, gardening, or other activities not because they are lazy, stupid, or inept, but because success, like grace, comes from the supernatural world. Frazer's primitive supernaturalism, magic, is also part of the cognitive system, consisting of a body of techniques whose mastery enables individuals to accomplish specific ends.

Malinowski, Magic, Science, and Religion

Other anthropologists have discussed religious beliefs and actions in the context of human emotions. On the basis of his ethnographic field work in the Trobriand Islands, Bronislaw Malinowski (1948, 1958) addressed himself to some of the same questions that occupied Frazer. Malinowski distinguished between magic, science, and religion. He disagreed with Frazer that magic was the science of nonindustrial peoples, for Malinowski actually found science (actually technology and techniques) among the Trobriand Islanders.

Thus nonindustrial people have developed techniques that enable them to deal with everyday problems involved in making a living. But there are certain aspects of their lives over which they have no control; it is when they are confronted with these, according to Malinowski (1958), that they turn to magic.

> But however much knowledge and science help man in allowing him to obtain what he wants, they are unable completely to control chance, to eliminate accidents, to foresee the unexpected turn of natural events, or to make human handiwork reliable and adequate to all practical requirements.

Malinowski pointed out that among the Trobrianders magical activities were usually associated with sailing, a very hazardous activity. Humans have no control over winds, rough weather, or the availability of fish. In such situations they turn to magic. "Magic is to be expected and generally to be found whenever man comes to an unbridgeable gap, a hiatus in his knowledge or in his powers of practical control, and yet has to continue in his pursuit" (Malinowski, 1958).

Religion, on the other hand, "is not born out of speculation or reflection, still less out of illusion or misapprehension, but rather out of the real tragedies of human life, out of the conflict between human plans and realities" (Malinowski, 1958). Malinowski (1958) stressed religion's role in giving comfort to individuals at certain times during their lives, particularly when they faced crises. "Primitive religion is largely concerned with the sacralization of the crises of human life. Conception, birth, puberty, marriage — as well as the supreme crisis, death — all give rise to sacramental acts" (Malinowski, 1958).

Malinowski emphasized the roles of magic and religion in reducing anxiety. Magical solutions resolve anxiety that develops when events are beyond human control; religion provides a familiar way of getting through the crises of life and facing death.

Radcliffe-Brown and the Social Functions of Ritual Acts

Malinowski stressed the roles of magic and religion as means of reducing anxiety, of allaying fears, but British social anthropologist A. R. Radcliffe-Brown (1965) argued for what he considered an opposite interpretation. He asserted that rites may actually create anxiety and a sense of insecurity and danger in participants.

Radcliffe-Brown was being argumentative. In fact, there is no necessary incompatibility between his and Malinowski's interpretations; they are complementary. Different kinds of explanations may be given for the same rites in a society. For an individual raised within the cultural tradition of a particular society, performance of the rite does relieve anxiety; often, it is the socially approved means of doing so. But Radcliffe-Brown was also right. In many cases anxiety may arise *because* a rite exists. As examples, Radcliffe-Brown discussed certain ritual acts he observed in the Andaman Islands, where he did field work. The Andamanese customarily prohibit

Hopi kachina dolls, carved from cottonwood root, represent ancestral spirits. Ancestor worship, which Spencer believed to be the most elementary form of religion, is actually more characteristic of food producers with descent-group organization — like the matrilineal Hopi — than hunters and gatherers. (Robert Davis/Photo Researchers)

expectant parents from eating certain foods. They also taboo the use by others of the personal names of the expectant father and mother. The individual may be anxious about carrying out culturally required ritual actions in the culturally appropriate way.

Radcliffe-Brown's major interest was in specifying the social functions of certain rites and attitudes encountered among non-Western populations. Like Malinowski, he was more concerned with the functions of religion in society than with its origin. Because of this, both have been called *functionalists*. Malinowski was interested in the psychological functions that magic and religion serve for the individual — allaying fears and anxiety; Radcliffe-Brown was interested in the social functions of religion. For him, the social function of institutionalized behavior consisted of the part that behavior played in maintaining a stable orderly society.

Spencer and the Ancestors

For Herbert Spencer (1896), a nineteenth-century sociologist, the earliest form of religion was ancestor worship, based on the continuing emotional involvement of living individuals with their departed kin.

The major objection to this thesis is that ancestor worship is not normally associated with very simple societies. Most hunters and gatherers do not worship their human ancestors. The Australian aborigines hold ceremonies honoring totems, stipulated ancestors who are plants or animals rather than humans. Most hunters and gatherers do not even remember their ancestors more than two generations back. Ancestor worship is typically found in populations where descent groups are important. The ancestors of living members of the descent group once enjoyed access to the group's estate. One of them may be remembered as founder of that estate. Worship of the ancestors serves to reinforce the continuing solidarity of the descent group by creating a link between the world of the living and the world of the dead.

Society Worships Itself

Many of the theories on religion just discussed are psychological. They refer to attempts by humans to explain the world, to the cognitive systems of different human groups, to their techniques for accomplishing individual ends, to their emotions, and to their psychological adjustment to the external world. French sociologist Emile Durkheim argued that religion should be studied as a social rather than a psychological phenomenon. He thought that much could be learned about the origin of religion by examining the religious beliefs and practices of the most primitive contemporary human populations.

Durkheim focused on totemism, important in the religions of aboriginal Australia. He argued that since the aborigines are technologically so primitive, totemism must be the simplest form of religion. *Totems* are animals, plants, and geographical features. Members of each totemic group assert that they are descended from their totem and customarily neither kill nor eat it. This taboo may be suspended once a year, when people assemble to take part in ceremonies dedicated to their totemic animal or plant. These annual ceremonies are believed necessary for the maintenance and continued reproduction of the totemic population.

In explaining the origins of totemism, and thus of religion, Durkheim asserted that the main role of religious rites and beliefs is to affirm and thereby maintain the social solidarity of the adherents of that religion. When people worship their totem, a sacred emblem that symbolizes their common social identity, they are actually worshiping society—the moral and social order without which, according to Durkheim, individual life would be impossible. In Durkheim's argument, such a moral and social order is too abstract to be worshiped in itself, and something less abstract must be substituted. Thus the totem. In totemic rites, people come together to worship their totem, which stands for their own social unity, and in so doing, they maintain that unity that the totem symbolizes. There is, as virtually everyone who has read Durkheim points out, a certain amount of circularity in his argument.

Radcliffe-Brown (1952) attempted a modification of Durkheim's interpretation of totemism. Like Durkheim, who influenced his own anthropological approach, Radcliffe-Brown also viewed the annual ceremonies as functioning to maintain social solidarity and the social order. But his analysis is easier to grasp. Groups—subdivisions or segments of society—have different totems. The totems are animals and plants, which are part of nature. Humans are members of social groups; as such, they relate themselves to nature through their totemic association with natural species. Each group has a different totem. Groups are thereby divided as are species of

Native Australian totemism, which Durkheim viewed as religion's most elementary form. Here a man affirms his membership in a totemic group by mimicking its totem—a magpie. (American Museum of Natural History)

plants and animals. Diversity in the natural order becomes a model for specialization in the social order. Yet although totemic plants and animals occupy different niches in nature, on another level they are united because all are part of nature. In the same way, social groups are united and made solidary in the human social world. Thus the unity of the social order is preserved by symbolic association with, and imitation of, the natural order. Note that Radcliffe-Brown was again not interested in the origin of religion. He specifically avoided conjecture about the past. His concern was with ascertaining the social functions of totemism and other religious practices and beliefs. (For a similar treatment of totemism, see Lévi-Strauss, 1963).

SOCIAL CORRELATES AND FUNCTIONS OF RELIGION

State Religions

In previous chapters we have examined contrasts between state-organized and stateless societies involving kinship groups, modes of exchange, conflict resolution, and other aspects of culture. Some comparable observations can be made about religion. Many nonindustrial states have had a state religion managed by specialized and elite religious functionaries. In some nonindustrial states with writing, literate priests preserved sacred lore and texts as well as more obviously utilitarian information. In ancient Mesopotamia, priests kept records of agricultural production, exchanges, and other economic transactions. In nonindustrial states with writing, the priesthood was distinguished from the masses by virtue of its privileged access to sacred lore and, along with other members of the elite, to the skills necessary to record the history and culture of that society. Though members of the priesthood often actively engaged in promoting state religion, folk religious beliefs and rites persisted in the countryside. Ancestor worship and beliefs in sacred attributes of certain spots in the countryside might exist alongside a monotheistic or polytheistic state religion.

On many occasions and in diverse populations, state religion has served as a means of supporting the state structure. Like the other attributes of state organization, it often functioned to maintain the general social order, including socioeconomic stratification. Subjugation, subordination, and slavery could be borne more easily if the unfortunate believed, for example, that there was an afterlife that held better things in store. Citizens' belief in all-knowing, all-powerful deities certainly helps priests and other members of the elite group maintain social control.

Religious doctrines can, then, serve as ideological struts of state organization, maintaining the status quo. However, this is not true in all states, for some of them lack state religions. The Merina of Madagascar provide an instructive example. During the eighteenth and nineteenth centuries they developed a state that covered approximately 150,000 square miles and ruled over approximately 2 million people. All the attributes of state organization mentioned previously were present, but not state religion. In the early nineteenth century Protestant missionaries began to arrive in Madagascar from England. They brought writing skills and, naturally, religion to the Merina elite. Christianity was rapidly accepted by members of the Merina nobility and promulgated among its subject population. So ripe was Madagascar for a state religion that today 6 million out of a total population of more than 8 million are nominal Christians—representing one of the most successful missionary endeavors in sub-Saharan Africa. Of course, as is true in other nonindustrial states, elements of the prestate religions of Madagascar, ancestor worship and indigenous ceremonials, remain. Some of the same factors at work in Madagascar were probably involved in the rapid spread of Islam among states in West Africa.

Religion and General Evolution

Leslie White's observations about the evolution of religion in *The Evolution of Culture* (1959) relate to state religions. White argues that there is a characteristic difference between the ideologies and pantheons of non–food-producing and food-producing populations. Foragers, according to White, generally have *zoomorphic* gods—animals and plants; or they may worship natural phenomena—the sun, moon, stars. On the other hand, as humans gain greater control over their environment through food production, their greater mastery is reflected in their deities. Anthropomorphic gods appear. They are supermen and -women who control certain natural phenomena, such as thunder and lightning, soil fertility, or the earth itself. White also discusses some of the attributes of state religions. In imperial, expansive states, according to White, gods serve as sacred arms of imperialism. There are gods of war or, as was the case during a certain epoch in ancient Egypt, gods of all the universe. Throughout history, religion has been used to justify the policies of nation-states. Religious fervor inspired Christians on crusades against the infidel and led Moslems to undertake *jihads*, holy wars against non-Islamic peoples. I can remember being told as a boy that God would not let the United States lose a war.

Another general evolutionary view comes from Guy Swanson, a sociologist whose book *The Birth of the Gods* (1960) is one of the most carefully documented works on comparative religion. Swanson confirmed the hypothesis that there is a relationship between general evolutionary status and conceptualization of deities. Analyzing data from several

Type of religion (Wallace)	Contains these types of cult institutions	Religious practitioners; conception of supernatural	General evolutionary continuum
Monotheistic	E, C, S, I	priesthood; supreme being	State
Olympian	ecclesiastical (E) and C, S, I	priesthood; hierarchical pantheon with powerful high gods	Chiefdom
Communal	communal (C) and S, I	occasional, community-sponsored rituals; several major deities with some control over nature	Food-producing tribe
Shamanic	shamanic (S) individualistic (I)	part-time practitioners	Foraging band

FIGURE 9.1 Wallace's typology of religious types, cult institutions, and general evolution. Associations with areas of the general evolutionary continuum are only approximate. Communal religions, for example, are found among Australian foragers as well as tribal food-producers, where such religions are more typical.

societies, he found that there was a correlation between level of social complexity and belief in high gods. Generally, high gods, whose attributes included omnipresence, omniscience, and omnipotence, were found in complex societies and were absent in primitive groups.

Wallace (1966) and Robert N. Bellah (1972) also find evolutionary associations between social contexts and certain religious forms. In developing a general evolutionary typology of the world's religions, Wallace views a society's religion as made up of all its *cult institutions*—its rituals and the beliefs associated with them. After examining the cult institutions of several societies, Wallace proposed a fourfold typology of religions: shamanic, communal, Olympian, and monotheistic religions (see Figure 9.1).

Shamanic religions contain two types of cult institutions, individualistic and shamanic. Individualistic cults lack religious specialists; people do not need intermediaries to enter into a relationship with the supernatural. Since no existing society has individualistic cults only, Wallace views the most elementary religions as shamanic, which includes both individualistic and shamanic cult institutions. Shamans are part-time religious practitioners who serve as intermediaries between ordinary people and supernatural beings and forces. They come in a variety of forms in different societies: diviners, curers, mediums, spiritualists, astrologers, and palm readers. Wallace identified shamanic religions among Eskimos and other northern latitude hunters and gatherers and among foragers of forested regions of Africa and Asia.

Communal religions add to individualistic and shamanic cults the communal type of cult institution. In communal cults, groups of ordinary people seasonally or occasionally organize, sponsor, and/or perform community rituals. Communal cult institutions include harvest ceremonials, other seasonal rituals, and rites of passage from one social status to another, for instance, puberty and other initiation rites. Societies with communal religions also lack full-time religious specialists, but their pantheons typically consist of several major deities who are seen as controlling, at present or in the past, various aspects of nature. Communal cults manage such calendrical or cyclical religious activities as seasonal or life-crisis rites. Although communal religions are found among some foragers, for example, Australian aborigines, they are more typical of populations whose economies involve pastoralism or labor-extensive cultivation, for example, horticulturalists.

To individualistic, shamanic, and communal cults, *Olympian* religions add what Wallace calls ecclesias-

A baptismal ceremony conducted by a shaman (woman with stick). All societies have both individualistic and shamanic cult institutions. Faith healers—one form of shaman—are found in our own society. (E. Cole/Rapho/Photo Researchers, Inc.)

tical cult institutions: rituals and beliefs managed by a professional priesthood that itself is hierarchically and bureaucratically organized. Associated with Olympian religions is a pantheon that includes many powerful high gods. Wallace's fourth type of religion, *monotheism*, includes all the cult institutions of the Olympian type, but it conceptualizes the supernatural differently. In monotheism, all supernatural beings and forces are controlled by, or are alternative manifestations of, one continuously active and important supreme being. Ecclesiastical cult organization, and thus both Olympian and monotheistic religions, are associated with state organization. Olympian pantheons have been prominent in the religions of a host of nonindustrial states—the Aztecs and Incas of the New World, several sub-Saharan African kingdoms, many Asian societies, and classical Greece and Rome. Hinduism, Buddhism, Islam, Judaism, and Christianity are examples of monotheistic religions that arose with the growth and expansion of state organization.

Bellah's (1972) evolutionary classification of religions is less detailed than Wallace's for nonindustrial societies. Bellah identifies five types of religion: primitive, archaic, historic, early modern, and modern. People identify with, rather than worship, the mythical people and animals who are the spiritual entities of *primitive* religions. In rituals, people act out events associated with the mythical beings whose identities they assume. As in Wallace's individualistic cult institutions, in primitive religions, as Bellah depicts them, religious roles are unspecialized; they are fused with other social roles. Complex societies in sub-Saharan Africa, Polynesia, the native New World, and in ancient China, India, and the Near East have *archaic* religions. Archaic religions have a complex of deities, priests, and rituals involving worship and sacrifice. In some, kingship is divinized and rulers assume priestly duties. Bellah's archaic religions seem therefore to correlate with Wallace's Olympian type. Spiritual entities are becoming gods: they are viewed as actively concerned with, and sometimes as arbitrarily controlling, aspects of the natural world. In each archaic pantheon, deities are hierarchically arranged—mirroring the political and administrative structures of the chiefdoms and nonindustrial states in which they are found.

Bellah links the rise of *historic* religions to the emergence, in ancient states, of literacy and a specialized priesthood. For the first time, religious ideology rejects the natural world and focuses on an entirely different realm of reality. Historic religions retain the hierarchical structure of the archaic religions. Moreover, the supernatural world is no longer viewed as superior simply because its beings and forces are more powerful than humans. It now also becomes a plane of exalted morality to which humans can only aspire. Salvation—fusion with the supernatural—becomes the major preoccupation of historic religions. Typically, religious specialization goes even further than in archaic religions. Political figures are no longer priests, and a dual hierarchy of church and state competes for primacy in social control.

Bellah's *early modern* religions are those that emerged during and after the Protestant Reformation. The hierarchical structure of the archaic and historic religions collapses, and salvation is directly available to individuals. As in Wallace's individualistic cult institutions, individuals, regardless of their social status, have direct access to the supernatural; however, there is a different conception of the supernatural, and the role of priestly intermediaries declines.

Bellah characterizes the historic religions and the early modern religions as *world-rejecting religions*. They sharply separate the profane material world of here and now from the sacred realm. Notions of the afterlife, and of the salvation that it offers, dominate the ideologies of world-rejecting religions.

Bellah calls the religions that are now emerging in the industrial world *modern* religions. Because they are so new, their generalized characteristics are less easy to identify. These religions continue to focus on individual relationships with the supernatural, but their ideologies are diverse. The gap between sacred and profane decreases. Interaction between the self, which is emphasized, and the supernatural is their major concern.

Religion and Stability

Having examined several scholarly contributions to this study of religions, we may now summarize some of the functions that religion serves. Religious beliefs and doctrines function within cognitive systems of human populations. The supernatural doctrines of a population often provide solutions to problems and queries that cannot be solved in terms of ordinary experiences. Religious doctrines provide explanations for individual success or failure. As Malinowski contended, religion also functions to allay anxieties and fears of individuals. Yet the existence of rites and ritual prohibitions that must be performed or observed in prescribed ways itself creates insecurities and anxieties that can be allayed only through ritual observance. Common religious sentiments and ritual activity promote and maintain social solidarity and thus preserve the cohesion of society. In nation-states religion often functions to maintain a stratified social order, to discourage rebellion against, and questioning of, the social and economic order.

It is obvious that religion creates and maintains social solidarity; yet perhaps less obvious is the fact that it also creates and maintains divisions. In a population subdivided into multiple social groups on the basis of religion, there may be conflict. You are familiar with social divisions between Christians and Jews, Catholics and Protestants, in your own society. You have heard about the conflict between Protestants and Catholics in Northern Ireland, between Christians and Moslems in Lebanon, and, of course, between other religious groups in other places and at other times. Often, religious divisions are institutionalized, as they are, for example, in the different totems of the Australian aborigines.

Religion and Change

Religion plays a role in maintaining the established social order, but it can also be an instrument of change, sometimes even of revolution. Anthropologists Ralph Linton (1943) and particularly Wallace (1956, 1966, 1970) have examined such religious phenomena, which Linton called *nativistic movements* and Wallace, *revitalization movements*. Especially in times of rapid social change, religious leaders may emerge and undertake to alter or revitalize a society in some way. Jesus, for example, was one of several prophets who preached new religious doctrines while the Near East was under Roman rule. All these doctrines represented rearrangements of preexisting religious doctrines, but usually with some new overall orientation. This was a time when foreign powers ruled the land, a time of social unrest and upheaval. Jesus, of course, succeeded in inspiring a new, enduring, and major religion; his contemporaries were not so successful.

Wallace (1966) has recounted the genesis in 1799 of the Handsome Lake religion among the Iroquois Indians of New York State. Handsome Lake, the prophet and founder of the revitalization movement, was a chief of the Seneca, one of the Iroquois tribes. By the end of the eighteenth century the Iroquois had been adversely affected by their support of the French against the British during the French and Indian War. Warfare and the British victory produced a major change in the Iroquois environment. In response to expanding European colonization, the Iroquois were dispersed among several small reservations. Unable to pursue their traditional way of life, horticulture and hunting, in their ancestral homeland, they became heavy drinkers and frequently quarreled among themselves.

Handsome Lake himself had been a drunkard until he began to receive a series of visions that he and his followers believed to be from heavenly messengers. He related his visions and the supernatural messages they contained to others. The spirits had told him that unless the Iroquois changed their ways, they would eventually suffer total destruction. Handsome Lake's visions contained specific moral injunctions to be followed if destruction was to be averted, a plan for adjusting to the new moral and social order. Witchcraft, quarreling, and drinking were to be forsaken. The Iroquois were told to copy the Europeans' farming techniques, which, unlike traditional Iroquois horticulture, stressed male rather than female work in the fields. Furthermore, Handsome Lake preached that the Iroquois should abandon the communal houses and matrilineal descent groups of their ancestors in favor of more permanent marriages and residence in individual family households. The teachings of Handsome Lake formed the basis for a new church and a new religion, one that still has adherents in New York and Ontario. As a result of this revitalization movement, the Iroquois survived in a drastically modified environment and have gained a reputation among their non-Indian neighbors as sober family farmers.

Events in the life of Handsome Lake were recorded by missionaries who actually witnessed the formation of the new religion as well as by his own followers. Recalled only in myth is another Iroquois revitalization movement that, according to Wallace, took place around 1450. The name of its leader and prophet — Hiawatha — is familiar. According to myth, Hiawatha lived at a time of great social conflict, of blood feud and warfare among different Iroquois tribes. His wife and children were killed by raiders; he then took refuge in the forest and became a cannibal, preying on travelers. Like other revitalization leaders, Hiawatha underwent moral regeneration as a result of contact with a deity, an Iroquois god born to a virgin mother. Hiawatha became the spokesman of the deity and traveled from village to village attempting to establish intertribal peace. According to myth, Hiawatha was responsible for the formation of a political confederation by the formerly warring tribes, the famous League of the Iroquois. The five major tribes, whose members spoke related languages and had similar cultural traditions, thereafter settled grievances through compensation rather than the blood feud. Later, during the seventeenth and eighteenth centuries, the league provided a basis of political unity for the Iroquois in their dealings with the European invaders.

CARGO CULTS   Throughout the world, revitalization movements have arisen in response to the spread of colonialism, European domination, and a world cash economy. Such movements often appear when natives come into direct or indirect contact with citizens of industrial societies, but are deprived access to their wealth, technology and living standards. Often, revitalization movements are native attempts to *explain* European domination and wealth and to achieve similar success magically by mimicking European behavior and by manipulating symbols of the desired life style. Well-known recent examples of such revitalization movements are the several cargo cults of Melanesia. The cults take their name from their focus on cargo, European goods of the sort natives have seen unloaded from the cargo holds of ships and airplanes. Like Iroquois revitalization movements, cargo cults have often developed around charismatic prophets. As originally defined by sociologist Max Weber (1947), *charisma* describes a specific quality that sets certain individuals apart from ordinary people. Charismatic individuals are treated as if they possessed unusual and extraordinary powers and qualities, often superhuman or supernatural (cf. Worsley, 1970).

One of the earliest cargo cults developed around a charismatic prophet living on an island in the Torres Straits. Cult members came to believe that spirits of the dead would arrive in a steamer. They would bring manufactured goods for the natives and would

Cargo cult in the New Hebrides, Melanesia. Participants use magico-religious means to gain access to cargo— European goods. Here they look to the sky for airplanes bearing desired possessions. (Kal Muller/Woodfin Camp & Assoc.)

kill all whites. Around 1920 a similar cult thrived in New Guinea. Ancestors would come in a steamship bearing cargo; their skins would be white. More recent cults have replaced steamers with airplanes. In many cults, elements of European culture have been manipulated as sacred objects. The native rationale is that Europeans have wealth and therefore know the secret of cargo; they also use these objects. By mimicking the ways Europeans use or treat objects, natives hope to hit upon the secret of how to gain cargo. Thus, having observed Europeans' reverent treatment of flags and flagpoles, some cultists began to treat flagpoles as sacred objects, reinterpreting them as communication towers capable of transmitting messages from dead to living. Peter Worsley (1977) reports that even before face-to-face contact between Europeans and New Guineans of interior territory had been established, these native populations were constructing airstrips to attract cargo planes bearing canned foods, portable radios, clothing, wristwatches, and motorcycles. Near the airstrips were crude effigies of beacon towers, airplanes, and tin cans magically used to establish radio links between cult members and supernatural pilots and crews.

Often cargo cult prophets promised revitalization through an eventual reversal of relations of European domination and native subjugation. The day was near, prophets preached, when natives, aided by God, Jesus, or native ancestors, would turn the tables, when native skins would turn white and those of Europeans brown, or when Europeans would die or be destroyed. In almost all the cults the ideology of the eventual millennium blended Christian doctrine with aboriginal beliefs. Melanesian myths told of mythical ancestors shedding their skins and being transformed into powerful beings and of dead people returning to life. Missionaries who had been spreading Christian doctrine in Melanesia since late in the nineteenth century spoke of an eventual millenarian resurrection. In cargo cult ideology, masters would become slaves and slaves, masters; chiefs, commoners and common people, chiefs; the white, brown and the brown, white. The meek would inherit the earth.

Such students and interpreters of Melanesian

cargo cults as C. S. Belshaw (1972), Harris (1974), Peter Lawrence (1964), and Worsley (1970, 1977) link the emergence of cults to the interaction of native social structure and ideology with the changing environment resulting from European contact, domination, and exploitation. As stressed in previous chapters, cultural responses to environmental changes depend on the raw material at hand when the change began. In attempting to adapt to the European presence, Melanesians used native social structure and ideology — for example, compatible aspects of Christian millenarian doctrine and native beliefs were fused in cargo cult ideology. Similarly, Harris (1974) links the cults' preoccupation with cargo to obligations traditionally associated with Melanesian big men. Recall from Chapter 3 that the Kapauku *tonowi,* and Melanesian big men in general, were expected to be generous. Horticulture and other forms of Melanesian cultivation supported basically egalitarian sociopolitical structures — tribal societies rather than chiefdoms and states. People worked for big men, aiding them to amass wealth. Eventually, the big man was expected to sponsor a huge feast in which all the wealth that had been amassed would be given away. Deprived of permanent wealth necessary to support a higher living standard, the big man would, after the giveaway feast, be leveled to the norm. Big men who shirked the social obligation of generosity, who tried, in an egalitarian society, to arrogate status and reputation, were subject to severe social censure, including death.

The giveaway was the only model of appropriate behavior for wealthy people the Melanesians had. For decades they were willing to attend Europeans' missions and to work on their plantations, but eventually the fruits of their labor had to come back. That is, wealthy Europeans were expected to act like wealthy Melanesians — like big men. When Europeans refused to distribute cargo or to let natives know the secret of its production and distribution, cargo cults, predictably, emerged. Like arrogant big men, Europeans would be leveled, by death if necessary. However, natives lacked the physical means of doing what their cultural traditions said they should do, and thwarted by better armed and organized colonial forces, they resorted to magical leveling. Supernatural beings would intercede, killing or otherwise deflating the European big men and redistributing their cargo. Protestant missions taught that salvation came through hard work. Melanesians, who were only recently exposed to such a world-rejecting religion as Christianity interpreted "salvation" to mean cargo. Yet natives could plainly see that Melanesians — not Europeans — were the plantation and dock *workers,* and they had to reject the missionary explanation for success. The only possible explanation for European access to material wealth was supernatural: Europeans, not natives, knew the magical secret of cargo.

Just as religious revitalization inspired by a charismatic prophet had changed Iroquois political organization (namely, formation of the League of the Iroquois), cargo cults eventually provided Melanesian society with a model for large-scale political integration. Previously separated by geography, language, and customs, Melanesians began forming larger collectivities as members of the same cults and as followers of the same prophet. Cargo cults gave previously diverse and isolated Melanesians a basis for common interests and activities, and thus helped pave the way for the emergence of political parties and economic interest organizations. Thus although cargo cults began as magical solutions, they did eventually help Melanesians respond, in terms that Europeans could understand, to their subordinate and exploited condition.

TABOOS AND ADAPTATIONS

Some of the functions that religious beliefs and practices may serve for societies and for individuals have already been indicated. The remainder of this chapter will be concerned with religion from a different point of view, namely, what it does for humans as *biological* organisms. That is, what functions do beliefs and rituals serve in the adaptations of human populations to specific environments?

Totems and Taboos

Consider first interpretations of food taboos, important religious prohibitions in many human populations. In interpreting the totemism of the Australian aborigines, Durkheim and Radcliffe-Brown attempted to show its role in maintaining social solidarity. Might totemism also aid Australian populations in adapting to their natural environment? Noting that different social groups have taboos on killing and consuming different plants and animals, an anthropologist might investigate the possibility that such a system of taboos functions as a primitive conservation device. Might not taboos protect certain species otherwise in danger of dying out? Could not annual ceremonies during which totemic animals are killed be a means of reducing these same animal populations if their increase had been too rapid? Since, as far as I know, no one has investigated the ecological functions of totemism to test these hypotheses, it is impossible to assess the ecological relevance of Australian totemism.

The Adaptive Significance of Sacred Cattle in India

The adaptive significance of a ritual prohibition against slaughter and consumption of a certain animal is more easily demonstrable, however, in the case of India's sacred zebu cattle. Indians worship their cattle, which are protected by the Hindu doctrine known as *ahimsa*, a principle of nonviolence that forbids the killing of animals generally. Several

anthropologists, economic developers, and economists have cited this taboo as an example of the extent to which the non-Westerner is culture bound. After all, Indians are ignoring a potentially valuable economic resource because of cultural or religious traditions, when, as any American knows, beef is not only good but nourishing. The economic developers also tell us that Indians do not know how to raise proper cattle. To illustrate their contention they point to the scraggly Indian zebus that wander about in town and country. Western techniques of animal husbandry, they assert, could certainly improve the size of Indian cattle, yielding more beef and more

An Indian worshipper prostrates himself before a sacred zebu while others crawl up the steps to a shrine. The Hindu doctrine of *ahimsa*, which taboos the killing of living things, protects cattle, worshipped as sacred beings, and thus preserves a vital resource in the Indian economy. (P. R. Shinde/ Black Star)

milk. But, they lament, Indians are set in their ways. Bound by culture and tradition, they will not change.

An anthropologist could identify errors in these assumptions and thereby warn the economic developers against potentially disastrous interference in an Indian ecosystem that represents the present culmination of millenniums of specific evolution. Harris (1966, 1974) has demonstrated some of the adaptive functions of ahimsa as it applies to sacred cattle. Most Indian peasants are poor agriculturalists. They employ some of their cattle—bullocks—as draft animals to pull plows and carts. The use of cattle as cultivating machines is an essential part of the technology of traditional Indian agriculture. Thin cattle pull plows and carts well enough, yet they do not eat the peasant out of house and home. The larger animals that many European developers want Indians to breed would require more food per animal. But how could Indian peasants, whose diets are already marginal and whose land, and therefore productive potential, is limited, feed supersteers without taking food away from themselves and their families?

Furthermore, Indians collect a portion of the dung from their cattle and use it to manure their fields. Not all dung is collected, however, since Indians do not carefully superintend their cattle, but allow them to wander around the countryside during certain seasons. As they wander, the zebus deposit dung. When the rains come, some of the dung from the hillsides is swept into fields below. Cattle are thus direct and indirect fertilizing machines. India's supplies of fuel coal are very low, and slow-burning, dry cattle dung is one of India's most basic cooking and heating fuels.

Far from being economically useless, the sacred cow is, in fact, vital to the Indian ecosystem. Biologically adapted to poor pasture land and a marginal environment, the zebu provides fertilizer and fuel, is indispensable in farming, but can still be supported by the peasant. There are good ecological reasons for maintaining the religious doctrine of ahimsa. It is a sociocultural means of adaptation to the Indian environment.

Yams for the Ancestors

Another frequently cited example of economically irrational, culture-bound behavior is based on ethnographic data from Melanesia. The yam-growing horticulturalists of the Trobriand Islands customarily overproduce. At harvest time they consecrate surplus yams to the ancestors and store them in a yam

In Hinduism, the doctrine of *ahisma* protects not just sacred zebu cattle, but living things in general. Here, a devout Indian shows his faith by worshipping rats in the Rat Temple of Deshnoke, western India. (Thomas Höpker/Woodfin Camp & Assoc.)

house, where they are left to rot. Westerners have regarded this cultural practice as irrational behavior. It is obvious that gods and dead ancestors cannot eat yams. Clearly, Trobrianders overproduce because they are slaves to their cultural rules, to their religious beliefs.

But wait, says the ecologically oriented anthropologist. Might seemingly irrational production of more yams than can possibly be eaten be a means of adaptation to the environment? Long-term study would be necessary to answer this question, but on the basis of what we already know about the Trobrianders, the argument would seem to have some merit. Most years do bring good harvests to the Trobrianders, with sufficient yams for the ancestors. But islands are particularly vulnerable to environmental fluctuations such as drought and natural disasters such as typhoons. At least once every ten years a drought destroys a good portion of the normal Trobriand yam crop. In these lean years, people have only a token sacrifice to give to the gods. Yet they cannot anticipate when they plant how large a crop they are going to get. If conditions are normal, they will have a surplus for the ancestors. If not, they will slight the ancestors that year but — because they have planted so many yam gardens — still have enough yams to eat themselves. This practice, then, may be viewed as a cultural means of adaptation to minimal conditions. These conditions are present only occasionally, yet if the people gave up their overproduction of yams they would face starvation when the limiting event took place.

RITUAL AND ECOLOGY

In some cases, ritual *action* serves a function in mediating relationships between human populations and their immediate environments. This behavior will now be examined, whereas in the previous section the emphasis was on ideology. Of course, people engage in specific rituals because they hold certain beliefs. But in the following discussion the ecologically relevant results of these rituals, rather than the beliefs that underlie them, will be emphasized.

Betsileo Ceremonial

The first example comes from my field work among the Betsileo, who grow rice using cattle as draft animals. The Betsileo settlement pattern is one of dispersed hamlets and villages. Formerly, hamlets were small settlements with an average of two or three households, but over time many have grown into villages. All Betsileo settlements have ancestral tombs.

The tomb is extremely important to the Betsileo; its construction usually represents a much larger investment of capital than a house. After all, the Betsileo say, it is right to spend more on the tomb, for this is where one spends eternity. One's house, on the other hand, is a temporary residence. Betsileo have the culturally recognized right to be buried in the same tomb as any one of their eight great-grandparents. If a Betsileo woman bears children, she also has the right to be buried in her husband's tomb, and most wives are. Most Betsileo men affiliate with their father's descent group, live in his village, and are buried in the tomb of their agnates. However, throughout their lives Betsileo participate in ceremonials involving all the tombs of their ancestors, because they have potential rights to be buried in all of them.

There are several kinds of Betsileo ceremonials that focus on the tomb. Most rice is harvested in April and May. The Malagasy winter, our summer, the time of year when agricultural work is least, is the ceremonial season. The major ceremonials honor the ancestors. The Betsileo open their tombs and do one of two things: simply rewrap the corpses and bones of their ancestors in new shrouds; or remove all the corpses and bones from the tomb, dance awhile with them, and then wrap them in new shrouds and return them to their beds in the tomb. When a new tomb is constructed, ancestral remains are moved to it from one or more of the old tombs. Transfer of remains is also a winter activity.

During these ceremonials, cattle are slaughtered, and part of the meat is offered to the ancestors. The participants in the ceremonial consume the rest. After the beef has been consecrated to the ancestors, the living remove it from the ancestral altar and eat it, too.

The ceremonial slaughter of cattle evolved among the Betsileo at a time when there were no markets in Betsileo country and population was dispersed among small hamlets. It is in this context that we must seek its ecological origin. Though cattle are used for sacrifice, they still provide animal protein important in the Betsileo diet. In the past, such ceremonial events represented the only source of beef available to the Betsileo. It was not feasible to

The ceremonial opening of a Betsileo tomb, a joyous occasion of winter—witness the dancing—in which living and dead are temporarily reunited. Ancestral remains will soon be transferred from two old tombs to this new one. (Conrad P. Kottak)

slaughter and consume a whole steer in a small hamlet. There were simply too few people to eat it up. Betsileo could not buy meat in markets. They obtained meat by attending ceremonials in villages where they had ancestral connections, relations by marriage, or fictive kinship.

Betsileo also slaughter cattle in a ceremonial context when there are funerals. Again, part is dedicated to the ancestors and eventually consumed by the living. Betsileo have the right to attend funerals of neighbors, kin, relatives by marriage, and fictive kin. Because the funerary slaughter of cattle takes place throughout the year, Betsileo have access to beef and thus to necessary animal protein on a fairly constant basis.

Although deaths occur throughout the year, they tend to cluster in certain seasons, and especially from November to February, the rainy season. It is also a lean period, because the rice stored in the granary following the harvest in March or April has dwindled and, for some peasants, may be virtually exhausted. Of interest to the study of Betsileo ecology is the fact that a large number of funerals, occasions on which beef and rice are distributed ceremonially, occur at precisely that time of the year when Betsileo are hungriest. Funerals tide people through the lean season.

Related to the ceremonial slaughter of cattle at funerals is another Betsileo ceremonial. Traditionally, when a Betsileo gets sick, he or she, or a close relative, consults a curer, who normally prescribes some native medicine. If the health of the afflicted individual does not improve, and if ancestral displeasure is diagnosed as the cause of the illness, the curer may advise the household head to slaughter a steer as an offering of appeasement. To this event one invites kin, affinals, fictive kin, and neighbors. Again, sicknesses cluster in the hungry period; some may be nutritional in origin, others involve greater susceptibility to disease because of nutritional inadequacies. The ceremonial distribution of beef and rice as a response to illness is also a means of getting the Betsileo through the lean season.

Today, though Betsileo settlements are larger and there are now markets in the Betsileo homeland, the ceremonials persist. However, I am told that there are fewer big winter ceremonials now than in previous years. Naturally, any discussion of the ecological functions of Betsileo ceremonials raises the question of whether Betsileo began the ceremonials because they recognized these functions. The question is instructive. The answer is that Betsileo take part in these ceremonials to honor, commemorate, or appease their ancestors, relatives, fictive kin, affines, and neighbors. However, all Betsileo have the right to attend several ceremonials throughout the year. They choose to attend some ceremonials but not others. If a distant relative or acquaintance dies at a time of the year when granaries are full and people are eating well, they may decide not to go. On the other hand, if an equally distant relative dies during the lean period, many Betsileo, especially the poorer people, may decide that they would enjoy nothing more than a day or two of communal feasting on rice and beef, with a little Malagasy rum thrown in. Some of my Betsileo informants, usually those with small parcels of land, were veritable funeral hoppers during the lean season, activating virtually all their personal ties to attend funerals and other ritual events throughout the countryside.

Ritual Regulation of Environmental Relations

Roy Rappaport has documented another example of the ecological functions of ritual action. Rappaport conducted field work among the Tsembaga Maring of the highlands of New Guinea. In his book *Pigs for the Ancestors* (1968) and in several articles (1967, 1971), he has been concerned with the ecological significance of their ceremonial slaughter of pigs. He points out that the ritual slaughter of pigs functions within two levels of ecosystems in which Tsembaga Maring are involved: the first level is the *local ecosystem,* consisting of the Tsembaga, their territory, and its plants and animals; the second is a wider or *regional ecosystem,* consisting of the Tsembaga and other Maring groups, along with the territory and plants and animals of a wider geographical region. Rappaport focuses attention on the Maring as a human ecological population jointly participating with other, nonhuman populations in these ecosystems.

Maring ritual functioned in local and regional ecosystems in several ways. Until the Australian government brought them under control in 1962, the Maring, like the Yanomamo but with less intensity, engaged in intratribal warfare. That is, Maring groups such as the Tsembaga warred on other Maring, generally their neighbors. Usually, a period of fighting between two Maring groups ended in a truce. Occasionally, however, one group prevailed, and the other vacated its ancestral territory.

When the fighting ended, either because a truce had been established or one group had withdrawn, the group or groups remaining in ancestral territory performed a ceremonial act known as planting the rumbim plant. Associated with this was a ceremonial slaughter of all nonjuvenile pigs in the group's herd. Their meat was distributed among the allies of the group, to repay them for their aid in war. The slaughter also had a ritual dimension. The Tsembaga believed that they were killing pigs to repay their ancestors for military assistance.

But their obligations to their ancestors and allies were not fulfilled by this pig feast. When they planted the rumbim, the Tsembaga vowed to the ancestors that they would hold a *kaiko,* a larger pig festival, when the pig herd was once again sufficiently numerous. This could take as long as twenty years.

The kaiko was more a ritual period than a single feast; pigs were slaughtered ceremonially throughout the year of the kaiko. The period terminated when the people uprooted the rumbim. By doing this, they signalled that they had repaid their ancestors and their allies. They also were ready to fight again. A Maring group could not fight another group as long as the rumbim stayed in the ground. Rappaport argues that this taboo on battle until the ancestors were repaid limited the frequency of hostilities among the Maring. Thus it functioned to introduce periods of relative peace within a society that lacked state organization. Recalling the Yanomamo, we might speculate that they could benefit from such a ritual device.

This function of the taboo was significant within the regional ecosystem because it regulated interrelationships between different Maring groups. However, the local ecosystem must be examined in order to ascertain what factors determined when the kaiko was held and also to discover how the local ecosystem articulated with the regional ecosystem. In addition to the ceremonial slaughter of large numbers of pigs, the Maring also killed individual pigs when members of their group fell ill or were injured. Rappaport argues that illness and injury bring physiological and psychological stress to individuals and increase their protein needs. Afflicted individuals and members of their own and related households consumed the pork. Not only did the custom contribute to the recovery of sick individuals if their illnesses had nutritional origins, it also made available high-quality animal protein to those closest to sick people. If sufferers' diets had been inadequate, it is likely that the diets of individuals whose crops came from the same or nearby gardens were also deficient. Remember that there is an analogous custom involving cattle among the Betsileo.

The rate of increase in the pig herd was affected by ritual demands of this sort. The pig herds of healthier populations increased faster. Maring women fed the pigs substandard yams and sweet potatoes from their gardens. Pigs were allowed to roam through the village and its territory during the day; they were collected at night. As the pig herd grew, Maring found that there were simply not enough substandard crops for their pigs to eat. They were forced to take some of the crops destined for human consumption and give them to pigs, and also to plant additional plots to satisfy the dietary needs of the human population. At this point, the Maring, especially Maring women, were working for the pigs.

Another problem arose as the pig herd grew. Pigs began to invade gardens. Again they were competing with humans for food. The owner of the garden might shoot a pig that had ravaged the crops. The pig's owner might then shoot the garden owner or the garden owner's spouse or pig.

At this point disputes between inhabitants of the same village were frequent. Women were also complaining to their husbands that they had more pigs than they could handle. Horticultural labor demands had increased. It was time for the kaiko. Usually, it was the women's complaints and demands for a kaiko that led their husbands to meet to plan the festival The men issued invitations to their allies. The kaiko lasted a year. During this time, groups of allies arrived in the territory of the local group; they danced, traded, arranged marriages. They ate pork and took it home to their own local groups. Once all but the juvenile pigs had been sacrificed to the ancestors, the men uprooted the rumbim. They could now engage in war again.

You now have enough information to understand the role of the ritual cycle in regulating the relationship between humans and their environment in the larger, regional ecosystem. Once it uprooted the rumbim, the local group could occupy any territory vacated by its adversaries in the last fighting period. Planting rumbim was a way of validating a claim to a territory. Since the adversary had vacated its territory, it was unable to plant rumbim. Its members had dispersed into other local groups, where they had joined relatives and affines. By this time, they might have participated with members of their new local

groups in rumbim planting. According to Rappaport (1967), "if one of a pair of antagonistic groups is able to uproot its rumbim before its opponents can plant their rumbim, it may occupy the latter's territory." The Maring believed that the ancestors of the vanquished group, like the group itself, had left its former territory. Among the Maring, then, the ritual cycle gradually adjusted the distribution of the human population over Maring territory. Note, too, that a period of between twelve and twenty years normally intervened between the cessation of war, the planting of rumbim, and the occurrence of the kaiko. In the Maring horticultural economy, based on shifting cultivation, it took abandoned fields this same amount of time to recover their fertility. The taboo against occupying neighboring territory until the victors' kaiko had been held therefore also reflected the time necessary for the fields of the vanquished to regain their productive capacity. Thus the timing of the Maring ritual cycle was also adapted to the optimal functioning of their productive system.

The Ecological Approach

An ecological approach to the material (real world) effects of religious beliefs and ritual actions does not replace other interpretations. It simply provides an additional dimension to our understanding of religion as one domain of human behavior. By adopting this approach, anthropologists have been able to suggest new interpretations for religious beliefs and practices. The ecological approach focuses attention on the human population as a biological unit. It demands that we consider basic biological variables. It places humans in the animal kingdom and shows that many of the laws and generalizations that apply to other animals also apply to human populations. By taking a new look at many practices formerly regarded as irrational and wasteful, ecological anthropology has shown that principles of Darwinian evolution apply to the study of cultural as well as biological adaptation and evolution. Taking specific human populations as units of analysis and focusing on their local and regional ecosystems, ecological anthropologists have been able to identify sociocultural means—ritual, for example—whereby these populations have learned to adapt to their environments.

Of course, not all sociocultural traits are adaptive. However, it is possible to evaluate whether a trait is adaptive or maladaptive with reference to biological and demographic variables. If a population is dying out because of some aspect of its culturally determined behavior, that aspect of behavior can well be called maladaptive. On the other hand, many traits that anthropologists formerly called economically wasteful or irrational turn out, when subjected to closer analysis, to have specific, demonstrable, selectively determined and maintained functions in adaptation.

SUMMARY

Religion, a cultural universal, designates human belief in supernatural beings, powers, and forces, and ritual behavior associated with such belief. Speculation about the origin of religion was a dominant concern of early anthropologists. Although it is impossible to discover when, why, and how religion first appeared, the comparative studies of early anthropologists help us to understand some of the functions of religion in varied sociocultural contexts. Tylor speculated that the most rudimentary form of religion was animism, belief in souls. For Tylor, religion functioned principally to explain, and it evolved from animism through polytheism to monotheism. He believed that as science provided better explanations for things and events, religion would decrease in importance and eventually disappear. Marett disputed Tylor's contention that belief in spiritual beings was the most elementary form of religious conception. Instead, he speculated that animatism, conceptualization of the supernatural as a domain of raw, impersonal power that under certain conditions could be controlled, was more fundamental. Frazer argued that religion evolved out of magic, attempts by primitives to control the supernatural through rites and spells. Malinowski argued that magic originated as an attempt to deal with potentially hazardous situations over which humans had no control. Religion, he argued, surrounded major life crises—birth, puberty, marriage, and death—and functioned to relieve anxiety caused by transitions from one life condition to another. Another functionalist anthropologist, Radcliffe-Brown, disputed Malinowski's contention, maintaining instead that the existence of customary rites and observances actually created anxiety—anxiety that only the observance of these rites could dispel. Both Malinowski and Radcliffe-Brown were addressing themselves to the psychological contexts of religion. Eschewing individual psychology, Durkheim offered a sociological approach to the origin of religion, considering the totemism of native Australians the most elementary religious form.

Though the reasons for the origin or origins of religious behavior will never be known, anthropologists, through their comparative research, have demonstrated several of the correlates and functions of religion. Swanson, Wallace, Bellah, and others have demonstrated relationships between religious forms and general evolutionary status. Religion's role in social change, particularly through such revitalization movements as cargo cults, has been clarified.

Anthropologists have traditionally stressed functions of religion for individuals and for societies, but religious beliefs and practices also function in the adaptation of human populations to their environments. For example, ecological explanations have been offered for several food taboos, such as the taboo on slaughtering cattle for food in India.

The effects of ritual action on ecology have also been described. Among the Betsileo of Madagascar several rituals centered around tombs maintain stable relationships between a human population and its environment. Ritual involving the ceremonial slaughter of pigs among the Tsembaga Maring of New Guinea also demonstrates the function of ritual prohibitions in regulating such ecological relationships. Although ecological explanations are not the only or even necessarily the best explanations for religious behavior, they do place in comparative, evolutionary terms many practices that hitherto have been called irrational. In this way they serve to increase our respect for the diversity of human customs.

SOURCES AND SUGGESTED READINGS

BANTON, M., ED.
1966   *Anthropological Approaches to the Study of Religion.* London: Tavistock. Excellent compilation of articles.

BELLAH, R. N.
1972   Religious Evolution. In *Reader in Comparative Religion: An Anthropological Approach,* ed. W. A. Lessa and E. Z. Vogt. 3rd ed., pp. 36–50. Evolutionary-comparative approach to religion.

BELSHAW, C. S.
1972   The Significance of Modern Cults in Melanesian Development. In *Reader in Comparative Religion: An Anthropological Approach,* ed. W. A. Lessa and E. Z. Vogt. 3rd ed., pp. 523–527. New York: Harper & Row. Cargo cults and socioeconomic change in Melanesia.

BERREMAN, G. D.
1972   *Hindus of the Himalayas: Ethnography and Change.* Berkeley, Calif.: University of California Press. Epilogue to this excellent study of a Himalayan foothill village includes fascinating data on religious practitioners.

CODRINGTON, R. H.
1891   *The Melanesians: Studies in Their Anthropology and Folklore.* Oxford: Clarendon Press. Early, very rich account of tribal life and customs in the South Pacific.

DOUGLAS, M.
1966   *Purity and Danger.* Middlesex: Penguin. Influential comparative study of taboos, polluting acts, substances, etc.

DURKHEIM, E.
1961   (orig. 1912). *The Elementary Forms of the Religious Life.* New York: Collier Books. Major figure in French sociology and social anthropology tried to find the most primitive form of religion among the Australian Aborigines, and in doing so developed a sociological analysis of religion which has influenced anthropologists Radcliffe-Brown, Lévi-Strauss, and many others.

FRAZER, J. G.
1911–1915 *The Golden Bough: A Study of Magic and Religion.* 3rd ed. 2 vols. London: Macmillan. Monumental collection of data from around the world on religion, myth, magic, and other rituals. The abridged version is recommended.

FURST, P. T., ED.
1972   *Flesh of the Gods: The Ritual Use of Hallucinogens.* New York: Praeger. The role of mind-altering substances in ritual, with a focus on New World societies.

GEERTZ, C.
1960   *The Religion of Java.* New York: The Free Press. Sensitive portrayal of religion in Indonesia.

GEERTZ, C., ED.
1974   *Myth, Symbol, and Culture.* New York: W. W. Norton. Eight articles examine ritual, myth, and other forms of human expression.

GENNEP, A. L. VAN
1960   (orig. 1909). *The Rites of Passage,* translated by M. B. Vizedom and G. L. Caffee. Chicago: University of Chicago Press. Influential early comparative study.

GODELIER, M.
1975   Towards a Marxist Critique of Religion. *Dialectical Anthropology* 1: 81–85. French structural Marxist comments on the anthropology of religion.

HARNER, M. J.
1973   *Hallucinogens and Shamanism.* New York: Oxford University Press. Interesting anthropological study of ritual specialists and their use of mind-altering substances.

HARRIS, M.
1966   The Cultural Ecology of India's Sacred Cattle. *Current Anthropology* 7: 51–66. Adaptive functions of the Hindu doctrine of *ahimsa.*

1974   *Cows, Pigs, Wars, and Witches.* New York: Random House. In a readable style, Harris explains seemingly curious religious customs, including cargo cults, and taboos on eating beef by Hindus, pork by Jews and Moslems.

LAWRENCE, P.
1964   *Road Belong Cargo.* Manchester: Manchester University Press. Well-done, detailed case study.

LÉVI-STRAUSS, C.
1963   *Totemism,* translated by R. Needham.

Boston: Beacon. A structural approach, continues a line of thought originated by Radcliffe-Brown and Durkheim.

LINTON, R.

1943   Nativistic Movements. *American Anthropologist* 45: 230–240. The use of religion to forge social solidarity in times of crisis, particularly of social change.

MAIR, L.

1969   *Witchcraft*. New York: McGraw-Hill. Analysis of social contexts and functions of witchcraft and witchcraft accusations; relies heavily on African data.

MALINOWSKI, B.

1948   *Magic, Science and Religion, and Other Essays*. Boston: Beacon Press. Includes distinctions between and discussions of science, magic, and religion.

1961   (orig. 1922). *Argonauts of the Western Pacific*. New York: Dutton. Myth and ritual in sailing and on the land.

1972   (orig. 1931). The Role of Magic and Religion. In *Reader in Comparative Religion: An Anthropological Approach,* ed. W. A. Lessa and E. Z. Vogt. 3rd ed., pp. 63–72. New York: Harper & Row. Differences between functions of magic and religion.

MARETT, R. R.

1909   *The Threshold of Religion*. London: Methuen. Argues that animatism is the most primitive form of religion and examines its expression in several societies.

MARWICK, M.

1975   *Witchcraft and Sorcery*. Baltimore: Penguin. Useful comparative study.

MIDDLETON, J., ED.

1967a   *Gods and Rituals*. Garden City, N.Y.: The Natural History Press. Articles on religion by anthropologists.

1967b   *Magic, Witchcraft and Curing*. Garden City, N.Y.: The Natural History Press. Articles on sorcery, witchcraft, dreams, curing, and divination in several societies.

1967c   *Myth and Cosmos*. Garden City, N.Y.: The Natural History Press. Articles on symbolism, myth, and aspects of world view.

NORBECK, E.

1961   *Religion in Primitive Society*. New York: Harper & Row. Introduction to the anthropology of religion; discussions of

major theorists are balanced with case analysis.

RADCLIFFE-BROWN, A. R.

1964   (orig. 1922). *The Andaman Islanders*. New York: The Free Press. Field study of role of religious observances and ceremonies in maintaining social solidarity.

1965   (orig. 1952). *Structure and Function in Primitive Society*. New York: The Free Press. Includes essays on totemism and taboo.

RAPPAPORT, R. A.

1967   Ritual Regulation of Environmental Relations among a New Guinea People. *Ethnology* 6: 17–30. Ecological interpretation of ceremonial slaughter of pigs in a highland New Guinea society.

1968   *Pigs for the Ancestors: Ritual in the Ecology of a New Guinea People*. New Haven: Yale University Press. Demonstrates the role of ritual in regulation of local and regional ecosystems; also includes impressive field data on diet and work.

1971   Ritual, Sanctity and Cybernetics. *American Anthropologist* 73: 59–76. General theoretical treatment of some of the ecological and other functions of ritual and various aspects of religion.

SPENCER, H. L.

1896   (orig. 1876). *Principles of Sociology*. 3 vols. London: Williams and Norgate. This nineteenth-century sociologist includes speculations about the origin of religion.

SWANSON, G. E.

1960   *The Birth of the Gods: The Origin of Primitive Beliefs*. Ann Arbor: University of Michigan Press. Statistical approach to comparative religion; demonstrates relationship between general evolutionary type and conceptualization of high gods.

TYLOR, E. B.

1873   *Primitive Culture: Researches into the Development of Mythology, Philosophy, Religion, Language, Art, and Custom*. 2nd ed. 2 vols. London: John Murray. In the second volume of this classic, Tylor offers a minimal definition of religion as belief in spiritual beings, and examines animism in several societies.

WAGLEY, C.

1968   (orig. 1943). Tapirapé Shamanism. In

Readings in Anthropology. 2nd ed., vol. 2, ed. M. H. Fried, pp. 617–635. New York: Crowell. Case analysis of behavior of practicing shamans among an Indian tribe in interior Brazil.

WALLACE, A. F. C.
1956 Revitalization Movements. *American Anthropologist* 58: 264–281. Religious movements as means of revitalization of societies at times of social crisis.

1966 *Religion: An Anthropological View.* New York: Random House. Excellent survey of anthropological approaches to religion.

WEBER, M.
1947 *The Theory of Social and Economic Organization.* London: Hodge. Sets forth basic theoretical framework of this major figure in social science; a taut thriller.

WHITE, L. A.
1959 *The Evolution of Culture.* New York: McGraw-Hill. Relates religious conceptions to general evolutionary type of society.

WORSLEY, P.
1970 *The Trumpet Shall Sound: A Study of Cargo Cults in Melanesia.* New York: Schocken. Basic history and ethnography of these millenarian movements.

1974 (orig. 1959). Cargo Cults. In *Readings in Anthropology 75/76.* Guilford, Conn: Dushkin. Readable, brief account.

"HUMAN NATURE"
and SOCIOCULTURAL
DIVERSITY

Culture and Personality: Human Psychology in Comparative Perspective

10

The examination of cultural diversity in previous chapters has focused on kinship, marriage, economics, politics, and religion—universal principles that organize human life and activity in all societies. Differences in these systems have been linked to such sociocultural correlates as general evolutionary type and strategy of adaptation. Reasons for sociocultural variation—in kinship groups, for example—have been identified and discussed. The discussion now turns to another arena of human variation: personality. Anthropologists are interested not only in how people are organized, but also in how they, as individuals, think, feel, and act in particular situations.

Anthropology and psychology intersect in the study of culture and personality, or psychological anthropology. To understand fully the nature and implications of this research, it is necessary to define personality and describe its relationship to culture. According to anthropologist Victor Barnouw (1973), "personality is a more or less enduring organization of forces within the individual associated with a complex of fairly consistent attitudes, values, and modes of perception which account in part for the individual's consistency of behavior." In our own society and in others, the consistency of an individual's personality reveals itself in a wide variety of situations and settings—work, rest, play, creative activities, and interaction with others.

In every society, people have different personalities because, except for identical twins, all are genetically unique. Furthermore, from conception on, no two individuals, not even identical twins, encounter exactly the same environment. Freud as well as other psychologists believed that childhood experiences are critical in determining one's adult personality. The environment of childhood and of later life combines with the individual's genetic predispositions to form the psychological attributes of the adult—his or her personality phenotype—which may change further as the adult encounters new problems, situations, and experiences. Genetic predispositions are hard to identify, however, since environment always contributes to phenotype, and even in the womb the environment begins to affect the child. Many psychologists believe that certain universal psychological traits link all humans. These common characteristics are not necessarily biologically based. They may result instead from universal or nearly universal experiences after conception, for instance, birth itself, stages of physiological development, interaction with parents, siblings, and others, and experiences with light and dark, heat and cold, and wet and dry objects.

Psychological anthropologists only occasionally comment on, usually to question or disprove, the universality of certain psychological attributes. Instead, in the study of culture and personality, they pursue the traditional anthropological interest in human diversity. By considering psychological data from a wide range of societies, anthropology places personality in a wider, cross-cultural perspective. Psychological anthropology has complemented psychology by showing how, in diverse contexts, cultural and other environmental factors influence personality.

The perspective of the psychological anthropologist differs from that of both psychologists and other sociocultural anthropologists. Other anthropologists study the behavior and thought of individuals in order to build a picture of the social and cultural systems in which they participate. And many psychologists focus on individuals as individuals. Psychological anthropologists, however, study individuals both as individuals and as representatives of their culture and its significant subdivisions. Through a variety of techniques, many of them developed by or shared with psychologists, psychological anthropologists document personality variation within a given society, between social groups in the same society, and in different societies. Techniques include observing individuals' verbal and nonverbal behavior in a variety of settings, conversing at length on wide-ranging topics, administering psychological tests, analyzing dreams, and collecting life histories. Because many anthropologists accept certain psychologists' insistence that child rearing is crucial in personality formation, they have conducted studies of child training in several societies. Considering

data gathered in a host of societies, they have generalized about the cultural and other environmental factors that produce certain types of personality. Psychological anthropology, then, shares with its parent field an overarching interest in explaining cultural variation, this time with reference to how individuals think, feel, and act.

Interest in variation also leads psychological anthropologists to examine environmental reasons for personality variation within a given society. In the United States, for example, regional, ethnic, and socioeconomic variation, as well as other environmental variables, affect patterns of child rearing, individual opportunities and limitations, and thus personality formation. In relating personality to culture, anthropologists must therefore examine personality traits common to all members of the society and those associated with subdivisions of that society. They must also look at personality variation that is atypical both of society at large and its subdivisions.

EARLY CONTRIBUTIONS TO CULTURE AND PERSONALITY RESEARCH

Margaret Mead: Child Training and Sex Roles

Margaret Mead, one of the leading anthropologists of this century, is perhaps best known for her comparative studies of culture and personality in the South Sea Islands. Like many other psychological anthropologists, she has focused on enculturation during childhood and adolescence. One of her earlier works, *Coming of Age in Samoa* (1949, orig. 1928), involved a nine-month study of adolescent Samoan girls. Her goal was to compare Samoan adolescence with the stressful adolescence characteristic of American youth. Mead's hypothesis was that the psychological changes associated with puberty were not inevitable but were culturally conditioned. She found, as anticipated, that Samoan adolescence was a relatively easy period; sexual frustrations imposed in American society were absent.

Like other early culture and personality researchers, Mead relied heavily on her own impressions of the feelings and emotions of Samoan girls. Although she reported several cases of deviant individuals, Mead was more interested in the *typical* adolescent experience. She does not present use of statistical data, so that the ratio of normal to deviant

faults of research

Margaret Mead, well known for her studies of enculturation and personality formation in Oceania, visits Tepoztlan, Mexico. Studies of the peasant community by Robert Redfield and Oscar Lewis described its residents' personalities very differently. (Ken Heyman)

behavior cannot be established. In commenting on her method of culture and personality research, Mead (1949) stated that "the student of the more intangible and psychological aspects of human behavior is forced to illuminate rather than demonstrate a thesis." Different approaches to culture and personality research, including a more "scientific" one, are discussed later.

In another study, Mead examined cultural variation in personality types of men and women. *Sex and Temperament in Three Primitive Societies* (1950, orig. 1935) is a comparative study based on her field work among three different groups in New Guinea. According to Mead, Arapesh men and women act much as Americans have traditionally expected women to act—in a mild, parental, responsible way. Mundugumor men and women, on the other hand, act as she believed we expect men to act—fiercely and aggressively. Finally, Tchambuli males suggested to Mead an American female stereotype—they were catty, wore curls, and went shopping—whereas Tchambuli women were energetic and managerial and placed less emphasis on personal adornment than did the men (see also Chapter 11).

Ruth Benedict: Cultures as Individuals

Like Mead's contributions, Ruth Benedict's widely read *Patterns of Culture* (1959, orig. 1934) influenced much subsequent research on culture and personality. Unlike Mead's work, this study drew on published materials rather than personal field ex-

periences. Benedict contrasted what she perceived as broadly different cultural orientations among the Dobu of the Pacific, the Kwakiutl of the Northwest Coast of North America, and the Zuñi of the American Southwest. Her descriptions of the Zuñi and the Kwakiutl have proved the most provocative. The Kwakiutl, whose potlatch system was described in Chapter 8, are atypical foragers. They inhabit a relatively rich environment and possess tribal or chiefdom rather than band organization. The Zuñi, tribal agriculturalists, are one of the Pueblo groups of the American Southwest.

Benedict saw entire cultures as integrated by one or two dominant psychological themes, and she proposed that cultures, in this case the Zuñi and the Kwakiutl, might be labeled in terms of these psychological attributes. *Dionysian* describes the psychological character of the Kwakiutl and most other Native American cultures, and *Apollonian* describes the Zuñi and other Pueblo groups. Benedict took these labels from *The Birth of Tragedy,* the study of Greek drama by the German philosopher Friedrich Nietzsche. She portrayed the Kwakiutl as constantly striving to escape the ordinary limitations of existence, to achieve excess, which would allow them to break into another order of experience. Given these strivings, Dionysians valued drunkenness, the use of drugs, fasting and self-torture, and frenzy and other forms of religious intoxication. The Apollonian Zuñi, on the other hand, were described as noncompetitive and retiring, gentle and peace-loving. Benedict found Dionysian traits, including strife and factionalism, painful ceremonials, and disruptive psychological states, to be absent among them. Instead, the Zuñi preferred a middle-of-the-road existence and distrusted drunkenness and other forms of excess.

The type of approach used by Benedict in her study of culture has been termed *configurationalism*. In Benedict's view, cultures were integrated wholes; each was uniquely different, and cross-cultural comparison was less feasible than the demonstration of a particular culture's unique patterning. She represents perhaps the most extreme position of cultural relativism, which asserts that particular cultures are comprehensible only in their own terms. Her descriptions of the Northwest Coast and the Pueblos have been disputed by several authorities, who point out that she ignored more cooperative and amiable aspects of Kwakiutl life, while overlooking evidence of factionalism, strife, suicide, painful whipping ceremonies, and actual incidences of alcoholism among the Zuñi and other Pueblo peoples. Others have very aptly criticized Benedict for her "shreds and patches" characterization of most Native Americans. In exempting only the Pueblos from the Dionysian category she ignored considerable cultural variation in the Americas. In ironic contrast to what the title of her work purports, only the Kwakiutl and Zuñi were treated as integral wholes. The behavior of other groups could be ripped from its cultural fabric and used to bolster the Dionysian stereotype. Benedict's use of individual psychologistic labels to characterize whole cultures influenced, in particular, later descriptions of national character.

National Character

Studies of national character enjoyed considerable popularity in the United States during World War II and through the early 1950s. Those conducted by anthropologists Benedict, Mead, and Geoffrey Gorer used only a small number of informants to generalize about shared personality traits of entire nations. During World War II several anthropologists involved in the war effort attempted to provide clues to the personality structure and patterns of customary response of the Japanese people. Naturally, due to the war, these were studies of culture at a distance. Some techniques used were interviewing Japanese living in the United States or other areas outside

their homeland, viewing Japanese films, and reading Japanese books, magazines, and historical works.

Since their aim was to describe *common* behavior patterns and personality traits, the anthropologists engaged in national character research often ignored significant variation in personality and behavior. They relied on the assumption that each individual samples, to an extent at least, groupwide patterns. Examination of individuals could therefore contribute to the composite pattern insofar as differences attributable to special status and peculiarity of experience were taken into account.

Some conflicting notions of culture have emerged in the debate over the value of national character studies: Should culture be viewed as a more or less autonomous force that influences individual personality and behavior patterns? Or should a culture be described by observing the behavior of numerous individuals, with their variations in socioeconomic status and differences in life experiences? The national character researchers never drew a sample that could satisfactorily encapsulate the entire range of variation in a complex nation.

Freud's influence is also apparent in many national character studies. The most famous example involves a proposed relationship between severe early toilet training and a compulsive Japanese personality preoccupied with ritual, order, and cleanliness. According to Gorer (1943), toilet training and the compulsion it engendered led to aggressive feelings that expressed themselves in warfare. Other anthropologists concurred with Gorer. Weston LeBarre (1945), for example, found the Japanese to be the most compulsive people in the world and linked this to sphincter control. In *The Chrysanthemum and the Sword* (1946), Benedict also accepted the toilet-training hypothesis. Subsequent research on Japanese both in Japan and elsewhere questions this compulsive stereotype. In fact, many researchers have found that toilet training is less of a preoccupation among Japanese than among Americans.

Under the auspices of a program known as Columbia University Research in Contemporary Culture, Gorer and Rickman produced *The People of Great Russia* (1949), a study of Russian national character. Gorer subsequently defended a much vilified hypothesis proposed in this book linking certain aspects of Russian national character and events in twentieth-century Russian history to the restrictive swaddling of Russian infants. He associated an alleged manic-depressive Russian personality struc-

APOLLONIAN

Interactions between adults and children vary widely from culture to culture. In American public schools there is usually more social distance between student and teacher — one more expression of the impersonality that often accompanies industrialism — than in the Turkish classroom shown here. A student kisses her teacher's hand in greeting. (© Louis Goldman/Rapho/Photo Researchers)

sonality school, would write in a professional report that "the Betsimisaraka are stupid and lazy, and insolent unless kept in check. . . . The Tsimahety are moderately straightforward and courageous, and are courteous to whites, but indifferent. . . . The Sakalava are by far the bravest of the Madagascar tribes, and are also fairly intelligent." If it is this difficult to maintain scholarly objectivity in ethnographic research in a strange land, how much more difficult it is to balance a description of enemy nations. This reveals one of the basic flaws in national character studies.

Basic Personality Structure

The idea of *basic personality structure* was first proposed in 1936 by the psychoanalyst Abram Kardiner. He conducted a series of culture and personality seminars in which participating anthropologists gave reports, generally on their own ethnographic field work. After this, Kardiner provided psychoanalytic interpretations, which were then discussed by the seminar.

Kardiner's work is dominated by a theoretical framework that is probably more useful than those of other early contributors to culture and personality study. He asserted that a basic personality structure typifies the members of a given society. This structure functions within a series of *cultural institutions*, patterned ways of doing things, found in that society. Kardiner divides such institutions into two categories: primary and secondary. *Primary institutions* may include patterns of family organization, feeding, weaning, child care, sexual training and taboos, and subsistence patterns. Although the primary institutions vary from one culture to another, they operate with sufficient uniformity in a given culture to develop certain similar psychological traits in all members of the society. Kardiner argued that in adapting to primary institutions, individuals acquire their personality or ego structure. Since the primary patterns are similar throughout the society, personality traits will be shared. These shared traits make up the society's basic personality structure.

A culture's *secondary institutions* arise as individuals strive to cope with the primary institutions. Conceptualization of gods, for example, may be modeled on a primary institution — children's relationship to their parents. Although secondary institutions also vary from society to society, Kardiner

ture with alternate swaddling (constraint) and unswaddling (freedom); and he attributed a host of events in Russian history, including the Russian Revolution and the confessions of intellectuals at Stalinist purge trials, to the guilt and anger fomented by such treatment. Among the criticisms leveled against the swaddling hypothesis is Harris's (1968), which points out that the Stalinist confessors may not even have been swaddled. Anger, guilt, and revolutions have also appeared in countries where swaddling is absent. Obviously, a better explanation than infant or childhood training must be found for major historical events.

Often when anthropologists attempt to describe typical personality structures of human groups, what they really do is offer personal impressions. Objective field work is put aside and canons of cultural relativism seem somehow to dissipate. It is difficult to believe that anthropologist Ralph Linton (1927), himself a major contributor to the culture and per-

In South Africa, a Zulu man and his children. Family structure, encompassing the relationship between father and child, is a primary institution that molds ego structure in most societies. (Keystone Press Agency)

felt that they would often include aspects of religion, rituals, folk tales, and other aspects of ideology.

Kardiner, like other students of culture and personality, argued for a form of childhood determinism, but his theoretical framework could accommodate limited comparative studies. It not only described cultures and personalities, but also incorporated a theory of change. On the basis of Linton's reports on the Tanala and Betsileo of Madagascar, Kardiner attempted to link change in certain aspects of basic personality structure and secondary institutions to the economic change from horticulture to agriculture.

BASIC PERSONALITY OF TANALA AND BETSILEO The Tanala, literally "people of the forest," inhabit a forested escarpment immediately to the east of the Betsileo. The Tanala are tribal horticulturalists who base their subsistence on cultivation of nonirrigated rice and several other crops. The Betsileo use artificial irrigation systems to cultivate wet rice. Linton correctly perceived a close linguistic relationship between the Tanala and Betsileo. Noting, too, certain similarities in their cultures and their close proximity, he argued that they were closely related. The Betsileo had formerly been horticulturalists like the Tanala and, but for subsistence, their cultures were similar. Linton claimed that the Betsileo had for-saken dry rice horticulture for irrigated rice agriculture. Therefore, deduced Kardiner, one must attribute differences in their basic personality structures and secondary institutions to the subsistence shift.

On the basis of my own field work, I find several factual errors in Linton's account. Foremost among them is the lack of evidence that the Betsileo were ever horticulturalists. All evidence I have examined suggests that they shifted gradually from mixed pastoralism to agriculture. Despite the incorrect observation on the part of Linton and Kardiner, it is true that the major contrast between the two is one of subsistence and that they come from the same ancestral population. A comparison in terms of basic personality structure and secondary institutions is therefore appropriate and may illuminate some of the psychological correlates of subsistence contrasts.

Among their primary institutions Kardiner found Tanala family organization similar to the United States in the 1930s in terms of the supreme position of the father and the nature of childhood discipline. These similarities to American culture are debatable, but the differences in primary institutions are clear; they include polygamy, the privileged position of the oldest son, the relatively low and immobile status of younger siblings, differences in the nature of the prestige system, and differences in the basic economy. To each of the primary institutions Kardiner attributes elements of basic personality structure and secondary institutions. For example, the values associated with the patriarchal family (primary institution) allowed the father to discipline his children at will, especially his sons; to exploit them by laying first claim to their labor; to frustrate their subsistence needs by controlling access to land and overseeing distribution of food to children still residing in the parental household. Various personality traits arose in response to patriarchal family organization, including repression of hatred for the father and patterns of submission to elders. These basic personality traits were then expressed in secondary institutions, such as the belief that ghosts caused illness, ancestor worship and the cult of patrilineal ancestors, and other patterns of behavior demonstrating loyalty to the dead.

Kardiner then contrasts Betsileo and Tanala cultures and basic personality structures, attributing differences to a change in one of the primary institutions—subsistence. According to Linton and Kardiner, the shift to irrigation resulted in several contrasts between Betsileo and Tanala, including new uses of labor to ensure water supply for irrigation and change in village descent-group structure from one named descent group to many. Personal ownership of land replaced communal rights to corporate estates, and the significance of patrilineal ties gradually declined. A stratum of slaves grew up in Betsileo society. The basis of social and political unity shifted from family organization to tribal associations of allied descent groups and finally to a kingdom, and new types of class interests and conflicts were engendered. The contrast obviously involves a difference between tribal and state organizations, and Kardiner indicates that in the new stratified structure different personality types—for example, those of slaves and nobles—developed.

With the subsistence shift, argues Kardiner, the role of the father changed. Since the Betsileo father, according to Kardiner, had less to dispense than the Tanala father, there was a limit to what sons could gain through submission. As private property replaced communal land, conflict among brothers increased and was extended to neighbors and more distant relatives. Hostility was openly expressed in adult life rather than being repressed. New loyalties were forged to kings and nobles. Given these changes, Betsileo personality placed a high emphasis on individual enterprise, skill, cunning, treachery, aggression, plunder, and subjugation of others. Political institutions partially checked these tendencies.

The general impression of Betsileo compared with Tanala is unfavorable. Kardiner's evaluation of their personality types is biased, however, by Linton's inadequate field work—based on only two months' research among the Tanala and even less time with the Betsileo. Kardiner sees wet rice cultivation as resulting in a host of new needs and new anxieties and a great increase in insecurity among the Betsileo. He states that certain contrasts in Betsileo secondary institutions, including greater emphasis on destructive magic and severe cases of possession by spirits, had their origins in the anxiety caused by the change in basic personality structure. Though he was dealing with a contrast of social and economic types rather than with an actual change, Kardiner made the interesting and probably valid generalization that once a basic personality structure is established, any change in primary institutions will lead to personality changes, but these changes will move only in the direction of the already established psychic constellations. In other words, personality does not change randomly but by modifying the evolutionary material at hand. This recalls evolutionary principles discussed previously, particularly in the discussion of Melanesian cargo cults in Chapter 9.

Although factual errors in Linton's reports mar Kardiner's interpretation, Kardiner nonetheless produced a valuable comparative study of two related cultures. He attempted to place his psychological analysis within an evolutionary framework, linking personality changes to economic change and, more generally, to changes in basic institutions. Kardiner also warned students of culture and personality that diversity of personality types in a given culture increases with social and political complexity, and he pointed to some of the anxieties associated with social stratification, private property, warfare, and state organization.

CROSS-CULTURAL AND COMPARATIVE STUDIES

Since the 1950s culture and personality studies have tended to employ data from several different societies instead of just two. Scholars like John and Beatrice Whiting have attempted to improve the quality of data on child training in different societies and to generalize about personality variables on a cross-cultural basis.

Limited Comparison: Concern for Improvements of Techniques

In a project conducted in the early 1960s, six research teams used similar techniques to investigate aspects of child training in six different societies (see B. B. Whiting, 1963). The researchers worked among the Gusii of East Africa, in a New England community, in a village in northern India that was inhabited by a land-owning caste, in a peasant community in Okinawa, in a lower-class ward of a Mexican community, and in a Philippine neighborhood. Their emphasis was on comparability of field methods and data rather than on similarities, differences, or relationships between the societies chosen for study. Prior to the field work, the time range of which was between six and fourteen months, John Whiting and his associates prepared a field guide to be used by all the field teams.

In each community the researchers studied between fifty and one hundred families, concentrating on the interaction between mothers and young children. They conducted interviews and actually observed behavior, paying particular attention to patterns of nurturance and succorance, degree of self-reliance, stress on achievement, degrees of responsibility, dominance, obedience, aggression, and sociability. The six societies were rated on the basis of psychological tones of child rearing; for example, mothers in some societies were found to be more affectionate than those in others.

On the basis of the comparative data, Beatrice Whiting noted more homicide, assault, and disputes in the northern Indian village and among the East Africans. She suggested a relationship between these patterns and the fact that husbands and wives did not eat, sleep, or work together regularly. In the other four communities, married couples had greater contact. As Barnouw (1973) has suggested, however, both the East Africans and the northern Indians lived in societies where militarism, including raiding, was an established part of cultural adaptation, and historical rather than child-training variables might better explain assault, homicide, and disputes. When dealing with data from a single society, or a small number of haphazardly chosen societies, it is often difficult to discover cause and effect relationships. As we shall see, comparative studies involving a greater number of more carefully selected societies make greater contributions to our understanding of causation in the field of culture and personality.

Limited Areal Comparison: Personality

In the early 1960s Walter Goldschmidt organized a research project to investigate cultural, psychological, and ecological variation among four groups in East Africa: the Hehe, Kamba, Pokot, and Sebei. All four groups have mixed economies. In each, some communities are cultivators, others are pastoralists, and some both cultivate and herd. Anthropologist Robert Edgerton, a participant in this project, gathered comparable, quantifiable psychological information in eight communities, one pastoral and one agricultural for each group. He drew a sample of at least thirty adults of each sex for each community, and interviewed a total of 505 people.

Statistical analysis of their responses to a set of eighty-five questions and their descriptions of ten Rorschach (ink-blot) plates and twenty-two color slides revealed basic personality configurations that differentiate the four groups (Edgerton, 1965). The Kamba, for example, were characterized by extreme male dominance, fear of poverty, and restrained emotions. Hehe responses suggested that they were impulsively aggressive, concerned with formal authority, profoundly mistrusting, and secretive. Other constellations marked the Pokot and the Sebei.

Similarities were found that reflected closeness of linguistic relationship. The Pokot and Sebei speak closely related languages of the Kalenjin group; the Hehe and the Kamba speak more distantly related languages of the Bantu group. Edgerton found that the Bantu speakers were more concerned with sorcery and witchcraft and valued land over cattle. The Kalenjin speakers valued sons and daughters; the Bantus preferred sons. The Bantu groups respected wealthy people; the Kalenjins, prophets.

Edgerton also investigated the roles of gender and acculturation in the various value systems and personalities. Contrary to expectation, he found differences in responses of males and females to be insignificant. Furthermore, he could find no significant relationship between degree of contact with European culture and patterns of responses.

Ecological differences, however, did produce different constellations. The eight communities could be placed on a continuum from pastoral to cultivating. Edgerton found that the cultivators consulted with sorcerers and with one another, whereas the pastoralists acted more individually. The farmers valued hard work; the herders did not. The cultivators were more hostile and suspicious. In terms of personality, the responses showed the farmers to be more indirect, given to fantasy, abstract, and anxious, and also less able to deal with their emotions and control their impulses. The herder's personality, on the other hand, was more direct, open, and bound to reality, with more effective control over emotions.

Edgerton's study is important for several reasons. His description is based on comparable, quantifiable data, collected according to definite and objective standards. Analysis of these data makes it possible to evaluate the relative contributions to overall personality of distinctive cultural traditions, historical relationships, gender, exposure to acculturation, and economy. If personality differences reflect ecological differences in East Africa, can we generalize that similar ecology-personality interrelationships are important on a worldwide scale? Several anthropologists have argued in the affirmative.

Worldwide Comparisons

H. H. Barry, M. K. Bacon, and I. L. Child (1959), for example, linked child rearing to subsistence economy on a cross-cultural basis. They found that populations with large accumulations of food resources (generally herders and cultivators) usually stressed responsibility and obedience in their child-rearing patterns, whereas foragers and other populations with little or no food accumulation emphasized achievement, competition, self-reliance, and independence. They did not, like Edgerton in his East Africa research, differentiate personalities of cultivators from those of herders.

Irvin Child and especially John Whiting have been major contributors to statistical cross-cultural generalizations about culture and personality, particularly about child rearing. Since Whiting's influence on cross-cultural studies has been profound, his theoretical assumptions will be briefly described. Whiting's framework of cross-cultural studies bears a noteworthy resemblance to Kardiner's scheme. Whiting and Child (1953) argued that child-training practices originate in different *cultural maintenance systems*. Like Kardiner's primary institutions, these maintenance systems include the economic, social, and political organizations of society, especially patterns of nourishment, shelter, and protection. Similar maintenance systems produce the same kinds of child-rearing practices and subsequently adult personality types (Kardiner's basic personality structures but on a cross-cultural basis). Such personality configurations then lead to similar *ideological projective systems* (Kardiner's secondary institutions).

As Raoul Naroll (1970) has pointed out, many of the explanations of cultural variables provided by Whiting and his associates are *psychogenic* explanations, so called because they regard cultural variables as delayed reactions to earlier experiences, most notably those of childhood. At times, however, Whiting has offered *biogenic* explanations, linking cultural variables to physiological, genetic, climatic, dietary, or pathological causes. An example is the link between the tropics, protein malnutrition, and circumcision (Whiting, 1964), established through the statistical study of comparable quantitative data from 177 societies around the world. In

certain parts of the tropics, low-protein diets are provided by cultivation of root crops and fruits, and cultivation is more important than hunting, fishing, or herding. Young children in such areas are especially susceptible to kwashiorkor, a condition caused by lack of protein. If a mother becomes pregnant while still nursing an infant, the quality of her milk may decline, and the child may be in danger of protein malnutrition. Certain populations, including many in tropical South America, attack this problem through abortion, and there are professional abortionists in such societies.

In many parts of Africa and in the islands of the Pacific, however, the problem is solved by tabooing sexual relations between wife and husband for a year or more after childbirth, and sometimes until the child is weaned. Often, the child sleeps in the mother's bed while the postpartum taboo is in effect, and the father sleeps in a separate bed or room or outside the maternal household altogether. Whiting (1964) found that sleeping practices are also associated with climate. The custom of husband and wife sleeping in the same bed occurs when winter temperature falls below fifty degrees. However, presumably because it is cooler to sleep with an infant than with a husband, in tropical areas women often sleep with their babies, but not their husbands.

Given the postpartum taboo and the prolonged mother-child sleeping arrangement, Whiting suggests that several consequences follow. Since the father is deprived of sexual access to his wife, he is likely to try to become polygynous. After all, a man may have sexual relations with his other wife or wives while one wife is still nursing and therefore tabooed.

Whiting argued that a strong cross-sex identification may be produced in the male infant from sleeping with his mother. Furthermore, the mother may derive physical gratification from her child's proximity at a time when she is deprived of sexual attentions from her husband. Polygyny is commonly found in societies with virilocal postmarital residence patterns, since males bring their wives to their own village rather than moving themselves. Virilocal residence demands more solidarity and cooperation and strong masculine identification in sons. Yet sons, having slept with their mothers, develop strong identifications with the opposite sex. To establish male sex identification in sons and to divert incestuous feelings between mothers and sons as puberty approaches, such societies often have severe male initiation rites, of which the most common is circumcision. Thus, through an intricate and roundabout series of associated customs, climate and diet contribute to the practice of circumcision.

COOPERATION, COMPETITION, INDIVIDUALISM, AND SOCIAL TYPES

Peasant Society and the Image of Limited Good

Using comparative techniques less rigorous than Whiting's statistical correlations, other anthropologists have also argued for worldwide links between economy and personality type. George Foster (1965), for example, has described a general cognitive orientation that he believes to be characteristic of all "classic" peasant societies—presumably, nonindustrial communities that farm and are included within a nation-state. Rather than relying on quantitative data from ethnographic samples, Foster discusses evidence from several peasant societies in different world areas to confirm the existence of a dominant theme of peasant orientation, or world view, which he calls the "image of limited good." Foster argues that this cognitive orientation was unconscious and never verbalized. However, he felt that such an unconscious structure did exist and served to explain a great deal about similarities in peasant behavior in different areas.

According to Foster, the image of limited good views all desired goods as finite in quantity. These would include land, wealth, health, love and friendship, honor, respect and status, power and influence, safety and security. Because all goods within the social, economic, and natural worlds are regarded as scarce, peasants believe that one member of a community can only profit by taking more than his or her rightful share of goods from the common pool and therefore depriving others. To the image of limited good Foster links several of what he regards as general attributes of peasant societies: emphasis on luck, fatalism, quarreling within and between families, stress on individualism, difficulties in cooperating; lack of emphasis on achievement, hard work, or thrift; and disposal of wealth in ritual expenses rather than in creating new wealth. Foster pictures peasant communities as consisting of individualistic persons and households who never cooperate for the welfare of the community but only to satisfy obligations.

When certain individuals improve their position over others, through increased wealth, for example, peasant ideology deals with these improvements in several ways. Differential wealth may be allowed, Foster suggests, if it comes from outside the community and does not require dipping into the finite pool of good. Individuals may prosper by external wage work, by favors from external patrons, or by sheer luck, and still leave the community's supply of good intact. If, however, wealth differentials reflect activ-

Collective rites of passage from boyhood to manhood help establish male solidarity and sexual identity in many patrilineal, virilocal, polygynous societies. Here, younger men play an important role in initiating younger members of their community. (Lewis/Anthro-Photo)

ity within the community, certain informal and un-organized forces of community opinion come into play as mechanisms of leveling differences. Individuals are forced to undertake ceremonial obligations, expenses that take away their wealth and leave them with prestige, which is not regarded as dangerous. Or they may become targets of community censure, character assassination, gossip, backbiting, envy, ostracism, and sometimes physical violence.

Given these sanctions, individuals who prosper try to hide their good fortune. Their dress, homes, and diet reflect the general standards. People who suffer ill fortune and fall below the community norm are also distrusted, for they are thought to be envious and potentially dangerous to all above them.

Although Foster's image of limited good is intriguing, it may be questioned. He finds his best evidence for such a cognitive orientation among peasants in Latin America and Europe. Peasants in other parts of the world, notably in African states, are often considerably less individualistic, and competition is normally expressed in rivalries between descent groups rather than between individuals or families. Foster finds love and friendship, like wealth, to be conceived as finite, and he links widespread sibling rivalry in peasant societies to competition for mother's love. We know, however, that sibling rivalry is not confined to peasants. Older children the world over are weaned to make way for younger siblings, thus precipitating much hostility. Rivalry for parental affection is basic to Freudian theory.

It seems that Foster's image of limited good is most characteristic given certain cultural traditions. Many Latin American communities share with Europeans an emphasis on nuclear family organization. Surely, ideology will differ if other social units, like corporate descent groups, are important. An image of limited good, as Foster himself points out, is also a response to the typical structural and economic position of peasants within the larger, national societies that include them. As Foster states, often good *is* limited by outsiders. Among the externally imposed limitations to peasant mobility are land ownership patterns and lack of access to adequate medical attention, government services and benefits, and the national power hierarchy. In concluding his article, Foster suggests—and there is considerable evidence to support him—that where access to wealth, power, and influence is more open, the image of limited good declines.

The Protestant Ethic and the Spirit of Capitalism

Consider now an argument for change from a peasant mentality operating on the principle of limited good to a personality structure valuing hard work, thrift, and capital accumulation. This rational, entrepreneurial type has been immortalized by sociologist Max Weber in a controversial but influential book *The Protestant Ethic and the Spirit of Capitalism* (1920). Weber argued that capitalism involving rational industrial organization attuned to a regular market demanded an entirely new personality type, and he linked this personality type to values inculcated by the ascetic Protestantism of Luther, Calvin, and other early Protestant leaders.

Weber noted that European Protestants were more successful financially than European Catholics, and he attributed this to religion. He characterized Catholics as more traditional, more concerned with happiness and security than Protestants, whose faith substituted other-worldly concerns for enjoyment of this life. Modern industrial capitalism, according to Weber, demanded that traditional attitudes, such as those typically expressed by European Catholic peasants, be replaced by others, more compatible with profit seeking and capital accumulation. (In an illustration of traditionalism, which recalls Foster's limited good, Weber described the case of a wealthy farmer who, in an attempt to increase the productivity of his hired workers, raised their piece rates, only to find that rather than working more to earn more, they actually decreased productivity to maintain their previous earnings.) Early Protestantism, according to Weber, provided a different ethos, one that valued hard work, an ascetic life, and profit seeking.

Associated with early Protestantism were notions that people's success on earth was a barometer of divine favor. In some versions of Protestantism, individuals could gain divine favor through a life of good works. Other Protestant sects stressed predestination, the doctrine that only a few mortals had been selected by God for eternal life, and that individuals could not change their fate. However, material success, achieved through hard work, could serve to indicate that an individual was one of the elect; and therefore, success, and its companion hard work, were valued because of their role in convincing individuals of their salvation.

English Puritanism continued the earlier Calvinist

The ancestors of the Amana of Iowa, like those of Dunkers, Hutterites, and Friends, were European Protestants who migrated to the United States and founded their own rural communities. Amana's settlers found an outlet for their "Protestant-capitalist" values in farming and in manufacturing refrigerators and freezers. In keeping with Weber's stereotype, the Protestants of Amana were sober and avoided ostentation. They were, however, less individualistic than other Protestant capitalists—sharing their wealth with church and community. Enculturation in the beliefs and traditions of Amana continues today. Shown here, three generations of Amana women. (Bradley Smith/Photo Researchers)

thrust in emphasizing hard work and asceticism. Puritanism stressed constant activity involving physical or mental labor, discouraged leisure and enjoyment of this life, called waste of time the deadliest sin, and placed no value on meditation. Labor came to be considered people's duty as ordained by God. This Protestantism valued the simplicity and asceticism of the middle-class home and condemned ostentation as a form of worldly enjoyment. The fruits of success, a sign of faith or preelection, could only be offered to the church or reinvested, for hoarded wealth might lead to temptation. Weber also attributes to early Protestantism a character of self-righteousness and a sober legality, consonant with the notion that people could expand their profit-making activity as long as they kept in mind the common good as well as their own and did not engage in harmful, illegal, greedy, or dishonest activity.

According to Weber, the change in the European world view that followed the Protestant Reformation resulted in modern, rational, industrial capitalism. Weber indicates that the transition from traditionalism to rational capitalism was checked at times by social and psychological factors, similar to the barriers to improvement that Foster has described for peasant communities. Early in the Reformation, those people who produced more than they needed for subsistence, who tried to make a profit, stirred up the mistrust, hatred, and moral indignation of others. Weber reports that successful Protestant innovators were people of unusually strong character, possessing definite and highly developed ethical qualities. Because of these attributes they could command the absolute confidence of their customers and workers, which was essential to their success. Furthermore, Weber argues that rational organization of capitalist enterprise depended on separation of business from the household, its core in peasant societies. Again Protestant doctrines made such a split possible. Protestantism emphasized individualism: persons, not families, were predestined to salvation, and individuals' good works could reveal their grace. The family, more important in Foster's peasant society, was a secondary matter for Weber's Protestants.

Controversy surrounds Weber's thesis. He dismisses economic forces, historical events, and political structures as causes of Western capitalism, but other scholars have simply demonstrated their importance. Today people of many religions and world views are successful capitalists. There are ample signs that Protestant asceticism has been replaced by a broad tolerance for the enjoyment of this life. In the United States, the need for hard and constant work has been replaced by the weekend football syndrome. Some of our Protestant politicians mouth the value of hard work to people on welfare while, like Europeans in Melanesia, themselves enjoying a leisured life style.

In fact, traditional Protestant emphasis on honesty and hard work often seems to have little relationship to modern capitalists' maneuverings. Regardless of just how much it can be considered a cause, rather than an effect of, Western capitalism, however, the

Protestant ethic did exist. Its individualistic focus was very compatible with the severance of ties to land and kin that accompanied the Industrial Revolution. Might such an ethic exist in nonindustrial areas, as an example of convergent evolution? In the case that follows, it is argued that it does.

The Spirit of Fishermen

Foster's image of limited good warns peasants against producing beyond their needs. Weber's Protestant ethic demands that they do so. To produce profits, however, one must dispense with certain social and ceremonial obligations that would otherwise limit accumulation of capital. The relationship between independent, achievement-oriented personalities and foraging economies has already been mentioned. Thus we might expect individualistic personality types to be found most characteristically at different ends of the evolutionary continuum, among foragers and industrialists. To illustrate such personality types among foragers, consider a fishing community in Brazil.

Arembepe is a village of some 800 people located near Salvador, capital of Bahia state in northeastern Brazil. Most Arembepeiros derive their income directly or indirectly from fishing in the Atlantic Ocean. However, Arembepe is not an isolated foraging community, but is tied to the Brazilian nation economically, politically, and socially. Arembepeiros sell their fish to marketers from outside their village, often to the detriment of their own subsistence needs. Some people in Arembepe farm small plots in addition to fishing. Although they do not live off the land, their behavior, ideology, and economic and political ties to the Brazilian nation are similar to those of peasants in nearby communities. Since they share cultural and structural features with peasants, we might expect to find some of the principles of Foster's image of limited good among them — and we do. On the other hand, since most Arembepe men fish, we can also expect them to be independent and achievement-oriented. Arembepeiros have no corporate descent groups, nor are social units larger than the household, which is generally inhabited by a nuclear family. Their social organization is individualistic and atomistic, though not to the extent that Foster leads us to expect in a peasant community.

Despite its inclusion within a stratified nation-state, Arembepe is a relatively homogeneous com-

In urban New York as in rural Iowa, America's religious sects and ethnic groups maintain their distinctive beliefs, traditions, and lifestyles. Shown here, a Hasidic Jewish grandfather and grandson in New York City. Subcultural differences help produce variation in personality type in multi-ethnic nations. (Bettye Lane/Photo Researchers)

munity socially and economically. All Arembepeiros belong to the national lower class. Although differences in wealth and status exist within Arembepe society, these are infinitesimal compared with the economic variations that exist in Brazilian society as a whole. For reasons that will be discussed in Chapter 13, achieved economic status is far more significant than ascribed status in Arembepe. Individuals have a relatively equal chance to ascend the local ladder of success, and social and economic advance often reflects success in the local fishing industry. Sailboats normally fish with crews of four or five men, one of whom is the captain. Often captains are full or half owners of these boats. In general, the Arembepe fishing fleet can be divided into four groups: (1) successful young captains; (2) older captains, who once belonged to the first group; (3) the least successful captains, who fish less regularly, primarily because of alcoholism; and (4) ordinary fishermen.

Arembepeiros hold different opinions about what determines success in fishing. Ordinary fishermen argue that captains must have good eyesight to espy distant landmarks that mark profitable fishing spots. They cite inadequacies in their own eyesight to justify their not becoming captains. They also say that — in addition to these skills — luck helps some captains and crews catch more than others. Older, but once successful, captains blame their declining catches on their failing eyesight, which prevents them from fishing as effectively as in the past. The third group of captains generally attribute differential success just to luck, refusing to admit that some captains are better than others.

The most successful, and generally the youngest, captains, those in group one, have a still different rationale for their success. They link it to factors that recall Weber's Protestant ethic. They cite their hard and constant work and sobriety, rarely mentioning luck or eyesight. My own analysis of determinants of success in fishing corresponds strikingly with this explanation. I found systematic differences in their behavior compared with less successful fishermen. First, because they are generally in their twenties and early thirties, they enjoy good health, which permits them to take their boats out more regularly than the others. Thus they attract hard-working crew members because they are dependable, are able to remain at sea longer, and can tolerate more work and weather conditions that are often unpleasant. Second, like Weber's Protestant entrepreneurs, they take calculated risks. Unlike other captains, they sometimes travel to further fishing zones during the winter, when there is always the danger of a sudden storm and rough seas. They experiment more, seeking new fishing zones. Often their risks pay off in terms of larger catches. Third, although unlike Weber's Protestants they are not teetotalers, they drink only on festive occasions, and they prefer the less intoxicating beer to the crude sugar cane rum that ordinary fishermen and less successful captains consume. Hence, young captains can drink more without getting drunk, and they miss no fishing days because of drunkenness. Because it is more expensive, beer is also a status symbol. Fourth, they command better crew allegiance (and attract better crew members). Fifth, they are respected within the community. They become officers of the local fishermen's society; other people are aware of their success and eager to join their crews.

Like Weber's Protestant entrepreneurs, they constantly strive to use profits derived from fishing to produce additional profits—by purchasing plots of land and livestock, by planting coconut trees, or by investing in new technology to increase their fishing productivity.

In contrast to the ideal peasant described by Foster, Arembepeiros do not rely on land, which is an easily limitable resource. Their subsistence comes from the sea, a more open frontier in which the assignment of property rights poses more difficulties. Hard work there does pay off. Furthermore, the high rate of inflation that plagues Brazil has also selected for reinvestment. With constant devaluation, hoarding would be disastrous.

As in the United States, kinship in Arembepe is relatively narrow. Only parents, siblings, "niblings" (nieces and nephews), aunts, uncles, and first cousins are important relatives. However, Arembepeiros do not normally restrict their kinship ties to the extent that we do, nor as severely as did Weber's Protestant capitalist. Since fishing demands hard work and youthful vigor, even the most successful fishermen know that their productivity will eventually decline. They attempt to anticipate their declining years by building up alternative sources of income on the land, but because there is no pension or social security system they can never be totally sure that they will not have to depend on their kin at some time in the future. Community opinion forces them to share a part of their present wealth with their relatives.

Arembepeiros do not appear to think of good as limited. No doubt this reflects their combination of an open economy and ties to an external economy. However, social mechanisms similar to those that Foster has described for the classic peasant community do operate in Arembepe to ensure that individuals do not stray too far from what is considered appropriate behavior. Consider the case of Laurentino, Arembepe-born son of a migrant from the Brazilian interior. Like his father, Laurentino has never been a fisherman but runs two stores in the village. Laurentino spent several years outside of Arembepe, and when he returned to the community he opened one of his stores. Arembepeiros say that during his absence he made a pact with the devil, and they attribute his initial business success in Arembepe to this pact. His store prospered; he bought four fishing boats; and he took over his father's store when the latter died.

Since his return, the social gap between Laurentino and other Arembepeiros has steadily widened. Villagers fear his devil, which, on the basis of his early success, they believe is powerful. They speak of nightly devil worship sessions in his house and of a demon kept in a cage somewhere in his store. They distrust him because, unlike other local storekeepers, he does not extend credit. Laurentino has played a major role in cultivating social distance, perhaps in an attempt to free himself from the obligations of kinship that all other Arembepeiros assume. He finds it amusing that other villagers think of him as a witch. Flouting Catholic doctrine, he bought birth control pills for his wife and demanded that she take them. When she did become pregnant, he let it be known that he would not have his child baptized.

He has suffered as a result of his unconventional behavior. Villagers avoid his stores because they fear him and he does not extend credit. No longer able to find men willing to serve as captains of his sailboats, he had to destroy all four of them. Not only is he the most isolated man in the community, but his efforts to increase his wealth have been blocked by community opinion. Obviously, it is possible to prosper in Arembepe, but only within the limits set by community opinion.

Detailed analysis of Arembepe illustrates that sev-eral different ideological themes can coexist in a single, relatively homogeneous community. The way that people explain things, like other aspects of their cognitive orientation, reflects their reference group. Yet the ideology of sharing with less fortunate relatives overrides differences in outlook among village subgroups and, as we shall see in Chapter 13, has social and economic implications. This analysis suggests that despite their demonstrated value, sta-tistical cross-cultural studies of relationships be-tween personality variables and cultural, social, and economic variables must be supplemented with in-tensive analysis of particular cases in order to clarify influences of culture on personality. Internal varia-tion within a community, cultural unit, or cross-cul-tural type may turn out to be as significant, and as explicable, as variation between types.

SUMMARY

Anthropologists have placed psychological findings in comparative perspective through culture and per-sonality research. In contrast to traditional eth-nography, which is principally interested in observed behavior and its results, the culture and personality approach is an attempt to explore the inner attributes of individuals and to determine personality types characteristic of different statuses and different cul-tures.

Early students of culture and personality often relied on personal impressions in gathering field data. Assuming that within any culture individuals share some personality traits, anthropologists also undertook studies of basic personality structure and national character. National character studies, pop-ular during World War II, have been criticized for various reasons, including their frequently impres-sionistic basis, their overemphasis on childhood de-terminism, and their lack of range. A similar, but theoretically more sophisticated approach was devel-oped by Kardiner, a psychoanalyst, in association with several anthropologists. Kardiner proposed that a culture's basic personality structure represents the end result of individual adaptations to certain primary institutions, including family organization and subsistence economy. The basic personality structure then influenced secondary institutions, in-cluding aspects of religion and ideology. Religious conceptions might be modeled after children's rela-tionship to their parents, for example. Statistically oriented anthropologists John Whiting and Irvin Child later applied a framework similar to Kardiner's to cross-cultural relationships between culture and personality variables.

The quality of culture and personality generali-zations improved as research teams undertook prob-lem-oriented field work, using objective techniques for gathering data on child training and other aspects of personality formation. Limited comparisons of personality configurations have been conducted in certain world areas, and ecological, cultural, histori-cal, and other correlates of personality structure have been specified. In world-wide studies using statistical techniques and quantitative data, anthro-pologists have demonstrated relationships between personality variables, on the one hand, and social evolutionary type and economy, on the other. Male initiation ceremonies, for example, have been associ-ated with polygyny, virilocal postmarital residence, temperature, and diet. Rationales for such relation-ships have been offered in terms of child rearing, dependency relationships, and cross-sex identifica-tions.

Other social scientists have taken a nonstatistical approach, arguing for relationships between person-ality and economy. Foster found an "image of limited good" to be part of the cognitive orientation of "classic" peasant societies. Weber attributed the emergence of industrial capitalism to rationality, asceticism, emphasis on hard and constant work, and profit seeking, all of which he believed to be associated with Protestantism.

Does this exist

A case study of Arembepe, a Brazilian fishing community, demonstrates that differences in explan-atory frameworks and other aspects of cognition may reflect reference group even in a relatively homogeneous community. Nevertheless, all Arembepeiros partook in a general ideology of sharing. Both individual studies of personality and cognition and larger, comparative studies promise to increase our understanding of the determinants and effects of psychological and cognitive variation.

SOURCES AND SUGGESTED READINGS

BARNOUW, V.
1973   *Culture and Personality.* Rev. ed. Homewood, Ill.: Dorsey Press. Most readable and complete introduction to the field.

BARRY, H., BACON, M. K, AND CHILD, I. L.
1959   Relation of Child Training to Subsistence Economy. *American Anthropologist* 61: 51–63. Describes similarities in child training and personality among herders and cultivators who are contrasted with foragers.

BENEDICT, R.
1946   *The Chrysanthemum and the Sword.* Boston: Houghton Mifflin. Description of national character based on the study of Japanese culture from a distance.

1959   (orig. 1934) *Patterns of Culture.* New York: New American Library. Popular handbook of configurationalism; examines Kwakiutl of Northwest Coast of North America, Melanesians of Dobu, and Zuñi of the American Southwest.

BERRY, J. W., AND DASEN, P. R., EDS.
1974   *Culture and Cognition: Readings in Cross-Cultural Psychology.* London: Metheun. Collection of 25 articles by anthropologists and psychologists.

DUBOIS, C.
1944   *The People of Alor: A Social Psychological Study of an East Indian Island.* Minneapolis: University of Minnesota Press. Best of the early field studies of basic personality structure.

EDGERTON, R.
1965   "Cultural" versus "Ecological" Factors in the Expression of Values, Attitudes and Personality Characteristics. *American Anthropologist* 67: 442–447. Analysis of quantitative data on culture and personal-ity variables among four neighboring East African societies.

FOSTER, G. M.
1965   Peasant Society and the Image of Limited Good. *American Anthropologist* 67: 293–315. Nonquantitative approach to cognitive orientation of peasants; influential and controversial article.

GORER, G.
1943   Themes in Japanese Culture. *Transactions of the New York Academy of Sciences* (Series II) 5: 106–124. Compulsive Japanese national character attributed to early and severe toilet training.

GORER, G., AND RICKMAN, J.
1949   *The People of Great Russia.* London: Cresset. Russian national character, including the swaddling hypothesis.

HARRIS, M.
1968   *The Rise of Anthropological Theory.* New York: Crowell. Chapters 15–17 contain lively evaluations of culture and personality research.

HSU, F. L. K., ED.
1961   *Psychological Anthropology.* Cambridge, Mass.: Schenkman. Basic reader, in which Hsu discusses why he prefers term "psychological anthropology" to "culture and personality."

KARDINER, A., ED.
1939   *The Individual and His Society.* New York: Columbia University Press. Framework of primary and secondary institutions and basic personality structure; uses Linton's incomplete accounts of Tanala, Betsileo, and Marquesas Islanders.

1945   *The Psychological Frontiers of Society.* New York: Columbia University Press. Reports by DuBois, Linton, and West on Alor, Comanche, and Plainville, U.S.A., respectively, and Kardiner's psychocultural analysis of each.

KLUCKHOLN, F., AND STRODTBECK, F.
1961   *Variations in Value Orientations*. Evanston, Ill.: Row, Peterson. Statistical evaluation of values among five ethnic groups in the modern American Southwest.

LABARRE, W.
1945   Some Observations on Character Structure in the Orient: The Japanese. *Psychiatry* 8: 326–342. Another attempt to link Japanese compulsion and anal training.

LEVINE, R. A.
1973   *Culture, Behavior, and Personality*. Chicago: Aldine. Original, fascinating, sophisticated text in psychological anthropology by an anthropologist-psychoanalyst.

LEVINE, R. A., ED.
1974   *Culture and Personality: Contemporary Readings*. Chicago: Aldine. Collection of 23 articles dealing with psychological universality, generality, and diversity.

LINTON, R.
1927   Report on Work of Field Museum Expedition in Madagascar. *American Anthropologist* 29: 292–307. Unusual combination of field data and character assassination of certain Malagasy peoples.

MEAD, M.
1939   *From the South Seas*. New York: Morrow. *New Guinea, Samoa,* and *Sex and Temperament* in one volume.

1949   (orig. 1928). *Coming of Age in Samoa.* New York: New American Library. Popular report of Mead's first fieldwork, a study of female adolescents in a Polynesian society.

1950   (orig. 1935). *Sex and Temperament in Three Primitive Societies.* New York: New American Library. Mead has called this examination of sex roles in three New Guinea societies her most misunderstood book.

MURDOCK, G. P.
1957   World Ethnographic Sample. *American Anthropologist* 59: 664–687. Test a hypothesis yourself! Includes coded data for 565 cultures on fifteen variables, including aspects of economy and social and political organization.

MURDOCK, G. P., AND WHITE, D.
1969   Standard Cross-Cultural Sample. *Ethnology* 8: 329–369. Quantified data on 186 well-reported cultures.

NAROLL, R.
1970   What Have We Learned from Cross-Cultural Surveys? *American Anthropologist* 72: 1227–1288. Survey of statistical cross-cultural studies of culture and personality and other areas of anthropology.

ROHNER, R. P.
1975   *They Love Me, They Love Me Not: A Worldwide Study of the Effects of Parental Acceptance and Rejection*. New Haven: HRAF Press. Data from a large sample of societies are used in this interesting study.

STEPHENS, W. N.
1962   *The Oedipus Complex: Cross-Cultural Evidence*. New York: The Free Press. Evaluation, through cross-cultural data, of the universality of Freud's most celebrated syndrome.

WALLACE, A. F. C.
1970   *Culture and Personality*. 2nd ed. New York: Random House. More specialized and theoretical than Barnouw, but highly original demarcation of the field and theory of psychological anthropology.

WEBER, M.
1958   (orig. 1920). *The Protestant Ethic and the Spirit of Capitalism*. New York: Scribners. Controversial explanation of rational industrial capitalism in terms of religious tenets of Protestantism.

WHITING, B. B., ED.
1963   *Six Cultures: Studies of Child Rearing.* New York: Wiley. Case studies including data gathered on comparable techniques of child training in Okinawa, India, New England, East Africa, Mexico, and the Philippines.

WHITING, J. W. M.
1964   The Effects of Climate on Certain Cultural Practices. In *Explorations in Cultural Anthropology: Essays in Honor of George Peter Murdock,,* ed. W. Goodenough, pp. 175–195. New York: McGraw-Hill. Intricate chain of statistical associations leading from tropical climate to circumcision.

WHITING, J. W. M., AND CHILD, I.
1953   *Child Training and Personality: A Cross-Cultural Study*. New Haven: Yale University Press. Influential comparative statistical study of relationships between child-training practices and conceptions of illness.

Biology, Society, and Culture

11

Because anthropology brings a comparative perspective to human biology, psychology, society, and culture, it is in a unique position to comment on nature (genes) and nurture (environment) as determinants of human behavior. For thousands of years people have speculated about the amount of control they have over their behavior. Notions that our lives are limited or determined by factors beyond our control probably have been more common than the belief in free will. In a variety of belief systems, individuals are denied control over their own fate and told that their destinies are supernaturally ordained. Scientists, on the other hand, argue that economic conditions, universal psychological drives, or genes determine or limit human action.

People's attitudes, values, and behavior *are* limited not only by genetic predispositions—which are difficult to identify—but by personal experiences during enculturation and by personality types valued and therefore fostered by the culture. Our biological attributes as adults are determined both by our genes and by our environments during growth and development. In stratified nations, people's opportunites are limited by their differential access to strategic resources and by legal, social, cultural, and political mechanisms that maintain inequality.

Flexibility, however, is as strong a theme in anthropology as determinism. In fact, the success of *Homo* rests on human plasticity, the tremendous adaptive potential that culture provides. Confronted with environmental change, human populations need not depend on genetic modification or physiological flexibility; they can also adapt by altering their customs—for instance, by changing descent rules, marriage patterns, or ceremonial organization. These solutions are sociocultural.

Debate about the relative impact of nature and nurture on human behavior and abilities continues today, involving both the scientific and public arenas. In this chapter we will examine the nature and nurture determinants of human aggression, altruism, and other psychological dispositions; behavior, attitudes, and abilities of males and females; human sexual expression; and intelligence. First, general themes that oppose naturists and environmentalists will be considered. Then specific areas of debate will be discussed.

Naturists assume that some—they differ about how much—human behavior and social organization is genetically determined and thus expresses universal human genetic traits. These traits, resting on chemical uniformities in *Homo*'s DNA, are fixed, inevitably expressed, and cannot be changed, except perhaps by mutation. Although nurturists, or environmentalists, usually do not deny in theory that some nonvariable aspects of human behavior may prove to have a genetic base, they do find most attempts to link behavior to genetics to be questionable or invalid and offer evidence for rejecting such theories. They use the variability in human behavior to counter naturist assertions of universal genetically based behavior. Environmentalists find few cultural universals, and interpret those that do exist as common responses to problems and experiences that affect all humans.

The basic environmentalist assumption is that *Homo*'s evolutionary success rests on flexibility, on the ability to mold biological traits in various ways. Because the human adaptive apparatus is based so strongly on learning, we can change our behavior more readily than members of other species. Whereas most naturists offer genetic explanations for *universal* behavior and social forms, some believe that *differences* in behavior and social organization among human groups may reflect corresponding genetic differences. This idea has been applied to performance on intelligence tests by groups of contemporary Americans and is examined below. Environmentalists interpret major differences in behavior and social organization among human groups as responses—often adaptive solutions—to different environments, that is, as differences in learning experiences. The naturist-environmentalist debate about possible determinants of human behavior and social organization is joined, therefore, in explaining both similarities and differences between human groups.

SOCIOBIOLOGY

Since 1961, when Robert Ardrey's *African Genesis* appeared, anthropological data have been used—often inappropriately—to support naturist arguments addressed to and read by a mass audience. The most influential naturist works have been by Ardrey (1961, 1966, 1970, 1976), Konrad Lorenz (1966), Desmond Morris (1967, 1969), Lionel Tiger (1969), Tiger and Robin Fox (1972). These popular works can be grouped with the more scientific works of Richard Alexander (1974), Robert Trivers (1971), E. O. Wilson (1975), and other academics as examples of sociobiology, and as works that make the naturist assumption that some, and even much, of human social behavior has a genetic basis. In his monumental book *Sociobiology: The New Synthesis,* zoologist Wilson claimed that *sociobiology*, the study of the biological basis for social behavior, would bring together the subject matter of the biological and social sciences as well as the humanities (including ethics).

The Popular Sociobiologists

The popular sociobiologists see contemporary humans as animals whose behavior is motivated by instinct; they stress human biology and often ignore culture. By comparing real or supposed similarities between humans and other species, they argue that behavioral similarities are homologies genetically transmitted from our common ancestors.

Morris's *The Naked Ape* (1967) is less extreme than typical popular sociobiological treatises, but is a good example of how they stress biology and ignore the cultural diversity that would undercut their theories. For Morris, *Homo*, despite culture, remains an animal, a naked ape. Morris is right in noting that humans remain constrained by our biological needs, but in presenting fighting, status seeking, and hierarchy as biological tendencies, he is on shakier ground. He neglects cross-cultural information, even though his book discusses human nature. His data on human society are drawn almost exclusively from the United States in the 1960s. His rationale for this bias is extraordinary: the United States "is biologically a very large and successful culture and can, without undue fear of distortion, be taken as representative of the modern naked ape." Exclusive use of such data, which represent just one of thousands of cultural alternatives, is a totally inadequate basis for assessing human nature or for comparing humans with other animals. Note, too, the implicit suggestion that the reproductive success of Americans rests on biological fitness rather than on technology and other aspects of culture.

Ardrey (1961) links the purportedly universal human psychological traits of acquisitiveness and status seeking to animal instincts; he makes nationalism, a social trait, a reflection of generalized primate territoriality. He ignores evidence that acquisitiveness and status seeking are missing in many cultures and that many nonhuman primates are not at all territorial. In *The Social Contract* (1970) Ardrey attempts to prove, by comparing humans and animals, that social inequality is the natural state of society, as revealed both in the social stratification that accompanies state organization and the dominance hierarchies of savanna-dwelling baboons. Here Ardrey ignores considerable evidence, discussed in Chapter 2, that nonhuman primate social organization is flexible, reflects adaptation to specific environments, and may rest as much on learning as on DNA; and that just as inequality is not universal among humans (think of foragers), the significance of baboon dominance hierarchies also diminishes away from the threat of savanna predators.

In *The Territorial Imperative* (1966) Ardrey makes a similar mistake. As primatologist Vernon Reynolds (1976) points out, Ardrey argues that humans are territorial creatures, genetically programmed to threaten and, if necessary, fight to defend strategic resources. Ardrey maintains that war reflects DNA, which we share with animals, and not variable economic, political, and social conditions, as anthropologists have demonstrated. In establishing the territorial imperative, Ardrey picks his animals arbitrarily, using gibbons, for example, to establish primate territoriality and ignoring chimpanzees, gorillas, and orangutans. In the discussion of primate territoriality and aggression in Chapter 2, behavioral diversity in several primate species was linked to definite environmental conditions, which also varied. Instincts shared by all animals, all primates, or all humans have to be displayed everywhere. However, territoriality, ranking, social inequality, and such cultural traits as status seeking and acquisitiveness are universal neither among primates nor among humans. Thus Ardrey's specific arguments must be rejected along with his mode of analysis.

Ethologist Lorenz (1966) attributes a genetic basis to aggression, which he sees as linking, through common inheritance, humans and other animals. The universality of aggression reflects its generalized survival value and therefore its selection as a genetic trait. The aggression drive, declares Lorenz, serves several adaptive purposes when directed by one species against another: it promotes strength, protects the young, and it spaces—that is, distributes and balances access to vital resources. However, when turned inward—either against other members of the same species or, psychologically, by repressing its expression in behavior—its effects can be disastrous. Among humans, the effects of this "hereditary evil" (Lorenz, 1966) are particularly destructive. Beginning around 40,000 years ago, when, according to Lorenz, people had brought most of nature under their control, aggression turned inward, and wars between hostile tribes selected "warrior" genes that survive among people today. For Lorenz, aggressive genes are part of every human gene pool, but some groups are genetically more aggressive than others. He maintains that among the Ute Indians, several centuries (actually less than 100 years) of a life that consisted "almost entirely of war and raids" intensified selection for hereditary aggression. Their intense aggression was later thwarted when the Utes were forced to live on reservations. Lorenz attributes a high incidence of disease, alcoholism, and even reckless driving and automobile accidents among contemporary Utes to their inability to discharge through war their strong hereditary aggression drive.

Note that Lorenz uses a naturist position to explain both similarities and differences among human groups. Although the level of aggressive behavior does vary significantly from one human population to another, this is not necessarily explained by genetics. Anthropological studies demonstrate that aggression is related to the scarcity of resources in specific environments. Humans and other primates have the hereditary capability of being mild and docile when resources are abundant, or extremely aggressive when they are limited or threatened. Aggressive behavior varies with environment among members of the same species of baboon, chimpanzee, and orangutan, and—in a given group—over time as the environment changes. If humans share with other animals a capacity for aggression, it is expressed behaviorally only under environmental pressure. That individuals can be trained to be aggressive or docile, in accordance with their culture's values, negates Lorenz's arguments that variation in aggression reflects genetic differences.

Freud and his followers share with Lorenz a belief in universal human aggression. To explain why a universal drive is not always expressed in destructive behavior, they have suggested that it may be diverted (sublimated or displaced) through socially approved channels, for instance, sports, that do not endanger society. The displacement theory would lead us to expect that those societies with the most aggressive sports would have the lowest incidence of war and raiding. (This theme is elaborated in the futuristic film *Rollerball*.) However, in a cross-cultural study anthropologist Richard Sipes (1973) found that war, raiding, aggressive sports, and other aggressive behavior were usually associated. He concluded that aggression is variable and culturally determined. If a society stresses aggression in some areas, that emphasis will be generalized throughout the culture. Yanomamo society, for example, is permeated by aggression, expressed in war, raids, and violent combative contests. Nations that combine aggressive sports with a large-scale military apparatus illustrate this point as well.

Scientific Sociobiology

Linking the popular works of Ardrey, Lorenz, and Morris with the scientific sociobiology of Alexander, Trivers, and Wilson is the assumption that human social behavior is genetically determined. Evolutionary theory stresses that natural selection, operating on manifest traits (phenotypes) gradually changes a population's pool of genetic material. The *population* thereby adapts to environmental change. Sociobiology, in contrast, maintains that *individuals* in a population compete with one another to maximize their genetic contribution to future generations. In sociobiology genes seem to have lives of their own, simply residing temporarily in bodies as they perpetuate themselves across the generations.

At the 1976 meeting of the American Anthropological Association, scholars offered sociobiological interpretations of aspects of primate and human behavior. For example, a few cases in which outside male monkeys killed off infants soon after entering a new troop were interpreted sociobiologically as attempts by invaders to maximize their own reproductive contribution (Hrdy, 1976). Wilson (1976), who had in 1975 argued that division of labor on the basis of sex is genetically based, characterized humans as self-centered and human society as internally competitive.

Sociobiologists say that in addition to competition, DNA may maximize itself through apparently unselfish behavior because of *inclusive fitness*. Individuals share their DNA with close relatives, for whom they may be willing to lay down their lives, and thus sacrifice personal reproduction. In so doing, they may actually increase the proportion of their (shared) DNA in future generations. If the altruistic act sends more of the shared genes to the next generation than does the sacrificing individual's own direct reproduction, self-sacrifice becomes adaptive in sociobiological terms. Trivers (1971) argues similarly about the genetic determinants of what he calls *reciprocal altruism*. By cooperating, even unrelated members of a population may mutually improve their life chances and thereby increase their reproductive success. Trivers argues that genes determining reciprocal altruism and cooperation will spread in a population if they maximize the reproductive success of individual organisms.

Marshall Sahlins (1976) clarifies a major error in applying such arguments to humans. Surveying the ethnographic literature, he shows that human kinship systems are not based on biological relationship. Bifurcate merging and generational kinship terminologies, for example, skew the correspondence between cultural categories and biological kin types. Furthermore, adoption and fosterage are common human institutions. Among the Betsileo, for example, virtually all boys are raised by people other than their biological parents, and women leave home when they marry. Throughout the world since the advent of universal group exogamy, humans have lived in local groups where some people are their biological relatives and others are not. One may live with or near some biological kin, but many members of a local group will lack any genealogical connection.

These observations are particularly important since Wilson has argued that people share with all other animals an unconscious and instinctive knowledge of their blood ties with others. This instinctive awareness of where common DNA is found is basic to sociobiology. To increase one's DNA by altruism toward kin, one must be able to identify biological relatives. Cross-cultural evidence refutes the sociobiological argument on several fronts. For one thing, people often cooperate and share more with distant kin or nonkin (in a genetic sense) than with genealogical relatives. Second, kinship systems, fosterage, adoption, and other purely social relationships muddle whatever "instinctive" genealogical knowledge people might have.

Sahlins makes another telling point against sociobiology. Sociobiologists posit that genes—determined to reproduce themselves—directly cause the psychological dispositions and behavior of the individual, which are then expressed in social interactions. Popular and scientific sociobiology both assume that a genetically determined individual psychological tendency will be directly revealed in a social institution of similar character. Thus individual aggressiveness will manifest itself in war; genetically programmed altruism will be expressed in food sharing, a social act. Sahlins argues convincingly against attributing the form of *social* institutions to *individual* psychological drives. The causes of war, are, he says, not the reasons people go to war. Various political, economic, and social conditions can lead to war, but the individuals who fight have a variety of drives and motives. Some may be aggressive; some may not. As we saw during the Vietnam War, many American soldiers were forced to fight in spite of their personal inclinations and dispositions. The same individual motivations, says Sahlins, appear in many different cultural forms, and different motives find expression in the same forms. Sahlins asserts that culture is not ordered by the emotions; the emotions are organized by culture.

Science, like myth, religion, and kinship systems, exists in and reflects a particular cultural setting. Sociobiology has arisen with an individualistic, competitive, stratified society as only one way of looking at data—no one has ever discovered an altruistic or a competitive gene. Sociobiologists have interpreted animal behavior in Western capitalistic terms, then thrown this culturally distorted picture back on human society. Their view of evolution, with individual rather than group as the evolving unit, is unorthodox. Anthropology's subject matter and focus on the plasticity permitted by culture disprove sociobiology, the most recent example of a naturist attempt to explain social behavior.

MALE AND FEMALE IN COMPARATIVE PERSPECTIVE

It has been argued that differences between males and females in attitudes, behavior, and capabilities are biologically caused. The Hagen, patrilineal horticulturalists of highland New Guinea (Strathern, 1972), for example, view women as naturally inferior creatures incapable of reasoning clearly. Many Americans believe that hormonal changes associated with the menstrual cycle affect women's personalities and muscular coordination. Tiger (1969), a sociologist with training in anthropology, views women as less sociable than men. He attributes a tendency for men to form all-male groups to male pair-bonding, an "underlying biologically transmitted 'propensity' with roots in human evolutionary history."

It is possible in theory that some genetically determined physiological differences may determine sex-role differentiation; however, current attempts to link male and female anatomy and destiny are highly suspect. Anthropologists, however, have demonstrated tremendous variability in the roles of men and women in a variety of social contexts. Anthropologist Ernestine Friedl (1975) states succinctly the anthropological position on sex roles and biology; she views "the biological nature of men and women not as a narrow enclosure limiting the human organism, but rather as a broad base upon which a variety of structures can be built."

Following the general strategy we have previously followed, in this chapter we will relate differences and similarities in sex roles to specific environments, strategies of adaptation, and levels of sociopolitical complexity. However, to review adequately the roles of men and women in cross-cultural perspective, we must first discuss the effects of general social conditions on both the history of women as anthropologists and the study of women by anthropologists. Historically, women in anthropology have had marginally better proportional representation and positions than in other disciplines. Women continue to be some of the field's best known and most productive scholars. Nevertheless, although today approximately equal numbers of men and women are entering graduate programs in anthropology, traditionally most anthropologists have been men. Before the revival of feminism, anthropological field work, whether conducted by male or female ethnographers, focused on men and their activities. Because of this, even after decades of ethnographic studies, anthropologists know less about women and sex roles in cross-cultural perspective than we should know, or now would like to know. In recent years feminism has directed both male and female

Women of Colombe, Ecuador work on the main road leading to their community. Women are no strangers to hard physical labor in many societies. (Guido Falconi/Rapho Photo Researchers, Inc.)

anthropologists toward reinterpretation of sex roles in societies and has produced new data that enlarge anthropological knowledge of women in varied cultural settings.

Anthropologists' traditional neglect of women's activities and opinions reflected their own values and class backgrounds as participants in American culture. Most anthropologists have come from middle- and upper-class families, and as such many have held the notion that "a woman's place is in the home." Not only have women's activities been relegated to a sideline of ethnographic research, anthropologists often interpret the position of women in other cultures in terms of the clear dichotomy between domestic and public sectors found in industrial society. American anthropologists unconsciously and inappropriately may have imposed this division on the nonindustrial societies they have studied.

Accepting the "inside-outside" dichotomy (Martin and Voorhies, 1975) as universal, Dorothy Ham-

mond and Alta Jablow (1976), for example, speak of a universal "relegation" of women to the domestic sphere: "Public life, which confers power and authority, is the concern of men. Male activities, interests, and attitudes tend to dominate the values and ethos of every society." Michelle Zimbalist Rosaldo and Louise Lamphere (1974) concur: "All contemporary societies are to some extent male-dominated, and . . . sexual asymmetry is presently a universal fact of human social life." Setting the domestic world of women in opposition to the public world of men, Rosaldo (1974) finds that everywhere men are the center of cultural value. Arguing that woman's secondary status is one of the true cultural universals, Sherry Ortner (1974) sees females as universally subordinate: "Everywhere, in every known culture, women are considered in some degree inferior to men." Although she stresses the wide variation in sex roles from culture to culture, Friedl (1975) finds "a degree of male dominance . . . in all human societies," male dominance being defined as "a situation in which men have highly preferential access, although not always exclusive rights, to those activities to which the society accords the greatest value, and the exercise of which permits a measure of control over others." These anthropologists accept that some degree of male dominance is universal, but also concur that, given contemporary technology and social conditions, even partial female subordination should not continue. Generally, they deny that male dominance is based on genetically determined psychological or physical differences between men and women. They link woman's domesticity to aspects of her reproductive role.

Other anthropologists are less sure of universal male dominance. Rayna Reiter (1975a), for example, recognizes that "cultures seem to display a wide range of variation in the amount of sexual equality or inequality expressed consciously or unconsciously by members of both sexes." Jane Fishburne Collier (1974), while viewing women as generally disadvantaged in competing with men for power and prestige, sees their handicap as "least in those political systems where leadership rests on ability and where there is little separation between the domestic and public spheres." Lamphere (1974) makes a similar point, noting that in societies where domestic and political spheres are integrated, authority is shared by men and women. Whether a degree of male dominance is universal is an arbitrary judgment. A much more profitable comparative approach to sex roles focuses on the tremendous cross-cultural variation (denied by none of the anthropologists mentioned above) in the behavior, rights, and obligations of men and women.

Sex Roles among Foragers

Similarities and differences in sex roles can be related to the strategies of adaptation (foraging, plant cultivation, pastoralism, industrialism) and levels of sociopolitical complexity (band, tribe, chiefdom, state) discussed in previous chapters. Within any one of these categories variation also reflects natural selection operating on learned behavior within specific environments. The degree of equality and symmetry in sex roles reflects economy. Among most foragers, particularly those in tropical and semi-tropical environments, gathering contributes more to the diet than either hunting or fishing. Gathering is generally, though not necessarily, women's work, while men are the usual hunters and fishers. We may generalize that where gathering is prominent, foragers' sex roles will be more equal and symmetrical than where hunting and/or fishing are dominant subsistence activities, as among certain northern and

temperate populations. This is a corollary of Sanday's (1974) finding that cross-culturally—and not just among foragers—women's status will be higher when they contribute about *as much* to subsistence as men do. Among food producers, in contrast to foragers, women's status appears to fall if they contribute either substantially more or substantially less to subsistence. Among foragers, status appears to fall only when women contribute substantially less, as among the Eskimos and other northern hunters and fishers.

Another generalization applies to both foraging and other strategies of adaptation: sex roles are more equal and symmetrical when domestic and public spheres are not sharply differentiated. Since the inside-outside dichotomy is less marked with foraging than with other adaptive strategies, foragers' sex roles tend toward equality.

A division of economic labor on the basis of sex has been an attribute of all human societies. The tasks that are assigned on the basis of sex do not reflect universal physical differences in strength or endurance between men and women. !Kung women, in the course of gathering on two or three days every week, travel some 1,500 miles in a year. For about half that distance, they carry not only children but up to thirty-three pounds of produce (Friedl, 1975). Among food producers, the onerous tasks of carrying water and firewood and pounding grain are often assigned to women. In the Soviet Union in 1967 women filled 47 percent of all factory positions, and women held many of the unmechanized positions that required the greatest amount of physical labor (Martin and Voorhies, 1975). Most sanitation workers as well as most physicians and nurses in the Soviet Union are women (Martin and Voorhies, 1975). Many tasks that in some societies are assigned to men are in others assigned to women, and vice versa.

Cross-culturally, however, some activities are usually assigned to one sex only. Generalized male activities, particularly in nonindustrial societies, include warfare and hunting. Divale and Harris (1976) have argued that, given hand weaponry, the greater average size and strength of males favors their role as warriors and defenders. Friedl (1975), however, suggests that the assignment of hunting and fighting to men reflects their greater average mobility. She argues that woman's hunting role is limited for demographic reasons. Given small band size and a high rate of infant mortality, Friedl suggests that, if the band is to maintain a stable population, all its women need to be either pregnant or nursing throughout their childbearing years. During the late stages of pregnancy and after childbirth, carrying the baby interferes with the woman's balance and can limit even her gathering activity. Given reproductive requirements and the effects of late pregnancy and lactation on mobility, it is not feasible, Friedl says, for foragers to make women regular hunters.

Despite these impediments, women do hunt in a variety of foraging societies. Among the Tiwi of northern Australia (Goodale, 1971) females hunt small and medium-sized game and gather resources of the land, while men concern themselves with the products of the air and sea, and with the largest land animals. Friedl (1975) found that while women fish and take part in communal hunts in many foraging societies, the hunting of large game animals in groups of four or five is universally a male activity. Woman's contribution to hunting appears to affect her symbolic identity among foragers. When women never hunt, foragers regard their menstrual blood as polluting, symbolically associating blood with the wounds and death of game animals. However, in foraging populations where women participate in communal hunts, the Mbuti of Zaire, for example, menstrual blood is not viewed as polluting, and sexual intercourse during menstruation is considered beneficial for both partners (Friedl, 1975).

Warfare, which also requires mobility and therefore may be generally assigned to males for the same reasons as hunting, is not prominent among foragers. Although exchanges take place between individual members of different bands, neither organized interregional exchange nor intergroup trade is typical of foraging societies. The absence of warfare and trade deprives men of two public arenas that contribute to status inequality of males and females among food producers.

The !Kung, as described by Patricia Draper (1975), illustrate the degree to which the activities and spheres of influence of men and women may overlap when foraging is the economic base. Draper found that !Kung male and female roles were interdependent and interrelated. During gathering, women amassed information about movement and availability of game and passed it on to the men. Neither men nor women worked more than three days a week. They spent about the same amount of time away from camp, where between one-third and one-half of the band's people remained while the others were working. Draper found !Kung willing to do the work of the other sex; men often gathered food and collected water, normally women's jobs. A general sharing ethos dictated that men distribute meat, a highly valued food because of its relative scarcity in the diet, and that women share beans and other gathered produce. Children of both sexes and all ages regularly played together. Fathers took an active role in raising children. Competition and aggression were discouraged since resources were more than adequate. Draper argues that interchangeability and interdependence of roles are adaptive in such small groups.

Draper's research is especially useful for evaluating relationships between economy and sex roles since it included not only a study of !Kung foragers, but field work among a group of former foragers who had recently adopted sedentary life. Today only a few thousand !Kung continue the foraging pattern of their ancestors; most now live in sedentary and semisquatter status near the settlements of Bantu-speaking food producers or European ranchers. Draper studied sedentary !Kung at Mahopa, a village at a permanent water source. Sex roles at Mahopa, where !Kung supported themselves by herding, horticulture, wage work for Bantu speakers, and a small amount of gathering, were more rigidly defined than in the bush. An inside-outside dichotomy was developing, as men traveled farther than women, who, with limited gathering, were more confined to their more permanent and private dwellings. Boys gained mobility through herding, while girls' work in subsistence was more limited. The open, egalitarian, communal world of the bush was being replaced by attributes of sedentary life. Replacing bush sharing and equal distribution to all was differential ranking of individual males according to their possessions — herds and houses — and the number of their sons, now seen as differentially valued producers.

If, as some anthropologists argue, there is some degree of male dominance in every contemporary society, this may reflect such recent changes as those that have affected the !Kung. Among populations who still cling to a foraging life, however, egalitarianism extends to relations between the sexes, and the social spheres, activities, rights, and obligations of men and women overlap. Foragers' kinship systems stress bilateral kinship calculation rather than unilineal descent, and a variety of residential choices are available to individuals and couples. Compared with people with other subsistence strategies, foragers treat males and females equally in cases of premarital sex, adultery, and divorce—which is common. Friedl (1975) generalizes that social concern with female sexuality—expressed in double or restrictive sexual standards—is linked to substantial property transactions at marriage, particularly bridewealth, rare or absent among foragers. This suggests an association between patrilineal descent and virilocal residence and the subordination of women's rights, an association that does exist.

In arguing for a genetic basis for aspects of contemporary human social behavior, sociobiologists typically stress the importance of hunting to our ancestors prior to 12,000 B.P. Ironically, study of contemporary foragers, whose skills, activities, and social patterns are closest to our pre–food-producing ancestors, casts greatest doubt on sociobiology. It is among foragers that public and private spheres are least distinct, that hierarchy is least marked, that aggression and competition are most discouraged, and that rights, activities, and spheres of influence of men and women most overlap. Foragers even contradict Tiger's (1970) hypothesis of men's naturally greater sociability. Draper describes !Kung women as vivacious and sociable. Gathering, most often done by groups of three adult women, was an occasion for social contact, and not solitary drudgery. Anthropologists have typically focused on the associations and ceremonials of males, slighting those of women. Native Australian women, however, who were excluded from all-male ceremonials, identified with female totemic ancestors and held their own rituals (Rohrlich-Leavitt, Sykes, and Weatherford, 1975). In northwestern Australia women held secret collective ceremonies, paralleling those of the men. The ceremonies were organized by middle-aged and older women and involved joking, teasing, song, dance, drama, and celebration of the clitoris as a sexual organ (Rohrlich-Leavitt, Sykes, and Weatherford, 1975). Again ethnography confirms variability, not genetically ordained universals.

Sex Roles among Cultivators: Horticulturalists

Sex roles in plant-cultivating societies vary widely, but they are linked to economy and social structure. Martin and Voorhies (1975) generalize that the status of women falls as cultivation becomes more intensive and as the percentage of cultigens in the diet increases. They find female status particularly low

with agriculture, where reliance on crops is great and where men tend to be the principal producers. Martin and Voorhies (1975) and Friedl (1975) also link the status of women to prevailing rules of descent and postmarital residence. Surveying tribal horticultural societies, Martin and Voorhies find the status of women almost universally high when descent is matrilineal and postmarital residence uxorilocal. But with patrilineal descent and virilocal residence, the status of women falls. Among intensive cultivators, they find it low regardless of descent or residence rule. To understand the implications of these generalizations, some figures must be examined.

Martin and Voorhies chose a sample of 515 horticultural societies, representing all geographical regions of the world, from Murdock's (1967) *Ethnographic Atlas,* a codification of cross-cultural data. They focused on several variables within the sample: rules of descent and postmarital residence, the percentage of the diet derived from cultivation, and the productivity of men and women. Overwhelmingly, women were the main horticultural producers. In 41 percent of the horticultural societies women dominated cultivating activities; in 37 percent, the contributions to cultivation by men and women were equal; and in only 22 percent did men dominate cultivation. Martin and Voorhies found that women contributed slightly more to horticulture in matrilineal than in patrilineal societies. Women dominated cultivation in 64 percent of the matrilineal societies, but in only 50 percent of the patrilineal ones. Note, however, that women's dominance of subsistence does not necessarily lead to uxorilocality, matrilineality, or high status. Women dominate horticulture in 50 percent of all patrilineal societies, while males work more in only 36 percent, yet the status of women under patriliny tends to be low.

Comparing the geographic and ecological distribution of matriliny and patriliny, Martin and Voorhies find the latter associated with dense forests and other habitats that are less favorable for cultivation. Patrilineal farmers, accordingly, have to work harder than matrilineal ones to obtain similar yields. Dietary dependence on cultivation is also greater for patrilineal cultivators, 68 percent of foods consumed compared with 55 percent with matriliny. Martin and Voorhies note that where critical resources are scarce, localization of males, and therefore virilocal residence and patrilineal descent, are adaptive. Divale and Harris (1976) find patriliny and virilocality associated with tribal warfare and with social devaluation of women expressed through polygyny, female infanticide, and a pervasive male supremacist complex.

MATRILINY, UXORILOCALITY, AND HIGH FEMALE STATUS The effects of matriliny and uxorilocality, which disperse rather than consolidate related males, are very different from those of patriliny and virilocality, and are adaptations to dissimilar ecological niches. Surveying the worldwide distribution of matrilineal horticultural populations, David Aberle (1961) found them generally located outside of, or bordering, forested areas, and in areas where large domesticated animals were absent. In the ecological niches of matrilineal-uxorilocal systems, population pressure on strategic resources is minimal. Warfare is infrequent or totally absent, as are its psychological and social results — aggression, competition, strong differentiation between public and private, devaluation of women, and female infanticide. Martin and Voorhies follow Keith Otterbein and Charlotte Swanson Otterbein (1965) in associating matriliny and uxorilocality with sociopolitical stability and habitats that allow it. Such habitats, however, have become decreasingly common over the past few centuries. Although matrilineal societies constitute only 24 percent of their horticultural sample, Martin and Voorhies suggest a higher frequency under more stable conditions in the past. They say that matrilineal descent tends to disappear when it confronts problems of expansion, competition, or intensification of production.

Why do women enjoy high status in matrilineal, uxorilocal societies? Descent-group membership, succession to political positions, allocation of land, and overall social identity are all based on links through females. Women thus become the focus of the entire social structure. Although positions of public authority may be assigned to older males, actual power and decision making may be concentrated in the hands of senior women. Anthropologists have yet to discover a matriarchy, a sociopolitical system in which women totally dominate men, but some matrilineal systems, particularly the native Iroquois (Brown, 1975) of the northeastern United States, demonstrate that women's political and ritual influence can equal or surpass that of men.

It was previously noted that sex roles among foragers tend to be more nearly equal when there are no sharp distinctions between male and female activities or between public and domestic spheres. However, this generalization does not hold for the Iroquois. Sexual equality may also be favored if differentiation between male and female activities is extreme — if females play a major role in subsistence production while males are removed from their home community for long periods, as among the Iroquois. The status of women is lowered when male and female spheres are sharply differentiated *within* the local community. As is true of matrilineal, uxorilocal societies generally, *internal* warfare among the Iroquois was uncommon, but men did wage war against distant groups, which might keep them away from home for years. Men also hunted and did most of the fishing, but women controlled the local economy. They did some fishing and were not barred from the hunt, but their major productive role was in cultivation. Horticulture in a stable, favored environment was highly organized under female leadership. Women owned the land, which they inherited from matrilineal kinswomen, and controlled both production and distribution.

Iroquois women resided with their husbands and children in family compartments of a communal longhouse. Women born in a longhouse would remain there throughout their lives. The senior women (matrons) of the localized matrilineage arranged marriages, deciding which men would be allowed to join the longhouse as husbands. In the event of incompatibility, matrons might evict husbands. Iroquois women therefore controlled the creation and termination of alliances between lineages, a vital aspect of sociopolitical organization among food producers. Matrons, as producers and guardians of crops, also dominated distribution, allocating food to men and children, and supplying dried meat to men embarking on war expeditions. They also controlled the exchange of moveable wealth.

In a society in which women managed production and distribution, and in which social identity, succession to office and titles, and property were all transmitted through the female line, woman's place loomed large in ritual and formal politics. Linguistically and culturally related tribes made up a political confederacy, the League of the Iroquois. Within this formal political organization of chiefs and councils, women held socially recognized and institutionalized authority. Individuals gained places on the council of chiefs, which managed external military operations, through matrilineal succession. A descent group's matrons, surveying their group's eli-

Archeologically reconstructed Iroquois longhouse of the fourteenth century A.D. Located on a hilltop near Syracuse, New York, the longhouse was 22 feet by 210 feet. These longhouses were inhabited by matrilineally related women who resided uxorilocally with their husbands and children. The matrons of the longhouse controlled cultivation and the distribution of food, arranged marriages, and could evict unpopular husbands. (Courtesy James Tuck, University of Newfoundland)

gible males, nominated one to replace their last council representative. Should the chiefs reject the matrons' first nominee, the women proposed others until one was finally accepted. The matrons had their own representative to the council, a man who took part in its deliberations and reported to the women. Matrons constantly monitored the behavior and decisions of chiefs and held the power to impeach. Women could veto proposed war declarations and initiate peace efforts. In religion, too, women shared power. Half the tribe's religious practitioners were women, and the matrons helped select the others. Control of production and distribution, and the removal of males from regular participation in community affairs, therefore supported power and prestige for Iroquois women.

Surveying the "matrifocal" (mother-centered) social organization of certain groups in Indonesia, West Africa, the Caribbean, and the contemporary United States, anthropologist Nancy Tanner (1974) also found that the absence of men, when combined with a major female role in subsistence, promoted high women's status. Among the Atjehnese and Minangkabau of Indonesia and the Igbo of West Africa the mother role was central in kinship, women participated equally in economy and religion, and the rights and obligations of men and women tended toward equality. Matrifocal societies are not necessarily matrilineal. The Atjehnese of northern Sumatra, for

example, lacked descent groups, but practiced uxorilocal residence. Women owned houses and dominated cultivation. Men owned other property, but they migrated easily, seeking cash outside the village. The marital link was weak; 39 percent of Atjehnese marriages ended in divorce. Women managed subsistence production, house, and children, and retained their independence. Among the matrilineal Minangkabau of western Sumatra male and female spheres of activity were sharply separated. Men represented their matrilineage to outsiders and contributed cash to its support, but they left home for long periods for trade and education. Women controlled cultivation and home industry, and sold their products in markets. As among the Atjehnese, marital ties were brittle. Women, possessing the means to retain their social independence, participated in economic, religious, and legal affairs.

Among the patrilineal, virilocal, polygynous—but still matrifocal—Igbo of eastern Nigeria each wife had her own quarters, where she lived in a matrifocal social unit with her children. Women planted crops on land next to their houses and traded any surplus. In fact, they controlled local markets, while men spent extended periods away from home as long-distance traders. In some Igbo areas, women joined influential all-female political associations based on their common economic interests. Their leaders controlled major market activity. Very successful women could become socially recognized husbands, paying bridewealth to acquire wives—not as sexual partners but to take over domestic responsibilities. Igbo lineages segmented not between brothers, as among the Nuer (Chapter 7), but between wives of a single ancestor. The Igbo remembered their great women as founding ancestors of their lineage segments. The central position of women in Igbo society rested on the separation of males from local subsistence, on the absence of males, and on a marketing system that allowed women to leave the domestic sphere and gain prominence in extradomestic redistribution and—through these accomplishments—in regional politics.

THE PATRILINEAL-VIROLOCAL COMPLEX AND LOW FEMALE STATUS   The Igbo are unusual among patrilineal-virilocal societies; in most, female status is much lower. Martin and Voorhies (1975) link the decline of matriliny and the spread of the patrilineal-virilocal complex to scarcity of strategic resources. The findings of Divale and Harris (1976) are complementary to this. Both studies show that patrilineal-virilocal societies share several contexts, characteristics, and results. Faced with scarce resources, patrilineal-virilocal cultivators often adopt the interrelated cultural responses of warfare and polygyny. Warfare, as Divale and Harris have shown, regulates population growth indirectly by encouraging or intensifying female infanticide. Warfare socially devalues women and favors the localization of

related men, and thus virilocality and patriliny. Martin and Voorhies argue that polygyny is a social response to the economic necessity of increasing production. Women remain the dominant producers of subsistence crops among patrilineal cultivators. According to Martin and Voorhies, polygyny increases household production since it brings together many working women.

Crops contribute more to the diet among patrilineal than among matrilineal horticulturalists (Martin and Voorhies, 1975), and cultivating techniques are more intensive, involving more work for a given yield. Surpluses may, however, be generated, and the polygyny may reflect men's wish to produce this surplus. In multicentric economies that assign the subsistence sphere to women and the prestige sphere to men, women thus generate surpluses for men. Throughout the world, patrilineal-virilocal cultivators exchange surplus crops for cattle, pigs, sheep, or goats—prestige items that can differentiate status, and that can be reconverted into food when need dictates. Through bridewealth these prestige items can be converted into a still higher sphere—women, who, as Martin and Voorhies point out, may be viewed socially as valuable moveable property. Not only are women the major subsistence workers, they also produce the children that make a man a descent-group ancestor, given patrilineality.

Among patrilineal-virilocal cultivators, men and women have sharply differentiated activities and concerns, but both sexes reside in the same commu-

Matrifocal families like the one shown here arise for varied reasons. In some cultures, they reflect marital instability and women's prominent role in religion, economics, and politics as well as in family life. In others, like Italy, female-headed households arise in the context of poverty and a shortage of males who migrate seeking wage work. (Constantine Manos/Magnum Photos)

nities. The private-public, domestic-extradomestic dichotomy is there for all to see, and men use their public roles in extradomestic distribution to symbolize and reinforce their oppression of women. Friedl generalizes that control over the channels for distributing goods and services is a critical factor in explaining differences in men's and women's power. In patrilineal-virilocal societies worldwide, men govern the extradomestic distribution of prestige items, whether prestige crops, animals, or alliance-forming marriages.

In many parts of highland New Guinea, the patrilineal-virilocal complex has extreme social repercussions. Women raise pigs, but men control their distribution and use in ritual. Men also raise and distribute prestige crops, and arrange strategic marriages. They even dominate food preparation for feasts, as among the patrilineal, virilocal, male supremacist Yanomamo. Women do domestic cooking, deal with subsistence crops, and tend pigs before they are slaughtered and cooked; generally, they are isolated from the public domain.

In the most densely populated parts of the New Guinea highlands, the separation of men's and women's worlds is institutionalized as severe sexual antagonism. Shirley Lindenbaum (1972) associates such hostility with population pressure on strategic resources, linked previously to patrilineality, male supremacy, and the need to limit reproduction. Given high population density, sexual contact with women is believed to weaken men, and all aspects of woman are viewed as polluting. Males segregate themselves in men's houses, guarding their sacred ritual paraphernalia from women. They fear contacts, including sexual intercourse, with women; they delay marriages, and some never marry. However, in the absence of population pressure—for example, in recently settled areas—taboos on male-female contacts lapse. The social view of woman as polluter fades; heterosexual intercourse is valued; men and women live together; and reproductive rates are high.

The Hagen, a group of some 75,000 densely populated cultivators of highland New Guinea (Strathern, 1972), illustrate institutionalized sexual antagonism and the full effects of the patrilineal-virilocal complex. Although men always provide access to land, women are the major subsistence workers, farming plots both in their husband's community and, at the behest of a kinsman, in their native village. A Hagen woman retains ties with her agnates, and the brother-

Women grinding maize, a daily cooperative activity. Women do most of the work to produce food, as well as prepare it, among many patrilineal-virilocal cultivators. (Victor Englebert/Photo Researchers)

sister bond is particularly strong. This gives her somewhat more independence than in those patrilineal societies where women join their husband's descent group at marriage. Yet the woman's link to her own descent group further weakens the marriage bond and increases husband-wife hostility, and hence community male-female antagonism. Male agnates live together in a large men's house. Women's residence patterns are less sociable. A wife moves into her husband's mother's hut. Her pigs and children also sleep there, until her sons join the men. Some men are polygynous, and relations among cowives are typically hostile and competitive. A woman's social allegiance remains with her kin and not with her affinals or cowives.

Men, as expected, control extradomestic distribution—of pigs, valuables made from shells, and women in marriage. Strategic marriages can convert minor enemies into friends. However, since wives often come from formerly hostile groups, the marital bond is strained and sexual antagonism is again reinforced. Men fear female bodies and their products. During menstruation women are secluded in huts and must not come into contact with food. Although the Hagen view heterosexual intercourse as pleasurable, they limit it to certain times and places. Hagen women respond to male oppression by exercising power and influence in the supernatural realm. Female ghosts are most feared, by men and women alike. Women use threats involving their polluting bodies and products as a means of partially controlling the men.

Despite the generalized links between patriliny, virilocality, polygyny, and female oppression, in some situations women can improve their lot. The Igbo of eastern Nigeria are not alone in allowing women access to extradomestic distribution. In many other patrilineal, polygynous societies, particularly in West Africa, women have access to careers in trade. Polygyny may even help the aspiring trader. Since all wives contribute to the common household, a woman can leave her older children with cowives while she pursues a business career. She will repay them with cash and other assistance.

All these generalizations about sex roles always specify a particular set of economic and sociopolitical conditions. Given tribal sociopolitical organization, patriliny and virilocality conspire to isolate women and devalue them socially. Friedl (1975) points out, however, that in the context of chiefdoms and states, new horizons open up, at least to some women. Given stratification, some men, women, and children have privileged access to strategic resources, while other whole groups of men, women,

and children have more limited opportunities. In such contexts, elite women can manipulate wealth and power as effectively as men. They can become queens, chiefs, and headwomen. They can assume central places in rituals, convoke and sponsor regional ceremonials, trade, exchange, and arrange marriages. Tribal society, under some conditions, discriminates against *women*. In stratified society, not only does discrimination against women continue, but some women join some men in discriminating against *people*.

Sex Roles among Cultivators: Agriculturalists

Agriculture, associated with state organization in 35 percent of Martin and Voorhies' (1975) sample of 93 agricultural societies, continues trends involving greater reliance on cultigens, intensification of production, and decline in women's status. The average agricultural population has about 10 percent greater dependence on cultigens than does the average horticultural population. Martin and Voorhies argue that as the need to increase production intensified, men were forced to participate in cultivation. New techniques, including use of the plow, called for male rather than female labor. Plowing was assigned to men, argue Martin and Voorhies, because of their greater average size and strength. Except with irrigated agriculture, plowing eliminated the need for constant weeding, an activity usually associated with women.

Data from a cross-cultural sample of horticulturalists and agriculturalists (Martin and Voorhies, 1975) illustrate the different productive roles of men and women. Women were the primary farmers in 50 percent of the 104 horticultural societies, but in only 15 percent of the 93 agricultural groups. Male labor was dominant in 81 percent of the agricultural societies, but in only 17 percent of the horticultural populations. Men and women assumed equal productive roles one-third of the time under horticulture, but only 3 percent of the time under agriculture (see Figure 11.1).

For the first time in cultural evolution, women were divorced from production. A conceptual distinction between women's domestic work and men's extradomestic, productive labor reinforced the contrast between the private role of women and the public role of men. Changes in social organization also affected woman's status. Both unilineal descent

FIGURE 11.1 Male and female contributions to production in cultivating societies.

	Horticulture (percentage of 104 societies)	Agriculture (percentage of 93 societies)
Women are primary cultivators	50	15
Men are primary cultivators	17	81
Equal contributions to cultivation	33	3

In most peasant societies with plow agriculture, men are the primary producers. Women, when isolated from relatives and cowives in nuclear family households, are often victims of the inside-outside dichotomy—deprived of political and legal importance as well as a major role in production. But there are exceptions. Shown here, a married couple in northern India harvest wheat to feed their family. (Marc & Evelyne Bernheim/Woodfin Camp & Assoc.)

and polygyny declined under agriculture; often women in nuclear family households were isolated from kinswomen, cowives, or other female affines. Martin and Voorhies find women's sexuality stringently controlled in agricultural societies, with differential rights in divorce and pre- and extramarital sex for men and women. Women's overall status under agriculture, they conclude, is one of institutionalized dependency, subordination, and political immaturity.

Woman's status under agriculture is not inevitably as bleak as Martin and Voorhies picture it. Low female status may be associated with plow agriculture rather than with intensive cultivation per se. For instance, recent studies of women's roles in France (Reiter, 1975b) and Spain (Harding, 1975), both mechanizing peasant societies with plow agriculture, do demonstrate that the house is conceived of as woman's and the fields as man's. But such a dichotomy is not inevitable, as my own research among agriculturalists in Madagascar shows.

Betsileo women play a major and indispensable role in agriculture; they contribute about one-third of the total hours annually invested in rice production and have their own assigned tasks in the traditional division of labor. Women's work in rice production is more seasonal than men's. Neither sex has much field work to do during the ceremonial season be-

tween mid-June and mid-September. Men work almost daily in the fields during the rest of the year. Women's cooperative work is required during transplanting (mid-September through November) and at harvest time (mid-March through early May). Like other household members, women weed each day during December and January. Women and men also work equally in winnowing unhusked rice and transporting it to their granary after the harvest. If the strenuous daily tasks of setting rice out to dry and husking it by pounding are also considered, women actually contribute slightly more than 50 percent of the labor devoted to producing and preparing rice prior to cooking.

Not just economy, but traditional social organization enhances female status among the Betsileo. While postmarital residence is almost always virilocal, descent groups are ambilineal, though with a tendency toward patriliny. When women marry they retain membership and rights in, and a strong allegiance to, their own descent groups. A woman assumes obligations to her husband, his kin, and their wives, but he and his closest relatives are also obliged to her and her relatives. Often accompanied by their husband and children, women pay regular visits to their home villages. The husband and his close relatives help the wife's kin in agriculture, and attend ceremonials involving her kin and ancestors.

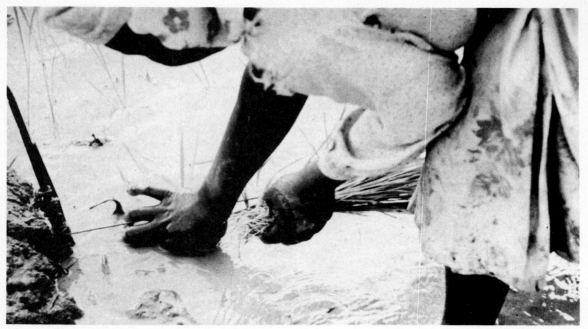

A Betsileo woman transplants rice seedlings in rows (note string for lining seedlings up), rather than haphazardly, as in traditional Betsileo cultivation. Row planting saves weeding time, since rotary weeding machines can be used. However, Betsileo women are resisting the new technique, perhaps wisely, since women do about half the traditional weeding. When women are isolated from production, their status usually falls. (Conrad P. Kottak)

When a woman dies, she is normally buried in her husband's ancestral tomb; however, a delegation from her own village always comes to request that she be buried at home. Since kinship is broadly and bilaterally calculated, women often marry into villages where some of their kinswomen have also married. Thus, even after marriage, a woman remains in contact with her relatives.

Betsileo women can inherit rice fields; thus men do not have exclusive control over the means of production. However, most women, on marriage, relinquish their share of the ancestral estate to their brothers. Sometimes a woman and her husband cultivate her field, eventually passing it on to their children. Betsileo society has been stratified and state-organized for more than 250 years. Women have rights to hold land and to invest their surpluses in cattle. They could also hold political office. Traditionally, men have had greater participation in public activity than women, but women engage in market trade, sponsor ceremonials, and are remembered when ancestors are worshiped. Women have used their own wealth, prestige, generosity, and cash to get men to work their rice fields. Arranging marriages, an important extradomestic activity, is as much or more women's concern than men's. Sometimes Betsileo women seek their own kinswomen as wives for their sons, thus reinforcing their own prominence in village life and continuing kinship-based female solidarity in the village.

The Betsileo illustrate that intensive cultivation per se does not entail a degraded status for women. Sex roles reflect not just type of adaptive strategy, but also specific environmental variables and cultural attributes. Betsileo women continue to play a significant role in their society's major economic activity, rice production. Plowing has only recently become prominent in Betsileo agriculture, but irrigation means that weeding, in which women participate, remains a problem. If new tools and techniques do eventually reduce women's roles in transplanting, harvesting, and weeding, female status may fall. In the meantime, descent-group organization and cultural stress on kinship, along with traditional female rights in inheritance, trade, and arranging marriages, continue to draw the Betsileo away from the stereotype of the degraded woman in agricultural or virilocal societies.

Sex Roles among Pastoralists

Pastoralism, because it rarely occurs as a "pure" adaptation, has diverse social correlates, including sex roles. In a sample of forty-four pastoral (dairy products and meat provided more than 50 percent of the diet) societies examined by Martin and Voorhies (1975), only ten lacked any dependence on cultivation. Of the remaining thirty-four, more than half were intensive cultivators, while the rest used horticultural techniques. Women's status reflected both herding patterns and type of plant cultivation. Among pastoralists practicing intensive cultivation or descended from agricultural parent communities, women's status reflected the inside-outside dichotomy characteristic of many agricultural societies. When pastoralists practiced horticulture, women's status might also be low; however, women's role in production was greater, and—reflecting their subsistence contribution to the household—polygyny was also more prevalent. The patrilineal-virilocal complex also characterized pastoralists. Of the forty-four societies in the sample, thirty-six were patrilineal and thirty-three virilocal. Martin and Voorhies also relate economic roles to herding patterns. Women milk when the entire community travels together throughout the year (nomadism) or when herds are grazed on pasture surrounding sedentary communities. Men, however, milk when herding

is transhumant. A male dairying role with transhumance is an economic necessity, since men and boys accompany the herds, while women, girls, and old men remain at home. Martin and Voorhies found the economic contribution of women lowest among transhumant pastoralists who relied little on cultivation.

Pastoralists residing in the Balkan peninsula of Greece, Yugoslavia, Albania, and Bulgaria (Denich, 1974) illustrate some of these points. In addition to men's movement between summer and winter pastures in transhumant herding, Balkan pastoralists practice plow agriculture. Both herding and plowing are male activities, although women contribute to cultivation, in addition to their domestic work, crafts, and carrying the heaviest burdens of firewood and water. The inside-outside dichotomy and the patrilineal-virilocal complex are fully expressed in what Denich calls "patricentric" social organization. Women may inherit neither land nor sheep and goats, the herd animals. Men control all property.

Balkan pastoralists belong to patrilineal-virilocal tribes, clans, and minimal, coresident lineages. The father is patriarch in a joint household including his wife, his married sons and their wives and children, and his own unmarried children. Joint households split sometime after the father's death, and the sons become patriarchs in their own right. Subordination of women is extreme. When naming their children, men mention only their sons; male ancestors, but never women, are remembered—for as many as twenty generations. Men arrange all marriages and attempt to establish broad-based alliances with their co–fathers-in-law. Convention dictates that brothers' wives come from different descent groups; thus women, on marriage, enter a totally alien social

A Betsileo woman tends pigs. Men tend cattle but women tend pigs among the Betsileo as in many other cultures, including the Tsembaga Maring (Chapter 16). Terraced rice fields, some flooded for transplanting, are shown in the valley and hillside beyond. (Conrad P. Kottak)

world, away from their own kinswomen. Men have total authority and power, and women lack any basis for autonomy. They are expected to defer to their husband and his kinsmen in a hundred ways; they may be beaten, and, if adulterous, killed; their premarital sexual activity is rigidly controlled. Exclusion of women from a dominant contribution to production acts to maintain patricentric organization among these pastoralists.

Sex Roles and Industrialism

The inside-outside dichotomy, which developed most fully among many agricultural and pastoral populations, has affected the status of women even in industrial societies. However, opinions about what women's roles are, and should be, are changing now and have been since the seventeenth century, as our own society illustrates. Maxine Margolis (1976) and Martin and Voorhies (1975) have indicated some of the social and economic reasons why. They link the American attitude that women's place is in the home to the emergence of industrialism. Martin and Voorhies, along with Margolis, note that pioneer women in the Midwest and West were perceived as fully productive work partners in a preindustrial economic life that rested on farming and home industry. Confirming this, Western frontier women were among the first of their sex to receive the right to vote.

As industrialism emerged, attitudes about woman's place varied with class and region. To poor people, women's paid work is usually proper.

Martin and Voorhies observe that lower-class men, women, and children in early industrial Europe flocked to factories as wage laborers. Elite Europeans justified unsafe, unhealthy working conditions and long, grueling labor by their belief in the genetic inferiority of working-class people. Americans used a similar rationale to justify enslavement of Afro-Americans. They exploited male and female slaves equally; following abolition, black women continued to work along with men as field hands and as domestics. Poor white women worked in the early cotton mills of the South, and during the 1890s more than 1 million American women held the most menial, repetitious, and unskilled positions in the country's factories. Martin and Voorhies note that a constant influx of European immigrants, along with better machinery and improving financial security, conspired to remove women from factory work early in this century. As the need for female labor declined, the idea that women were unfit for factory work and other menial jobs increased.

Margolis links attitudes about women's place and their actual participation in extradomestic labor to general economic needs. Wartime shortages of male labor traditionally promote the idea that extradomestic labor is woman's patriotic duty. During World Wars I and II the notion that women were biologically unfit for hard physical labor was suspended. Margolis also found that inflation has favored female extradomestic labor. When prices rise more rapidly than wages, additional income helps maintain the family's, particularly the poor family's, living stan-

In the Soviet Union, women like those shown here hold many physically demanding jobs. Soviet women outnumber men as both physicians and sanitation workers. Societal forces like war and inflation determine division of labor by gender in industrial societies. (Fred Mayer/Woodfin Camp & Assoc.)

dard. Margolis attributes a steady increase in female paid employment since World War II to industrial expansion and to the need for *female* labor per se. American culture has traditionally defined many jobs, including much clerical work and such professions as teaching and nursing, as female occupations. With postwar business expansion the demand for women to fill such jobs grew steadily, even though returning World War II veterans were also seeking work. Employers were able to increase their profits by paying women lower wages than men for the same jobs.

Business expansion, inflation, increasing demand for female labor, and the profit motive have all acted to increase steadily women's overall role in extradomestic employment since World War II. In 1950 only 28 percent of all mothers with school-age children held outside jobs, but in 1975 the figure had risen to 54 percent. In 1975 about three times as many mothers of pre-school-age children worked outside the home as in 1950. Only 18 percent of cash-earning spouses were women in 1950, compared with 34 percent today (*Washington Post,* January 2, 1977). Margolis's major point is that changing *attitudes* toward women do not increase their participation in public life or extradomestic labor. Rather, changes in the *economy* lead to changes in attitudes toward women. Woman's role in the home is typically stressed during periods of high unemployment, although if inflation occurs simultaneously, her working may still be accepted. Today's feminism results from the steadily increasing participation by American women in extradomestic labor, and is more a result than a cause of this increase.

What Determines Variation?

Sex roles vary widely from culture to culture. This reflects adaptive problems associated with specific environments and, more generally, particular adaptive strategies and levels of sociopolitical complexity. Neither the degradation of woman, male dominance, nor sharp differentiation between public and private spheres is a cultural universal. Among many foragers and matrilineal cultivators, the public-private contrast has little meaning and sex roles are symmetrical. Competition for scarce resources selects for both warfare and intensification of production, and each condition favors patriliny and virilocality. To the extent that women are removed

Anatomy is not destiny. Like this copper smelter in Montana, women customarily perform hard physical labor in many cultures. Men's customary role in hunting and warfare may reflect their greater mobility, freed as they are from pregnancy and lactation, rather than sheer size and strength. (Craig Aurness/Woodfin Camp & Assoc.)

from productive roles in agricultural and pastoral societies, the inside-outside dichotomy becomes complete and the degradation of woman is extreme. With industrialism, new forms of family organization and attitudes about woman's place rest on the ever-increasing participation of women in extradomestic employment. The variability of sex roles in time and space suggests that they will continue to change. Like the social mobilization of aggression or altruism, sex roles reflect culture, society, politics, and economics—not genetics.

SEXUAL EXPRESSION IN COMPARATIVE PERSPECTIVE

Scholars and the public alike have linked variant forms of sexual expression to biological factors, arguing, for example, that hormonal balance differentiates heterosexuals from homosexuals. But are whole cultures that value homosexuality over heterosexuality, at least for certain people at certain times and in certain places, characterized by hormonal abnormalities? The best evidence is that they are not. Differences in sexual preferences and behavior reflect environmental and cultural differences, not biological variation. In their cross-cultural study, *Patterns of Sexual Behavior*, Clellan S. Ford and Frank A. Beach (1951) found wide variation in culturally approved forms of sexuality.

To understand how sexual expression reflects learning, we will contrast sociocultural variation in attitudes about masturbation, bestiality (interspecific sex), and homosexuality. Even in the United States, attitudes about sex differ according to socioeconomic status, region, and rural or urban residence. In general, in the United States there has been less intense social disapproval of and fewer social sanctions against masturbation than bestiality or homosexuality. Even in the 1950s, before the "age of sexual permissiveness" began, researchers determined that 92 percent of American men and 54 percent of American women admitted to masturbation (Ford and Beach, 1951). Between 40 and 50 percent of boys raised on farms had engaged in interspecific sex. In the Kinsey report 37 percent of the American men sampled admitted at least one homosexual experience culminating in orgasm (Kinsey, Pomeroy, and Martin, 1948). In a subsequent study of 1,200 unmarried women, 26 percent reported homosexual activities (Ford and Beach, 1951).

Social treatment of homosexuality, masturbation, and bestiality in other cultures differs from that in the United States. Ford and Beach found that in only twenty-eight (37 percent) of seventy-six societies for which data were available were adult homosexual activities reported to be totally absent, rare, or carried on in secrecy. In the other forty-nine (63 percent) various forms of homosexual expression were considered normal and socially acceptable, at least for certain members of the community. Ford and Beach found data on female homosexual behavior reported for only seventeen of the seventy-six societies in their sample; this once again reflects anthropologists' general neglect of women's activities.

Often, but not always, sexual relations between people of the same sex involved the transvestism of one of the partners. Among several Native American populations of the western plains, for example, biological men could reject the usual male role of bison hunter, raider, and warrior, and become *berdaches*. Among the Crow (Lowie, 1935) berdache

was a third gender. Berdaches dressed, spoke, and styled their hair like women, and pursued such traditionally female activities as cooking and needlework. Certain ritual duties were reserved for berdaches, suggesting their regular and normal place in social life. Among the Siberian Chukchee (Bogoras, 1904), whose coastal populations fished and interior groups herded reindeer, men might become powerful shamans by copying the dress, speech, hair arrangements, and general life styles of women. These shamans took other men as husbands and sexual partners, and enjoyed considerable community respect for their supernatural and curative expertise. Women, similarly in connection with shamanism, could join a fourth gender, copying men and taking wives.

Anthropologist E. E. Evans-Pritchard (1970) has described institutionalized homosexuality among the Azande of the Sudan, a herding society that valued the warrior role. Boys between twelve and twenty were separated from their families and shared quarters with adult fighting men. These men paid bridewealth for, wed, and had sexual relations with the apprentice boys, who, during their apprenticeship years, performed the domestic duties of women. As males moved to warrior status, they took their own boy-wives. On retiring as warriors, Azande men married women and, flexible in their sexual expression, had no difficulty in performing coitus. Among the Etoro of New Guinea, to be described below, homosexual preference persists for life, though heterosexual intercourse does occur.

Ford and Beach (1951) found greater cross-cultural acceptance of homosexuality than of either bestiality or masturbation. Almost all societies in their sample discouraged masturbation, and in only five societies were human-animal sexual contacts permitted. Note that their data involve only the social approval or disapproval of forms of human sexual expression, not the actual frequency of the acts. As in our own society, socially disapproved alternatives to heterosexual intercourse are likely to be more widespread than people are willing to admit. Flexibility in sexual expression seems an aspect of our primate heritage. Both masturbation and homosexual behavior are widely encountered among chimpanzees, other nonhuman primates, and animals in general. Our sexual potential is plastic and is molded by the environment and reproductive necessity. Heterosexuality is natural and widespread among humans and other animals—which, after all, must reproduce themselves—but so are alternatives. Just how humans will express their "natural" sexual urges is a matter that culture and environment determine and limit.

The Etoro of New Guinea (Kelly, 1976, 1977), a population of 400 who subsist through hunting and horticulture, provide an extreme case of the impact of culture on human sexual plasticity. Sexual attitudes form a consistent part of the Etoro culture's symbolic structure and ideology. The following account is limited to Etoro males and their beliefs. Etoro cultural norms restrain a male anthropologist from gathering information from females or about their attitudes. Etoro opinions about homosexuality and heterosexuality are linked to their beliefs about the cycle of birth, physical growth, maturity, senescence, and death.

A man's semen, through his intercourse with his wife, gives life force to the child, planted by ancestral spirits within the woman. Yet the loss of semen, of which men are believed to have a finite store, depletes the men, sapping their vitality. The birth of children, nurtured by semen, symbolizes a man's necessary sacrifice that will lead to his senescence and eventual death. Heterosexual intercourse, needed only for reproduction, is thus discouraged. Women who entice their husbands to sexual excess are socially disapproved of; they are seen as potential or actual witches. Etoro culture taboos heterosexual intercourse for between 205 and 260 days a year, and the seasonal clustering of births suggests that taboos are obeyed. Heterosexuality is also removed from normal community life. Coitus cannot take place in either the communal longhouse, where men and women occupy separate quarters, or the gardens where the Etoro grow their food. It is restricted to the forest, but even there it is considered dangerous, since deadly snakes, Etoro say, are attracted to such activity.

Frequent heterosexual coitus is discouraged, but regular homosexual acts are considered a necessity of life. Etoro believe that boys possess no semen at birth. In order to acquire semen and to grow into men, they must be inseminated orally by older men. The transmission of semen is therefore needed not just to create, but to transform, life. From the age of ten to their mid-twenties, boys are continually inseminated by older men, one of whom is usually the principal inseminator. Unlike heterosexual intercourse, no taboos about time and place are attached to this activity. Homosexuality may be expressed in longhouse or in garden. Every three years a group of boys around the age of twenty is formally initiated into manhood. With the previous group of initiates, they withdraw to a secluded mountain lodge, where they are visited and inseminated by several older men.

Etoro homosexuality is governed by a strict code of propriety. Although homosexual relationships between older and younger males are culturally essential, those between boys of the same age are severely discouraged. A boy receiving semen from other youths is sapping their life force and preventing their proper development. A boy's especially rapid maturation confirms such illicit activity, and earns him the label of witch.

From a cross-cultural perspective, Etoro sexual attitudes and behavior are extreme, although they are common among some neighboring groups in New Guinea. For the Etoro the sexual relationship between older and younger male is a fact of life, an integral part of an elaborate symbolic system that orders and explains inevitable conditions of human existence. The transmission of semen symbolizes the creation, maturation, decline, and eventual end of life. Etoro homosexuality rests not on hormones or genes, but on cultural traditions. Etoro sexual behavior and associated symbolism represent one extreme of a male-female avoidance pattern that is widespread in New Guinea and, more generally, in patrilineal-virilocal societies. The Etoro provide further illustration of the range of behavior that cultural diversity promotes.

CULTURE, BIOLOGY, PSYCHOLOGY, AND LEARNING ABILITY

Over the centuries groups with power have attempted to justify their own privileged and dominant social positions by declaring minorities to be innately inferior. The Nazis argued for the superiority of the "Aryan race." European colonialists proclaimed the "White man's burden"; to justify the exploitation of native peoples they argued that these populations were inferior. In the United States the supposed superiority of the white race was standard segregationist doctrine. Belief in the biologically based inferiority of Native Americans has been used as an argument for their slaughter, confinement, and neglect.

In view of these historical patterns it is not surprising that many people equate deprivation with lack of ability. Nor is it surprising that the doctrine of innate superiority should occasionally be defended by scientists, who, after all, are steeped in the cultural traditions of the favored stratum.

Twenty years ago most anthropologists would have considered it unnecessary to write this section. In the early decades of the twentieth century, anthropologist Franz Boas, usually considered to be one of the founders of American anthropology, clarified the independence of genetic makeup of human groups and their learning ability. Since the time of Boas, it has become standard anthropological doctrine that behavioral variation among contemporary human populations reflects culture rather than biology. It is also standard anthropological doctrine that genetically determined capacities for cultural advancement are equivalent in all human populations; and that within a single stratified society, differences in performance among economic, social, racial, and ethnic groups reflect unequal opportunities rather than genetic makeup.

In view of these doctrines, which the overwhelming majority of professional anthropologists regard as basic to their discipline, why should we continue to concern ourselves with the question of genetic versus cultural determination? The answer is that during the past decade racist doctrines have been revived by a small group of scholars and have gained some currency—and thereby a measure of respectability—in the United States. The newest "scientific" racist doctrine has been called Jensenism, after educational psychologist Arthur R. Jensen, who has been its leading proponent. Jensenism was first brought to the attention of academics in a lengthy article in the *Harvard Educational Review*. Simply stated, Jensenism is the belief that "intelligence" is mostly determined by the genes. It is an interpretation of the observation that black Americans, on the average, perform less well on standard intelligence tests than white Americans. According to Jensenist doctrine, blacks are incapable of performing as well as whites on these tests because of their genetic makeup. Related interpretations have been advanced by R. J. Herrnstein (1971) and physicist William Shockley (1972).

There is, however, an environmental explanation for this difference between mean (average) scores on intelligence tests, which the great majority of social scientists accept. This can be stated simply: test performances of human groups reflect environmental conditions—social, economic, educational,

nutritional, and cultural factors—and not genetic attributes.

This does not deny that some individuals are inherently smarter than others. In any human society specific abilities of individuals vary from high to low. An environmental explanation does deny, however, that these differences can be generalized to whole human groups. In other words, *within-group* differences in native intelligence are recognized, but there is no scientific evidence that *between*-group differences exist. Even when talking about individual intelligence, however, we still have to decide which of several culturally nurtured abilities are to be regarded as a basis for evaluating or measuring intelligence.

Perhaps in some human societies hereditary differences among individuals find complete expression in culturally valued achievements. In the case of many foraging populations, a relatively egalitarian social structure assigns prestige on the basis of age, sex, personal abilities, and achievements. However, as indicated in Chapter 4, the situation is very different in stratified societies, where ascribed status is important in determining access to strategic and culturally valued resources. By definition, a stratified society is not egalitarian. Some people must be superordinate, some subordinate. Ascribed status is important in assigning individuals to each group. In every stratified society, mechanisms—social, economic, and other environmental limitations—operate to keep members of the subordinate stratum "in their place."

The relationship between achievement and membership in different stratified groups is confirmed by the fact that lower-class American whites, Mexican-Americans, and members of other deprived ethnic groups usually perform well below members of the middle class on standard tests. Of course, Americans who believe that success is determined by rugged individualism would argue that people become or remain members of the lower class because of low intelligence or lack of ambition. The same argument of genetic limitations is applied, then, to class differences and to ethnic differences. However, abundant evidence supports environmental rather than genetic explanations for poorer test scores by members of disadvantaged groups in stratified societies. Let us consider some.

To determine relationships between class or ethnic status and intelligence, it is necessary to measure intelligence. Psychologists have devised several kinds

WHAT KIND OF EVIDENCE WOULD BE ACCEPTABLE?

of intelligence tests, but there are problems associated with all of them. Most of the intelligence tests devised early in this century were based on verbal ability, skill in manipulating words. Tests based on skill with words are not accurate measures of innate intelligence or learning ability for several reasons. For example, it has been found that individuals who learned two languages as children, *bilinguals*, do not perform as well on verbal intelligence tests as individuals who were taught a single language. It would be preposterous to suppose that people who have learned as children the art of communicating in two languages have inferior intelligence. The explanation seems to be that because such people have acquired vocabularies, concepts, and verbal skills in both languages, their ability to manipulate either suffers a bit. Certainly, this may be offset by the tremendous advantage of being fluent in two languages.

Furthermore, most intelligence tests have been developed by middle- or upper-class scientists in Europe or the United States and naturally reflect the experiences of the people who devised them. It is not surprising that middle- and upper-class Europeans and Americans perform better on these tests than lower-class people in the same societies. They share with the test makers a common orientation and world view, the result of similar opportunities and experiences in their stratified societies.

In fact, no intelligence test is free of class, ethnic, and cultural biases. IQ tests in the United States, for example, often require familiarity with old American proverbs (for example, "Robbing Peter to pay Paul") and with kinship terms as used by members of the middle class. Subjects may be asked to solve problems most typically encountered in middle-class settings. Subjects may be scored on their ability to define words that do not occur in certain class, ethnic, or regional linguistic variants of American English (Kagan, 1975). Such instruments invariably test what has been learned, not one's potential for learning, and they use middle-class performance as a standard for determining what features of middle-class culture should have been learned by a given chronological age. Consider, too, that tests are typically administered by middle-class people who give instructions in a dialect that may not be totally familiar to the child being tested. Test performance improves when subcultural, socioeconomic, and/or linguistic backgrounds of subjects and test personnel are similar. Several studies (cf. Watson, 1972) demonstrate that the tested IQ of black schoolchildren, for example, rises an average of six points when the person administering the test is black.

Some of the tests developed by middle-class Americans and Europeans have been translated into foreign languages. Anthropologists and others have given such tests to people in different cultures. Usually, average scores of people outside the country where the test was developed are lower. This reflects the fact that although the words and phrases of the tests are translated, the concepts are nonetheless ones that are appropriate to European or American culture and unfamiliar to people with other cultural traditions. It is thus not surprising that such people do not do as well on the tests. It would be interesting to know how well a group of middle-class Americans would do on a verbal intelligence test composed by New Guineans and translated into English.

Psychologists are aware of the difficulties involved in devising a culture-free intelligence test based on verbal skills, and have developed several other types, hoping to find an objective measure of intelligence that will not be bound to a single culture. In one of these, individuals achieve higher scores as they add more and more body parts to a stick figure. Another is a maze test, in which subjects must trace their way out of various mazes. The score increases with the speed of completion. Other tests also base scores on speed. Placing round pegs into round holes and fitting other geometric objects into holes with the same shape have been used as other measures of intelligence.

But these tests are also culture-bound. American culture places an emphasis on speed and competition. Most nonindustrial cultures do not. American culture is individualistic; individuals are expected to compete with others in many areas of everyday life, and individuals are expected to solve problems by themselves. In many nonindustrial societies, problems are typically solved by groups rather than individuals. In solving everyday problems, a person asks the advice of kin and neighbors. Many cultures stress cooperation rather than competition. Otto Klineberg (1951), in what is still one of the most important articles written for the lay reader on race and psychology, relates several instances of this. For example, a white teacher attempting to test the problem-solving abilities of a group of Native American children wrote several arithmetic problems on a blackboard. The teacher then asked each student to stand in front of one of the problems, to solve it, and to turn around when he or she had finished. The teacher observed that no child put down the chalk until all the other children had finished. Each child, on completing the problem, looked at neighbors on either side to see their progress. The line of children turned around together.

Klineberg describes many other cases in which performance on intelligence tests varied in different cultures because people stressed cooperation and group problem solving rather than competition. A social scientist working among Australian aborigines had recently been incorporated into one of the local groups as a fictive kinsman. When he gave the maze test to some of his new kin, he found that the aborigines looked up after each move out of the maze for the tester's approval. When they encountered a problem they asked their foreign kinsman, who, after all, was familiar with the problem, for assistance. The social scientist refused to help and told other members of the group not to give their advice. The aborigines were surprised, since they were accustomed to learning from the experience of their kin and to group deliberation in decision making.

Many other examples could be given of failures to eliminate cultural biases from intelligence tests. As we have seen, such bias will not only affect performance by people in other cultures, but also by different groups within the culture of origin. This is the major reason why many Native American groups do so poorly on verbal tests of intelligence. Add to this the fact that many Native Americans have grown up in environments that are completely foreign to other Americans. On reservations, for example, or under conditions of urban or rural poverty, they have suffered social, economic, political, and cultural discrimination. According to Klineberg, Native Americans score lowest of any minority group in the United States on intelligence tests. In a more recent study by George Mayeske (1971), they scored ahead of Mexican Americans and Puerto Ricans, but still behind Oriental Americans (who had the highest mean scores), American whites, and American blacks. A score of about 100 is supposed to be average for test performance. According to Klineberg the mean for Native Americans was 81.

Studies of Native Americans who have not grown up in deprived environments demonstrate that when the environment offers opportunities equivalent to those available to middle-class Americans, test performance is also equal. One study examined the test performance of Native American children who had been raised in homes of white foster parents. The average IQ for this group was 102. These children were compared with their brothers and sisters who had remained on the reservation. It was found that the average IQ among the reservation children, born to the same sets of parents, was only 87.

Another illustration of the relationship between improved environment and IQ test scores comes from the Osage Indians, on whose reservation oil was discovered. They were able to profit economically from their wealth in oil. Their diet was nutritionally adequate; they did not experience the psychological stresses of poverty, and they developed a good school system. Their average IQ was tested at 104. In this case the relationship between intelligence test performance and environment is particularly clear. The Osage did not settle on the reservation because oil was there. It was discovered after they were established. There is no justification for believing that these people were innately more intelligent than others living on different reservations. They were merely more fortunate.

Similar relationships between social, economic, and educational environment and performance on intelligence tests come from comparison of different groups of blacks and whites in the United States. When considering these relationships it is important to remember that white and black are social rather than biological categories. Neither group is genetically "pure"; individuals are placed in either "race" not on the basis of their genes or their phenotypes but according to the cultural rule that — totally neglecting biology — arbitrarily classifies anyone with black ancestry as black. The black and white social groups have experienced several generations of unequal access to wealth, education, power, and prestige. Variable performance, therefore, reveals correlations merely between social categories specific to American culture, on the one hand, and achievement norms specific to the white middle-class majority, on the other.

At the outbreak of World War I, intelligence tests were given to approximately 1 million army recruits. Analysis of the results showed that, on the average, blacks from some northern states scored better than whites from some southern states. It is ironic — but understandable given the racist bias of many Americans — that people never focused on these results to argue that blacks were innately superior to whites. Northern blacks in the first two decades of the twentieth century enjoyed better educational opportunities than many southern whites. Their better average performance on intelligence tests is not surprising.

On the other hand, southern whites as a group performed better than southern blacks. This is also not surprising, considering the separate and tremendously unequal school systems then open to white and black Southerners. It is also not surprising that segregationists proclaimed that the test results demonstrated innate white superiority.

Some people tried to avoid the environmental explanation for the superior performance of northern blacks over southern whites by suggesting selective migration, that the smarter blacks had moved north. Note that since northern whites also did better than southern whites, smarter whites would also be expected to have moved north. Fortunately, it was possible to test this suggestion about the selective migration of blacks, and it was found to be false. If smarter blacks had moved north, their superior intelligence should have been revealed while they were still attending schools in the south. It was not. Furthermore, subsequent studies conducted in New York, Washington, and Philadelphia showed that as length of residence in the northern cities increased, intelligence scores also increased. Finally, we might question the premise that smarter people are more likely than less intelligent people to move away from their homes. Smart people would probably be more successful and hold positions of greater prestige in their home communities. They would therefore be less likely to move away. On the other hand, we know that many blacks have moved north seeking employment. In other words, they have not been especially successful, economically at least, in their homeland. Selective migration has also been used (Eysenck, 1971), and can be similarly criticized (Gordon and Green, 1975), to explain IQ test performance by the Irish, whose average scores are the same as those of American blacks.

IQ scores do not measure innate intelligence. Rather, they test, with reference to white middle-class standards, phenotypical intelligence; and the interaction between environment and genotype begins in the womb. In some cases, prenatal dietary deficiencies have effects that persist through adulthood. Environmental influences, such as nutritional quality of the diet, continue to affect development in infancy, throughout childhood, and in young adulthood. For example, IQ scores of poor black children in Norfolk, Virginia, who had received a daily supplement of B complex vitamins for several years averaged 8 points above a socioeconomically similar control group (Biesheuvel, 1975).

In another study, conducted at Yale University during the 1940s, the psychological and physical development of groups of black and white infants were compared and found to be equal. The explanation was clearly environmental. Because of dietary controls introduced during World War II, mothers of black and white infants had similar diets during pregnancy. The income of the black parents was also relatively good, because of opportunities to work in war-related industries during the period.

Educational opportunities represent an obvious factor that can affect performance on intelligence tests. The parents' economic status, the extent to which their values and expectations for their offspring accord with middle-class norms, and their general outlook on life are others. Children who grow up in homes where toys, books, and art are present tend to do better on standard intelligence tests than individuals who come from homes without these things.

In a study involving more than 900 Mexican-American and black elementary school children, Jane Mercer (1971) found a systematic relationship between social, economic, and educational attributes of the home environment and performance on intelligence tests. The average IQ score both for the black and the Mexican-American school children was 90, 10 points below the national average. However, when socioeconomic differences were taken into account, the influence of home environment on test performance became very clear. A subgroup of black children was also studied. These came from families who owned their homes and had households with five or fewer members; moreover, the head was married and pursued a certain type of occupation, and the mother expected her children to obtain at least some education beyond high school. These children were found to have an average intelligence test score of 100, the national average. Among the Mexican-American children, a similar subgroup was found to have an average IQ score of 104.

Studies of identical twins raised apart illustrate the impact of the environment on (identical) heredity. In one study of nineteen pairs of twins, IQ scores varied directly with number of years in school. The average difference in IQ was only 1.5 points for the eight twin pairs with the same amount of schooling, 10 points for the eleven pairs with an average of five years difference in schooling. One subject, with fourteen years more education than his twin, scored 24 points higher (Bronfenbrenner, 1975). In another study (Skodak and Skeels, 1949), natural mothers of 100 foster children had an average IQ of 86, their children 106. All these findings seriously undermine the Jensenist assertion that an average difference of 15 points in IQ test scores of whites, compared with blacks or Native Americans, reflects genetic rather than environmental limitations. Still another environmental factor—the amount of parental attention—has been linked (Record, McKeown, and Edwards, cited in Bodmer, 1975) to IQ scores. Average scores of 49,000 single births, 2,200 twins, and 33 triplets were 100, 96, and 92, respectively. Bodmer suggests that division of parental care between twins and triplets is responsible.

These and similar studies (Montagu, ed., 1975; Richardson and Spears, eds., 1972) provide overwhelming evidence that performance on intelligence tests measures such factors as education, social, economic, and nutritional status, and cultural orientation, rather than genetically determined intelligence. Racists have developed doctrines of racial superiority to justify, first, enslavement, then, social, educational, and economic discrimination against Native Americans and Africans and their descendants.

During the past 500 years Europeans and their descendants have gradually extended their political and/or economic control over most of the world, radiating into environments that they reached in their ships and conquered with their weapons. Today there are two major world powers: the United States and the Soviet Union, with a third bloc of industrially important nations in western Europe. China, Japan, Israel, and the OPEC nations are increasing their influence economically and politically. The majority of the populations of the most powerful nations have light skin color. It is understandable that people in these presently powerful and technologically advanced countries incorrectly believe that their world position results from innate biological superiority. Anthropology teaches us, however, that there is no relationship between group genotype or physical characteristics and the ability to learn or to advance technologically, and that all contemporary human populations seem to have the same average innate learning abilities.

Remember that we are living and viewing things at a particular time. In the past there were far different associations between centers of power and general evolutionary advance and phenotypes. While Europeans were barbarians, advanced civilizations were thriving in the Near East. While Europe was in the Dark Ages, states and civilizations existed in the interior of West Africa, on the East African coast, in Mexico, and in Asia. Before the Industrial Revolution, ancestors of many present-day Europeans and Americans were living much more like precolonial Africans than like present-day members of the American middle class. Their average performance on twentieth-century IQ tests would have been abominable.

SUMMARY

Anthropology is uniquely qualified to evaluate arguments for genetic determinism of human behavior. Most naturists offer genetic explanations for behavioral universals; environmentalists use cultural diversity to counter their assertions. Rather than being genetically determined, cultural universals may be common responses to problems and experiences that affect people everywhere. When considering "human nature," environmentalists typically stress flexibility and the adaptive significance of human learning; they view major behavioral differences between human groups as cultural rather than genetic responses—often adaptive solutions—to different environments.

Such popular sociobiologists as Ardrey, Lorenz, Morris, and Tiger see human behavior as determined by our animal instincts. They assert that fighting, status seeking, hierarchy formation, acquisitiveness, nationalism, social inequality, and aggression rest on a genetic foundation. Typically, they mention only those animals and cultures that support their theories, ignoring cross-cultural data that show that their purported human behavioral universals are not universal at all. Scientific sociobiology also assumes that social behavior is genetically determined. The individual members of any population are viewed as competitors trying to maximize their genetic contribution to future generations. The sociobiological

"Human Nature" and Sociocultural Diversity

concept of inclusive fitness, based on the fact that individuals share their DNA with their relatives, is used to explain individual self-sacrifice and "altruism." However, kinship systems, fosterage, adoption, exogamy, and other social institutions muddle whatever "instinctive" genealogical knowledge people might have. Sociobiologists may also be criticized for making the unwarranted assumption that an individual psychological trait—for instance, aggression—even if it were genetically determined, would be directly revealed in a social institution of a similar character—for instance, warfare.

Until recently, anthropologists have failed to study adequately women's activities and opinions. Furthermore, they often interpret women's positions in other societies in terms of a distinction between private (domestic) and public spheres—the inside-outside dichotomy—which is particularly marked in industrial societies. The universality of male dominance is subject to speculation, and anthropologists can more profitably focus on cross-cultural variation in the behavior, rights, and obligations of men and women.

Sex roles may be related to specific environmental variables as well as to strategy of adaptation and level of sociopolitical complexity. Where gathering is the prominent subsistence activity among foragers, sex roles are more equal and symmetrical than when hunting or fishing is dominant. Sex roles tend toward equality and symmetry when domestic and public spheres are not sharply differentiated. Among foragers, neither warfare nor organized interregional trade are typical; this deprives men of two public arenas that contribute to status inequality among food producers. Among foragers like the !Kung, public and private spheres are least distinct; hierarchy is least marked; aggression and competition are most discouraged; and rights, activities, and spheres of influence of men and women most overlap.

The status of women falls as cultivation becomes more intensive and as the percentage of cultigens in the diet increases. Female status is also linked to rules of descent and postmarital residence. Patrilineal and matrilineal systems appear in different ecological niches. Matrilineal-uxorilocal systems tend to arise where population pressure on strategic resources is minimal and warfare infrequent. Women's status is high in such societies, since descent-group membership, succession to political positions, allocation of land, and overall social identity

are based on links through females. Anthropologists have never discovered a matriarchy, but women in many societies wield considerable power and make important decisions. The matrilineal-uxorilocal Iroquois and other "matrifocal" societies illustrate that if females play a major role in subsistence production while males are removed from their home communities for long periods, sexual equality may be favored. Women's status is lowered when male and female spheres are sharply differentiated *within* the local community.

Where critical resources are scarce, patriliny and virilocality tend to arise. The localization of males is adaptive; and warfare and polygyny represent cultural responses to scarcity of strategic resources. Warfare may regulate population growth indirectly by producing a male supremacist complex, social devaluation of women, and, thereby, an intensification of female infanticide. Women have low status in these societies and remain the dominant subsistence workers. Polygyny brings several female workers under the control of one man's household. It may thus intensify production and generate surpluses, which male household heads can then invest in the prestige and marriage spheres of multicentric economies. In such societies, men use their public roles in extradomestic distribution to symbolize and reinforce their oppression of women.

Agriculture continues trends of greater reliance on cultigens, intensification of production, and decline in women's status. With plow agriculture men assumed major responsibility for subsistence; thus women were, for the first time in cultural evolution, divorced from production. The conceptual distinction between women's domestic work and men's extradomestic, "productive" labor reinforced the contrast between men as public and women as domestic creatures. The Betsileo illustrate, however, that intensive cultivation per se does not mean a degraded status for women.

Pastoralism, since it rarely occurs as a "pure" adaptation, has diverse sex roles. Most pastoralists are patrilineal and virilocal, but women's economic contribution and social status are lowest among transhumant pastoralists who rely little on cultivation.

Consider sex roles in industrial societies. Americans' attitudes about woman's place vary with class and region. Historically, the attitude that woman's place is in the home can be linked to the emergence of industrialism. As the need for female labor declined, the idea that women are unfit for factory work and other menial jobs increased. Such general economic forces as wartime needs, inflation, and the demand for female work per se account for actual extradomestic employment of women and Americans' attitudes toward it. Today's feminism reflects increasing participation by American women in extradomestic labor. Neither the degradation of women, male dominance, nor sharp differences between public and private spheres appear to be cultural universals.

Wide variation among culturally approved forms of sexual expression demonstrates that sexual attitudes and practices reflect cultural rather than biological differences. Attitudes about homosexuality, bestiality, and masturbation differ cross-culturally. Humans, like other primates, seem biologically capable of pursuing varied forms of sexual expression. Etoro sexual behavior and associated ideology represent one extreme of a male-female avoidance pattern that is widespread in patrilineal-virilocal societies, particularly in densely populated areas of New Guinea.

There have been attempts recently and in the past to demonstrate a relationship between innate learning abilities and the "races" of the United States. Anthropologists, on the other hand, explain differential performance on intelligence tests with reference to differences in environments — including economic, educational, social, and nutritional opportunities. Intelligence tests reflect the cultural orientations and life experiences of the people who devise and administer them. Even when tests devised by Americans and Europeans are translated into foreign languages, they generally retain concepts appropriate to, and in some cases peculiar to, Western culture. All intelligence tests are to some extent culture-bound. Many stress competition and speed of completion, values of a society that emphasizes individualism rather than the group decision-making process. When environmental opportunities are equalized, this is reflected in improved performances by formerly disadvantaged groups. The anthropologist's conclusion is that intelligence test results reflect socioeconomic and other environmental variables and tell nothing about innate abilities of different human groups.

SOURCES AND SUGGESTED READINGS

ABERLE, D.
1961   Matrilineal Descent in Cross-Cultural Perspective. In *Matrilineal Kinship,* ed. D. M. Schneider and K. Gough, pp. 655–727. Berkeley: University of California Press. Good comparative article in indispensable volume on matriliny.

ALEXANDER, R. D.
1974   The Evolution of Social Behavior. *Annual Review of Systematic Ecology* 4: 375–383. Sociobiologist uses selected anthropological terms and data to argue for common elements of animal, including human, social behavior.

ARDREY, R.
1961   *African Genesis.* New York: Atheneum. Playwright Ardrey interprets the early human fossil record in terms of the street gang conflict in *West Side Story;* trendsetting popular work linking human behavior to biology and our animal heritage.

1966   *The Territorial Imperative.* New York: Atheneum. Ardrey's second attempt to link human behavior (defense of property) to genes we supposedly share with other animals.

1970   *The Social Contract.* New York: Atheneum. Here Ardrey suggests a biological basis for social inequality.

1976   *The Hunting Hypothesis.* New York: Atheneum. How the genes of our "hunting" ancestors influence contemporary human behavior.

BAXTER, P., AND SANSOME, B., EDS.
1972   *Race and Social Difference.* New York: Penguin Books. Excellent reader considering race relations and stereotypes in cross-cultural perspective.

BIESHEUVEL, S.
1975   An Examination of Jensen's Theory Concerning Educability, Heritability and Population Differences. In *Race and IQ,* ed.

A. Montagu, pp. 59–72. New York: Oxford University Press. Good refutation.

BOAS, F.
1966   (orig. 1940). *Race, Language, and Culture*. New York: Free Press. Collection of articles asserts the independence of race, language, and culture.

BODMER, W. F.
1975   Race and IQ: The Genetic Background. In *Race and IQ,* ed. A. Montagu, pp. 252–286. New York: Oxford University Press. A geneticist counters Jensen's assertions.

BOGORAS, W.
1904   The Chukchee. In *The Jesup North Pacific Expedition,* ed. F. Boas. New York: Memoir of the American Museum of Natural History. Shamanism, fishing, and reindeer herding — an old-time ethnographic classic.

BOSERUP, E.
1970   *Women's Role in Economic Development.* London: Allen and Unwin. Woman's changing role as cultivation intensifies, including plow agriculture and the inside-outside dichotomy.

BRACE, C. L., AND LIVINGSTONE, F. B.
1971   On Creeping Jensenism. In *Race and Intelligence,* ed. C. L. Brace, G. R. Gamble, and J. T. Bond. Anthropological Studies, no. 8. Washington, D.C.: American Anthropological Association. This article is one of several in this volume offering scientific evidence contradicting Jensen's assertions.

BRONFENBRENNER, U.
1975   Nature with Nurture: A Reinterpretation of the Evidence. In *Race and IQ,* ed. A. Montagu, pp. 114–144. New York: Oxford University Press. Detailed presentation of the environmentalist position.

BROWN, J. K.
1975   Iroquois Women: An Ethnohistoric Note. In *Toward an Anthropology of Women,* ed. R. Reiter, pp. 235–251. New York: Monthly Review Press. Factors underlying women's rights in a matrilineal, uxorilocal society.

COLLIER, J. F.
1974   Women in Politics. In *Woman, Culture, and Society,* ed. M. Z. Rosaldo and L. Lamphere, pp. 89–96. Stanford: Stanford University Press. A cross-cultural consideration.

DENICH, B. S.
1974   Sex and Power in the Balkans. In *Woman, Culture, and Society,* ed. M. Z. Rosaldo and L. Lamphere, pp. 243–262. Stanford: Stanford University Press. Women's oppression in a patricentric, pastoralist, plow-agricultural society.

DIVALE, W. T., AND HARRIS, M.
1976   Population, Warfare, and the Male Supremacist Complex. *American Anthropologist* 78: 521–538. Links widespread warfare among horticulturalists to population regulation through female infanticide.

DRAPER, P.
1975   !Kung Women: Contrasts in Sexual Egalitarianism in Foraging and Sedentary Contexts. In *Toward an Anthropology of Women,* ed. R. Reiter, pp. 77–109. New York: Monthly Review Press. Excellent study of relationship between economy, settlement, and gender roles.

EVANS-PRITCHARD, E. E.
1970   Sexual Inversion among the Azande. *American Anthropologist* 72: 1428–1433. War, boy-brides, and sexual plasticity among a Sudanese tribe.

EYSENCK, H. J.
1971   *The IQ Argument: Race, Intelligence, and Education.* New York: Library Press. This appraisal contains controversial arguments.

FORD, C. S., AND BEACH, F. A.
1951   *Patterns of Sexual Behavior.* New York: Harper Torchbooks. A cross-cultural perspective; how culture molds human sexual plasticity.

FOX, R., ED.
1975   *Biosocial Anthropology.* Association of Social Anthropologists Study, no. 1. New York: Wiley (Halsted). Lays out some of the major sociobiological and ethological assumptions; a taut thriller.

FRIEDL, E.
1975   *Women and Men: An Anthropologist's View.* New York: Holt, Rinehart & Winston. Short but interesting study of sex roles among foragers and horticulturalists; some intriguing hypotheses.

GOODALE, J.
1971   *Tiwi Wives.* Seattle: University of Washington Press. Case study of north Australian foragers, with focus on women — major figures in Tiwi society.

GORDON, E. W., AND GREEN, D.
1975   An Affluent Society's Excuses for Inequality: Developmental, Economic, and Educational. In *Race and IQ,* ed. A. Montagu, pp. 73–103. New York: Oxford University Press. Anti-Jensenist argument.

HAMMOND, D., AND JABLOW, A.
1976   *Women in Cultures of the World.* Menlo Park, Calif.: Cummings. Brief, mainly descriptive, account of women in different cultures.

HARDING, S.
1975   Women and Words in a Spanish Village. In *Toward an Anthropology of Women,* ed. R. Reiter, pp. 283–308. New York: Monthly Review Press. The inside-outside dichotomy among Spanish peasants.

HERRNSTEIN, R. J.
1971   IQ. *The Atlantic* 228(3): 43–64. A Jensenist view.

HRDY, S. B.
1976   Infanticide as a Private Reproductive Strategy. Paper read at 75th Annual Meeting of the American Anthropological Association, Washington, D.C. Do a few cases confirm that monkeys are genetic crusaders?

JACOBS, S-E.
1974   *Women in Perspective: A Guide to Cross-Cultural Studies.* Urbana: University of Illinois Press. Useful bibliography for the study of gender, women, and men cross-culturally.

JENSEN, A.
1969   How Much Can We Boost I.Q. and Scholastic Achievement? *Harvard Educational Review* 29: 1–123. This article achieved considerable notoriety because of its unfounded conclusion that American whites are smarter than American blacks.

1971   Can We and Should We Study Race Differences? In *Race and Intelligence,* ed. C. L. Brace, G. R. Gamble, and J. T. Bond. Anthropological Studies, no. 8. Washington, D.C.: American Anthropological Association. Defense of author's 1969 study against attacks in this volume and elsewhere.

KAGAN, J.
1975   The Magical Aura of the IQ. In *Race and IQ,* ed. A. Montagu, pp. 52–58. New

York: Oxford University Press. Problems with IQ testing situations spelled out.

KELLY, R. C.
1976   Witchcraft and Sexual Relations: An Exploration in the Social and Semantic Implications of the Structure of Belief. In *Man and Woman in the New Guinea Highlands,* ed. P. Brown and G. Buchbinder, pp. 36–53. Special Publication, no. 8. Washington, D.C.: American Anthropological Association. Links homosexual behavior among the Etoro of New Guinea to an elaborate set of beliefs about birth, growth, parenthood, senility, and death.

1977   *Etoro Social Structure: A Study in Structural Contradiction.* Ann Arbor: University of Michigan Press. Kinship, ideology, and sexual expression in a small New Guinea group.

KESSLER, E. S.
1976   *Women: An Anthropological View.* New York: Holt, Rinehart & Winston. Some discussion of theory and explanation along with case studies.

KINSEY, A. C., POMEROY, W. B., AND MARTIN, C. E.
1948   *Sexual Behavior in the Human Male.* Philadelphia: W. B. Saunders. Classic statistical study of male sexuality in the United States.

KLINEBERG, O.
1950   Race Differences: The Present Position of the Problem. *International Social Science Bulletin* 2: 460–466. A social psychologist examines environmental causes of variable performance on intelligence tests.

1951   Race and Psychology. In *The Race Question in Modern Science.* Paris: UNESCO. An especially important demonstration of cultural, linguistic, and class biases in intelligence testing, and the effects of social, economic, and cultural differences on performance on such tests.

KUPER, L., ED.
1975   *Race, Science and Society.* New York: Columbia University Press. Articles view race from biological, social, and cultural perspectives.

LAMPHERE, L.
1974   Strategies, Cooperation, and Conflict among Women in Domestic Groups. In *Woman, Culture, and Society,* ed. M. Z. Rosaldo and L. Lamphere, pp. 97–112. Stanford: Stanford University Press.

LINDENBAUM, S.
1972 Sorcerers, Ghosts, and Polluting Women: An Analysis of Religious Belief and Population Control. *Ethnology* 11: 241–253. Links antagonism between the sexes to population density in the New Guinea highlands.

LOEHLIN, J. C., LINDZEY, G., AND SPUHLER, J. N., EDS.
1975 *Race Differences in Intelligence.* San Francisco: Freeman. Very thorough review of Jensenism, evidence, and counterarguments.

LORAINE, J. A.
1974 *Understanding Homosexuality: Its Biological and Psychological Basis.* New York: American Elsevier. The contributions of several disciplines to understanding male and female homosexuality.

LORENZ, K.
1966 *On Aggression.* New York: Bantam. In this popular work, a prominent ethologist, citing studies of other animals, argues that human aggression is universal and genetically based.

LOWIE, R.
1935 *The Crow Indians.* New York: Farrar and Rinehart. Matrilineality among Native Americans of the Plains.

MARGOLIS, M.
1976 From Betsy Ross through Rosie the Riveter: Changing Attitudes toward Women in the Labor Force. Paper read at 75th Annual Meeting of the American Anthropological Association, Washington, D.C. How economic forces affect women's paid employment and Americans' attitudes about it.

MARTIN, K., AND VOORHIES, B.
1975 *Female of the Species.* New York: Columbia University Press. Indispensable work on sex roles and gender in comparative and evolutionary perspective.

MAYESKE, G. W.
1971 *On the Explanation of Racial-Ethnic Group Differences in Achievement Test Scores.* Washington, D.C.: U. S. Government Printing Office, Office of Education. Effects of social environment on intelligence test performance.

MERCER, J. R.
1971 Pluralistic Diagnosis in the Evaluation of Black and Chicano Children: A Procedure for Taking Sociocultural Variables into Account as Clinical Assessment. Paper presented at the meetings of the American Psychological Association, Washington, D.C. Controlled comparison of intelligence test performances of whites, blacks, and Chicanos; demonstrates that as social and economic opportunities are equalized, so are intelligence test scores.

MONTAGU, A.
1975 *The Nature of Human Aggression.* New York: Oxford University Press. Well-known anthropologist refutes the popular sociobiologists' arguments for instinctive human aggression.

MONTAGU, A., ED.
1975 *Race and IQ.* New York: Oxford University Press. Scientists from several disciplines review and counter naturist reasoning.

MORRIS, D.
1967 *The Naked Ape.* London: Jonathan Cape. Writing for a lay audience, a zoologist focuses on behavior in the United States of the 1960s to illustrate humans' animal heritage.

1969 *The Human Zoo.* London: Jonathan Cape. A host of contemporary social ills are attributed to overcrowding, as in experiments with rats.

MURDOCK, G. P.
1967 *Ethnographic Atlas.* Pittsburgh: University of Pittsburgh Press. Comparable cross-cultural data; test your own hypothesis and advance anthropology.

ORTNER, S. B.
1974 Is Female to Male as Nature is to Culture? In *Woman, Culture, and Society,* ed. M. Z. Rosaldo and L. Lamphere, pp. 67–68. Stanford: Stanford University Press. Is she? Yes! Read on.

OTTERBEIN, K., AND OTTERBEIN, C. S.
1965 An Eye for an Eye, a Tooth for a Tooth: A Cross-Cultural Study of Feuding. *American Anthropologist* 67: 1470–1482. Bionics, robotics, and transplants—and the human emotions that boil up around them—cross-culturally.

PESCATELLO, A., ED.
1973 *Female and Male in Latin America.* Pittsburgh: University of Pittsburgh Press. Sex roles south of the border, where machismo got its start.

REITER, R.
1975a Introduction to *Toward an Anthropology*

of Women, ed. R. Reiter, pp. 11–19. New York: Monthly Review Press. Seventeen articles in this excellent anthology examine gender and sex role theory in comparative perspective.

1975b Men and Women in the South of France: Public and Private Domains. In Toward an Anthropology of Women, ed. R. Reiter, pp. 252–282. New York: Monthly Review Press. Sex roles among plowing peasants.

REYNOLDS, V.
1976 The Biology of Human Action. San Francisco: Freeman. Well-done refutation of pop sociobiology; good discussion of human biological constants, including maturation.

RICHARDSON, K., AND SPEARS, D.
1972 Race and Intelligence: The Fallacies behind the Race-IQ Controversy. Baltimore: Penguin. In this anthology, psychologists, biologists, and sociologists provide a basis for evaluating Jensenist reasoning.

ROHRLICH-LEAVITT, R., SYKES, B., AND WEATHERFORD, E.
1975 Aboriginal Women: Male and Female Anthropological Perspectives. In Toward an Anthropology of Women, ed. R. Reiter, pp. 110–126. New York: Monthly Review Press. Argue that male bias has blinded anthropologists to rights of Australian women.

ROSALDO, M. Z.
1974 Woman, Culture, and Society: A Theoretical Overview. In Woman, Culture, and Society, ed. M. Z. Rosaldo and L. Lamphere, pp. 17–42. Stanford: Stanford University Press.

ROSALDO, M. Z., AND LAMPHERE, L.
1974 Introduction to Woman, Culture, and Society, ed. M. Z. Rosaldo and L. Lamphere, pp. 1–16. Stanford: Stanford University Press.

SAHLINS, M. D.
1976 The Use and Abuse of Biology: An Anthropological Critique of Sociobiology. Ann Arbor: University of Michigan Press. This short paperback exposes some of sociobiology's weaknesses, particularly its interpretations of kinship.

SANDAY, P. R.
1974 Female Status in the Public Domain. In Woman, Culture, and Society, ed. M. Z. Rosaldo and L. Lamphere, pp. 189–206. Stanford: Stanford University Press. Good comparative article examining several factors that affect woman's status.

SHOCKLEY, W.
1972 Sysgenics, Geneticity, Raceology: A Challenge to the Intellectual Responsibility of Educators. Phi Delta Kappan 53: 297–307. A physicist speculates about genetic determination of intelligence.

SIPES, R. G.
1973 War, Sports, and Aggression: An Empirical Test of Two Rival Theories. American Anthropologist 75: 64–86. Cross-cultural data negate common assumption that violent sports help fend off warfare; rather, war, aggressive sports, and violence throughout culture go together.

SKODAK, M., AND SKEELS, H. M.
1949 A Final Follow-up Study of One Hundred Adopted Children. Journal of Genetic Psychology 75: 85–125. IQ's of adopted children and their biological mothers; shows environment's impact.

STRATHERN, M.
1972 Women in Between. New York: Seminar Press. Sex roles among the patrilineal, virilocal, polygynous Hagen of New Guinea.

TANNER, N.
1974 Matrifocality in Indonesia and Africa and among Black Americans. In Woman, Culture, and Society, ed. M. Z. Rosaldo and L. Lamphere, pp. 129–156. Stanford: Stanford University Press. Good survey.

TIGER, L.
1969 Men in Groups. New York: Random House. The sociability of men—here seen as greater than that of females—is linked to human biology.

TIGER, L., AND FOX, R.
1972 The Imperial Animal. New York: Delta Books. Sociologist and anthropologist collaborate in another pop sociobiology effort.

TRIVERS, R. L.
1971 The Evolution of Reciprocal Altruism.

Quarterly Review of Biology 46: 35–57. Prominent sociobiologist tries to show that apparently unselfish behavior actually maximizes reproductive advantage.

WATSON, P.

1972   Can Racial Discrimination Affect IQ? In *Race and Intelligence: The Fallacies behind the Race-IQ Controversy,* ed. K. Richardson and D. Spears, pp. 56–67. Baltimore: Penguin. Environmental (class, subcultural) factors in test performance.

WILSON, E. O.

1975   *Sociobiology: The New Synthesis.* Cambridge, Mass.: Belknap Press of Harvard University Press. Classic statement of the controversial field that links so many aspects of human behavior to maximizing reproductive advantage.

1976   Sociobiology: The New Synthesis. Paper read at the 75th Annual Meeting of the American Anthropological Association, Washington, D.C. Argues for genetically based division of labor by sex and competition among humans.

Uniformity and Diversity in Language

12

In earlier chapters language, an aspect of culture, was cited as one of the major adaptive advantages of the genus *Homo*. Differences in the communication systems of human and nonhuman primates were discussed, and call systems of nonhuman primates were contrasted with language. We may speculate that by the *Homo erectus* stage of human evolution some means of communication more advanced than a call system was an adaptive advantage associated with human cooperation and learning. There is no way of actually ascertaining, however, whether the communication systems of *Homo erectus* would qualify as language. In fact, all statements about the ultimate origin of language are speculative. During the nineteenth century, linguists and other scholars occasionally tried to explain the origin of language. Some proposed what has been called the "bow-wow" theory, according to which humans first began to speak by imitating the sounds they encountered in their environment, the calls of various animals, the sounds made by moving objects. In other words, human speech originated as imitation of sounds heard in nature. Others have linked the emergence of language to changes in posture and locomotion, arguing that as upright bipedalism developed, the burden of exploring the environment and carrying things shifted from the mouth to the hands. With their mouths freed from other activities, our ancestors' chattering was ultimately converted into language.

Although speculation about the origin of language is not fashionable among contemporary linguists, it seems reasonable to argue that in the evolution of *Homo*, call systems similar to those found among other primates gradually developed more and more in the direction of language. Although we cannot determine the ultimate origin of language, and, in fact, there may have been no single origin, it *is* possible for historical linguists to document gradual changes in form among languages of the recent past.

Linguistics is divided into the study of language at a single time (descriptive linguistics) and over time (historical linguistics).

THE STRUCTURE OF LANGUAGE

Until the late 1950s descriptive linguists advocated that the study of a language proceed through a sequence of separate stages of analysis. The first stage involved *phonology,* the study of sounds used in speech. Phonological analysis would determine which sounds *(phones),* out of a host represented in the languages of the world, were present and significant in the particular language being studied. The next analytic stage was *morphology,* the study of how sounds combined to form *morphemes*—words and their meaningful constituents. Thus the word "cats" would be analyzed as containing two morphemes, *cat,* the English language name for a kind of animal, and *-s,* a morpheme meaning plurality. The language's *lexicon* was a dictionary containing all its morphemes and their meanings, translated for analysis into the linguist's native language. At the next stage the arrangement and order of words in sentences—*syntax*—were examined. Such stage-by-stage analysis presented languages as static systems and implicitly created the erroneous impression that phonology, morphology, lexicon, and syntax were themselves unrelated.

Techniques of descriptive linguistics have been especially helpful to ethnographers. Many of the populations studied earlier in this century had spoken languages only. Imagine that you are an ethnographer arriving in the field and confronted with learning an unwritten language. You need to know the most rapid and efficient means of acquiring that language. Your linguistic task may be made easier if a missionary, say, has preceded you and compiled a dictionary of the language, with some of the rules of sound and organization included. Otherwise, you must yourself undertake to translate the strange cacophony you hear at first into understandable form.

Experiences in daily life can help you to picture the dilemma ethnographers face when they arrive at the scene of their field work and hear an unfamiliar language. You have probably heard radio broadcasts in languages other than your own. At first, the broadcast seems to be a garbled stream of sounds with no apparent pattern and no discernible meaning. As you listen longer and more carefully, you begin to notice that some of these sounds are similar or identical to those in your native language; others, however, remain totally foreign, and you cannot even pronounce them. Merely by listening long enough to a broadcast or sample of speech in a foreign language, linguists and trained ethnographers are able to list many of the sounds they hear. They discover that some have English equivalents, whereas others do not. They can record all sounds using the international phonetic alphabet (IPA), a series of symbols devised after wide experience to describe virtually any sound that occurs in a language.

By consulting native speakers, you obtain information about the relationship between sound and meaning in the language. Eventually, you will determine the sounds significant to the language you are learning, and those sound contrasts that differentiate meaning between two utterances that are otherwise very much the same. Simultaneously, you will be learning how to combine sounds into structured sequences—morphemes, words, phrases, and sentences—that convey meaning.

As you learn the language you will also be recording its lexicon, compiling a list of things, events, and notions named in the language. You will begin to understand more of what is said to you and around you, and your own speech in the new language will become more fully comprehensible and more pleasing to native ears. If your study continues long enough, you will also learn some of the subtleties of the language, some of its elegance: how to avoid misunderstandings; how to vary your speech with different people and in different social situations; how to use emphasis and gestures as the natives do.

Consider now some of the concepts, definitions, and techniques most basic to traditional descriptive linguistic analysis. You will grasp them more readily if, as you read, you try to apply them either to your native language or to a foreign language that you know. The contributions of descriptive linguistics will be discussed in the context in which they are most useful to most anthropologists, in a field situation in which a new language is being learned. Again, assume the role of a linguistically trained ethnographer learning a previously undescribed language.

Once you arrive in the field, perhaps the easiest way to start learning the language is to point to things you see and to ask people to name them. By writing

A linguist using a tape recorder for field work in Peru. (Cornell Capa/Magnum)

these names down, you are beginning to amass a dictionary. As your dictionary grows, some patterns begin to emerge. You find that some forms resemble others. Two names may resemble each other in all but one sound; a single contrast may serve to differentiate their meaning. Linguists call such pairs of words *minimal pairs*. The sounds that differentiate them are known as *phonemes*.

Phonemes and Phones

No single language employs, or even includes, all the sounds designated by the symbols in the IPA. Nor is the number of phonemes—significant sound contrasts—infinite. Standard American English (the "region-free" dialect spoken by most television network newscasters, for example) has about three dozen phonemes—twenty-four consonants (Figure 12.1) and at least eleven vowels (Figure 12.2). The number of phonemes varies markedly from language to language, from fewer than fifteen to more

			Organs involved						
			Bilabial	Labiodental	Dental	Alveolar	Alveopalatal	Velar	Glottal
Stops	voiceless		p			t		k	
	voiced		b			d		g	
Affricates	voiceless						č		
	voiced						ǰ		
Fricatives slit	voiceless			f	θ				h
	voiced			v	ð				
groove	voiceless					s	š		
	voiced					z	ž		
Lateral	voiced					l			
Nasals	voiced		m			n		ŋ	
Semivowels	voiced		w			r	y		

FIGURE 12.1 English consonants. Consonants differ in the organs that are used to produce them (articulators) and the shape or direction of the passage the air takes as it is expired (manner of articulation). See text for the meaning of terms used here.

Diversity in Language 267

than sixty, with the average between thirty and forty. In contemporary American English, the number of phonemes, vowels particularly, varies from dialect to dialect.

The number of phonemes is limited to a certain extent by the human articulatory apparatus, the organs of speech. Sounds differ according to the organs involved in their articulation and manner of that articulation. Some of the phonological contrasts that distinguish meaning differ in only one feature. For example, the only difference between the phonemes /b/ and /p/ in English (conventionally, phonemes are enclosed in slashes) is that /b/ is *voiced* and /p/ is *voiceless*. Voiced sounds, which include all vowels and some consonants, are produced when the vocal cords—two bands of elastic tissue enclosed in the larynx, or voice box—vibrate. Voiceless sounds produce no such vibration.

Vowels and consonants are produced as the tongue, lips, and other speech organs assume different positions. The shape of the passage between the larynx and the outside is modified, and thereby the quality of the sound. The English *nasal* consonant phonemes /m/, /n/, and /ŋ/ (as in "bam," "ban," and "bang") are produced when the expired breath takes the passage through the nose. If the passage involves an opening at one or both sides of the tongue while it is pressed against the upper gums, a *lateral* is produced. The English lateral phoneme is /l/.

Any very narrow opening can produce friction at different points in the air passage, and sounds known as *fricatives* are then emitted. Variations in the shape of the narrow opening produce differences in the sounds of the fricatives. (See Figure 12.1 for identification of the fricatives and other English consonants.) Other sounds, called *stops*, are produced by complete closure of the air passage.

Consonants differ according to their point of articulation and the articulators that meet to produce them. The articulators that produce the English *bilabials*, /p/ and /b/, are the upper and lower lips. *Labiodental* consonants, /f/ and /v/, are produced as the lower lip meets the upper teeth. *Dental* consonants, the initial sounds in "thy," /ð/, and "thigh," /θ/, are produced as the tip of the tongue meets the upper teeth. When the tip of the tongue meets the upper gums, several *alveolar* consonants are produced: English /t/, /d/, /s/, /z/, /l/, /n/, and /r/. Five English consonants are known as *alveopalatals* because to produce them the front of the tongue must

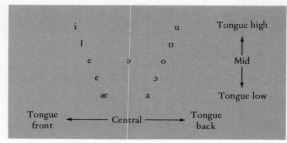

high front (spread)	[i] as in *beat*
lower high front (spread)	[ɪ] as in *bit*
mid front (spread)	[e] as in *bait*
lower mid front (spread)	[ɛ] as in *bet*
low front	[æ] as in *bat*
central	[ə] as in *butt*
low back	[a] as in *pot*
lower mid back (rounded)	[ɔ] as in *bought*
mid back (rounded)	[o] as in *boat*
lower high back (rounded)	[ʊ] as in *put*
high back (rounded)	[u] as in *boot*

FIGURE 12.2   Vowel phonemes in Standard American English shown according to height of tongue and tongue position at front, center, or back of mouth. Phonetic symbols are identified below by English words that include them (note that most are minimal pairs). (Adapted from *Aspects of Language*, Second Edition, by Dwight Bolinger, Copyright © 1975 by Harcourt Brace Jovanovich, Inc., and reproduced by their permission.)

meet the far front of the palate (roof of the mouth). Finally, the English *velar* consonants, /k/, /g/, and /ŋ/, are produced as the back of the tongue meets the velum, or soft palate.

As Figure 12.1 documents, some English phonemes are very much alike in terms of their articulation: /b/ and /p/, /d/ and /t/, /g/ and /k/, all differ only in that the first member of each pair is voiced, while the other is not. The initial sound of "the," indicated by the symbol /ð/, differs from /v/ by point of articulation: /v/ is labiodental; /ð/ is dental. Other English phonemes, however, are very dissimilar, sharing few or no features. The only similarity between /ŋ/ and /ð/, for example, is that they are both voiced.

Consonants (except for /h/) are produced by obstructing the passage of expired air; vowels are made by shaping it. Vowels are classified along a height axis (high, mid, or low) according to the distance between the tongue and the palate. Vowels are also differentiated by whether the highest point of the tongue is front, central, or back and by whether the lips are rounded or spread (Figure 12.2).

If, as you learn a foreign language, you have a good ear and are linguistically expert, you may learn to pronounce native sounds like a native. You will learn whether you are succeeding by asking for and watching native reactions to your speech. On the other hand, there may be some sounds that you will never learn to pronounce as the natives do, and so you will speak with an accent. Yet this will not necessarily be a barrier to communication if you have learned the phonemic system well. Although native speakers of French may always pronounce the English /r/ in the Parisian manner, the fact that they do so consistently means that English speakers who talk with them for a while will have no difficulty understanding them. English speakers will recognize that although they are hearing a Parisian sound, it is being used as an English phoneme. If the French natives never confuse their [r] (sounds are characteristically enclosed in brackets to distinguish them from phonemes) with another English phoneme, they will be understood. However, if the contrast between two English phonemes, for example, /b/ and /v/ or /l/ and /r/, is missing in the foreigners' own language, and if they do not recognize the contrast in English, they will have difficulty communicating. "Bet" and "vet," "craw" and "claw, will be pronounced in the same way. In other words, linguistic analysis aims to describe the sound contrasts that differentiate meanings in a given language. If the significant contrasts are mastered, deviations in pronunciation may be accepted and understood by natives, and ethnographers may never learn that they have a foreign accent.

Shifting our attention from *phonemics* to *phonetics,* from the study of sounds that are significant within a particular language to the study of human speech sounds in general, we see that phonemes normally incorporate and gloss over a number of phonetic contrasts. In English, /b/ and /v/ are phonemes, occurring in minimal pairs like "bat" and "vat," "jibe" and "jive." They differ in point of production and manner of articulation: /b/ is a bilabial stop; /v/ is a labiodental fricative. In many languages, however, the contrast between [b] and [v] does not serve to distinguish meaning, and there is a single phoneme, normally pronounced either [b] or [v]. There can therefore be variation between [b] and [v] in the pronunciation of this phoneme. In a language like Spanish, where there is no phonemic contrast between [b] and [v], and in which [b] is the normal pronunciation, a linguist may find that occasionally a native speaker will pronounce the phoneme as [v]. Such pronunciation does not obscure

meaning because the contrast between [v] and [b] is not phonemic.

In English the phonetic distinction between the [pʰ] in "pin" and the [p] in "spin" is not phonemic. Most English speakers don't even recognize the phonetic difference. [pʰ] is aspirated—a puff of air follows the [p]—while the [p] in "spin" is not. The contrast between [pʰ] and [p] is, however, phonemic in some other languages. Other English phonemes involve not consonants or vowels but how a sequence of sounds is said. In the minimal pair "ímport," "impórt," for example, *stress* is phonemic. When the first syllable is stressed, we have a noun; when the second is stressed, a verb. Varied intonation can also change meaning and is thus also phonemic in English.

Linguists have at their disposal a machine known as a sound spectrograph, which can actually measure the acoustic properties of human speech. Study of the spectrographic records shows wide acoustic variation among native speakers in their pronunciation of certain phonemes. This variation is important in understanding the evolution of language, for if shifts in pronunciation did not take place there could be no sound change in language. The social significance of such phonetic variation and its relationship to the evolution of phonology are examined in the discussion of sociolinguistics below.

Morphology and Syntax

Study of *grammar,* the formal organizing principles that link sound and meaning in a language, has been revolutionized over the past two decades by an approach known as *transformational,* or *generative, grammar.* But first let us review some basic concepts in the more traditional approach to morphology and syntax. Learning and describing a new language involves mastering phonology and phonemics; extending vocabulary; learning how sounds combine in morphemes and words; and mastering rules of syntax from conversations, oral narratives, and intensive work with individual informants. Morphemes— words and their meaningful constituents—are minimal forms that carry meaning in themselves; they cannot be broken down into smaller units that contribute to their meaning. For example, the English word "blackberry" contains two morphemes, *black* and *berry.* One can see other meaningful forms in "black"—namely, *lack* and *a.* However, since these constituents do not contribute to the meaning of "black" as *black* contributes to "blackberry," they are not constituent morphemes.

In the case of "blackberry," the constituent morphemes are capable of standing alone. However, this is not the case with several common English morphemes. The word "cats," for example, contains two morphemes, *cat* and *s* (phonemically transcribed /kæt/ and /s/). Such *bound* morphemes as /s/ are always included in words that contain another morpheme as well.

Note, too, that there are many cases in English in which different sounds have the same meaning and thus represent the same morpheme. Several suffixes convey the meaning of plurality in English, the /s/ at the end of "cats," the /z/ at the end of "cads," the *-es* at the end of "dishes," the *-en* at the end of "oxen" and "brethren." Where such phonologically different forms convey a single meaning, each of the phonetically different forms, or *morphs*, is called an *allomorph* of the same morpheme.

In most cases in English, the occurrence of one allomorph rather than another is phonologically conditioned. When nouns end in voiceless phonemes like /t/ or /p/, a voiceless phoneme forms their plural, -/s/. When the terminal sound of the singular is voiced—/d/ or /b/, for example—a voiced phoneme, -/z/, follows and marks plurality. When the word ends with *ch* (/č/) or *sh* (/š/) as in "church"/ "churches," "knish"/"knishes," the suffix *-es* forms the plural. The rules that automatically produce these phonologically different allomorphs are called *morphophonemic* rules.

Ethnographers and linguists must also master the syntactic patterns whereby words are arranged to form phrases and sentences. How do languages convey similar meanings by varying rules of syntax? Is it possible to formulate analytical rules to cover all the grammatical sequences permissible in the language? These questions involve the analysis of syntax and, more generally, of grammar as a formal system that provides a structure for verbal communication.

Transformational-Generative Grammar

Noam Chomsky's *Syntactic Structures* (1957) brought a dynamic, inclusive, and abstract approach to the study of syntax and to the study of language in general. His approach—called transformational, or generative, grammar—started a revolution in linguistic analysis that continues today. For Chomsky, a language is more than the surface phenomena—sounds, morphemes, words, and word order—studied by traditional descriptive linguists. It is, rather, an abstract system of rules—a grammar—that any native speaker acquires during childhood. Chomsky and other transformational-generative linguists enlarge the meaning of "grammar" to include not just morphology and syntax but to designate the entire set of abstract rules or principles that make up any language.

Chomsky (1972) views language as a uniquely human possession, qualitatively different from primate call systems (Chapter 2) and the communication systems of other animals. Furthermore, language is not only a distinct human ability, but a universal one. For Chomsky, the child's mastery of language is not just a matter of learning during enculturation, but is the fulfillment of an innate, genetically specified program for acquiring language. Any normal child who grows up in a social environment will inevitably develop language. This facility in language comes easily and automatically. Chomsky believes that this is because any human brain contains a genetically encoded blueprint, or basic linguistic plan, for building a language—a *universal grammar*. When children begin to learn a particular language, they do not have to build up a linguistic structure from scratch, because they already know the basic outline. As they learn their native language, children experiment with different parts of the blueprint. In so doing, they find that certain sections of it are used in their language, whereas others are not. They gradually reject the organizational principles used in other languages and accept the rules incorporated in their own.

Chomsky's theory of universal grammatical processes is supported by the fact that children in every culture begin to demonstrate linguistic ability at about the same age. Furthermore, they show similar rates of progress in mastering particular aspects of language. Such universal features of language acquisition as overgeneralizations ("foot," "foots"; "hit," "hitted"), and their eventual correction, illustrate the process whereby the child experiments with rules, eventually accepting and refining some, while rejecting others. Chomsky believes that beneath the surface variety represented in the world's languages, linguists may uncover a limited set of formal organizing principles that rest on universal attributes of the human brain. Viewed in this way, the study of language becomes a subdivision of psychology, concerned with human intellectual abilities in general. Universal features of language are sought as clues to universal mental processes.

As we learn to use our native language to communicate, we master a *particular* set of rules—those our language has selected from the universal set—that enable us to translate our intentions or meanings (what we want to say) into structured sequences of sounds (what we do say). Those who hear us and speak our language instantaneously retranslate our sounds to decipher their meaning. Mastery of grammatical rules enables us to use language creatively, to *generate* an infinite number of grammatical sentences from a finite number of rules. Under appropriate circumstances, we, as speakers, can produce sentences that have never before been uttered. As hearers, we can immediately understand the original utterances of others.

Chomsky distinguishes between a native speaker's linguistic *competence* (what the individual must know about language to engage appropriately in verbal interaction) and *performance* (what the individual actually says). Competence in a particular language develops during childhood as an abstract unconscious structure that underlies the ability to communicate through language. The linguist's job is to discover this unconscious structure by looking at deep structures, surface structures, and the transformational rules that link them.

When a speaker wishes to express a particular thought, a sentence is formed at what Chomsky calls the level of *deep structure* in the speaker's mind. That sentence is then channeled by a *transformational rule* to the speaker's *surface structure*. The message, expressed through sound, then passes from speaker to hearer. When a sentence (roughly defined as a complete thought) is pronounced, the hearer deciphers its meaning by translating it back into his or her own deep structure. The surface structure of most sentences clearly reveals their deep structure, since only one meaning is possible. For example, when you hear the sentence "The women are cooking rice," you have no trouble understanding its meaning since it has just one possible deep structure. With ambiguous sentences, however, the distinction between deep and surface structures is clearer. Consider the sentence "They are barbecuing chickens." Here the single surface structure masks the fact that the sentence has two different deep structures that convey two different meanings. One of the deep structures means that people are

doing something, preparing a meal; they are barbecuing chickens. "Barbecuing" is a verb and "chickens" is the object of that verb. In the second deep structure "chickens" is a noun and "barbecuing" is an adjective; barbecuing chickens are being distinguished from other kinds of chicken, for instance, frying or roasting chickens. The meaning of the sentence—that is, which of the two deep structures the single surface structure is expressing—must be inferred from the context. For example, if the conversation is about patios or backyards, the first deep structure will be apparent. If, on the other hand, it is about products displayed in supermarkets, the second deep structure is suggested.

Deep and surface structures are linked by transformational rules. We have just examined a sentence whose ambiguity results from the fact that one surface structure expresses two deep structures. Conversely, a single deep structure may be expressed by several surface structures. In other words, there are different ways of saying the same thing. Thus there is a single deep structure for these two sentences:

The women are cooking rice.
Rice is being cooked by the women.

In this case, a single deep structure is transformed into two surface structures by transformational rules that produce active and passive constructions. The same transformational rules can convert into active or passive form any deep structure that includes a transitive verb and its object.

Replacement is another way of transforming a single deep structure into multiple surface structures. Look at this deep structure:

The book is on the shelf.

In it, "the book" can be replaced by "it" and "on the shelf" by "there." When the replacement transformation is applied, we have

It is there.

A further transformational rule is *deletion*. If you say, "Sally went to the museum," the person who hears you may respond, "I know." A transformational view of this snippet of conversation involves several steps. As the speaker, you begin with a meaning or idea you want to convey (the *semantic component* of the sentence). Drawing on your linguistic competence, you put together a deep structure sentence, "Sally went to the museum." As you then transform your sentence to the surface structure, as the simple declarative statement "Sally went to the museum," you put together a specific sequence of sounds that your hearer immediately decodes into first a surface structure and then a deep structure. The hearer grasps your meaning and wishes to respond that he or she knows that Sally went to the museum. From the deep structure sentence "I know that Sally went to the museum," the transformational rule of deletion produces "I know" in the surface structure. Your mutual understanding of the response reflects your shared ability as speakers of the same language to recognize a single deep structure in "I know that Sally went to the museum" and merely "I know." A finite number of additional transformational rules in English generate surface structures from deep structures (see Figure 12.3).

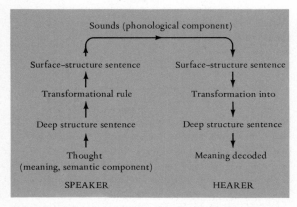

FIGURE 12.3 How a message passes from speaker to hearer according to the transformational-generative model. The speaker translates meaning (the semantic component) into sound (the phonological component), through deep structure, a transformational rule, and a surface-structure sentence. The hearer decodes to find meaning in reverse order.

The intricacy of the last example may suggest to you that the transformational-generative approach to language overanalyzes the obvious. This reaction probably rests on your own proficiency as a native speaker of English and on your intuitive knowledge of how grammatical rules in English work. In contrast to the descriptive linguistic techniques it has replaced, transformational-generative theory views any language not as a static structure built on discrete levels, but as a dynamic, creative, flexible system that enables meanings to be communicated through an abstract set of grammatical rules and a

structured code of sounds. Transformational grammar proposes that there is much more to a language than what appears on the surface. It can show that different surface structures actually communicate a smaller number of deep structures, and that a finite set of grammatical rules suffices to enable speakers and hearers to generate and understand an infinite number of sentences, many of which they have never spoken or heard before. The transformational approach argues that surface structures — the object of traditional descriptive linguistic study — make languages seem more different than they really are. The similarities of languages lie deeper. By studying the deep structures of different languages we may eventually discover universal principles that compose a universal grammar, the building blocks of which any language is necessarily constructed.

LANGUAGE, THOUGHT, AND CULTURE

Note that Chomsky advocates a naturist position — a DNA-coded basis for similarities among languages. However, since he is arguing for genetic determinism only on the most general level, Chomsky's position is considerably less extreme and much more plausible than those of the sociobiologists and other naturists discussed in Chapter 11. Chomsky's genetic determinism refers to an indisputably universal human capacity, language acquisition, rather than to any specific psychological trait, like aggression or altruism, that varies widely among cultures and individuals. All people share, in Chomsky's view, a predisposition for language, though not for any particular language. Common organizational features of the brain provide a large but finite number of principles for organizing any language. By knowing the rules of our own language, however, we can creatively generate an infinite number of sentences. That people can learn other languages, and that terms and concepts can be translated from one language into another, tend to support Chomsky's position that the same linguistic underpinnings and similar thought processes characterize all humans.

Other linguists and anthropologists have a very different view of the relationship between language and thought. Rather than seeking universal linguistic structures as clues to universal mental processes, they argue that different languages produce divergent patterns of thought. This position is sometimes known as the Sapir-Whorf hypothesis after linguists

Edward Sapir (1931) and Benjamin Lee Whorf (1956), its prominent early advocates. Sapir, Whorf, and others argue that the lexicons and grammars of particular languages may lead their speakers to think about their own experiences and aspects of their world in distinctive ways. Third-person singular pronouns of English (he, she; him, her; his, hers), for example, distinguish gender, whereas those of the Palaung, a small tribe in Burma, do not. This distinction is coded in our language, although a fully developed noun gender and adjective agreement system, as in French and other Romance languages (la belle fille, le beau fils), is not. The Sapir-Whorf hypothesis might suggest, therefore, that English speakers pay more attention to differences between males and females than the Palaung, but less than French or Spanish speakers.

To support his hypothesis, Whorf (1956) examined differences in the tense systems of English and Hopi, a language of the Pueblo region of the Native American Southwest. English divides time into past, present, and future. Hopi does not; its grammar, rather, distinguishes between events that indisputably exist or have existed (what we use past and present to discuss) and those that do not (our future events, along with the imaginary, hypothetical, and fanciful). Whorf then argues that from this grammatical difference, which leads English and Hopi speakers to different perceptions about time and reality, come differences in Hopi and English thought.

In the view of Whorf and others, lexicon—a language's names for things—can also produce different perceptions of reality and thus cause differences in thought and action. Thus Eskimos have three short and distinct words for different types of snow that in English are all called "snow," and the Nuer have an elaborate vocabulary to deal with cattle. The argument runs that Eskimos recognize, think about, and respond to differences in snow that English speakers cannot even see because our language provides us with just one word. The same for the Nuer and their cattle. Carol Eastman (1975), however, follows Roger Brown (1958) in suggesting that Eskimos have multiple words for snow, and Nuer for cattle, because of their environmental needs. When need arises, English speakers can also elaborate their snow and cattle vocabularies. Skiers, for example, regularly recognize and name varieties of snow that are missing in the lexicons of Miami retirees. Similarly, the cattle vocabulary of Texas ranchers is much more extensive than that of a salesperson in a New York City department store.

As you will see in the discussion of historical linguistics, vocabulary and lexical distinctions belong to the area of language that changes most readily. New words and new types of distinctions—if needed—can appear and rapidly spread among the speakers of any language. Brown (1958) notes that words that are most important to speakers, those that are needed most and thus used most often, are usually single words (monolexemes) rather than phrases (for instance, "rain" versus "tropical storm"). Names for items get simpler as the items themselves become more important. In the late 1970s, a television has become a "TV," an automobile, a "car," and a citizen's band radio, a "CB."

Language, culture, and thought are indisputably interrelated. However, it seems more reasonable and accurate to say that changes in culture produce changes in thought and in language (at least its surface structure) than the reverse. Robin Lakoff (1975) points out differences between female and male Americans in the color terms they use and the color distinctions they make. Distinctions implied by such terms as "salmon," "rust," "peach," "beige," "chartreuse," "mauve," and "dusky orange" are rarely found in the American male's lexicon. Most of them, however, weren't even in American women's lexicons fifty years ago. Here lexical changes rest on changes in American economy, society, and culture—in this case, the proliferation of women's fashion and cosmetic industries. A parallel and even more recent gender-based difference in Americans' vocabularies shows up in football, basketball, and hockey vocabularies. Fans—more often males than females—use more terms and make more elaborate distinctions in the games they watch. We see, then, how cultural differences and social changes are expressed in changes in vocabulary and in lexical distinctions (for instance, "peach" versus "salmon") within semantic domains (for instance, color terminology).

The Study of Meaning

Several recent studies demonstrate that speakers of different languages and dialects do categorize their experiences and their perception of the world around them in different ways. Differences in kinship terminology of the sort described in Chapter 5 provide examples of cross-cultural differences in folk taxonomies—how people classify their relatives. The study of folk taxonomy, also called *ethnoscience* or *ethnosemantics*, involves analysis and description of the ways in which different cultures customarily categorize the world through distinctions involving lexicon. It examines contrasts and classifications significant in various cultures that are incorporated into their language.

Anthropologists and linguists have described several ethnosemantic domains recognized in languages. *Domains* are classes of things, events, and ideas viewed as in some way similar, and thus as different from other such classes. Some of the most frequently and thoroughly studied domains have been kinship terminology and color terminology. Others include native categorization of disease, including causes, symptoms, and cures (see Frake, 1961); native astronomy (see Goodenough, 1953); and the folk taxonomy *(ethnobotany)* of plant life (see Conklin, 1954; Berlin, Breedlove, and Raven, 1974). Other studies have examined native classification of animals *(ethnozoology),* firewood, and foods.

The contributions of ethnosemantic analysis to linguistics, and particularly to anthropological linguistics, have been great. In particular, ethnosemantic studies have demonstrated that, like phonology, morphology, and syntax, meaning, too, can be analyzed systematically. Consider, for example, Robbins Burling's formal semantic analysis of the domain of personal pronouns in Palaung, a Burmese language. Burling has demonstrated differences between Palaung and English in the way the pronouns of these languages classify people. Palaung has eleven personal pronouns, which can be translated into English as follows (Burling, 1970):

1. I
2. you (singular)
3. he, she
4. he or she, and I
5. you (singular) and I
6. they and I
7. you (singular), I, and he, she, or they
8. he or she, and you (singular)
9. they and you (singular)
10. they two
11. they, three or more

There are some obvious differences between Palaung and English in the way in which people are perceived and classified. For example, English has "he" and "she," but the Palaung pronoun (item 3) makes no distinction for sex in the third person singular. Furthermore, Palaung does not lump the second person singular and plural under a single term, as the English "you" does. What are the significant dimensions of contrast involved in the domain of Palaung pronouns? There appear to be three, and they are summarized in Figure 12.4. First, like English pronouns, Palaung pronouns reflect distinctions in number. However, in contrast to English, Palaung has three numbers: singular, dual, and plural. Dual, as the term suggests, means that the pronoun refers to two and only two people. Second, like English, which distinguishes between "I" and "we," the first person forms, and all other personal pronouns, Palaung distinguishes between pronouns that include the speaker and those that do not. There is, however, a third dimension of contrast that Palaung shares with many other languages but not with English. Palaung pronouns indicate whether the person spoken to is included or excluded from the remark (see items 6 and 7, for example).

	Speaker Included	Speaker Not Included
Hearer Included	5. (dual) 7. (plural)	2. (singular) 8. (dual) 9. (plural)
Hearer Not Included	1. (singular) 4. (dual) 6. (plural)	3. (singular) 10. (dual) 11. (plural)

FIGURE 12.4   Palaung pronouns.

Figure 12.4 demonstrates that these three dimensions of contrast are sufficient to distinguish the meaning of each Palaung personal pronoun from every other. The meaning of each represents a unique combination of three different components, one from each dimension. Because it isolates the components that are minimally sufficient to distinguish the meaning of each item within the domain, a formal semantic analysis such as Burling's is also known as a *componential analysis.*

The same procedure that Burling used in his componential analysis of Palaung pronouns has been used by anthropologists in describing other domains in languages.

As we have seen, the way in which people divide

up the world, the contrasts they perceive as significant, reflect their daily lives and their specific adaptations to their environments. As you saw in Chapter 5, kinship terminology is related to forms of social organization. Language reflects distinctions that are socially important. Some anthropologists have even suggested that general evolutionary statements can be made about the lexical systems of specific languages. Brent Berlin and Paul Kay (1969), for example, have suggested that there is a relationship between color terminology and general evolutionary status. After examining the color terms in more than one hundred languages, they found that although different languages varied in the number of color terms in their vocabularies, there were only eleven basic color terms for all languages. Significantly, the number of basic color terms in a specific language appeared to vary directly with general cultural complexity. Representing one extreme were the languages of New Guinea horticulturalists and Australian foragers, which used only two basic terms that translate as "black" and "white" or "dark" and "light." At the other end of the continuum were languages with all eleven color terms. These were languages of Europe and Asia. Measures of general evolutionary complexity are still relatively crude. However, on the basis of Berlin and Kay's research, anthropologists and linguists should certainly investigate the possibility of other relationships between lexical domains and general cultural complexity.

VARIATION IN SPACE: SOCIOLINGUISTICS

Language and culture merge in the ethnosemantic study of how people in other cultures perceive and treat, through classification and lexical distinctions, aspects of their experience. Detailed and systematic ethnosemantic research has provided data that demonstrate links between language and culture and reveal cross-cultural differences and similarities within such domains as color and kinship terminology. Despite these contributions, ethnosemanticists have neglected variation within particular cultures. We have already seen, for example, differences in the sports and color vocabularies of contemporary American males and females. This semantic variation reflects broadly different activities and experiences of men and women in American society. Ethnosemantics needs to investigate systematically the

ways in which such semantic diversity among speakers of a given language mirrors their overall social diversity.

Competence and Performance

The field of *sociolinguistics* is concerned with investigating and explaining interrelationships between social and linguistic variation. William Labov (1972b), a prominent figure in the field, charges that linguists in general have neglected variation in different speakers' use of the same language. Traditional linguists and members of the transformational-generative school have viewed any language as a uniform system of rules shared by all its speaker-hearers. Chomsky and other generativists make linguistic *competence,* the unconscious, abstract system of generative rules and processes mastered by all speaker-hearers of the same language, the object of linguistic study. In focusing on uniform, invariant linguistic norms, linguists create the erroneous impression of speech communities as homogeneous systems in which everyone speaks alike by mastering the same rules.

Linguistic *performance*—the actual use of language in concrete social situations—is neglected by generativists but is the main concern of sociolinguists. Sociolinguists do not deny that people who speak the same language share common deep structures and sets of rules that permit mutually intelligible communication. Most linguistic rules are of this sort. However, sociolinguists focus on those linguistic elements that lie closer to the surface and that vary systematically with social context. If linguistic variation is socially recognized and differentially evaluated, it provides a sensitive index of many other social processes.

The technique of linguistic analysis used will follow from whether uniformity or variation is stressed. For linguists who see language as a shared, invariant system, any informant is as good as any other. Working with any one native speaker will enable the trained linguist to identify all the important rules of the language being investigated. Furthermore, when their task is to analyze their own language, linguists' own intuitive knowledge of the language can be substituted for work with informants. Sociolinguists, however, to investigate how speech varies with social position and situation, must actually enter the speech community. A few infor-

According to Chomsky, children easily and naturally learn whatever language is spoken around them because their brain contains a genetically coded blueprint for language acquisition—a universal grammar. Schools teach children prestige dialects, not how to speak grammatically, a talent that all children develop naturally as they grow up in society. (Arthur Tress)

mants will not suffice. Variable aspects of language must be defined, observed, and measured. The frequency of their use by different speakers must be quantified; to demonstrate covariation of linguistic and social factors, social attributes of speakers must also be assessed.

One of the main assumptions of sociolinguistics is that variation within a speech community at a given time represents linguistic change in progress. Labov (1972b) states this as the principle of *linguistic uniformitarianism:* the same mechanisms that have operated to produce the large-scale linguistic changes of the past can be observed operating in the current changes taking place around us. Linguistic change does not occur in a vacuum; only when social meaning is assigned to variations in speech will they be imitated, spread, and begin to play a role in linguistic change.

Linguistic Diversity in Nation-States

As an illustration of the linguistic variation encountered in a nation-state, consider the contemporary United States. Ethnic diversity is revealed by the fact that 32 million Americans learn first languages other than English; Spanish is the most common. Most of these people eventually become bilinguals, adding English as a second language. Not just in the United States, but in other multilingual nations, peo-

ple may automatically use their two (or more) languages on different occasions—one in the home, for example, and the other on the job or in public. Because we learn and customarily use the two languages in different contexts, we may maintain separate semantic domains for them. Anthropologist Robert Lowie's native language was German, and although he eventually spoke, wrote, and used English in most contexts, he still had difficulty thinking of cooking—of the entire semantic domain surrounding the kitchen—in any language other than German. In certain parts of Europe people must similarly switch not from one language to another, but between two dialects of the same language. This phenomenon, known as *diglossia,* applies to "high" and "low" variants of the same language. The "high" variant is used in writing and for communication in such formal contexts as universities, certain occupations, and the mass media. The "low" variant is used for ordinary conversation with family members and in egalitarian social relations.

Whether bilingual or not, all of us vary our speech on different occasions. According to Labov (1972a), in our ordinary casual speech, our *vernacular,* we pay least attention to how we are saying things and speak *most* grammatically. When we give lectures, have a job interview, have a conference with a teacher, or read aloud, we pay more attention to how we are speaking; our style becomes increasingly formal, and we make more grammatical mistakes. These are called *style shifts,* variations in speech in different contexts. Linguists interested in this phenomenon find that their informants, when interviewed, speak most formally—paying most attention to pronunciation, for example—when asked to read isolated word lists.

Just as the contexts we speak in modify our phonology, morphology and syntax, so do geographical, cultural, and socioeconomic differences—for instance, region; city, town, suburban, or rural residence; ethnic background; education; and socioeconomic class. Associated with such contrasts, which are found in all stratified nations, are the dialects that coexist in our country alongside Standard (American) English (SE). SE is itself a dialect of English that differs, say, from RP (Received Pronunciation, or BBC English)—the preferred linguistic variant or dialect in Great Britain.

A major contribution of sociolinguistics—and one that jars our popular stereotypes about language—is that all dialects are, as linguistic systems, equally effective systems for communication—which is, after all, language's major function. Our tendency to think of particular dialects as better or worse than others is social evaluation. We differentially rank certain speech varieties because we recognize that they are used by certain social or regional groups that we also rank. For example, people who normally say "dese," "dem," and "dere," instead of "these," "them," and "there," can communicate effectively with one another, and indeed with anyone who recognizes that the alveolar stop systematically replaces the dental fricative in their speech. Yet this form of speech, which does not block effective communication, is disapproved of because it has become a linguistic indicator of low social and educational rank. Labov points out that the use of "dems," "deses," and "deres" is one of many phonological differences that Americans recognize and stigmatize. Other examples are negative stereotypes held by non-Bostonians of Boston speech, and by non-Southerners of the so-called Southern drawl. We also know that these regional variants can gain new respectability as a result of social and political changes, for instance, by electing a President who represents such a regional variant.

Phonological Change in Progress

Other variable linguistic features may escape our notice. Many Americans, for example, are replacing

The foods offered at this multi-ethnic food stand illustrate culture contact and borrowing in language and cuisine. Linguistic variation based on regional, rural-urban, class, and ethnic contrast is encountered in any nation-state. Particular speakers also shift their styles, dialects, and even language in different situations. (Timothy Eagan/Woodfin Camp & Assoc.)

the initial [t] of such words as "tiger" with a [ts] similar to the German sound written *z* and pronounced [ts] in such words as *zu* ("to") and *zeit* ("time"). In a sociolinguistic study carried out in the 1960s on the island of Martha's Vineyard, Massachusetts, Labov found that fourteen phonological contrasts differentiated two groups of Vineyarders who held different attitudes about relations between their native island and the outside world. One group used higher, more constricted phonological variants as a social indicator of their solidarity against tourists and other outsiders who spent their summers on the island and were buying up land from natives. In areas of the island (down island) where Vineyarders had more contact with the summer people, among people who relied most on the influx of tourist dollars, and among those natives who planned careers on the mainland, accent included lower, more open phonological forms.

In particular, Labov (1972b) contrasted the two groups of Vineyarders in terms of articulatory position of the first phonetic element in the diphthongs /ay/ and /aw/ (the sounds of *i* in "fight" and of *ou* in "house," respectively). *Diphthongs* are sounds made by combining a vowel such as /a/ with one of the semivowels such as /y/ or /w/. Up-island natives with positive attitudes toward residing in Martha's Vineyard and retaining its integrity against outsiders were shifting toward higher and more centralized pronunciation of the /a/ in these diphthongs (approaching the /ə/ in b*u*t, *a*bout, and th*e*). Down-island speech approached the mainland pattern, the SE pronunciation of /a/. Other phonological changes were accompanying this shift, since, as the pronunciation of one phoneme changes, other shifts may follow to allow those distinctions between vowel phonemes indicated in Figure 12.2 to be retained. Although people whose attitude toward the island was positive recognized that their speech was not the same as that of the down islanders and mainlanders, they were not aware of the particular phonological differences, including greater /a/ centralization, which were producing an increasing dialect contrast.

Labov was able to measure this and other phonological changes in progress on Martha's Vineyard by collecting quantitative data. He interviewed several informants representing the contrasting social groups and analyzed their tape-recorded phonetic variation with a sound spectrograph. The phonological contrasts between Vineyarders were not absolute, but involved significant differences in the *frequencies* of the contrasting phonological features. Labov was seeing linguistic change in progress and—through information about his informant's plans, life histories, education, residence, and jobs—he could relate linguistic change to social variation.

Women, Men, and Linguistic Diversity

As with other phonological changes, some linguistic contrasts between men and women may lie close to the consciousness of native speakers, but not be fully recognized. Peter Trudgill (1974), for example, reports that several studies of American speakers have found women's vowels to be more peripheral (more front, more back, higher, or lower) than men's. Studies carried out in British and American cities demonstrate that, when other social contrasts are held constant, women use forms closer to the standard or prestige dialect. Consider the data in Figure 12.5 gathered in Detroit. Throughout all the strata, but particularly in the lower working class, men use multiple negation more often than women. These findings, along with similar results from other studies, suggest that women are more sensitive to socially stigmatized forms than men and are more likely than men to incorporate standard forms in their own phonology and syntax. This trend shows up consistently in both the United States and Great Britain, but the social and cultural reasons for it are imperfectly understood. Trudgill suggests that men may adopt speech forms that are social indicators of working-class status more than women because they associate working-class occupations—and thus speech—with cultural stereotypes of greater masculinity. Perhaps women pay more attention than men to mass media, where standard dialects are employed. Also, women may compensate for the social and economic barriers they have traditionally encountered in stratified nations by copying the linguistic norms of upper-status groups.

Considering differences in the speech patterns of American men and women, Lakoff (1975) suggests that lexical disparity reflects inequity in women's status in the United States. Lakoff finds that expletives used by women ("Oh dear," "Oh fudge," "Goodness!") are less forceful than those used by men ("Hell," "Damn," *Expletive deleted*). She relates men's greater use of such "forceful" expletives

	Upper Middle Class	Lower Middle Class	Upper Working Class	Lower Working Class
Male	6.3	32.4	40.0	90.1
Female	0.0	1.4	35.6	58.9

FIGURE 12.5 Multiple negation ("I don't want none") according to class and sex (in percentages). (From Peter Trudgill: *Sociolinguistics: An Introduction* (1974), p. 91. Copyright © 1974 by Peter Trudgill.)

to their traditionally greater public power and presence. She also notes that certain words that belong to "women's language" ("adorable," "charming," "sweet," "cute," "lovely," "divine") cannot be used by men without raising doubts about their masculinity as American culture has typically defined it. Lakoff also finds differences in men's and women's intonation patterns. Consider the following fragment of conversation:

Man: When will dinner be ready?
Woman: Oh . . . around six o'clock . . . ?

Lakoff suggests that the second sentence's intonation pattern—a declarative answer that is hesitant and that has the rising inflection typical of a question—differentiates American women and men. In Lakoff's analysis, the woman is actually saying to the man, ". . . if that's all right with you."

Linguistic Diversity and Socioeconomic Stratification

As these examples illustrate, language reflects social contrasts and is used, evaluated, and changes in accordance with *extralinguistic factors*—that is, larger political, economic, and social forces. Although aspects of phonology, syntax, lexicon, and meaning vary from group to group, linguistic traits of low-status groups are negatively evaluated. This is not because these traits are intrinsically deficient, but because they are associated with and come to symbolize, mark, or indicate low-status groups. Consider, for example, variation in pronunciation of *r* when it occurs in certain positions in words—for instance, "yard," "fourth," "car," "floor," "carry," "Barbara." In some parts of the United States today *r* is regularly pronounced, and in other (*r*less) areas, it is not. Originally, *r*less speech was a pres-

tige form modeled on the fashionable speech of southern Britain and was adopted in many parts of the United States, where it continues as the norm in areas around Boston, Richmond, Atlanta, and Charleston, South Carolina. In New York City people emulated *r*less speech and lost their *r*'s in the nineteenth century after having pronounced them during the eighteenth, but today New Yorkers are in the process of reverting to the eighteenth-century pattern. Clearly, what matters, and what governs the linguistic change, is not the sound of pronounced *r* but its social evaluation, whether *r*'s are "in" or "out."

Studies on *r* pronunciation in New York City clarify, for one phonological feature, the mechanisms of linguistic change. Labov (1972b) focused on whether or not *r* was pronounced after vowels in such words as "car," "floor," "card," "fourth." To obtain information on how this linguistic variation related to socioeconomic class, he used a series of rapid and anonymous speech encounters with employees in three of the city's department stores, each of whose prices and locations attracted a different socioeconomic group. Saks Fifth Avenue (68 speech encounters) catered to the upper middle class; Macy's (125) attracted middle-class shoppers, and S. Klein's (71) had predominantly lower-middle-class and working-class customers. The class affiliations of store personnel reflected those of the clients. Having already determined that a particular department was located on the fourth floor, Labov approached ground-floor salespeople and asked where that department was. After the salesperson had responded "fourth floor," Labov said, "Where?" and *fourth floor* was repeated. The second response given was more formal and emphatic, the salesperson presumably thinking that the first response had not been understood. For each salesperson, therefore, Labov had two samples of /r/ pronunciation in two words.

Labov calculated the percentage of store personnel who pronounced /r/ at least once during the interview: 62 percent at Saks, 51 percent at Macy's, and 20 percent at S. Klein's. Labov also found that personnel on upper floors, where he obtained information by asking "What floor is this?" pronounced *r* more often than ground-floor salespeople. Pronunciation of *r* was clearly associated with prestige. It varied from store to store as expected, but within each store, salespeople on the upper floors, where the more expensive goods were located, also pronounced *r* more often.

Style Shifting and Hypercorrection

In a subsequent, more detailed study of linguistic variation on New York City's Lower East Side, Labov (1972b) found a similar association between *r* pronunciation, other phonological features, and indexes of class, including occupation. In the Lower East Side study, Labov and his associates conducted interviews that lasted from four to eight hours. Through these lengthy interviews with informants whose socioeconomic attributes were known, they were able to collect information on a range of speech styles for each informant. Although an interview is an artificial situation in which a speaker usually adopts a formal speech pattern (style B), Labov, by shifting the informant's attention away from the actual interview, was also able to gather information on casual speech (style A). Speech increasingly more formal than style B was also obtained by having informants read passages (style C, reading style), read lists of isolated words (style D), and read lists of minimal pairs (style D').

These detailed data enabled Labov to show linguistic changes that took place when informants paid more and more attention to their speech. His results for just one phonological variable — *r* pronunciation — will be considered; the others follow roughly a similar pattern. As expected from the department store study, only upper-middle-class (UMC) speakers under age forty showed any sizable amount of *r* pronunciation in casual speech (style A). Older UMC speakers — whose favored socioeconomic position gave them more secure prestige — were more likely than younger UMC speakers to have *r*less speech — the prestige pattern more than forty years ago. Although most of Labov's lower-middle-class (LMC) and working-class (WC) informants did not pronounce *r* in their own ordinary casual speech, all informants, regardless of class, seemed to have positive evaluation of *r* pronunciation. Such evaluations were obtained by playing a tape recording of twenty-two sentences, spoken by people with a variety of speech characteristics, and asking informants to rank each speaker according to suitability for a scaled series of occupations. All informants, regardless of class, assigned the *r* pronouncers to more positively valued occupations, suggesting their acceptance of *r* pronunciation as the prestige norm.

Labov found another significant pattern. Although his LMC informants did not pronounce *r* in their everyday speech, their sensitivity to *r* pronunciation as a marker of prestige was revealed when they shifted from casual to more formal speech styles. In styles D and D' LMC informants' *r* pronunciation actually surpassed that of UMC speakers, the only ones who used it regularly in ordinary speech. This mechanism — called *hypercorrection* — along with linguistic insecurity by members of the LMC were potent agents of linguistic change. LMC speakers tended to adopt, even in middle age, the prestige forms used by the youngest members of the highest ranking class. LMC children, exposed to their parents' changing speech, as well as to the speech of their teachers and peers who were attending college, would eventually become *r* pronouncers, too. Thus, given differential social evaluation, and as one form spreads as the prestige norm, linguistic variation at one time becomes the basis for a historical change.

Black English Vernacular (BEV), Standard English (SE), and Other Dialects

Labov and many other linguists have analyzed the relation of sociolinguistic variation to ethnic background. In particular, Labov (1972a) and several associates, both white and black, conducted a detailed study of what they call Black English Vernacular (BEV), the "relatively uniform dialect spoken by the majority of black youth in most parts of the United States today, especially in the inner city areas of New York, Boston, Detroit, Philadelphia, Washington, Cleveland, . . . and other urban centers. It is also spoken in most rural areas and used in the casual, intimate speech of many adults." Researchers collected comparable data for six adolescent peer groups and several adult populations in New York City, as well as several samples of speech in other cities.

Labov's definition of BEV refers specifically to the speech of inner-city boys from eight to nineteen years old — people who participate most fully in the "street culture" of urban areas. Labov analyzes BEV as a fully coherent and complex linguistic system closely related to SE and other American English dialects. He concludes that the dialect differences between BEV and SE are not *in themselves* the reasons for reading difficulties encountered by many black youths in inner-city schools. Rather,

Black English Vernacular (BEV) and Standard English (SE) are two dialects of contemporary American English. According to Labov, BEV is most characteristically spoken by black youths in American cities. Most of its contrasts with other dialects involve surface structure rather than deep structure. (Ken Heyman)

dialect differences have come to symbolize the political and cultural conflicts present in the classroom. An understanding of BEV and how if differs from, and is similar to, SE may help school personnel work toward improving educational opportunities of black Americans. However, large-scale political, economic, and social changes are necessary to guarantee full access by all social groups to our nation's resources.

The historical origin of BEV is open to debate. Many linguists feel that the similarities BEV has to the creole languages of the West Indies suggest that it has a creole base. Creoles develop out of *pidgins:* languages that form as the speakers of two or more different languages come into continuous firsthand contact—typically, in the context of trade. By incorporating elements of two or more languages, pidgins facilitate communication. Once they become linguistic systems with grammatical rules of their own and acquire native speakers, they become full languages—called *creoles*. Linguists disagree about the extent to which early BEV rested on a creole base or formed as a variant of certain British dialects. Nevertheless, in the American South BEV developed as a variant of southern speech, with a phonology and syntax similar to those of other southern dialects. No doubt their influence was mutual. Almost every feature that distinguishes BEV from SE can also be found in the everyday speech of at least some southern whites, although with less frequency than among people who have fully mastered

BEV. BEV was perfected in the South but has since emerged as the relatively uniform dialect of black youths in northern cities.

Labov finds that most of the grammatical rules of BEV are the same as those of SE and other English dialects. BEV does, however, have certain subsets of rules absent from the grammar of SE and other dialects. With a few exceptions, most of the contrasts between BEV and other dialects lie at or near the level of surface structure, but when these forms are examined at deeper levels they do not contrast.

Because of phonological differences between BEV and SE, speakers of the two dialects have different homonyms. Labov (1972a) discusses some of the main phonological contrasts. BEV speakers are less likely than SE speakers to pronounce *r*. Even though many SE speakers fail to pronounce *r* as a consonant before other consonants (ca*r*d) or at the end of words (ca*r*), most do pronounce *r* as a consonant before a following vowel, either at the end of a word (fou*r* o'clock) or within a word (Ca*r*ol). Although the difference is one of degree (some BEV speakers do pronounce *r* as a consonant in all environments in certain formal styles of speech), BEV speakers are much more likely than SE speakers to omit the *r* before a vowel or between vowels. Among the homonyms produced: Carol = Cal; Paris = pass; terrace = test. The last example occurs because of another BEV phonological rule that deletes certain consonants at the end of words. Other homonyms are produced by the fact that many BEV speakers drop pronunciation of *l*. Thus: toll = toe; help = hep; Saul = saw. BEV also reduces certain consonant clusters at the end of words, giving such homonyms as past = pass; rift = riff; mend or meant = men. In combination with the previous rule of *l* dropping, "told," "toll," and "toe" may also become homonyms for a BEV speaker.

Because of these and other systematic phonological contrasts between BEV and SE, BEV-speaking students will systematically pronounce certain words differently from SE-speaking students. Since the BEV-speaking students' homonyms will differ from the SE-speaking teacher's, in evaluating reading accuracy, the teacher must note whether the meanings of such homonyms as "told" and "toe," "passed," "past," and "pass," are being recognized by students. The teacher should make sure that students grasp what they are reading and not that they are pronouncing words "correctly" according to the SE norm.

Phonological contrasts between BEV and SE speakers often have grammatical consequences. One of these is *copula deletion*, absence of SE forms of the verb "to be" in the present tense and auxiliary (is, are . . .-ing). For example, any of the following may contrast BEV and SE:

BEV	SE
you tired	you are tired
he tired	he is tired
we tired	we are tired
they tired	they are tired

In its deletion of the present tense of "to be," BEV is similar to several languages—for instance, Russian, Hungarian, and Hebrew—but contrasts with SE. Labov has shown that this contrast is one of surface structure rather than deep structure. BEV copula deletion is the grammatical result of BEV's phonological rules, some of them already discussed. BEV omits the copula only where SE contracts. Thus SE contracts "you are tired" to "you're tired." Through contraction SE produces "he's," "we're," and "they're." The phonological rules of BEV dictate that *r*'s and word-final *s*'s be dropped. Note that since no BEV phonological rule omits *m*, the contracted copula is present in the BEV first person singular, "I'm tired." Thus when BEV omits the copula, it is merely carrying the SE contraction rule one step further—an automatic result of BEV's phonological rules.

Similarly, BEV speakers, because of the *l*-dropping rule, may say "I be there" for SE "I'll be there." Commonly, however, BEV speakers distinguish present from future by uncontracted forms—for instance, "I will be there"—or by auxiliaries derived from "going to"—for instance, "gonna," "gon," or "gwin be there." Also, whereas phonological rules may lead many BEV speakers to omit *-ed* as a past tense marker and *-s* as a marker of plurality, these differences involve contrasts between SE and BEV at surface rather than deep structure. Some BEV speakers do pronounce *-ed* and plural *-s* in certain linguistic environments, and all BEV speakers draw a clear conceptual distinction between past and present verbs and singular and plural nouns. This is confirmed by irregular verbs—those that do not use *-ed* to form the past (for instance, BEV "he tell," "he told")—and by irregular plurals (for instance, "child," "children").

Another BEV grammatical rule, often erroneously stigmatized as "illogical" by SE-speaking teachers, is *negative concord*, or use of double negatives. Sentences such as "He don't know nothing" or "Can't nobody do nothing about it" are not illogical. Negative concord is a feature of languages as diverse as French, Spanish, Portuguese, Russian, and Hungarian. The evaluation of negative concord as illogical by SE-speaking teachers rests on sociolinguistic and not on linguistic factors. The presumed illogical aspect of "he don't know nothing" is that it really means "he knows something." However, a BEV speaker can easily express whether the person he or she is describing knows *something* or *nothing* by emphasis, context, or a different sentence entirely. Anyone who hears BEV—or any other English dialect in which "he don't know nothing" is grammatical—immediately understands its meaning.

Most contrasts between BEV and SE therefore lie at or close to the surface. Many surface grammatical differences are consequences of such phonological rules as *r*lessness, *l* dropping, and reduction of consonants at the ends of words. A few differences between BEV and SE, however, do appear deeper. Even if not used regularly by all BEV speakers, the differences are aspects of their competence and are immediately understood by BEV, but not by SE, speakers. One of these is the remote perfect "been," as in "I been know your name." Translated into SE, this means "I've known your name for a long time and still do." Another is invariant "be," a

form that is regularly associated with "usually" and "sometimes" and that indicates habitual action. Invariant "be" refers to events that are repeated but continuous.
Compare:

BEV	SE
He busy right now.	He's busy right now.
Sometime he be busy.	Sometimes he's busy.

BEV speakers have access to a verb for which no equivalent single form exists in SE. To express the meaning of BEV's invariant "be," SE would have to say "Sometimes he's busy, and sometimes he isn't."

This necessarily brief discussion of some of the major differences between BEV and SE — most at the surface-structure level — demonstrates that BEV, like SE and other dialects, is a fully developed, complex, rule-governed grammatical system. Because BEV is so close to SE, speakers of the two dialects often fail to recognize that some of the grammatical rules and subsets of rules of the two dialects differ. SE-speaking teachers need thorough knowledge of BEV's phonology and grammar if they are to teach its speakers successfully. BEV-speaking students must be shown specifically how SE — used by the mass media, in writing, and in many public contexts — differs in phonology and syntax from BEV.

Any rule-governed language or dialect is a coherent, complex, and perfectly effective means of communication for its speakers. Evaluation of particular languages or dialects as "better" or "worse," or as more or less "correct," than others has nothing to do with language per se. These "linguacentric" judgments reflect social prejudices and the particular social contexts in which linguistic variants are used. "Ain't" communicates meaning as effectively as "isn't." The social value of pronouncing consonantal *r* changes from century to century. Some languages include the copula; others delete it. Some require double negatives; others exclude them. Any language or dialect always has phonological and grammatical variation. It is only when particular aspects of linguistic variation come to speakers' attention that they are positively or negatively evaluated. In this way, *given socioeconomic stratification,* differential evaluation of social groups, when applied to linguistic variation, can lead to linguistic change over time.

VARIATION IN TIME: HISTORICAL LINGUISTICS

Sociolinguistics examines contemporary variation — historical change in progress; historical linguistics deals with the results, over longer time periods, of variation in phonology, grammar, and meaning. Historical linguists can, for example, reconstruct phonology, grammar, and vocabulary of past languages by examining *daughter languages,* contemporary languages that, after hundreds or thousands of years of separation and linguistic change, are the diversified descendants of a common linguistic ancestor called the *protolanguage.* With related techniques historical linguists also classify contemporary languages according to their degree of relationship.

A close relationship between languages does not necessarily mean that their speakers are also closely related, since people may shed one language and adopt another. In the equatorial forest of central Africa, many groups of foragers have discarded their ancestral languages and adopted those of their horticultural neighbors, relatively recent arrivals in the forest. Immigrants to the United States spoke many different languages on their arrival, but today their descendants speak English as their native tongue. In nation-states people who are otherwise very different socioculturally may speak a single language. On the other hand, people who are culturally similar over a large area, like central African foragers, may speak different languages.

Despite certain parallels to be noted below, there are important differences between the evolution of life and of languages. In the evolution of diverse species, borrowing of genetic material stops once they can no longer interbreed. But in language and in culture complete speciation never occurs. Linguistic items and cultural items can pass from one speech community to another, from one human population to another. Like sociocultural means of adaptation, linguistic evolution may be, and usually is, influenced by contact with others.

Historical Linguistics and Other Anthropological Concerns

Let us now explore how historical linguistics has been useful in other studies. Knowledge of linguistic relationships is often valuable to anthropologists interested in the recent past, in events that have taken place, say, during the past 5,000 years. Many ethnological studies have focused on areas of the world where multiple language families are represented. Certain other sociocultural features may be correlated with the distribution of language families. Groups who speak related languages may be more similar to one another in their sociocultural means of adaptation than they are to populations whose speech patterns derive from different traditions.

Similar sociocultural traits and patterns may not be limited to groups who speak related languages. Such traits may have spread by diffusion. Even groups whose members speak unrelated languages may have contact with one another—through trade, intermarriage, or war. Ideas, inventions, and other cultural baggage will diffuse among the groups. For example, many items of vocabulary and even some sounds included in contemporary English come from French. Even if there were no written historical documentation of France's influence on England following the Norman Conquest in 1066, linguistic evidence in contemporary English would reveal a long period of important firsthand contact.

Historical information about nonliterate populations is often absent. In this case, linguistic evidence alone may reveal cultural contact and borrowing. By considering which forms and meanings have been borrowed, we may be able to learn about the nature of the contact. All the people of Madagascar, for example, speak related Malagasy languages. Despite the nearness of Africa, the Malagasy languages are members of a widespread language family, the Malayo-Polynesian stock, which also includes the languages of Polynesia, Indonesia, and the Philippines, as well as some languages spoken in Southeast Asia.

Although Madagascar's earliest colonizers were Indonesian traders, contact between Madagascar and East Africa has continued throughout the history of the island. The Malagasy languages provide extensive clues to the nature of this contact. Malagasy words for several species of economically useful plants and animals have clearly been borrowed from languages spoken in East Africa, suggesting that these items come from East Africa. Many of the terms used by Malagasy in commercial activities, particularly in the marketplace, have been borrowed from Swahili, a widely spoken East African language that is a member of the Bantu linguistic group. Such evidence suggests a long period of trade between Madagascar and East Africa. Further, it suggests that Swahili-speaking peoples were important in this trade.

The Evolution of Language

That language changes form over time, that it evolves—varies, spreads, splits, or otherwise segments into subgroups—is implicit in the preceding sections. Distinct daughter languages grow out of a single parent, especially if they are isolated from one another. Some of these may then segment, and new languages will develop. If some people remain in the ancestral homeland, however, their speech patterns will also change over time. It is appropriate, therefore, to consider the evolving speech patterns that occur in the ancestral homeland as a daughter language like the rest. This perspective contradicts an American myth that pockets of people who speak "pure Elizabethan English" still survive in the mountains of Tennessee, a belief similar to the one that people are descended from contemporary apes or monkeys. Daughter languages and dialects, wherever they are spoken, are the end results of specific evolutionary sequences. They are collaterals, cousins or sisters, rather than ancestors and descendants. Certain archaic forms of speech may have been preserved in particular daughter languages and dialects and not in others, but other innovations have taken place that distinguish the daughter from the protolanguage. This does not deny that it is possible, through written records, to preserve languages. Latin, Sanskrit, and ancient Greek all exist as living fossils inscribed on stone or paper and are spoken and understood in special, primarily ritual, contexts. Latin does not live in its ancient form; if it is spoken today, it is as French, Spanish, Portuguese, Italian, or Roumanian—one of its many divergent descendants.

Consider now some of the longer-term results of language variation in time and space. Vocabulary seems to be the aspect of language least resistant to change. In most languages it is fairly easy to coin or borrow new words for new concepts and new things. Innovations in vocabulary reflect modifications in the daily lives of members of the speech community. That the vocabularies of contemporary human groups are more complex—that is, include more words and recognize a wider range of concepts—than the vocabularies of *Homo erectus* and the Neanderthals cannot be demonstrated, but most anthropologists would probably accept it. Furthermore, languages spoken in more complex societies tend to have larger and more extensive vocabularies than those spoken in nonindustrial societies. Note, however, that the larger vocabulary applies to the *language* of the complex society and not to its individual speakers. The average American's vocabulary may be no greater than that of a person chosen at random from a tribal society.

SOUND SHIFTS Although we have examined several cases of phonological change in progress, the sound system of a language does appear to be more resistant to change than its vocabulary. This means simply that phonological changes typically take longer to accomplish. Major long-term phonological changes in English are obvious from written documents. Shakespeare is often difficult for many American students because of differences in English grammar, pronunciation, and meaning from his time to ours. When contemporary pronunciation is used, some of Shakespeare's apparent rhymes don't rhyme at all. This frequently reflects phonological change—many of those words did rhyme in his day.

Although shifts in pronunciation take time, linguists have noted that long-term shifts are not haphazard. If the pronunciation of a phoneme changes in one word, corresponding changes in pronunciation will also occur in all words in which that phoneme occupies the same phonological environment (for instance, after a vowel, between vowels). A new phoneme may also enter a language, but this occurs far less frequently than sound shifts. Because sound shifts are regular rather than capricious, and because phonetic change may proceed independently of phonemic change, historical linguists can extend their analyses back in time. As daughter languages differentiate from a common protolanguage, they change phonologically. The shifts in pronunciation that take place in one may not be the same as those that take place in another. By comparing the phonologies of several daughter languages, however, it is possible to work back in time and reconstruct much of the phonological system of the protolanguage.

THE COMPARATIVE METHOD The comparative method involves identifying homologous forms in related languages and then reconstructing the original form. It was developed in Europe during the nineteenth century, and the bulk of the historical linguistic work carried out then was concerned with Indo-European languages and their parent language, proto–Indo-European (see Figure 12.6). The Indo-European family is widespread. Its name is derived from India and Europe, the easternmost and westernmost areas in which such languages were spoken prior to European explorations. Proto–Indo-European was probably spoken in northern Europe around 5,000 years ago. Over time, through population growth, dispersions, migrations, and conquests, linguistic differentiation occurred and the present-day distribution of the Indo-European languages was accomplished.

French, a member of the Italic subgroup of the Indo-European family, and English, a member of the Germanic subgroup, are distantly related languages whose most recent common ancestor may be proto–Indo-European itself. English and German, on the other hand, both belong to the Germanic subgroup and are thus more closely related. This means that it is easier for an English-speaking student to learn the phonology and grammar of German than of French. On the other hand, because of the long period of common French and English history following the Norman Conquest, French and English vocabularies have as many similarities as German and English vocabularies do. The closer relationship of English to German is much more obvious in deep structure than in surface structure.

Many of the phonemic contrasts and some of the phonetic contrasts that exist in modern English can be traced back to proto–Indo-European, and the same is true of French phonology. Knowledge of the corresponding pronunciations of phonemes in related languages facilitates language learning. For example, there is a regular correspondence between the German phoneme written *z* (as in *zu*) and pronounced /ts/ and the English phoneme /t/ (as in "to"). Consider some pairs in the two languages that have the same or similar meanings and show phonetic correspondence: *zu*, "to"; *zwei*, "two"; *sitz*, "sit." When the relationship is more remote, as in the case of English and French, it is more difficult, but still possible, to trace the shifts that have taken place in the daughter languages. Since it is impossible to hear proto–Indo-European spoken, of course, linguists must examine several daughter languages and consider their interrelationships in order to guess about pronunciation of a phoneme in the parent language.

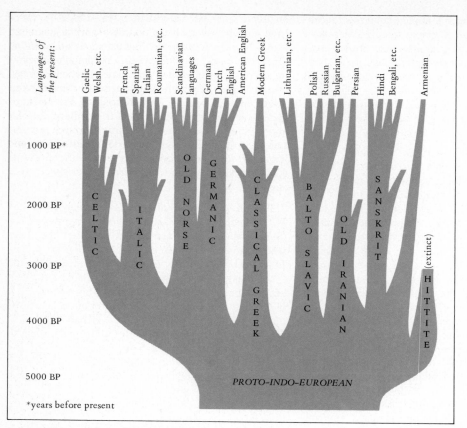

Languages of the present:

Gaelic
Welsh, etc.
French
Spanish
Italian
Roumanian, etc.
Scandinavian languages
German
Dutch
English
American English
Modern Greek
Lithuanian, etc.
Polish
Russian
Bulgarian, etc.
Persian
Hindi
Bengali, etc.
Armenian

1000 BP*

2000 BP

3000 BP

4000 BP

5000 BP

CELTIC

ITALIC

OLD NORSE

GERMANIC

CLASSICAL GREEK

BALTO SLAVIC

OLD IRANIAN

SANSKRIT

(extinct)
HITTITE

PROTO-INDO-EUROPEAN

*years before present

FIGURE 12.6 Main languages and subgroups of the Indo-European language stock, showing approximate time of their divergence. (From *Modern Cultural Anthropology*, Second Edition, by Philip K. Bock.)

SUBGROUPING Languages, like life forms, can be differentiated into subgroups by degrees of relationship. As in biological taxonomy, linguistic subgrouping reflects differences in recency of common ancestry. All the Germanic languages share certain innovations, indicating a period of common history when a proto-Germanic speech community existed apart from other Indo-European languages whose descendants now belong to other linguistic subgroups. *Shared innovations* in certain related languages indicate a separate connection—something that ties them to each other but not to any other languages.

LEXICOSTATISTICS Traditionally, historical linguistics has relied on phonological and morphological ev-

idence to indicate relationships and degrees of relationship in language. More recently, however, a different technique has received attention. It is called *lexicostatistics* because it deals with vocabulary (lexicon) in a statistical, or quantitative, manner. Such analysis is based on the distinction in any language between *basic vocabulary* and *cultural vocabulary*. The assumption is that while changes in cultural vocabulary may be rapid and unpredictable, changes in basic vocabulary occur more slowly and regularly. The notion that some lexical domains are more resistant to change than others seems reasonable. Contrast, for example, the difficulty in getting Americans to adopt the Japanese word for the number one with the ease with which they have accepted words such as sukiyaki, hari-kari, and other items of nonbasic vocabulary.

The second assumption of lexicostatistics is that the same meanings are basic in all languages, that is, that the same list of items applies equally well to all languages, present and past. Lexicostatistics uses a list of one hundred basic items assumed to be encountered and named in all languages. They include parts of the body, actions common to human existence (walk, sleep), features of animals and plants (tail, bark), and other universal parts of human experience.

The third assumption is that changes in basic vocabulary occur at a constant rate, and that the rate is the same in all languages. Change—due to borrowing, internal innovation, and various other reasons—is assumed to occur among the items in the one hundred-word list at a rate of 14 percent per 1,000 years. This means that if we look at a language spoken 1,000 years ago and its contemporary descendant, we can expect to find that 14 percent of the basic vocabulary items have changed and 86 percent have been retained.

To determine how closely related two languages are, we must examine the basic vocabulary of each. We must look for *homeosemantic cognates,* items similar both in phonological form and in meaning. This similarity is assumed to reflect development from a common ancestral form with the same meaning. If two contemporary languages developed from a common ancestral tongue, and if their divergence took place 1,000 years ago, each of the daughter languages is assumed to have been changing independently of the other. In each, because of separate histories, we can expect to find that 14 percent of the basic vocabulary items have changed and that 86 percent have been retained—and also that the changes have not necessarily been the same in each. According to lexicostatistics, these languages are separated by 2,000 years of separate history—1,000 for language A and 1,000 for language B. Lexicostatisticians therefore expect the percentage of shared cognates to be the square of 0.86, or about 74 percent. On the basis of the number of shared cognates, and by using a simple formula, some lexicostatisticians have argued that it is possible to date the divergence of any two related languages.

Although few linguists accept the assumptions of lexicostatistics uncritically, many have used basic vocabulary lists as a quick means of seeing relationships between languages and of defining the subgroups of those languages. If certain daughter languages share a large number of homeosemantic cognates, a period of separate history, and thus a linguistic subgroup, can be assumed. In a sufficiently large sample of contemporary languages drawn at random, some will show remarkable similarities, others will show less obvious but still perceptible similarities, and still others will hardly be alike at all. More traditional linguistic analysis will be able to refine the results of lexicostatistical comparison by determining sound correspondences between related languages and tracing daughter forms back to original forms. For sociocultural anthropologists or archeologists who have not received extensive training in linguistics, lexicostatistics represents the quickest and easiest way to spot relationships and degrees of relationships in language.

LANGUAGE AND ADAPTATION

In previous chapters language was discussed as a major adaptive advantage that differentiates *Homo* and *sapiens* from other genera and species and that has been responsible for the evolutionary success of humans. However, precisely because it is a generic advantage, because all contemporary human populations speak languages, language cannot be viewed as an adaptive advantage that distinguishes one contemporary human population from another. The adaptive status of language in human evolution is like that of the large and complex brain, which has been a specific advantage that contributed to the evolutionary success of humans compared with other genera. Yet, precisely because all contemporary human populations have complex brains and display equivalent potentialities for learning, variable brain complexity is no longer a factor in adaptation of contemporary human populations. Speechless hominids with small and simple brains have long since vanished from the earth; their descendants evolved into *Homo sapiens* and their languages into ancient languages. Chomsky, recall, has argued that human linguistic ability is rooted in specific brain structures, and that any normal child born in the contemporary world will have encoded in the brain a universal grammatical blueprint on the basis of which his or her particular language will be constructed. Just as there are no documented differences in brain complexity or intelligence among contemporary human populations, no one has ever been able to demonstrate the absolute superiority of certain languages or dialects over others.

Linguistic relativity has been accepted as one of the basic tenets of twentieth-century anthropology and linguistics. Any language or dialect is interpreted, according to this view, as an instance of specific evolution, just one of many potential variants on a universal base. All languages and dialects evolve within speech communities and provide equally effective means of communication.

This doctrine of linguistic relativity goes against popular stereotypes. French people who believe that theirs is the only appropriate language for civilized discourse would reject it. And there are many British and Americans who would assert the superiority of their language in commercial negotiations. These claims, however, reflect sociocultural variables rather than linguistic facts. They reflect events in the history of world politics and economy rather than anything about the inherent properties of particular languages. In establishing a world empire, the French spread their culture through the medium of their language, and, since they asserted to the people they conquered that they were engaged in a civilizing mission, they came to equate the French language with civilization itself. English became dominant as a commercial language because English—and now American—influence has been widespread.

The extent of contemporary use and distribution of particular languages reflects factors other than intrinsic features of the language itself. One language spoken in China has more native speakers than English, not because it is a superior language but because the population that speaks it has grown, due to ecological and sociopolitical factors. English is the native language of British, North Americans, Australians, New Zealanders, and many South Africans because of vast English colonization and conquest. The success of such colonization and conquest had nothing to do with language. Weapons, ships, and sociopolitical organization played decisive roles.

Between 2,000 and 3,000 years ago a small population lived in a confined area of West Africa in what are now the nation-states of Nigeria and the Cameroons. Today the linguistic descendants of this language, proto-Bantu, cover most of central and southern Africa. The Bantu languages did not expand because of any intrinsic superiority they had as a vehicle of communication. Rather, population growth and territorial expansion of proto-Bantu speakers appears to have taken place because of an adaptive advantage, early reliance on iron tools and weapons, and cultivation of certain highly productive food crops.

Linguistic relativity is well established and, as we saw in the discussion of sociolinguistics, its demonstration is clear. No particular language or dialect can confer, by virtue of its purely linguistic qualities, a differential adaptive advantage on the group that speaks it. Only a positive or negative social evaluation of its speakers and, by extension, of the language itself can do this. Languages are flexible and, at the surface level, constantly changing systems. Languages or dialects can accommodate new items or new concepts in their vocabularies fairly easily: old forms may be combined, a foreign name may be borrowed, or an entirely new form may originate. One of the principles expressed in Chapter 11 should also be applied to the study of links between languages and the people who speak them. Languages, like gene pools and phenotypes, are not in themselves impediments to social change, nor do they determine social and cultural forms. In Chapter 11 it was pointed out that in many respects the daily lives of rural Europeans before the Industrial Revolution were more similar to those of precolonial West Africans than to those of their contemporary descendants. Yet linguistic change in English or in French has proceeded very slowly compared with the rate of economic, political, and social change. Particular languages, through modifications in their surface structures, retain their effectiveness as vehicles of communication in the face of rapid cultural change. Yet the central core of a language, its deep structure, may remain virtually intact while its speakers' lives are revolutionized.

SUMMARY

Anthropological linguists, like other anthropologists, are interested in uniformity and variation in time and space. Descriptive linguistics examines speech communities at specific times, generally the present; historical linguistics studies linguistic change. Also, new fields of anthropological linguistic study—meaning systems, relationships between language and culture, research on linguistic universals, and sociolinguistics—are now attracting considerable attention.

Language has three interrelated subsystems, or components: phonology, syntax, and semantics. Sounds are combined in structured sequences—morphemes, words, phrases, and sentences—to convey meaning. Phonology focuses on sound contrasts (phonemes) that distinguish meaning in a given language. No language distinguishes between, or even includes, all the sounds (phones) that the human vocal apparatus can produce. In sociolinguistics, patterned variation in pronunciation is related to social contrasts and is viewed as historical change in progress.

The transformational, or generative, approach advocated by Noam Chomsky and other linguists has revolutionized the study of grammar—the formal organizing principles that link sound and meaning in a language. Generative grammar views any language as an abstract system of rules, a grammar, that any native speaker masters during childhood. Chomsky argues that mastering a language fulfills an innate, genetically specified program, a blueprint in the brain for building a language. He calls this blueprint—a universal set of organizing principles—a universal grammar. In his view, all people share a genetically determined capacity for language, though not for any particular language. Each language's grammar is a particular set of rules selected from the universal set. Once we master our language's particular rules we can creatively generate an infinite number of grammatical sentences from a limited number of rules. Generative grammarians attempt to define competence in a given language by discovering deep and surface structures and transformational rules. The transformational-generative approach argues that surface structures—the object of traditional descriptive linguistic study—make languages seem more different than they really are. Their similarities lie deeper.

Unlike Chomsky, other scholars stress particular, rather than universal, relationships between language and thought. Sapir and Whorf, for example, argued that the lexicons and grammars of particular languages lead their speakers to perceive and think in distinctive ways. Casting doubt on the Sapir-Whorf hypothesis and similar views is the fact that vocabulary and lexical distinctions change readily. A more reasonable argument is that cultural changes lead to changes in thought and in language—at least in surface structure. Nevertheless, studies of such ethnosemantic domains as kinship and color terminologies and pronouns show that speakers of different languages do categorize their experiences and their perception of the world around them differently.

Sociolinguistics investigates relationships between social and linguistic variation; it focuses on performance (the actual use of language) rather than competence (rules shared by all speakers of a given language). Sociolinguists enter speech communities, work with several informants, and quantify their observations. Only when social meaning is assigned to variations in speech will the variations be imitated, spread, and begin to play a role in linguistic change. In nation-states people vary their speech on different occasions, shifting styles from vernacular to formal, and, in many nations, from one language or dialect to another. Sociolinguistics recognizes that, despite their social evaluation, all languages and dialects are—as linguistic systems—equally complex, rule-governed, and effective systems for communication.

Language usage reflects social contrasts and is used, evaluated, and changes in accordance with political, economic, and social forces. Linguistic traits of a low-status group are negatively evaluated not because of their intrinsic qualities, but because they are associated with—and come to symbolize—low status. Hypercorrection, revealed by lower-middle-class informants in Labov's study of *r* pronunciation and other linguistic variation in New York City, can contribute to linguistic change. BEV, a dialect of contemporary American English most characteristically spoken by black American males between eight and nineteen, shares, despite certain surface phonological and syntactic differences, most of its deep structural rules with SE and other American English dialects. Both SE and BEV are fully developed, complex, rule-governed grammatical systems; neither dialect can communicate meaning more effectively than the other.

Some of the techniques employed by descriptive linguists to describe and analyze the phonology, syntax, and lexicon of specific languages are also used by historical linguists. In addition, knowledge of basic linguistic techniques aids ethnographers in learning their field language. Also, for the ethnologist, archeologist, or biological anthropologist interested in relationships between nonliterate populations of the present and recent past, historical linguistic information is often very useful. For example, similarities and differences in other aspects of culture are often associated with linguistic similarities and differences. Linguistic clues can suggest past contact between now distinct populations.

Also, two populations may speak different languages that are descended from an original protolanguage. Thus historical linguistics may reveal information that will help to explain differences and similarities in cultural patterns and to unravel past relationships for which no written records exist.

Application of general evolutionary principles to language is more doubtful than in the case of other sociocultural phenomena. Only a few linguists and anthropologists have demonstrated plausible links between linguistic phenomena and general evolutionary status of human populations. When languages are compared, a position of linguistic relativity is essential: each language should be viewed as an instance of specific evolution, a human communication system as adequate as any other for enabling people to exchange essential information.

Despite the difficulty of applying evolutionary principles to the study of language, we know that languages change, and we also know a great deal about how they change. Vocabularies, for example, appear to change more easily and rapidly than grammars and phonemic systems. Within vocabulary, however, there appears to be a basic vocabulary that is most resistant to change. Lexicostatistics, a means of evaluating degrees of interrelationship between closely related languages, assumes the existence of this basic vocabulary. Using this and other techniques, historical linguists have studied linguistic divergence, the gradual development of separate languages out of ancestral speech communities. Relationships between languages do not necessarily reflect genetic relationships between their speakers, since languages and speech habits can be adopted or shed independently of phenotypical or genetic changes. However, certain kinds of linguistic similarities, if not evidence for common genetic ancestry, indicate a period of common history and thus may explain some other differences and similarities of interest to anthropologists.

SOURCES AND SUGGESTED READINGS

BAUMANN, R., AND SHERZER, J., EDS.
1974 *Explorations in the Ethnography of Speaking.* New York: Cambridge University Press. Twenty-one papers analyzing speech in its social context; a useful anthology.

BERLIN, B.
1970 A Universalist-Evolutionary Approach in Ethnographic Semantics. In *Current Directions in Anthropology: A Special Issue,* vol. 3 (3), part 2, ed. A. Fisher, pp. 3–17. Washington, D.C.: American Anthropological Association. Argues for the possibility of a comparative evolutionary approach to the study of meaning.

BERLIN, B., AND KAY, P.
1969 *Basic Color Terms: Their Universality and Evolution.* Berkeley: University of California Press. Partial correlation between number of basic color terms recognized and general evolutionary status of cultures.

BERLIN, B., BREEDLOVE, D. E., AND RAVEN, P. H.
1974 *Principles of Tzeltal Plant Classification: An Introduction to the Botanical Ethnography of a Mayan-Speaking People of Highland Chiapas.* New York: Academic Press. Thorough, model technical report of field research project in ethnoscience.

BLOUNT, B. J.
1975 Studies in Child Language: An Anthropological View. *American Anthropologist* 77: 580–600. Useful article reviewing six books and numerous articles encompassing recent research on how children acquire different languages.

BLOUNT, B., ED.
1974 *Language, Culture, and Society: A Book of Readings.* Cambridge, Mass.: Winthrop. Seventeen papers dealing with language, culture, and society, and the historical development of anthropological linguistics; a useful reader covering major issues.

BOLINGER, D.
1975 *Aspects of Language.* 2nd ed. New York: Harcourt Brace Jovanovich. Very thorough, up-to-date introduction to linguistics.

BROWN, R. W.
1958 *Words and Things.* Glencoe, Ill.: The Free Press. Insightful comments on the study of meaning.

BURLING, R.
1970   *Man's Many Voices: Language in Its Cultural Context.* New York: Holt, Rinehart & Winston. Role of language in social life, and the cultural context of variations in grammar, phonology, and meaning.

CHOMSKY, N.
1957   *Syntactic Structures.* The Hague: Mouton. A revolution in linguistics toward the construction of transformational grammars was prompted by this technical book.

1972   *Language and Mind.* 2nd ed. New York: Harcourt Brace Jovanovich. Transformational-generative theory and the cerebral basis of a universal grammar.

CONKLIN, H. C.
1954   *The Relation of Hanunóo Culture to the Plant World.* Unpublished Ph.D. dissertation. Yale University. Detailed study of classification of plant life by the Hanunóo, a group of Filipino horticulturalists; great influence on students of ethnoscience and componential analysis of folk domains.

DAVIS, F.
1973   *Inside Communication: What We Know about Nonverbal Communication.* New York: McGraw-Hill. This book by a popular science writer presents in a readable and generally accurate way the major theories and approaches in nonlinguistic communication.

EASTMAN, C. M.
1975   *Aspects of Language and Culture.* San Francisco: Chandler & Sharp. Brief but useful treatment of language and culture, sociolinguistics, transformational grammar, and other linguistic topics and approaches.

FARB, P.
1974   *Word Play: What Happens When People Talk.* New York: Alfred A. Knopf. Nontechnical, competent treatment of human communication.

FRAKE, C. O.
1961   The Diagnosis of Disease among the Subanun of Mindanao. *American Anthropologist* 63: 113–132. Ethnodiagnosis; how members of Filipino tribe classify and treat their illnesses.

GOODENOUGH, W. H.
1953   *Native Astronomy in the Central Carolines.* Philadelphia: University of Pennsylvania Press. Field study of ethnoastronomy; how a group of islanders in Micronesia classify the planets and stars.

GREENBERG, J. H.
1972   Linguistic Evidence Regarding Bantu Origins. *Journal of African History* 13: 189–216. Recent conclusions about area of origin of the proto-Bantu speech community.

1975   Research on Language Universals. *Annual Review of Anthropology* 4: 75–94. Survey of the literature with useful bibliography.

GUDSCHINSKY, S. C.
1967   *How to Learn an Unwritten Language.* New York: Holt, Rinehart & Winston. Brief manual applies techniques of linguistic science to learning a foreign language; intended for college students.

HALL, R. A., JR.
1960   *Linguistics and Your Language.* 2nd ed. Garden City, N.Y.: Doubleday. Entertaining paperback that explodes some myths about correctness in language taught by generations of English teachers.

HARMAN, G., ED.
1974   *On Noam Chomsky: Critical Essays.* Garden City, N.Y.: Doubleday/Anchor. Several authorities evaluate Chomsky's profound influence on linguistics and philosophy.

HOIJER, H.
1954   The Sapir-Whorf Hypothesis. In *Language in Culture,* no. 79, ed. H. Hoijer, pp. 92–104. Washington, D.C.: American Anthropological Association. Extent to which language, particularly grammar, determines patterns of thought in different cultures.

HYMES, D., ED.
1964   *Language in Culture and Society: A Reader in Linguistics and Anthropology.* New York: Harper & Row. Excellent reader; strong in ethnoscience and other linguistic developments of the early 1960s.

LABOV, W.
1972a   *Language in the Inner City: Studies in the Black English Vernacular.* Philadelphia: University of Pennsylvania Press. Model sociolinguistic study; phonology and syntax of BEV and its differences with SE.

1972b   *Sociolinguistic Patterns.* Philadelphia: University of Pennsylvania Press. Sociolinguistic theory and practice on Martha's Vineyard and in New York City.

LAKOFF, R.
1975   *Language and Woman's Place.* New York: Harper & Row. Readable, nontechnical discussion of how women use and are treated in Standard American English.

LEHMANN, W. P.
1972   *Descriptive Linguistics: An Introduction.* New York: Random House. Many of the new approaches to linguistics developed during the 1960s.

SAPIR, E.
1931   Conceptual Categories in Primitive Languages. *Science* 74: 578–584. Early statement of the controversial Sapir-Whorf hypothesis.

TRUDGILL, P.
1974   *Sociolinguistics: An Introduction.* Baltimore: Penguin. Nontechnical, well-written short introduction.

WEITZ, S.
1974   *Nonverbal Communication: Readings with Commentary.* New York: Oxford University Press. Theory and data about means of communicating other than language.

WHORF, B. L.
1956   A Linguistic Consideration of Thinking in Primitive Communities. In *Language, Thought, and Reality: Selected Writings of Benjamin Lee Whorf,* ed. J. B. Carroll, pp. 65–86. Cambridge, Mass.: MIT Press. Illustration of the Sapir-Whorf hypothesis and other papers on language and culture.

FOCUSING on
CONTEMPORARY SOCIETY

The Anthropology of Complex Societies: Peasants and Cities

13

Although many anthropologists still prefer field work in small communities where they can get to know most of their informants personally, they no longer study primarily isolated, nonindustrial societies. One of the principal reasons for this is that there are simply not many such societies left. Some 10,000 years ago food production began to absorb and replace foraging adaptations in environments where they had reigned supreme. More recently, the state and, today, industrialism, have had a similar impact on previous social forms. If anthropologists wish to study an isolated primitive society, they must journey to the highlands of New Guinea or to the tropical forests of South America. In faraway Madagascar one finds motels run by AGIP, a hotel chain based in Italy. In Australia sheep owned by speakers of English graze where totemic ceremonies once were held.

For a variety of reasons, technologically advanced adaptations tend to replace simpler ones. Food production typically supports larger and denser populations than foraging. Cultivation and domestication have spread throughout most of the world not just through population growth and expansion from food-producing areas, but also as foraging populations have gradually added domesticates to their diets to supplement hunting, fishing, and gathering. Similarly, states have spread at the expense of tribal societies. States have brought stateless populations under their control or within their spheres of influence through superior arms, military organization, larger and denser populations, and economic specialization, which increases the pace of technological innovation. States and industrial adaptations are not necessarily better than or superior to the forms they are replacing. In fact, several inhumane results have accompanied the emergence and spread of state

Air pollution, traffic noise, and wasteful use of finite energy sources accompany contemporary industrialism. States, while displacing other forms of sociopolitical organization throughout the world, typically leave ecological destruction in their wake. (Elliott Erwitt/Magnum Photos)

METROPOLE-SATELLITE RELATIONSHIPS

As Europeans took to ships, developing a trade-oriented, mercantile strategy of adaptation, populations in many world areas were gradually brought under European control. The Industrial Revolution brought people everywhere into a growing world economy based on capitalism. In the early years of exploration European ships landed on foreign shores and engaged in reciprocal trade—albeit characterized by negative reciprocity—with people strange to them. With colonization, however, exchange became a facsimile of redistribution, with colonial populations, *satellites*, providing goods and services for a European center, the *metropole*. Typically, there was more siphoning than redistribution in this form of exchange. Natives in colonial areas rarely got back what they had given up. Nor, in a multiethnic society, was the relationship between European superordinates and native subordinates phrased in the same terms as, for example, that between ruler and subjects in nonindustrial states, or between chiefs and their relatives of lower rank in chiefdoms.

As the Industrial Revolution spread in Europe and North America, raw materials from the colonies were transported on European ships to manufacturing areas in the metropole. Finished products were largely consumed in the metropole. However, some of these manufactured goods were sold in colonial areas, at prices that reflected the cost of transportation and manufacture, plus a margin of profit. England, France, Spain, Portugal, and other European nations all became metropolitan centers of empires managed by colonial administrations. Colonial officials, who wanted to avoid duplication of effort and products in their different colonies, were overseers of territorially dispersed empires, as chiefs and their advisers had been overseers of different areas of their chiefdoms. They encouraged economic specialization—a colonial gold coast, an ivory coast, a slave coast, areas that exported spices or particular kinds of wood.

In the colonies of the New World plantation economies based on the cultivation of a single crop (*monocrop production*) developed during the seventeenth, eighteenth, and nineteenth centuries. Europeans established plantation colonies in other areas—for example, in the Indian Ocean—but the New World plantations bear responsibility for the largest forced migration of human beings in world history.

organization. Because states are always stratified societies, they create and maintain social inequality. Compared with people in stateless societies, and particularly with foraging populations, many or most citizens of states enjoy less leisure time, eat less well balanced diets, and are forced to relinquish to impersonal figures their time, energy, labor, and wealth. Increasing exploitation of the earth's finite store of natural resources, particularly through industrial technology and modern life styles, is achieved at great cost. Thus industrial states—which might in the short run seem to represent general evolutionary progress (by virtue of numbers and range)—may in the long run prove disastrous because of the ecological destruction they leave in their wake. Through studies in a variety of settings, anthropologists are providing concrete data on a variety of human problems encountered in complex societies.

Living in states and cities involves stresses and problems missing in unstratified and nonindustrial societies. State organization also means harder work for most of the population. Shown here, four people in Brooklyn, New York spend weekend leisure hours playing cards. (Arthur Tress)

possessions, and trade areas, so that each empire had specialized sources of sugar, slaves, spices, and coffee. Throughout the period of European colonization in the New World, the influence of different metropolitan powers waxed and waned; empires contracted and expanded. There was, however, always more than one metropole.

During the nineteenth century plantation economies based on slave labor became, in many parts of the world, monocrop economies based on free but poorly paid labor. In the twentieth century many former colonies gained their political independence. However, economic control of an underdeveloped nation does not generally end with its political independence. The specialization promoted under European colonialism remains the basis for much of the poverty in the world today. Former colonies remain economic satellites of metropolitan powers and continue to provide raw materials, crops, and other produce for consumption in these nations. In many cases the items exported are the same ones that flowed from satellite to metropole under colonialism, and the same system of distribution still prevails. In addition, underdeveloped areas in different parts of the world often produce the same item because each was formerly a specialized appendage of a metropolitan empire. Brazil provided sugar to its metropole, Portugal, while islands in the West Indies grew sugar for Britain and France. As long as underdeveloped nations continue to specialize in traditional cash crops and raw materials, the economic situation of, say, a cacao worker in Brazil will be affected by what happens to the cacao crop in Ghana.

Today there are new metropoles: Japan, the OPEC nations, West Germany, the Soviet Union, China, and other members of the "Communist" bloc. Some, of course, wield greater political and economic power than others; for example, U.S. economic policies can affect the economies of Western Europe. In the context of such economic colonialism, isolated, nonindustrial societies have become few and far between. Isolation has broken down as metropolitan powers have sought, and still seek, new markets and new possessions. The means whereby the United States, for example, maintains its range of control include legal agreements with other governments, designed to protect American interests; one of the world's most technologically sophisticated means of gathering information; a mobile and widely

To the lowlands of the West Indies and Latin America, generally areas where native population densities had been low, European slave ships brought Africans, whose labor built the lowland economies of the New World. The plantation monocrops differed from century to century and from area to area. In Brazil's early colonial history its major export crop was sugar; subsequently, it became coffee. Cotton, of course, was the principal plantation crop in the southern United States.

The metropolitan interests of each empire planned and promoted productive diversity in its colonies,

Production for subsistence rather than profit characterizes this closed community in the highlands of Guatemala. (Max Hunn/Frederic Lewis)

dispersed military apparatus with an extensive arsenal of weapons; and social and political relationships that protect the interests of the metropole in its many satellites. Of course, each of the other metropoles duplicates these means, though usually on a smaller scale.

Although the isolated ways of life that represent anthropology's traditional concern are disappearing, the subject matter open to the discipline is, in fact, expanding. This book has been oriented around a major interest that unifies the different subdisciplines of anthropology—the study of evolution. The definition of environment employed here has never been limited to the immediate natural surroundings. Alterations in the wider environments of contemporary human populations—that is, in their relationships with foreigners—represent changes to which formerly isolated populations must adapt. Although the process of metropolitan incorporation is proceeding today on a larger scale and more rapidly than ever before, it is not new. It began on a large scale with the European voyages of discovery and grew during the period of colonialism in the New World. But

there were empires in ancient civilizations, too. Their capitals served as metropoles to economically and ecologically specialized satellites, and in this way also changed the wider environments to which many tribal populations had to adapt.

Since the 1940s many anthropologists have become interested in the changes that accompany or follow contact between industrial and nonindustrial populations. Published results of research concerned with "social change," "cultural change," "socioeconomic change," or "acculturation" are now abundant. Specific studies have been guided by larger questions: What kinds of social, cultural, and economic changes have accompanied sustained contact between metropolitan nations and satellite areas? Have satellite populations been able to survive their incorporation within larger systems through changes in their sociocultural means of adaptation? Have sociocultural changes been major or minor? Have some populations been able to adapt more easily or rapidly than others?

In short, because complex societies are expanding, anthropologists are studying problems in these societies and problems associated with their expansion. The study of peasants, small-scale rural farmers living in state-organized societies, is flourishing. Peasants may be found today both in "backward" rural areas of such industrial nations as France and Italy and in weakly industrialized states. Nonindustrial states themselves, like band and tribal societies, have been incorporated into metropoles. Many such states have become *satellite states*—weakly industrial or nonindustrial, internally stratified, economically specialized appendages of metropolitan nations. In addition, some stratified societies—for example, in Latin America—that were originally founded as satellites have become satellite states. Some of the results of anthropological studies of populations that live in satellite states will be presented here.

The remainder of this chapter is intended to provide some idea of the research problems and field methods that have recently engaged anthropologists working in peasant communities and cities. An exhaustive summary of recent anthropological research will not be presented here. Rather, I will confine the discussion to the two areas of the world I know best: Latin America and Africa. The list of readings at the end of this chapter mentions many similar studies done in other parts of the world.

THE STUDY OF CONTEMPORARY PEASANTRIES

Community Studies: Variation Within Complex Societies

Ethnographers working among foragers, tribal peoples, and peasants usually survey several communities before choosing one for intensive field work. After they have made a long-term study of everyday life, usually lasting at least a year, ethnographers describe and treat this community as representative of the larger society. But any anthropologist will recognize that even in the most homogeneous and egalitarian society, there are differences between communities. An occasional ethnographic report will take account of such variations, relating them perhaps to differences in physical or social environments. However, variation in complex societies is not so easily explained. Obviously, no single community can serve as a microcosm of an entire nation with its many regional, ecological, class, ethnic, and subcultural contrasts.

Two pioneering examples of anthropological research in complex societies were carried out in Latin America. In the early 1950s Julian Steward (1956) and several of his students did research in Puerto Rico, involving coordinated study of several areas with different economies and historical backgrounds. Charles Wagley (Wagley, ed., 1952) directed graduate students in communities in northern Brazil, sampling different economic and ecological conditions. These community studies employed traditional anthropological techniques of participant observation, firsthand observation of behavior, formal and informal interviewing and other questioning, gathering of genealogical information, and census taking.

In their published reports, the ethnographers also viewed these communities historically. Comparison produced a picture of regional ecological and economic variation in northern Brazil: the Amazon community (Wagley, 1976) with its early twentieth-century rubber boom and subsequent decline; the plantation economy (Hutchinson, 1957); the interior community settled originally by gold miners (Harris, 1956); the subsistence-oriented community of pastoralists and horticulturalists in the backlands (Zimmerman, 1952). None of these communities provided a microcosmic view of Brazilian society, but

together the studies clarified historical and contemporary variation in Brazilian society. Subsequent work by Wagley (1971), Harris (1964), and their students has increased still further our knowledge of Brazilian society. Through community studies, anthropologists have learned about peasant life in different world areas.

Peasant Communities in Latin America

Anthropologist Eric Wolf has written extensively about peasants. In a 1955 article he distinguished between two types of communities in Latin America, the "closed, corporate peasant community" and the "open, non-corporate peasant community." Another anthropologist who has written extensively on Latin America (Wagley, 1968) drew a similar distinction between Indian and mestizo communities there. Both were pointing to a difference between Indian communities located in the highlands (Wolf's closed, corporate type) and non-Indian communities located in the lowlands (Wolf's open type). Closed, corporate peasant communities are found in the highlands of Mexico, Guatemala, Ecuador, Peru, Bolivia, and, to a lesser extent, Colombia.

The highlands of Latin America were generally areas of high population density and sophisticated political development, chiefdoms and states, prior to the arrival in the New World of the *conquistadores*. With the arrival of European diseases, aboriginal populations declined considerably. However, Indian influence has remained significant in the highlands, and in each of the countries where closed, corporate peasant communities are found, a large percentage of the national population is Indian.

In the precolonial Latin American lowlands, on the other hand, where horticultural and foraging strategies of adaptation and tribal forms of sociopolitical organization were characteristic, aboriginal population densities were very much lower. Here foreign diseases, slave raids, and warfare with Europeans proved more devastating, and in some cases completely eliminated populations. In the lowlands of contemporary Latin American nations the Indian population is smallest and their cultural contribution least marked. Here, too, the open community is the characteristic rural settlement.

Wagley has used the term "mestizo" ("mixed") to describe the communities of the lowlands because their populations generally represent mixtures of Europeans, Indians, and/or Africans. In Brazil and other Latin American nations with plantation economies, large numbers of slaves were imported from Africa during the seventeenth, eighteenth, and nineteenth centuries. These Africans left their mark, both phenotypically and culturally, on the Latin American lowlands, as they did on the British West Indies and the United States. In Brazil the populations of most peasant communities represent a wide array of phenotypes—a result of the intermingling of Europeans, Africans, and Indians.

THE HIGHLAND PEASANT COMMUNITY The peasant community of highland Latin America is *corporate*. Like descent groups in many parts of the world, it has an estate, which usually consists of land. In general, closed, corporate communities are located in marginal lands in the Latin American highlands, areas that the European invaders and their descendants could not profitably exploit for cultivating plantation crops. In Peru and Guatemala, as in other nations that include both highlands and lowlands, plantation economies developed in the lowlands. In the closed, corporate community of the highlands, peasants use their estate to grow the crops that make up their daily diet. Production for subsistence rather than for cash is characteristic here.

Highland communities are also *closed*. In other words, status as a member of a community is usually ascribed at birth and cannot be shifted. For further isolation, endogamy is emphasized; most marriages take place between members of the community. All members of a community have access to its estate.

Corporate economically and closed socially, highland communities maintain a feeling of solidarity and distinctiveness from other, similar communities. In some areas of Latin America, people in neighboring communities speak different dialects and sometimes even different languages. Communities are also distinguished by differences in costume. In a marketplace it is often possible to identify people's homes by their dress. Finally, although the Indians who live in these communities are all Roman Catholics, each community has its own patron saint. In the course of the year fiestas are held to honor each particular saint. Thus the saint of the closed, corporate peasant community serves a function analogous to that of the totem in corporate descent groups. It is an emblem of internal solidarity and a ritual marker of social differentiation.

THE LOWLAND PEASANT COMMUNITY Lowland and highland communities differ in several ways. First, inhabitants of a lowland community do not typically farm a joint estate. If the economy is based on plant cultivation, individuals and nuclear families own or manage the land they farm. Second, the lowland community is not closed. Membership in a particular community is not determined at birth and it may be shifted. Finally, there is no cultural preference for endogamy. Marriages can involve people from inside or outside the community. We speak of the community as an *agamous unit;* it has no marriage rule.

The lowland community, not being corporate, has few of the features of community solidarity and distinctiveness characteristic of the highlands. Like neighboring communities, Arembepe, an open peasant community in Brazil, has a patron saint. Each year, in February, a festival is held in his honor. However, the typical lowland festival is less of a blowout than the highland fiesta, and its functions are different. The patron saint is not an important means of identifying communities in the lowlands. Many of the people who live in Arembepe, for example, were unable to identify the patron saints of villages located only a few miles away.

Peasants in lowland areas work and produce for profit as well as subsistence, cultivating cash crops that they sell in regional markets or to marketers who come to the community from the outside. Wolf estimated that between half and two-thirds of what is produced in open communities is sold for cash. This does not mean that people eat better; it merely means that they can buy more than highland Indians, that they are more dependent on the outside world. In fact, I found that in the fishing community of Arembepe, people would often sell their fish to buy manioc flour and sugar, which are high in calories but lower in protein and most other nutrients than fish. Peasants also use cash profits to purchase clothing, household items, and other goods manufactured outside the community.

All inhabitants of the lowland community speak the national language—Portuguese in Brazil, Spanish in other Latin American countries. Because lowland peasants speak the national language, they are better able to participate in national life than are highland peasants. Politicians come to the community to woo voters, and people who know how to write their names vote in national elections. Some lowland peasants avidly follow national events. In Brazil, lotteries, soccer, and the Miss Universe contest are national pastimes. Lowland peasants also celebrate national holidays.

Thus, the inhabitants of the open peasant community feel less attached to the community and more attached to the nation than do peasants in the highlands. Yet it would be wrong to suppose that the Indian populations of closed communities are totally isolated from their nation-states and from the world economy; and it would be equally erroneous to suppose that life in open communities is necessarily better, happier, or more fulfilling. People in open communities are often just as poor as those in the highlands. They may eat as poorly; they are just as illiterate; their health conditions are as bad; and their life expectancies are equally short. Furthermore, the impediments to progress are frequently just as great in both lowlands and highlands. Some of these impediments will now be examined.

Poverty in Highland Latin America: The Cargo System

In the absence of a permanent political structure like that found in chiefdoms and states, redistribution of wealth among local groups in *tribal* societies may be accomplished through such mechanisms as the ceremonial feast (see Chapters 8 and 9). Ceremonial feasting in highland Latin America, however, operates within the context of a political and religious hierarchy characteristic of each community — the *cargo system*. (This term derives from the Spanish *cargo,* meaning "charge" or burden. It should not be confused with the cargo cults discussed in Chapter 9.) Males in highland communities move up in the cargo system by undertaking more and more onerous burdens to gain the respect of other members of their community. Young men enter the cargo system by undertaking menial burdens, for example, running errands for older men. As they grow older, however, they hold political offices in the community; they are the highland equivalents of sheriffs, city council members, mayors, or community leaders. Associated with each political office are religious burdens. Highland communities celebrate several saints' days throughout the year, often culminating in a large fiesta designed to honor the patron saint of the community. As individuals move up in the political

hierarchy, they are expected to contribute more and more of their time and wealth to these religious celebrations. In return for conformity they are awarded prestige by other members of their community.

Several anthropologists who have studied highland communities have pointed out that the burdens associated with office and with religious celebrations act as a *leveling mechanism* in terms of intracommunity wealth differences. The amount of time and wealth invested by an Indian in organizing fiestas is great, and among community members, the wealthiest individuals are chosen to fill the most important offices and perform the major cargos. In *Patterns of Race in the Americas* (1964) Harris describes some of the expenses that devolve on the fiesta organizers. They must dispense considerable quantities of food and liquor. Additional expenses involve special church services, candles, costumes for dancers and players, musicians' fees, fireworks, and bulls and bullfighters. Harris also points out that since fiesta organizers are also expected to serve on the village council, they are required to be away from their fields during most of the year. Thus they give in time as much as or more than they give in money.

The cargo system recalls another leveling device: the potlatch. However, although the institutions are similar, their effects are quite different. Closed, corporate peasant communities exist within satellite states, within stratified, multiethnic nations where Indians are usually members of the lowest stratum. Such nations also include mestizos. The principal difference between Indians and mestizos is not genetic but cultural. Indians are people who live in Indian communities, speak Indian languages, wear Indian costumes, and take part in the cargo system. Mestizos are individuals who are not members of closed, corporate peasant communities, who speak the national language, who wear modern dress, and who are either members of, or have strong ties with, the national elite. They do not participate in the cargo system, but indirectly they benefit from it.

The cargo system helps to maintain inequalities in wealth and social status between Indians and mestizos; it reinforces systems of stratification in which Indians are socioeconomic subordinates. To understand this, recall the economy of the highland community. Indians expend most of their productive energy in growing crops for subsistence rather than for profit. Since they sell little, they also buy little.

However, fiestas require large expenditures of cash on goods produced outside the community. Here mestizos profit, since they are generally the storekeepers and merchants who supply nonfood items consumed during the fiesta.

Mestizos profit from the cargo system in still another way. Nations with highlands generally also include lowland zones, often areas of plantation or cash crop economies. Highland Indians are a source of cheap labor for these plantations. But how, in view of the solidarity of the closed, corporate peasant community, do plantation owners get the Indians to leave their homes to work for wages? The cargo system provides an answer. Recruiters from the lowlands regularly travel through highland communities seeking out Indians who have assumed some of the heaviest cargos that year. Since these often leave the Indian with a great deal of prestige but destitute, former *cargueros* are often willing to sign labor contracts or accept loans from mestizos. They can only get the cash to repay these loans by selling their labor on the national market. The cargo system, then, functions to provide cheap labor for the national economy and to maintain the status quo.

Thus in the satellite states of highland Latin America, there are institutions that are similar in form to those in tribal society. However, rather than functioning to maintain a nonstratified society by leveling temporary fluctuations in wealth and subsistence resources between communities, these institutions preserve a stratified society by transferring wealth and labor from the lower-stratum Indians to the upper-stratum mestizos. Ceremonial burdens function similarly in stratified nations throughout the world.

Understandably, highland Indians are sometimes extremely reluctant to assume religious and civil burdens. Ruth Bunzel (1952), in her study of a highland community in Guatemala, describes cases of Indians so reluctant to fill the offices to which other members of their community have elected them that they literally have to be dragged into office. Members of the community often apply pressure on one another to assume cargos. Indians who have themselves assumed cargos are not eager to excuse others from the same cultural obligations. Church and government officials, too, compel compliance. (For a more extensive discussion of the cargo system, see Harris, *Patterns of Race in the Americas*.)

Poverty in Lowland Latin America: Kinship in Brazil

In the rural mestizo community of lowland Latin America, the kinship system serves functions analogous to those of the cargo system in the highlands. Like the cargo system, it levels out wealth differences between members of a subordinate stratum. It also provides cheap labor for the national economy, and it preserves social and economic stratification within the satellite state.

The following analysis of kinship is based on my own field work in Brazil. It applies to Brazil's most underdeveloped area—the northeast, a region where a plantation economy based on sugar flourished from the seventeenth to the nineteenth century. Whether or not kinship also serves the same leveling function in other parts of lowland Latin America may be determined by future research.

Arembepe is an open community with a population of about 800 people, most of whom derive their livelihoods from fishing in the Atlantic Ocean. The community is mestizo; but because this was an aboriginal region of low population density, the Indian contribution has not been great. Most of the people of Arembepe are mixed descendants of Europeans and slaves brought from Africa to work on the sugar plantations.

For lower-class Brazilians the functions of kinship in impeding vertical mobility and limiting social and economic advancement may overshadow its adaptive functions. All the people who live in Arembepe are members of the Brazilian lower class. However, no completely homogeneous human communities exist. In all societies there are, at least, differences in social position related to age, sex, and personality. This is true in Arembepe, where adult males are able to increase their wealth and social position within the community through hard and constant work. Although Arembepe has no class divisions, it does have differences in wealth.

Certain aspects of Brazilian social structure impede the economic advancement of lower-class individuals. Most obvious are obligations associated with kinship. Men who through hard work have become more successful within the community are expected to share their wealth with a larger number of people. First of all, a man must share his wealth with his close kin. As he becomes more successful, earns more from the sale of his fish, he can provide his family with a better diet. This means that more of his children survive than do those in poorer households. The people of Arembepe do not practice birth control, so their families are often large. Furthermore, as a man's wealth increases, he is likely to find himself supporting other relatives — his widowed mother, a few aunts and uncles, and some cousins perhaps.

Obligations associated with marriage also drain wealth from the enterprising man. In Brazil the union with most prestige is that which has been sanctified by both church and state. The poorer couples in Arembepe are generally involved in common law unions. Upwardly mobile young men may add to their reputations by having civil and religious ceremonies when they marry. If they do this, however, they undertake obligations to affinals that do not exist with the common law union. In a common law union there is no socially recognized obligation to share wealth with the wife's relatives, but a formal bond does create such obligations. Since divorce is difficult in Brazil, these obligations are usually for life.

Finally, as wealth increases, a man will accumulate more fictive kin, godchildren, and coparents (*compadres*). A couple asks a man and a woman to stand as godparents at the baptism of their child. The two couples become coparents to each other, and the child has godparents. Two of the wealthiest men in Arembepe each had more than one hundred godchildren. By agreeing to become a godparent a Brazilian assumes a special obligation to share with both his godchild and his coparents.

Kinship thus acts in several ways to level wealth differences and impede individual vertical mobility among the lower classes. The harder a man works, the more successful he becomes within the community, but the greater the number of dependents he must support. If he wishes to spend his life within the community, he must fulfill his obligations to relatives in the socially prescribed way, since in the future he may have to rely on them. The people of Arembepe, like most other lower-class Brazilians, have no recourse to any form of government-provided social assistance. Hard work, reinvestment of meager profits, and reliance on relatives are the only avenues to social security open to them.

One further observation should be made. People who are successful in fishing usually also buy or create estates on the land, generally coconut groves. You might think, then, that if a man worked very hard at accumulating an estate, his children would benefit. This is not the case. Inheritance is equal among all children in Brazil. As a man's wealth grows, the number of his children also grows, and the estate is severely fragmented when he dies. His children cannot rely on their inheritance to give them a head start in life. Their success must again be based on individual hard work.

Kinship in the upper class has different functions. Upper-class Brazilians usually consider as relatives a far larger number of individuals than do lower-class Brazilians. Yet the extended kindred system of the upper class does not serve to drain wealth. Members of the upper class are not expected to support their distant kin; however, if they are in a position to help a relative get a job, this they certainly must do.

As long as massive poverty and inadequate public assistance persist, lower-class Brazilians will continue to respect obligations based on kinship, marriage, and fictive kinship. Differential advantages within the lower class will go on being leveled out. The lower class will keep its members, and Brazilian society will retain its highly stratified form.

URBAN ANTHROPOLOGY

Topical fields called "rural sociology" and "urban anthropology" suggest that the interests and techniques of anthropology and sociology are converging. Today, the United States provides an especially popular arena for urban anthropological research. To understand why, consider that research problems and theoretical concerns of American anthropology, like other academic disciplines, reflect a larger context of issues, events, and movements in and beyond American society. Tax dollars that funded anthropological research during the early and middle 1960s were later diverted toward the war in Southeast Asia or toward more "practical" problems. For a variety of reasons, some of which are discussed in Chapter 14, political events in foreign lands have closed many areas to research by anthropologists and other social scientists. Increasing interest in the United States also reflects growing awareness by anthropologists and by society in general of social and economic problems and grievances, particularly those of minority groups. American minority problems and movements have directed anthropologists to certain areas of research — the study of poverty and class and subcultural variation. The 1960s war on poverty, for example, bred anthropological studies of poverty in the United States and cross-culturally. The cross-cultural study of social problems affecting the poor remains a major concern of contemporary anthropology.

The Culture of Poverty

In *Five Families,* anthropologist Oscar Lewis (1959) coined the phrase "subculture of poverty," which he often shortened to "culture of poverty." Lewis listed seventy economic, social, and psychological traits characteristic of this subculture of Western society. Economically, the poverty culture is marked by a constant struggle for survival; reduced family income reflecting unemployment and underemployment; low wages; unskilled and unspecialized occupations; frequent change of jobs; low purchasing power; reliance on child labor; the absence of food reserves in the home; a pattern of spending money freely when some is on hand; little saving; and frequent pawning. Some of the social and psychological attributes include crowded living quarters; lack of privacy; gregariousness; a high incidence of alcoholism; frequent use of physical violence; corporal punishment for children; wife beating; early initiation into sex; free or consensual marital unions; marital instability; a relatively high incidence of abandonment by family heads; a trend toward mother-centered households; a much greater knowledge of matrilateral relatives; the predominance of small kinship units; a strong predisposition to authoritarianism; and a great emphasis on family solidarity, as the ideal.

Among the psychological traits that Lewis viewed as particularly important are a feeling of marginality, of not belonging to something; critical attitudes toward the institutions of society and toward government and political figures; and, in general, a feeling of insecurity and desperation. However, the culture of poverty also includes cultural and psychological traits that are compensatory and rewarding—a capacity for spontaneity and adventure, enjoyment of the sensual, and the indulgence of impulse.

In various works Lewis asserted that to an extent the subculture of poverty transcends regional, rural-urban, and national differences. The existence of a subculture of poverty in different nations represents convergent evolution; the traits recur as common adaptations to common problems. Lewis linked the appearance and persistence of the subculture of poverty to certain historical conditions: a cash economy of wage labor and production for profit; a consistently high rate of unemployment and underemployment for unskilled labor; low wages; and the failure of society to provide social, political, and economic organization for the poor. Furthermore, the subculture of poverty, according to Lewis, depends on the existence of a set of values in the dominant class that stresses the accumulation of wealth and property, allows for the possibility of upward

Slum life in Mexico. According to Lewis, the subculture of poverty is most characteristically found in Latin America and the contemporary United States. The subculture of poverty is actually founded on objective conditions of poverty. (Arnold Weichert/D.P.I.)

social and economic mobility, stresses thrift as an ideal, and views low economic status as the result of personal inferiority. The values of members of the subculture of poverty represent their attempts to cope with feelings of hopelessness and despair.

Although poverty exists in different nations, Lewis denied that it inevitably produces the subculture of poverty. Lewis asserted that when the poor become class conscious, when they become active in trade organizations, or when they adopt an internationalist outlook on the world, they remove themselves from the culture of poverty—although they may still be desperately poor. Lewis believed that the culture of poverty does not exist in such socialist countries as postrevolutionary Cuba, which he visited both before and after Castro's revolution. In postrevolutionary Cuba he found slums where the people did not complain about the government or talk in a fatalistic manner, where they showed some hope for the future. Slum life now seemed to be highly organized, with block committees, education committees, and political party committees. The people had a sense of power and importance. They had been armed and given a revolutionary doctrine that glorified the lower class as the hope of humanity.

In addition to field work among Mexicans and Puerto Ricans, Lewis conducted earlier ethnographic field work in India, where he found the culture of poverty to be absent. His Indian experience convinced him that there was no direct relationship between poverty and the culture of poverty. In Indian villages he observed greater poverty than in the slums of Mexico City and San Juan, but the Indian caste system seemed to contribute a sense of identity and organization lacking in Latin American nations. All the Indian castes were highly organized, and caste organization transcended communities and villages. Lewis reported that sometimes members of the sweeper caste representing as many as sixty villages met to decide how they were going to modify the system of ceremonial obligations. Lewis attributed the absence of the culture of poverty in India not only to the organization and therefore the power of its castes, but also to the fact that India remained a civilization in the sense that all people were incorporated into a single social system— even members of the lowest castes felt that they were still Hindus.

Lewis argued that the culture of poverty in Western nations developed in the context of real poverty as well as the lack of such a feeling of belonging.

The subculture of poverty appeared in Europe and the New World with the breakdown of old feudal structures and the migration of people from rural zones to cities. In this process the poor had no organization and therefore no power. Lewis also linked the subculture of poverty to the bilateral kinship systems of European and New World cultures, stating that the prior existence of descent-group organization would also impede its development. In areas where social organization includes corporate descent groups, specifically in India and Africa, Lewis predicted that the subculture of poverty would fail to appear, even though poverty was great. Lewis saw something positive in the nature of descent-group organization, the feeling that one corporate body continues to exist though individuals come and go. This gives a sense of the past and of the future even to the desperately poor. As we shall see, through descent and other social mechanisms, African town dwellers usually maintain village ties. Descent groups and other forms of social and political solidarity are of diminished importance among the poor in Latin America.

Linking the subculture of poverty primarily to the early stages of capitalism and to colonialism, Lewis located its most typical expressions in Latin America. He found the culture of poverty to be considerably less prevalent in the contemporary United States, and he calculated that while between 40 to 50 million Americans live in poverty, only about 8 million of them exhibit the cultural and psychological traits of the culture of poverty. The American welfare apparatus, he suggested, had successfully eliminated many of the conditions that produce the culture of poverty. Nevertheless, it might be characteristic of certain American ethnic minorities, including poor blacks and urban Indians, Mexican Americans and Puerto Ricans, as well as some poor whites. At the time of his death in 1970, Lewis was planning research among poor white and black families in Chicago's slums, to determine the presence or absence of the subculture of poverty.

When Lewis announced in 1968 that he would begin his work among American whites and blacks, it was with a sense of trepidation that reflected the controversy surrounding this somewhat touchy area. Former Harvard professor, Nixon adviser, U.N. ambassador, and current senator from New York, Daniel Patrick Moynihan, for example, in *The Negro Family* (1965) and elsewhere, argued for the existence of a self-perpetuating subculture of poverty

In unstratified societies, anyone who wants to work can work. The means of producing a livelihood are open to all. In industrial America, joblessness is a major problem, affecting Hispanic and black Americans more than other ethnic groups. Poverty and a scarcity of jobs force these migrant workers in Texas to work for low wages. (Michal Heron/Monkmeyer Press)

among American blacks. Moynihan viewed this subculture as consisting of distinctive norms and values that are transmitted through enculturation and that do not simply represent responses to situations of extreme poverty. This view echoes Lewis, who believed that, because the subculture of poverty was a real culture, it would be more difficult to eradicate it than the objective conditions of poverty.

The views of Lewis and Moynihan have been criticized by Charles Valentine (1968), Carol Stack (1975), and by several others. Valentine has proposed that there are no significant differences between the cultural norms of the poor and the more affluent in the United States. The poor are merely unable to live up to the dominant norms of the society because of the severe social and economic disadvantages to which they are exposed. Valentine admits, however, that the poor may have some specific alternative values that enable them to adapt to the necessities of their situation. Seymour Parker and Robert Kleiner (1970) have suggested that the poor hold two sets of values and attitudes simultaneously, one shared with the larger society and the second developed in response to the objective conditions of poverty. The latter help poor people to make necessary psychological adjustments and preserve their sanity.

In *Tally's Corner* (1967) Elliot Liebow describes the results of extended participant observation of street-corner behavior in a Washington, D.C.,

ghetto. Liebow's research convinced him that poor blacks do internalize many of the dominant values of the larger society, but, because their hopes are often frustrated, which contributes to deep feelings of failure, they also develop alternative values. On the basis of field research in a middle-sized midwestern city, Stack (1975) provides good information on poor blacks' strategies for survival.

In attempting to reconcile the opposing views about the relationship between culture and poverty, Seymour Parker (1973) suggests, reasonably, that ongoing social behavior results from both enculturation and the constraints imposed by the objective situation. He notes that the crucial questions for future research involve the relative contributions of enculturation and real constraints to the perpetuation of poverty in the United States. Parker proposes that middle-class social scientists often focus on only a narrow range of the attitudes and values of poor people—for example, those that Lewis makes diagnostic of the subculture of poverty—while ignoring the many values that they share with the larger society.

Drug Addict Subculture

In a discussion of drug addicts, based on research among patients at the National Institutes of Mental Health Clinical Research Center in Lexington, Kentucky, anthropologist Michael Agar (1977) argues that addicts, like poverty victims, simultaneously relate both to general and subcultural values. Agar's work confirms previous anthropological studies that have identified an addict subculture, an alternative cultural system with its own goals, values, rewards, and rules of appropriate behavior. As members of a particular subculture, addicts' behavior is not random, but purposive, reflecting the standards and demands of their peers.

At the same time, addicts belong to a larger social system. In treatment centers they meet its agents in the person of psychiatrists, psychotherapists, and other treatment personnel, who see them as criminally deviant and produce in them a different self-image: they become social failures, miserable creatures enslaved by a physical addiction.

On the basis of his study, Agar criticizes orthodox treatment techniques, pointing out that treatment personnel are more interested in interpreting addicts' behavior in terms of psychological theory than in terms of its meaning in addict subculture. He found, for example, that psychologists and psychiatrists typically labeled addicts "paranoid" or "alienated" when they were reluctant to open up to treatment personnel. Agar, on the other hand, pointed out that suspicion, secrecy, and great care in personal relationships were adaptive characteristics in the addict subculture. In the streets, addicts are, after all, under constant threat of arrest. Furthermore, if addicts are robbed or cheated in business transactions, they cannot turn to the police—they must resolve their dilemmas themselves. Given such isolation from benefits of the larger social system, their secrecy is comprehensible. As in the case of poverty, therefore, addicts' behavior reflects their objective condition of powerlessness. Addict subculture does not replace the larger social system, but it offers addicts a way to keep a positive self-image and a degree of psychological security in the context of a larger system that condemns their behavior as deviant.

From Country to Town

In the United States and elsewhere a major problem confronts anthropologists who want to work in cities: how are field methods and procedures that were originally developed to describe and analyze small, isolated communities to be elaborated or altered to deal with apparently more complex, less obviously structured situations?

Robert Redfield has been prominent—although certainly not alone—among anthropologists in indicating contrasts between rural communities, whose social relations are on a face-to-face basis, and larger, socioeconomically heterogeneous urban populations, where impersonality characterizes many aspects of everyday social life. In *The Folk Culture of Yucatan* (1941) Redfield argued that cultural change could be studied along a rural-urban continuum, and he described certain differences in values and social relations in four settings spanning that continuum. He compared an isolated Maya-speaking Indian community, a rural peasant village, a small provincial city, and a large capital. Redfield suggested that similar studies could be conducted elsewhere in the world. Several recent studies in Africa have been influenced by Redfield's view that cities are centers through which cultural innovations are introduced into tribal areas. Kenneth Little (1971), for example, writes of the diffusion of values and behavior patterns from city to countryside, stating that the farmer-villager may become urbanized as urban culture is incorporated into the ideational and behavioral patterns of the rural resident.

Pointing out that scholars in Africa have concentrated particularly on contrasts between tribal and urban life and on diffusion of urban patterns to tribal areas, J. Clyde Mitchell (1966) and other students of African urbanization have argued that major unsolved research problems require intensive study of urban social systems. Mitchell argues that migrants do not bring their rural institutions with them to town, for urban and rural institutions are parts of different social systems and individuals may move back and forth from one to the other. Continuing this reasoning, Mitchell suggests that it is a mistake to view urban institutions as variants of rural institutions. Rather, urban people develop new institutions to meet their specific needs.

Mitchell is right in suggesting that there are problems and cultural adaptive responses, in the form of institutions and behavior patterns, specific to cities. However, it would be fallacious to assume that the enculturative experiences of home do not affect the adjustment of individuals to urban situations and that social forms developed in rural settings do not influence adaptation to city life. Lewis made exactly this point when he argued that descent groups and other forms of tribal organization provide migrants to African cities with adaptive mechanisms that many Latin American peasants lack. Some examples are given in the discussion of ethnic associations in cities.

Since urban research has been especially prominent in recent anthropological studies of Africa, some of the methods of research and its results may profitably be examined.

Methods of Studying African Cities and Towns

While at present less than 25 percent of the total population of sub-Saharan Africa lives in cities of 100,000 or more people, African cities may be growing faster than those of other continents. Scholars frequently distinguish between two types of African city. Aidan Southall (1961), for example, argues that type A cities, found in Tanzania, Uganda, the Sudan, and throughout equatorial and West Africa, are old, established centers. Very large towns existed in some of these areas long before European commercial expansion into Africa. Many such towns originated as administrative centers in pre-European states. Generally supported by traditional economic pursuits, urban populations in these areas tend to be ethnically homogeneous, and their rate of increase is slower than that in the towns of type B. In this group Southall classifies the newer African towns whose rapid population increase is based on industrial and commercial development. Many of these originated with European expansion in Africa during the latter half of the nineteenth century. Most type B towns have resulted from African involvement in colonialism and the international economy. Located mainly in South Africa, Zimbabwe (Rhodesia), Zambia, Kenya, and Zaire, these towns tend to be ethnically heterogeneous.

Both types of cities share common features of urban life. These include high settlement density, geographical mobility, social heterogeneity, economic differentiation, and concentration of political power and administrative apparatus. Both types also show demographic disproportions, although in type B cities especially there is a preponderance of young people over old and of men over women, reflecting demands and opportunities of the cash labor market.

Reviewing the literature of African urban studies, Mitchell (1966) suggests that anthropologists should investigate both structural and personal or egocentric relationships in cities. Since similar investigations are being employed in anthropological studies in cities outside of Africa, let us consider these methods in greater detail.

ANALYSIS OF STRUCTURAL RELATIONSHIPS Mitchell argues that several types of urban institutions and relationships represent areas for fruitful investigation by anthropologists. Among the African urban institutions that have been studied anthropologically are voluntary associations, burial societies, social clubs, and marital relationships.

Voluntary associations have been investigated by several anthropologists. Kenneth Little (1965) and Michael Banton (1957) have suggested that voluntary associations in West African towns are adaptive institutions that help newly arrived migrants to understand urban norms of behavior and to construct, through membership in such organizations, a network of supportive relationships for themselves. There are several sorts of voluntary associations in Africa. There are, for example, secular social clubs, some of whose members have university educations. There are religious organizations associated with Christianity and with other religions. Some associations concern themselves with their members' occupational or commercial activities; others sponsor various forms of entertainment.

Anthropologists have also investigated ethnic associations, which build for the rural migrant a kind of bridge between one social system and another. Frequently called "tribal" associations, ethnic associations are common both in West and East Africa. Associations like that of the Luo in Kampala, Uganda, studied by David Parkin (1969), are segmented first into regions or subtribes, which are internally segmented into clan groups. Similarly, in Nigeria, voluntary associations of the Ibo and other groups are segmented, with extended families or lineages organized into clan associations; the clan associations unite in district associations, which combine to form the total ethnic association (Banton, 1957). The Ugandan Luo association concerns itself with urban problems that directly affect the individual and provide economic as well as moral support, including transportation of the destitute to the rural area. In Nigeria, although most members of a given ethnic association are illiterate day laborers, the membership inevitably includes doctors, lawyers, and other professionals. The ideology of the association is that of a gigantic kinship group; members are expected to address one another as brothers and sisters. As in an extended family, richer people are obligated to help the less fortunate. When their own members are involved in a dispute, voluntary associations often assume arbitration functions characteristic of

courts. Such associations control their membership through the financial help they offer, and their ultimate sanction is expulsion, usually an unhappy fate for a migrant in an ethnically heterogeneous city.

Other types of associations play analogous roles in allowing individuals to adapt to city life. Trade associations, for example, help their members to acquire and save capital; occupational societies often guarantee members that their burial expenses will be paid.

The existence of voluntary associations as means of adaptation to urban life is not confined to Africa. Paul Doughty (1970), for example, has investigated associations of urban migrants in a region of Lima, Peru, and notes that these organizations serve a variety of important functions for the individual and the nation. Doughty documents ways in which they help to reduce the stress of social and cultural changes on the migrant. Associations involved in organized crime in the contemporary United States are examined below.

ANALYSIS OF PERSONAL RELATIONSHIPS: NETWORK ANALYSIS Organizing field data gathered during community studies in Norway and London, John Barnes (1954) and Elizabeth Bott (1957) developed the concept of social network analysis. They distinguished two broadly different types of social networks: the contained, small-mesh, close-knit network characteristic of the rural community; and the dispersed, large-mesh, loose-knit network characteristic of urban society. Network analysis is a form of egocentric analysis; it focuses on specific individuals and determines their patterns of association with others. Individual networks are then compared, and generalizations about networks in particular social settings are made. In the small-mesh, close-knit network, many of ego's friends, neighbors, and relatives know one another; in the large-mesh, loose-knit network, this is not so. Bott argues that with more closely knit networks it is easier to reach agreement on norms, and because of tight association, people exert consistent and final pressure on network members to conform to those norms. Close-knit networks can exist in cities, too. Stack (1975) demonstrates the importance of small-mesh, kin-based networks among the urban poor in the contemporary United States.

American Ethnic Groups, Poverty, and Organized Crime

Francis Ianni (1977) identifies both associations and personal networks in his description of criminal activities involving segments of certain ethnic groups in contemporary American cities. He has analyzed research data on the organization of criminal activi-

Alone, with hundreds of other people, on an American subway. In American cities, men, women, and children—particularly in the middle class—are often isolated in houses or apartments from personal contact with others. In contrast, the ethnic, tribal, and clan associations of many African cities provide social ties for rural migrants. Social networks in American urban ghettos serve similar functions. (Burk Uzzle/Magnum Photos)

ties by black and Hispanic Americans, and views organized crime as an integral and long-time part of American economic life — an adaptive response to the persistence of poverty and differential power. Indeed, the criminal organizations that Ianni describes stand at one end of an economic continuum that has legitimate business enterprises at the other. Black and Hispanic criminals are merely the most recent urban migrants and immigrants to have found in organized crime an established route to socioeconomic advancement.

Federal census data confirm the socioeconomic inequality that continues to deny blacks and Hispanics full access to advantages that most other Americans routinely enjoy. In 1975 median family incomes for whites, Hispanics, and blacks were $14,268, $9,551, and $8,779, respectively. Nearly 27 percent of the country's 11 million Hispanics were below the federally defined poverty level of $5,500 for an urban family of four, compared with 31.3 percent of blacks and 9.7 percent of whites. Cuban Americans had a median family income of $11,772; this raised the figures for Hispanics slightly. However, the situation of other Hispanics, particularly the country's 6.6 million Mexican Americans and 1.8 million Puerto Rican Americans, actually deteriorated between 1974 and 1975, with median family income falling from 71.2 percent to 67 percent of that of white families. Legitimate economic opportunities are also limited. March 1975 unemployment figures were 13 percent for blacks, 11.5 percent for Hispanics, and 6.8 percent for whites.

I am not suggesting that most blacks and Hispanics who confront severe poverty pursue criminal careers. They do not. Historically, however, some poor people have used organized crime as a route to financial and psychological security. This is not just true in the United States; generally, in stratified nations, crime develops when access to legitimate economic opportunity is blocked. State organization — particularly industrialism — creates unemployment. In prestate societies no one who wants to work is denied access to the means of production, distribution, and consumption. Crime in state societies is a matter of socioeconomic need. It may also be a from of social protest. Indeed, the formation of the Mafia and other clandestine groups in southern Italy early in this century bears some resemblance to the genesis of the Melanesian cargo cults examined in Chapter 9. Ianni explicitly cites poverty and powerlessness — not an ethnic group's cultural norms or the subculture of poverty — as the causes of crime. Successive ethnic groups with very different cultural heritages have, after all, used organized crime to better themselves economically.

Ianni found that several types of personal relationships serve to introduce black and Hispanic criminals to each other and to crime. Links between adult criminals are often based on childhood friendships or membership in the same youth gang. Commonly, however, boys begin their apprenticeship in crime through relationships with older men. Established criminals, who later serve as role models, recruit boys or groups of boys for criminal ventures. Links established in prison also form a basis for later criminal association. Sometimes these relationships are interethnic. Ianni also found that, occasionally, women join criminal organizations through their male friends or husbands. Among neither blacks nor Puerto Ricans, however, is kinship a common link in criminal networks.

Once individuals become fully committed to organized crime, their common activity holds the networks together. Established networks involve such relationships as partners, employers and employees, and buyers and sellers of goods and services. As in legitimate business, criminal networks are cemented by social solidarity — an esprit de corps. The stronger this spirit, the more successful criminal ventures are likely to be.

Ianni also describes such crime-related groups as childhood gangs and "prison courts," ethnically segregated groups of prisoners made up of a strong leader and followers. Like associations generally, both gangs and courts are based on close personal relationships and mutual trust. Each has a code of rules and sanctions that regulates membership and members' behavior toward one another and toward outsiders. Gang members might not actually engage in crime, but gang membership often serves as a first step toward participation in crime. The rules of both gangs and courts stress members' personal qualities and require bravery, loyalty, and intelligence on their part.

Ianni describes another type of criminal association, the entrepreneurial organization, which he compares to a legitimate business enterprise. It is composed of a head, the criminal entrepreneur, and his agents in illegal activity; it maintains a code of rules designed to foster and protect the organization and its activities. The rules stress secrecy (don't tell the police or other nonmembers), honesty (don't cheat on members), and competence.

Ianni analyzes the ethnic succession of organized crime in American cities. Segments of Jewish, Italian, Cuban, black, Puerto Rican, and other ethnic groups have used crime to escape poverty and powerlessness. However, Ianni did find certain differences in the criminal networks of each ethnic group. The most obvious difference involved kinship. Whereas the networks of Italian and, to a lesser extent, Cuban criminals were organized by kinship, those of Puerto Ricans, and particularly of blacks, were not. Ianni suggests that if black and Puerto Rican criminals are to wrest domination of organized crime from Italians, they need to develop an equivalent organizational principle. Ianni indicates that they may be doing this already through links established in prisons. Also, they might use ethnic militancy and a fictive kinship model including such terms as "brother" and "sister" as means of establishing solidarity.

However, most differences between Italian American criminal organizations and those of blacks and Hispanics reflect the former's longer period of development. Ianni contrasts hierarchically structured Italian American crime syndicates, with diverse activities and many layers of authority, with the less structured criminal organizations of black and Hispanic Americans. As with legitimate enterprises, small criminal operations need time to grow into larger ones and eventually to join with other operations to control rich market areas. At the time of Ianni's study, neither blacks nor Hispanics had begun to supply major services to other criminals. He notes that until Prohibition, which provided a rich source of extra-ghetto profits and thus favored the expansion of organized crime, Italian American criminals were not suppliers either. Ianni speculates that blacks and Hispanics could best hope to compete with the Italian syndicates by dealing in cocaine. In this way, they might be able to develop a national or international base of operations, which might, in turn, support expansion into other profit-making activities, illegal and, eventually, legitimate.

American cultural norms condemn crime, but view some illegal acts as more reprehensible than others. Similarly, subcultures in the United States view crimes as having different degrees of seriousness. Whereas the larger society overlooks or lightly punishes white-collar, corporate, and Presidential crimes, ghetto residents often excuse such activities

as prostitution, loan sharking, and gambling. Ianni found ghetto opinion about narcotics ambivalent. On the one hand, local pushers are condemned; on the other, many ghetto residents see drugs as part of a plot by the larger society to destroy ghetto youth. Local drug sources are not considered to be as bad as suppliers, who live outside the ghetto while draining profits from it.

Ianni's study of criminal networks and associations again illustrates the application of anthropological techniques to the study of behavior in complex societies. It also places crime in the larger framework that orients this book. Through modifications in behavior and social organization, people attempt to adapt to environmental conditions. Deprived of access to wealth and power, some representatives of ethnic minorities have found economic and social mobility in organized crime. Like other urban associations, criminal associations — based on various principles of social organization — help people adapt to urban life in stratified societies.

Other Units of Analysis in Urban Anthropology

Interest in urban life has forced anthropologists to develop new techniques and units of study. For example, a series of specifically anthropological field techniques may be used in conjunction with quantitative, survey techniques in analyzing city life. Mitchell, Ianni, and several others have demonstrated that anthropologists can profitably examine urban associations, structural relationships, and individual networks. Anthropologists Victor Turner (1957), Max Gluckman (1958, orig. 1940, 1942), Ronald Frankenberg (1966), and others have stressed the value of studying unusual events. Aspects of urban life may, for example, be perceived and studied at large gatherings, including ceremonials, political events, and plays.

Oscar Lewis was responsible for other innovations in the study of urban life. His research led him away from traditional anthropological holism and toward the study of personal experience. In *Five Families* (1959), Lewis described a day in the life of each of five families. In his well-known book *The Children of Sanchez* (1961) he focused on individual experience, using information provided by members of a single Mexican family. Here Lewis added a novelistic dimension by having the same events described by different family members. His next book, *Pedro*

Martinez (1964), viewed changes in Mexican society principally through the eyes of a Mexican peasant.

By the time Lewis began the research that culminated in *La Vida* (1966), studying the culture of poverty had become his major research objective. To determine whether this culture existed among other Hispanic populations, he shifted his study of the poor from Mexicans to Puerto Ricans in San Juan and New York City. *La Vida* combines an autobiographical technique, with the characters narrating their own lives, and objective description. Lewis started this work by interviewing one hundred families from four suburbs of San Juan. After the general survey he selected ten extended families for more concentrated study.

Lewis' techniques of urban anthropological research have been severely criticized. Other scholars have pointed out that his concentration on specific families and individuals inevitably required him to ignore considerable variation, and they fault him for often skimping on his own anthropological analysis in favor of informants' accounts. Some critics have characterized his books as literature rather than anthropology. None of his critics can deny, however, the uniqueness, sympathy, and value of his accounts of poverty as actually experienced by the poor.

SUMMARY

Continuing metropolitan dominance of satellite areas threatens the existence of populations that sociocultural anthropologists have traditionally studied. The effects of this domination on underdeveloped nations have expanded the range of problems amenable to anthropological investigation. The study of contemporary peasantries has grown enormously, as have investigations of other areas within sociocultural anthropology: urban anthropology, applied anthropology, and studies of acculturation.

This chapter has concentrated on variations in Latin American and African peasant societies. Anthropologists have pointed out the existence of two basic types of rural peasant communities in Latin America: the closed, corporate (generally Indian) community of the highlands; the open, noncorporate (generally mestizo) community of the lowlands. Both communities include some sociocultural institutions that are formally similar to those described previously for tribal societies. Yet, comparing similar forms — for example, ceremonial, kinship, and marriage forms in states and nonstates — we find that functions may be very different. The role of the cargo systems of highland Latin America in leveling wealth differentials within communities and maintaining poverty among the national lower class has been contrasted with the adaptive, intercommunity leveling associated with blowouts in tribal societies. Similarly, the functions of the kinship system in lowland Latin America in impeding individual vertical mobility and maintaining poverty there have been contrasted with adaptive functions of kinship and marriage in band and tribal organization.

Poverty, however, is not confined to rural areas of the Third World. It extends to the slums of San Juan, Mexico City, New York City, and a thousand other cities. Oscar Lewis, well known for his studies of urban poverty, created great controversy because of his popularization of the "subculture of poverty," a set of behavioral and ideological traits that he believed characterized the poor in certain areas of the world. Lewis believed that through enculturation the subculture of poverty became self-perpetuating, and that it would be more difficult to eradicate than poverty itself. However, he also asserted that poverty did not always breed the culture of poverty. Poor people whose history or social organization provided a sense of belonging to some larger, more enduring unit would not exhibit the fatalism associated with the culture of poverty. For example, Lewis discovered no culture of poverty in India, where its formation was impeded by caste solidarity and a feeling of historic participation in Hindu civilization. Similarly, solidarity associated with corporate descent-group organization would combat the culture of poverty in African cities. And in revolutionary Cuba he found it replaced by a feeling of active participation by the poor in a new social order.

Criticism of Lewis points to research that shows

that America's poor share many values with the national majority, but that their deprivations prevent them from actualizing all these values. Some scholars have asserted that in adapting to poverty, the poor develop alternative values that help them preserve their sanity. It may be that social scientists have concentrated too exclusively on a narrow range of the values of the poor, while ignoring a much larger set of values shared with the larger society. Anthropological study of drug addicts shows that they, too, must relate both to subcultural and to larger social norms.

Although ethnographic techniques have been employed in research in the United States for several decades, anthropological research in American cities is currently booming. In the United States and elsewhere, anthropologists encounter difficulties in applying their traditional field methods to urban situations. In Africa, for example, where statistical data on social characteristics of cities are usually lacking, many anthropologists have employed social surveys as means of gathering quantitative data. Yet more traditional qualitative techniques have also been used successfully in studies of urban life. Anthropologists have studied structural relationships in cities, examining, for example, the role of voluntary associations in enabling migrants from rural zones to adapt to urban life. Anthropologists have also developed social network analysis as a tool for urban research. They have found that there are characteristic differences in the social networks, the web of personal ties, of town and rural dwellers. In Ianni's anthropological study of the succession of various ethnic groups in organized crime, he found that both associations and informal networks are important in black and Hispanic criminal operations. He linked crime to objective conditions of poverty and powerlessness, not to subcultural norms of ethnic groups.

Anthropologists have used still other methods in urban studies. Social events have been described and analyzed. Lewis has combined intimate field study with tape recordings of his informants' life histories and observation of their daily lives in several studies of urban poverty and its cultural manifestations.

SOURCES AND SUGGESTED READINGS

AGAR, M.
1977   Ethnography and the Addict. In *Readings in Anthropology*, pp. 59–65. Guilford, Conn.: Dushkin Publishing Group, Inc. How addicts relate to norms of American society and their own subculture.

BENNETT, J. W.
1976   *The Ecological Transition: Cultural Anthropology and Human Adaptation.* Fairview Park, Elmsford, N.Y.: Pergamon. The implications of anthropology's ecological approach for the environmental movement and other contemporary issues.

COHEN, A.
1969   *Custom and Politics in Urban Africa.* London: Routledge & Kegan Paul. A major contribution to the anthropology of urban life in Africa.

DALTON, G., ED.
1971   *Economic Development and Social Change: The Modernization of Village Communities.* Garden City, N.Y.: The Natural History Press. Articles on development and cultural change in several Third World countries.

DOUGHTY, P.
1970   Behind the Back of the City: "Provincial" Life in Lima, Peru. In *Peasants in Cities: Readings in the Anthropology of Urbanization,* ed. W. Mangin, pp. 30–46. Boston: Houghton Mifflin. Discusses role of voluntary associations in adaptation to urban life in Peru.

FOSTER, G. M., AND KEMPER, R. V., EDS.
1974   *Anthropologists in Cities.* Boston: Little, Brown. A collection of ethnographic studies from several continents.

FRANK, A. G.
1969   *Capitalism and Underdevelopment in Latin America: Historical Studies of Chile and Brazil.* New York: Modern Reader

Paperbacks. Metropole-satellite relationships with reference to Latin American underdevelopment.

FRANKENBERG, R.
1966 British Community Studies: Problems in Synthesis. In *The Social Anthropology of Complex Societies,* ed. M. Banton, pp. 123–154. London: Tavistock. Problems in adapting anthropological field techniques to life in cities and other areas of complex society.

FRIEDL, J., AND CHRISMAN, N. J.
1975 *City Ways: A Selective Reader in Urban Anthropology.* New York: Crowell. Good collection of articles examining contemporary issues in urban anthropology.

GLUCKMAN, M.
1958 (orig. 1940, 1942). *Analysis of a Social Situation in Modern Zululand.* Manchester, England: Manchester University Press. Analysis of a bridge opening as a key to modern Zulu life in South Africa.

GUILLEMIN, J.
1975 *Urban Renegades: The Cultural Strategy of American Indians.* New York: Columbia University Press. Study of the urban Micmac, Native Americans in Boston.

HARRIS, M.
1956 *Town and Country in Brazil.* New York: Columbia University Press. Field study of urban ethos in a former gold-mining town in the Brazilian interior.

1964 *Patterns of Race in the Americas.* New York: Walker. Determinants of different patterns of race and ethnic relations in North and South America.

HEATH, D. B., ED.
1974 *Contemporary Cultures and Societies of Latin America.* 2nd ed. New York: Random House. Most complete collection of anthropological research on Latin America.

HUTCHINSON, H. W.
1957 *Village and Plantation Life in Northeastern Brazil.* Seattle: University of Washington Press. Ethnographic and historical study of a sugar plantation town in Bahia, Brazil.

IANNI, F.
1977 New Mafia: Black, Hispanic and Italian Styles. In *Readings in Anthropology,* pp. 66–78. Guilford, Conn.: Dushkin Publishing Group, Inc. Poverty, ethnic succession, and organized crime.

JORGENSEN, J. G.
1972 *The Sun Dance Religion: Power for the Powerless.* Chicago: University of Chicago Press. An American Indian religious movement as an adaptation to political and economic events in the larger society.

KOTTAK, C. P.
1967 Kinship and Class in Brazil. *Ethnology* 4: 427–443. Lower-class kinship and relationship between kinship and class.

LEACOCK, E. B., ED.
1971 *The Culture of Poverty: A Critique.* Anthropologists and other social scientists examine arguments of Lewis, Moynihan, and others.

LEWIS, D.
1973 Anthropology and Colonialism. *Current Anthropology* 14: 581–602. A historical overview, with implications for applied anthropology.

LEWIS, O.
1958 The Culture of the *Vecindad* in Mexico City: Two Case Studies. *Actas de XXXIII Congreso Internacional de Americanistas,* San José, 20–27 julio, pp. 387–402. Anthropological research in an urban neighborhood.

1959 *Five Families.* New York: Basic Books. A day in the life of each of five Mexican families.

1961 *The Children of Sanchez.* New York: Random House. Family life as perceived by five members of the Sanchez family in a Mexico City slum.

1964 *Pedro Martinez: A Mexican Peasant and His Family.* New York: Random House. A peasant views the Mexican revolution.

1966 *La Vida: A Puerto Rican Family in the Culture of Poverty—San Juan and New York.* New York: Random House. Controversial study of Puerto Rican family life.

1968 Poverty, Bourgeoisie, Revolution, translated by R. U. Ballesta. From a conversation between O. Lewis, K. S. Karol, and C. Fuentes which appeared in *Mundo Nuevo,* no. 11. May, 1967. Courtesy of Dr. Nan Pendrell. Informal discussion of some of the characteristics of the culture of poverty and reasons why it is not a national universal.

LIEBOW, E.
1967   *Tally's Corner.* Boston: Little, Brown. Field study of a Washington, D.C., ghetto.

LITTLE, K.
1965   *West African Urbanization: A Study of Voluntary Associations in Social Change.* Cambridge, England: Cambridge University Press. Role of voluntary associations in adaptation to urban life.

1971   Some Aspects of African Urbanization South of the Sahara. Reading, Mass.: Addison-Wesley, McCaleb Modules in Anthropology. Review article.

LUNDSGAARDE, H. P.
1977   *Murder in Space City: A Cultural Analysis of Houston Homicide Patterns.* New York: Oxford University Press. Anthropological study of murder and its consequences in Houston, Texas in 1969.

MANGIN, W., ED.
1970   *Peasants in Cities: Readings in the Anthropology of Urbanization.* Boston: Houghton Mifflin. Articles on urban life in several countries; reprints and originals.

MINER, H.
1953   *The Primitive City of Timbuctoo.* Princeton: Princeton University Press. Field study of a small city in the West African interior.

MITCHELL, J. C.
1957   *The Kalela Dance: Aspects of Social Relationships among Urban Africans in Northern Rhodesia.* Rhodes-Livingstone Paper no. 27. Manchester, England: Manchester University Press. Analysis of urban life through field study of a dance association.

1966   Theoretical Orientations in African Urban Studies. In *The Social Anthropology of Complex Societies,* ed. M. Banton, pp. 37–68. London: Tavistock. Comprehensive review of techniques of urban anthropological study in Africa.

MOYNIHAN, D. P.
1965   *The Negro Family: The Case for National Action.* Washington, D.C.: U.S. Government Printing Office. The much maligned Moynihan report, linking family organization and other attributes of some members of the American black population to a subculture of poverty.

NIETSCHMANN, B.
1973   *Between Land and Water: The Subsistence Ecology of the Miskito Indians, Eastern Nicaragua.* New York: Seminar Press. Account of foragers (turtle-hunters and sellers) in the modern world.

PARKER, S., ED.
1973   Poverty and Culture. In *To See Ourselves: Anthropology and Modern Social Issues,* gen. ed., T. Weaver. Glenview, Ill.: Scott, Foresman. Articles on poverty and the culture of poverty and Parker's prefatory comments and concluding synthesis.

PARKER, S., AND KLEINER, R.
1970   The Culture of Poverty: an Adjustive Dimension. *American Anthropologist* 72: 516–527. Cultural values and mental illness among Philadelphia blacks.

PARKIN, D.
1969   *Neighbours and Nationals in an African City Ward.* London: Routledge and Kegan Paul. Analysis of ethnic associations among the Luo of Kampala, Uganda.

PIVEN, F. F., AND CLOWARD, R. A.
1971   *Regulating the Poor: The Functions of Public Welfare.* New York: Random House. Stratification, political unrest, and economic forces as they affect welfare assistance.

POTTER, J. M., DIAZ, M. N., AND FOSTER, G. M., EDS.
1967   *Peasant Society: A Reader.* Boston: Little, Brown. Peasant society in many world areas.

REDFIELD, R.
1941   *The Folk Culture of Yucatan.* Chicago: University of Chicago Press. The rural-urban continuum as exemplified in four Yucatan communities.

1953   *The Primitive World and Its Transformations.* Ithaca, N.Y.: Cornell University Press. Growth of heterogeneity from homogeneous folk societies.

1956   *The Little Community.* Chicago: University of Chicago Press. Good introduction to community study techniques in traditional ethnography.

RYAN, W.
   1971   *Blaming the Victim.* New York: Random House. How contemporary American society, like other stratified nation-states, relies on and perpetuates poverty, then blames the poor for their plight.

SERVICE, E. R.
   1968   War and Our Contemporary Ancestors. In *War: The Anthropology of Armed Conflict and Aggression,* ed. M. H. Fried, M. Harris, and R. F. Murphy, pp. 160–167. Garden City, N.Y.: The Natural History Press. Brilliant delineation of problems in extrapolating past conditions from contemporary primitive populations in the wake of European disruption of native life in many world areas.

SOUTHALL, A.
   1961   Introductory Summary. In *Social Change in Modern Africa,* ed. A. Southall, pp. 1–46. London: Oxford University Press. Good introduction to social change and urban anthropology in Africa; includes a classification of African towns.

STACK, C. B.
   1975   *All Our Kin: Strategies for Survival in a Black Community.* New York: Harper Torchbooks. Well-done ethnographic study of fluidity in household and residence patterns and the importance of non–nuclear-family kin in an urban ghetto.

STEWARD, J. H.
   1956   *People of Puerto Rico.* Urbana: University of Illinois Press. Pioneering research by anthropological field team of variation in a complex society.

TURNBULL, C. M.
   1972   *The Mountain People.* New York: Simon and Schuster. Controversial, impressionistic study of an uprooted population in Uganda.

TURNER, V. W.
   1957   *Schism and Continuity in an African Society.* Manchester, England: Manchester University Press. Analysis of social drama as a tool for anthropological study of complex societies.

VALENTINE, C.
   1968   *Culture and Poverty.* Chicago: University of Chicago Press. Controversial critique of the culture of poverty.

WAGLEY, C. W.
   1968   *The Latin American Tradition.* New York: Columbia University Press. Collected essays on unity and diversity in Latin American culture.

   1971   *An Introduction to Brazil.* Rev. ed. New York: Columbia University Press. Introduction to history, society, and culture of Latin America's largest nation.

   1976   *Amazon Town: A Study of Man in the Tropics.* 2nd ed. New York: Oxford University Press. Classic Brazilian community study; an ethnography of the boom and bust of rubber in the Amazon region; original 1948 research updated with data gathered in 1974.

WAGLEY, C. W., ED.
   1952   *Race and Class in Rural Brazil.* Paris: UNESCO. Studies by Wagley and his students of social stratification and race relations in four areas of Brazil.

WAGLEY, C., AND HARRIS, M.
   1958   *Minorities in the New World: Six Case Studies.* New York: Columbia University Press. Qualitative descriptions of native Americans in Brazil and Mexico, Afro-Americans in Martinique and the United States, and Euro-Americans (French Canadians and Jews) in the United States.

WALLERSTEIN, I.
   1974   *The Modern World-System: Capitalist Agriculture and the Origins of the European World-Economy in the Sixteenth Century.* New York: Academic Press. How a world political economy affects the formerly isolated people anthropologists traditionally study; an influential work.

WILLEMS, E.
   1975   *Latin American Culture: An Anthropological Synthesis.* New York: Harper & Row. General anthropological overview; strong on Brazil.

WOLF, E. R.
   1955   Types of Latin American Peasantry. *American Anthropologist* 57: 452–471. Classic article defining closed, corporate and open, noncorporate as basic types of peasant communities in Latin America.

   1966   *Peasants.* Englewood Cliffs, N.J.: Prentice-Hall. Best introduction to cross-cultural study of peasants.

1969   *Peasant Wars of the Twentieth Century.*
New York: Harper & Row. An anthropologist examines revolutionary movements
in Mexico, Russia, China, Vietnam,
Algeria, and Cuba.

ZIMMERMAN, B.
1952   Race Relations in the Arid Sertão. In *Race
and Class in Rural Brazil,* ed. C. Wagley,
pp. 82–115. Paris: UNESCO. Race relations in the Brazilian backlands.

Uses and Abuses
of Anthropology

14

Many anthropologists would agree with Kathleen Gough (1973) that anthropology is rooted in the Enlightenment's humanistic vision of a science that could liberate us and improve human welfare by expanding human knowledge. Anthropologists show justifiable pride in the contributions of their discipline toward reducing ethnocentrism by instilling appreciation for cultural diversity, and in questioning racist attitudes and the validity of race as a scientific concept. Presumably, this broadening, educational function affects the knowledge, values, and attitudes of those exposed to anthropology. Now we must ask: What is anthropology's role with respect to contemporary practical and political questions? What are the ethical components of the anthropologist's involvement in practical and political matters?

Ralph Piddington (1960) has divided attitudes toward the appropriate role of the anthropologist in practical affairs into three schools of thought. The first, characteristic of many contemporary anthropologists, is an ivory tower conception. This attitude maintains that anthropologists should remain aloof from practical matters and should devote themselves to research, publication, and teaching.

The second attitude is held by a large number of social scientists in addition to anthropologists. It represents what Piddington calls the "schizoid interpretation" of the role of the social scientist. According to this viewpoint, anthropologists may appropriately employ concepts and methods of their discipline in collecting facts related to conduct of a given policy. They may then report their findings to the client who has commissioned the study. However, the anthropologist should play no role in formulating or criticizing policy and should refrain from advocating decisions that would only reflect the anthropologist's personal value judgment. Value judgments and scientific investigation, in this view, should be kept strictly separate, although social scientists have a right to express their own values when not engaged in professional work. Bronislaw Malinowski and several other anthropologists considered below exemplify this attitude.

The third attitude maintains that since anthropologists are most aware of the human problems involved in carrying out policies, they are entirely correct in advocating certain policies. Furthermore, they should supply facts needed to accomplish only those policies of which they approve.

Kathleen Gough, Gerald Berreman, and many other anthropologists (Weaver, ed., 1973) hold opinions characteristic of the third group. Gough suggests that no one is more qualified to propose and evaluate guidelines for human society than those who study it. She argues that anthropologists, as scientists, have the responsibility to present their knowledge and the inferences they can draw from such knowledge as clearly, thoughtfully, and responsibly as possible. Gough (1973) laments the fact that many anthropologists have been unwilling to do this, stating that "it is as though the more we study the world's cultures, the less capable we feel of making judgments as citizens." Berreman (1973) similarly stresses the anthropologist's responsibility to actively combat politicians' and policy makers' widespread ignorance about comparatively simple aspects of social existence that have been described, analyzed, understood, and amply demonstrated by anthropologists. Those adhering to the third attitude thus reject both the ivory tower and schizoid interpretations of the anthropologist's role. Not only do they feel their duty is to propose and advocate guidelines for society, they feel their professional responsibility is to communicate as widely and effectively as possible the findings of their research.

Piddington finds the third view attractive; however, he questions its effectiveness, since anthropologists do not normally occupy important policy-making positions, and since many administrators have a low opinion of social scientists. It seems that anthropologists can increase their effectiveness. They can draw on their knowledge, awareness, and opinions of contemporary social and political problems, and then express themselves collectively through the American Anthropological Association. Also, anthropologists would appear to have a duty to popularize findings related to current issues through wider publication in nonprofessional books and journals.

Finally, more anthropologists can follow the example of those of their colleagues who have expressed their knowledge of and concern for human problems through participation in contemporary social and political movements.

Perhaps we should add a fourth group to Piddington's classification—anthropologists who concern themselves with practical matters, not on behalf of government or other clients, but because of their own research goals. The research and development approach and the action anthropology approach to applied anthropology (both discussed below) exemplify attempts by anthropologists to introduce changes by helping the people they study as part of their own research goals.

PRACTICAL AND APPLIED ANTHROPOLOGY

James A. Clifton (1970) defines *applied anthropology* as "the use of anthropological findings, concepts and methods to accomplish a desired end." As he has defined it, it played a role in European colonialism in Africa and other areas. In 1929 Malinowski advocated a new branch of anthropology and called it "practical anthropology." Chiding his colleagues for their antiquarian emphasis on singular, quaint, and exotic institutions and customs rather than description of behavior and process in social life, he argued that anthropology should begin to study "the changing Native" and the impact of Westernization on traditional African societies, especially the diffusion of European culture into "savage" communities.

Malinowski, clearly expressing Piddington's second attitude, argued that the anthropologist could serve the "practical man," that is, the administrator or missionary, by investigating such matters as law, economics, and other customs and institutions. He believed that anthropologists could easily avoid politics by concentrating exclusively on facts and processes. He asserted that decisions about how to apply the results of anthropological investigations should be left to diplomats and journalists. According to Malinowski, anthropologists should be free to pursue their "impartial cold-blooded passion for sheer accuracy."

Jacques Maquet (1964) and several others have pointed to direct and indirect associations between anthropologists and colonial administrations, and many Africans feel that anthropologists and their findings were tools of colonial regimes. It seems that Malinowski saw nothing wrong with this role. As examples of ways in which the anthropologist could help the "practical man," Malinowski advocated training of cadets (trainees) in the British colonial service in the languages and cultures of Africa. The anthropologist working in Africa could also help the colonial regime by studying such matters as land tenure and determining traditional land use patterns as well as the indispensable minimum of land to be reserved for native groups in the face of European land claims.

Although Malinowski argued for a separation of anthropology and politics, his own political values as expressed in these statements cannot be ignored. He did not question either the legitimacy of the colonial regime or the role of the anthropologist in bolstering it by helping it function smoothly. He cautioned against too rapid attempts to undo or subvert traditional African value systems with external moral codes on the grounds that "black bolshevism" would inevitably result. Malinowski's assumption that rebellion against colonial authority is to be avoided certainly bears witness to his own value judgments and political biases.

Although his comments represent perhaps an extreme view of the appropriateness of collaboration between anthropologists and officials of their own government, Malinowski's conception of the practical role of anthropology in colonial regimes is certainly not unique. The Rhodes-Livingstone Institute of Central African Studies, located in Zambia, was created to study the impact of European culture on traditional African societies and began research activities in 1938. Godfrey Wilson (1940), who participated in its research, felt that the fact that the Institute was responsible neither to any government nor for any government policies guaranteed intellectual freedom to its anthropologists. Wilson partially adopts the schizoid view; on the one hand, he asserts that the social scientist cannot judge good and evil, but only objective social fact and its implications; at the same time, he suggests the potential value of general social understanding in inspiring governmental actions.

Anthropologists have played a variety of applied roles both during and after the period of European colonialism. In addition to advising administrators, they have actually held positions in colonial regimes, serving as community development advisers; working as researchers, cultural interpreters, and intermediaries between natives and communities and government officials; working in mental hospitals, public health programs, and educational programs; and, as we shall see below, undertaking research roles on behalf of the military.

Although the formal colonial structure of the United States has never been as well developed as in England, France, and other European nations, anthropologists have held government positions in U.S. trust territories and acted as consultants for U.S. government programs abroad. In almost all these cases, anthropologists involved in administration or technical assistance programs have willingly or unwillingly adopted the schizoid view of the social scientist's role.

The association of practical anthropology and government was a response to U.S. involvement in World War II. In 1943, reflecting the war effort in the Pacific, the United States Office of Naval Intelligence contracted with Yale University for a research program on Micronesia, under an anthropologist's direction. The relationship between anthropology and government continued in the Trust Territory of Micronesia even after control passed from the Navy to the Interior Department in 1951. In this project, a staff anthropologist and five district anthropologists were employed to gain information useful to administrators. Like Malinowski's colonial anthropologists, the Americans were to have no say in determining or implementing policies, nor were they charged with control or enforcement. Theoretically freed of administrative responsibilities, they were to become experts on Micronesian attitudes and behavior, and to devise and recommend techniques to accomplish objectives decided upon by the administrators. The staff anthropologist was to organize and conduct research and to maintain professional relationships with other anthropologists interested in Micronesian research. All the anthropologists were expected to confine themselves to analyses of means and results rather than concern themselves with objectives. On the basis of their familiarity with village life, they were expected to assess prospects for success of specific programs and to evaluate results. They were expected to serve as intermediaries between the Micronesians and the U.S. government. For example, they were to interpret U.S. legal norms and educational standards for natives, and to indicate problems and cultural incompatibilities to the administrators (Barnett, 1956).

Despite the limitations placed on them by certain types of government sponsorship and by policies over which they have no control, many anthropologists have attempted to use the findings, concepts, and methods of their discipline for some purpose they regard as worthy. Undoubtedly, the anthropologists who participated in the Micronesian project were motivated by their humanitarian concern over problems inflicted by Japanese occupation and other effects of war on these island societies.

Other anthropologists have intervened in the lives of their subjects in order to bring about what they regard as beneficial economic and social changes. In some cases the U.S. government sponsored their intervention; and in certain instances, the long-range benefits of these programs are doubtful. In other cases anthropologists have been able to devise their own intervention programs.

Research and Development: The Vicos Project

One of the best examples of independent anthropological intervention is found in the *research and development approach* to applied anthropology. In 1952 Cornell University, jointly with the Peruvian Institute of Indigenous Affairs, initiated an experimental five-year program of induced social and economic change (Holmberg, 1958, 1965). The project focused on the transformation of Vicos, one of Peru's most unproductive and highly dependent

manor (or *hacienda*) systems, into a productive, self-governing community, adapted to the realities of surviving in modern Peru. This intervention in the social and economic life of Vicos reflected anthropologist Allen Holmberg's humanitarian awareness that peasants, who represent more than half the world's population, often live with natural and social conditions that deny them effective participation in modern life.

The manor of Vicos spanned some 40,000 acres with a population of about 1,700 Quecha-speaking Indians and was located between 9,000 and 20,000 feet above sea level. Since colonial times the inhabitants of Vicos, like many other Peruvian Indians, had been bound to the land as serfs, or peons. Title to Vicos, a public manor, was held by a Public Benefit Charity Society, which rented it out to the highest bidder at public auctions for periods ranging from five to ten years. When the industrial firm that was running Vicos on a ten-year lease went bankrupt in 1952 after five years, Cornell was able to sublease the manor and use its serfs for the remaining five years.

Part of any Peruvian hacienda, usually the most fertile bottom lands, is reserved for commercial exploitation by the renter. Rental of a manor, always by outsiders who are mestizos, also entitles them to the labor of the manor's serfs for a certain number of days each week. In return for their work, the renter is, in theory but often not in practice, legally bound to provide them with sufficient marginal land to support

This Brazilian street scene offers a glimpse of the poverty—urban and rural—encountered in Peru, Indonesia, Brazil, and other stratified, satellite nations. (Ken Heyman)

their households. Representing the renter locally is a mestizo administrator; under the administrator, depending on the size of the estate, are one or more work supervisors, also mestizos, whose job is to mobilize Indian labor. Indian straw bosses organize the work of the serfs.

The idea of a research and development approach to anthropology reflects the desire of Holmberg and his colleagues to change the conditions just discussed, and to study the nature and results of their intervention. The major goal of Cornell's acquisition of Vicos was transference of power to members of the community, in an attempt to promote the production and distribution of greater wealth, the introduction of new and modern skills, the encouragement of general health and well-being, and the formation of a modern system of education. Holmberg believed that all Vicosinos should have, if they so desired, the right and the opportunity to take part in decisions affecting their community; to enhance their own knowledge, health, esteem, and talents; and to preserve the dignity of their private lives. Holmberg described the Cornell personnel as using their own power to share power to the point that they no longer held power.

The changes that they promoted were guided by two principles. First, they assumed that people would be most likely to accept innovations in areas where they felt most deprived. Second, they believed that an integrated approach to change is usually better than a piecemeal approach. The anthropologists formulated about 130 specific lines of research and development. Each line was matched to a specific goal such as the development of community leadership, the diversification of agriculture, the improvement of educational opportunities, and the reduction of social distance between Indians and mestizos.

In the last case, they began a project to test the hypothesis that prejudice will be reduced by conditions of social equality. They scheduled social events to draw mestizos from neighboring communities into Vicos and then conducted the events so as to break down the traditional segregation. Their hypothesis was confirmed in more equal social relations between Vicosinos and mestizos by the time the project ended.

In contrast to the old system, in which profits from the renter's commercial land were removed from the community, Cornell's profits were reinvested in the community to improve agricultural productivity, to construct health and educational facilities, and to increase the Indians' skills. Simultaneously, new agricultural techniques were introduced and adopted by the Indians for use in their own fields.

There are several indications of the success of the Vicos project. In 1958 the Peruvian Institute of Indigenous Affairs began conducting five similar experiments in other areas of the country. Attached to each of these were Peruvian anthropologists, many of whom had participated in the Vicos project. In addition to the specific hypotheses it tested in the field, the Vicos project is also of scientific interest. It demonstrates that significant social, political, and economic change can be produced quickly using this model of intervention. Furthermore, contradicting the common view that peasants are intrinsically reluctant to adopt new ways, Vicos suggests that under favorable conditions, attitudes and behavior patterns can be changed very rapidly indeed.

In addition, events in the late fifties, as Cornell's lease ran out, suggest that obstacles to changes in peasant attitudes and behavior do not lie primarily in peasant world view but in forces external to the community. Vicos has been called an "experiment in revolution in microcosm." How did vested interests view this experiment? During the project Peruvian media gave favorable publicity to Vicos. However, the power elite in this area of Peru — which consisted of mestizos, businesspeople, landed families, political figures, and so on — paid little attention to the experiment, believing that any benefits would eventually return to future renters, members of the mestizo elite. When the Cornell project ended, the Vicosinos applied for the right to buy the estate themselves. Hearing of this, vested interests resisted and attacked with a variety of legal maneuvers. Because of its own elitist ties, the Peruvian government avoided action in favor of the Vicosinos, while paying lip service to their cause. Finally, through the intervention of the Institute of Indigenous Affairs and certain U.S. government officials in Peru, an agreement was reached between the Public Benefit Charity Society and the Vicos community for direct sale at a price and on terms that the Vicosinos could realistically afford. The community actually became economically independent in July 1962, and since that time Cornell's role has involved research, consultation, and advice (Holmberg, 1965).

As Holmberg points out, the major lesson of Vicos is that a suppressed population of peasants, once freed from external exploitation and given encouragement, technical assistance, and learning, *can* succeed by their own efforts and become productive citizens of their nation. Although the achievements of Cornell and the Vicosinos have been impressive, one must remember that the Vicosinos represent only 1,700 people among several million Peruvian Indians bound to such manor systems. Experiments modeled after Vicos are going on in other areas of Peru, but, although change in Vicos was rapid, change throughout the Peruvian nation requires massive governmental action. If we view Vicos as a revolution in microcosm, then the intensity of the opposition of vested interests to freedom there, when seen on a national scale, must be viewed as an enormous opposition to major social and economic change.

Action Anthropology: The Fox Project

A less ambitious example of intervention by anthropologists to promote community change began in 1948 among the Fox Indians living in the town of Tama in central Iowa. Under the direction of Sol Tax, six anthropology graduate students from the University of Chicago went to central Iowa as part of a field-training program involving research on processes of acculturation, adjustment, and community organization. The students eventually asked Tax if they could help their study population try to solve some of its problems. Tax accepted their proposal, and coined the term "participant interference" to describe this new role of the anthropological researcher (Tax, 1958). The anthropological techniques used in the Fox project were also called *action anthropology* by those involved.

As with the research and development approach in the Vicos project, action anthropology fully involves residents of the community in directing change. In contrast to Vicos, however, the Fox anthropologists had absolutely no power; they were not estate lords, nor were they affiliated with the government. Their approach to change was considerably vaguer than in Vicos, and all evidence indicates that the effects of participant interference were fewer. The action anthropologists assumed that new behavior should entail neither loss of Fox identity nor violation of Fox moral beliefs. The objective of their action was to free the Indians to make only those changes that they wished and that also appeared to be in their interests.

The action anthropologists correctly perceived the genesis of the Fox problem to lie in their relationships with white society, and thus attempted to increase both Fox self-confidence and understanding of the Fox by whites. To instill self-confidence, their first target was education. They introduced adult education courses in civics and in them examined historic relationships between Indians and whites, including the nature of certain treaties. Following from their assumption that people most readily accept changes that they understand, perceive as relevant, and play a part in planning, education was a necessary initial target. They eventually instituted a scholarship program to train young people for professional careers and tried to help the Fox develop a cooperative project to design and produce crafts.

Action anthropology as undertaken among the Fox represents what Art Gallaher (1973) has described as the *clinical* rather than the *utopic* model of intervention. With a clinical model of intervention, community residents are actively involved in promoting change; ends are often vague and the outsiders are more concerned with means than ends. The Fox researchers attempted, through discussion with the Fox, to suggest plausible alternatives that the Fox could freely choose; they tried to impose as few restrictions as possible and never made decisions for the Fox. They acted merely as catalysts, helping the Fox develop and clarify goals, and, in the process of doing so, promoting compromises among conflicting ends and values within the Fox community. The objectives of the action anthropologists tended to be open-ended goals like growth of understanding and clarification of values (Gearing, Netting, and Peattie, 1960).

The Vicos project also represents clinical intervention, although it includes some utopic elements. Utopic intervention, which guides many technical assistance programs, assumes that intervention is necessary to gain the acceptance of change, and that results are best achieved by doing things for people rather than involving them in the action. Utopic intervention is more concerned with ends than means.

ECONOMIC DEVELOPMENT AND TECHNICAL ASSISTANCE PROGRAMS

Anthropologists, using the ethnographic method, have traditionally studied people directly at the local level. This places them in a unique position to view the effects of national and international development and aid programs on the populations the programs are supposed to help. Community research by an-

Women in a Mexican village await the arrival of a doctor. Some anthropological studies stress related attitudes and beliefs rather than basic material causes of poor health. (Arnold Weichert/D.P.I.)

thropologists often reveals severe inadequacies in the yardsticks that economists and political scientists use to measure economic development and a nation's economic health. Measures like per capita income and gross national product tell us nothing about the distribution of wealth. Although these measures may reveal an increase in overall wealth, since the first is an average and the second a total, what may really be happening is that the rich are getting richer and the poor poorer.

What is to be the role of the anthropologist who is in a position to evaluate results of economic development schemes? Several agencies of the U.S. government and private foundations are encouraging and funding research on aspects of economic development. Yet, in addition to doing research on development, many anthropologists have chosen to actually participate in such programs. In the Vicos and the Fox projects, anthropologists were free to formulate intervention strategies. However, when they hire themselves out to clients such as the U.S. government, other governments, or private foundations, their capacity for criticism and direction of policy is severely limited.

Robert Manners (1956) suggests that attempts by the United States and the United Nations to introduce fundamental change in underdeveloped countries through technical assistance, health education, and other programs have involved even more anthropologists than the British and others used in their colonial activities. What are the implications of such heavy involvement of anthropologists in these and similar programs? There are notable similarities in the roles of such practical anthropologists and their colonial office prototypes. Both have been expected to instruct government agents in means of introducing change with the least difficulty. According to Charles Erasmus (1954), the anthropologist's role in studying technical change is to indicate the implications of cultural patterns for the successful and economical operation of such programs.

In practice, the anthropologist helps administrators make wise decisions in the context of a broad policy over which the anthropologist normally has no control and which determines larger social and cultural consequences. Laura Thompson (1965) suggests that the role of the applied anthropologist is to scrupulously refrain from making decisions, leaving that function to the client. The applied anthropologist appropriately provides the client with decision-making tools, relevant information including the probable consequences of alternative courses of action. Piddington's schizoid attitude about the role of the social scientist reemerges here. Thompson states that the applied anthropologist must avoid commitment to values other than those of the scientific method, formulating specific action alternatives in a value-neutral framework. Richard Schaedel (1964) suggests the dilemma of the hired action anthropologist even more clearly, stating that however much one feels that a series of measures being carried out in a host country may do more harm than good, once the policy has been set, and once the anthropologist has participated in the program, he or she is no longer free to criticize it.

Thus severe ethical dilemmas may trouble many anthropologists who become involved in action anthropology for governments and other clients. The anthropologist's traditional appreciation of cultural diversity may be offended by the fact that efforts to extend industry and technology entail profound cultural modifications. Or perhaps action anthropologists will find that their most serious dilemma is their association with U.S. interests that may not, in the long run, coincide with the best interests of the people they are trying to change. For more than two decades, U.S. aid has not necessarily been channeled where need and suffering are most intense, but in accordance with political, economic, and strategic priorities as national leaders perceive them. Manners (1956) points out that in President Truman's inaugural address in January 1949, he launched the Point Four program of technical assistance with the assertion that one of the major aims of technical assistance was to create favorable conditions for the investment of U.S. capital overseas.

The applied anthropologist may also be troubled by the common tendency of Western powers to bolster feudal and reactionary regimes through their aid programs rather than to help the progressive forces opposing these regimes. The realization of the disproportionate amount of U.S. foreign aid destined for military dictatorships has begun to trouble a number of our elected representatives during the past few years. Manners (1956) suggests that when aid is channeled through political and administrative agencies within the underdeveloped country, officials are often reluctant to interfere with existing political arrangements and social conditions. The case of trying to bring the "green revolution" to Java, analyzed below, illustrates this. Thus the United States lends moral and financial support to the groups in power. As a result, most of the changes that are financed with U.S. aid maintain and even strengthen the status quo. If they did not, Manners suggests, they would

undoubtedly be resisted by the controlling elements.

Action anthropologists may find that people are reluctant to accept innovations not because of an unreasonably conservative attitude, but because of their relationship with vested interest groups. Vicos demonstrates the intensity of resistance of elites to land reforms. Many of the sharecroppers and tenants who populate underdeveloped nations have learned from bitter experience that if they raise their incomes, their taxes and rents will also be raised. Ignoring for a moment the major impediment to radical change, that is, vested interest groups, Charles Erasmus (1954) and others have suggested that changes will be most readily received if there is clear and immediate proof of their effectiveness and desirability. These changes usually achieve a more rapid and widespread acceptance than those with only long-range benefits that cannot be immediately recognized.

The Brazilian Sisal Scheme

Consider now a change that took place rapidly because of perceived immediate benefits and that was widely believed to have helped an underdeveloped population, but that, in fact, has had a negative effect on this population. This case occurred in Brazil, in a fairly arid area of the northeastern interior called in Portuguese the *sertão*. Until the mid-twentieth century, the economy of the *sertão* was based on cultivation of corn, beans, manioc, and other subsistence crops. The *sertão* was also a grazing region for herds of cattle, sheep, and goats. During most years the peasants were able to derive a living from their plots; however, on an average of once every eleven years, major droughts came to the area, drastically reducing yields and forcing people from the interior to migrate to the coast in search of nonexistent jobs. As part of a scheme to develop the northeast and to dampen the effects of drought, the Brazilian government began encouraging peasants in the *sertão* to plant sisal, a plant naturally adapted to arid areas.

Peasants began to plant sisal on a large scale. Sisal is a cash crop—no part of it can be eaten. Furthermore, the sisal grown in the *sertão* is exported, most of it to the United States where the fiber is used in binding and baling, especially of animal fodder. To ready sisal for export, preparation in the field is necessary. Thus there arose throughout the *sertão* local centers with decorticating machines, devices that strip water and other residue from the sisal leaf, leaving only the salable fiber. Decorticating machines are expensive; small-scale sisal cultivators cannot afford them and must rely on machines owned by members of the local elite.

The decorticating operation involves a small team of workers with a marked division of labor. Two jobs are especially arduous, both done by adult men. One is that of disfiberer—the person who feeds the sisal leaf into the machine—a demanding and dangerous job because the machine exerts a strong pull with the possibility of getting one's fingers caught in the press. The other job is that of residue man, who shovels the residue that collects under the machine onto a heap at some distance from the press and brings new leaves to the disfiberer.

Anthropologist Daniel Gross (1971) studied the effects of sisal on the lives of the people of the *sertão*. He observed that most peasants who have begun to grow sisal have turned over most of their land to this cash crop and have completely abandoned subsistence cultivation. Furthermore, since it takes four years for sisal to mature, after planting peasants must seek wage work, often as members of a decorticating team, to sustain themselves until they can harvest their own crop. When they do harvest, they often find that the price of sisal on the world market is less than when they originally planted. Moreover, once sisal has been planted in a plot, it is

virtually impossible to return to food crops. The land and the population of the *sertão* were hooked on sisal.

How did the new strategy of adaptation based on a cash crop affect the population? Gross was fortunate to have the collaboration of a professional nutritionist, Dr. Barbara Underwood, in his field study. They were interested in the effects of a sisal economy on nutrition. The nutritional requirements of a population are specific to that population. In order to subsist, the calories expended in daily activity must be replaced by calories in the daily diet. To determine if the energy consumed and energy expended are balanced, the caloric content of the daily diet and the cost in calories of work must be determined. Gross was able to calculate the energy expended in two of the jobs on the sisal decorticating team: disfiberer and residue man. Observing one disfiberer and one residue man over an extended period of time, he was able to show that the disfiberer expended an average of 4,397 calories per day and the residue man an average of 3,642 calories per day.

Gross then examined the diets of the households headed by each man. The earnings of the disfiberer were the equivalent of $3.65 U.S. per week; those of the residue man were $3.24 U.S. per week. The disfiberer's household included only himself and his wife, but the residue man had a pregnant wife and

In Petrolina, Bahia, Brazil, workers tie up bundles of decorticated sisal fiber. Since most sisal is grown for export, variation in its price on the world market has brought a boom and a bust to the Brazilian sertão. (United Nations)

	Calories		
Age of Child	Minimum Daily Requirement	Actual Daily Allotment	Percentage of Standard Body Weight
8 (M)	2,100	1,112	62%
6 (F)	1,700	900	70
5 (M)	1,700	900	85
3 (M)	1,300	688	90

Adapted from Gross and Underwood, 1971, p. 733.

FIGURE 14.1 Malnutrition among children of a Brazilian sisal residue man.

four children aged three, five, six, and eight. By spending most of his income on food, the disfiberer was obtaining at least 7,145 calories a day for himself and his wife, ample to supply his own daily needs of 4,397 calories and to leave his wife a comfortable allotment of 2,748 calories.

However, the situation of the residue man was less favorable. With more than 95 percent of his meager income going for food, he was only able to provide himself, his wife, and his four children with 9,392 calories per day. Of this, he consumed 3,642 calories, sufficient to enable him to go on working; his wife consumed 2,150 calories. His children, on the other hand, were clearly being nutritionally deprived. Figure 14.1 compares the minimum daily requirement in calories for his children with their actual daily caloric intake.

Long-term malnutrition has physical and psychological results that are still incompletely understood. Clearly though, sustained malnutrition will be revealed in body weight. As Figure 14.1 shows, average weight of malnourished children will be inferior to that of their better nourished peers. The longer the malnutrition continues, the greater will be the disparity between the nutritionally deprived and those with a normal diet. The oldest children, who have been malnourished longest, compare least favorably with the standard body weight.

Although the children of sisal workers were being undernourished to enable their fathers to continue to work for wages that could not feed them, Gross and Underwood suspected that the children of members of the local economic elite, businesspeople, and owners of decorticating machines, were faring better. They found that malnutrition was much less

severe among these children. Finally, Gross and Underwood thought that the nutritional condition of poor sisal workers today might actually be considerably worse than those of subsistence cultivators before the introduction of sisal. To confirm this, they compared the body weights of people in the generation who had grown up before the conversion to sisal with those of the generation that had grown up following the shift. They found that the weights of the older generation were actually closer to the norm than was true for the post-sisal generation.

The conclusions drawn by this pioneering collaboration between an anthropologist and a nutritionist are extremely important for understanding problems that beset most people in the world today. An irreversible shift from a subsistence economy to a cash economy devised as part of an economic development scheme led to an improvement neither in diet nor in leisure time for the mass of the population. Rather, it produced a situation in which, in concrete caloric terms, the rich got richer and the poor got poorer. This is certainly not an isolated example of the effects of economic development programs and of shifts from subsistence to cash production.

Fortunately, Gross undertook his study as an independent researcher rather than as an adviser to any client organization. Thus in publishing his findings he was unhampered by any reluctance to criticize a program or policy he helped to execute. Through studies such as that of Gross and Underwood anthropologists will be able to evaluate the effects, in terms of basic biological variables affecting human populations, of economic development programs.

The Greening of Java

Like Gross, anthropologist Richard Franke (1977) conducted a study—independent of sponsorship by economic development agencies—of discrepancies

A Brazilian mother holds her malnourished son. Increased malnutrition was one of the results of the shift from subsistence to cash crop production in the Brazilian interior. (Ken Heyman)

between goals and actual results in an ambitious scheme to promote social and economic change. Throughout the world, economic development experts and government officials have assumed that as small-scale peasant farmers gain access to modern technology and more productive crop varieties their lot will improve. The popular media regularly carry accounts of new, high-yielding varieties of wheat, maize, and rice. These new crops, along with chemical fertilizers, pesticides, and new cultivation practices, have been hailed as the bases of a "green revolution" that will increase the world's food supply and thereby improve the diets and living conditions of peasants and other victims of poverty, particularly in land-scarce, overcrowded regions. Through the labors of scientists at the International Rice Research Institute in the Philippines, established in 1962, a genetic cross between strains of rice from Taiwan and Indonesia produced a high-yielding "miracle" rice known as IR-8, capable of increasing by at least half the productivity of a given plot. Subsequently, cultivation of IR-8, along with use of chemical fertilizers and pesticides, has been encouraged by governments throughout mainland and insular southern Asia, including the Indonesian government.

The Indonesian island of Java—with its 80 million people, one of the world's most densely populated agricultural areas—became a prime target of the green revolution. The total crop of Java was, and remains, insufficient to supply its people with mini-

mal daily requirements of calories (2,150) and protein (55 g); thus it certainly needed to increase its food supply. In 1960 the Javanese economy supplied only 1,950 calories and 38 g of protein per capita. By 1967 these figures had fallen to 1,750 calories and 33 g. Might not IR-8, by increasing agricultural yields by 50 percent, reverse the trend?

Java shares with Brazil and with many other underdeveloped nations a history of socioeconomic stratification and colonialism. Precolonial contrasts in wealth and power were intensified under Dutch colonialism. Although Indonesia gained political independence from the Netherlands in 1949, internal stratification continued. Today contrasts between the wealthy (government employees, businesspeople, large landowners) and the poor (small-scale peasants) are present even in small farming communities. The persistence of stratification, even on the village level, is one of the main reasons for the failure of Java's green revolution and will be discussed below.

Programs intended to improve Javanese agricultural productivity, initiated during the early 1950s, began to succeed a decade later. In 1963 the College of Agriculture of the University of Indonesia began a program in which students went to live in peasant villages, to work with peasants in the fields, to observe their lives and problems firsthand, and to share their knowledge of innovative agricultural techniques while learning from the peasants. The program was a tremendous success; yields in affected villages increased by half. The program, now directed by the Department of Agriculture, was expanded in 1964; nine universities and 400 students joined. These intervention programs were succeeding where others had failed because the outside agents recognized that economic development rested not only on technological change, but on political change as well. As participants in the program, students could observe firsthand how established interest groups resisted attempts by peasants to improve their lot. On one occasion, when local officials stole fertilizer destined for peasant fields, elite students got it back by threatening in a letter to turn well-documented evidence of the crime over to higher-level officials if the fertilizer was not returned.

The combination of new work patterns and such political action was achieving promising results when, in 1965–1966, Indonesia fell victim to an antigovernment insurrection. In the eventual military takeover, Indonesia's President Sukarno was ousted and replaced by pro-Western, anticommunist President Suharto. Between 200,000 and 1 million people were massacred; in the face of this, little agricultural reform remained. Although efforts to

A harvest in Indonesia, where the "green revolution" failed because of vested interests and peasants' lack of political clout. New technology alone does not guarantee economic development, particularly when it is opposed by social and political inpediments. (United Nations/UNESCO/D. Roger)

increase agricultural production resumed soon after Suharto took control, Indonesia's new government assigned the task to multinational corporations based in such industrial countries as Japan, West Germany, and Switzerland rather than to students and peasants. These industrial firms were to supply IR-8 and other miracle seeds, fertilizers, and pesticides. Peasants adopting the whole green revolution kit were eligible for loans, which they could use to buy food and other essentials in the lean period just before harvesting.

Java's green revolution soon encountered major obstacles. One of the pesticides, for example, had never been tested in Java. When used in flooded rice fields, it proved lethal to fish in the irrigation canals and thus destroyed a major source of protein. Furthermore, one of the multinational corporations was revealed as a ghost organization set up fraudulently to benefit members of the military and other high officials of the new government.

In addition to these national-level obstacles, Java's green revolution was also failing on the village level, again because of entrenched interests. Franke found that members of the local elite in a Javanese village were blocking access by peasants to a program that might threaten an established system of debt-bondage and cheap labor. Traditionally, during the lean preharvest season, peasants had fed their families by taking temporary cash jobs or by borrowing from wealthier villagers. Since jobs were scarce, loans from local patrons enabled most peasants to

The lessons of the Brazilian sisal scheme and the failure of Java's green revolution can help explain why, despite ever increasing world population, family planning programs often fail. Given high infant and child mortality rates and the need for children's labor, peasants are often reluctant to limit births. Illiteracy, poverty, and lack of access to health care centers are other reasons birth control often fails. Anthropologists can point out the local level effects of such programs, and, if the anthropologist approves of such a program, can help reform it to meet people's actual needs. (United Nations)

survive this period. But having accepted loans, peasants were obligated to work for their patrons throughout the year at wages considerably lower than those paid on the open market. The low-interest loans made available as part of green revolution reform might have freed peasants from their customary dependence on wealthy villagers, thus depriving the latter of cheap labor. Since local officials and other elite villagers were to spread details of how the program worked, the wealthy could limit peasant access by withholding information. Furthermore, Franke found that wealthy villagers also discouraged peasant participation more subtly, by raising doubts about the effectiveness of new techniques and about the wisdom of accepting government loans when familiar patrons were at hand. Faced with the thought that starvation might follow should innovative behavior fail, peasants were reluctant to take risks, an understandable reaction.

Franke found that as a consequence of obstacles to peasant involvement in the program, wealthy villagers, not small-scale subsistence farmers, were reaping the benefits of the green revolution. Only 20 percent of the village's 151 households were participating in the program. Yet, because these were the households of the wealthiest villagers, 40 percent of the land was cultivated by the new techniques. In other parts of Java, Franke found development attempts equally ineffective in improving diets and living standards of most peasants. In some areas, large-scale landowners were systematically using

their green revolution profits at peasants' expense, buying up small plots and purchasing such labor-saving machinery as home milling machines and tractors. As a result, the poorest peasants lost both means of subsistence—their land—and local work opportunities. Their only recourse was to flock to cities, where a growing pool of unskilled labor further lowered already depressed wages.

Like Gross's analysis of the Brazilian sisal scheme, Franke's study of the local implications of the green revolution in Java reveals results very different from those foreseen by the national and international agents of economic development and the news media. Franke's study again illustrates that utopian economic development programs that ignore traditional social, political, and economic divisions on both the national and local levels are doomed to failure. Merely introducing new technology, no matter how promising, will not inevitably help its intended beneficiaries—and may very well hurt them—if vested interests are allowed to interfere. The Javanese student-peasant projects of the 1960s worked because it was recognized that peasants need not just technology but also political clout. The two ambitious programs in Brazil and Java, although designed to alleviate poverty, actually increased it by causing peasants to cease relying on their own labor in subsistence and instead to depend on a much more volatile and fickle economic pursuit—cash sale of labor. Brazil and Java remain *underdeveloping* countries; they retain—indeed increase—their supply of cheap labor; the rich get richer, and the human implications of poverty become ever more anguishing.

Conditions for Development

Not all contemporary governments are equally committed to improving the lot of their people. Moreover, even if such aims exist, interference by major powers often prevents their realization. This commitment is lacking, or exists in an extremely rudimentary form, in many contemporary nation-states and highly stratified societies, like Brazil. In these states the class structure has a castelike rigidity, mobility from the lower into the middle class is very difficult, and it is equally hard to raise the living standards of the lower class as a whole. Such societies have a long history of powerful private-interest groups who control the government and run it for their own aims. On the other hand, one may also find some nation-states in which the government views itself as an agent of the people, in which, for various reasons, private economic interest groups have developed to a lesser extent. As one example of such a society, consider Madagascar.

DEVELOPMENT AND DESCENT-GROUP ORGANIZATION As in many areas of continental Africa, state organization emerged in Madagascar prior to its conquest by the French in 1896 and the satellite status that it has subsequently occupied. Furthermore, as in many parts of Africa, the people of Madagascar were organized into descent groups even before the origin of the state. Imerina, the major native state of Madagascar, incorporated descent groups into its structure, making members of important commoner descent groups advisers to the king, giving them authority in government. The Merina state made provisions for the people it ruled. It required that they work for the state; it collected taxes; and it forced labor in public works projects. In return the state redistributed some of what it had collected to peasants in need. It also granted them relative safety against war and slave raids, and it allowed them to cultivate their rice fields in peace. It supplied and maintained the water works necessary for rice cultivation. It opened to ambitious peasant boys the chance of becoming, through hard work and study, state bureaucrats.

Thus, historically, among the Merina there have been strong relationships between the individual, the descent group, and the state. Local communities, in which residence is often based on descent, have also been more solidary in Madagascar than in Java or Brazil. Madagascar gained its political independence from France in 1960. Although its economic dependence on France and other Western European nations was still strong when I did research there in 1966–1967, the Malagasy administration, like the regimes that have succeeded it, appeared to be committed to a form of socialist development. Economic development schemes were increasing the ability of the Malagasy to feed themselves; they emphasized more productive cultivation of rice, a subsistence crop, rather than any cash crop. Furthermore, local communities, with their traditional cooperative patterns and solidarity based on kinship and descent, have been viewed as partners in—and not obstacles to—the development process.

In a sense, the corporate descent group appears to be preadapted to socialist national development. In Madagascar members of local descent groups have customarily pooled their economic resources to educate their especially intelligent members. Once educated, these men and women gain responsible and economically secure positions in the national economy and polity. They share the advantages of their new positions with their kin, for example, by giving room and board to rural cousins while they attend school and by helping them to find jobs.

Recent Malagasy administrations appear to have shared a commitment to meaningful economic development, perhaps because government officials are of the peasantry or have strong personal ties to the peasantry. This has never been the case in Brazil, where the controllers and the lower class have different origins and no strong connections of kinship, descent, or marriage. Furthermore, Madagascar and other African societies with descent-group organization contradict an assumption that many economists and sociologists seem to make. These instances show that it is not inevitable that, as nations become more and more tied to the world cash economy, aboriginal forms of social organization will break down into nuclear family organization with concomitant impersonality and alienation. There is every indication that descent groups, with their traditional communalism and corporate solidarity, have important roles to play in meaningful economic development. Some of their effects on social life in African cities have already been mentioned in the discussion of the culture of poverty in Chapter 13.

The Underdeveloped Talk Back

In a provocative critique that echoes the thoughts of many colleagues in the Third World, Mexican anthropologist Guillermo Batalla (1966) presents "an anguished analysis" of six "conservative and essentially ethnocentric assumptions" that he believes underlie much of the applied anthropology in Latin America. Batalla criticizes many North American anthropologists for their failure to see the relationship between the troubles of people and the political circumstances that nurture and perpetuate these problems. His characterization of applied anthropology as conservative reflects the tendency of certain anthropologists to favor gradual change and to discourage conflict. The result, he claims, is an applied anthropology that favors, intentionally or unintentionally, maintenance of the status quo.

Batalla discusses several expressions of such thought in applied anthropology. One is the heavy psychological emphasis of many studies, assertions that applied anthropology should investigate and deal with attitudes and beliefs about such matters as health and nutrition rather than with the basic material causes of poor health and malnutrition. A second component is anthropologists' belief that their main function is to avoid rapid changes because the resulting maladjustments and conflicts often lead to social and cultural disorganization. Because of this attitude, the anthropologist promotes only small and partial reforms and neglects changes in basic social institutions.

A third aspect of conservative thought that Batalla finds is the misuse of the anthropological doctrine of cultural relativism among certain applied anthropologists, who feel disinclined to interfere in existing social situations because of the inappropriateness of judging or guiding. He suggests that such opinions should be rejected in favor of greater anthropological attention to the study of history, which provides patterns and laws of change that can be used in formulating development programs.

Fourth, Batalla faults the multiple causation theory, which, because it assumes that there are countless small and diverse causes of any social event, cannot isolate as targets for attack major social and economic inequities. Fifth, he criticizes applied anthropologists for viewing communities as isolated units. As has been shown previously, changes within communities are accepted or opposed in a larger context. Batalla suggests that applied anthropologists pay greater attention to regional, national, and international frameworks of communities. Finally, he criticizes applied anthropologists for assuming that diffusion, usually of skills from the United States to the underdeveloped nation, is the only, or the only significant, process involved in change.

Batalla certainly does not argue that all applied anthropology in Latin America has suffered from these faults. Many aspects of the Vicos project, for example, can stand up to his criticisms. However, there is validity in his arguments. More important, many social scientists in the Third World would agree, and are becoming increasingly critical of American anthropology, not only because of static theory, but because of connections between some anthropologists and agencies of the U.S. government.

ANTHROPOLOGISTS AND GOVERNMENT

Remarks by anthropologist Ward Goodenough in 1962 present striking parallels to Malinowski's 1929 comments. They exemplify some of the theoretical assumptions that Batalla has criticized. According to Goodenough (1962), much of the government's need for research "has to do with some form of intelligence gathering that calls for the behavioral scientist's professional skills in data collection and interpretation." Like Malinowski, Goodenough allots only an advisory role to the anthropologist. He states that after government officials have decided on the classes of phenomena they must consider in developing a policy, they may ask behavioral scientists what is known about these phenomena. He mentions the role of the anthropologist as "trouble shooter" in community development projects to determine what is going wrong and why.

In addition to the usefulness of the ethnographic skills of anthropologists to officials of the U.S. Agency for International Development (AID) and the Peace Corps, Goodenough suggests that "the Army is another potential market," since "the successful conduct of modern guerrilla warfare obviously requires both extensive and intensive ethnographic intelligence." Goodenough (1962) further suggests that ethnographic skills are vital "if one is to enlist people's cooperation in economic development or in guerrilla warfare, and if one is to assess reliably the way in which people are likely to respond to changed conditions in the future."

How is the anthropologist to serve the government? In 1962 Goodenough perceived a shortage of anthropologists. To remedy this, he suggested establishment of special programs to train people to do competent ethnography. These people would have some knowledge of the cultural and psychological aspects of social process, but would not be academic scholars. In a phrase that recalls Malinowski, he suggests a master's degree program in "practical ethnography."

Instruction would involve the "kind of ethnography that has the greatest utility for people engaged in overseas action programs that require the cooperation of local populations in order to succeed." Assuming positions that Batalla has criticized, Goodenough regards the community as a self-contained unit and advocates study of the psychological manifestations of social problems rather than the problems themselves. Thus, "what is vital is not the material state of affairs that characterizes a community as a *more-or-less self-contained system* [my italics], but the ideas and values of the people in the community." Goodenough (1962) suggests that what AID officials want is a "dictionary" and a "grammar" of social conduct. That is, they desire "good accounts of the local codes of manners and etiquette, the kinds of roles that people can play in dealing with one another, and the acts and avoidances symbolic of these roles."

Like Malinowski (1929), Goodenough suggests that the association of anthropology and government will have the potential to improve the scientific rigor of anthropology. Thus "if we are effectively to fill our government's need for our ethnographic skills by developing training programs in practical ethnography, we are again challenged to develop methods of descriptive ethnography capable of producing the kind of ethnographic intelligence that is practically more needed." As to the specifics of the associaton between anthropology and government, Goodenough (1962) suggests that "at present, it is impossible to say what requests, if any, for our ethnographic services may emerge from government agencies, but there are straws in the wind suggesting

that we may be called upon. If this should happen, how are we to respond?"

Project Camelot

Project Camelot was the outgrowth of U.S. Army concern over revolutions in Cuba and Yemen, insurgency movements in the Congo, now Zaire, and Vietnam, and guerrilla warfare elsewhere. As conceived by the army in 1963, the project was intended to measure and forecast the causes of such movements for social change. In addition, it was to find ways of eliminating these causes or coping with them if they did occur. Project Camelot was to take three to four years, was funded at $4 to $6 million, and was to involve social science research carried out by a Special Operations Research Organization. Latin America was the first area chosen for study, but there were plans to include countries in Asia, Africa, and Europe.

In a recruiting letter sent to scholars all over the world in late 1964, the aims of the project were defined as a study to "make it possible to predict and influence politically significant aspects of social change in the developing nations of the world." This would include devising procedures for "assessing the potential for internal war within national societies" and "identify[ing] with increased degrees of confidence those actions which a government might take to relieve conditions which are assessed as giving rise to a potential for internal war." The letter also stated that "the U.S. Army has an important mission in the positive and constructive aspects of nation-building in less developed countries as well as a responsibility to assist friendly governments in dealing with active insurgency problems [quoted in Horowitz, 1965]." Such army activities were described as "insurgency prophylaxis."

A well-known Latin American specialist, a sociologist, was recruited to direct the project. An anthropologist who ultimately became involved was primarily responsible for the blow-up that followed widespread discovery of the project's existence and aims. In the early days of Camelot, he had asked to be officially connected with the project. Although never given a regular Camelot appointment, he was commissioned to prepare a report on the possible cooperation of scholars in Chile. Presenting himself as a Camelot official, he interviewed the vice-chancellor and a professor of a Chilean university. During the interview, the professor, who had received from an outraged Norwegian sociologist a copy of the 1964 recruitment letter, confronted the anthropologist with his knowledge of the aims of the project, its army sponsorship, and its military implications. When the true nature of the project was revealed, the specter of U.S. military intervention in the internal affairs of Chile was debated in the Chilean Senate, decried in the Chilean press, and ultimately provoked a debate in the U.S. Senate and academic community. The Johnson administration canceled Project Camelot in July 1965.

Senator William Fulbright recognized the conservative implications of the army's research goals and stated his objection to Project Camelot's "reactionary, backward-looking policy opposed to change. Implicit in Camelot, as in the concept of 'counter-insurgency,' is an assumption that revolutionary movements are dangerous to the interests of the United States and that the United States must be prepared to assist, if not actually to participate in, measures to repress them [quoted in Horowitz, 1965]." On the day that the project was canceled, a congressional committee was told by the Special Operations Research Organization that the project had taken its name from King Arthur's domain because "it connotes the right sort of things—development of a stable society with peace and justice for all [quoted in Horowitz, 1965]."

Although the project died, Camelot's repercussions still haunt anthropologists. Batalla's critique of conservative thought in applied anthropology, published a year after the revelation of Camelot, echoes Fulbright's concern with the assumption that the United States should promote order and stability. In more practical ways, the revelation of Camelot and of other associations of anthropologists with U.S. government agencies has hampered legitimate anthropological research by creating suspicion of American anthropologists as possible agents of their government. In the Camelot instance, the Chilean press and academic community expressed outrage at scholars being recruited for spying missions. The *New York Times* noted the harm done to legitimate anthropological research in the wake of Camelot; it cited the difficulty anthropologists face in providing acceptable evidence that they are not involved in clandestine research, when it is known that the CIA has engaged in funding established agencies and in creating new illicit ones (Sahlins, 1967). In 1965 Professor Ralph Beals was named by the American Anthropological Association to chair a committee on research problems and ethics, necessitated by the Camelot controversy.

The Camelot social scientists undoubtedly believed that their participation in the project would accomplish some worthy goals, for example, education of the more progressive elements of the military. However, in the final analysis, social scientists who sell their skills to powerful clients do not, as the discussion of applied anthropology demonstrates, make final policy, nor do they determine the ultimate uses of the information they collect.

Other Government-Sponsored Research

Normally, anthropologists design their own research projects and apply for funding to such nonmilitary government agencies as the National Science Foundation and the National Institutes of Health, or to private foundations such as the Social Science Research Council. In violation of the usual procedure, the Camelot social scientists were recruited by the military to participate in a preestablished research plan. Sponsorship by a U.S. military agency, aside from the ethical considerations discussed below, is often perceived as a threat in less-powerful nations, where people are familiar with examples of U.S. intervention.

Gerald Berreman (1973a) decries involvement of social scientists in clandestine research, their acceptance of military funding, and covers adopted by intelligence agents who claim that they are anthropologists engaged in standard ethnographic research. He points out that the people who are most affected by such activities are the scholars who regard their work as the legitimate and sympathetic pursuit of knowledge, who attempt to contribute to international understanding, and who believe that the results of their research should be open to all rather than classified for exclusive government use. As a specialist in South Asia, Berreman experienced firsthand the damaging results of collaboration between anthropologists and the U.S. military.

In the summer of 1968 American scholarship in India was jeopardized by the disclosure that the University of California Himalayan Borders Project was to be financed for three years at almost $300,000 by the U.S. Department of Defense. The immediate result was that Indian officials delayed all applications for permits to conduct anthropological research and examined them closely. After considerable outrage by Indian scholars and in the Indian press, the

Indian government decreed that no further social science projects supported by U.S. government funds would be approved. Individual scholars with other sources of support would, however, be allowed into India if their proposals were approved by the Indian government.

Additional damage was done to the academic freedom of legitimate researchers by the more recent revelation of involvement of American anthropologists and other social scientists in army-sponsored research on counterinsurgency in northern Thailand. In the wake of Camelot, India, and Thailand, anthropologists have recently begun to concern themselves more intensely with their ethical responsibilities not only toward their colleagues, but toward the public, and, most important, the people they study.

ETHICS AND ANTHROPOLOGY

In 1967 the American Anthropological Association adopted a Statement of Problems of Anthropological Research and Ethics. A Committee on Ethics appointed in 1968 published a draft version of a Code of Ethics in the association's newsletter in April 1969 and proposed the election of a standing committee on ethics in anthropology. In 1970 a draft of a code prepared by the standing committee became a focus of debate but was eventually adopted. Examination of this code, entitled "AAA: Principles of Professional Responsibility," reveals fundamental differences between the attitude of a majority of contemporary anthropologists and the viewpoint that holds that anthropologists' ethical and value judgments should be totally distinct from their scientific work.

The preamble to the code suggests that anthropologists should avoid research that can potentially damage either the people studied or the scholarly community. The code covers six areas of the anthropologist's professional responsibility: to those studied, to the public, to the discipline, to students, to sponsors, and to governments, one's own and those of host countries.

1. RESPONSIBILITY TO THOSE STUDIED Anthropologists' paramount responsibility in research is to those whom they study. Anthropologists must do everything they can to protect informants' physical, psychological, and social welfare, and to honor their dignity and privacy. If interests conflict, these people come first. The rights, interests, and sensitivities of those studied must be protected. Specifically, anthropologists should make known to informants the aims and the anticipated consequences of their investigation; they should ensure that informants preserve their anonymity in all forms of data collection. Individual informants should not be exploited for personal gain. Anthropologists must anticipate and take steps to avoid potentially damaging effects of the publication of their research. In accordance with the AAA's official disapproval of clandestine or secret research, no reports should be provided to sponsors that are not also available to the general public.

2. RESPONSIBILITY TO THE PUBLIC Anthropologists owe a commitment to candor and to truth in disseminating their research results and in stating their opinions as students of human life. Anthropologists should make no secret communications, nor should they knowingly falsify their findings. As people who devote their professional lives to understanding human diversity, anthropologists bear a positive responsibility to speak out publicly, both individually and collectively, on what they know and what they believe as a result of their professional expertise. They bear a professional responsibility to contribute to an "adequate definition of reality," upon which public opinion and public policy can be based. In public discourse anthropologists should be honest about their qualifications and aware of the limitations of their discipline's expertise.

3. RESPONSIBILITY TO THE DISCIPLINE Anthropologists bear responsibility for the good reputation of their discipline and of its practitioners. They should undertake no secret research or any research the results of which cannot be freely derived and publicly reported. They should avoid even the appearance of engaging in clandestine research by totally and freely disclosing the objectives and sponsorship of all research. They should attempt to maintain a level of rapport and integrity in the field such that their behavior will not jeopardize future research there.

4. RESPONSIBILITY TO STUDENTS Anthropologists should be fair, candid, nonexploitative, and committed to the welfare and academic progress of their students. They should make them aware of the ethical problems of research.

5. RESPONSIBILITY TO SPONSORS Anthropologists should be honest about their qualifications, capabilities, and aims. They should be especially careful not to promise or to imply acceptance of conditions in violation of professional ethics and competing commitments. They must require of the sponsor full disclosure of the sources of funds, personnel, and aims of the institution and the research project, and the disposition of the research results. They must retain the right to make all ethical decisions in the research. They must enter into no secret agreement with a sponsor regarding the results or reports.

6. RESPONSIBILITY TO ONE'S OWN AND TO HOST GOVERNMENTS Anthropologists should be candid and honest. They should demand assurance that they will not be required to compromise their professional responsibilities and ethics as a condition of permission to pursue the research. Specifically, they should engage in no secret research, should write no secret reports, nor agree to debriefings of any kind.

The authors of the code stressed that this statement of principles of professional responsibility was not designed to punish anthropologists but to provide guidelines. However, the code has a provision for censure of unprofessional conduct. When the actions of an anthropologist jeopardize the people studied, professional colleagues, students, or others, or if the anthropologist otherwise betrays professional commitments, colleagues may legitimately inquire into the propriety of those actions and take such measures as lie within the legitimate powers of the AAA, as the members deem appropriate. A committee on ethics is now a permanent part of the struc-

ture of the American Anthropological Association.

THE CONTINUANCE OF DIVERSITY

Anthropology teaches us that populations respond to environmental changes through modification of the evolutionary material at hand. Adaptive responses of human populations can be more flexible than in the case of other biological populations because the principal adaptive means are sociocultural. However, the sociocultural forms of the past always influence subsequent adaptation, producing continued diversity and imparting a certain uniqueness to adaptive responses of specific human populations. Anthropology focuses attention on similarities and differences among human populations in their sociocultural means of adaptation. Because evolution through natural selection must always accommodate itself to and proceed on the basis of the material at hand, populations with different traditions and different adaptive means have reacted to, and will continue to react to, metropolitan incorporation differently. Because of this, among human populations who manage to survive and to adapt successfully to events of the twentieth century, the diversity that has intrigued students of anthropology since its inception may be expected to endure. Let us hope that adaptive divergence will continue to provide a major obstacle to what some social scientists see as a bland convergence of the future and that free and open anthropological investigation of human diversity will be decreasingly imperiled by the actions of a few. With our knowledge and with awareness of our professional responsibilities, let us work to keep anthropology the most humanistic of all the disciplines.

SUMMARY

Anthropologists hold different opinions about the relationship between their personal values and their scientific research and its application. Some adopt an ivory tower position, maintaining that anthropologists should confine themselves to teaching, research, and publication, avoiding practical and political issues. Others believe that anthropologists may appropriately offer their techniques and findings for practical tasks; however, they should strictly separate personal values from endeavors in research or in

applied anthropology. According to this second view, anthropologists may work for governments, colonial administrations, and other clients; however, their role is not to set or to influence policy, but to determine how policies, once set, can be carried out effectively or to investigate reasons for acceptance or rejection of changes inspired by policy makers. A third group argues that anthropologists, because of the discipline's familiarity with many aspects of the human condition, and especially of human problems, should actively seek to influence government positions and policies and should participate only in those projects of which they approve.

Anthropologists traditionally have been interested in social and cultural change, and many such changes have accompanied the incorporation of formerly autonomous populations into modern nations and metropole-satellite webs. In addition to the three views mentioned above, a fourth group, including many applied anthropologists, have used techniques and findings of anthropology to introduce changes on their own, rather than for a client, and to study the nature and effects of such changes. Holmberg and colleagues were instrumental in introducing beneficial economic and social changes in Vicos, Peru, formerly a rented manor on which impoverished Indians lived as serfs. Over the course of the five-year period during which Cornell University rented Vicos, project personnel introduced several economic and social changes along specific lines of development with predetermined goals. Holmberg characterized the Vicos project as a "research and development approach" to the study of change. Directions of development had been hypothesized in the early stages of the project, and not only could the nature and effects of the changes be studied as research problems, but deviations away from the hypothesized developments could be studied as well.

University of Chicago students followed the techniques of "action anthropology" among Fox Indians in central Iowa. This approach to applied anthropology was guided by what anthropologist Sol Tax calls "participant interference." The students attempted to help the Fox formulate their own goals for change aimed at improving Fox material conditions, self-esteem, and the image of them held by white Iowans. Since they wielded no power, the action anthropologists confined their efforts to the rather vague objectives of improving the economic and social position of the Fox in the larger society and of getting the Fox to help themselves.

In European colonial regimes, in U.S. experiments in colonialism, and in development and technical assistance programs sponsored by the United States, the United Nations, and others, anthropologists have been hired to apply their skills in projects aimed at economic and cultural change. Anthropologists who are so employed often face both practical and ethical problems reflecting their subordination to the larger goals of the client, their inability to set or to influence

policy, and the difficulty in criticizing programs in which they have participated.

Some anthropologists, however, have made independent investigations of the results of economic development schemes. Gross, for example, studied changes that accompanied a shift from subsistence farming to cultivation of a cash crop in the interior of northeastern Brazil. Gross found that material conditions of most people affected by the change had actually worsened. His research demonstrates some of the unfortunate and unforeseen consequences that often accompany development schemes, particularly those aimed at replacing subsistence economies with economies that must rely on the vagaries of the world cash economy. Similarly, through a study in Java, Franke found that the green revolution was failing because it stressed new technology rather than the combination of technology plus peasant political organization. The green revolution was actually increasing poverty, rather than eradicating it.

For historical, political, and economic reasons, not all governments are committed to the improvement of the material conditions of the lower classes of their countries. Social forms of the past, including the nature of the relationship between elites and masses, affect the potentiality and course of economic development.

Many of our colleagues in Third World nations criticize North American anthropologists for a conservative bias in the research problems they choose to investigate and in their approaches to economic development and social change. They point to a tendency on the part of anthropologists to stress gradual change and to fear social disorganization, which therefore leads them to sanction only minor changes rather than the major institutional ones often necessary to rapid material improvement. Perhaps as a result of the traditional field methods of their discipline, many anthropologists have viewed communities as isolated units, ignoring the ties these communities have with region, nation, and world. They have been criticized for such views, since many of the major impediments to development lie in relationships that link community and outside world.

Anthropologists have shown this conservative bias in areas beyond research and publications. Some have participated in projects actually designed to combat rapid social changes and sponsored by the U.S. Army and Department of Defense. Not surprisingly, revelation of this participation has imperiled access to certain countries by the majority of independent anthropologists who desire only to conduct free and open research. Worse still, by their participation in research sponsored by certain governmental agencies, anthropologists have collected data that potentially or actually damage the people they have studied.

In recognizing the dangers of such participation, the American Anthropological Association has issued a statement of professional conduct, indicating the responsibilities of anthropologists to informants, universities, colleagues, students, sponsors, and governments. The AAA has also committed itself to action against breaches of professional ethics.

It is hoped that greater attention to professional responsibilities will ensure that anthropologists can continue a free and open study of human diversity and that anthropology can remain the most humanistic of all the sciences.

SOURCES AND SUGGESTED READINGS

AMERICAN ANTHROPOLOGICAL ASSOCIATION
Newsletter. Published ten months a year; best source of news and controversy affecting anthropologists.

ANGROSINO, M. V., ED.
1976 *Do Applied Anthropologists Apply Anthropology?* Athens, Ga.: Southern Anthropological Society. The application of anthropological findings and techniques to contemporary problems; eleven contributors write about this increasingly important area of anthropology.

BATALLA, G. B.
1966 Conservative Thought in Applied Anthropology: A Critique. *Human Organization* 25: 89–92. A Latin American colleague views North American anthropologists.

BARNETT, H. G.
1956 *Anthropology in Administration.* New York: Harper & Row. Uses of anthropology in administration, including Micronesia.

BELSHAW, C. S.
1976 *The Sorcerer's Apprentice: An Anthropology of Public Policy.* Fairview Park, Elmsford, N.Y.: Pergamon. Possibilities and problems that anthropologists face when they confront matters of public policy.

BERNARD, H. R., AND SIBLEY, W. E.
1975 *Anthropology and Jobs: A Guide for Undergraduates.* A Special Publication of the American Anthropological Association. Washington: American Anthropological Association. Information about varied jobs open to undergraduates who have majored in anthropology.

BERNARD, H. R., AND PELTO, P. J., EDS.
1972 *Technology and Social Change.* Eleven cases of implications of technological innovations on social life.

BERREMAN, G. D.
1973a (orig. 1969). Academic Colonialism: Not So Innocent Abroad. In *To See Ourselves: Anthropology and Modern Social Issues,* gen. ed. T. Weaver, pp. 152–156. Glenview, Ill.: Scott, Foresman. Repercussions of U.S. Defense Department support of anthropological research in India.

1973b Foreword to O. C. Stewart, The Need to Popularize Basic Concepts. In *To See Ourselves: Anthropology and Modern Social Issues,* gen. ed. T. Weaver, pp. 55–57. Glenview, Ill.: Scott, Foresman. Need for anthropologists to make the concepts and findings of their discipline more widely known.

CLIFTON, J. A., ED.
1970 *Applied Anthropology: Readings in the Uses of the Science of Man.* Boston: Houghton Mifflin. Reader on applied and "practical" anthropology. Includes several of the articles discussed in this chapter.

DOBYNS, H. F., AND DOUGHTY, P. L.
1976 *Peru: A Culture History.* New York: Oxford University Press. How its precolonial culture and historical forces influence the behavior and thought of today's Peruvians.

ERASMUS, C.
1954 An Anthropologist Views Technical Assistance. *Scientific Monthly (Science)* 78: 147–158. Some reasons for acceptance of or resistance to externally induced technical change.

1961   *Man Takes Control.* Minneapolis: University of Minnesota Press. Role of economic motivation in change.

FOSTER, G. M.
1962   *Traditional Cultures and the Impact of Technical Change.* New York: Harper & Row. A standard textbook in applied anthropology.

1969   *Applied Anthropology.* Boston: Little, Brown. Updated expansion of his 1962 book.

FRANKE, R.
1977   Miracle Seeds and Shattered Dreams in Java. In *Readings in Anthropology,* pp. 197–201. Guilford, Conn.: Dushkin Publishing Group, Inc. Technology and miracle crops must be coupled with peasants' political clout for economic development to take place.

GALLAHER, A.
1973   Introduction and Conclusion to Intervention: Changing the System. In *To See Ourselves: Anthropology and Modern Social Issues,* gen. ed. T. Weaver, pp. 436–437, 475–478. Glenview, Ill.: Scott, Foresman. Comments on current problems in applied anthropology.

GEARING, F., NETTING, R. M., AND PEATTIE, L. R.
1960   *Documentary History of the Fox Project.* Chicago: Department of Anthropology, University of Chicago. The first experiment in action anthropology.

GOODENOUGH, W.
1962   The Growing Demand for Behavioral Science in Government: Its Implications for Anthropology. *Human Organization* 21: 172–176 (also in Clifton, ed., 1970). How ethnographers can modify their field methods to meet needs of the American government.

1963   *Cooperation in Change.* New York: Russell Sage Foundation. Manual for technical assistance workers and the anthropologists who help them.

GOUGH, K.
1973   (orig. 1968). World Revolution and the Science of Man. In *To See Ourselves: Anthropology and Modern Social Issues,* gen. ed. T. Weaver, pp. 156–165. Glenview, Ill.: Scott, Foresman. The role and responsibilities of the anthropologist in the context of contemporary colonialism and imperialism.

GROSS, D.
1971   The Great Sisal Scheme. *Natural History,* March, pp. 49–55. Failures of an economic development scheme in northeastern Brazil.

GROSS, D., AND UNDERWOOD, B.
1971   Technological Change and Caloric Costs: Sisal Agriculture in Northeastern Brazil. *American Anthropologist* 73: 725–740. More technical presentation of anthropological and nutritional data included in Gross, 1971.

HOLMBERG, A.
1958   The Research and Development Approach to the Study of Change. *Human Organization* 17: 12–16 (also in Clifton, ed., 1970). Strategy of an applied anthropology project in Vicos, Peru.

1965   The Changing Values and Institutions of Vicos in the Context of National Development. *American Behavioral Scientist* 8: 3–8. Results of the Vicos project (also in Clifton, ed., 1970).

HOROWITZ, I. L.
1965   The Life and Death of Project Camelot. *Trans-action* December (also in T. Weaver, gen. ed., 1973, pp. 138–148). History of Project Camelot and some of its implications.

KIMBALL, S. T., AND WATSON, J. T., EDS.
1972   *Crossing Cultural Boundaries: The Anthropological Experience.* San Francisco: Chandler. Twenty ethnographers discuss their personal encounters with field work.

LEACOCK, E., GONZALEZ, N., AND KUSHNER, G.
1974   *Training Programs for New Opportunities in Applied Anthropology.* Washington: American Anthropological Association, Society for Applied Anthropology. Of interest to students; discusses prospects for social involvement and non-academic work using anthropological insights.

MALINOWSKI, B.
1929   Practical Anthropology. *Africa* 2: 23–38. Anthropology for cadets in the British colonial administration (also in Clifton, ed., 1970).

MANNERS, R.
1956   Functionalism, Realpolitik and Anthropology in Underdeveloped Areas. *America Indigena* 16 (also in T. Weaver, gen. ed., 1973, pp. 113–126). Some of the political and ethical problems that beset "practical anthropologists."

MAQUET, J.
1964   Objectivity in Anthropology. *Current Anthropology* 5: 47–55 (also in Clifton, ed., 1970). Formal and informal connections between anthropologists and colonial administrations in Africa.

MEAD, M., ED.
1955   *Cultural Patterns and Technical Change.* New York: New American Library. Changes in nutrition and medical and maternal care in underdeveloped countries.

PEACOCK, J. L.
1975   *Consciousness and Change: Symbolic Anthropology in Evolutionary Perspective.* New York: John Wiley (Halsted Press). Symbols, creative expression, and social change.

PIDDINGTON, R.
1960   Action Anthropology. *Journal of the Polynesian Society* 69: 199–213 (also in Clifton, ed., 1970). Three contrasting conceptions of the role of the values of the social scientist in his work.

PELTO, P. J.
1973   *The Snowmobile Revolution: Technology and Social Change in the Arctic.* Menlo Park, Calif.: Cummings. Effects of introduction of snowmobiles on reindeer-herding Lapps in Finland; interesting case study of social change.

RYNKIEWICH, M. A., AND SPRADLEY, J. P.
1976   *Ethics and Anthropology: Dilemmas in Fieldwork.* New York: Wiley. Focuses on ethical problems encountered by anthropologists when teaching, writing, and in the field.

SAHLINS, M. D.
1967   The Established Order: Do Not Fold, Spindle or Mutilate. In *The Rise and Fall of Project Camelot: Studies in the Relationship between Social Science and Practical Politics,* ed. I. L. Horowitz. Cambridge, Mass.: M.I.T. Press (also in T. Weaver, gen. ed., 1973, pp. 148–152). Sahlins, an anthropologist, is one of several scholars who discuss Camelot's implications for their disciplines in this book.

SCHAEDEL, R. P.
1964   Anthropology in AID Overseas Missions: Its Practical and Theoretical Potential. *Human Organization* 23: 190–192 (also in Clifton, ed., 1970). Anthropology's practical value in overseas development programs.

SPICER, E. H.
1952   *Human Problems in Technological Change.* New York: Russell Sage Foundation. Includes case studies of agricultural development schemes.

SPINDLER, G., ED.
1974   *Education and Cultural Process: Toward an Anthropology of Education.* New York: Holt, Rinehart & Winston. Anthropology's comparative perspective and concern with problems arising from ethnicity and poverty in the contemporary United States make its findings applicable to evaluating education in the U.S., as this collection shows.

TAX, S.
1958   The Fox Project. *Human Organization* 17: 17–19 (also in Clifton, ed., 1970). Some results of action anthropology and participant interference.

THOMPSON, L.
1965   Is Applied Anthropology Helping to Develop a Science of Man? *Human Organization* 24: 277–287. Draws distinction between "engineering" and "clinical" approaches to technological and culture change, and discusses examples of the latter.

WAX, R. H.
1971   *Doing Fieldwork: Warnings and Advice.* Chicago: University of Chicago Press. Problems anthropologists encounter in getting acquainted with informants and collecting data.

WEAVER, T., GEN. ED.
1973   *To See Ourselves: Anthropology and Modern Social Issues.* Glenview, Ill.: Scott, Foresman. Timely anthology of articles on the social responsibility of the anthropologist, anthropology and the Third World, race and racism, poverty and culture, education, violence, environment, intervention, and anthropology in the contemporary United States.

WILSON, G.
1940   Anthropology as a Public Service. *Africa* 13: 43–60. The inception and research of the Rhodes-Livingstone Institute of Central African Studies.

Anthropological Perspectives on Contemporary American Culture

15

In previous chapters both divisive and unifying factors in a variety of societies have been examined. People in nonindustrial societies are often divided on the basis of their residence in different villages and their membership in different descent groups. With state organization, and particularly with industrial society, nations are divided by such factors as ethnicity; class; region; religion; rural, suburban, or urban residence; political party affiliation; and neighborhood. Descent groups and other social divisions in nonindustrial societies may be linked together through exchange relationships based, for example, on marriage or trade, or they may temporarily unite through a segmentary lineage structure. Common beliefs and participation in the same cultural tradition also provide a basis for uniformity. In states, incorporation within and subjugation to a governmental structure link diverse groups.

Compared to such contemporary nations as China and the Soviet Union, and also to many nonindustrial states, the U.S. government interferes relatively little in the affairs of its citizens and has only limited success in regulating even antisocial schemes and activities. Whatever unity American culture may have does not, then, rest on a particularly strong central government. Nor is it a function of segmentary lineage structure, marital exchange networks, or adherence to codes of appropriate behavior sanctified by the traditions of several generations. In this chapter, I will try to demonstrate that many of the commonalities of behavior, belief, and activity that enable us to speak of "contemporary American culture" are relatively new, more or less peculiar to the United States, and founded on and perpetuated by twentieth-century industrial developments, particularly those in business organization, transportation, and the mass media.

ANTHROPOLOGISTS AND AMERICAN CULTURE

In previous chapters, particularly Chapters 13 and 14, you have seen that anthropologists are increasingly studying social and economic conditions and problems in the United States and other industrial nations. The reasons for greater concentration in these areas reflect both a decrease in funds from agencies to study Third World nations as well as political developments there. Examples of anthropological analyses of ethnic groups in urban centers and of relationships between socioeconomic class and kinship, marriage, and household patterns have been presented in earlier sections. Such studies exemplify the highly important anthropological concern with *variation* and its causes and consequences.

Anthropology traditionally has been as concerned with cultural uniformity as variation. "National character" studies of the 1940s and early 1950s foreshadowed the growing interest by anthropologists in unifying themes in contemporary American culture. Unfortunately, these studies, which tried to identify the distinctive psychological attributes of Americans, Japanese, Russians, and citizens of other nations, usually focused excessively on the cognitive and emotional characteristics of *individuals*. Culture, however, is an attribute of groups rather than of individuals. Shared cultural themes— beliefs, values, ways of thinking and acting—override many differences between individuals and between groups. Whereas Chapters 13 and 14 emphasized differences among people, this chapter focuses on unifying factors in American life—common experiences, actions, and beliefs that compose contemporary American culture.

It is appropriate that anthropology should study American society and culture. Anthropology aims, after all, at being a science of human behavior that is concerned with social and cultural universals, generalities, and uniqueness. American culture is a particular cultural variant, as interesting, as exotic, and as unique as any other. Americans are similar to members of other cultures in some ways, different in others. Anthropological techniques developed in smaller-scale societies, where sociocultural uniformity is more marked, can nonetheless contribute to an understanding of American life.

In describing and analyzing American culture and society, American anthropologists enjoy an advantage. Although their training in anthropology and their familiarity with other cultures grant them a certain degree of removal and objectivity in studying American culture that most American natives lack, American anthropologists *are* Americans. Anthropologists from various Third World nations have correctly asserted that their life experiences as natives, combined with their scientific training and objectivity, give them an added advantage in anthropological studies in their own countries. The same applies to American anthropologists studying American culture. As native anthropologists we are frequently full participants as well as observers, often emotionally and intellectually caught up in the events and beliefs we are describing.

One irony of the historical expectations of anthropology is striking. Anthropologists write extensively about foreign areas in which they have spent several years doing field work. Yet is it not even more appropriate for them to use their knowledge of anthropology to try to comprehend a culture they have lived in and observed for a lifetime—a good part of it as an anthropologist? The examples in this chapter demonstrate that I and several of my colleagues deem such native anthropology a challenge and a pleasure.

Native anthropologists must be particularly careful to resist their own emic biases (their prejudices as natives) and to be as objective in describing their own cultures as they are in analyzing others. Thus many of the following examples incorporate an etic, or observer-oriented research strategy (see Chapter 1). Native anthropologists must be aware that natives often see and explain their behavior very differently from the anthropologist. In Chapter 9, in the etic analysis of pig festivals among the Tsembaga Maring and Betsileo tomb-centered ceremonials, you saw that such rituals serve a variety of economic, nutritional, demographic, and other functions that natives do not recognize.

In most of the examples that follow, the etic perspective is taken. Most Americans have probably never considered the possibility that such apparently secular, commercial, and recreational institutions as football, rock music, Walt Disney Enterprises, and fast-food restaurants have things in common with religious beliefs, symbols, and behavior in our own and other societies. Most Americans have probably thought little about why so many young Americans simultaneously appreciate such apparently different events as football games and rock concerts. Yet anthropological techniques usually used to deal with, say, myths of South American Indian tribes and rituals of matrilineal horticulturalists in Zambia, East Africa, can show not only how football and rock are related, but how each relates to equally significant aspects of American ideology. Similarly, techniques developed to analyze rituals and myths in nonindustrial societies can enlighten us about "Star Trek" and its devoted following, science fiction, the Disney organization's contributions to American culture, and our behavior at what most Americans consider the most ordinary places we frequent—fast-food restaurants.

Anthropology textbooks often stress the discipline's value for understanding ourselves; by studying other cultures, they say, correctly, we learn to appreciate, understand, and question our own. However, since only recently has the United States become an area significant to anthropologists, this assertion usually remains undemonstrated. In the following examples it is shown that the very same techniques that anthropologists use in describing and analyzing other cultures can be applied to our own. This chapter will also raise another intriguing possibility. By examining whatever resistance you as an American native may have to accepting these anthropological analyses of your own beliefs, values, and behavior, you may come to see that any natives, in any culture, may have similar reactions to an anthropologist's account of their culture.

Furthermore, Americans may not find the arguments in this chapter convincing. In part this may be because you are a native and know so much more about your own culture than any other. But in part it may also be because in trying to extract culture (*shared* programs for behavior) from a variety of individual opinions, acts, and experiences, we, as anthropologists, depart from areas that can be quantified—such as household composition, population density, poverty, wealth, and socioeconomic variation in general—and enter a more impressionistic domain, one in which analysis sometimes seems as akin to philosophy or to the humanities as to science. Certainly, you will be right in questioning some of the conclusions set forth here. Some are surely debatable, some perhaps just plain wrong. But if they illustrate how anthropology can be used to shed light on aspects of your own life and experience, and used to revise and broaden your understanding of your own culture, they will have served a useful function.

A final word, about culture, ethnocentrism, and native anthropologists is needed on the application of anthropological techniques to American culture. For anthropologists, *culture* means much more than refinement, cultivation, education, and appreciation of the fine arts—its popular usage. Curiously, however, when some anthropologists confront their own culture, they often seem to forget this. They carry an image of themselves as adventurous and broadminded specialists in the unusual, the ethnic, and the exotic and, like other academics and intellectuals, tend to regard aspects of American "pop" culture as trivial and unworthy of serious analysis. In doing so, they demonstrate their own ethnocentrism as American natives and reveal a bias that comes with being members of the academic-intellectual American subculture. According to the values and norms of this subculture, certain aspects of American life are trivial. Afternoon soap operas, which deal with ordinary human problems and attract a daily audience of 18 million, three-fourths of them women

Televisions, which now outnumber toilets in American households, carry the same messages and themes to millions of Americans. Television plays a major role in creating, maintaining, and spreading American national culture. Here, Native American children watch a television program depicting Native Americans. (Michal Heron/Woodfin Camp & Assoc.)

(Bean, 1976), are defined as trivial. In this subculture, fast food, rock, and football are scorned, in that degree of decreasing intensity, but "Masterpiece Theatre" and public broadcasting stations are approved of.

As these examples show, in examining American culture, native anthropologists must be particularly careful to overcome the subcultural bias associated with their own status as academics and intellectuals. That 18 million Americans, mostly women, watch soap operas daily is surely a highly significant sociocultural fact of American life. That 79 million people tuned their televisions to the first annual Super Bowl game (Arens, 1976) is almost as impressive and as important in understanding American culture as the fact that televisions now outnumber toilets in American households. My own research on Michigan college students may be generalizable to other young Americans. They visit McDonald's more often than houses of worship. No more than 5 percent of them had *never* seen a Walt Disney movie. In each case, the number of University of Michigan college students questioned who had never entered a Protestant, Catholic, or Jewish house of worship far exceeded the number who had never eaten at McDonald's, seen an episode of "Star Trek," or attended a rock concert. If true of young Americans generally, as I suspect they are, these highly significant facts about Americans and their culture suggest major twentieth-century modifications in American enculturation patterns. Certainly, any extraterrestrial anthropologist doing field work in the United States would stress them. They represent major, perhaps dominant, themes in contemporary American culture. Surely, they merit anthropological study.

Now that we have given the general problems associated with any anthropological study of American culture, some background information about several aspects of ritual is needed. In American culture, with its many social divisions, certain events, beliefs, and activities, on the surface, appear ordinary and mundane, even profane. However, these components of American culture have some functions and aspects analogous to religious rites and doctrines in our own and other cultures.

Rites of Passage

Early in this century Arnold van Gennep (1960, orig. 1909), a Belgian anthropologist, studied rites of passage in a variety of societies. Passage rites are encountered in every society; they are exemplified by such phenomena as vision quests of certain Native American populations in North America. As boys moved from boyhood to socially recognized manhood, they temporarily separated themselves from their communities to journey alone to the wilderness. After a period of isolation, often accompanied by fasting and drug consumption, the young men would see a vision, which would become their personal guardian spirit. On return to their communities they would be reintegrated as adults. In contemporary societies, rites of passage include confirmations, baptisms, bar mitzvahs, and fraternity hazing. Passage rites do not refer only to such changes in social status as from boyhood to manhood, or from nonmember to fraternity brother, but apply more generally to any change in place, condition, social position, or age. Examining data from a variety of societies, van Gennep generalized that all rites of passage have three phases: separation, margin, and aggregation. Separation is exemplified by the initial detachment of individuals from the group or their initial movement from one place to another; aggregation, by their reentry into society after completion of the rite. More recently, anthropologist Victor Turner (1974) has focused on the marginal period, the position between states, the limbo during which individuals have left one place or state but have not yet entered or joined the next. Van Gennep (1960) used the Latin term *limen* (threshold) to refer to this in-between period, and Turner's designation of it as the *liminal* phase of a passage rite will be used here.

On the basis of data from several societies, Turner (1974) identified generalized attributes of liminality. Liminal individuals occupy ambiguous social positions. They exist apart from the status distinctions and expectations of normal social life, living in a time out of time. They are cut off from normal social intercourse. In contrast to the vision quest, which is individualistic, passage rites are often collective. A group of people — boys undergoing circumcision, fraternity initiates, men attending military boot camps, football players at summer training camps, women becoming nuns — pass through the rites together. Turner points out that liminal periods are ritually demarcated by a variety of contrasts with normal social life. Among the Ndembu of Zambia, whom Turner studied, a newly chosen chief had to undergo a passage rite before taking office. During the

Liminality in a U.S. Marine Corps basic training camp. A collective rite of passage in which initiates are separated from normal society, subjected to a uniform dress (or undress) code, humiliated (harsh haircuts, drawing of blood), and insulted. For other attributes of liminality, see Figure 15.1. (Thomas Höpker/Woodfin Camp & Assoc.)

FIGURE 15.1 Oppositions between liminality and normal social life. (Adapted from Victor W. Turner, *The Ritual Process.* Copyright © 1969 by Victor W. Turner. By permission of Aldine Publishing Co., Chicago.)

Liminality	Normal Social Structure
transition	state
homogeneity	heterogeneity
communitas	structure
equality	inequality
anonymity	names
absence of property	property
absence of status	status
nakedness or uniform dress	dress distinctions
sexual continence or excess	sexuality
minimization of sex distinctions	maximization of sex distinctions
absence of rank	rank
humility	pride
disregard of personal appearance	care for personal appearance
unselfishness	selfishness
total obedience	obedience only to superior rank
sacredness	secularity
sacred instruction	technical knowledge
silence	speech
simplicity	complexity
acceptance of pain and suffering	avoidance of pain and suffering

liminal period, his past and future positions in society were ignored, even reversed, and he was subjected to a variety of insults, harangues, instructions, and humiliations.

Turner lists a number of contrasts or oppositions between liminality and normal social life (see Figure 15.1). Most notable is a social aspect of collective liminality that he calls *communitas.* People who experience liminality together characteristically form an egalitarian community; whatever social distinctions have existed before, or will exist afterwards, are temporarily forgotten. Liminal individuals experience the same treatment and conditions and are expected to act alike. Liminality may be marked ritually and symbolically by reversals of ordinary behavior. Sexual taboos may be intensified or, conversely, sexual excess may be encouraged.

Turner points out that not only is liminality always a temporary part of any passage rite, it may, in certain social contexts, become a permanent attribute of particular groups. This will occur, Turner suggests, in the most socially diverse societies, presumably state-organized societies and particularly modern nations. As in political and economic organization, aspects of behavior that are embedded in, or emerge only temporarily as aspects of, social behavior in nonstate societies emerge as permanent attributes of special-purpose groups in stratified, state-organized societies. Thus, within socially diverse states, religious sects often use liminal characteristics to set themselves off from the rest of the society. Such requirements as humility, poverty, equality, obedience, sexual abstinence, and silence may be conditions of sect membership. The ritual aspect of persons, settings, and events may also be communicated through liminal attributes that set them off as extraordinary—outside normal social space and regular time. Turner's examination of liminality contributes to a useful framework for examining many ritual and quasi-ritual aspects of American culture, including those associated with football.

Football

Football, Americans say, is only a game. Yet it has become one of the most popular spectator sports in the United States. From August to January, from Friday to Monday, Americans can follow football. In places as diverse as Ann Arbor, Michigan, and Los Angeles, California, people spend Saturday traveling to and from, and attending, college football games. Smaller congregations meet for high school games. Vast audiences watch televised football; indeed, more than half the adult population of the United States regularly watches the annual Super Bowl. As anthropologist William Arens (1976) points out, football is clearly not simply a preoccupation of "Middle America," but of all America, and as such is a major aspect of American culture. An interest in football unites Americans regardless of ethnic group; region; state; urban, suburban, or rural residence; religion; political party; job; status; wealth, gender; or sexual preference.

While football originally may have become popular as a vehicle of college spirit, the popularity of contemporary college football and particularly of professional football depends directly on the mass media, especially television. Arens (1976) analyzes reasons for this popularity. Questions often asked are: Is football, with its territorial incursion, hard hitting, and physical violence—occasionally resulting in injury to players—popular because Americans are a violent people? Are Americans naturally bloodthirsty? Are football spectators vicariously realizing their own hostile, violent, and aggressive tendencies? Arens discounts this approach. He points out that football is an almost uniquely American pastime. Although a similar kind of football is played in Canada, it is considerably less popular than in the United States. Baseball has become a popular sport

Football simulates prominent features of contemporary American culture. It also provides an outlet for the frustrations of modern life and reaffirms "traditional American values." Football's emphasis on aggression, shown in this dressing-room photo, echoes American cultural values, not genes. (Ken Heyman)

in the Caribbean, some areas of Latin America, and in Japan. The popularity of basketball is also spreading. And throughout most of the world, soccer is the most popular sport. Arens argues that if football were a particularly effective channel for expressing aggression, it would have spread to many other countries, where people have as many aggressive tendencies and hostile feelings as Americans. Furthermore, he suggests that if a sport's popularity really rested on a bloodthirsty temperament, boxing, a far bloodier sport, would be America's national pastime. Arens concludes that the explanation lies elsewhere, and I agree.

Arens contends that of all the sports, football best represents, or symbolizes in a public context, certain major features of American life. In particular, it echoes group coordination through elaborate variation, specialization, and division of labor—pervasive features of American society and economy. Susan Montague and Robert Morais (1976) take his analysis one step further. They argue that Americans appreciate football because they can recognize in it a miniaturized and simplified version both of the structure of modern industrial organizations and of the behavior deemed appropriate by such business enterprises, and they can master it as such. Bureaucracies, whether in business, universities, or government, are indeed perplexing and mysterious. Ordinary workers, faculty members, and students find it difficult to understand the structure of such organizations as businesses and universities, and to comprehend how decisions are made and rewards allocated.

Montague and Morais link values extolled in football to those associated with success in business. Ideal characteristics of football players, like success-oriented businesspeople, include hard work, diligence, dedication, and denial of individual self-interest for the good of the team ("teamwork"). But, the anthropologists argue, rewards for such behavior in business are not always forthcoming. Because of the complicated and often capricious nature of decision making within large organizations, workers are not always assured that they will be rewarded for their dedication and good work. For precisely this reason football is popular. Any fan can, through careful study and observation, become an expert on the rules, teams, scores, individual statistics, and patterns of play in football.

Even more important, football demonstrates to fans that the values stressed by business really do pay off. Teams whose players and coaches work hardest, show the most team spirit, and best develop and coordinate the talents of their players can be expected to win more often than others. Both teams and players receive large bonuses. Classic capitalist values, which are still presented as guides for success in American business, are represented by and affirmed through football. Football is popular therefore because it is so well suited to the American economy, society, and traditional values.

FOOTBALL AND ROCK MUSIC

Many young Americans are equally devoted to football and to rock music. How can this common interest in such diverse areas be explained? Montague and Morais (1976) attribute the popularity of football

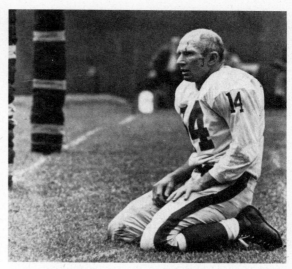

Although football is a team effort, individual achievement is ultimately rewarded, and individual mistakes require atonement. Shown here, dejected quarterback Y. A. Tittle experiences personally the agony of defeat. (Wide World Photos)

and rock, often among the same people, to the association of each phenomenon with an opposite but equally important theme of American life. Football is associated with the *technical* side of American society and the American economy; it provides a simplified model of American industrial organizations and illustrates that business values and appropriate capitalist behavior are rewarded in the end. Rock, on the other hand, can be linked to a long-existing but more recently articulated theme in American culture —the desirability of *creative* expression, the value of doing one's "own thing." Whereas in football, teamwork, diligence, talent, and self-denial are rewarded, in rock, creative expression is rewarded, not only materially (a fact that many rock stars try to play down), but also in the communitas, communion, even love, between audience and star.

Rock and football can coexist in American society and be appreciated by the same people because, despite their contrasting nature, both are essentially "as American as apple pie." The popularity of both rests on changes in the mass media in the mid-twentieth century. Both are totally compatible with the individualistic focus of American society, with the decline of kinship values and a shift to social interactions and associations with nonrelated individuals. Both exalt individualistic values: the individual football player, along with the team, is rewarded for working well with others with money, fame, and fans' appreciation; the individual rock star is rewarded with fans' affection and devotion as well as with wealth and renown.

Rock music and football, although opposites in several concrete ways, are also linked, since both depend on and express common themes and values in contemporary American culture. Consider a series of contrasts or oppositions that, by making rock and football seem like totally different institutions, mask in our minds their common relationship to individualism and other American values. They involve behavior of performers and audiences; symbolism associated with performances and games; and ritual aspects, including liminality. The analysis of similarities and differences between rock and football that follows exemplifies *structural analysis,* a technique of comparison that has recently found favor among American anthropologists.

Structural Analysis

During the past decade, Claude Lévi-Strauss, a prolific French anthropologist, has become a major figure in both European and American anthropology. First in *Structural Anthropology* (1967), and subsequently in several other books, Lévi-Strauss has advocated an approach to social and cultural data known as the structural method of analysis. Lévi-Strauss's *structuralism* rests on his assumption that the human mind has certain universal characteristics and that they reflect common structures of the human brain. Accordingly, he believes that similarities in the brain structures of people everywhere lead them to think similarly no matter what their society or cultural background. Among the universal characteristics are the need to classify: to impose order and arrangement on aspects of nature, on people's relationship to nature, and on the relationships between people. According to Lévi-Strauss, a universal aspect of the need to classify is opposition or contrast. Although many, perhaps most, phenomena are continuous rather than discrete, Lévi-Strauss argues that the mind, because of its need to impose order, makes them more discrete and different than they really are. Things in nature that are continuous, that are quantitatively rather than qualitatively different, are made by classification to seem absolutely different and discrete. Scientific classification, including zoological taxonomy and such

schemes as band-tribe-chiefdom-state, are merely Western academic versions of the universal need to impose order by classifying. One of the most common means of classifying is by *binary opposition.* Good and evil, white and black, old and young, high and low are oppositions that, according to Lévi-Strauss, reflect the human need to convert continuous contrasts into absolute contrasts.

Binary Oppositions between Rock and Football

In contemporary American culture, as Montague and Morais (1976) have pointed out, several binary oppositions differentiate rock and football. Yet rock and football are also similar because they exaggerate, although in different directions, the *same* set of prominent themes in contemporary American culture. Rock and football are associated with polar ends of several contrasts significant in American life. By converting differences of degree into differences of kind — binary oppositions — rock and football set themselves off from each other and from ordinary life. Let us consider some of these binary oppositions. (See Figure 15.2).

Individual versus group. We all do some things alone, others in groups. We are neither total loners nor totally social creatures. However, the contrast between individual and group is converted into a binary opposition, like the other differences that differentiate rock and football. Rock musicians perform individually or in small groups, whereas a football team is a coordinated, highly specialized, tightly integrated group. Football players are regularly replaced during a game; substitutions are allowed. Rock focuses on the individual, even in small groups. The Rolling Stones have become Mick Jagger; the Grateful Dead have become Jerry Garcia. The Beatles began as a group of individual artists and writers but eventually dissolved to allow each to follow his own career.

Creative versus technical. All of us sometimes "do our own thing," sometimes carefully mesh our activities with those of others. But the creative-technical distinction — one of degree — has also become a binary opposition separating rock and football. Rock stresses the individual artist and exemplifies the American value of individual fulfillment through creative expression. Football involves coordination, teamwork, and self-denial, and the submergence of the individual in the social; it reflects the

Rock	Football
1. individual or small-group activity; focus on individual performer even in small groups	1. coordinated, highly specialized, tightly integrated group activity
2. expresses individualistic, creative theme of American culture	2. stresses technoeconomic basis of American industrial society
3. deemphasizes "masculinity" of males and "femininity" of females	3. exaggerates "masculinity" of males and "femininity" of females
4. deemphasis of sexual differences permits heterosexual acts to be mimicked or imitated in performances	4. exaggeration of sexual contrasts permits quasi-homosexual behavior on the field
5. stresses performer's illicit behavior; sexual license; promiscuity expected	5. stresses performers' clean living; sexual prohibitions; abstinence expected
6. audience participates in performance, interacts with performer	6. audience observes performance, rigidly separated from performers
7. performers allowed to consume drugs and alcohol, to behave obscenely	7. audience permitted to consume drugs and alcohol, to behave obscenely
8. preparation stresses technical skills	8. preparation stresses physical skills
9. social, affective rewards	9. individual, material rewards

FIGURE 15.2 Binary oppositions represented in rock concerts and football games.

values of technique, endurance, and skill in American society and economy.

Deemphasis of gender differences versus exaggeration of gender differences. There are contrasts in the typical personalities, dress, and behavior of American males and females, but they are quantitative rather than qualitative. Rock and football deny this, but in opposite ways. Rock tends to deny gender differences, while football exaggerates them. The dress, posture, and gestures of some male rock stars often disguise the fact that they are males. Alice Cooper and David Bowie are the most notable examples of such performers. Female rock performers also depart from traditional American feminine cultural norms; sometimes this is expressed in dress, but it is more obvious in behavior, including loudness and exuberance. Arens (1976) has pointed out that the uniforms of football players exaggerate male anatomy. Shoulder pads are the cultural equivalent of the shoulder manes of adult male baboons. Skin-tight trousers and metal codpieces complete the supermasculine effect. As much a part of the football ritual as the game itself are the ultrafeminine cheerleaders and "pom-pom girls," who are selected more because they meet American standards of beauty and appropriate feminine personality than because they are effective in rousing fan support. An obligatory aspect of a football telecast is the camera pan of attractive young women spectators. In football the differences between male and female are celebrated symbolically; in rock they are hidden or denied.

Heterosexual versus homosexual. By denying sexual differences, rock allows performers to include sexually explicit material in their songs and gestures. A variety of sex acts are imitated, mimicked, and simulated on the stage. Such behavior has evolved from the late Elvis Presley's mild pelvic gyrations of the fifties to Tina Turner's use of the microphone to imitate oral sex (Montague and Morais, 1976). In contrast, because football players exhibit such exaggerated masculinity, their hand holding, hugging, and bottom patting, which in other contexts might suggest homosexual behavior, are socially acceptable. Joe Namath, but not David Bowie, can wear women's panty hose in a television advertisement without raising questions about his sexual preference.

Illicit versus licit. In another binary opposition, rock and football create stereotypes of socially disapproved and approved behavior. Football players are expected to be clean-livers; this is an aspect of their self-denial. Smoking, drinking, drug consumption, and gambling are taboo (Montague and Morais, 1976). Arens (1976) has pointed out similarities between sexual taboos associated with football and ritual prohibitions against sexual relations in other societies. In many societies, men are expected to be sexually continent before a hunt or a raid; even sexual relations with their wives are tabooed for a period established by convention. Football players observe similar sexual taboos. During summer training camp—a liminal period prior to the start of the football season—professional players are isolated from their wives or other women. Both college and professional players are also expected to abstain from sex on the night before a game. Like liminal figures generally, they observe a variety of taboos on eating particular foods, smoking, and drinking. At the University of Michigan, football players, coaches, and staff spend the Friday nights before home games in a local hotel. They read, participate in prayer groups, and watch such movies as *Patton*, which provide lessons in the values associated with football: discipline, teamwork, coordination, dedication, and submission to authority.

A rock star's life style is touted as just the opposite of that of the football player. Rock stars are expected to consume a variety of drugs and to be sexually promiscuous. The teen-age groupie, available for sex after performances, fills a functionally specialized role within this set of expectations. Expression through drugs, sexual excess, and other behavior condemned by the larger society is an aspect of the individualistic, creative focus of rock. Whereas football players symbolize their submersion in society and submission to authority by watching *Patton* and praying together, rock performers use drugs and sex to symbolize their transcendence of society and freedom to do their own thing.

Incorporation versus separation. Both football games and rock performances share with many religious rituals certain aspects of liminality — namely, in being set off from ordinary time and space — but again they do it in different ways. This aspect of football is particularly obvious. Football games normally take place in special-purpose structures intended primarily or exclusively for sports events.

Home games are scheduled at more or less invariant hours on specific days of the week. Football players' liminality is not limited to their separation from ordinary social life the night before the game, but lasts until the game is over. Audience and players are physically and ritually separated in the football stadium. Barriers of grass or astroturf clearly demarcate the field from surrounding stands, and the actual playing surface is marked off by lines. Total separation of audience and players is expected. Television commentators serve as guardians of the game's morality, scolding fans who throw paper, smoke bombs, and liquor bottles on the field. Nets behind goal posts protect the game's most sacred object from defilement by contact with the audience. Only at game's end, and particularly after a very important game or at the conclusion of the season, are fans allowed on the field. The separation of players and spectators finally ends as fans congratulate the players; the end of the separation is symbolized by tearing down the goal posts.

In contrast to football, where players are temporarily isolated from normal social life at specified times of the year and days of the week, in rock, performers are more *permanently* isolated from society by the expectation of individualism and excess in their life styles. Yet the separation of spectators and performers in football is inverted in the rock concert, which, if successful, becomes a true communion of performer and audience (Montague and Morais,

Fans' emotional reactions, fully comparable to the emotional effervescence that often arises when rituals are performed, at a rock concert in Shea Stadium in New York. (Ken Heyman)

1976). Ideally, the audience and rock performer become one; the performer is rewarded in love and community for creative achievements. Stars sometimes move into the audience, touching their fans and letting their fans touch them. The emotions generated during a rock concert are more sensual, and through the performer's instigation, more sexual than during a football game.

Performers' excess versus audience's excess. In football—at least in college football—players and fans are expected to show opposite types of behavior. For the players, the game is a time to demonstrate that clean living translates into victory, but for spectators it is conventionally a time of excess, expressed through continuous ingestion of consciousness-altering substances—mostly alcohol and marijuana. Turner (1974) reports that among the Ndembu of Zambia, customary parts of certain rituals are collective expressions of obscenity. So, too, at University of Michigan football games, spectators are allowed to violate normal taboos against certain words, shouting in mass "Ah, Shit" when the home team fails to gain necessary yardage. Other four-letter words are sometimes spelled out ("Gimme an F . . ."). The contrast between the expressive behavior of performer and audience is less marked in a rock concert, aiding the communion that is supposed to develop. Still, stars often consume drugs as part of their performance. Although spectators may smoke or drink, especially at outdoor concerts, they have come to be "turned on" more by the performance than by drugs.

How the Oppositions Are Inverted

Following an observation by Montague and Morais (1976) it can be seen that certain of these oppositions between football and rock are inverted (turned around) in events and behavior before and after the performances themselves. Football as technical has been opposed to rock as creative. Yet preparation for the season—summer training camp—stresses football's *physical* rather than technical aspects. Sports reporters dwell on the exercises and physical preparation of training camp. Technical aspects of football—gameplans, well-executed plays, and analysis through instant replays and statistics—are stressed only during the actual football season. A rock performance projects an image of a spontaneous happening, of a bunch of creative people getting it together, that masks the hours and years of training

necessary to produce effective musicians and performances. Indeed, the affective, creative feeling of a rock performance is built in part on much *technical* labor involving setting up and testing sophisticated electronic equipment (Montague and Morais, 1976). In preparation rather than performance, then, the opposition is partially inverted: rock as technical opposes football as physical, if not creative.

Montague and Morais (1976) point out that a similar partial inversion applies to what occurs after the actual performances—to the rewards given to successful performers. The football team is a *social* unit, the rock star an *individual*. Yet the rewards for individual creativity in rock are social—that is, rock stars aim to create a community of self and audience. For football players, social demands are temporary and seasonal; during training and the actual season, they intensify as each game approaches. The life style of rock stars is more permanent; to satisfy their cultural image they must always surround themselves with others—groupies, managers, technicians, and assorted hangers-on. The formal association of football player–pompom girl ends with the game, whereas the formal role of the groupie comes after the concert is over. The opposition of football as social and rock as individual is thus inverted outside the performance, where rock becomes social and football more individualistic. The best player on the team is ultimately rewarded as an individual. He becomes a superstar, and reaps benefits from television commercials, movie roles, and other business interests.

In an industrial, stratified, individualistic society, for the very talented, rock and football are, finally, alternate routes to the same ends—money, fame, and perhaps power. The symbols, rituals, and values associated with football make Joe Namath and O. J. Simpson effective salespeople. The image of the rock performer as a creative, liminal individualist makes David Bowie a most appropriate choice for Nicholas Roeg's film *The Man Who Fell to Earth*. In it Bowie is an extraterrestrial visitor who becomes an iconoclastic Howard Hughes, ultimately corrupted by the excesses of American life—particularly gin and television.

Broader Themes of Opposition in American Life

Lévi-Strauss has shown how specific oppositions contained in the myths and social structures of nonindustrial peoples can be linked to larger-scale oppositions that reverberate throughout their lives and cultures. Consider briefly now how the specific structural analysis of rock and football just given might be enlarged to reveal broader themes of opposition in American life.

We might say, for example, that rock is to football as night is to day. This opposition is derived from a number of material and symbolic aspects. Football games are usually played—at least in colder areas of the United States—during the day; rock concerts are usually held at night. Americans symbolically associate day with cleanliness and propriety, night with impropriety, illicit activity, and murkiness. Or we might say that football is to rock as cold is to hot. Football is a cold-season game, whereas rock concerts, particularly those held outdoors, are associated with summer and California. Rock— symbolically stressing affect, sexuality, vibrant colors, loud music, and psychedelic patterns—seems, in Marshall McLuhan's terms, a "hot" medium. Football—with its technical aspects; its exclusion of women from the game, and of fans of both sexes from the playing field; its limited, traditional, and clearly bounded field and uniform colors; and its emphasis on clean living—suggests a "cold" medium, again in McLuhan's terms. Surely a rock concert comes closer to most Americans' image of hell than does football.

Rock is left and football is right. Americans classify political positions on a scale of left-right opposition. Republicans are supposed to represent right, Democrats left. (Americans' fondness for binary oppositions can be seen in the labels we use for people whose politics differ from our own. The opinions of people that we label "wild-eyed commie bastards" or "fascist pigs" are not as different from our own as these terms imply.) Rock stars tend to support Democrats or positions to the left of Democrats; football players are thought more likely to support Republicans and to take right-of-center stands. Republican Richard Nixon cultivated ties with football coaches and used football terms to describe nonfootball situations. Republican Gerald Ford was a college football player. Republican Ronald Reagan's most famous movie role was as a football player. On the other side, during the 1976 Presidential campaign, Democrats Jimmy Carter and Jerry Brown both actively sought the public support of rock stars.

Less easy to demonstrate is the opposition of rock as feminine and football as masculine. In our culture, men seem traditionally to be more concerned than women with stressing differences between the sexes and with keeping sex roles distinct. Rock breaks down traditional symbols of sex differences, whereas football exaggerates them. In our conventional images of male-female distinctions, women are seen as more emotional, affective, and creative— warmer—and men are seen as more rational, distant, and technically oriented—colder. Again this suggests that football and rock are associated with oppositions prominent in contemporary American culture—in this case, masculine versus feminine, respectively.

Thus the specific binary oppositions that differentiate rock and football link up with larger themes of opposition in American culture. Through association with opposite ends of the same contrasts, rock and football are set off from each other and from other domains of American life, granting to each its own special niche in our culture. Although rock and football symbolize different extremes, we should not lose sight of the similarities that explain their popularity and significance to contemporary Americans. Both rock and football exaggerate—differently—the same cultural themes. Both express the individualistic focus of contemporary American society. Both rock and football are big business, and the popularity of both rests on mid-twentieth century changes in the mass media, as is true in the examples that follow.

As an American native, you probably question this structural anthropological perspective on football and rock, just as South American Indian informants might doubt a structural analysis of their important myths. Structural analysis aims not at *explaining* otherwise hidden relations, themes, and connections among aspects of culture, but at uncovering them. It thus differs sharply in its aims and results from the methods of gathering, interpreting, and explaining data used in previous chapters. Structuralism is as akin to the humanities as to science. In fact, structuralist techniques are now widely used in literature and art as well as in anthropology, again illustrating anthropology's holism—its links to other disciplines. Any structural analysis is difficult to confirm. How one chooses which of two or more structural analyses is more accurate or more revealing usually reflects personal opinion. But after thinking about rock versus football and their relationships to American culture in terms of structural analysis, one can never again view rock as merely a form of entertainment or of football as only a game. Structural analysis can, I believe, be enlightening as one among many tools available to the anthropologist.

WALT DISNEY AS CREATOR: WALT DISNEY WORLD AS SHRINE

American natives think of football as "only a game" and rock music as one among many forms of entertainment. Along the same lines, most also think of Walt Disney as a highly successful businessman whose commercial empire has been built on movies, television programs, and amusement parks. Again, however, etic analysis reveals that there is much more to Walt Disney Productions than most Americans have recognized. Specifically, our common exposure to Disney products provides a highly significant common enculturative experience for contemporary Americans, particularly for those born after 1937, when *Snow White and the Seven Dwarfs*, Disney's first full-length cartoon, was released. Furthermore, there is a quasi-religious aspect to our relationship to Disney and his works; this emerges most clearly in Americans' behavior at the two Disney amusement parks, Disneyland, in Anaheim, California, and Walt Disney World, near Orlando, Florida. The following account is intended to illustrate certain similarities between visits to these amusement parks and pilgrimages to such religious shrines as Mecca, the holy city of Islam; Lourdes in France; Fátima in Portugal; and, particularly, Bom Jesus da Lapa in the arid *sertão* of northeastern Brazil (see Gross, 1971). Since I have never been to Disneyland, my observations are based on several trips—as participant and observer—to Walt Disney World.

The quasi-religious attributes of Walt Disney World rest on Americans' prior exposure to other, nationally available products of the Disney organization. As a whole these products, transmitted through our mass media, constitute one of the most powerful sets of quasi-mythological symbols found in American culture. Their symbolic position rests in part on a quasi-deification, aided by Disney Enterprises, of Walt Disney himself. Disney became, for many Americans, one of our country's greatest geniuses. In one person were combined the contrasting themes of creativity (as in rock) versus coordination and technical skills (as in football). Walt Disney, in Lévi-Strauss's (1967) terms, mediates the American cultural opposition between creativity and technicality. Animation, an extremely technical art

involving precise coordination and teamwork, became the primary medium for his creativity.

For many American children, Walt Disney's death in 1966 occasioned feelings of sorrow and emptiness that could have been rivaled, perhaps, only by the demise of Santa Claus. Childhood's principal mythmaker was dead. In fact, Disney's death is sometimes even denied, as in the continuing rumor that he is not dead, but frozen, cryogenetically preserved, set to rise again once an effective cure for cancer has been found.

Disney's influence on Americans has survived his death. His classic movies are regularly rereleased; noncartoon full-length films have been shown on national television; cartoon characters live on in short features, television programs, advertising, and—in the flesh—at the Disney amusement parks. Though the creator was mortal, his vision has posthumously guided the organization; indeed, he left his successors a plan. This scheme included future movies and other entertainment projects, as well as completion, to his specifications, of an obvious shrine to his memory—Walt Disney World. The willingness of Americans to journey hundreds or thousands of miles to Disneyland or Walt Disney World reflects decades of work in preprogramming our populace in Disney lore.

Particularly important in Disney lore are the images of childhood fantasy—the cartoon characters, often unusual humans and humanlike animals—that continue as very important components of the mythology of American childhood. A common vision of a witch is Snow White's stepmother, particularly as she holds a poisoned apple. *Snow White* again provides our image of dwarfs, Peter Pan's Tinkerbell of fairies, Captain Hook of pirates. Perfect princes and princesses are modeled on those in *Snow White*, *Cinderella*, and *Sleeping Beauty*. Our fears of a mother's death are partially molded by *Bambi*.

The Disney Mythology

The mythology disseminated by the Disney organization shows many similarities with myths of other cultures, and can be analyzed in the same anthropological, particularly structuralist, terms. In applying the structural method to Native American (that is, North and South American Indian) myths, Lévi-Strauss shows that binary oppositions are often resolved by mediating figures—entities that somehow link opposites. Consider an opposition, of nature to culture, that is a concern of humans everywhere. It was shown in Chapter 2 that many differences between humans and other animals are differences of degree rather than differences of kind, but religions and myths, for hundreds of thousands of years and throughout the world, have been concerned with demonstrating the opposite—that humans stand apart from nature, that people are unique. The opposition between the human—the cultural—and nature may be modeled in myth or religion on any one of the major attributes of culture: speech ("In the beginning was the word"), technology (Prometheus stole fire from the gods), thought (the soul), or knowledge (the fall of Adam and Eve). Human knowledge of good and evil is opposed to the innocence of animals. Many anthropologists overlook similarities between other primates and humans and still try to render us distinct by arguing that only *Homo* has culture.

In the myths that Lévi-Strauss has analyzed, oppositions are often resolved mythically by mediating figures. Animals, for example, are given human abilities, thus bridging the opposition between culture and nature. In Genesis a cultural, bipedal, talking, lying snake brings culture and nature closer together. Adam and Eve are, in the beginning, innocent parts of nature, yet they are unique because of their creation in God's image. The snake encourages original sin, which keeps humans unique, but in a far less exalted way. The punishment for eating forbidden fruit is physical labor; people are pitted in a struggle with nature. That humans are a part of nature, while at the same time different from other natural beings, is explained by the serpent-mediator's role in the fall. Note that the fall of humanity is also paralleled in the fall of the serpent—from culture-bearing creature to belly-crawling animal.

In Lévi-Strauss's terms, the principal purpose or function of myth may be to mediate an opposition, to resolve a logical contradiction. Mediating figures and events may resolve such oppositions or contradictions as culture versus nature by showing that just as mythical animals can have human abilities and thus be cultural, people, while different from nature, are also part of nature. They are like animals in many ways, dependent on natural resources and participants in natural systems.

Walt Disney himself bridged the American cultural opposition between creativity and technicality, and the universal human concern with explaining and overcoming a perceived opposition between culture and nature is manifest in Disney creations. Humans stand in opposition to other animals. We have culture, we make things, talk, rely on learning, have souls, laugh, smile, joke, lie—these are some of the contrasts used by scientists, theologians, and ordinary people to distinguish humans from "dumb animals," to assert our uniqueness. The way that contemporary Americans think about animals, not so much by denying our own superiority to them as by raising them to our own level—a cultural level—owes much to the Disney organization. Americans, told by traditional religions about souls, animistically confer souls on their pets, sending their remains to animal cemeteries and their spirits, some children suppose, to animal heavens.

Interacting with larger trends of American life, Disney creations bridge the opposition between culture and nature. Disney confers a host of human attributes on his animated (*anima*, Latin "soul") nonhuman characters—talking, laughing, tricking, bumbling, lying, singing, friendship, family life. In most of his movies, in fact, the animals—and witches, dwarfs, fairies, pirates, and other not-quite-human characters—deny the opposition of culture and nature by having more human qualities than the stereotypically perfect heroes or heroines. Such "supporting characters" are remembered best because they are used not just to personify, but usually also to exaggerate, basic human imperfections. In *Snow White* a disguised and distorted witch-stepmother is evil incarnate. The dwarfs' names—Bashful, Sleepy, and the rest—read like a sanitized, child's version of the Seven Deadly Sins. *Lady and the Tramp* is a story about dogs who exaggerate American sex-role stereotypes of the 1950s.

In *Cinderella* the nature-culture opposition is inverted; mice—natural (undomesticated) animals that are ordinarily considered pests and inimical to humans—are endowed with speech and other cultural attributes and become Cinderella's loyal friends. The cat, ordinarily a part of culture (domesticated) becomes a dark creature of evil (named Lucifer) who almost blocks Cinderella's own transformation from domestic servant into princess. The transformation of Cinderella, a woman, is aided by *man's* best friend —a dog.

The reversal of the normal opposition, that is, cat-culture-good versus mouse-nature-evil—demonstrates how, through Disney characterization, the opposition of culture and nature is overcome. Similarly, just as natural animals in Disney films are depicted as cultural creatures, people are often represented as closer to nature than we normally are. In several Disney films human actors are used to portray close relationships between children and such undomesticated animals as raccoons, foxes, bears, or wolves. His choice of Kipling's *The Jungle Book* as subject matter for a cartoon feature illustrates the second means of dealing with the nature-culture opposition.

A Pilgrimage to Walt Disney World

With Disney as quasi-deified creator and mythmaker for so many Americans, his shrines could hardly fail. A variety of distinct religious systems focus on particular sacred sites. Infertile Betsileo women in the highlands of central Madagascar seek fecundity by spilling the blood of a sacrificial cock before particular phallic stones. Australian totems are associated with holy sites where, in mythology, they first emerged from the ground. Sacred groves are shared reference points that provide symbolic unity for otherwise dispersed clans among the Jie of Uganda (Gulliver, 1974, orig. 1965). A visit to Mecca is an obligation of Islam. Miraculous cures are sought at shrines like Lourdes and Fátima associated with the mythology of Roman Catholicism. In the arid *sertão* of northeastern Brazil, more than 20,000 pilgrims journey each August 6 to fulfill their vows to a wooden statue in a cave—Bom Jesus da Lapa. During the Bicentennial year, millions of Americans flocked to Philadelphia's Independence Hall, Washington's Lincoln and Jefferson Memorials and Washington monument, to worship national ancestors, remember their achievements, and reaffirm national solidarity. Thousands of Americans waited in line in front of the National Archives to view a historical artifact—the Declaration of Independence—and to sign their names on a register to be put in a time capsule that will be opened in the twenty-first century. And virtually every day of every year, thousands of American families travel long distances, and often invest significant amounts of time and money, to experience Disneyland and Walt Disney World.

A conversation with anthropologist Alexander Moore first prompted me to think of Walt Disney World as analogous in some respects to the pilgrimage centers of the world's major religions; and the behavior, demeanor, and experiences of the millions of Americans who have visited or will visit it as comparable to the behavior of religious pilgrims. On the basis of his field work at Disney World, Moore pointed out, for example, a striking similarity between that center and Mecca: division of the shrine into two distinct domains, an inner, sacred center and an outer, more secular domain. In Walt Disney World, appropriately enough, the inner, sacred area is known as "The Magic Kingdom."

Non-Disney motels, restaurants, and camping grounds dot the approach to Disney World; they become increasingly concentrated as one nears the park. As you enter the park, a few miles along World Drive, a sign on the right side of the road in-

The Bicentennial celebration was an unusual unifying experience in American culture, with celebrations throughout the United States, an Independence Day marathon on national television, and millions of pilgrimages to Washington, D.C. Here, natives imitate national ancestors. (Lucien Aigner/Monkmeyer Press)

structs you to turn to a specified AM radio station. A recording played continuously throughout the day gives information about where and how to park and how to proceed on the journey to the Magic Kingdom. It also promotes new Magic Kingdom activities and special attractions such as "America on Parade" and "Senior American Days." Travelers enter the mammoth parking lot by driving through a structure like a turnpike toll booth. As they pay the parking fee, they receive a brochure describing Disney attractions located both inside and outside the central area. (Camping grounds, lakes, islands, and an "international shopping village" are located in the park's outlying areas.) Sections of the parking lot bear totemlike designations: Minnie, Goofy, Pluto, and Chip 'n' Dale, each with several numbered rows. Uniformed attendants direct drivers to parking places, making sure that cars park within the marked spaces and that every space is filled in order. As visitors emerge from their cars, they are directed to open-air, trainlike buses called "trams." Lest they forget where their automobiles are parked, they are told, as they board the tram, to remember Minnie, Pluto, or whichever mythological figure has become temporary guardian of their car. Many travelers spend the first minute of their tram ride ritually reciting "Minnie, Minnie, Minnie, Minnie," memorizing their automobile's location. Leaving the tram, visitors hurry to booths where they purchase ticket booklets granting entrance to the Magic Kingdom and its attractions ("adventures"). They then pass through turnstiles behind the ticket sales booths and prepare to be transported, by "express" monorail or ferryboat, to the Magic Kingdom itself.

Because the approach to the central area occurs in gradual, definite stages, the division of Walt Disney World into outer, secular space and inner, sacred space is not clear-cut. This gradual entry into the center of Walt Disney World can be compared to Judaism's conception of the zonation of sacred space radiating out from Jerusalem. In orthodox Judaism, Jerusalem is conceived as the center (navel) of the world. In the center of Jerusalem is the Temple, in the center of which is the altar, in the center of which is the ark, and in front of which is the foundation stone through which humans are linked to heaven. (An interesting discussion of the relationship between this religious world view and the Sunday morning bagel ritual of many Jewish Americans can be found in Regelson, 1976.) Sanctity is concentrated at the center, and the zones closing concen-

trically inward become gradually, rather than abruptly, more sacred. In the central Disney World area, even after one has passed parking lot and turnstiles, a still secular zone, where central hotels, beaches, and boating areas are located, intervenes before the Magic Kingdom. Visitors can take a "local" monorail to a hotel, but most choose the express monorail to the Magic Kingdom, a futuristic mode of transportation, rather than the alternative, the ferry boat.

Aboard the express monorail, which accomplishes for most visitors the transition between outer, more secular areas and the Magic Kingdom, similarities between Walt Disney World pilgrims and participants in passage rites become especially obvious. Rites of passage, remember, involve transitions in space as well as in age or social status. Disney pilgrims who ride the express monorail exhibit, as one might expect of a transition from secular to sacred space (a magic kingdom), many of the attributes that Turner (1974) associates with liminal states. Like liminal periods in other passage rites, during the transition aboard the monorail all prohibitions that apply anywhere else in Disney World are intensified. In the secular areas and in the Magic Kingdom itself, people are allowed to smoke and eat, and in the secular areas they can consume alcohol, have sexual intercourse (in hotel rooms), and go shoeless—but all these things are tabooed aboard the monorail. Like liminal travelers through other passage rites, Disney pilgrims temporarily relinquish control over their own destinies. Herded like cattle through gates leading to sections of the monorail, passengers enter a place apart from ordinary space, a time out of time, in which social distinctions disappear, in which everyone is reduced to a common level. As the monorail departs, a voice prepares the pilgrims for what is to come, enculturating them in the lore and standards of Walt Disney World.

Typical, too, according to Turner (1974) of liminal periods are reversals of the sexual aspects of everyday secular life and, at the end of liminality, the appearance of symbols of the passenger's ritual rebirth. Extraterrestrial anthropologists studying behavior on the monorail might note that although sexual abstinence is prescribed, major sexual and rebirth symbolism is an aspect of the ride. As the express monorail speeds *through* the Contemporary Resort Hotel, travelers facing forward observe an enormous tiled mural that covers an entire wall of the hotel. Just before the monorail reaches the hotel, but much more clearly after it emerges, travelers espy Walt Disney World's primary symbol, Cinderella's castle. In Freudian terms, this juxtaposition of castle and penetration might well be seen as a symbolic representation of sexual intercourse; and the emergence from the mural into full view of the Magic Kingdom might be viewed as a simulation of rebirth. The monorail, one might note, is simultaneously male and female. It is phallic-shaped, yet at the same time is the womb in which passengers are carried from a secular state to rebirth in the sacred domain.

Many readers may find this symbolic analysis far-fetched, but it is included to illustrate, using American natives as examples, techniques that anthropologists use to describe symbols associated with religious rituals in our own and other societies. As in the structural analysis of rock and football, such analyses of symbols permit a variety of alternative interpretations, and it is difficult to judge which is best. However, even if this analysis of monorail symbolism is rejected, other parts of the analysis confirm similarities between visits to Walt Disney World, on the one hand, and "religious" pilgrimages and passage rites, on the other.

Within the Magic Kingdom

Once the monorail pulls into the Magic Kingdom station, the transition is complete. Passengers emerge on their own; direction by attendants, so prominent at the other end of the line, is conspicuously absent. Walking down a ramp, travelers pass through another turnstile; a transit building where lockers, phones, rest rooms, strollers, and wheelchairs are available; and a circular open area. They find themselves in the Magic Kingdom, walking down "Main Street, U.S.A."

The Magic Kingdom itself invites comparison with shrines and ostensibly religious rites. A. R. Radcliffe-Brown (1965, orig. 1952) and several other anthropologists have argued that the major social function of religious rites is to reaffirm and thus to maintain social solidarity among participants, members of the congregation. Radcliffe-Brown's arguments about the anxiety-producing and dispelling aspects of rituals have been discussed in Chapter 9. Turner (1974) suggests that certain rituals among the Ndembu of Tanzania serve a *mnemonic* function (they make people remember). Women's belief that they can be afflicted and made ill by spirits of their deceased matrilineal kinswomen leads them to take part in rites that reaffirm the values of matrilineality by reminding women of their ancestors. Ancestor worship in any society serves a similar mnemonic purpose.

Similar observations can be made about Walt Disney World. Frontierland, Liberty Square, Main Street, U.S.A., Tomorrowland, and Fantasyland—the major sections of the Magic Kingdom—not only remind pilgrims of the important historical values on

Walt Disney and his works mediate the American cultural oppositions between the creative and the technical and between nature and culture. Shown here, Disneyland pilgrims photograph humans who are portraying the Seven Dwarfs. (Georg Gerster/Rapho/Photo Researchers, Inc.)

which America is purported to be founded, but also juxtapose and link together, through the creative vision of Walt Disney, the past, present, and future; childhood and adulthood; the real and the unreal. Many of the adventures, or rides, particularly Space Mountain—an innovative but frightening roller coaster—can be compared to anxiety-producing rites. This anxiety is ultimately dispelled when pilgrims realize that they have survived simulated speeds of ninety miles an hour.

Detaching oneself from American culture, one might ask how a Betsileo visitor would view Disney World adventures, particularly those based on fantasy. Among the Betsileo, and in other nonindustrial societies, witches are actual people—parts of reality rather than of fantasy. Peasants in Brazil and elsewhere *believe in* witches, werewolves, and nefarious creatures of the night. A Betsileo would probably find it difficult to understand why Americans voluntarily take rides designed to produce uncertainty and fright.

Pilgrims agree implicitly, during their visit to Disney World, to constitute a temporary community, to spend a few hours or days observing the same rules, sharing experiences, and behaving alike. They share a common social status as pilgrims, waiting for hours in line, presenting tickets to attendants.

Yet the structure and attractions of the Magic Kingdom also relate to higher levels of sanctity, representing, recalling, and reaffirming not only Walt Disney's creative acts, but values of American society at large. In the Hall of Presidents, considered one of the Magic Kingdom's major attractions, people silently and reverently view a display of our national ancestors—moving, talking, lifelike dummies. Like Ndembu rites, aspects of the Magic Kingdom make us remember. Not only are we made to recall presidents and American history, but such familiar characters in children's literature as Tom Sawyer are brought to mind. And, of course, we meet the cartoon characters who, in the person of costumed humans, walk around the Magic Kingdom, posing for photographs with children. The juxtaposition of past, present, future, and fantastic represents eternity and argues that our nation, our people, our technological expertise, and our beliefs, our myths, and our values will endure. Even dress codes for Disney World employees reaffirm the stereotype of the clean-cut American. The whole ambience of Disney World reiterates the value of coupling industrial technology with such character traits as clean living, enthusiasm, imagination, creativity, and vision. Disney propaganda uses Walt Disney World itself to illustrate what American creativity joined with technical know-how can accomplish. Students in American history are told how our ancestors carved a new land out of wilderness; similarly, Walt Disney is presented as a person who created cosmos out of chaos, a structured world out of the undeveloped chaos of Florida's central interior.

A few other links between Walt Disney World and religious and quasi-religious symbols and shrines should be examined. Disney World's most potent symbol is Cinderella's castle, complete with a moat where pilgrims throw coins and make wishes. On my first pilgrimage to Walt Disney World I was surprised to discover that the castle has a largely symbolic function—as a trademark or logo for Walt Disney World—and little utilitarian value. A few shops on the ground floor are open to the public, but the rest of the castle is off-limits. In thinking about the function of Cinderella's castle, I recall a lecture given at the University of Michigan in 1976 by British anthropologist Sir Edmund Leach. In describing the ritual surrounding his dubbing as knight, Leach noted that Queen Elizabeth stood in front of the British throne and did not, in accordance with our stereotype of monarchs, sit on it. Leach concluded that the primary value of the British throne is to represent, to make concrete, something enduring but abstract—the British sovereign's right to rule. Similarly, Cinderella's castle offers concrete testimony to the eternal aspects of Walt Disney creations.

A Pilgrimage to a "Religious" Shrine

A brief comparison of Walt Disney World with Bom Jesus da Lapa, a shrine center in the arid backlands of Bahia state, Brazil, will point out further similarities between the former and "religious" pilgrimage sites. Normally a town of some 8,000 people, Bom Jesus da Lapa is isolated like Walt Disney World in the interior of its state but experiences an annual influx of more than 20,000 pilgrims on August 6. The patron saint, Bom ("Good") Jesus, is represented by a wooden statue that stands atop an altar in a cave. Like Cinderella's castle, a well-known landmark—a gray limestone outcrop pitted with caves—identifies Bom Jesus to pilgrims. Gross (1971) compares this symbol to a medieval fantasy.

Gross found that most pilgrims had come to Bom

Pilgrims worshipping at Mecca, the holy city of Islam. As at Mecca, Jerusalem, and other religious centers, there is a gradual transition from secular to sacred space (the Magic Kingdom) at Walt Disney World. (Marc & Evelyne Bernheim/ Woodfin Camp & Assoc.)

Miraculous cures are sought, and reported, at Lourdes, just as during performances by itinerant faith healers in the contemporary United States. Interviews with visitors to Walt Disney World would probably reveal a similar variety of motives for making the trip. "Pleasing the children" would probably be a frequent reason. Also, parents offer a trip to Disney World as a major reward for children's behavior and achievements or, perhaps, as an incentive to help them recover from long illness. Most Americans probably visit Walt Disney World for amusement, recreation, and vacation. In this sense, they differ from pilgrims to religious shrines. They do not appear to believe that a visit to Disney World has curative properties, although they may feel that vacations are good for their health. Nonetheless, local television news programs have presented human interest stories about communities pooling their resources to help terminally ill children and their families visit Disney World or Disneyland. Thus, although a visit to Walt Disney World is not conceived by Americans as curative, it is regarded as being an appropriate last wish.

Even when people undertake "religious" pilgrimages, however, their motives may not be exclusively or even primarily "religious," as Gross's account of the Bom Jesus da Lapa pilgrimage illustrates. Be-

Pilgrims to Disneyland. Within the Magic Kingdom, Cinderella's castle serves no utilitarian function, but symbolizes the enduring nature of Walt Disney and his creations. (American Airlines)

Jesus da Lapa to fulfill vows, usually concerned with health. They pray to Bom Jesus and promise to make the pilgrimage to his shrine if their request is granted. Prayer requests are varied. Bom Jesus may be asked to help cure a specific malady, to guarantee a safe journey, to enable lovers to stop quarreling. To further fulfill their vows, pilgrims make offerings at the altar. If the prayer concerned a successful marriage, a photograph of the happy couple may be offered. People who have prayed for a broken leg to heal may leave X-rays or casts of the leg at the altar of Bom Jesus. (Transfers of body parts also go on at Disney World. Children bring home hats representing Mickey Mouse's ears and Donald Duck's beak.)

The kinds of reasons people give for making pilgrimages vary from shrine to shrine. Most people go to Bom Jesus da Lapa to fulfill vows made in prayers. A visit to Mecca is an obligation of Islam.

cause there are so many pilgrims to Bom Jesus, most have no chance to accomplish the ostensible purpose of their journey, to worship the wooden statue of Bom Jesus da Lapa. They are rapidly herded by chapel officials past the altar, just as Disney visitors are corralled into tram and monorail. Many pilgrims are forced to move on to make way for others before they have a chance to kneel. Furthermore, Bom Jesus and Disney World have similar commercial and recreational aspects. A variety of souvenirs, not limited to church-related icons, are sold to Bom Jesus pilgrims, as in Disney World. In fact, the Bom Jesus pilgrim spends little time in religious contemplation. Several kinds of entertainment come to Bom Jesus along with the pilgrims: traveling circuses, trained boa constrictors, vaudeville acts, roulette wheels and other gambling devices, and singing troubadors. During the height of the pilgrimage, Bom Jesus sports more than a dozen brothels. In fact, Americans might find Walt Disney World, with its celebration of the values of clean living, more ascetic and religious than the Bom Jesus "religious" shrine. It is not unlikely that similar nonreligious activities and a similar representation of other-than-religious motives characterize popular shrines and pilgrims elsewhere.

Many Americans believe that recreation and religion are distinct and incompatible domains. On the basis of my own field work in Brazil and Madagascar, and from reading about other societies, I believe this separation to be both ethnocentric and false. Betsileo tomb-centered ceremonials are times when the living and the dead are joyously reunited; when people get drunk, sing and dance, gorge themselves, and enjoy sexual license. Perhaps the gray, sober, and ascetic aspects of many religious events in the contemporary United States, in taking the fun out of religion, force us unwittingly to find our religion in fun—to seek in such apparently secular contexts as Disney amusement parks, rock concerts, and football games what other people find in their rites, beliefs, and ceremonies.

This account of Disney World exemplifies an etic analysis. Walt Disney has not been viewed as a merely commercial figure nor his amusement parks as simply recreational domains. Rather, through a measure of anthropological detachment, a deeper level of attachment between Americans, Walt Disney, and his creations has been described. The implication is *not* that Americans' relationship to Disney constitutes a religion. But through observa-

tion of behavior and beliefs, and through comparison with pilgrims in other parts of the world, similarities between passage rites, religious pilgrimages, and rituals, on the one hand, and our relationship to Disney, on the other, have been noted. Disney, his amusement parks, and his creations constitute a powerful complex of enculturative forces in contemporary American society. Still another example of common American ritual can be found in an even more unlikely commercial setting, the fast-food restaurant chain.

MCDONALD'S AS MYTH, SYMBOL, AND RITUAL

Each day, on the average, a new McDonald's restaurant opens somewhere in the world. The number of McDonald's outlets today surpasses the total number of fast-food restaurants in the United States in 1945. In barely more than twenty years McDonald's has grown from a single hamburger stand in San Bernardino, California, into today's international web of outlets—more than 4,000 of them—located throughout the United States and in such foreign countries as Japan, Hong Kong, Mexico, France, Sweden, England, Germany, and Australia. In 1972, annual sales of $1.3 billion propelled McDonald's past Kentucky Fried Chicken as the world's most successful fast-food chain, a position it has held ever since. Today's sales exceed $3 billion a year.

Have factors less obvious to American natives than relatively low cost, fast service, cleanliness, and taste contributed to McDonald's success? Could it be that natives—in consuming the products and propaganda of McDonald's—are not just eating or watching television, but are experiencing something comparable in certain respects to participation in religious rituals? To answer this question we must briefly consider the nature of ritual.

Anthropologist Roy Rappaport (1974) mentions several features that distinguish rituals from other behavior. Rituals, first, are formal—stylized, repetitive, and stereotyped. They are performed in special (sacred) places and occur at set times. Rituals include liturgical orders—set sequences of words and actions laid down by someone other than the current performers. All these features link rituals to plays, but there are important differences. Plays have audiences rather than participants; actors are only *portraying* something, whereas ritual performers—who make up congregations—are *in earnest*. Rituals also convey information about participants and their cultural traditions. Performed year after year, generation after generation, rituals translate into observable action enduring messages, values, and sentiments. Rituals are social acts. Although inevitably some participants are more strongly committed to the beliefs on which the rituals are founded than others, just by taking part in a joint public act, the performers signal that they accept an order that transcends their status as mere individuals.

In the view of some anthropologists, including Rappaport himself, such secular institutions as McDonald's are not at all comparable to rituals. Rituals, they argue, involve special emotions, nonutilitarian intentions, and supernatural entities, which are not characteristic of Americans' participation in McDonald's. But other anthropologists define ritual more broadly. Writing about football, Arens (1976) points out that behavior can simultaneously have sacred and secular aspects. Thus, on one level, football can be seen as simply a sport, while on another it can be seen as a public ritual. On one level McDonald's is a mundane, secular institution—just a place to eat—but on another it assumes some of the attributes of a sacred place. And, in the context of comparative religion, why should this be surprising? The French sociologist Emile Durkheim (1954; orig. 1915) pointed out long ago that almost everything, from the sublime to the ridiculous, has in some societies been treated as sacred. The distinction between sacred and profane does not depend on the intrinsic qualities of the sacred symbol. In Australian aboriginal totemism, for example, Durkheim found that sacred entities were generally such humble and nonimposing creatures as ducks, frogs, rabbits, and grubs—beings whose inherent qualities could hardly have been the origin of the religious sentiment they inspired. If frogs and grubs can be elevated to a sacred level, why not McDonald's?

Behavioral Uniformity at McDonald's

For several years, like many other Americans, I have frequently had lunch and occasionally had "dinner" at McDonald's. Recently, I have begun to observe carefully certain ritual-like aspects of Americans' behavior at these fast-food restaurants. Tell your fellow Americans that going to McDonald's is similar in some ways to going to church or temple and their emic bias as natives will reveal itself in laughter, denial, or questions about your sanity. Just as football is a game and Walt Disney World an amusement park, McDonald's, for natives, is just a place to eat. However, comparison of what goes on in McDonald's outlets in this country will reveal a very high degree of formal, uniform behavior from store to store on the part of staff and customers alike. Particularly interesting is that this invariance in act and utterance has developed in the absence of any theological doctrine. McDonald's ritual aspect, rather, is founded on twentieth-century technology, particularly on automobiles, television, work away from home, and the one-hour lunch break. It is striking, nevertheless, that one commercial organization should be so much more successful than other businesses, the U.S. Army, and even many religious institutions in producing behavioral invariance. Factors other than low cost, fast service, and the taste of the food—all of which are approximated by other chains—have contributed to our acceptance of McDonald's and our adherence to its rules.

Remarkably, when Americans travel abroad, even in countries noted for distinctive cuisines, many visit the local McDonald's outlet. It seems that the same factors that lead us to return to McDonald's again and again in our own country are responsible. Because Americans are thoroughly familiar with how to behave, what to expect, what they will eat, and more or less what they will pay at McDonald's, in its outlets overseas they have a kind of home-away-from-home. In Paris, whose natives are not especially renowned for making tourists, particularly Americans, feel at home, McDonald's offers sanctuary. It is, after all, a uniquely American institution, where only natives, programmed by years of prior experience, can feel completely at home. Americans, if they wish, can temporarily reverse roles with their hosts; if American tourists can't be expected to act like the French, neither can the French be expected to act in a culturally appropriate manner at McDonald's.

This devotion to McDonald's rests in part on uniformities associated with almost all its outlets, at least in the United States: food, setting, architecture, ambience, acts, and utterances. For example, the McDonald's symbol, its golden arches, is an almost universal landmark, just as familiar to Americans as Mickey Mouse, Joe Namath, and the Beatles. Only about a dozen McDonald's outlets in this country lack golden arches as outside markers. One of them, where a significant portion of my field work has been done, is in Ann Arbor, a block and a half from the University of Michigan. However, the absence of this symbol does not reduce the outlet's impact as a quasi-ritual setting. Although the restaurant is a contemporary brick structure, it has stained-glass windows, with golden arches as their central theme. Sunlight floods in through a skylight that recalls the clerestory of a church. The golden arches are uniform symbols that are universally recognized by, and have special significance for, participants. Thus analogies between religious symbols and the arches are not, I think, far-fetched. And in Ann Arbor, where the golden arches are absent, McDonald's stained-glass windows and clerestory certainly conjure up religious connotations among natives I have interviewed.

Americans enter a McDonald's restaurant to perform an ordinary, secular act—to eat, usually lunch. Yet the surroundings there tell us that we are somehow apart from the variety, disorder, and variability of the world outside. We know what we are going to see, what we are going to say, what will be said to us, what we will eat, how it will taste, and how much it will cost. Behind the counter at McDonald's, agents are differentiated into three categories: male help, female help, and managers. Members of each group wear similar attire. Permissible utterances by customer and worker alike are liturgically specified above the counter. Throughout the United States, with only minor variation, the menu is located in the same place, contains the same items, and has the same prices. The food, again with only minor regional variation, will also be prepared according to plan, and will vary little in taste. Obviously customers are limited in what they can choose; less obviously, they are also limited in what they can say. Each item has its appropriate McDonald's designation: "large fry," "quarter pounder with cheese." The neophyte customer who innocently asks, "What kind of hamburgers do you have?" or "What's a Big Mac?" is out of place.

Other ritualized phrases are uttered by the person behind the counter. If a man asks for a quarter-pounder, the automatic response is, "Will that be with cheese, sir?" After the customer has completed his order, if no potatoes have been requested, the agent ritually incants, "Will there be any fries today, sir?" Once food is presented and picked up,

the agent conventionally says, "Have a nice day." Nonverbal behavior of McDonald's agents is programmed as well. Before opening the spigot of the drink machine, workers fill paper cups with ice exactly to the bottom of the golden arches that decorate them. As customers request food, agents look back to see if the desired sandwich item is available. If not, they tell you, "That'll be a few minutes" and prepare your drink, after which a proper agent will take the order of the next customer in line. McDonald's lore of appropriate verbal and nonverbal behavior is even taught at a "seminary," called Hamburger University, located in Illinois. Managers who attend pass the program they have learned on to the people who work in their restaurants.

It is not simply the formality and regularity of behavior at McDonald's but its total ambience that invites comparison with sacred places. Like the Disney organization, McDonald's image-makers stress clean living and draw on an order of values— "traditional American values"—that transcends McDonald's itself. Agents submit to dress codes and are uniformly and cleanly attired. Their hair length, height, and complexions are scrutinized by management. McDonald's kitchens, grills, and counters sparkle. Styrofoam food containers that promise to haunt the world for eons are used only once. Understandably, the chain's contributions to worldwide product pollution (along with labor practices that have been questioned) evoke considerable hostility. In 1975 the Ann Arbor campus McDonald's was the scene of a ritual rebellion—desecration by the Radical Vegetarian League, who held a "puke-in." Standing on the second-story balcony just below the clerestory, more than a dozen vegetarians gorged themselves on mustard and water and vomited down on the customer waiting area. McDonald's, defiled, lost many customers that day.

The formality and relative invariance of behavior in a ritually and symbolically demarcated setting thus suggests some analogies between McDonald's and the sacred. Furthermore, like performance of a ritual, participation in McDonald's occurs at specified times fixed by clock, calendar, or specified circumstances. In American culture our daily food consumption is supposed to occur as three meals: breakfast, lunch, and dinner, of which dinner is stressed as the major meal. Americans who have traveled abroad are aware that cultures differ in which meal they emphasize. In many parts of the world, the midday meal is primary. Americans are away from home at lunchtime because of their jobs, and are usually allowed only an hour for lunch; they view dinner as the main meal, and lunch as a lighter meal symbolized by the sandwich. McDonald's provides relatively hot and fresh sandwiches and a variety of subsidiary fare that many American palates can tolerate.

The ritual of eating at McDonald's is confined to ordinary, everyday life. Eating at McDonald's and religious feasts are in complementary distribution in American life; that is, when one occurs the other does not. Most Americans would consider it inappropriate to eat at a fast-food restaurant on Christmas, Thanksgiving, Easter, Passover, or other religious and quasi-religious feast days. Such feast days are often holidays from work and are regarded in our culture as family days, occasions when relatives and close friends get together. However, although Americans neglect McDonald's on holidays, television reminds us that McDonald's still endures, that it will welcome us back once our holiday is over. The television presence of McDonald's is particularly obvious, in fact, on such occasions — whether through a float in the Macy's Thanksgiving Day parade or through sponsorship of special programs, particularly of "family entertainment."

McDonald's Advertising

Although such chains as Burger King, Burger Chef, and Arby's compete with McDonald's for the fast-food business, none rivals McDonald's success. The explanation probably lies in the particularly skillful ways in which McDonald's advertising plays up the features just discussed. Its commercials are varied to appeal to different audiences. On Saturday morning television, with its steady stream of cartoons and other children's features, McDonald's is a ubiquitous sponsor. The McDonald's commercials for children's shows usually differ from the ones that adults see in the evening and during football games. Children are introduced to, and reminded of, McDonald's through several fantasy characters, headed by the clown Ronald McDonald. These commercials often stress the enduring aspects of McDonald's. For example, Ronald has a time machine that enables him to introduce hamburgers to the remote past and the distant future. Anyone who noticed the McDonald's restaurant in the Woody Allen film *Sleeper*, which takes place 200 years hence, will be

aware that the message of McDonald's as eternal has gotten across. As in Disney films, but on a limited and less dramatic level, representations of conflict between good (Ronald) and evil (Hamburglar) are gently portrayed. Children can meet the "McDonaldland" characters again at McDonald's outlets. Their pictures appear on McDonaldland cookie boxes and, from time to time, on durable plastic cups that are given away with the purchase of a large soft drink. Even more obvious are children's chances to actually meet Ronald McDonald. Actors portraying Ronald scatter visits, usually on Saturdays, among McDonald's outlets throughout the country. One can even rent a Ronald for a birthday party.

McDonald's adult advertising has a different but equally effective theme. In 1976 and 1977 breakfast at McDonald's was promoted by a fresh-faced, sincere, happy, clean-cut young woman, inviting the viewer to try a new meal in a familiar setting. In other commercials, healthy, clean-living Americans gambol on ski slopes or in mountain pastures. The single theme, however, that runs throughout all the adult commercials is personalism. McDonald's, the commercials drone on, is something other than a fast-food restaurant. It is a warm, friendly place where you will be graciously welcomed and will feel at home, where your children won't get into trouble. Other chains have copied McDonald's incessant emphasis on the word *you:* "You deserve a break today"; "You, you're the one"; "We do it all for you." McDonald's commercials tell you that you are not simply an anonymous face in an amorphous crowd. You can find respite from a hectic and impersonal society, the break you deserve. Your individuality and dignity will be respected in McDonald's. McDonald's backpacks take up the theme. "Me, I'm the One," they say. You become an individual — one with yourself — you are told, by becoming one with McDonald's. Verbally and nonverbally you demonstrate your participation in the subculture of McDonald's. You load your books in a McDonald's backpack, you impress your friends by your ability to recite "Two all beef patties, special sauce, lettuce, cheese, pickles, onions on a sesame seed bun."

McDonald's advertising tries to deemphasize the fact that the chain is, after all, a commercial organization. In the jingle, you hear, "You, you're the one; we're fixin' breakfast for ya"—not, "You, you're the one; we're makin' millions off ya." McDonald's is presented as much more of an American

McDonald's advertising—one of the main ingredients in the chain's phenomenal success—presents McDonald's as much more than a fast-food restaurant; in fact, as an all-American institution, upholder of our values and the American way of life. (Charles Gatewood)

tain the values of American family life. They have even suggested a means of strengthening what most Americans conceive to be the weakest link in the nuclear family: father-child. "Take a father to lunch," kids are told; love your father at McDonald's.

As with the Disney organization, the argument here is certainly *not* that McDonald's has become a religion. Rather, it is merely being suggested that specific ways in which Americans participate in McDonald's bear analogies to religious systems involving myth, symbol, and ritual. Just as in rituals, participation in McDonald's involves temporary subordination of individual differences in a social and cultural collectivity. By eating at McDonald's we communicate information about our current physical state (hunger). Even more important, by going to McDonald's, or by wearing McDonald's backpacks, we convey information about ourselves to others. In a land of tremendous ethnic, social, economic, and religious diversity we demonstrate that we share something with millions of other Americans. Furthermore, as in ritual performances, participation in McDonald's is linked to a cultural system that transcends McDonald's itself. By eating at McDonald's we say something about ourselves as Americans, about our acceptance of values and ways of living that belong to a social collectivity. By returning to McDonald's over and over again, we affirm that certain values and life styles, developed through the collective experiences of Americans before us, will continue.

institution than the apple pie it serves. Commercials make it seem like a charitable organization by stressing its program of community good works. During the Bicentennial year, commercials reported that McDonald's was giving 1,776 trees to every state in the union. How big the trees were, or what the states did with them, was never specified. Brochures at outlets echo the television message that, through McDonald's, you can sponsor a carnival to aid victims of muscular dystrophy. Again in 1976, McDonald's sponsored a radio series documenting contributions to American history of Afro-Americans. Such "good, clean" family television entertainment as the film *The Sound of Music* was brought to you by McDonald's, complete with a prefatory sermonlike address by its head, Ray Kroc. On this occasion, special commercials united Ronald McDonald (shown picking up after litterbugs) with the adult commercial themes. McDonald's commercials tell us that it supports and works to main-

ANTHROPOLOGY AND AMERICAN "POP" CULTURE

The examples presented in Chapter 9 demonstrated that in addition to whatever emically recognized and ostensibly religious considerations may motivate participants, such customs as ritual pig slaughter in New Guinea or taboos on consumption of beef in India have material causes and effects. In this chapter it has been argued that, correspondingly, consumption of the propaganda and products of such manifestly commercial organizations as McDonald's involves ritual behavior and mythological and symbolic components that go unrecognized by native participants. Just as etic analysis of religious ceremonials in nonindustrial societies may demonstrate the latent ecological and economic functions of these ceremonials, etic analysis of Americans' participation in, and beliefs and feelings about, football, rock music, Disney creations, and McDonald's fast-food outlets reveals unsuspected analogies with religious rituals, myths, and symbols.

Some examples of the growing anthropological interest in American society were given in Chapter 13. These studies, however, related *variation* in the United States and other complex societies to such factors as socioeconomic class, poverty, ethnicity, and rural versus urban residence. In this chapter the examination of aspects of American *culture* has stressed some experiences and enculturative forces common to most Americans, particularly the young. In so doing several points have been emphasized.

We have seen that anthropology is not simply the study of nonindustrial populations. Many techniques that anthropologists have applied to other cultures—including structural, symbolic, and etic analyses—can be used just as easily to interpret American culture. In studies of their own cultures, native anthropologists can contribute uniquely by coupling detachment and objectivity with their own experience and understanding as natives.

This chapter has also demonstrated that structural and symbolic analyses of aspects of culture share as much with the humanities as with the sciences. In contrast to concerns of previous chapters, these approaches often seek primarily to *discover, interpret,* and *illuminate* otherwise hidden dimensions or deeper meanings of phenomena rather than to explain them. Structural and symbolic analyses of any culture are, therefore, difficult to confirm or to falsify. They can be evaluated emically: Do natives accept them or prefer them to alternative interpretations? Do they enable natives to make more sense of familiar phenomena? They can also be evaluated etically: Do they fit within a comparative framework provided by data and analyses from other societies? Previous chapters have included several anthropological observations about associations between, say, socioeconomic class position and household composition, or between population density and political organization. Such relationships can be evaluated statistically and can be confirmed or denied by researchers independently examining the same data. However, structuralist hypotheses, although relying more on the anthropologist's impressions, can be revealing as well, addressing different aspects of the same phenomena. They explain little about *why* cultural phenomena developed as they

did, but they may enlighten us about otherwise unsuspected coherence and contradictions in cultural forms.

The examples considered in this chapter are new and uniquely American shared cultural forms that have appeared and spread rapidly during the twentieth century because of major changes in the material conditions of American life—particularly in work organization, communication, and transportation. Late-twentieth-century Americans deem at least one automobile a necessity, and televisions now outnumber toilets in American households. Through the mass media, such institutions as football, rock music, Disney creations, and McDonald's have become powerful elements of American national culture, providing a framework of common expectations, experiences, and behavior that overrides region, class, formal religious affiliation, political sentiments, gender, ethnic group, and place of residence. Although some of us may not like these changes, we certainly can't deny their significance.

The rise of fast-food restaurants, Disney, rock, football, and similar institutions is related not just to the mass media but also to the decreasing participation in traditional organized religion, and the weakening of ties based on kinship, marriage and community within industrial society. Neither formal religion, strong centralized government, nor segmentary lineage structure unites most Americans. Cars, movies, television, stereo, and their by-products do, and in this we provide a uniquely exotic example in the realm of cultural diversity.

These aspects of contemporary American culture are perhaps viewed as merely passing, or "pop," culture by certain segments of American society, but they are highly significant features of our culture, shared by millions of Americans. As such, they certainly deserve, and are receiving, the attention of anthropologists and other scholars. Anthropologists have provided analyses similar in some respects to those included in this chapter of such aspects of American culture as "Star Trek" (Claus, 1976); motion pictures, including *The Exorcist* (Burton and Hicks, 1976) and the Marx Brothers' *Duck Soup* (Karp, 1976); teen-age literature, including Nancy Drew mysteries (Montague, 1976); soap operas (Bean, 1976); and television commercials (Kirkpatrick, 1976). Such studies are fulfilling the traditional promise offered in textbooks that by studying anthropology we can learn more about ourselves. Americans can view themselves not just as members of a varied and complex nation, but also as a population united by distinctive shared symbols, customs, and experiences. Although American culture resembles others in certain respects, like any other cultural system, it also makes its own unique and original contributions to the realm of cultural diversity. And that, after all, is the subject matter of anthropology.

SUMMARY

Such factors as ethnicity, class, region, religion, place of residence, political party affiliation, and neighborhood make American society diverse, yet it is also unified by certain shared aspects of American culture. Many of the commonalities of behavior, belief, and activity that enable anthropologists to speak of contemporary American culture are relatively new, more or less peculiar to the United States, and founded on and perpetuated through twentieth-century industrial developments, particularly in business organization, transportation, and mass media. Anthropological techniques developed in studying nonindustrial societies can also be used to investigate both socioeconomic variation and cultural uniformity in the contemporary United States. Anthropologists who study their own culture are *native* anthropologists who can draw on their experiences and understanding as natives as well as on their scientific training and cross-cultural comparative perspective. Native anthropologists must, however, be particularly careful to resist their own emic biases—their culturally conditioned frames of reference. As anthropologists, we must be aware that natives often see and explain their behavior very differently from the way anthropologists do.

Most Americans, for example, have probably never thought that such apparently secular, commercial, and recreational institutions as football, rock music, Walt Disney Enterprises, and fast-food restaurants have things in common with religious beliefs and symbols in our own and other societies. But there are, for example, similarities between these institutions and passage rites, which may develop to mark any change in social status, age, place, or social condition. Passage rites universally have three phases: separation, margin or liminality, and aggregation. Turner's discussion of the liminal period, during which individuals occupy ambiguous social positions, is particularly important in identifying many ritual and quasi-ritual aspects of common American institutions.

Arens asserts that football is the sport that best symbolizes such major features of American life as group coordination through elaborate variation, specialization, and division of labor. Montague and Morais argue that football provides a miniaturized and simplified version of the modern industrial organization and of the behavior that business inculcates. Football demonstrates to fans that the values stressed by business really do pay off. Montague and Morais also argue that football and rock are both popular, often appealing to the same people, because they represent equally important themes in American life. Football—which stresses teamwork, diligence, talent, and self-denial—is linked to the technical emphasis of American life. Rock, on the other hand, expresses the American theme of creativity. However, since both exalt individualistic virtues, identify with different poles of the same contrasts, and have ritual aspects, they are more similar than they would seem on the surface. In several binary oppositions, their similar values are hidden: they are made to seem more different than they really are.

Structural anthropologist Lévi-Strauss argues that people universally tend to classify aspects of nature and culture by opposition or contrast. Phenomena that in reality are continuous rather than discrete are made, through binary opposition, to seem absolutely different. In his analyses of myths in several societies, Lévi-Strauss shows that binary oppositions are often resolved by such mediating figures as the serpent in Genesis. Structural analysis—which aims not at explaining, but at uncovering, otherwise hidden relations and connections among aspects of culture—links anthropology to the humanities rather than the sciences.

Common exposure to the products of Walt Disney Enterprises—particularly by Americans under forty—provides another highly significant common enculturative experience. Walt Disney combined in a single person the contrasting themes of the American fulfillment formula: creativity and technical skills; in

Lévi-Strauss's terms, he mediated the cultural opposition between them. His cartoon characters continue to provide an important component of the mythology of American childhood. Disney creations, like myth, bridge the opposition between culture and nature by depicting animals as cultural creatures and by representing people as closer to nature than we normally are.

The success of Disney's amusement parks, and their similarities to religious shrines, reflect his status as quasi-deified creator and mythmaker. Walt Disney World, like shrines and sacred cities, is divided into an outer, more secular space and an inner, sacred domain called The Magic Kingdom. The passage from secular to sacred is gradual and liminal. The Magic Kingdom itself recalls shrines and religious rites in several ways: by reaffirming and thus maintaining social solidarity among participants; by recalling the values on which America is purported to be founded; by linking together past, present, future, real, and unreal; by creating and dispelling anxiety; and by creating a community of people observing the same rules, sharing similar experiences, and behaving alike. However, the reasons why people undertake pilgrimages are often not exclusively or primarily "religious." Shrines and pilgrimage centers also have recreational and secular aspects. Americans ignore similarities between what we consider religious and nonreligious institutions because, unlike other cultures, we view recreation and worship as distinct, incompatible domains.

Anthropological analysis of another familiar fixture of contemporary American life, the fast-food chain McDonald's, also turns up analogies with ritual. Although Americans' relationships to McDonald's lack the emotional component present in religious rituals, and although our visits to fast-food chains are motivated by practical rather than supernatural ends, some of the key elements of ritual remain. Our behavior at McDonald's involves an astonishing degree of formality and uniformity on the part of staff and customers alike. This relative invariance in act and utterance has developed in the absence of any theological doctrine. McDonald's ritual aspects are founded on automobiles, television, work away from home, and the one-hour lunch break. As in religious rituals, Americans' participation in McDonald's subordinates individual differences in a common public act. The business organization itself, through its advertising, ambience, and codes of behavior, recalls and reaffirms traditional values of the society of which it is a part. McDonald's sells its products by creating a fantasy world for children and by using personalism to attract adults. Like formal religious organizations, it sponsors community good works. Americans return to McDonald's not just because they like the food and the prices, but because they have learned exactly what to do, say, and expect, because—as in a familiar house of worship—they feel at home.

Anthropologists working in other cultures have demonstrated that religious performances have material causes and effects that participants may not recognize. Similarly, Americans' consumption of the propaganda and products of certain manifestly commercial organizations involves ritual behavior and mythological and symbolic components ignored by natives. Although American society is varied and complex, Americans are united by distinctive shared symbols, traditions, and experiences. Many of the shared features of contemporary American culture are new and rest on twentieth-century technological developments. They influence millions of people and thus merit anthropological attention.

SOURCES AND SUGGESTED READINGS

ARENS, W.
1976   Professional Football: An American Symbol and Ritual. In *The American Dimension: Cultural Myths and Social Realities,* ed. W. Arens and S. P. Montague, pp. 3–14. Port Washington, N.Y.: Alfred. Football's popularity related to features of American work organization and division of labor.

BEAN, S. S.
1976   Soap Operas: Sagas of American Kinship. In *The American Dimension: Cultural Myths and Social Realities,* ed. W. Arens and S. P. Montague, pp. 80–98. Port Washington, N.Y.: Alfred. Kinship, marriage, and morality on afternoon television.

BOAS, M., AND CHAIN, S.
1976   *Big Mac: The Unauthorized Story of Mc-
        Donald's.* New York: Dutton. Popular
        account of the chain's growth; they don't
        quite do it *all* for us.

BURTON, J. W., AND HICKS, D.
1976   Chaos Triumphant: Archetypes and Sym-
        bols in *The Exorcist.* In *The American
        Dimension: Cultural Myths and Social
        Realities,* ed. W. Arens and S. P. Mon-
        tague, pp 117–123. Port Washington,
        N.Y.: Alfred. Whatever possessed
        Regan? William Friedkin received an
        Academy Award nomination for directing
        the movie made from the book on which
        this article is based.

CLAUS, P.
1976   A Structuralist Appreciation of "Star
        Trek." In *The American Dimension: Cul-
        tural Myths and Social Realities,* ed. W.
        Arens and S. P. Montague, pp. 15–32.
        Port Washington, N.Y.: Alfred. Kirk and
        Spock as mediators of several binary op-
        positions.

DE VOS, G. A., AND ROMANUCCI-ROSS, L.
1975   *Ethnic Identity: Cultural Continuities and
        Change.* Palo Alto: Mayfield. Fourteen
        anthropologists of different ethnic back-
        grounds adopt the perspective of the na-
        tive anthropologist.

DURKHEIM, E.
1954   (orig. 1915) *The Elementary Forms of the
        Religious Life,* translated by J. W. Swain.
        New York: The Free Press. Influential
        work. Examines Australian totemism,
        which Durkheim considered religion's
        most primitive form; contains good recipe
        for steak tartare.

GARDNER, H.
1974   *The Quest for Mind: Piaget, Lévi-Strauss,
        and the Structuralist Movement.* New
        York: Vintage. Very readable introduc-
        tion to structuralism in anthropology and
        psychology.

GARRETSON, L. R.
1976   *American Culture: An Anthropological
        Perspective.* Dubuque: Wm. C. Brown.
        Brief introduction.

GENNEP, A. VAN
1960   (orig. 1909) *The Rites of Passage.*
        Chicago: University of Chicago Press.
        Classic comparative study.

GROSS, D. R.
1971   Ritual and Conformity: A Religious Pil-
        grimage to Northeastern Brazil. *Eth-
        nology* 10:129–148. Analysis of Bom
        Jesus da Lapa.

GULLIVER, P. H.
1974   The Jie of Uganda. In *Man in Adaptation:
        The Cultural Present.* 2nd ed., ed. Y. A.
        Cohen, pp. 323–345. Chicago: Aldine.
        Ugandan pastoralists; shrines and sacred
        groves.

KARP, I.
1976   Good Marx for the Anthropologist: Struc-
        ture and Anti-Structure in *Duck Soup.*
        In *The American Dimension: Cultural
        Myths and Social Realities,* ed. W. Arens
        and S. P. Montague, pp. 53–68. Port
        Washington, N.Y.: Alfred. Structural
        analysis of a Marx Brothers movie.

KIRKPATRICK, J. T.
1976   Homes and Homemakers on American
        TV. In *The American Dimension: Cul-
        tural Myths and Social Realities,* ed. W.
        Arens and S. P. Montague, pp. 69–79.
        Port Washington, N.Y.: Alfred. Anthro-
        pologist looks at depiction of women in
        commercials and television programs.

LEACH, E.
1976   *Culture and Communication: The Logic
        by Which Symbols Are Connected.* New
        York: Cambridge University Press. Dis-
        cusses sign, symbol, and meaning, and in-
        troduces reader to Lévi-Strauss's structur-
        alism.

LÉVI-STRAUSS, C.
1967   *Structural Anthropology.* New York:
        Doubleday. No matter what you say
        about his anthropology, he still makes a
        good pair of pants.

LUCKMANN, T.
1967   *The Invisible Religion.* New York: Mac-
        millan. Religion, mass media, and con-
        temporary American culture.

MONTAGUE, S. P.
1976   How Nancy Gets Her Man: An Investiga-
        tion of Success Models in American Ado-
        lescent Pulp Literature. In *The American
        Dimension: Cultural Myths and Social
        Realities,* ed. W. Arens and S. P. Mon-
        tague, pp. 99–116. Port Washington,
        N.Y.: Alfred. Analysis of cultural themes,
        including sex roles, as reflected in Nancy
        Drew and the Hardy Boys, etc.

MONTAGUE, S. P., AND MORAIS, R.

1976   Football Games and Rock Concerts: The Ritual Enactment. In *The American Dimension: Cultural Myths and Social Realities,* ed. W. Arens and S. P. Montague, pp. 33–52. Port Washington, N.Y.: Alfred. Binary oppositions and links between these two institutions and contrasting themes in American life.

RADCLIFFE-BROWN, A. R.

1965   (orig. 1952) *Structure and Function in Primitive Society.* New York: The Free Press. Religious observances reaffirm values and maintain stable, orderly society.

RAPPAPORT, R. A.

1974   Obvious Aspects of Ritual. *Cambridge Anthropology* 2:2–60. Distinguishing ritual from other behavior.

REGELSON, S.

1976   The Bagel: Symbol and Ritual at the Breakfast Table. In *The American Dimension: Cultural Myths and Social Realities,* ed. W. Arens and S. P. Montague, pp. 124–138. Port Washington, N.Y.: Alfred. Lox, cream cheese, bagels, and Jewish religious symbolism.

ROSSI, I., ED.

1974   *The Unconscious in Culture: The Structuralism of Claude Lévi-Strauss in Perspective.* New York: Dutton. Excellent reader on structuralism compiled by an anthropologist who is sympathetic to this controversial approach.

SPRADLEY, J. P., AND RYNKIEWICH, M. A.

1975   *The Nacirema: Readings on American Culture.* Boston: Little, Brown. Nacirema is *American* spelled backward; articles, some rather dated, focus on a broad range of American social and cultural features.

TURNER, V. W.

1974   *The Ritual Process.* Harmondsworth, England: Penguin. Liminality among the Ndembu and in comparative perspective.

ZARETSKY, I. I., AND LEONE, M. P.

1974   *Religious Movements in Contemporary America.* Princeton: Princeton University Press. Lengthy and useful collection of articles on assorted religious groups and beliefs in the United States today.

GLOSSARY

acculturation Changes in behavior patterns involving continuous firsthand contact between one or more cultures.

achieved status Position that individuals occupy through their own efforts, abilities, and achievements; for example, role of the big man.

adaptation Process whereby a population establishes means of existing and surviving in a specific environment.

adaptive radiation Development of an array of diverse types out of a relatively homogeneous ancestral population as a result of population increase and adaptation to a variety of different environments.

adjudication The legal process; judging.

affinal, affine A relative by marriage, an in-law.

agnates Members of the same patrilineal descent group.

agriculture Nonindustrial system of plant cultivation characterized by intensive use of land and human labor.

ahimsa Hindu doctrine prohibiting the slaughter of zebu cattle; more generally, of harming life.

alleles Chemical differences at the same genetic locus.

allomorph Phonetically different form or morph of a single morpheme, produced automatically by morphophonemic rules.

alluvial desert Arid area of rich soil deposited by flowing water.

ambilineal Principle of descent that does not automatically exclude from descent-group membership the children of either sons or daughters. Descent-group membership is achieved rather than ascribed.

ambilocal Nonunilocal postmarital residence pattern in which couples may reside with either the wife's or the husband's group.

Ameslan American Sign Language, a medium of communication for deaf and mute hominoids.

amino acid Any one of twenty constituents of protein. A diet including all twenty is needed for adequate nutrition.

analogies Similarities produced independently by natural selective forces operating in similar environments.

Andes Major mountain range in South America; in Peru, Bolivia, Ecuador, and Chile. Site of Inca civilization.

anima Latin for *soul;* root of animism and animation.

animatism Concept of the supernatural as a domain of raw, impersonal power that influences humans but can be controlled. According to Marett, the most rudimentary form of religion.

animism Belief in spiritual beings, souls or doubles. According to Tylor, the most primitive form of religion.

Anthropoidea One of two traditional suborders of the Primate order. Classification includes New World and Old World monkeys, apes, and humans.

apical ancestor Ancestor common to all members of a given descent group. Called "apical" because the ancestor stands at the apex of the common genealogy.

applied anthropology Use of anthropological findings, techniques, or methods to accomplish some desired practical purpose.

arable Able to be farmed.

arboreal Pertaining to trees.

archaic state A nonindustrial state.

archipelago A chain or group of islands, such as Indonesia.

artifacts Manufactured items.

ascribed status Position occupied involuntarily by an individual; for example, sex, age.

asymmetry Inequality.

Australopithecus africanus Hominid species that existed in Africa between 6 and 1 million years ago. Ancestral to *Homo.*

autonomous Independent.

Aztec Late postclassic empire in the Valley of Mexico, centered on Tenochtitlan.

balanced reciprocity See *generalized reciprocity.*

band Basic social unit in many foraging populations. Normally includes one hundred or fewer people, all related by kinship or marriage.

Bantu Group of closely related languages spoken over a large area of central, eastern, and southern Africa.

basic vocabulary Notion fundamental to lexicostatistics. As distinguished from cultural vocabulary, it is the area of lexicon that is most resistant to change.

berdache Third gender among Crow and other Native Americans of the Plains—a biological male who dressed and spoke like a woman and had a special role in Crow society.

373

bifurcate collateral   System of kinship classification on the parental generation employing separate terms for M, F, MB, MZ, FB, and FZ.

bifurcate merging   System of kinship classification on the parental generation whereby M and MZ are called by the same term, F and FB are called by the same term, and MB and FZ are called by different terms.

big man   Figure often found among tribial horticulturalists and pastoralists. The big man occupies no office but creates his own reputation through entrepreneurial expertise and generosity to others. Neither his wealth nor his position passes to his heirs.

bilateral kinship calculation   Kinship ties that are calculated equally through kin of both sexes; that is, through mother and father, sister and brother, daughter and son, and so on.

binary opposition   Pairs of opposites, such as good-evil and old-young, produced by converting continuous contrasts into qualitative distinctions. Important term in structuralism.

biomass   (of a species, population, or other group). Average weight per individual multiplied by total number of individuals in the group.

biotic   Referring to *biota*, or life forms—plants and animals.

blood feud   Feud between families in a nonstate society.

blowout   Tribal adaptive distribution of resources, usually in ceremonial context.

B.P.   Before the present; 1000 B.P. = 1000 years ago. To convert B.C. dates to B.P. dates, add 2000 years. For example, 10,000 B.C. = 12,000 B.P.

bride price   See *progeny price.*

bridewealth   See *progeny price.*

broad spectrum revolution   Gradual evolutionary shift from specialized foraging economics oriented around big-game hunting to more generalized foraging that incorporated hunting and gathering of a variety of plant and animal resources. Began in Europe around 17,000 B.P. and in the Near East around 20,000 B.P., where it culminated in food production around 10,000 B.P.

call systems   Systems of communication among nonhuman primates composed of a limited number of acoustically distinct sounds that vary in intensity and duration. Tied to specific environmental stimuli.

caloric staple   Basic source of calories; main food crop, such as rice, maize, millet, or plantains.

canines   Eye teeth; project in apes and terrestrial monkeys but not in humans.

cargo cults   Revitalization movements that attempt to gain European goods (cargo) by magical imitation of European behavior and technology; typical of Melanesia.

cargo systems   A series of obligations associated with the political and religious hierarchies of Latin American communities, generally in the highlands.

carrying capacity   The largest number of people or other animals that a particular environment could support, given the population's needs and its techniques of satisfying them.

caste system   Stratified groups in which membership is ascribed at birth and lifelong.

catastrophism   Doctrine stating that extinct life forms met their end through catastrophic events. Often combined with creationism.

cerebral cortex   The outer layer of the brain. Concerned with memory, association, and integration of information, and therefore with learning.

ceremonial fund   Investment of scarce resources within a ceremonial or ritual context.

charisma   A quality, coming from a person rather than from an office, that inspires intense loyalty and devotion; often has religious significance—linking prophet and followers.

chiefdom   Form of sociopolitical organization based on food production, usually agriculture or intensive horticulture, in which kinship remains important and generosity is associated with political office. Often a transitional form between tribal society and state.

chromosomes   Long, threadlike structures contained in the nucleus of each cell of a living being and normally occurring in homologous pairs. Human cells generally contain twenty-three pairs, or forty-six chromosomes.

chronology   A system for determining time; a dating framework.

city   Population of 10,000 or more concentrated in a small, continuous, compact area. Characterized by intense internal social differentiation based on variations in wealth, economic specialization, and power.

civilization   Variety of state with writing, exact practical sciences, full-time artists, and sophisticated art styles.

clinical model of intervention   Intervention in which people are actively involved in planning a change that affects them; outsiders promoting change are more concerned with means than with ends, which are usually vague.

closed, corporate peasant community   Generally Indian, located in the highlands of Latin America. Corporate in sharing an estate and closed by birth and through endogamy.

collateral household   See *expanded family household.*

collateral relative   A relative who is neither a lineal nor an affinal relative.

common history   That which results when two or more populations are divergent descendants of a common ancestral population; also occurs with borrowing or contact.

commoner   Neither noble nor slave.

communitas   The egalitarian, communal ideology, behavior, and social relations that often accompany liminality.

compadre   Coparent. The godparents of a child and the child's parents become coparents.

comparative method   Historical linguistic technique. Reconstructs protolanguages by comparing their divergent descendants; for example, proto–Indo-European from French, English, and the other contemporary Indo-European languages.

competence What a native speaker or hearer must know about his or her language to engage in verbal interaction.

competitive exclusion Principle that if two species rely on the same ecological niche, any advantage on the part of one of them, even though minor, will eventually force the other from that niche.

componential analysis Technique important in the study of meaning systems of different languages. Examines certain domains in the folk taxonomies of different speech communities and attempts to identify dimensions of contrast and their components.

conservative Acting to maintain the status quo.

conspecifics Members of the same species.

convergence Development of similar structural traits or behavior patterns among distantly related populations, resulting from adaptation to similar environments and natural selective forces.

conversion Exchange of items from different spheres of a multicentric economy.

conveyance Exchange of items from the same sphere of a multicentric economy.

corporate groups Groups that exist in perpetuity and manage a common estate. Includes some descent groups and modern industrial corporations.

correlation An association between two or more variables, such that when one changes (varies), the other(s) also change(s) (covaries); for example, temperature and sweating.

creationism Doctrine of divine creation. Opposed to transformism.

creoles Pidgins that have acquired native speakers and complex grammatical rules of their own.

crime Act that is prohibited by law.

cross cousins Children of siblings of the opposite sex.

Crow kinship terminology Manner of classifying kin on ego's own generation, usually associated with matrilineal descent-group organization.

cult institutions Phrase coined by A. F. C. Wallace to refer to a set of rituals and associated beliefs.

cultigens Cultivated plants.

cultural vocabulary Portion of the vocabulary of any speech community that is least resistant to change. Contrasted with basic vocabulary.

culture That which is transmitted through learning, behavior patterns, and modes of thought acquired by humans as members of society. Technology, language, patterns of group organization, and ideology are aspects of culture.

daughter languages Different languages that have developed from the same parent language; for example, Ger-

man and English are daughter languages of proto-Germanic.

demography The study of population.

demonstrated descent Basis for lineage membership. Members of the same lineage demonstrate their descent from their common apical ancestor by citing the actual or accepted descendants in each generation from the ancestor through the present.

descent group Social unit found among horticultural, pastoral, and agricultural populations. All members of a descent group maintain that they are descendants of the founder of that group and share access to the group's territory and estate.

descriptive linguistics Subdivision of linguistics that deals with languages at a single time.

developmental type Category based on convergent evolution and environmental similarity. Includes human populations located in geographically different but ecologically similar environments who have evolved in analogous fashion. Associated with Julian Steward.

differential access Access to strategic and other socially valued resources; basic attribute of chiefdoms and states. Superordinates enjoy favored or unimpeded access to such resources, while subordinates have their access limited by the former.

diffusion Process whereby aspects of culture pass from one group to another.

domestic Within or pertaining to the home.

dominance hierarchy Social means of adapting to terrestrial life among baboons and macaques. Involves superordinate-subordinate relationships.

dowry Offering made by bride's group to the new couple, the groom, or the groom's kin when a marriage takes place.

ecclesiastical Pertaining to a professional clergy or priesthood that is hierarchically and bureaucratically organized.

ecology The study of plant and animal populations and communities and their relationships with one another and with their environment.

economic determinism The assumption that economic changes produce other sociocultural changes and that, in the long run, the form of the economy determines the form of the society.

economizing The allocation of scarce means to alternative ends. Often given as the subject matter of economics.

economy A population's system of production, distribution, and consumption of material resources.

ecosystem A patterned arrangement of energy flows and exchanges; composed of variables, each one of which influences every other.

egalitarian "Equal," with few status distinctions, such as those between male and female, rich and poor, powerful and subordinate.

ego Latin for *I*. In kinship charts, point at which one enters an egocentric genealogy.

egocentric See *ego;* viewed from the individual's perspective.

emic A research strategy that seeks the native viewpoint; relies on informants to say what is and is not significant; actor-oriented.

enculturation Process whereby individuals learn, through experience, observation, and instruction, their population's culture.

endogamy Marriage of individuals within the same social group.

environment Surroundings to which a human population adapts, including physical, biotic, and social components.

environmentalist position See *nurturist position.*

Eskimo kinship terminology Way of classifying kin on ego's own generation whereby cousins are distinguished from brother and sister. Associated with nuclear family organization.

estate Strategic resources administered, say, by an industrial corporation or a descent group.

estrus cycle Period of sexual receptivity in some female primates signaled by swelling and coloration of the vaginal skin.

ethnic group People whose particular customs and cultural heritage differ from other such groups and from the main body of society.

ethnocentrism Universal human tendency to interpret and evaluate foreign beliefs and practices in terms of one's own cultural tradition.

ethnography Field work by a sociocultural anthropologist.

ethnohistory The study of native oral traditions and genealogies.

ethnology Comparison and generalization in sociocultural anthropology.

ethnoscience The study of classification systems of populations. Often used as a synonym for ethnosemantics.

ethnosemantics See *ethnoscience.*

ethology The study of animal behavior, usually assuming that such behavior is biologically based.

etic A research strategy that relies on the scientist's criteria of significance; shows reasons and results of behavior and beliefs that natives may not recognize; observer-oriented; views ethnographic data in comparative and/or historical perspective.

evolution Change in form over generations. According to Charles Darwin, descent with modification: in anthropology, change in form of *Homo* as a biological organism or change in form of human adaptations to the environment.

exogamy Cultural rule that requires members of a group to marry outside of that group.

expanded family household Group that may include siblings and their spouses and children (a *collateral* household) or three generations of kin and their spouses (an *extended* family household) that reside together in the same household; larger than the nuclear family.

extended family household See *expanded family household.*

extradomestic Outside the home, within or pertaining to the public domain.

family of orientation Nuclear family in which one grows up.

family of procreation Nuclear family established when one marries and has children.

fiscal Pertaining to finances.

fission To split up.

folk taxonomy The division of aspects of life into categories specific to members of a particular culture; the American and Brazilian systems of racial classification.

food production Plant cultivation and annual domestication.

foraging Hunting and gathering.

fraternal polyandry Marriage of a group of brothers to the same woman or women.

functionalism School of sociocultural anthropology associated with Bronislaw Malinowski and A. R. Radcliffe-Brown, both of whom avoided speculation about origins and advocated study of psychological and social functions of institutionalized behavior in human societies.

functional alternative Social form that serves the same function as another social form.

functional explanation Explanation that relates a specific practice to other aspects of behavior in the society being examined. When aspects of human behavior are functionally interrelated, if one of them changes, the others will also change.

gene Position on a chromosome, often called a genetic locus or place.

general anthropology Incorporates the four subdisciplines: biological, archeological, linguistic, and sociocultural anthropology.

general evolution Study of formal changes, biological and sociocultural, in the genus *Homo,* abstracted from a variety of times, places, and specific populations.

generalized exchange Prescriptive marriage system in which women of descent group B always marry men from descent group C, while men of descent group B always marry women from descent group A.

generalized reciprocity Principle that characterizes exchanges between closely related individuals; as social distance increases reciprocity becomes *balanced* and, finally, *negative.* All three refer to points along a continuum.

general-purpose money Currency that functions as a means of exchange, a standard of value, and a means of payment; opposed to special-purpose money.

generational kinship terminology System of classification of kin on the parental generation whereby there are only two kin terms, one designating M, MZ, and FZ, the other designating F, FB, and MB.

genetic explanation Demonstration that the presence of a similar item or behavior pattern in two or more populations reflects inheritance from a common ancestral culture. A homology.

genetic relationship in language Development from a common ancestral language. Describes the relationship between languages rather than between speakers of the languages.

genitor Biological father of a child.

genotype Genetic composition of an organism as programmed by genes and chromosomes.

grammar The formal organizing principles that link sound and meaning in a language. The entire set of abstract rules or principles that make up any language.

green revolution Agricultural development based on chemical fertilizers, pesticides, twentieth-century industrial technology, and new crop varieties like IR-8, "miracle rice."

hacienda Estate or manor in highland Latin America.

Hawaiian kinship terminology Manner of classifying kin on ego's own generation whereby brothers and male cousins are called by one term and sisters and female cousins are called by another.

headman A village leader in a tribal society who has limited authority, leads by persuasion and example, and who is expected to be generous.

hectare Basic unit of land area in metric system; 1 ha. = 2.47 acres.

historical explanation Demonstration that a social institution or cultural practice exists among two or more different populations because they share a period of common history or have been exposed to common sources of information. Includes diffusion.

historical linguistics Subdivision of linguistics that studies languages over time.

history The ongoing process whereby individuals live and die, migrate in and out of populations or social systems. May proceed without evolution.

holistic Applied to anthropology: concerned with the whole human condition — biology, psychology, society, and culture in all times and places.

homeostasis Equilibrium, or stable relationship, between population and environment.

homeostat Mechanism that operates to maintain equilibrium.

Hominidae Zoological family that includes fossil and living humans of at least three genera, *Ramapithecus*, *Australopithecus*, and *Homo*.

Hominoidea Zoological superfamily that includes fossil and contemporary apes and humans. Composed of three contemporary families: *Hylobatidae*, *Pongidae*, and *Hominidae*.

Homo erectus Second of the stages of human evolution. Occurred between about 1,500,000 and 300,000 B.P.

homologies Similarities present among related species or populations because of inheritance from a common ancestor.

homonym A word pronounced just like another word, such as *bear* and *bare*.

Homo sapiens Sapiens Second of the subspecies of *Homo sapiens*, appeared circa 37,000 B.P. Includes all contemporary humans.

horticulture Nonindustrial system of plant cultivation in which plots are fallowed for varying lengths of time.

hydraulic systems Systems of water management, including irrigation, drainage, and flood control. Often associated with agricultural societies in arid and riverine environments.

hypercorrection Exaggerated imitation of a valued speech pattern, such as *r* pronunciation by lower middle class speakers when reading minimal pairs.

hypodescent Descent rule, characteristic of the United States and certain other stratified societies, that always associates offspring of mixed marriages with the parent of the poorer group.

Incas Creators of one of the major empires of the tropics, in the Peruvian Andes. Conquered by the Spanish in the sixteenth century.

incest Act of mating with or marrying a close relative.

inclusive fitness Concept in sociobiology; fitness includes not just individual's genes, but those he or she shares with close relatives.

infanticide The act of killing a baby; a socially approved form of population control in some societies.

inside-outside dichotomy Contrast between women's role in the home and men's role in public life, with a corresponding social devaluation of women's work and worth.

integrated Tied together; interlinked.

interlacustrine Between lakes.

intermontane Between mountains.

interspecific Between two species, such as interspecific aggression or sex.

interview schedule A series of questions asked of several informants. Whereas questionnaires are filled out by informants or respondents, ethnographers fill in the interview schedules. Interview schedules provide comparable, quantifiable information for several informants.

intraspecific Within a particular species.

inverse correlation As one variable increases in value, another decreases in value, such as temperature and total cost of furnace fuel.

invert To turn around; reverse

invertebrates Animals without backbones, such as snails.

Iroquois kinship terminology Manner of classifying kin of ego's own generation whereby the same term designates parallel cousins and siblings, and a different term is used for cross cousins.

Jensenism Doctrine that intelligence of human groups is determined in great measure by differences in their genetic characteristics. Largely discredited.

kaiko Pig festival among Maring of New Guinea.

kilogram Basic unit of weight in metric system; 1 kg. = 2.2 lbs.

kinship calculation The system by which individuals in a particular society reckon kin relationships.

lactate To produce milk.

latent function Underlying function served by some behavior pattern in a society.

law A legal code and legal machinery—adjudication and enforcement.

leveling mechanism Sociocultural form that acts to even out wealth differences within a social unit.

levirate Custom whereby a widow marries the brother of her deceased husband.

lexicon Vocabulary.

lexicostatistics Historical linguistic technique for evaluating degree of relationship between languages on the basis of quantitative comparison of their basic vocabularies.

licit Socially approved or acceptable.

limited good, image of Phrase coined by George Foster to refer to characteristic peasant ideology that views all desired things as finite; when one peasant takes too much from the finite pool, everyone else is deprived.

lineage Descent group based on demonstrated descent.

lineal kinship terminology Manner of classifying kin on the parental generation whereby there are four terms: one for M, one for F, one for FB and MB, and one for MZ and FZ.

lineal relative Any of ego's ancestors or descendants; on the direct line of descent that leads to or from ego.

linguistic relativity Anthropological and linguistic doctrine that states that each language should be regarded as an instance of specific evolution.

liturgical order A set sequence of words and actions laid down by someone other than the current performer of the ritual in which the liturgical order occurs.

localized (or local) descent group All the members of a particular descent group who live in the same place, as in the same village.

longitudinal study A long-term study; research over several years, as of a primate group or human growth and development.

macroregional Spanning several regions; a large territory.

maize Indian corn; a major domesticate of the New World.

mana Sacred force associated with Polynesian nobility, causing their persons to be taboo.

manifest function Reasons that people in a society give for a custom.

manioc Cassava, a tuber, abundant in South American tropical forests. Along with maize and white potatoes, it became one of the three major caloric staples of the aboriginal New World.

marriage Socially recognized relationship between a so-cially recognized male (the husband) and a socially recognized female (the wife) such that children born of their union are socially accepted as their offspring.

matrifocal Families or households that are headed by a woman (*mater*), with no permanently resident husband-father.

matrons Senior women, as among the Iroquois.

Maya Civilization that arose in the tropical lowlands of Mexico and Guatemala. Flourished in classic form between about A.D. 300 and A.D. 900.

mediate To negotiate between parties in opposition over some issue; to bring closer together.

mercantile Trade-oriented; one of Cohen's strategies of adaptation.

Mesoamerica Middle America—Mexico, Guatemala, Belize.

Mesopotamia World's oldest state; first cities also developed there; included in modern nations of Iraq and western Iran. Sumer was in southern Mesopotamia.

mestizo Mixed; in Latin America, having a combination of European, African, and/or Native American ancestors; speaking national language.

metropole Phrase used by André Gunder Frank to refer to manufacturing and power centers of the world. In the past, these were capitals and ports of colonial nations. A city may serve as a metropole for the surrounding countryside, or a region may serve as a metropole for satellite regions.

Mexico, Valley of Highland area where Mexico City now stands. The site of Teotihuacan, great urban center of the Mesoamerican Classic, and Tenochtitlan, capital of the Aztec Empire.

millet Cereal grain that is dietary mainstay of one-third of the world's population; used in the United States as bird food.

moiety One of two descent groups in a given population. Usually intermarry.

monocrop production Economies based on the cultivation of a single crop, usually for sale.

monolatry Primary worship of a single deity.

monotheism Exclusive worship of a single, eternal, omniscient, omnipotent, and omnipresent deity.

morpheme Minimal meaningful form in a langauge.

morphology The study of form, used in linguistics (the study of morphemes and word construction) and for form in general; for example, biomorphology relates to physical form.

multicentric economy Exchange system organized into spheres of exchange.

multilinear evolution Study of evolution of human society "along its many lines" through examination of specific evolutionary sequences. Associated with Julian Steward.

multivariate Involving several variables.

mutation Chemical change in genetic material; principal source of variety essential to natural selection.

mutualism See *symbiosis*.

namesakes People who share the same name; a form of fictive kinship among the !Kung, who have a limited number of personal names.

natal Pertaining to birth, as in natal village — the village where one was born.

national character Constellation of personality attributes shared by inhabitants of a nation.

nation-state Sociopolitical system with a government and sharp contrasts in wealth, prestige, and power.

native anthropologist An anthropologist who is studying his or her own culture.

natural selection Doctrine that nature — the sum total of natural forces associated with a specific environment — selects the forms most fit to survive and reproduce in that environment, and thus perpetuates those forms. Charles Darwin's major contribution to evolutionary theory.

naturist position Argument that human behavior and social organization are genetically determined.

negative reciprocity See *generalized reciprocity*.

Neolithic The New Stone Age, characterized by the grinding and polishing of stone tools.

Neolithic Revolution Proposed by V. Gordon Childe to describe the repercussions of food production.

neolocal Rule of postmarital residence; establishing a new place of residence.

network analysis Method of egocentric analysis. Social relationships are plotted for specific individuals and constitute their social networks. Networks are then compared for linking and overlapping.

New World North and South America.

Nilotes Populations including the Nuer, Dinka, and others that inhabit the upper Nile region of eastern Africa.

nomadism Movement throughout the year by the whole herding group (men, women, children) with their animals. More generally, such constant movement in pursuit of strategic resources.

nonunilinear See *ambilineal*.

nuclear family Coresident group consisting of a married couple and their children. Also called elementary family or biological family.

nurturist position One that links behavior and social organization to distribution of strategic resources and other environmental factors; focuses on variation rather than universals; stresses learning and culture's role in human adaptation.

Oaxaca, Valley of One of the highland areas of Mexico where urbanism, the state, and civilization developed.

Oedipus complex From Sigmund Freud's theories about stages of childhood development. During the Oedipal or genital period, which follows the oral and anal stages, boys wish to kill their father and marry their mother, like Oedipus, a king in classical Greek drama. In normal development, the complex is resolved as boys eventually identify with their fathers and look for sexual gratification outside the nuclear family.

office Permanent political status.

Omaha kinship terminology Manner of classifying kin on ego's own generation; usually associated with patrilineal descent organization.

open peasant community Located in the lowlands of Latin America; populations represent admixtures of Indians, Europeans, and Africans. Noncorporate; members do not generally farm a joint estate. Not closed; flexibility in admitting new members.

osteology The study of bones.

Paleolithic Old Stone Age, traditionally divided into Lower (early), Middle, and Upper.

paleontology The study of ancient life, the fossil record; a branch of geology.

pantheon A collection of supernatural beings in a particular religion.

parallel cousins Children of siblings of the same sex.

parallelism The development of traits or behavior patterns among related species or populations as a result of adaptation to similar natural selective forces and environments.

participant observation Common ethnographic technique; ethnographers participate in some of the events that they are observing and describing in an attempt to improve their rapport with informants.

pastoralism Food-producing strategy of adaptation based on care of herds of domesticated animals.

pater Socially recognized father of a child, but not necessarily the genitor.

patrilineal parallel cousin marriage Marriage of the children of brothers.

patrilineal-virilocal complex Patrilineality, virilocality, warfare, male supremacy, female infanticide, polygyny, generally with a horticultural economy.

peasant Rural inhabitant of state.

perennial Bearing fruit or flowers year after year; not planted each year (annually).

performance What people actually say; the use of speech in concrete social situations.

personalty Items other than strategic resources that are indelibly associated with a particular person; contrasts with property.

phenotype Manifest biology and behavior of an organism. Opposed to genotype.

phone Any speech sound.

phoneme Minimal sound contrasts that serve to distinguish meaning, as in minimal pairs. One of several categories within the phonemic system specific to any language.

phonology Study of the sound system of a language.

phylogeny Genetic relationship; related through common ancestry.

physiological anthropology Subfield of biological or physical anthropology. Studies long-term and temporary individual biological reactions to stress.

pidgin A linguistic system that forms when the speakers of two or more languages come into continuous first-hand contact, incorporating features of both languages.

plantain Bananalike staple of Yanomamo and Ganda.

plant-cultivating continuum Or PCC, a continuum based on the comparative study of nonindustrial cultivating societies in which labor intensity increases and fallowing decreases.

plural marriage Marriage involving more than two spouses.

polity An independent political unit, such as a particular chiefdom or state; the political order.

polyandry Variety of plural marriage in which there is more than one husband.

polygamy Any marriage involving more than two spouses.

polygyny Marital relationship involving multiple wives.

Polynesia Large group of islands in the Pacific Ocean; included in a triangle with Hawaii to the north, Easter Island to the east, and New Zealand to the southwest.

polytypic species A species that is highly variable in phenotypical and genetic characteristics of its subpopulations.

positive feedback Ecosystems consist of several variables that affect each other. Changes in one lead to changes in the others. With negative feedback, a change in one variable is corrected by changes in others so that the system returns to its original state (as a thermostat would maintain a more or less constant temperature). With positive feedback, also called *deviation amplification,* a change in one variable feeds back on several others; subsequent changes in several variables magnify the independent effects of each, and the whole system changes rather than being restored to its original state.

potsherds Fragments of pottery.

precision grip Grasping an object between index finger and opposable thumb; anthropoid ability important in tool manufacture.

primary group Permanently bonded male and female and their preadolescent offspring; basic social unit among gibbons and siamangs.

primatology The study of apes, monkeys, and prosimians.

primitive Populations with band or tribal organization.

primogeniture Inheritance rule that makes oldest child (usually oldest son) the only heir.

progeny price A gift from the groom and his kin to the wife and her kin prior to marriage. Legitimizes children born to the woman as members of the husband's descent group.

Protestant ethic World view associated with early ascetic Protestantism, which values hard and constant work as a sign of salvation. Concept developed by Max Weber.

protolanguage Extinct language ancestral to several *daughter languages.*

Ramapithecus punjabicus Regarded by many scientists as ancestral to the genus *Homo.* A fragmentary fossil record of *Ramapithecus* includes bits of jaw and teeth, 14 to 8 million B.P.

reciprocal altruism Cooperation that, according to sociobiologists, improves the life chances and reproductive potential of a whole group.

reciprocity One of three principles of exchange identified by Karl Polanyi; governs exchange among social equals. The most characteristic mode of exchange in relatively egalitarian societies. Eventually grades into the market principle.

redistribution One of three principles of exchange identified by Karl Polanyi. Major exchange mode of chiefdoms, many archaic states, and states with managed economies.

regulation Management or control of variables within a system of interacting variables. Regulation assures that variables stay within their normal ranges, corrects deviations from normal, and thus maintains the system's integrity.

religion Human behavior involving belief and ritual concerned with supernatural beings and forces.

rent fund Term used by anthropologist Eric Wolf to describe scarce resources that a subordinate is required to render to a superordinate.

replacement fund Term used by Eric Wolf to describe scarce resources that people invest in technology and other items essential to production and everyday life.

research and development Approach to applied anthropology, as exemplified by the Vicos project; anthropologists learn from changes that they have promoted and test hypotheses about change against change as it actually occurs.

revitalization movements Movements that occur especially in times of rapid social change, in which religious leaders emerge and undertake to alter or revitalize a society.

rites of passage Culturally defined activities associated with the transition from one stage of life to another.

ritual Behavior that is formal, stylized, repetitive, stereotyped, and performed earnestly as a social act. Rituals are held at set times and places and have liturgical orders.

rural-urban continuum Term used by Robert Redfield to describe progressive change in certain attitudes and features of social organization as people move from rural to urban communities.

sanction Positive sanctions are rewards; negative sanctions are punishments.

Sapir-Whorf hypothesis Theory that different languages,

particularly their morphology, syntax, and lexicon, lead their speakers to think differently.

satellite Subsidiary of metropole; may be fully political or principally economic; provides raw materials for consumption and manufacture in metropolitan center; usually economically and ecologically specialized to meet the needs of the metropole.

satellite states Weakly industrial or nonindustrial, internally stratified, economically specialized nations that are appendages of metropolitan nations.

savanna Open grasslands; *Homo*'s earliest ecological niche.

sedentary Remaining in one place; a sedentary village is one in which people remain together year-round and for several years.

segmentary lineage system Sociopolitical organization based on descent, usually patrilineal, in which individuals belong to multiple descent segments that form at different genealogical levels and function in different contexts.

selective migration Theory that smart members of minority groups will usually move to urban areas. A largely discredited notion used to explain superior performance of Northern blacks on intelligence tests.

semantics Meaning; in Chomsky's view language's semantic component is linked to the phonological component through deep and surface structure and transformational rules.

serial monogamy Marriage of a given individual to several spouses, but not at the same time.

sertão Arid interior of northeastern Brazil; backlands.

settlement hierarchy A ranked series of communities differing in size, function, and type of building.

sexual dimorphism Marked differences in male and female anatomy and temperament, in addition to the contrasts provided by breasts and genitals.

shaman A part-time religious practitioner who serves as intermediary between ordinary people and supernatural beings and forces, such as Ben (Obi-Wan) Kenobi.

slash and burn Form of extensive horticulture in which the forest cover of a plot is cut down and burned before planting to allow the ashes to fertilize the soil.

social fund Investment of scarce resources to assist kin, fictive kin, affinals, or neighbors.

social race A category of a specific folk taxonomy. Defined socially, culturally, and legally rather than with reference to biological factors.

society Organized life in groups.

sociobiology Popular and scientific—the study of the biological basis of social behavior.

sociolinguistics Study of relationships between social and linguistic variation; of language (performance) in its social context.

sororate Custom whereby a widower marries the sister of his deceased wife.

Southwest Asia The Near East or the Middle East.

special-purpose money Currency that serves only one or two of the three functions associated with general-purpose money.

species Population that consists of organisms capable of interbreeding and producing viable and fertile offspring that are themselves capable of producing viable and fertile offspring.

specific evolution Studies of formal changes in relationships over time between specific human populations and their environments.

speech community Total number of speakers of a given language or dialect.

spheres of exchange Exchangeable goods are organized into separate categories, and items within a given category are normally exchanged only for other items within that category. Constitutes a multicentric economy.

state Form of sociopolitical organization whose principal function is preservation of general order and the order of socioeconomic stratification.

status A position within a social structure.

steppe Plain with few or no trees.

stereoscopic vision Ability to see in depth.

steward A representative of a chief.

stipulated descent Basis for clan membership. Clan members claim that they are descended from the same apical ancestor, but they do not trace the genealogical links between themselves and that ancestor.

strategic resources Resources necessary to sustain life; for example, food and water.

stratigraphy The study of earth layering and sedimentation (deposition of soils); a branch of geology.

stratum One of two or more duosexual, multi-age groups that contrast in social status and economic prerogatives, including access to strategic resources.

structuralism Structural analysis; technique developed by French anthropologist Claude Lévi-Strauss. Naturist position that assumes uniformities in human thought, particularly classification, resting on universal features of the human brain. Aims not at explaining sociocultural similarities and differences, but at uncovering cultural themes and relationships and cross-cultural similarities.

style shifts Speech varying in different contexts.

subgroups Those languages within a taxonomy of related languages that are most closely related.

subordinate Below; under the control of or victimized by others.

subsistence fund Term used by Eric Wolf to describe the fact that most people have to work to eat—to replace the calories they expend in everyday activities.

sumptuary goods Items whose consumption is specific to the life styles of chiefs, kings, and other members of the elite.

superordinate Enjoying privileged or favored access to wealth, power, and other valued resources.

swidden A horticultural plot; swiddening is a synonym for slash-and-burn cultivation.

symbiosis An obligatory interaction between groups that is beneficial to each.

symbol Something that stands for something else, both arbitrarily and by convention.

syntax The arrangement and order of words in phrases and sentences.

taboo Prohibition; interdiction backed by supernatural sanctions.

taxonomy Zoological taxonomy is the assignment of organisms to categories (*taxa;* singular, *taxon*) according to phylogenetic relationship and structural resemblance.

Tenochtitlan Capital of the Aztec Empire; located in the Valley of Mexico.

Teotihuacan Classic urban center in the Valley of Mexico with a population of over 100,000; was the capital of a major Mesoamerican empire.

terrestrial Pertaining to the earth; on the ground, as *Homo sapiens* is a terrestrial species.

territoriality A group's behavior in defending its right to exclusive use of a tract of land.

totems Stipulated ancestors of human groups. Generally plants or animals; more rarely, inanimate objects.

transformational-generative grammar Approach associated with Noam Chomsky; views language as set of abstract rules; deep and surface structures linked through grammatical transformations, such as active-passive.

transformism Doctrine that species have arisen gradually from other species over time. Same as evolution.

transhumance One of two variants of pastoralism; part of the population moves seasonally with the herds, while the rest remain in home villages.

tribal society See *tribe.*

tribe Form of sociopolitical organization generally based on horticulture or pastoralism, more rarely on foraging or agriculture. Socioeconomic stratification and centralized rule are absent in tribes, and there is no means of enforcing political decisions.

troop Basic unit of social organization among nonhuman primates. Composed of multiple adult males and females and their offspring.

tropics Zone bounded by the Tropic of Cancer to the north and the Tropic of Capricorn to the south. Extends for twenty degrees on each side of the equator.

tundra Vast, nearly level, treeless plain characteristic of arctic environments.

typology A system of classification into types.

unicausal Having a single cause.

unilineal Type of descent and descent group, either patrilineal or matrilineal. Children of descent-group members of one sex are automatically included as descent-group members, while children of members of the opposite sex are excluded.

unilocal Either virilocal or uxorilocal postmarital residence; requiring that a married couple reside with the relatives of either husband (*vir*) or wife (*uxor*) depending on the society.

universal grammar According to Chomsky a genetically encoded blueprint for language, a basic linguistic plan in the human brain.

urban anthropology The anthropological study of cities and towns.

uterine Kinship through female links.

utopic model of intervention Assumes that intervention is necessary to gain the acceptance of change, and that results are best achieved by excluding the people whose lives are being changed; concerned with ends rather than with means.

uxorilocality A couple's residence with the wife's group.

variable Any factor or characteristic that varies or changes; for example, temperature, rainfall, food supply.

vernacular Ordinary, casual speech.

vertebrates Animals with a backbone. Taxonomic status —a subphylum of the kingdom *Animalia.*

vertical economy Economic system of a population living in environmental zones that differ in rainfall, temperature, and other features but are located close together.

virilocality A couple's residence with the husband's group.

voiced Sound produced by vibration of the vocal cords; includes all vowels and many consonants.

voiceless Sound produced with no vibration of the vocal cords; includes many English consonants.

voluntary associations Organizations like burial societies, social clubs, and trade associations that people join, usually in cities. Basic adaptation to urban life.

world-rejecting religions Religions that sharply separate the profane, material world of here and now from the sacred realm; typically include notions of an afterlife and salvation.

zebu Humped cattle kept, for example, in India, East Africa, Madagascar.

INDEX

Disney mythology, 355–357
Disneyland, 355, 361
Divale, William, 152–154, 181, 237, 239–240
Divorce, 102, 134, 138, 303
DNA (deoxyribonucleic acid), 27
Dobu, of the Pacific, 215
Domestication of animals, 49. *See also* Food production
Dominance hierarchy
  among baboons, 4
  among chimpanzees, 38
Doughty, Paul, 309
Draper, Patricia, 238, 239
Drug addiction, 306–307, 311
Durkheim, Emile, 193, 200, 363

Eastman, Carol, 273
Ecological differentiation, 37
Ecology
  archeological anthropology and, 14
  descent groups and, 111–113
  multicentric economies and, 177–180
  origins of the state and, 85
  rituals and, 206–207
Economic organization
  anthropological approach to, 17–18, 167–168
  anthropologist's role in, 324–333
  in archaic states, 80
  in Buganda, 90–92, 95
  in chiefdoms, 78
  of corporate communities, 300–301
  and crime in U.S., 309–311
  distribution and exchange, 174–176
  economizing and maximization, 168–170
  future anthropological studies of, 180–181
  industrial vs. nonindustrial, 172, 176–177
  in Java, 328–332
  among kinship groups, 106
  metropole-satellite relationships, 296–298
  money and, 177–178
  multicentric exchange and, 177–180
  in peasant societies, 170–172
  along plant-cultivating continuum, 64–66
  plantation, 297
  production and, 170–174
  in *sertão,* Brazil, 326–328
  in subculture of poverty, 304–305
  Vicos manor, 322–324
Economics, anthropology and, 17–18
Ecosystem, defined, 14
Edgerton, Robert, 220, 221
Education vs. enculturation, 106–108
Elam, of Iran, 85
Emic approach, of anthropology, 5–7
Enculturation, 5, 18, 231, 270, 306
  education vs., 106–108
Endogamy, 79
  functions of, 129–130, 131–132
  in peasant communities, 300
  postmarital residence rules and, 110–111
Environment, 298
  biological anthropology and, 15

circumscription of, 86–87
intelligence testing and, 253–256
natural selection and, 27, 50
predation and, 37–39
primate behavioral adaptation to, 37–40
sociocultural behavior and, 231–232
Erasmus, Charles, 325, 326
Eskimos, 55, 273
  adaptation of, 4
  kinship terminology of, 118
  language of, 273
  political organization of, 149–150, 153
  religion of, 195
  status of women among, 237
"Essay on the Principles of Population" (Malthus), 27
Ethics, in anthropology, 326, 336–337
Ethiopia. *See specific group and place names*
Ethnic associations, 308
Ethnobotany, 274
Ethnocentrism, 6–7, 101, 319, 345
Ethnographic Atlas (Murdock), 239
Ethnography, 12–13, 14, 17, 19
Ethnohistory, 88–89
Ethnology, 13, 14
Ethnoscience, 274
Ethnosemantics, 273–275
Ethnozoology, 274
Ethology and anthropology, 8–9
Etic approach, of anthropology, 5–7
Etoro, of New Guinea, 9, 154, 250–251
Evans-Pritchard, E. E., 154, 155, 250
Evolution
  anthropological approach to, 12
  as basis for taxonomy, 25–26
  convergent, 29, 50, 53–55
  cultural adaptation and, 4, 5
  of culture, 52–53
  Darwinian theory of, 26–27, 50
  descent groups and, 112–113
  environment and, 27, 50
  genetics and, 27
  human, 5, 50–55
  of language, 284–287
  multilinear, 53
  natural selection, 15, 26–27, 50–55
  parallel, 29, 54
  religion and, 194–197
  sociobiology and, 232–235
  transformism, doctrine of, and, 26
  trends in, 25–27
  unilinear, 52
Evolution of Culture, The (White), 52, 194
Exchange
  modes of, 176–177
  spheres of, 177–178
Exchange systems. *See also* Marriage
  coexistence of various modes within, 176–177
  generalized, 132–133, 177
  market principle of, 174–175, 177
  metropole-satellite relationships, 296–298
  reciprocal, 175–176, 177
  redistribution in, 78, 80, 175, 177

About the Author

Conrad Phillip Kottak is Professor of Anthropology at the University of Michigan, where he has taught since 1968. He received his Ph.D. from Columbia University in 1966. In 1966 and 1967 he conducted field work among the Betsileo of Madagascar. In 1962, 1964, 1965, and 1973, he undertook ethnographic research on the social effects of "modernization" in northeastern Brazil. He is the author of the forthcoming *From Bias of Nature,* an ethnographic and historical study of Betsileo cultural adaptation. Professor Kottak has contributed articles to many journals, including *American Anthropologist, American Ethnologist, Comparative Studies in Society and History, Ethnology, The Journal of Anthropological Research,* and *Natural History.* He is a Fellow of the American Anthropological Association and the Royal Anthropological Institute of Great Britain and Ireland.